本书为教育部重点研究基地西南边疆少数民族研究中心文库——非物质文化遗产研究系列丛书
"云南大学哲学社会科学创新团队"项目资助成果
云南大学"中国-东南亚、南亚贝叶文化传承与保护研究"创新团队成果

贝叶文化

与区域文化遗产传承保护：
中国—东南亚、南亚的认知与实践

Palm-leaf Culture & Regional Cultural Heritage Inheritance and Protection

周娅　郭山 ◎ 主编

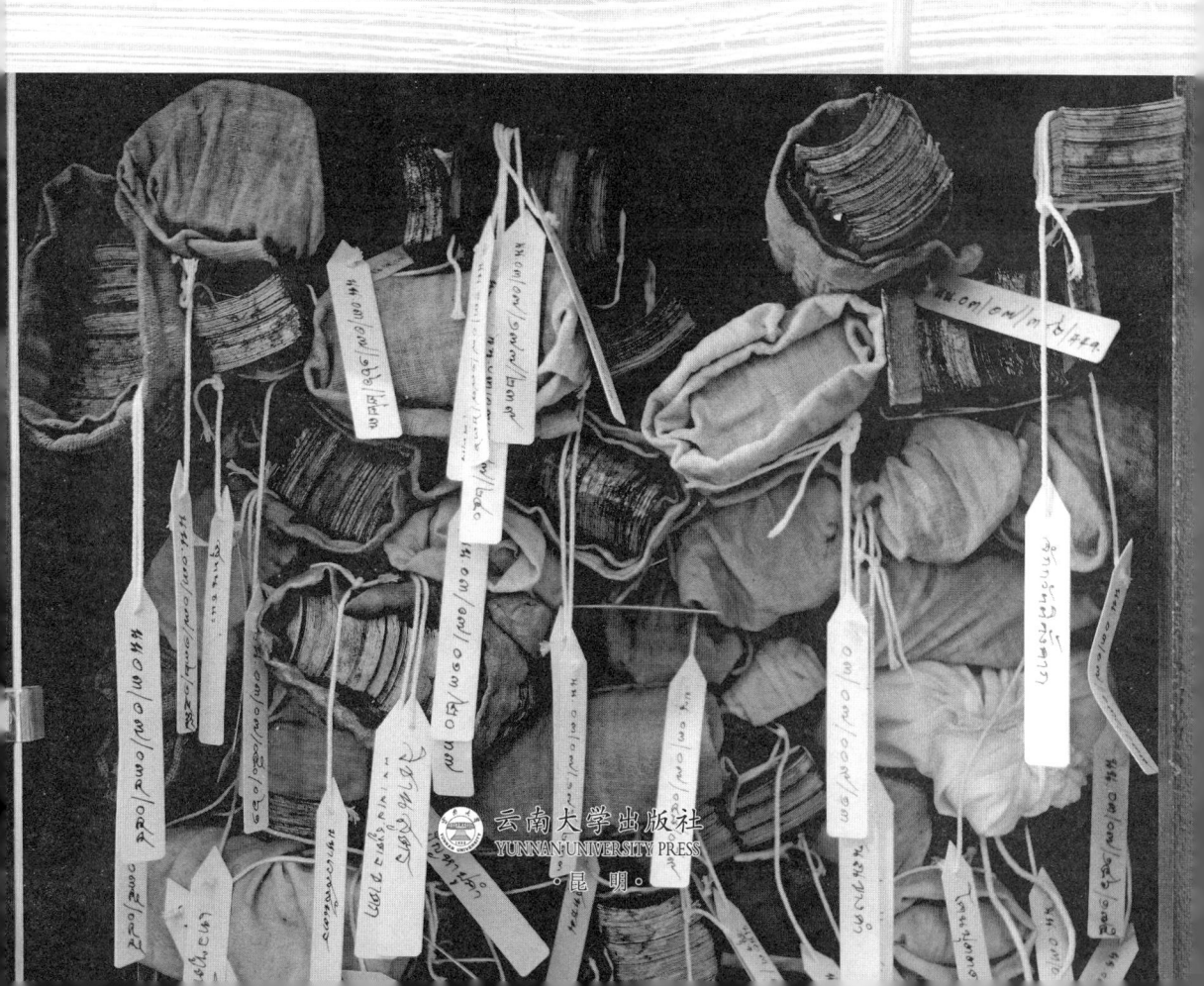

云南大学出版社
Yunnan University Press
·昆 明·

图书在版编目（CIP）数据

贝叶文化与区域文化遗产传承保护：中国—东南亚、南亚的认知与实践 / 周娅，郭山主编. -- 昆明：云南大学出版社，2022

ISBN 978-7-5482-3944-4

Ⅰ. ①贝… Ⅱ. ①周… ②郭… Ⅲ. ①傣族—民族文化—文化遗产—保护—研究—中国②民族文化—文化遗产—保护—研究—东南亚③民族文化—文化遗产—保护—研究—南亚 Ⅳ. ①K285.3②K330.03③K350.03

中国版本图书馆CIP数据核字(2020)第224853号

策划编辑：张丽华
责任编辑：张丽华
封面设计：任 微

贝叶文化
与区域文化遗产传承保护：
中国—东南亚、南亚的认知与实践

BEIYE WENHUA YU QUYU WENHUA YICHAN CHUANCHENG BAOHU:
ZHONGGUO—DONGNANYA NANYA DE RENZHI YU SHIJIAN

周娅　郭山 ◎ 主编

出版发行：云南大学出版社
印　　装：昆明埕煌印务有限公司
开　　本：787mm×1092mm 1/16
印　　张：23.75
插　　页：4页
字　　数：590千
版　　次：2022年8月第1版
印　　次：2022年8月第1次印刷
书　　号：ISBN 978-7-5482-3944-4
定　　价：96.00元

地　　址：昆明市一二一大街182号（云南大学东陆校区英华园内）
邮　　编：650091
发行电话：0871-65033244　65031071
网　　址：http://www.ynup.com
E-mail：market@ynup.com

若发现本书有印装质量问题，请与印厂联系调换，联系电话：0871-64167045。

"中国—东南亚、南亚贝叶文化传承与保护"国际研讨会期间"老挝贝叶经数字图书馆"项目负责人David Wharton博士讲座现场，2019年（摄影 刘艳雪）

2019年云南大学"东南亚—南亚贝叶文化传承与保护"创新团队在泰调研（摄影 【泰】Direk Injan）

2021年西双版纳州图书馆工作人员在布朗山曼兴龙（佛寺）进行古籍普查（摄影 玉罕为）

老挝保存完好的贝叶经及藏经柜（摄影 【英】David Wharton）

缅甸掸邦文化精英在Lik Loung国际研讨会手稿分类工作坊中，2015年（摄影 【英】David Wharton）

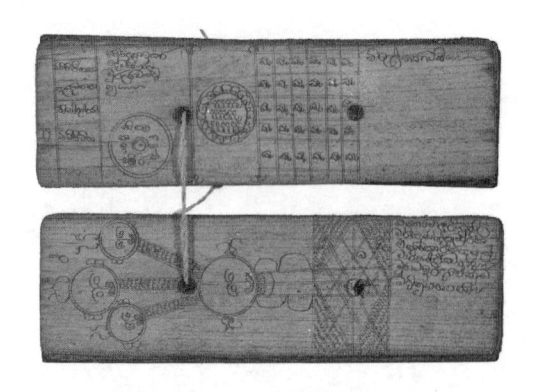

斯里兰卡僧伽罗文贝叶经（【斯】Premakumara de Silva 供稿）

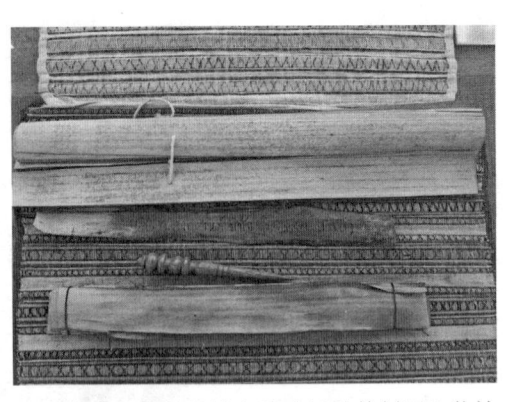

泰国北部的兰纳文贝叶经及其刻写和装帧器物（中间绿色贝叶刻写的为现代泰文）（摄影 都坎章拉）

泰国楠府文化精英收藏的贝叶经（摄影 周娅）

泰北贝叶经数字图书馆项目网页（【德】Harald Hundius 供稿）

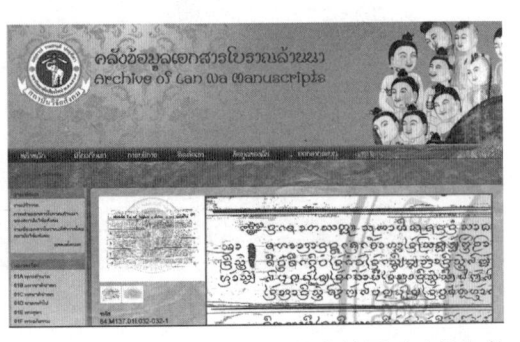

清迈大学兰纳手稿网络档案馆网页（都坎章拉 供稿）

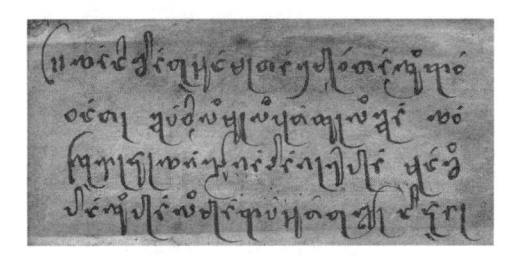

在中国发现后被带到老挝的19世纪中叶的抄本页面及豆芽文字体（摄影 【英】David Wharton）

西双版纳贝叶经保护传承实践者在贝叶文化展览活动现场（摄影 玉罕为）

西双版纳小和尚学习刻写贝叶经（周寒丽 供稿）

泰国帕府Wat Songmen佛寺内的藏经柜及其可二维码检索信息的贝叶经及抄本（摄影 周娅）

泰国清迈皇家大学组织学生志愿者参与当地贝叶经保护整理（摄影 【泰】Direk Injan）

中国德宏五云寺的贺路照看佛寺藏经柜内的抄本，2019年（摄影　周娅）

中国德宏的长休傣文（豆芽文）抄本（摄影　张云）

中国文化与旅游部非遗司领导在西双版纳贝叶文化传习中心调研，2019年（摄影　张玲）

中—泰贝叶文化传承保护研究团队在泰国清迈皇家大学举办工作会议后合影，2019年（摄影　张海）

中国—东南亚、南亚贝叶文化传承与保护国际研讨会参会代表合照（摄影　武有福）

前　言

过去一百多年，人类的现代化生产和生活方式席卷全球。尤其近半个世纪以来，以计算机和互联网为标志的科技风暴席卷全球，推进了全球一体化的进程。面对社会加速变迁的"大时代"，"文化折叠"现象频发——世界上很多角落和族群的人们历经诸多"小时代"才累积形成的文化体系，在全球化和现代文明的双重浪潮冲击下，正以令人难以置信的速度消失乃至消亡！"文化折叠"现象频发，也导致了很多文化形态迅速遗产化的并发症——它们正默然地淡出当地人鲜活的社会系统，从原先的社会结构中迅速边缘化甚至脱出，成为一种遥远的集体记忆、一种文化的"遗存"，或者一种族群文化认同的熟悉而又陌生的象征。

在这个科技裹挟一切的大时代，人类群体正汲汲于对宇宙外太空的"向外探寻"。然而，对于人类本身来说，随着全球范围内地缘边界的模糊，不同地方、地域的不同文化、文明的碰撞、挤压与融合，人类应如何"向内探索"，让世界不同地方、地域、国家的人类群体成为一个休戚相关、荣辱与共的"共同体"，而无关其区域、种族、族群、宗教信仰和价值观，成为人类社会在21世纪亟需共同应对的问题。在此过程中，人类不仅要能学习、尊重和适应当下"共时性"的你、我、他者群体之间的文化差异（尤其是价值观差异），实现相互学习、整合和转化、融合，以便共同应对当下人类面临的资源短缺、气候恶化、生化危机、核武器威胁，避免冲突和战争；而且要有历史眼光，在"历时性"的人类社会发展长河中，汲取先人们的智慧，并立足当下，实现一种转化和整合，形成跨越国家或地缘边界、跨越种族或宗教信仰、跨越时空或价值观差异的"更高层级和形态的人类共同体文化"，以共同应对未来人类面对自然、人类社会、非人类社会和宇宙的种种问题，引导人类文明的未来。

华裔美籍历史学家许倬云先生曾言："在历史的过程中，最短的是个人，其次是政治，更长一点的是经济，然后是社会，更长的是文化，而最长的是自然……现代人类要有人心之自由，胸襟开放，拿全世界人类曾经走过的路，都要算是我走过的路之一，要有一个远见，能超越你未见……"

许先生的这一人文主义理念是弥足珍贵的，尤其在当今这个人类以科技主义壮大一切的时代。虽然人文主义并不能解决现今大量的现实问题，但它仍是人类社会继续前行中的精神依托和乡愁复归之所。

由联合国教科文组织倡导，在全球范围内践行的对人类文化遗产的记录、传承和保护，正是人类社会对其历史发展中珍贵的人文遗产的系统性"识遗"和"拾遗"。在此过程中，不仅各种有形的自然与文化遗产得到了识别与保护，那些蕴含着人类集体记忆、文化认同与文化基因的无形的人类文化遗产也获得了更多的关注与珍视。更重要的是，这些文化遗产的价值超越了时间、地域和国家等狭隘界限，为全人类共同的文化财富遗产。

然而，和能被列入《世界遗产名录》的"幸运儿"们相比，全球范围内还存在着巨量的自然与文化财富，值得人类共同珍视。其中的文化财富由于相较自然资源来说，其形成、发展、成熟和消亡的"生命"历程相对较短，尤其是那些已呈现出濒危性的文化遗产，一旦消亡，便是人类文化多样性理念与实践的损失。因此，文化遗产的保护工作，更需要引起各国和相关国际组织的重视。

中国于2019年成为全球拥有世界遗产数量最多的国家。但总体上看，除中国本土自然与文化资源之外，中国仍有不少与周边区域国家共同享有的世界级的区域性文化遗产值得进一步地发掘和整理，甚或今后可共同申报世界遗产名录项目。这就需要我们对中国边疆省份及其联通的周边的东北亚、东亚、东南亚、中亚等相关区域的共享文化资源投入更多的关注，从而更大限度、更深层次、更广领域地推动"一带一路"倡议合作，丰富和提升中国与周边区域国家的人文交流与合作实践。

本文集聚焦中国西南边疆云南省西部和西南部的若干少数民族地区与南亚、东南亚国家共有共享的"贝叶经和贝叶文化"这一重要区域人文遗产资源的传承与保护，希望通过文集收录的相关研究成果，促进该区域国家间在该领域及其他文化遗产保护实践方面的合作。

中国的云南省与西藏自治区的边疆地区地处中华文化圈与东南亚文化圈、南亚文化圈的交汇之地，在"文化的地缘边界"上有"跨界"性，属于亨廷顿"文明冲突论"中的"文明的断层线"。亨氏认为，在这条断层线上尤其容易出现文化的撞击和冲突，从而相当不稳定；但换个角度看，它们不也正是"文明的联结区点"吗？不同的文化在这里汇聚、碰撞、交流、交融，这里的人们习惯于相互学习、相互尊重、互相包容，从而形成一种跨越主权国家边界，超越种族、族群和宗教信仰的多元文化和谐共存的区域性文化生态。由于西藏受特殊地理环境的限制，在某种程度上说，云南面向东南亚、南亚的地缘通达性较其更有优势，因此成为中国面向南亚、东南亚的陆路门户和通道中心。云南这片神奇的土地，孕育了多元的族群生态和人类文化形态以及众多独特的世界级自然与文化景观。无论是澄江化石遗址、南方喀斯特地貌石林或"三江并流"，还是"丽江古城""东巴文古籍文献""红河哈尼梯田"，它们都成为令世人瞩目的世界遗产。然而，云南境内除了本土资源外，还存在着跨国乃至跨区域的珍稀文化遗产资源。其中，贝叶经及贝叶文化，就是其中很有代表性的一例——跨越时空和国家边界的人类区域性共同文化遗产。

贝叶经和贝叶文化是中国、东南亚、南亚区域的重要文化遗产。它承载了该区域作为"东方文明"的重要组成部分的佛教文明及其成文经典，反映了佛教在上述区域的传播及其深受佛教文化影响的人类区域文明史。大量的贝叶经和巨量的相关纸质抄本中记载了博大精深的佛教经典和哲学、天文学、医药学、文学、语言学等内容，乃至书面的或口传的历史和地方知识。这些珍贵的文献典籍曾经在历史上记录和见证了该区域人们生产、生活和劳动等物质财富创造的过程，并以文献的形式记录和保存了人们的思想与文化等精神财富，千百年来逐渐累积形成卷帙浩繁的该区域内若干族群群体的共有历史记忆和"传统文化的百科全书"，是现居于该区域的印度、斯里兰卡、尼泊尔、泰国、老挝、缅甸、柬埔寨和中国西南地区的诸多族群在长期的社会历史过程中不断创造积累的文化财富。它在历史上长期而持续地对该区域的上亿人口产生了重要的社会历史影响，至今仍有其独特的文化价值和意义，故而是该区域社群共同享有的珍贵文化财富，也是人类历史杰出而罕有的跨越千年留存至今的宝贵文化遗产。

然而，近几十年来，这些凝结区域社群智慧的典籍正面临日益显著的遗产化现象——大量散落于民间的文献没有被很好地收藏和保护，不少贝叶经和纸质古籍被损毁或散佚，其在当地社会生活中的使用频率也日益降低，濒危性日益加剧。更严重的是，熟悉和掌握贝叶经刻写制作技艺的传承人人数少、年龄大，真正愿意学习和持续实践贝叶经刻写制作或纸质经本抄写的年轻人寥寥无几。这项曾经对该地区社会生活有着重要意义和影响的技艺及其物质载体，正与当地的社会生活脱离，走向边缘化，难以实现技艺的代际传承。新抄刻的经本文献数量赶不上原有经本文献的自然或人为损毁速度，其总藏量也随着时间的推移而不断减少。诚然，在上述区域的局部地区（如泰国清迈、缅甸景栋、中国云南的西双版纳等地），贝叶经的抄写制作仍被当作一项神圣的地方文化传统而得以继承和保存下来，然而，在更多地方，历史上曾经神圣而鲜活的贝叶文化已经迅速遗产化。我的老朋友，德国帕绍大学 Harald Hundius 教授的博士生，英国人 David Wharton 博士，一位跑遍中国西南和东南亚多个国家，实地考察、研究和实践贝叶经保存和保护的数字技术专家曾感叹道："我们必须认识到，（贝叶经和纸质）手稿是当地丰富的无形文化的一部分，但这种文化消失的速度甚至比手稿本身还要快！"

上述贝叶经和贝叶文化迅速遗产化的现象，在中国、缅甸、泰国、老挝、柬埔寨、斯里兰卡、尼泊尔等国家都不同程度地存在着。这个现象和问题即是本文集论题的客观现实依据。贝叶经和贝叶文化已经成为中国和东南亚、南亚区域部分国家需要协同保护的重要区域文化遗产，应该得到更多的社会关注和保护实践。

基于推动对中国—南亚、东南亚贝叶经和相关纸质经典的持续保护及研究的初衷，云南大学贝叶文化研究中心于2018年年底在与泰国清迈大学、清迈皇家大学相关机构的合作协议中提出了出版这部文集的想法。2019年11月，我们与上述高校和机构合作，顺利地在云南大学举办了"中国—东南亚、南亚贝叶经与贝叶文化传承与保护国际研讨会",并于 2020 年 3 月间基本完成了书稿的组稿和翻译工作。

在本文集中,我们对中国—东南亚、南亚地区一些国家对贝叶经和贝叶文化的现状、遗产价值的基本认知,以及对其进行传承与保护的方法和具体实践、经验等内容进行了交流及探讨,并对未来区域内各国、各地方对其进行保护与传承提出了一些建议,作了展望。受篇幅所限,此次结集出版无法把所有的参会论文全部收录其中,但我们仍希望读者可以从这本文集有限的研究面向和成果中获得信息和启发。

此次论文翻译工作除一两篇由英语专业的老师翻译完成外,其余均由毕业于云南大学民族学与社会学学院、发展研究院等学院的社会学、宗教学专业的硕士或在读硕士研究生翻译。虽本着锻炼学生、让他们多参与专业研究工作,提升专业技能的初衷,但因学生以及编者受水平、学识所限,中英文稿件翻译质量仍存在不少不尽如人意之处,在此希望能获得读者和专家的谅解和批评指正。

最后,本文集名为"贝叶文化与区域文化遗产传承保护",是基于贝叶经与贝叶文化诸面向正在区域内各国不同程度地加速遗产化的客观现状。在我们呼吁和推动贝叶文化的区域文化遗产协同保护的背后,我们更想表达或呈现的,是中国、东南亚、南亚区域内自"轴心时代"以来,数千年存续至今的鲜活的贝叶文化习俗和传统,以及那背后人类的先人面对自然、社会和宇宙的认知与实践经验、思想和智慧的光芒!

编　者

2020 年 3 月,昆明

目 录

掌握以贝叶经为基础的仪式知识
　　——对斯里兰卡贝叶经传统的概述……………………… Premakumara de Silva　01
对傣泰族群佛教手稿文化的传承与保护的一些考察……………… David Wharton　08
贝叶经与西双版纳傣族的赕
　　——基于M村的田野调查 …………………………………………… 郭　山　14
傣文巴利语释读问题及建议……………………………………………… 戴红亮　20
珍贵的区域文化遗产
　　——贝叶经与贝叶文化：来自中国的传承与保护实践及认知……… 周　娅　28
贝叶经和纸质抄本对旅游业资料的贡献
　　——以清迈府市区的清曼寺为例…………………………… Direk Injan　38
傣泰民族佛教文学的跨界交流……………………………………………… 刀承华　45
傣族贝叶文化世俗经典中的诗歌修辞研究………………………………… 刀金平　54
中国贝叶经传承与保护概况………………………………………………… 张振伟　66
傣文贝叶经《佛祖巡游记》音译词的规范化……………………………… 保明所　71
西双版纳傣文古籍翻译整理初探…………………………………………… 陆云东　79
让贝叶文里的文字活起来
　　——德宏傣文古籍抢救保护翻译整理与开发利用……………………… 张　云　84
云南南部傣泐贝叶经的复兴、传播与发展 ………… Apiradee Techasiriwan　93
西双版纳南传上座部佛教傣文经典传承与发展现状研究………………… 康南山　99
贝叶经在斯里兰卡佛教文化中的传承………………… Wimal Hewamanage　108
傣民族医药古籍与师承教育模式探析
　　——以滇西应用技术大学傣医药学院为例……………………………… 玉喃哈　115
DREAMSEA项目概况及其抢救濒危手稿的经验介绍 …………………… 周寒丽　121
经典傣文的名称和使用分布初探…………………………………………… 岩坎章拉　126

贝叶文化与区域文化遗产传承保护

巴利语系贝叶文化典籍的保存、保护与研究
  ——以西双版纳傣族自治州古籍保护中心为例……… 岩温宰香 玉罕为 132
西双版纳傣族贝叶文化载体
  ——贝叶棕现存情况调查…………………………………… 玉楠叫 138
中国南传上座部佛教典籍中的"赕"主题故事及其阐释……… 田玉玲 143
贝叶文化传承的村寨支持模式探寻
  ——基于西双版纳州三个傣族村寨的调研…………… 玉万叫 王明姣 150
贝叶经籍文化交流是德宏沿边开放先行先试的重要路径
 ……………………………………………… 李茂琳 熊甜芳 蒋潞杨 157
中国—东南亚、南亚贝叶文化传承与保护国际研讨会综述……… 韩 帅 162
会议总结及闭幕致辞………………………………………………… 周 娅 168

Explorations of Lao Manuscript Culture: The Case of the Vat Maha That
  Collection ……………… Volker Grabowsky Khamvone Boulyaphonh 171
Palm-Leaf Manuscripts and the Dai People's Dan in Xishuangbanna
  —Based on Field Investigation in M Village …………………… Guo Shan 198
The Study on Palm-Leaf and Sa Paper Manuscripts to Support the
  Information for Tourism: A Case Study of Chiang Man Temple,
  Muang District, Chiang Mai ……………………………… Direk Injan 206
Precious Regional Cultural Heritage
  —Palm-Leaf Scriptures and Palm-Leaf Culture: Inheritance and
  Protection Practice and Cognition from China …………………… Zhou Ya 216
A Study on the Inheritance and Development of Dai Scriptures of
  Theravada Buddhism in Xishuangbanna ……………………… Kang Nanshan 231
Heritage of Palm-Leaf in Sri Lankan Buddhist Culture … Wimal Hewamanage 244
The Revival, Transmission and Development of Tai Lü Papsa
  Manuscripts in Southern Yunnan ……………… Apiradee Techasiriwan 253
Let the Words of Palm-Leaf Living
  —Rescue, Protection, Translation, Arrangement, Development
  and Utilization of the Ancient Dai Books ……………………… Zhang Yun 264
A Preliminary Study on the Names and Distribution of Tai Tham
 ………………………………………………………………… Yankan Zhangla 276
The DREAMSEA Project, an Overview: Critical Work in the Preservation of
  Endangered Southeast Asian Manuscript Cultures ……………… Zhou Hanli 284

Buddhism and Sexology Literature: The Observances from Thai Palm Scripts
.... Aphilak Kasempholkoon 291

***Kāraked*: The Overlooked Siamese Dance-Drama Play Manuscripts**
.... Sutheera Satayaphan 300

An Analysis of Ancient Books of Dai Medicine and the Education Mode of Teach-Inheritance
—A Case Study of Dai Medical College of Applied Science of West Yunnan .... Yu Nanha 317

The Village-Based Preserve-Support Model for the Dai Palm-Leaf Culture
—The Study of Three Dai Villages in Xishuangbanna
.... Yu Wanjiao Wang Mingjiao 326

Possession of Palm-Leaf Based Ritual Knowledge: An Overview of Palm-Leaf Manuscript Traditions in Sri Lanka .... Premakumara de Silva 335

Some Observations of the Inheritance and Protection of Tai Buddhist Manuscript Cultures .... David Wharton 345

An Overview of the International Seminar on the Inheritance & Protection of Palm-Leaf Culture in China, Southeast Asia and South Asia ...... Han Shuai 353

Conference Summary and Closing Speech .... Zhou Ya 361

后　记 365

掌握以贝叶经为基础的仪式知识

——对斯里兰卡贝叶经传统的概述

Premakumara de Silva[1] 文　刘艳雪[2] 译

导　言

在斯里兰卡岛屿上，悠久的土著社区习俗和传统知识在最早的时候是通过口头传统保存的，再者是碑文（sellipi）或石刻。早在公元前2世纪，僧伽罗人就有了书面文字，并且有刻写这一书面文字的铭文。当笔者提及"题刻"时，其意思为在石头上刻写文字。贝叶经在传统上被用来记录传统知识以及用于认知古代社会如何利用这些知识，包括传统医学、仪式、宗教、文化、本土技术、健康传统等。斯里兰卡和南亚大部分国家或地区拥有广泛传播的贝叶文化，其不仅局限于书面材料。这些贝叶经是宝贵的资料，其中包含大量的本地知识和智慧，这些知识和智慧是我们的祖先经过数千年的实践和经验而获得的。追溯到公元前5世纪，贝叶（puskola poth）仍是整个南亚国家（或者地区）的主要书写材料。到公元20世纪，棕榈叶手稿通常被称为贝叶经，它是使用传统的技术工艺结合文化习俗制备而成的，而棕榈叶的嫩叶（Borassus flabelliformis）可用于满足这些用途。也有写在贝叶上的书。现存的最古老的书籍，主要由佛教僧侣于12世纪篆刻而成，后来也有非专业人士篆刻的。

历史概要

这种贝叶书写系统一直延续到19世纪末。我们一定不要忘记这里的另一件事。即使到了现在，一个人所属的星座和生病孩子的护身符仍被刻在这些叶子上。通过研究斯里兰卡仍然可以购买到的贝叶经，就可以找到与传统医学、文化习俗、占星术、农业及古代技术有关的大量信息。目前，由于湿度、白蚁、鼠害和一些疏忽大意的人类活动，以及将这些手稿作为古董和艺术品卖给外国人，这些手稿很快就会

---

[1] 作者为斯里兰卡科伦坡大学社会学学院院长，教授，博士。
[2] 译者为云南大学民族学与社会学学院2018级宗教学硕士研究生。

贝叶文化与区域文化遗产传承保护

消亡。贝叶经上的文字和与之相关的传统技术和文化活动，在不久的将来将完全消失（Peiris，2018）。与此同时，在不久的将来，关于贝叶经的写作以及相关的传统技术和文化活动也将完全消失。在斯里兰卡，这些贝叶经中所刻写的大多数有关土著知识和适当做法是该国现代发展的宝贵资源。为了维护这种古老的贝叶经刻写传统，有必要通过传播制作这种手稿的技术知识，并重新定义其在当代社会中的潜在用途来复兴这种古老的传统。公元前 1 世纪后期，佛教僧侣通过口述传统来向佛教徒传播佛法，这是有记录以来第一次使用贝叶进行写作。[①]本地医生在贝叶上记载了许多处方和本土治愈方法，以保留和保护它们免于灭绝，并世代相传。像僧侣和本地医生一样，当地的仪式专家也通过贝叶传统记载方式保存他们的仪式知识。[②]这些不同类型的文本有很大部分未出版而被当作收藏品，保存在不同的档案中，例如寺庙、私人藏品、政府档案和外国博物馆中（Godakumbura，1980；Liyanaratne，1983）。

除此之外，Hugh Nevill（1955 年）[③]收集了数百本仪式文本，他是一位受过训练的印度学者，在锡兰（斯里兰卡）为英国殖民大国工作，从历史角度来看，他的工作是最富成果的工作之一。Nevill 收集了许多南部（Dondra）地区的仪式文本，并调查了其所构成的年份以及它们与更具广泛意义的南亚文化传统之间的关系。他从斯里兰卡各地收集的 2227 份贝叶经文本中，包括大约 931 份仪式文本（Deraniyagala，1954、1955；Kariyawasam，1989）。例如，在 931 份手稿中，大约有 500 份涉及传统仪式，其中各种神灵都受到赞美，恶魔也得到了供养。一些手稿还描述了今天已不为人知的各种仪式。[④]

焦 点

本文研究了斯里兰卡南部低地传统仪式专家的 Bali Tovil（行星仪式），及其对仪式知识的掌握，特别是占星术仪式知识的掌握。本文所依据的数据为在斯里兰卡南部省的 Berava 或鼓手种姓中收集的人种学数据，以及与该研究对象有关的档案资料。尽管鼓手种姓在其种姓等级中排名较低，但仍然是基于口头和贝叶经传统的大

---

① 僧侣在斯里兰卡文本产出中具有非常重要的历史作用，他们通过制作、翻译、评论、选集和朗诵的行为来保存和改造佛法（Berkwitz，2009）。
② Obeyesekere（2013）发现，"本地知识分子"（主要是有文化的村民）把在想象中的或真实的历史事件或过去的事刻写在贝叶上。这些手稿大部分尚未出版，被广泛称为"vitti pot"，即"过去的事"。除 vitti pot 外，还有一些相关文本，例如 bandaravaliyas 或贵族家庭的历史，它们是斯里兰卡版本的家庭谱系，在许多文化中都可以找到，但此处以书面形式记录下来。这为我们提供了有关 15 世纪后的新科提王国和康提王国的历史及社会组织的宝贵信息，补充了众所周知的编年史。其他此类工作称为 kadaim pot 或边界书，它们描绘了想象中的国家，其中包含了省和地区的边界。
③ 内维尔（Hugh Nevill）是英国的公务员，他在锡兰（斯里兰卡）服务近 30 年。他出生于 1848 年 6 月；在英国工作的确切位置未知。于 1865 年末抵达锡兰。他曾担任首席大法官的私人秘书，然后被任命为监狱委员会秘书。此后，他经常在马塔拉（Matara）担任地区代理法官，为期大约两个月，或在 Balapiti Modera 担任代理警司。他于 1897 年 10 月死于法国耶尔。他收藏了大约 2227 份贝叶手稿，其中有 932 篇诗歌作品。其中 911 篇由国家博物馆馆长 P. E. P. Deraniyagala 在 1953 年整理，并出版了三卷。其被列于斯里兰卡科伦坡国家博物馆手稿系列中。
④ 科伦坡国家博物馆图书馆收藏了 2400 多种手稿，并提供了相关的目录。佩拉德尼亚大学图书馆也有大量藏书，但缺少出版的目录。

量仪式知识和技能的载体及保管人。本文的重点是基于口头和贝叶经基础之上的知识机制的研究，这些机制使仪式专家群体能够一起执行驱魔和治疗的高度复杂的仪式，该岛的南部也因此而闻名。这种仪式的表演体现了非凡的知识和技能的融合，包括敲鼓、跳舞、喜剧表演、雕刻、唱歌、背诵和yantra（护身符）绘画，关于这些，我将在后面提供更多的信息。对于这种仪式传统而言，至关重要的是渴望尽可能忠实地再现每一个场合的行为、背诵、序列和表演。仪式之间有重复，今天执行的一种康复仪式与上周和前一周进行的基本上相同。在更大的范围内，重复发生在几代人的礼仪专家身上，每一位专家都运用他们的知识和技能，以便在不同的时间点创建相同的礼仪空间。

斯里兰卡仪式专家（aduro）及其在手稿传统方面的知识和技能

"Tovil 系统"引用了包括 Yak Tovils 在内的南方传统：Mahasona, Samayama, Sanni Yakuma, Rata Yakuma 和 Maha Kalu Kumare Samayama 以及 Shanti Karmaya 仪式：Suniyama, Deva Tovil, Gammaduva, Gara Yakuma 和 Bali Yage 以及不太复杂的 pidenis。Shanti Karmaya 仪式中提供的神灵优于 Yak Tovils 中的恶魔和神灵。在斯里兰卡，各种礼仪专家通过口头和手稿传统延续了大多数赞美各种神灵并招募魔鬼的传统仪式。Aduro 认为这些传统是从同一来源发展而来的，即大约3000年前印度人的 yage / homa 祭祀仪式。第一场 yage / homa 仪式是由来访的印度婆罗门在斯里兰卡表演的。关于仪式工作，居住在这些地区的 Aduro 社区保留的传统在具有独特宗教信仰的社会权力中心中得到了发展。Reed（2002）在康堤（Kandy）和 Simpson（1998）在加勒（Galle）工作时，他们的作品揭示了当代国家在乡村和低地传统之间的有趣差异。

Gurunanse 或首席仪式专家教他们的学生舞蹈、歌曲、面具姿势/舞蹈、咒语、面具雕刻、杂技、击鼓、阿育吠陀医学、仪式装饰品（gokkole）、喜剧对话、宇宙学/万神殿、诊断、占星术知识和治疗程序，以及所有"大师"的秘密。如此广泛的知识和技能，是通过师生关系系统代代相传的（Simpson, 1997：47）。[1]

Bali Tovil 或行星仪式中的手稿传统

在斯里兰卡，人们普遍相信，根据人的出生时间和地点，行星会对其产生好与坏的影响。在孩子出生时要做的第一件事就是占卜，以后在他（她）生活中所有重要的事情都要参考这个占卜结果。当一场灾难像一场严重的疾病降临到某人身上时，占卜结果不可避免地会被查阅，如果这个人受到了行星的不良影响，占星家会推荐某种供奉的仪式（De Silva, 2000 和 Kemper, 1979、1980）。这可能是一个小

---

[1] 在 Berava 仪式专家中，有正式的学徒制，其中有人声称是由特定的老师（aduro）教的。这种关系涉及一个男孩在老师家中的居住期，与老师的亲属关系，交换礼物和学生的终生债务。

的像切石灰仪式（dehi-käpīma）或一个大的 Bali 仪式，这取决于情况的严重程度。如果是 Bali 的仪式，他可能还会推荐适合这种仪式的特定类型的场合。占星术在斯里兰卡人生活的各个阶段都是很重要的，Bali Tovil 仪式（或行星仪式）[①]都是模仿占星术知识中关于行星的神力量（De Silva，2000）。

Bali Tovil 或行星仪式用来减轻由于经历了一个糟糕的占星期而导致的不幸或 apala kcālaya，意思为字面上的"无福期"。这些仪式的目的是在行星的保护薄弱且受到恶性影响而脆弱性相应较高的时候，为一个人祝福和强化。达到这一目的的方法是在一个通宵的仪式中向佛、神和魔献上无数的祭品。

Bali Tovil 传统中的大多数占星学知识都来自传统的古典教科书或手稿。[②]这里列出了十五种这样的文本：

（1）*Yagalankaraya*

（2）*Rathnalankaraya*

（3）*Posijanalankaraya*

（4）*Somigunaalankaraya*

（5）*Chandralankaraya*

（6）*Mahabali nidhanaya*

（7）*Wessanthara Mangallaya*（民间传说）

（8）*Subhasiri Mangallaya*

（9）*Ranakekulu Mangallaya*（最近在 Hatharaliyadda 发现）

（10）*Chandrawatharaya*（佛的颂歌）

（11）*Maha Sirasapadaya*（从头至脚的祝福歌）

（12）*Nawaguna Shanthiya*（祝福歌）

（13）*Maha Yamaka bandana Atakuru Sirasapadaya*

（14）*Lokarathna Malaya*

（15）*Daru Uthpaththiya*（Jinadasa，2009、2010）

这些教科书用僧伽罗语、巴利语和更多梵语混合编写而成。所依据的占星术的解释图和每个 Bali（图）的形成都在贝叶手稿中有相关的描述。这些 15 世纪的作品经常被联络人引用，为现今的 Bali Tovil 表演提供了背诵模式。

除此以外，还贴有众多的护身符（yantra）图表和占星术符号以及有关人员的详细信息。传统上，仪式专家（称为 Kattadiralas / Aduro）并未对贝叶经上的 yantra 绘画进行精心保存，因而我们所见的文化遗产是零散的。Aduro 是祭司，他们从事康复仪式和复仇仪式，同时也是民间艺术家，按照规定的规则准备相关的用具，并

---

① 在 Bali 的仪式中，行星的主要神灵（graha）被召唤和安抚，以抵御其邪恶的行星影响。在斯里兰卡，人们普遍相信行星对人的影响取决于出生的时间和地点（De Silva，2000）。

② Bali Tovil 被认为起源于佛陀时期的印度北部。联络人在交谈中揭示了仪式所唱诗中赋予仪式起源的事件的场所。无论 Bali 与这个特定地点和时间之间的实际历史联系如何，Bali 都具有悠久而成熟的佛教神话传统，赋予了 Bali 强大的合法性（Simpson，2004）。

通过祈祷和魔咒将其奉献给他们（Paul Wirz，1954；G. Obeyesekere，1969，1984；Kapferer，1983，1997；David Scott，1994 和 De Silva，2000）。"yantra"（护身符）一词源自梵语"yantr"，"去绑定"，源于"yam"，是宗教仪式中使用的神像、人物画像、图画或几何设计的总称。yantra 的模型出现在古代的贝叶手稿中。一些手稿已经彻底丢失了。其中一些形式是无法理解的，有些符号是无法识别的，因此，某些美学和哲学价值仍未得到解释。

根据 Peiris（2018）的说法，yantra 绘画构成了独特的艺术传统。这是对人类脆弱状况的承认，同时也证明了人们愿意为自己辩护；它是信仰的证明，就像所有仪式艺术一样，体现了人们渴望超越世俗。艺术表达了一种世界观，yantra 艺术也不例外。这些图纸与神话联系在一起，并通过它们与古代天文学、占星术、命理学和其他隐匿艺术联系在一起，形成了古代和中世纪世界中的形而上学思想体系。yantra 绘画具有保护和治愈性的目的，以及用于作为恩赐的护身符。它们还用于巫术（huniyam，kodivina）和反巫术仪式（suniyama）中，并为仪式专家执行巫术提供参考，并声称可以引导灵魂、伤害或消灭敌人，或充当保护性的仪式（Kapferer，1997）。

Yantra 提供各种图案和设计元素。Ananda Coomaraswamy 认为，僧伽罗（Sinhala）艺术比 19 世纪初在印度大陆上幸存的任何印度艺术都具有更多的印度早期艺术特征。他声称已经确定了僧伽罗艺术中的一些古老设计元素，这些元素与印度早期艺术中的埃及、亚述和希腊文化元素有关。他还确定了某些其他元素，他认为这些元素可能是从该岛上的前僧伽罗居民的艺术衍生出来的。Yantra 中的某些设计元素很可能是斯里兰卡本土的，但是只有在未来的比较研究中才能确定这一点（Coomaraswamy，2003）。祭司的贝叶刻本可能包含这方面的有用信息，因为某些仪式起源于很早的时期。最有可能进行富有成果的研究领域将是泥土图像、叶子祭坛和叶屏风的表现形式，它们是远古时代最早的肖像和仪式装饰形式的直系后裔，主要用于植物繁殖仪式中对树木神灵的调和。

根据 Peiris（2018）的说法，尽管我们从印度借来了许多文化元素，但它们在改编过程中得以改变并重新诠释。一些零散的人物通过对非理性、潜意识和梦想的探索暗示了超现实主义。失真和其他表现主义特征很突出。这一类的绘画作品在潜意识层面上起作用，并具有使人惊讶的能力。有些形式看起来像精神病艺术，是精神健康破裂状态的产物。这位画家在描述人类与死亡的斗争，以及与现实竞争时，创造了自己的宇宙。

除了我之前已经讨论过的贝叶绘画外，还有一些以贝叶传统文学书写的仪式诗，这些诗在斯里兰卡的 Bali Tovil 体系中被进行仪式性的吟诵（De Silva 2000）。根据 Kapferer（1983）的说法，仪式中使用了五种不同的诗歌。"Asirivada kavi 将神话与魔鬼的关系联系起来，并赞扬它们的力量以及神灵的力量；Ambun kavi 讲述了如何制作祭篮和其他仪式用品；Yadini kavi 基本上与 Asirivada kavi 相似，讲述了祖先和恶魔的起源；Atacona kavi 从八个方向召唤恶魔；Sirasapada（从头到脚）kavi 主要是治愈性的，唱歌能从患者身上祛除疾病。"（Kapferer，1983：198）。Kannalauva（召唤经文）与祝福的 kavis-verses 具有积极的保护作用。Kannalauva 是针对居住在"其他世界"中的超自然人而进行的，目的是吸引他们的注意力。应该注意的是，在 Tovil 仪式的任何供奉行为开始时，会经常引用 kannalauva 经文，就像在献祭之前一定要引起超自然者的注意一样。在整个 Bali Tovil 祭祀仪式中，引用的诗歌和歌曲以及在斯里兰卡南部进行的治疗中，描述了众神传给远古圣贤（reśi）的物品，例如金黄色的捣蛋器、镶有珠宝的公鸡、十六英里长的鼓。不用说，使用这些物体现实中的对应物进行的仪式，并不像它们所遭遇的令人难以置信的事件那样有效。

在我之前列出的十五份仪式文本中，描述了相关的准备工作、供奉的盘子的结构和仪式方式的广泛细节。在这方面至关重要，也是 Bali 仪式的核心，这是一个植物祭坛（mal baliya），其中包含 9、25 或 81 个正方形，分别放置有行星、各种其他神灵和恶魔的祭物。例如，Hugh Nevill（1956）科伦坡国家博物馆的收藏——Sinhala kavi Vols Ⅰ、Ⅱ & Ⅲ，使用声称已超过 200 年的贝叶手稿的诗词翻译，为我们提供了以下描述：祭坛由车前草茎、一个肘尺和四个手指宽度的正方形以及围绕它的正方形围栏组成。祭品有九种叶子、九种颜色的米饭、九种花、槟榔叶和九种祭品。九色米饭代表十二个 rasi 或黄道十二宫，颜色有红色、白色、黄色、灰色、黑色、蓝色、金色和蓝黑色。行星祭品应按其特殊方向放置。

诸如此类的谨慎而详细的处方被认为是古代印度圣人所制定的处方。在神圣的启示下，rei 也被称为婆罗门（bamuno）和"古代教师"（poranäduro）首先做出这些祭品，并将这些仪轨传递给他们的后代，作为对抗苦难的手段。上面相关的故事讲的是植物坛的起源（mal baliya）。但是，还有另一组故事讲述了许多大型 Bali 仪式中建造的泥塑图像的起源。按照先哲们的启示，他们认为其是以诗歌和故事的形式流传下来的，主要是以口头的方式传播，然后是以贝叶的书写方式传播，相信现在的受害者是可以被治愈的。

结　论

贝叶是世界上最早的书写载体之一，距今已有两千多年的历史，最早出现在公元前 5 世纪。这些手稿主要分布在南亚和东南亚，包括南印度、尼泊尔、斯里兰卡、缅甸、泰国、印度尼西亚、柬埔寨，它们不仅用作文字信息的载体，而且还用作艺术品、保护性护身符和宗教用品、礼物、礼拜对象。尽管大量的贝叶手稿是宗教和仪式文本，但它们还涵盖了天文学、艺术、建筑、医学和数学等主题。大约在 5 世纪，随着书面文本逐渐取代世界各地的口头传统，贝叶手稿的产出也有所增长。18 世纪开始，贝叶手稿迅速衰落，因为手工纸取代了贝叶作为书写介质。19 世纪，印刷机广泛使用，手抄本几乎过时了。贝叶手稿虽然不再普遍使用，但在塑造当代历史和文化方面继续发挥积极作用，并揭示有关斯里兰卡过去文化和宗教的重要信息。贝叶手稿的存在为斯里兰卡的文化、宗教、政治和知识史带来了重要的启示，它是我们历史的宝贵产物，对此类知识的保存刻不容缓。

本文研究了斯里兰卡贝叶传统中所呈现的仪式知识及其技巧的性质，特别是保留在民间的传统。当代的仪式表演者或 Aduro 通过特定的老师讲授来主张其合法性，这样，表演者的知识和技能就可以被称为 paramparāva 的谱系或以谱系的形式追溯。在这种表演中，仪式表演易于表现出万花筒的特征，将不同层面上的知识、技能和能力结合在一起，在斯里兰卡等国家创造独特的仪式传统。

貝叶文化与区域文化遗产传承保护

对傣泰族群佛教手稿文化的
传承与保护的一些考察

David Wharton[①] 文　李小辉[②] 译

傣泰族群手稿文化的持续危机和消失

　　20世纪上半叶以来，傣泰族群[③]手稿文化（Tai manuscript cultures）日渐式微，面临生存危机。除了在部分傣泰族群之中，这一传统不太可能再世代相传。傣族目前正致力于保护和复兴他们传统文化的民间运动，对他们来说，手稿文化传统仍然是其文化身份的重要特征。对于大多数傣泰族群，当然也包括泰国和老挝的，情况不再如此，[④]他们的手稿文化很可能会消失，而那些幸存下来的手稿将会被保存在国家或大学图书馆等主要馆藏中，而非如传统上将之存于寺庙里。

　　在我接受泰国山林派僧侣的训练期间，我被教导要尊重佛经典籍，不能把它们放在地板上，而应放在一个较高的位置。今天，我们经常看到一些杂乱的手稿如垃圾一般被丢弃在寺庙满是灰尘的地板上，这些代代相传的文化遗产现在被如此不尊重地对待，真是可悲。而看到整个地区寺庙里的僧人对佛陀的典籍如此不尊重，更为可叹。这是一个不幸的迹象，表明整个系统对曾经是傣泰文化根基和受人尊敬的特征的无知和忽视。我经常听到他们的借口，比如，"哦，僧人们通常不怎么读手稿了"，但这并不能作为手稿文化遗失的借口。对保护手稿文化，我们应该做得更好。总的来说，作为当地主要藏书者的僧侣和俗人的手稿文化保护工作做得极其欠缺，而我们忽视了其可能带来的严重后果。

　　这一严峻的评估来自我在老挝、泰国北部、缅甸北部和中国西南地区从事傣泰族群手稿收藏工作15年多的经验，同时我还在老挝国家图书馆工作过，并在帕绍大学（University of Passau）攻读过博士学位。以前我参与过的一些大型调查项目，如在泰国北部和老挝进行的，[⑤]也可以作为一条基线来评估这些地区手稿退化和丢失的程度。我将以泰国北部为主要的例子，因为这是我拥有第一手经验的地区，也是

[①] 作者为法国远东学院研究员，老挝国家图书馆"贝叶经数字图书馆"项目负责人。
[②] 译者为云南大学民族学与社会学学院2018级宗教学专业硕士研究生。
[③] 主要指中国、泰国、老挝等东南亚国家的傣族和泰族。
[④] 当然，也有相反的例子，贝叶经文化在当地的领导下得以延续，但我在这里说的是整个地区傣族社会的全貌。
[⑤] 其中，清迈大学保存泰国北部贝叶经项目（1987—1991年）和老挝国家图书馆保存老挝贝叶经项目（1992—2004年）是最大的。

清迈大学保存泰国北部贝叶经项目（1987—1991年）收录了大约120座寺庙的手稿的地方。从2013年开始，在当地大量的实地考察中，我目睹了所有手稿由于火灾、受潮而失去原貌，或是被白蚁、啮齿动物啃噬而破坏严重，很多手稿上覆盖着灰尘与鸟类、蝙蝠和老鼠的粪便，品相损毁已经相当严重，这些只是显性的"消失"，而一些未被人觉察的隐性消失也会发生在当地僧人和俗人的造作之中，例如已有相当多的手稿被贩卖。我参观过一个寺庙，一个僧人在那里卖手稿和储存手稿的箱子，当地人通知警察时，他已经离开。在过去30年里，①在泰国北部进行的调查中，据我估计，有多达50%的手稿可能已经佚失。我希望我的估算是错误的，希望真实的数字要少一些，然而这是我基于多年来对泰国最北端8个省每个省诸多寺庙的访问情况而得出的实际评估。在老挝，我们多年来一直试图获得资金，以便对20世纪90年代编目的收藏品进行系统的再调查，以揭示其损失的程度。这一趋势还在迅速发展，最近我听说，在泰国北部和老挝的许多地区的手稿收藏被偷了，储藏箱被丢弃在路边，因为窃贼对出售储藏箱不感兴趣。2019年年底，我们发现万象一座大寺庙的全部手稿收藏已经"消失不见"。傣泰族群文化遗产的这一宝贵财富正在被大量破坏。

　　这并不是要批评以前的保护项目。相反，它们非常成功，得到了应有的赞扬。但现实是，没有任何一个外部资助的项目能够在有限的时间内为这场危机提供一个可持续的长期解决方案。②当时进行这一项目我们制定了一个原则，就是把手稿保留在原处（即使有迹象表明它们在当地得不到保护），也不应把它们移走以妥善保管。显然上述手稿遗失的情状也是有些始料不及的意外和不可预见的结果。

迫切需要研究"贝叶经文化"而不是"贝叶经"

　　令我感到鼓舞的是，这次研讨会的主题是"手稿文化"，而不仅仅是"手稿"本身。我指的是会议主题是关于"手稿"的一切，从棕榈叶或纸支架的制作到贝叶经的制作和使用，也包括习诵的传统等等。几十年来，整个地区的手稿文化在很多方面都受到了威胁，使他们抄写的贝叶经得不到传播。事实上，这一过程始于印刷书籍的出现，远早于电视和互联网等现代电子媒体的出现，而这些电子媒体的出现又加速了书籍的衰落。在一些地区，数字手稿也供现代使用，这对传统手稿的使用产生了负面影响。因此，重要的是要记住，手稿是构成区域本土文化本身的重要部分，而它们正处于危机之中。电子媒体的出现直接导致并加剧了对传统手稿保护的忽视。当然，这些都是我们的力量无法控制的。我认识的人当中，没有人建议我们不使用互联网而回到听读背诵手稿的日子。但这是一种不公平的竞争，导致了手稿这种载体将在与现代科技传播媒介的竞争中逐渐消失。

---

①　真正的数字只有在使用以前的记录作为基线进行彻底调查后才能知道。
②　换句话说，除非它是一个简单地收集手稿以保存在其他地方的项目，在这里并没有被提议，而且无论如何只会加速当地手稿文化的消失。

贝叶文化与区域文化遗产传承保护

多年来，一直有调查、编目和数字化手稿的项目，但它们所涉及的相关文化却很少受到关注。与此同时，当地的手稿文化消失的速度甚至比手稿本身还要快。也只有这样关注整个贝叶文化/手稿文化的范畴，我们才能从一个地方的角度来真正理解这些贝叶经/手稿。那么，有办法保持和促进手稿文化吗？或者至少在它们消失之前记录下来。

我自己在老挝国家图书馆的大部分工作也集中于在大型寺院数字化其收藏的手稿，以及通过数字图书馆将它们放到网上。但与此同时，在过去的十年中，设计项目是集成音频、视听文档传统的概览和手稿的视觉文化的其他方面而发展出来的在线存储库手稿文化，而不是单独的手稿。除了保护濒危手稿文化的数字记录，研究结果还可以将这些传统知识及技能用于教学和研究。此外，在许多在线手稿收藏中发现的前现代脚本已不再日常使用，允许用户在观看数字图像时听录音将极大地帮助文本的研究和学习阅读脚本。我相信，每当一个项目被设计或资助来只对贝叶经进行数字化时，我们都失去了一个宝贵的机会，往往涉及重要的相关计划安排和与当地古籍持有者的会晤，而这些古籍持有者的知识和阅读技能都没有记录下来。因此，虽然手稿数字化是非常有价值的，我还是强烈建议手稿文化应该包含上述对古籍持有者知识和技能的记录，并将之作为数字化手稿项目的一个组成部分。

谁来传承？

本次研讨会的题目是关于手稿文化的"传承与保护"，但这似乎回避了一个问题："谁来传承？"

在过去的五六百年里，当地的学者和抄写者，僧人和俗人都保留了傣泰族群的手稿文化，但正如上文所述，当前这种地方关怀和责任的缺失对无数手稿收藏及其相关文化的生存与否产生了巨大的影响。那么谁应该来传承它们呢？当然有些是私人拥有的，它们被家庭中的年青一代传承，他们有时会传承得很好，但更多的情况通常是没什么兴趣。在这种情况下，新传承人显然可以随心所欲地处置它们，其中可能包括故意销毁、出售或让它们因无人照管而损毁腐烂。可能有关于保护文化遗产（其中也包括这些私人物品）的法律，但在这种情况下，它们似乎很少得到执行。当然，在寺庙收藏中，情况应该大不相同，僧侣是手稿的保管人（而不是所有者）。这很重要，因为他们没有权利出售或销毁寺庙里的手稿。与此同时，僧侣在其寺庙藏经阁中保管手稿的责任并没有得到明确的界定或执行，那些忽视手稿以至于将其销毁的人再一次不承担任何后果。这是一个不幸的情况，因为在过去，僧人在保护手稿方面强有力的措施可以对手稿的保护产生巨大的影响。然而，在今天的多数情况下，僧人连寺院普通的工作都难以做好，更不用说去保护他们从未使用过的手稿了，而且他们显然对这些贝叶经缺乏兴趣或耐心。

其他利益相关者包括负责文化遗产的政府部门、国家或地方图书馆、大学，当然还有一些海外在线馆藏数字化手稿的国际项目，这些项目往往没有试图解决当地的此类问题。这里的根本问题是，实际上没有人承担责任。当然，公平地说，没有人要求当地的保管人如僧人和世俗的主管机构，正式授权他们保管这些手稿。他们继承了这些收藏品，作为当地寺产的一部分，但没有明确了解这意味着什么，也没有承担责任所需的知识。一些手稿的保存工作中已经包含了努力训练当地的僧侣和俗人，但结果大多是短暂的，没有制度或设备来维持这样的工作。

在这里，"保护"是什么意思？

"保护"这个词也出现在这次研讨会的标题中，在这里它是什么意思呢？我们是在保护什么，保护谁？保护是否意味着保护和保存工作，使手稿得到安全的保存？不幸的是，正如上面概述的，这是一个正在进行的任务，而不是在一个有限的项目时间框架内完成的任务。它永远不会完成。即使在大规模、长期的手稿保存计划取得成功的地方，如泰国北部和老挝，资金和项目工作也有终止之时。当我们持续评估他们的成功时，很明显，即使他们取得了很大的成就，他们也只能暂时缓解对持续承诺的需要。我参观过许多书库，当地管理员怀着美好的愿望认为，保护手稿的最佳方式是锁上书库的门，但几年后才发现，大部分藏书都被白蚁吃掉了。

那么，当当地的僧人或世俗的所有者不保管（或不知道如何保管）他们的手稿时，该怎么办？泰国和老挝北部的政策从未从他们的立场把手稿保存工作和培训当地托管人的手稿保存看做一项非常专业的工作。在过去的25至30年中虽有世代交替的托管人训练，但仍有成千上万的手稿已经丢失。在我参观过的许多寺庙中，我怀疑任何额外的培训是否会有所帮助。但是，当地的僧人和负责寺院事务管理的俗人因疏忽导致丢失手稿时又该怎么办？总的来说，这个问题被完全忽视了，但它是造成手稿退化和丢失的主要原因。那么，是否存在这样的情况，手稿应该被移走，并由其他保管人保管（也许是能使其保存完好的方式）？这些问题没有简单的答案，但如果我们试图阻止手稿丢失的趋势，这些问题确实需要考虑。不幸的是，即使是周期性的外部资金支持开展的手稿保护项目被证明也难以使手稿得到长期性保存。

未来保护工作的综合模式

上述问题没有简单的答案，需要在各自的范围内寻求当地的解决办法。但有一些关键的教训和现状特点，可能有助于使未来的保存工作更全面。

首先，我们必须停止仅仅局限于手稿数字化的狭隘范围内的思考，并努力将手稿文化纳入其中。我们必须认识到，手稿是当地丰富的无形文化的一部分，它消失的速度甚至比手稿本身还要快。当在实地工作时，这样的手稿文献本身是非常有益的，而且比单调地触发相机快门将数千帧手稿图像数字化有趣得多。丰富我们对手稿本身的理解，记录它们的背诵风格等也是很重要的。然而，它并不是绝大多数手稿数字化项目的组成部分。

其次，广泛的手稿文化调查和编目是保存它们的一个潜在的重要工具，最好是

贝叶文化与区域文化遗产传承保护

由国家图书馆等机构维护的国家或省级数据库进行这项工作。没有这样的记录，也就没有采取适当行动的基础。例如，老挝国家图书馆计划重新调查全国各地的手稿收藏，使用25年前采录的目录（约8.6万份手稿）作为基准，以揭示这一时期手稿丢失的程度。现有的目录仅限于手稿收藏，但新的数据将成为更全面的"全国贝叶经文化数据库"的一部分。这将建立在现有的手稿目录数据，包括保护和保存数据（需要解决的问题，在过时的摄影记录及存储条件下，手稿退化和丧失的原因等），微型拍摄或记录数字化，仍在制作和使用的手稿的记录，以及如何联系本地资源人的细节。在中国云南省和泰国北部都对傣文手稿进行了大规模的调查，目前缅甸掸邦也在开展类似的调查。这些可以用类似的方式来记录，以利于努力为后代保护手稿文化，并促进他们的研究。

再次，应该重新评估我们对有时限项目的外部资金的依赖。在过去的四年里，我在缅甸的掸邦见证了一种非常不同的方式。那里有一个由僧人和抄写员组成的网络，他们在没有外部项目资金支持的情况下坚持从事手稿调查、编目和保存工作。之所以能这样，是因为它是由受人尊敬的高级僧人所倡导的，他们激发了人们对傣族手稿文化的尊重和自豪感，并提供了所需的地方资金和志愿者支持。虽然我非常欣赏这种模式，但我被告知，这种模式在其他地方几乎没有成功的机会。也许是我孤陋寡闻，但确实没听说或知悉在掸邦以外有任何高级别僧人显示出对保护他们的手稿文化有类似的兴趣。与此同时，必须承认的是，在一些国家有非常富有的寺庙，如果他们的一部分资金可以用于这样的工作——记住，手稿大部分也储存在寺庙里——那么这将是非常有益的。过去，类似的复兴手稿文化的地方性运动在泰国北部和该地区的其他地方取得了成功，但目前的趋势是依靠外部资金进行有时间限制的项目，很少有当地寺庙社区的直接参与。虽然可能无法大规模进行，但我仍希望能有一些僧人和寺庙有兴趣，并能得到鼓励和支持来保护手稿，促进手稿文化。但这不会是普遍的，当然将取决于这些僧人能否持续倡导。否则，任何全面的努力将需要地方官员与国家或省级机构（如政府部门、国家图书馆和大学）之间的合作，建立内部资源来管理大型项目，以维护手稿文化的保护合作，这与当前的仅外部资助小型项目以数字化海外在线收藏手稿的趋势相吻合。

最后，我们还必须回答以下问题：谁是手稿的保管者？他们的责任是什么？这还需要解决一个难题，即在当地保管人疏忽导致贝叶经和其他手稿丢失的情况下，就地保存是否可行。这并不容易，因为就地保护必须始终是第一选择。但过去30年的经验表明，在许多情况下，它已经失败，并将继续失败。一个相关的问题是，谁将做出这样的决定？希望来自调查的确凿证据能揭示出原稿遗失的程度（如计划在老挝进行的调查），这将激发关于未来制定保存傣文手稿文化的政策和实践的国家层面的进一步辩论。

结　论

　　以上对傣语手稿文化所面临的危机的描述可能确不令人愉快。但我强烈认为，我们需要提高人们对其严重性的认识。如果我们要解决这个问题，就必须立即采取行动。然后，我们可能会做出明智的决定，以最好的方式进行。似乎不可避免的是，除了个别情况，许多傣泰族群地区的傣文手稿文化将在这一代或下一代中大量消失。因此，我们能做的就是努力通过现代化的各种形式进行手稿保护工作（如在掸邦和其他地方），并尽我们所能来记录手稿文化的其他方面。我们仍有机会通过手稿数字化和视听录音这样的方式来抢救保护它。目前由海外资金和机构主导的努力，主要集中在为他们的在线收藏进行小规模的手稿数字化，这些努力既不是为解决这一危机而设计的，也没有声称正在解决这一危机。没有简单的标准答案，它们会依不同的本土环境而有所不同。但如果我们选择不采取行动，只是让目前的忽视趋势顺其自然，那么在一代人之内就不会再有这样做的机会。我希望这篇论文将有助于激发对这一宝贵遗产进行及时保护的思考，以及我们保护和保存它的合作行动。

贝叶经与西双版纳傣族的赕

——基于M村的田野调查

郭 山[①]

M村位于西双版纳州勐海县县城至澜沧县的214国道东侧，隶属勐遮镇景真村委会。截至2019年11月，有68户359人，除汉族7人、布朗族4人外，其余均为傣族，是一个标准的傣族村寨。2014年，村寨佛寺修缮完成，经书得到了更加有序的保存、保管。

一、M村佛寺所藏贝叶经的基本状况

据记载，过去"贝叶经的成文经本主要有叶质形和纸质形两种形式。叶质形一类是真正的贝叶经，傣语称'坦兰'。其规格有每页四行式、五行式、六行式和八行式等四种，前三种规格是贝叶经本最普遍的规格。纸质形一类是指绵纸经书，傣语称'薄嘎腊沙'。而规格有宽面页式和连折叠式两种，其中以宽面页式最为普遍"。[②]

根据笔者2019年11月在M村的田野调查，对于目前M村佛寺所收藏的经书，经过整理，笔者从以下几个方面来进行描述：

从材质上看，叶质形刻本的规格依然以每页四行式、五行式、六行式为主，纸质形经本的规格以宽面页式最为普遍，但数量已经远远多于叶质形刻本。并且，纸质形经本除传统的绵纸手抄经本、连折叠式经本外，出现了16开复印纸手抄经本、印刷折叠经本、印刷经本、复印手抄经本和复印印刷经本等多种形式。

从数量上看，可以分为以下七类，分别是：①叶质形刻本44部（函）；②绵纸手抄经本780余册；③手抄折叠经本22册；④印刷折叠经本66册；⑤印刷书籍形经本45册；⑥复印手抄经本38册；⑦复印印刷经本64册，共计一千余部（册）。

从时间上看，叶质形刻本中有15部（函）刻写于20世纪80年代（即改革开放）以前，绵纸手抄经本有240余册抄写于20世纪80年代之前。其余各类经本都

[①] 作者为云南大学教授，博士。
[②] 秦家华，周娅.贝叶文化论集.昆明：云南大学出版社，2004：12.

是改革开放以后制作、抄写的。

从内容上看，叶质形刻本中以"三藏经"（傣语称"三毕达迦"）、佛本生经（以《维先达腊》为代表）最为丰富。其中，"三藏经"7部，《维先达腊》6部，另外还有《涅槃经》（傣语称"涅帕那素"）、《波罗蜜经》（包含十波罗蜜、千句波罗蜜、十万波罗蜜等多部）、《念诵经》（玛哈巴坦、玛哈摩萨），等等；绵纸手抄经本中除包含上述叶质形刻本的内容外，以《佛本生故事经》最为丰富。另外，还有《清净论》（傣语称"维苏提雅"）、《生辰经》（坦木栽达）、《驱邪经》（罗迦乌提）、《念诵经》（玛哈巴坦、尊达素嘎里打素）、《教育经》（坦麻莱双罗），等等。

值得一提的是，除了传统的贝叶刻本和手抄绵纸经本外，现代印刷出版的南传上座部佛教典籍已经进入村寨佛寺，并逐步为人们所喜爱，M村佛寺大佛爷告诉笔者，诵读印刷的经本比较"省眼睛"，意思是印刷体的经本在诵读时比较好辨认，因此更容易识读，也更受人欢迎。

二、从"素栽达"看贝叶经在赕仪式中的地位

在当地傣族的语汇中，"素"的发音为"she-m"，其意思相当于洗礼、自省、内化、完善，他们说："就是一块石头，如果你每天'素'它，日久天长也会变成宝。""素"这个行为在日常生活中非常重要，傣族人一生都想着"素"。它在《傣汉字典》中的解释是"对八字做功德，使生命更长久"。而大佛爷给出的解释是"继续、接续"之意。"栽达"是巴利语，意思是生命，或称一个人一出生就带来的东西。"素栽达"的字面意思就是延续生命，使得生命能一帆风顺，什么都好。在他们眼中，世上的东西都有各自特定的这种生命。生下来的人有这种生命，组建的家庭有这种生命，修建起来的房屋也有这种生命，包括寨子、佛寺等也都有这种生命，总之，一切东西生产出来时都有这种生命，而有生命的东西在整个成长过程中，或随着时间的流逝，难免会有走偏的情况，于是要对其进行整理、修正，才可能让它继续成长得（或称走得）正确、顺利。每个人从出生到死亡都有各自的生命历程，人们相信这就是这种生命在左右着的表现，所以用"命中注定"来解释个人的生命事件。当某个人日常的生命足迹与命定的生命历程相吻合时，这个人的人生之路就"走得正，走得好"，否则就会出问题。于是人活一生就要时常进行修正、纠偏，赕"素栽达"就是进行这种修正、纠偏的仪式。经常纠偏能保证一个人更好地成长，不入歧途、不走邪路。因此，有对个人的赕，称"素栽达滚"；有对家庭的赕，称"素栽达很"；有对寨子的赕，称"素栽达曼"；有对佛寺的赕，称"素栽达瓦"；等等。于是，这个仪式在傣寨中比较频繁，尤其是人口数量大、家庭户多的寨子，在开门节后几乎每周都会举行。

笔者于2019年11月田野调查时参与观察的赕"素栽达很"仪式过程如下：

此次是赕"素栽达很"，也就是对家庭的赕。赕者是岩光夫妻及他们的儿子岩

香、儿媳玉光叫一家四人。仪式开始前，岩香已经将场地布置好。三副竹架顺序放置在长方形屋子的中央靠前部，后部放置着一个盆及一些小食品。

参加仪式的人每人带着一对蜡条、帕巾和一点祝福礼钱来到主人（赕者）家，进屋后将这些物品放在事先主人家已经准备好的一个盆中，然后找个地方坐下。坐的顺序为男性在前女性在后，老者在前年轻者在后。参加者都是已经达到"凹星"年龄的老年人。被访者告诉笔者，这些已经开始"凹星"的老年人能给主人家带来福气。

下午2:00，仪式准备开始，大佛爷手执佛扇面对大家坐于竹架前部，布章、康朗们分坐在两侧，他们的面前放着一个茶盘和一个篾桌，茶盘中放着少许蜡条、帕巾和一对燃着的蜡烛，篾桌上放着蜡条、帕巾、水果等。岩香已经将仪式用的白线"Maisu-mong"[①]（买素勐）从搭系于大佛爷面前的蜡烛、贝叶经等物的一端慢慢牵引出，先在竹架上绕几圈，然后将白线引到大门外。这样，从大佛爷手中引出的长长的白线就将屋内和屋外连在一起了。

一切就绪，布章宣布今天岩光一家的"素栽达"现在开始。首先由布章带领大家先向大佛爷礼拜，傣语称"su-ma-da-la"（苏麻达拉），然后，布章向大佛爷"gao-wen-dan"（告温挡），大意是说明今天是岩光一家为家庭而做的赕，他希望全家人能身体健康、诸事顺利，请大佛爷给予帮助等。布章念一段，大家跟念一段。念毕，大佛爷手持白线开始诵吉祥经《芒格拉》。开始时，大佛爷诵一段，大家跟着诵一段。然后是大佛爷一个人诵，大家听。诵毕，大佛爷、布章与两位康朗商量今天赕的五部经书《迪巴芒达素》《罗迦乌提》《三松细典》《雅尼》和《栽雅桑迦哈》的念诵人。分配完经书后，大佛爷开始诵第一部经。满屋的人都在安静地听，在中间一些段落处，坐在后面的咩涛会取米花向天空方向抛撒，大家齐声欢呼。待大佛爷诵完后，布章和两个康朗分别念诵各自拿在手上的经。在这个过程中，大佛爷会用竹条蘸银盆中的水向众人点撒。竹架子上的蜡条火不能熄灭。一位康朗带几根蜡条、一点钱从现场出去，把这些东西弄到屋外远处，表示已经把家里不好的东西驱出家庭、留置远处了。

待上述五部经书都诵毕，大家全体欢呼，并向天空撒米花。岩香将竹架上的买素勐白线拆下收好，同时将竹架也收拢。

接下来是"ya-nanm"（雅喃），即请大佛爷为岩光一家人诵经、滴水。此时，岩光一家人围拢坐于大佛爷、布章面前，并在自己的面前燃起蜡条，布章先向大佛爷"gao-wen-dan"（告温挡），然后大佛爷诵祝福语，大意是说：今天是岩光一家为自己的家庭做"shem-zai-da"赕，我们点上蜡条，滴下清水，请天上的神（diu-wa-la）和地下的神（nang-tuo-la-ni）记住我们赕的物品，请千万帮助把这些赕品送到应该去的地方。我们知道这些物品要经过千山万水才能到达要去的地方，请众神

[①] 大佛爷专用的白线团，平时存放在佛寺中，在为赕者做赕、避祸求福等仪式中使用。

帮助，让这些赕品掉到水里时也不丢失，掉到火中也不熔化，最终都能好好送到应该去的地方。同时，也求佛祖能让这些愿望都实现。最后，大佛爷诵《回向经》，此时，岩光一家人轮流将清水滴入盆中。诵经接近尾声时，众人集体跟随大佛爷诵一段经。此时布章站起身来，手执钵盂在屋内走着向众人洒水，象征大家共同沐浴佛的甘霖。在布章诵经过程中，屋外燃放鞭炮，象征将所有的邪气、晦事驱赶得烟消云散。

滴水完毕，大佛爷为岩光夫妻及儿子岩香夫妻四个人——拴线。至此，整个仪式结束。历时约3小时。

仪式结束后，大佛爷、布章和老人们就在楼上用餐，其余的人都去楼下吃饭。儿子岩香则将竹架送到村寨佛寺内的大青树下放置。今天赕的五部经书，除《三松细典》要置于主人家的供台上留存外，其余的戒律经《迪巴芒达素》和驱邪经《罗迦乌提》《雅尼》和《栽雅桑迦哈》四部经书都将赕到佛寺中留存。

西双版纳南传上座部佛教在民众中形成的功德积累的"嘎木"观念①决定了赕仪式供奉的赕品是与神佛的一次交换。赕或做赕——献出祭物——象征着献给神佛的礼物，当神佛收到这份"心拥有的礼物"（而非"手拥有的礼物"）后，②就会增加做仪式的人家好的"嘎木"，使其获得庇佑。正如利奇所说的，赕仪式使"献祭者在神界与人界之间架设了一座桥梁，神的能力通过桥梁能够通达到献祭者本人"。③村民们都清楚，获得福报的多少取决于献祭者赕的质与量，也就是功德的多少。村民说："做赕是为了下辈子好吃好在……一个人有这辈子，也有下辈子，这辈子过得好坏，自己还管得住（即能靠自己现实的理性行动来左右），而下辈子过得好坏，自己就无法左右了，只能靠神佛的护佑。而神佛的护佑又取决于这辈子做的赕，如果不在这辈子把赕做好，自己下辈子就不好吃不好在了。""赕多少要看自己，反正多赕多得，少赕少得，不赕嘛就什么也没有了。"对于赕者，做赕和供奉的赕品对自己的一生有着重要的意义，它涉及自己的声誉和社会地位。通过做赕，赕者的行为受到全体社会成员的评判，从而获得声誉，使村落的成员具有了更亲密的感情，重新整理或获得了新的社会关系。

从整个仪式过程可见，赕的过程，事实上是一个在经过布置的、有仪式感的空间中由大佛爷、布章和康朗向赕者、共同参与者诵经的过程。在此空间下，大佛爷、布章和康朗是老师，他们是傣族人心目中有地位的知识分子，是村寨里当然的教育者。赕者是受教育者，在仪式活动中经历一个反省自身既往行为、调整自己今

---

① 在西双版纳傣族的阐释中，"嘎木"由一个人过去的全部所为、所言、所想而生。依据佛教道德对善（功德）与恶（不善）计算之后，如余额为善，则产生好的"嘎木"，相反，则产生坏的"嘎木"。参见谭乐山. 南传上座部佛教与傣族村社经济——对中国西南西双版纳的比较研究. 赵效牛，译. 昆明：云南大学出版社，2005：72。
② 利奇在研究缅甸高地克钦社会结构时看到，克钦人在对待财产和所有权这类事情上会很清楚地区分"心拥有的礼物"和"手拥有的礼物"，前者在经济上是无用之物，但仍然使收受者对给予者负有义务。参见［英］埃德蒙·利奇. 缅甸高地诸政治体系. 杨春宇，周歆红，译. 北京：商务印书馆，2010：139。
③ ［英］埃得蒙·利奇. 文化与交流. 郭凡，邹和，译. 上海：上海人民出版社，2000：83—86。

后行为的过程。对于共同参与者，是一个受教育的过程。而这堂课所使用的教材，就是此次赕的贝叶经。正是在这个意义上，"和尚们向村民讲述的经文及其引申的故事，使乡村寺庙成为人民道德的课堂……佛教僧人的教化作用让佛教农村社会的精神生活同道德教育、娱乐活动以至感情交流不可分地融合为一体"。①

三、傣族日常生活仪式中常用的贝叶经

在当地傣族的日常生活中，赕是一项重要的仪式活动，而贝叶经在这些仪式活动中几乎是不可或缺的。据M村佛寺的大佛爷、本村布章和康朗所述，笔者将各种仪式所涉及和用到的贝叶经略记如下：

（1）赕逝者时用的经书：引路经《玛哈巴汤》《叠娃肚党当哈》，"三藏经"《三毕达咖》（Sam Bittaka），波罗蜜经《巴腊密》（Palami）、《维苏提雅》（Vissuthiya）、《爷竜》（Yelong，汉语译为"大仓库"），佛本生故事经《色提送号》（Setthi Songkhao，汉语译为"富翁送饭的故事"），涅槃经《尼八拿素》（Nippannasut）、《叠娃当哈》（Devadut Tangha）、《玛哈维娃》（Maha Vibak，又作《摩诃维拔》，汉语译为"大果报"）、《阿尼松》（Anisong Katamboonyak）和《甘纳瓦迪纳管》（Kannakavati）等。

（2）赕未来（即赕玛哈邦）时用的经书：佛本生故事《维先达腊》是必需的，"三藏经"（苏滇达、维奈、阿皮达玛）、故事经《麻莱》《迭迷牙贡曼》《麻贺萨塔》《麻哈维拨欢》《爷竜》、驱邪经《罗迦乌提》、波罗蜜经《巴腊密先果》《巴腊密板降》、戒律经《迪巴门打素》等。

（3）赕"素栽达"时用的经书：《雅尼》，用于赕房子（素栽达很）时，据说念诵它可以赶走鬼、蛇等不好的东西；《三松细典》；《栽雅桑迦哈》（也称"布塔滚竜"），人们认为鬼神比较怕它，因此念诵它可以赶走鬼神；戒律经《迪巴芒达素》《罗迦乌提》，在赕家时要用。

（4）赕生辰（豪乌咋）时用的经书：结合赕者个人的生辰情况（栽达），从传统三藏典籍中抄录佛语"编写"供其使用的"经书"。

（5）赕塔时：念诵《典达塔》《喃欢毫》。后者用于求谷神奶奶。

四、结论

M村佛寺的这些经书都是本村傣族信众的赕品，每一次赕都为村寨佛寺积累下几部经书，日积月累就形成了现有的存量。在笔者驻村访谈时，村民们表示，大多数信众都不能识、读这些经，但当佛爷、布章一诵读，他们就知道其中的基本内容，并能跟随着诵读。当问及读不懂为什么还要赕这些经书时，他们很明确地回答说这是傣家人的习俗。当问及既然村民们读不懂，怎么知道什么仪式应该赕哪部贝

---

① 宋立道.传统与现代——变化中的南传上座部佛教世界.北京：中国社科出版社，2002：45。

叶经书时，村民们的回答是可以通过询问布章或康朗而知晓。赕者赕什么经，是由其出生时的"栽达"（相当于汉族的生辰八字）决定的，而布章、康朗等能通过看他们的"栽达"，指导村民做什么仪式时应该赕什么经。

由于众所周知的原因，虽说当下能识读、书写贝叶经的普通傣族民众人数不多，但贝叶经在傣家人心目中的分量仍然是不可低估的，我们有理由将其比喻为是傣家人日常生活中用以滋养心灵、安顿生活的一剂"良药"。

贝叶文化与区域文化遗产传承保护

傣文巴利语释读问题及建议[①]

戴红亮[②]

一、引言

2002年，西双版纳州启动了《中国贝叶经全集》整理工程，经过8年多辛苦劳动，共整理了100卷傣文古籍。这在傣文古籍整理史上是一次影响深远的标志性事件。贝叶经以"六对照"形式（原件扫描图像、老傣文、新傣文、国际音标、汉文直译和汉文意译）进行翻译整理工作，既保留了傣文古籍原貌，又采用了现代化整理方法，特别是汉译和标注国际音标，让一些爱好傣族文化但不能直接阅读傣文古籍的人也能享受这一文化成果。

《中国贝叶经全集》在处理巴利语借词时，除了人们较为熟知的巴利词语外，其他词主要采用音译方式。从整理角度来看，这是一种权宜之计，从傣文古籍研究和提高傣文古籍整理质量角度来看，却是一个缺憾。这个拦路虎不解决，傣族贝叶经整理只能在意译加音译的模式中打圈而很难取得突破。

二、巴利语释读及存在的问题

傣文古籍中的巴利语借词释读问题，主要有识别和对应两个方面：一是识别出哪些是巴利语借词，然后按规则转写为巴利语；二是与巴利语原形对应，从音义相合两方面判断是否为巴利语。傣文古籍中巴利语主要以两种方式出现：一是偈颂，即整句或整段地采用巴利语，并携带巴利语各种时体格。这种巴利语翻译难度较大，但从识别角度看，它们都是巴利语词却是确信无疑的，关键是找出巴利语词根或原形并知晓其意义。二是借用巴利语词汇，一般不携带时体格，而是作为一般词借用，这部分借词有相当一部分融入语音体系中，一些常见借词的识别或对应较容易，但发生语音变异或不按转写规则的借词识别难度则很大，需专门总结特殊规律进行识别，然后才能对应。本文以《维先达腊》为例，结合个人释读傣文古籍中的

[①] 本研究是教育部人文社会科学规划基金项目"傣族佛经文献《维先达腊》词汇研究"（18YJA850002）成果之一。
[②] 作者为中央民族大学教授、博士。

20

巴利语心得，分析傣文古籍中巴利语的释读问题。

（一）偈颂的释读及存在的问题

下面是《维先达腊》大森林中的一段话，我们从这一段话中来看看相关问题吧。

这段话中从 ꩰꩰꩰꩰ（klāu²kā⁴vā⁵dang²ni⁶，告诉偈颂这样说）①之后，一直到 ꩰꩰꩰ（xā³de²，奴仆，在下）之前是一段偈颂。这一段话有个明显特征，就是没有任何显性声调，但傣语在念读时是需带调的，我们先转写再做分析。

kat¹tsi¹nu⁵	phon⁴to¹	kut¹sa¹laŋ⁴	kat¹tsi¹nu⁵	phon⁴to¹	ʔa¹nā⁴ma⁶jaŋ⁴
也许	诸尊者	给善业	也许	诸尊者	给无疾病（给健康）
kat¹tsi¹	un¹tse¹na⁶	yā⁴be¹si¹	kat¹tsi¹	mun⁴la⁶pha¹lā⁴	ba⁶hu¹
是否	存活	持续了	是否	根果	很多

上面这段话，《中国贝叶经全集》是这样整理的：

xău³suʰpha¹sāi¹miʰhoʰtsāi¹tsumʰtsɤn²mi¹vāi³jɤŋʰthāi¹san¹kauʰkthaʰdăŋʰnī¹vā⁵kāt¹tsī¹nŭ¹ pho⁴ to¹ kŭ¹sā¹lăŋʰkāt¹tsi¹
奔 向 打 招 呼 有 心 情 欣 慰 手 拜 举 献 言 词 讲 偈 语 这 样 " 旺 几 奴 破 多 故 夏 浪 旺 几

pho⁴ to¹ ʔa¹nā⁴ma⁶jăŋʰkāt¹tsi¹²un¹tse¹na⁶ ja⁴ be¹sī¹kāt¹tsi¹mun⁴la⁶phā¹ la⁴ pa⁶hu¹xa³ de² ta¹ băt¹sā¹ra¹ti¹xvam¹
破 多 啊纳马羊 旺 几 温 阶哪亚别西 旺 几 门腊怕 啦把互" 奴 才 修理工行者腊西 事

《中国贝叶经全集》采用了全音译形式。这种采用音译方式好处是翻译速度快，不存在巴利语疑难词翻译问题，保证了整理翻译的相对一致性和工程整理的进度。但从意义理解角度来说，没有带来任何新信息，从整理质量和科学研究角度来说，它是古籍整理中的一个缺憾和进一步研究的障碍。这段话由于是偈颂，携带了巴利语时体格，如 phon⁴to¹ 是"诸尊者、诸贤"的意思，在这里是复数主格，kut¹sa¹laŋ⁴，ʔa¹nā⁴ma⁶jaŋ⁴ 是名词与格复数。yā⁴be¹si¹ 表示动词过去式。此外ꩰꩰꩰ（mun⁴la⁶pha¹lā⁴）是 mulaphala 复数。

这段话从识别角度来说是简单的，它们肯定都是巴利语。难点在以下几个方面：

1. 偈颂携带了巴利语时体格，仅靠查字词典是不够的，需懂得巴利语语法，这样才能准确翻译出巴利语。从目前来看，解决偈颂问题，一靠字词典；二靠从巴利

---

① 为了更好地与《中国贝叶经全集》相一致，本文的国际音标只标注调类，而且按照傣族传统的六种调类标注。调类与调值对应关系是 1—55，2—35，3—13，4—51，5—33，6—11。

语"三藏"中寻找对应偈颂，如英文巴利语"三藏"，当然其与缅甸语和泰语"三藏"最为接近，可这需懂得这两种语言和文字。

2. 怎么处理这段话？这段话较简单，个别词重复率高，在这里主要是为了说明傣文古籍中偈颂翻译问题，所以还是比较合适的。问题是要准确地将这段话切分成一个个巴利语词，词切分错了意思就没法弄对，释读就很难进行。我个人在做这项工作时，吸收了现代计算机分词技术的一些做法，因为巴利语是文献语言，字词典是最主要工具，而正向最大匹配法和逆向最大匹配法分词就是基于字词典的，这两者精神是吻合的。具体做法就是先从左至右对偈颂巴利语词进行切分，然后又从右向左再对巴利语词做一次切分。这样双切分后，辅以语法知识，基本上就可保证分词是正确的，很少出现破读问题。

3. 傣语在转写时，由于傣语是单音节有声调，韵母发达，没有时体格变化的语言，而巴利语是多音节无声调，辅音发达，存在时体格变化的语言。两种语言语音结构差异很大。傣语在吸收巴利语时，会做各种调整。通常有些词会出现添加或减少，特别是巴利语的复辅音，有时会省略一个，而在韵尾化驱动下，有时又添加某个辅音，如 $mun^4la^6pha^1la^4$ 就添加了个 l，这就需懂得转写中可能出现的情况。

某些巴利语词由于转写中出现了讹误或语音变异，巴利语难以寻找。如 ဥဥ္စန un^{1}tse^{1}na^6 还原为巴利语是 uñcena，可是巴利语字词典中并没有这个词，如这个词携带了格的话，那么它就可能是 uñca，可是巴利语中也没有这个词。按傣语转写巴利语规则，它最有可能是 uñchā 了。这个词巴利语意思是"为生计聚集任何东西"，而 uñchena 是其工具格形式。从语义角度来说，这是通的，但这只是猜测。后来我咨询了一位懂缅甸语的高僧，他告诉我，我的还原是正确的。这段话实际上翻译如下：

Mahāvanavaṇṇanā

【罗马巴利偈语】

2008. Kacci nu bhoto kusalaṁ, kacci bhoto anāmayaṁ;

Kacci uñchena yāpesi, kacci mūlaphalā bahū.

【傣泐巴利偈语】

ကစ္စိ ႏု ေဘာေတာ ကုသလံ ကစ္စိ ေဘာေတာ ဘုဇဗယံ
ကစ္စိ ဥဥ္စန ယာေပသိ ကစ္စိ မူလဖလာ ဗဟူ ။

【中文翻译】

殿下您行何种善？殿下您为何无病？

为何食落果存活？为何树根果实丰？

这段话在《维先达腊》第八章"王子篇"再度出现：

除了 jaa⁴be¹tha¹ 时态有略微变化外，其他都几乎一样。

从分析中可看出，偈颂巴利语识别难度低，但因携带了巴利语时体格，需懂巴利语语法，找出巴利语原形，因而翻译难度大，尤其是一些转写不是一一对应的词汇，就需多语知识和考证了。如在转写过程中发生了讹误难度就更大了，而这种情况在傣文古籍中却也不少。

（二）借用巴利语借词释读及存在的问题

除偈颂外，傣文古籍中还存在借用巴利语词情况，也就是在傣语中间隔使用巴利语。这些巴利语一般不携带巴利语时体格，而且很多借词接受了傣语语音结构改造。从外形上看，除三音节以上借词尚好识别外，一些单音节或双音节融入度高，与傣语固有词形成同音词，甚至受傣语历时音变影响，如 ᨡᩬᩬᨦ 后面的 ᨲᨷᩈ（ta¹bat¹sa¹）它是一个三音节，从外形看，它很像是巴利语借词，这个词如转写为巴利语是 tapassa，可是巴利语词典中并没有这个词。按照上面我们说的，它很可能是添加或省掉了辅音，如增加了辅音就是 tasapa，如省调了辅音就是 tappassa，或一增加一减少就是 tappasa。由于傣语转写中同时允许两对复辅音的借词很少，实际上最有可能的是一、三两种形式。实际上它的词形是 tāpasa，傣语将第一个长元音转写成短元音了，它的意思是"苦行者"。我们之所以敢确认是这个词，一是因为它后面的 ᩁᩈᩥ（ra⁶si¹）在傣语中也是"苦行者"的意思，在傣语中，经常使用近义词来注释巴利语借词；二是从句子的意思来看，也是对的，它处于句子中，通过上下文比较容易确定它的意义范围，但如放在偈颂中难度就大了，还好另一个词形 tappasa 也不存在，这就从另一个侧面确认了。

傣语借用巴利语借词问题比较复杂，再举两个音变现象来说明。

1.《维先达腊》第一卷标题叫 ᨵᨾ᩠ᨾᩤᨾᩉᩣᩅᬯᩔᩢᨶ᩠ᨲᩁᩀᨹᩪᨠᨴᩦ（tham⁴ma⁶hā¹vet⁵san¹ta¹ra⁶ ta⁶sa¹pɔn⁴phuk²thi⁴nuŋ⁵），这个标题中 tham⁴ 是"经书"，对应着巴利语 dhamma（达摩，法），读音虽变化较大，字形却与巴利语一一对应。ma⁶hā¹ 对应巴利语 mahā，表示"大"，vet⁵san¹ta¹ra⁶ 对应巴利语"vessatara"，是佛祖成佛前最后一个化身，ta⁶sa¹ 是巴利语"十"，都是严格的一一对应。"pɔn⁴"是巴利语吗？如从外形判断，第一印象它肯定不是，因为巴利语没有 ɔ 这个元音。可是它确实是个巴利语借词，它的意思是"愿"，所以《维先达腊》第一卷译为"十愿经""十祷"。但这个词形发生了很大变化。傣语在转写巴利语 ara 音节时，在浊辅音后面将它作为一个整体，转写为 ɔn。它实际对应巴利语 vara，这个词巴利语意思是"高贵，最上；惠与；福利，愿望"，所以翻译成"十愿经"更符合巴利语意思。何以知道傣语这个词对应巴利语 vara 呢？这是因为，这不是一种孤立现象，而是有一批词也是这样的，详见下表：

巴利语	巴利语意义	傣语	傣文国际音标	傣语意义
nagara	城，市，都市		na⁶kɔn⁴	城市，都市
pavara	最顶尖的，最优秀卓越的		ba¹vɔn⁴	卓越，优秀
nāvara	歌手		(nā⁴vɔn⁴)	歌手
dharamāra	持续，继续，活着		thɔ⁵ra⁶mɔn⁴	持续
dīpaṃkara	燃灯佛		ti⁴baŋ¹kɔn⁴	燃灯佛

更可靠的证据是《维先达腊》也将 ၜၐသြာ 写成 ကဝန်ၐြ。但这种转写不是任意的，而是有条件的。剩下的词 phuk² 和 thi⁴nuŋ⁵ 前者是巴利语借词，后者是汉语借词，这都是来源清楚的。

2. 《维先达腊》第六章标题是 ၜၐမဟာဝေၑ်သန္တရစ္ဆၐေါက်ၑုလပုန်ကန်သွန်ဟောက် （tham⁴ma⁶hā¹vet⁵san¹ta¹ra⁶tsā⁴dok¹tsu¹la⁶pun⁴kan¹thon³hok¹），第七章标题是 ၜၐမဟာဝေၑ်သန္တရစ္ဆၐေါက်မဟာပုန်ကန်သွိစ်တ် （tham⁴ma⁶hā¹vet⁵san¹ta¹ra⁶tsā⁴dok¹ma⁶hā¹pun⁴kan¹thi⁴tset¹）。

tham⁴、ma⁶hā¹、vet⁵san¹ta¹ra⁶ 等前面分析过了。ၐြ 是"本生经"意思，可是巴利语形式是"jātaka"，ၐ 是"森林"的意思，可是巴利语形式是 vana（森林；欲林，欲望），从外形看，它们差别非常大，这都是傣语语音变异造成的。请看下表：

序号	巴利语	老傣文	傣文国际音标	意义	说明
1	jambu		tsum⁴bu⁴	阎浮树	音节 ja 中的 a 转写成 u；其他音节——对应
2	upagāmaṃ		ʔu¹ba¹ka⁶muŋ⁴	在村落的附近	maṃ 中 ma 转写成 u，其他音节——对应
3	nigama		ni⁶kum⁴	市镇	ga 音节中的 a 转写成 u，ma 韵尾化附着在前一音节上，其他音节——对应
4	samma		sum¹ma⁶	亲爱的	sam 音节中的 a 转写成 u
5	cūḷavana		tsu¹la⁶pun⁴	小森林	va 中的 a 转写成 u，na 韵尾化附着于前一音节上；va 中的 v 转写为 b（傣语中这种情况也多见）
6	dasabala		ta⁶sa¹bun⁴	十力尊者，佛陀的称号之一	ba 音节中的 a 转写成 u，la 韵尾化并附着在前一音节上
7	kusala		ku¹sun¹	善，善业	sa 中 a 转写成 u，la 韵尾化并附着在前一音节上
8	vaṅkatā		vaŋ⁴kot¹	曲折，歪曲；迷宫	vaṅ 中的 a 转写成 u，ka 中的 a 转写成 o，tā 韵尾化附着在前一音节上

24

续表

序号	巴利语	老傣文	傣文国际音标	意义	说明
9	yasa	ꨀ	jot[5]	名称，称誉，名声	ya 中的 a 转写成 o，sa 韵尾化附着在前一音节上
10	ratha	ꨀ	rot[5]	车，车子	ra 音节中的 a 转写成 o，tha 音节韵尾化附着在前一音节上
11	rasa	ꨀ	rot[5]	味道，汁，滋味	ra 音节中的 a 转写成 o，sa 韵尾化附着在前一音节上
12	jātaka	ꨀ	tsā[4]dok[1]	本生经	ta 转写成 do，ka 韵尾化附着于前一音节上
13	jujaka	ꨀ	tsu[4]tsok[1]	《维先达腊》中的婆罗门，是一个老乞丐	ja 中的 a 转写成 o，ju 高化为 tsu[4]，ka 韵尾化附着在前一音节上

这些词都遵循着相同变化，如不了解音变是很难识别出来的，关于具体转写规则及转写条件，我们将另文详细描写。

从上面分析中可看出，一些巴利语借词受傣语语音结构影响，加上语音演变及变异，使得巴利语的释读难度加大。不过只要是语音结构影响或语音演变及变异导致的还是有规律可循的，只要下功夫总结傣语转写巴利语规则，就可以释读文献中的巴利语借词。

三、系统整理巴利语时存在的问题及相关建议

从总体上看，目前释读古籍中的巴利语，还是一项难度很大的工作，主要是以下几个因素导致的：

一是傣文巴利语研究基础薄弱，没有一部合适的傣文巴利语词典，往往需借助其他语言的巴利语词典作为重要的辅助工具。其他语言的巴利语词典非常有用，特别是大规模的多语种巴利语电子词典作用更是巨大，但两者外形差异巨大，需进行转写和识别。

二是傣文转写巴利语时采用了复杂的转写规则，即使一一对应的借词，也需一定的转写知识，更为重要的是，很多借词在转写时采用了特殊转写规则，这就使两者对应关系不明显。

贝叶文化与区域文化遗产传承保护

ꨘꨮ ꨅ ꨆꨯꨮ ꨀꨱ ꨆꨮꨉꨵ ꨤꨪ꩑   ꨆꨯꨮ ꨘꨱꨉꨳ ꨕꨯꨮ ꨚꩃ ꨚꩂ ꨤꩀ ꨕꨫꩀ ꨟꩂꩄ   ꨦꨫꨱꨓ ꨤꨱꨳ ꨦꨫꨱꨓ ꨕꨱ   ꨆꨱꨳꨟꨮꨭꨚꨯꨵ ꨆꩄ ꨆꨳ ꨘꨫꩀ ꨕꨮꨳꩀ ꨚ ꨓ ꨤ ꨝ ꨓꩃ ꨚ ꨓꨱ
na¹ti¹ me⁵ kvaŋ³ li⁴   ke² xaŋ⁵ bāi¹ bo¹ bit¹ pok¹ ho¹ hɯ² hum³ jin¹ xu¹ tɬai¹ lok⁵ nām⁵ kum² peŋ⁶ xn¹ vān¹ nān¹ te¹ tā¹ mā¹ thāŋ⁶ bā¹ ka¹
水 河 宽 躲 于 旁 叶 荷 摘 盖 头 包 裹 立 在 处 水 深 平 脖 那 天 了 "大 玛 当 把 嘎

ꨦꨮꨱꨳ ꨓꨯꨵ ꨔꨱ ꨘꨬ ꩒ꨓꨱꨀꨯꨳ ꨦꨱꨳ ꨦꨱꨓ ꨔꨱ   ꨚꨰ   ꨎꨰ ꨕꨮꨉꨵ ꨚꨬꩂ ꨦꨮꩀ ꨤꨯꨱꩀ   ꨘꨱꩀ ꨦꨱꨳ ꨆꩃ ꨚꨱꨘꩃ ꨓꨱꩀ ꨜꨘ ꨎꨱꩀ ꨆꨮꨶ ꨈꨘꨮ ꨦꨯꨢ ꨦꨯꨱ
sen¹ to¹ sā¹ tha¹ ʔa⁴ hā¹ sā¹ tha¹ sā¹ pān¹ ju¹ tun¹ pin¹ xu¹ tɬai¹ lok⁵ nām¹ sā¹ xam³ pun⁵ tsak² ʔo² xa⁶ vā¹ tha¹ sok¹ suŋ¹ san¹ tsā¹ k¹
辛 喋 散 它 啊 哈 散 它" 萨 般 若 身 是 师 救 世 带 兽 渡 过 离 洪 流 人 间 悲 世 尘 要

ꨌꨰ ꨚ   ꨓꨱ ꨎꨮ ꨘꨬ ꨓꨮ ꨎꨯꨳꨟꨯꨱꨮꨳ   ꨆꨯꨵꨱꨳ ꩂꨕꨱ   ꨕ ꨆꨱꨳꨤꩀꨟ ꨇ ꨓꨯꨮ ꨗꨱ ꨓꨱ   ꨆꨮ ꨝꨱꩀ ꨠꨱ ꨛ ꨆꨮ ꨘ ꨦꨱꨀꨯꨵ
xāi¹ ʔā¹ thā¹ ni¹ tan¹ bot¹ lāŋ¹ ma⁴ hɯ¹ tseŋ² phā¹ kn⁵ seŋ³ te¹ sā¹ na¹ pin¹ ka¹ tha¹ va¹ tā⁵ to¹ kum¹ ma¹ ra⁴ pja⁶ thi¹ ta¹ sū¹ tva¹
解 内 容 历 史 段 后 来 给 清 楚 僧 就 故 说 教 成 偈 言 说"大 多 贡 麻 拉 巴 牙 替 达 苏 哒

这段话中一些转写采用了特殊规则，《中国贝叶经全集》在整理时，将 tlai¹ 这个词翻译成"救"是一种随文释义。它实际上是巴利语"taya"，是"三"的意思，应是"三世祖师"。suŋ¹sān¹ 对应的巴利语为 saṃsāra，是"轮回，流转"意思。再举一个有趣例子，傣语ꨝꨳ（bot¹）是"首、章"的意思，经常组成"课文 bot¹ren⁴"。这个词实际上对应巴利语"Pada"，巴利语 Pada 指"脚，脚步；一句话；位置，地方；理由，因素；一行诗节，最后的休息"。傣语还借进了另一个义项，转写为"bāt²"，如"ꨝꨳ（佛印 bla⁶bāt²）"傣语在转写时将它变成了两个不同的词，一个词按照一般规则转写，一个词按照特殊音变规则转写，两个词都很常见，但一般人已看不出两者联系了。

三是偈颂在口耳相传中出现了各种误读、误写和误抄，这就更使巴利语释读难度加大。这种现象是客观存在的，罗马体巴利语也存在这种现象，但在傣语巴利语的识别和释读中，我们也要注意三个问题：一是忽视偈颂中的巴利语时体格性变化，将字词典中查不到的巴利语借词认为是一种讹误；二是忽视傣文在转写巴利语时出现的语言变异，将语言变异认为是一种讹误；三是将傣文在转写巴利语复辅音时出现的变化认为是一种讹误。

四是缺乏综合性人才，傣文古籍巴利语释读需懂巴利语、古傣文、缅甸语、泰语方面的专家，但这种多语种人才培养起来难度大，需专门机构长期进行。

古籍巴利语识别和对应不仅关系到古籍整理质量和研究水平，也关系到对贝叶文化了解的深度和广度，是一项必须要处理的问题，只要持之以恒，久久为功，这件事迟早是可以逐步解决的。因此提几项建议，以促使这项工作得到有效开展。

一是对《中国贝叶经全集》进行再梳理，将巴利语词、语句、段落挑选出来，形成电子词典，先从容易的和准确无误的着手，采取先易后难的思路，先解决傣文古籍中百分之八九十的问题。从我们对《维先达腊》整理情况看，巴利语释读是可行的，经过总结转写规则，在语境和语言学知识的帮助下，前七章绝大多数巴利语借词都识别出来了，下一步需整理更多傣文古籍文献，形成规模化的巴利语借词电子词典，以便互相验证、互相启发，从而释读更多巴利语借词。

二是加强对傣文转写巴利语规则分析和研究，提出傣文转写巴利语的基本规则和特殊规则，为进一步释读有疑问的巴利语借词提供方法，如：

序号	巴利语	老傣文	傣文国际音标	意义	说明
1	sotaṃ		so¹taŋ¹	耳朵，听觉器官	一一对应
2	ārāma		ʔā⁴rām⁴	阿蓝摩，寺院，园林	ma 音节韵尾化附着在前一音节上
3	pūpa		bup¹bā¹	果子	傣文增加一个 p
4	ākāsa		ʔā⁴kāt²	天空，空间	音节 sa 韵尾化并附着在前一音节上，变成发音部位相近的 t
5	jāti		tsā⁴ti¹	出生，再生	一一对应
6	dhamma		tham⁴	达摩，法	取前一音节形式，书写上仍保留后一音节，用特殊符号表示，不用读出来
7	vessantara		vet⁵san¹ta¹ra⁶	维先达腊	一一对应
8	eka		ʔe³ka¹	一，一个，某个	一一对应
9	mukha		mu⁵xa¹	嘴，脸，入口	一一对应
10	Pāli		bā¹li⁴	巴利（语）	一一对应

目前最为紧要的是归纳和总结特殊规则并找出演变和变异条件，并与一般规则互相补充，互相验证，从而形成一个整体规则系统，为傣文转写巴利语的释读工作打基础。

三是编撰《傣文巴利语词典》，收集整理各种傣文巴利语形式，特别是通过各种特殊规则形成的巴利语借词，采取一国际音标对应多种傣文形式的方式，为文献中巴利语释读提供真实有效的释读方法。傣语在转写巴利语时，由于语音结构差异较大，在归化巴利语语音结构时，采用了多种方式，从而造成大量的异形词问题，这些异形词只有一种形式与巴利语存在着严格对应关系，其他则是书写异形词。这些异形词需结合意义才能确定它们是否为巴利语借词。如：

序号	巴利语	傣语1	傣语2	傣语3	傣语国际音标	词义及注释
1	puñña				bun¹	福，善，福德，功德
2	nigrodha				ni⁶xo⁴tha⁶	榕树，尼拘律，尼拘陀，诺瞿陀
3	pokkhara			—	bok¹xa¹ra⁶	荷花，莲
4	nibbāna				ni⁶pān⁴	涅槃。后一种更接近梵语 nirvāṇa
5	rāja				rā⁴tsa⁶	国王，统治者

四是采取联合攻关手段，综合结合老傣文、巴利语、缅甸语、泰语等人才，为未来的傣文古籍整理储备人才，并进一步解决巴利语疑难问题。傣语中巴利语只是一种转写，也就是说，这些巴利语都是有来源的，主要来自巴利语"三藏"，特别是第五次结集中确定下来的。因此，东南亚很多国家，特别是缅甸和泰国有较多的巴利语人才，可以采取联合攻关方式来解决傣语中的巴利语，特别是偈颂问题。

珍贵的区域文化遗产

——贝叶经与贝叶文化：来自中国的传承与保护实践及认知

周 娅[①]

一、导论

随着全球化进程的不断加深，世界在资本流动和经济、社会、文化交流深广频密的同时，也使地缘边界模糊，造成了地方性消解、地域文化特色衰微等问题，这客观上引发了全球范围内的一种逆文化多样性的"文化折叠"现象，即大量承载历史信息的地域传统文化被更强大的全球性现代文化所冲击而被消解甚至加速消失的文化现象。[②]

近半个世纪以来，中国—南亚、东南亚区域珍贵的"贝叶文化"就正在经历这一过程。"贝叶文化"以巴利语系贝叶经典籍（包含贝叶经刻本和各类纸质抄本）为核心，以该区域人们的佛教信仰和相关文化习俗为外延，是人类文明和世界文化多样性的重要组成部分。目前，在上述区域的部分地区，贝叶文化尚兼具鲜活性和遗产性。鲜活性，是指部分地区仍有一定规模和现实存量的文化资源（如大量现有的贝叶典籍刻本和抄本，以及一定量的新的贝叶刻本和纸质抄本仍在产生），并且有着与其相关的一系列传统文化习俗和活动在民间延续着。但同时，在区域内的多个地区，这一文化系统的很大一部分已经"遗产化"，表现为传统上支撑这一文化系统的各种传统社会因素正大量消解或消失，贝叶文化在较大程度上失去了其传统功能，并在现代社会中表现出诸多与现代社会格格不入的适应性问题，如被认知／被使用得越来越少，或者"没什么用"等。

在中国，贝叶经和贝叶文化迅速遗产化的问题尤为突出。这首先是由于中国在20世纪80年代工业化迅猛发展，广大城镇、乡村迅速现代化的社会变迁原因所造

[①] 作者为云南大学贝叶文化研究中心主任，云南大学民族学与社会学学院副研究员，博士，云南省非物质文化遗产保护研究基地专家委员，云南省宗教学会副秘书长。

[②] 周娅.傣泰民族研究的若干核心议题及价值发凡——郑晓云《傣泰民族研究文集》述评.湖北大学学报（哲学社会科学版），2020（2）.

成的。另外，相较于其他以南传上座部佛教为主流文化的国家，中国境内以傣族为代表的信仰南传上座部佛教、传承贝叶文化的边疆少数民族，难以避免地会受到国内主流文化汉文化的冲击和影响，这进一步加剧了贝叶文化的遗产化进程。近十余年来，以傣族为代表的族群，将传承和复兴"贝叶文化"作为其保持族群身份认同和文化认同的重要途径。除了民间的努力，中国政府也十分重视少数民族优秀传统文化的保护，并从民族语言教育、古籍文献保护、非物质文化遗产保护等方面为少数民族传统文化的传承与保护给予诸多政策倾斜和资助扶持，一定程度上起到了积极的作用。然而，最令人深思的是内源性的问题——当地的傣族和相关族群年轻人在全球化、现代化和剧烈的社会变迁面前的"自由选择"——很少有人还愿意高度投入地传承刻写贝叶经或是坚持到佛寺学习贝叶经和贝叶文化，大多数年轻人都主动地选择"投奔"/"拥抱"现代化的都市生活，他们和他们的家长也大都很支持现代国民教育，仅把贝叶经和贝叶文化视为一种在闲暇时间可以偶尔学习和"受一下熏陶"的传统（过时）文化。这一情形反映了中国傣族社会青年人当前的生活状态和社会价值观，并对贝叶经和贝叶文化在当地社会的传承与保护构成了巨大的挑战。

可以说，贝叶经和贝叶文化的遗产化加速趋势已经难以避免。我们需要更清晰地对其文化形态和遗产价值进行更深入的了解、认识，以便切合实际地在现阶段做好这一珍贵区域文化资源和遗产[①]的传承与保护工作。

二、珍贵的区域文化遗产——贝叶经与贝叶文化

贝叶经是世界佛教历史与文明的重要载体和表征。在佛教的传播发展历程中，早期佛教以口耳相传的方式持续了数百年。在那之后，将佛教义理用文字刻录在载体上的传播方式，是佛教在古代得以突破其地方性，向更大区域乃至世界范围传播的媒介基础。而贝叶经就是在这个漫长时期中佛教经典的主要载体和媒介。作为世界三大宗教之一的佛教，流传广深，在全球有约5亿教徒，约占全球总人口数的7%。[②]若考虑到世界一些佛教文化大国在宗教人口统计数据技术口径方面的因素，则全球实际信仰佛教的人数可能接近10亿。按全球人口数75.85亿计算，信仰佛教的人约占世界总人口的13%。因此佛教文明是人类文明的重要组成部分。而贝叶经和贝叶文化也成为佛教文化尤其是南传上座部佛教文化的重要标识之一。

在中国，贝叶文化多被看作一种西南边疆地区的少数民族特色文化。中国境内的贝叶经可以分为梵语系和巴利语系两大类。其中，梵语系贝叶经在中国的传播与翻译，自汉代以来较为频繁，在唐朝曾达到高峰，之后在中原地区便因汉语系佛典的出现、传播和普及而逐渐式微。现今，梵语系贝叶经大多已成为中国一些内地佛寺和收藏家或收藏机构的藏品，其刻写制作和传播传承现象已近绝迹。但在流传巴

[①] 本文对贝叶经和贝叶文化的讨论，包括"文化资源"和"文化遗产"两方面的意涵。笔者注。
[②] 根据皮尤研究中心2017年4月5日发布的《变化的全球宗教形势研究报告》（*The Changing Global Religious Landscape*）数据。

利语系佛教即南传上座部佛教的中国云南南部和西南部的傣族聚居区，巴利语系贝叶经的制作、刻写、使用和传承实践及与此相关的诸多文化现象仍在该区域内的部分地区鲜活地传承实践着。因此，在中国，"贝叶文化"也被视为一种地域性的少数民族特色文化。其地域范围大致包括云南省西南部和南部的西双版纳、德宏、临沧、普洱、保山等地的傣族聚居区域；其文化族群则包括傣族、布朗族、德昂族、阿昌族和少数彝族、佤族等信仰南传上座部佛教的族群。其中，尤以傣族为该文化的代表性群体。

综上所述，对于"贝叶经与贝叶文化"，我们大致可形成以下几点基本认知：

第一，贝叶经和贝叶文化的关系。贝叶经是贝叶文化的核心和表征，没有贝叶经，"贝叶文化"难以名副其实。

第二，"贝叶文化"有广义和狭义之别。广义上讲，贝叶文化当包含世界历史中关涉贝叶经及以其为载体的佛教传播的各种社会文化事项；狭义上看，贝叶文化是包括贝叶经（乃至纸质抄本）在相关族群社会中的传播、制作、刻写抄录、使用和以其内容传承为中心的各种仪式、习俗和礼俗活动等在内的文化系统。

第三，贝叶文化是跨国跨地区的区域性文化。鉴于目前人类对贝叶经和贝叶文化的现实性使用、刻写制作和内容的传承与保护实践活动主要集中于巴利语系佛教的传布地区，因此也可以说，贝叶经和贝叶文化是中国、东南亚、南亚区域范围内若干国家共享共有的文化资源和遗产。

第四，贝叶文化在中国有活态文化资源和文化遗产的双重属性。在中国，贝叶文化流布范围主要以云南南部和西南部傣族聚居区域为代表。在该区域内，因地方性差异，贝叶经和贝叶文化既有活态的文化资源的特征，也在一定程度上表现出文化遗产的属性。

第五，贝叶文化有世界级的文化遗产品位和价值。历经历史长河至今仍得以存续的贝叶经和贝叶文化，随着佛教的传播流传世界各地，它反映和象征着佛教文明，是具有跨国、跨区域、跨族群、跨语言文字、跨时空等特性的世界级文化事项，有着世界级的人类文化遗产价值。

三、贝叶经与贝叶文化的文化遗产价值

贝叶文化以贝叶经为象征。贝叶文化的核心载体是贝叶经（贝叶刻本），其次才是纸质抄本。但因为二者记录的内容有不少混杂的情况，难以截然区分，因此许多中国学者将二者统称为"贝叶经典籍"或"贝叶文化典籍"，国际学者则多将其统称为"手稿"。它们既反映和象征着佛教文明，又承载着该地域范围内许多族群的历史与传统文化。

（一）佛教文化遗产价值

贝叶经是由人用铁笔手工刻写在经特殊工艺制作而成的贝叶上的佛教经典。贝叶经一般分为巴利语系贝叶经和梵语系贝叶经两大类，分别是世界巴利语系佛教

（南传上座部佛教）和梵语系佛教（北传佛教）传播的源流性文字经典。作为佛教传播的主要文字媒介和重要象征性载体，贝叶经的出现扩大了佛教的传播区域，提高了佛教文化的传播速率和效能，为佛教成为世界性宗教打下了基础。从这个意义上说，贝叶经本身就是世界珍贵的佛教文化遗产。

巴利语系贝叶经，是南传巴利语系佛教传播的文字载体，其流布范围所覆盖的"贝叶文化区域"包含南亚的斯里兰卡、印度、尼泊尔，东南亚的缅甸、泰国、老挝、柬埔寨等国的大部或局部，以及中国云南南部和西南部的傣族地区。巴利语（Pāli-Bhāsā），即佛陀传法讲经时所使用的印度地方俗语。在贝叶经等文字载体出现之前，佛教的传播一直是用巴利语口耳相传的。公元1世纪，在斯里兰卡开始用贝叶作为载体用僧伽罗文拼写巴利语记录佛教经典。从此以后，南传上座部佛教一直保持着用巴利语来刻写记录佛经典籍的传统至今。南传上座部佛教传播中，各国用本国的文字来拼写巴利语，记录和保存佛陀传法时的教言（Buddha's Teaching）。因此，贝叶经承载的古老文字所记录的"历史信息"，真实地反映了佛陀的教言教义，对历史上佛教向更大范围、更多国家、更广区域的传播起到了其他媒介载体难以替代的独特作用，从而使贝叶经本身成为佛教"佛、法、僧"三宝中"法"的象征。

现今，这些贝叶经和纸质抄本仍大量保存于中国，东南亚和南亚区域国家的佛寺中，在文博机构和民间也有不少收藏。其中一部分具有百年以上甚至更久的历史，是该区域乃至全世界人类珍贵的历史记忆和佛教文化遗产。

（二）古文字库和古籍文献价值

巴利语系贝叶经的另一重要遗产价值，在于它对于古老文字的保护。此"古老"，是指记录在贝叶经的文字，都是在该国家/地区/族群中传承了数百上千年历史的文字。例如在中国，历史上，"佛经中相当一部分被傣族僧侣按原音转写成傣文，一部分被翻译成傣语"。[①]但随着时代和社会的变迁，这些文字现今已经只有比较少的人才懂得，从而显现出一种遗产化或"古老"性。例如，西双版纳地区刻写贝叶经使用的文字被当地人叫作"老傣（泐）文"，自从20世纪五六十年代经"简化"改革后，就被一种书写相对简易的"新傣文"取代。由于新傣文确实比老傣文简单易学，加之国民教育系统里对少数民族地区实行的"双语"教学中选用的民族语言也是"新傣文"，因此，书写优美、有着特殊韵味但比较难学的"老傣（泐）文"便逐渐淡出了西双版纳傣族的社会生活。然而，因为新傣文的一些局限性，民间一般不用它来刻写抄录佛教典籍尤其是贝叶经。故而，至今仍存在于贝叶经刻本上的那些"老傣文"，便成了保留和记录老傣文的文字库。

仅就文字方面来说，贝叶文化也因国别、使用族群和地方的差异而呈现出显著的多样性特征。例如，巴利语系贝叶经刻本和纸质抄本中用于记录佛经教义的文字

---

① 《傣族简史》编写组，《傣族简史》修订本编写组.傣族简史.北京：民族出版社，2009：305.

贝叶文化与区域文化遗产传承保护

就有很多种。若按现代国家来划分，这些文字来自斯里兰卡、缅甸、泰国、老挝、柬埔寨、中国等多个国家；若从历史观的角度看，主要的记录文字包括僧伽罗文、高棉文、缅文、兰那文、傣文等多种，其刻写与传承族群涉及斯里兰卡僧伽罗族、柬埔寨高棉族、缅甸掸族、老挝佬族、泰国泰族和中国傣族等多个主要族群；即便在一个族群内部，文字也可能有多种，如在中国，傣族用于刻写贝叶经或贝叶典籍的文字就分西双版纳（傣泐文）、德宏傣文（傣纳文）、耿马和瑞丽的傣绷文以及金平傣文（傣端文）等。其中德宏傣文和金平傣文只有纸质古籍，未见贝叶经。①

就贝叶经的历史价值来看，虽然在保存条件适宜的情况下，贝叶经刻本的保存时间可以长达数百上千年，但由于贝叶文化区域内大多数地区气候炎热，一些地区历史上甚至战乱频繁，加之保存不善所引起的虫蛀、风干脆裂等问题，影响了贝叶经典籍的实际保存时限。在泰国发现了历史逾四百年的贝叶经刻本；在泰国、缅甸、老挝等国也不乏历史超两三百年的贝叶古籍；在中国，由于20世纪下半叶"文化大革命"的冲击，加之傣族寺庙中也有以新刻经更换旧经的习惯，现在常见的大多是18世纪以后的贝叶经了。②

无论如何，中国、东南亚和南亚地区诸多国家的贝叶经典籍，都是承载着多种古老文字系统的文字库，是包含着海量历史信息和各族群珍贵传统文化的珍贵古籍文献。

（三）族群传统文化、集体记忆和地方知识价值

贝叶经典籍所保留与刻录的不仅只是记录于贝叶刻本上的佛教性内容，还包括了大量记载于纸质抄本的世俗性内容，如天文历法、医药医理、地方法规、地方史、技术技艺、伦理道德和文学如诗歌、传说、格言警句等。它们共同构成了该族群传统文化中的地方知识和集体记忆，蕴含着不同地方、族群的"文化基因"、精神气质和价值观念，对族群认同、地方文化的形成起到了重要的作用。中国、东南亚、南亚区域内海量的贝叶文化典籍无不具有上述特征。

中国傣族的贝叶文化典籍被视为"傣族传统文化的百科全书"。其蕴含的丰富内容涉及傣族社会生产生活的方方面面。篇幅所限，这里仅以傣族医药为例来说明。傣族医药与蒙古族、藏族和维吾尔族传统医药一起并称"中国四大民族医药"，它有着较系统的医学理论和丰富的实践经验，具有鲜明的民族特色和地方特点，是中国传统医学的重要组成部分之一。傣族历史上对于医药医理的理论和实践经验大都记录于贝叶典籍中流传于民间数百年。在西双版纳发现有一部名叫《腕纳巴特微》（《医经》）的贝叶刻本医书，其中不仅有丰富的处方，而且有对病理的阐述。此贝叶原作年代无可考，现在见到的本子是傣历1289年（1927年）抄刻的，是一部比较珍贵的傣文医学文献。③纸质抄本《档哈雅》（《药典》）中汇集了近千

---

① 张公瑾.中国少数民族文字古籍版本研究.北京：民族出版社，2018：63.
② 张公瑾.中国少数民族文字古籍版本研究.北京：民族出版社，2018：64.
③ 《傣族简史》编写组，《傣族简史》修订本编写组.傣族简史.北京：民族出版社，2009：338.

个药方。另两部抄本《嘎雅桑哈雅》(《医书》)和《康塔档细塔都档哈》(《医理》)论证了傣族诊治疾病的医理及其辩证思想。这些医书在当地有多种形制的版本,都较为系统、完整地记录傣族传统医药医理,是傣族族群和地方性知识的宝贵经典。它们中的一部分内容当前已被运用于傣族现代医药产业,对傣族人民的社会生活持续产生着影响和价值。

（四）"文化遗产"的叠加型价值

贝叶文化浩繁厚朴,其中还包括一些本身也是珍贵的地方性文化遗产的内容,或者在内容上与地方性文化遗产深度相关,而展现出一种"遗产之内含遗产"的叠加型价值。例如,贝叶经典籍中蕴含了不少古老的技艺,除了贝叶经的制作技艺,还包括佛像的制作技艺、孔明灯（"贡飞"）和高升的制作技艺、傣族大鼓的制作技艺和规程等,都在贝叶文化典籍的纸质抄本中有详细记录,如《中国贝叶经全集》100卷中的第75卷名为《制作大鼓、佛像的规矩及其它》,其母本就是一本19行式双面的纸抄本,在其中清楚地记载了制作大鼓和佛像时需要准备的物料器具、所需严格遵守的仪轨规程等。另外,很多纸质典籍本身的用纸也是"非物质文化遗产"级别的技艺性产物,如耿马县孟定芒团村的制纸工艺便在2008年被列入《国家级非物质文化遗产名录》。[①] 2006年,"傣族章哈"列入第一批《国家级非物质文化遗产名录》,而章哈们的很多唱本便源自贝叶经典籍。

上述这些地方知识和族群传统技艺等,反映了历史上傣族真实生活（authentic life）中人们的宇宙观、生态观、价值观等集体意识和认知,以及他们的个体或群体活动、技艺和实践,承载着傣族的民族心理和珍贵的集体记忆。

贝叶经典籍中这部分"遗产中的遗产"大都有非物质文化遗产的属性,值得加以重视,加强保护和传承。现今,这些地方知识和族群技艺只被极少数人了解和掌握,靠师徒相传的方式传承和实践,面临着后继乏人的情况。如不从文本保护和人的传承实践两方面加以重视和传承保护,这些宝贵的地方知识和文化经验将难以为继。

四、贝叶经与贝叶文化的传承与保护——中国的实践

贝叶经和贝叶文化对于体现云南省独特的地缘区位优势和文化多样性魅力有着非凡的意义和价值。云南省具有联结中国、东南亚、南亚大通道特殊的地缘位置,同时也是世界佛教文化区内汉传、藏传、南传三语系佛教在地理上的碰撞交汇融合之地,这是世界佛教文明三语系的一个汇聚型"文化节点"。贝叶经和"贝叶文化"跨越千年留存到现在,说明它有强大的生命力和文化力,不仅参与了过去该区域社会生产生活的方方面面,而且对当今区域的文化产业仍具有源源不竭的文化创造力和社会效益。例如在中国,贝叶文化就曾深度参与到西双版纳、德宏等地的文化产业发展中,为当地的影视产业、旅游业、制药业、文博业和文创工艺品等经济

---

① 张公瑾. 中国少数民族文字古籍版本研究. 北京：民族出版社,2018：64.

和文化产业的发展提供了源泉。

为了更好地体现它区域文化纽带的重要人文价值，我们还需对其传承与保护实践做阶段性的总结和认知。

大体上说，贝叶经和贝叶文化的保护与传承可以划分为两个大的面向：一是对"贝叶经"的保护，即对贝叶经和贝叶典籍抄本（包括纸质抄本）的实体性保护，改善和提升现有保存条件，以及可以采取的数字化等技术性保护等；二是对"贝叶文化"的保护，即地域内社会（民间）通过当地民众来实施的与贝叶文化相关的习俗性的传承与保护，包括对民间贝叶经刻写制作技艺的传承与保护，对赕经等仪式习俗的传承实践，以及借助各种资源和力量促进本土人群对这些习俗仪式价值的认知甚至认同，进而推动这些习俗仪式在当地的传承与保护等。

中国与东南亚、南亚国家一样，致力于对贝叶经及贝叶文化这一珍贵的区域文化遗产的传承与保护。目前，在中国境内，有关其保护的实践大体可分为形制性保护、传承性保护、制度性保护和研究性保护四类。

（一）形制性保护（Form Protection）

形制性保护指对贝叶经刻本和各类纸质抄本在实体、实物层面上的保护，包括对贝叶典籍文献的保护性搜集、整理、收藏和修护等。其保护实践主体主要是各相关地区的档案部门、文博部门（文化馆和博物馆等）、古籍文献部门（古籍办和图书馆等）以及佛寺和民间文化精英（如佛寺僧人、康朗/布章/贺路/安章等受过较高傣族传统文化教育的宗教事务人员和民间知识分子、收藏者等）。例如在贝叶经刻本存量较多的西双版纳，州档案馆、州博物馆、州图书馆等机构都有成规模的贝叶经刻本和纸质抄本典籍的收藏。德宏州图书馆也曾大量参与当地抄本古籍的整理保护工作。德宏州目前的贝叶典籍以纸质抄本为主，仅有极少量的象牙抄本、象骨抄本和贝叶经刻本。近年来搜集整理或查明收藏保护地的贝叶经典籍近4000册（卷），主要集中在州政府所在地芒市，其他的分散在瑞丽、梁河、盈江、畹町等县市的文化机构和佛寺中。

（二）传承性保护（Inheritance Protection）

传承性保护指当地政府部门和民间力量对贝叶经和贝叶文化的"活态"传承与保护实践及机制，包括贝叶棕的种植培育、贝叶经刻写制作技艺的保护与传承、鼓励民间传承或恢复有关传统习俗以增加贝叶经的现实使用，以及对贝叶经内容和贝叶文化的传播等。

贝叶文化的传承难主要是因为原先支撑其文化系统的一系列社会因素随社会变迁而消解甚至不复存在。在傣族传统社会，佛寺即是学校，贝叶经便为教材，贝叶经在传统社会中有着显著的教育功能和实用性，因而是傣族社会运行的重要链环，贝叶经的刻写制作是常规性的，不存在需要传承和保护的问题。但随着社会变迁，现代国民教育体系取代了传统教育方式，贝叶经的功能被大部分消解，失去了其现实实用性的贝叶经传承便成了"大问题"。因此，要真正做到保护和传承，还需要从"市场"需求、教育功能、价值认知、效益报酬等方面多管齐下来共同改善和缓解现在的"濒危"局面。中国南传上座部佛教界的多位高僧大德，如刀述仁居士、祜巴罕听长老、祜巴等傣长老、玛欣德尊者以及较年轻的如勐海县勐景来佛寺的都比坎章等，做了很多促进贝叶经和贝叶文化的"传统文化教育"适应当代社会发展的有益实践，如做公益演讲、组织教育界和民间精英开展贝叶经刻写技艺传习活动、开展跨境讲经交流和"塔玛扎嘎"诵经团活动、汉译巴利语系佛经以及开办"贝叶书院"等，有力地推动了贝叶经的保护和贝叶文化在傣族社会的传承。

（三）制度性保护（Institutional Protection）

制度性保护指通过申报中国各级政府机构所设立的文化保护资助项目来获得资源尤其是资金支持，进而推动贝叶经和贝叶文化传承与保护的实践活动。例如中国文化与旅游部设立的《中国非物质文化遗产名录》对于成功入列的项目，每年都会专门划拨款项资助其相关传承活动和传承人。此种保护形式主要以文化和旅游部非物质文化遗产司及其下属的省级文化与旅游厅非物质文化遗产处以及市（县）级的文化旅游局及其下属的文化馆等单位的"垂直管理系统"为保护主体来组织运行。2008年，"傣文贝叶经刻写技艺"申报该名录获得通过后，贝叶经刻写技艺的传承培训活动、传承人等每年都获得相应的资助。又如德宏州将古籍整理翻译工作作为州政府"十三五"期间重要工作，并向云南省民族宗教事务委员会申报入选云南省民族文化"百项精品"项目，目前该项目已获得专项资助资金（第一批拨付40万元），正在推动相关工作。

从国家和各级政府的制度性层面获得认定与扶持，激发了民间对贝叶文化的认同和主观能动性，有力地保障和推动了地方和民间的传承与保护实践。

（四）研究性保护（Research Protection）

研究性保护指通过与高校、研究机构等的合作来推动贝叶经和贝叶文化的保护与传承。如2002—2006年，云南大学人类学系尹绍亭教授在丰田基金资助下与唐立教授合作对德宏、西双版纳、耿马、孟连等多地的傣文古籍进行搜集、整理和摄录并编撰出版的《中国云南（地名）傣文古籍编目》，对傣文古籍主要是纸质抄本做了较早的研究性保护工作；再如西双版纳州政府与云南大学合作共建"贝叶文化研究中心"，用10年时间完成了对西双版纳州境内贝叶经和纸质抄本的搜集、整理、遴选版本、翻译和编撰工作，并采用原件影印、老傣文原文、国际音标、汉文直译、汉文意译和新傣文意译的"六对照"形式出版《中国贝叶经全集》（100卷）等，让更多人了解和读懂贝叶典籍。云南大学贝叶文化研究中心不仅直接通过调研和撰写申报文本的方式促成了"傣族贝叶经刻写技艺"申报入列第二批"中国非物质文化遗产名录"，而且数次召开国内国际贝叶文化研讨会，客观上促进了国际国内相关方面机构和民间力量对贝叶经和贝叶文化进行保护与传承的地方性共识和国际合作共识。

上述四种保护实践类型对中国境内的贝叶经和贝叶文化的传承与保护起到了一

定的推动作用。但由于诸多现实条件的制约，目前在保护范围、保护意识、保护合作以及保护技术性手段（如数字化保护）等方面的实践成效还十分有限，保护效率也有地区差别。尤其在技术性手段方面，还有待进一步提升。

近期，中国西藏古籍文献数字化工作提速，大批珍贵的藏文古籍近期实现了"云阅读"。作为文化多样性突出、民族文化和民族古籍资源丰富的省份，云南省也应加大在古籍文献数字化方面的技术和资金投入力度，扶持包括贝叶经古籍文献在内的古籍文献的数字化和"云储存""云阅读""云查询"等"云空间"相关工作。关于傣文古籍的数字化保护，包括云南省少数民族古籍整理出版规划办公室、云南省文化与旅游厅非物质文化遗产处、云南省博物馆、云南大学人类学博物馆、云南大学贝叶文化研究中心等单位前期曾进行了一些具体实践，但总体来说，都是规模小、投入少的零星工作，而且没有系统化、整体性的考虑与"顶层设计"。从长远来看，这些工作前期积累的一定经验和认知，为未来的国家政府层面的数字化工作和文化保护实践打下了一定基础。

同时，在推动数字化技术保护的同时，我们也要认识和处理好"贝叶文化"的传承与保护在人本与技术之间的关系问题。数字化保护仅只是贝叶文化传承与保护的一个方面。作为贝叶文化所代表的人文主义本身是不应也不会被科技主义所掩盖的。数字化只是贝叶文化保护的一个涉及内容、记忆与形制的技术空间层面，它不可能代替贝叶经刻写制作的传统在民间的传承与延续，更无法取代把贝叶文化内化为族群共有文化的人群本身所传递出的精神风貌与传统社会中长期形成的那些珍贵的人类的认知、技艺经验、精神和价值观等"集体观念"。技术是"末"，而人本是"本"；前者是"术"而后者乃"道"。因此，那些源自民间的传统应该得到更多的重视，"赕经"等与贝叶经和贝叶文化传承与实践密切相关的民间传统和习俗仪式应该得到更多的关注与实践。如此才能形成傣族社会内部对贝叶经刻写制作传统的"市场需求"，才会产生围绕贝叶经制作刻写的生产与消费，进而保证贝叶文化传承保护的民间内生性机制的良性发展。

五、结语

在全球化大潮的冲击下，一些地域性文化正在被快速消解，甚至被时代所埋葬或抛弃。这种逆"文化多样化"的"文化折叠"现象大量地发生于过去的一个世纪。随着时代的发展和科技的进步，过去数百年来广泛流布于东南亚、南亚地区多个国家和中国西南的贝叶经与贝叶文化，或许已经在很大程度上丧失了它原先所具有的实用性价值，但由于制作刻写贝叶经本身，以及其中包含的博大精深的文化内容，不仅是人类佛教文明的重要组成部分，而且记录和承载着相关族群的信仰、集体仪式、价值观念和精神追求，成为这些社会群体的共同记忆和文化基因。因此，虽然贝叶经与贝叶文化的实用性文化功能正在被时代和社会变迁大量消解，在近半个世纪以来其遗产化程度也在不断加深，但值得庆幸的是，包括中国西双版纳、泰国清迈、缅甸景栋、印度阿萨姆等在内的中国和东南亚、南亚国家的一些傣—泰—掸—佬民族地区,至今仍能看到大量的贝叶经刻本和纸质抄本,民间仍有贝叶经刻写制作技艺在传承,民众也仍将贝叶经典籍和贝叶文化视为他们"传统"文化的最重要的表征之一。

但正如法国远东学院研究员、老挝国家图书馆"贝叶经数字图书馆"项目负责人 David Wharton 博士所言:"我们必须认识到,手稿是当地丰富的无形文化的一部分,它消失的速度甚至比手稿本身还要快。"[1] 在全球化和现代化面前,贝叶经和贝叶文化的遗产化速度和"濒危性"程度已经亟须引起各方的重视和行动。

作为跨越国家和地区的人类重要的文化现象,相关国家和地区的文化部门,应对贝叶经和贝叶文化的传承与保护高度重视。建议通过"一带一路"倡议的契机,在国家间建立文化合作保护的区域性合作机制。通过互相信任与合作达成共识,为各国贝叶经和贝叶文化的传承与保护实践产生更有力的推动。

2020 年,中国已经超越意大利成为全球世界遗产名录数量最多的国家。中国的文化与旅游部等相关部门在文化遗产申报方面已经积累了相当的实践经验,可以在推动"一带一路"倡议过程中带动沿线国家,对双方乃至多国共享的文化遗产事项的传承、保护和申报建立合作机制,分享中国"申遗"的先进经验,助力东南亚、南亚国家的"申遗"保护工作,推动区域内部的文化合作与人文交流。例如通过共同申报世界文化遗产等,促进中国—东南亚、南亚国家在区域文化遗产保护方面的实质性合作。在这方面,作为该区域重要文化遗产的贝叶经与贝叶文化或许就为中国、东南亚和南亚国家联合申报"世界记忆遗产"提供了一个不错的选项。

---

[1] 源自 Wharton 博士 2019 年在云南大学召开的"中国—东南亚、南亚贝叶经与贝叶文化传承与保护国际研讨会"上的发言。

贝叶经和纸质抄本对旅游业资料的贡献

——以清迈府市区的清曼寺为例

Direk Injan[1] 文　韩帅[2] 译

清曼寺位于清迈老城墙内。它是一个重要的历史遗迹，是公元 1296 年清迈建立后，在芒莱王的命令下建造的第一座寺庙。寺庙值得注意的艺术品和建筑包括象群塔、主殿、池塘中的 Ho Trai（藏经阁）、Phra Sae Tang Khamani（水晶佛像）、Phra Sila（石雕佛像）、一块关于清迈建立的石碑，以及描绘芒莱王传记的绘画。

目前，清曼寺是清迈旅游计划中的热门目的地，泰国人和外国人都会来参观。然而，有趣的是，这两类游客的行为不同，并影响了他们参观寺庙和宗教场所的方式。一方面，泰国游客倾向在没有导游的情况下旅行，而且在参观之前很少研究这些地方。他们从阅读信息标志、小册子或其他形式的媒体中学习，因为他们对修行更感兴趣，比如功德，敬拜佛像以祈求好运，而不是历史。另一方面，外国游客会研究一些地方来计划他们的旅行。他们可能还会参观由导游带领的旅游计划中的地方，这给了他们比泰国游客更多了解重要事实的机会。这种现象导致了非本地的泰国游客不会重游宗教遗址。如何让自己或从导游那里了解这些地方的外国和泰国游客知道关于历史和艺术的重要信息？毕竟这些信息显然可以广泛获得。

对于那些从这些地方获利的人来说，"鼓励人们重游一个旅游景点"是一个挑战，因为他们必须给游客留下深刻印象，或者想出办法让游客有足够的兴趣在未来再次光临。大多数时候，重点都是方便和新奇，比如泰国旅游局为曼谷制订的"九大皇家寺庙之旅"计划。在这个旅行计划中，游客被引导去参观拉达那哥欣岛的重要寺庙。大多数人可能已经在不同的时间参观过它们，但这次旅行计划是一天的旅行，重点是向佛像致敬。这一概念现在在泰国各地广为流传。

例如在清迈，有"清迈老城墙内九大庙"旅游计划，也有"清迈九寺"旅游计划。"清迈九寺"计划包括参观清曼寺（求安定）、吉运寺（求好运）、大佛塔寺（求伟大）、帕辛寺（求"狮子"般的权势）、君威寺（求威望）、孟澜寺（求

---

[1] 作者为泰国清迈皇家大学文化艺术办公室学术协调员，清迈皇家大学贝叶经研究中心主任。
[2] 译者为云南大学民族学与社会学学院 2019 级宗教学专业硕士研究生。

财富)、消业寺(求避险)……这个旅游计划是鼓励游客重游旅游景点的一个例子。不过,清曼寺有多方面的吸引力。人们可能对学术感兴趣,或者想欣赏艺术品的美,或者想了解历史。还有一种新的观光风潮,就是利用历史、寺名和相关的故事,吸引广大民众到清曼寺参观。

本研究的主要目的是从贝叶经、桑皮纸手稿、碑文等资料中综合有关清曼寺的重要资料,以推广清曼寺为旅游胜地。这些信息将用于创建学习中心,或支持历史旅游。书面文本被认为是可信的,并且在一定程度上具有趣味性,因此被用作主要的史料。

一、研究目标

1. 研究清迈市区清曼寺的贝叶经、桑皮纸手稿和碑文的历史相关信息和重要性。
2. 利用贝叶经、桑皮纸手稿、碑文等资料,支持清迈市区清曼寺的历史旅游。

二、研究方法

(一)空间区域和文献种类

本研究仅对清迈市区清曼寺收藏的贝叶经、桑皮纸手稿和碑文进行研究。所研究的文献包括贝叶经1835份,桑皮纸手稿33份,碑文4份。

(二)内容范围

从收集到的内容来看,研究内容仅限于贝叶经、桑皮纸手稿、碑文中的文字文本,从历史、社会状况、知识等方面可以应用于导游讲解清曼寺的内容,或代表文献价值和重要性的内容。

(三)知识综合法

1. 从清迈市区清曼寺的贝叶经、桑皮纸手稿和碑文中选取了重要而有趣的信息。然后,这些文本被音译并翻译成泰语。
2. 按文件日期对内容和要点进行分类。
3. 收集和整理可用于支持历史旅游的信息,以展示清迈市区清曼寺古迹和古董的重要性。

三、结果

证据表明,位于清迈市区旧城墙内的清曼寺,是公元1296年清迈第一任国王芒莱王统治下,作为首都建立的第一座寺庙。广泛应用的寺庙历史版本简明扼要,主要的信息来源集中在艺术品和建筑上,如主要的佛堂及其描绘芒莱王传记的镀金绘画、Chedi Chang Lom(象群塔)、Phra Sae Tang Khamani(Phra Kaew Khao 白玉佛寺)和 Phra Sila(石雕佛像)以及关于清迈建成的碑文。然而,贝叶经、桑皮纸手稿和碑文中的信息并没有出现在寺庙的游客手册中。

贝叶文化与区域文化遗产传承保护

清曼寺目前藏有许多贝叶经、桑皮纸手稿和碑文。这些文件已经过检查，并列出了清单，有贝叶经 1835 份、桑皮纸手稿 33 份、碑文 4 份。它们中的许多已经被研究、音译和翻译，但大多数信息只有在学术界才能获得和使用。

（一）清曼寺发现的重要而有趣的贝叶经、桑皮纸手稿和碑文

清曼寺拥有的贝叶经大多是佛教教义和仪式的内容，但也有一些是历史、传说、法律、星象、巫术、天文、语言学、诗歌、地方仪式和民间药方、地方智慧等知识的内容。此外，还有一些后记和附加段并不是作者打算作为经文的主要内容，但是它们提供了关于他们写作时的历史、知识和社会状况的有趣信息。这些经文目前存放在 Ho Trai（藏经阁）和乌钵苏（戒堂）。

1. 重要而有趣的贝叶经

《沙门果经》写于公元 1870 年，参考了清迈僧伽委员会对僧侣和初学者的规定和限制的两个版本（公元 1868 年和 1870 年）。它规定，居住在此区域主要寺院的僧侣被命令抄写《沙门那卡塔》，并将抄写本送到下属寺庙。这份文件提供了统治清迈的年长僧侣的名单，清迈僧伽委员会统治的寺庙，以及从它被写的时候起僧侣和新手的职责和规则。

《芒莱法典》，制于公元 1874 年，包含了古老的法律和教义，声称是芒莱王所制定的律法。它揭示了不同社会阶层人民所适用的法律和惩罚，以及要承担的经济责任和社会角色。

《清曼寺庙名录》，写于公元 1874 年，其中包括清迈城墙内的 98 座寺庙和城墙外的 61 座寺庙。它包括了当时寺庙的数量和名称（今天，城墙区域内只剩下 38 座寺庙）。

清曼寺石碑的音译，写于公元 1874 年，包含了清迈建成时的石碑的音译，这是用酸角文写的。清曼寺的方丈将文本音译成泰语，告知清迈的统治者维查亚依王，清曼寺的戒堂正在建设中。

清迈纪年含重要事件的摘要记录，以及日期和时间。例如，有清迈和南奔统治者的死亡日期，清迈年长僧人的讣告，清迈统治者的加冕典礼，以及军队对缅甸耿东的两次进攻；还有一次是对老挝万象的袭击。

2. 重要而有趣的（桑皮纸）纸质手稿

清曼寺的桑皮纸手稿大多为祈祷和传统的兰那仪式的内容，都存放在方丈室里。下面几段是有趣的手稿的例子。

卡萨（咒语）集提供了巴利语咒语，用泰语书写，用于祈祷各种结果。例如，有 Khatha Sek Som Poi，它将给予祈祷者来自长者的爱；还有一种 Khatha，当一个人把它刻在贝叶上时，它将帮助这个人赢得女人的心；Khatha Fu Thoi Kham Ja，当一个人把它刻在一块木头上并跳过它时，Khatha Fu Thoi Kham Ja 将帮助这个人赢得一场官司；Khatha Sek Nam Lang Na，它将给予祈祷者来自他人的尊敬和来自敌人的顺从。

《养马与马药教科书》提供了如何使用草药作为马的药物来改善马的健康和治疗

马的疾病的说明。有保养马的药，也有治马大便带血的药。还有一本相马的手册。

高升（土火箭）配方书是一本由帕邀（Dok Khamtai）区的和尚撰写的土火箭手册的复印件。它提供了公式，用于制造土火箭的竹竿的尺寸，以及如何发射的说明。

《吉树种植手册》提供了如何种植不同种类树木的指导，根据指示，以获得好运。它还包含了一些建议，比如不应该种植在房子附近的树的种类，以及如果生长方向错误就会带来厄运的树，应该被砍掉。

《清盛镇平面图》是清盛镇平面布置图的手抄本，详细记载了清盛镇的城门、寺庙和重要场所的名称。据推测，该规划是在清盛成为一个废弃城镇之前制定的。它被认为是一个重要的历史来源，说明了在它被绘制的时候清盛镇的地理风貌。

天文现象和地震的记录包含了天文现象发生的日期，记录了在何时出现流星，同时还用插图记录了流星位置。记录还显示，已经发生过两次地震。

3. 重要而有趣的碑文

清曼寺的碑文分布在石碑、青铜佛像底座、金面和木面上。它们提供有关清迈历史的信息，以及清曼寺历史遗迹和古董的翻修和修复。

（1）关于清迈的建立与清曼寺的建造和翻修的石碑（公元1571年）

泰语的碑文创作于公元1571年。但它提供了有关清迈建立的信息，事件发生在公元1296年。同时碑文当中详细地提到了与这一事件有关的日期和时间，与这一事件有关的人名，以及清曼寺多次翻修的记录。此外，在碑文的末尾还提到了清迈统治者指派照看寺庙的人的名字。据说大约有68个家庭担任过这一角色。

（2）托钵佛像底座上的铭文（公元1465年）

清曼寺的僧堂中供奉着托钵的站立佛像。它是兰那地区已知的最古老的佛像。在雕像的底座上，有用泰文、巴利文和参与创作的长老僧侣和忠实的僧侣的名字，以及雕刻雕像的创作日期。这一碑文意义重大，因为它是清迈佛像底座上发现的最古老的泰文铭文。

（3）Phra Sila 铭文（公元1790年）

Phra Sila 是一尊用大理石雕刻的佛像，呈碑形，具有南印度的风格。这座雕像现在被供奉在清曼寺佛堂（Wihan Phra Kaew）内的 Khitchakut Mountain 中。他们为雕像做了一个漆和镀金的木框。画框上的泰文铭文提到，七君王朝的第一位国王嘎维拉国王、他的妻子和他的亲戚们在公元1790年创作了这幅画框。目的将功德奉献给其他家庭成员，并希望能给他们带来祝福。这个碑文提供了重要的资料，比如嘎维拉国王亲属的名字。另一个意义是巴利语中的"Ye Dhamma"咒语是如何书写的。同样的铭文在清迈只发现了两处，在清迈国家博物馆展出的嘎维拉国王统治期间修复的佛像脚上发现了另一个铭文。

（4）在 Phra Sae Don Khamani 或 Phra Kaew Kao（公元1873年）底座上的碑文

Phra Sae Tang Khamani 是一尊由水晶雕刻而成的佛像。传说在公元1296年，芒莱国王将这尊雕像从哈里奔猜带到清曼寺。底座下的碑文说，维查亚依王在公元

1873 年为供奉雕像制作了一个金色的底座和一把金色层次伞。

（二）贝叶经、桑皮纸手稿、碑文信息在支持历史旅游中的利用

清曼寺的贝叶经、桑皮纸手稿、碑文的年代、数量、内容等有趣的细节，都可以作为以前研究过的建筑、艺术品和历史相关资料描述的佐证资料。这将有助于提高公众对古代文献的重要性和价值的认识，以及了解如何在今天实际使用它们。

1. 佛堂（Main Wihan）

清曼寺的主体建筑采用典型的兰那建筑风格。这里供奉着主要的佛像和佛塔的模型。佛堂的一个突出特点是红色背景上的镀金绘画，描绘了芒莱国王的生平，描述是用泰文书写的。这些画是在寺庙管理者的领导下设计和绘制的，是为了纪念 1996 年清迈建成 700 周年（镀金艺术品在缅甸掸邦很受欢迎）。这些画作描绘了有关清盛传说的贝叶经、清迈民间传说、佛祖巡游记传说以及清曼寺石碑中记录的内容，这些都是在清曼寺发现的文献资料。

2. 玉佛城（Wihan Phra Kaew）

一座玻璃质的神龛是为了在僧堂中供奉 Phra Sae Tang Khamani（Phra Kaew Khao）和 Phra Sila 而建造的。根据清迈的民间传说，芒莱国王从哈里奔猜带来了 Phra Sae Tang Khamani。有一段碑文是关于在公元 1873 年维查亚侬国王、Thip Keson 王后、Ratchaphakhinai 王子和 Ubonwanna 公主统治期间创造的金色底座和金色层次伞。碑文是由敲击的小孔和线条雕刻而成的字母形状。

此外，在清曼寺版本的"Phra Sila 传奇"中提到了 Phra Sila，据说它是在佛陀结束生命后的 7 年零 7 个月零 7 天后由印度拉吉尔的阿贾塔沙特鲁国王创造的。这尊雕像随后被带到了南邦，并被供奉在南邦，直到公元 1476 年，三界王将雕像带到清迈并将其供奉在那里。Phra Sila 的另一个重要特征是在雕像上有巴利铭文。

僧堂中还有一座托钵的青铜站立佛像，在其底座上刻有泰文。这是已知最古老的泰文铭文（公元 1465 年）。

3. 象群塔

清曼寺最古老的佛塔——象群塔，就在佛堂的后面。它是以兰那—素可泰风格建造的，塔周围有"莲花形"的底座和 15 个大象雕塑。清曼寺的碑文说，原来的佛塔是由芒莱王在修建寺庙的同时建造的。在那之后，在三界王统治期间，建造了一座新的佛塔来覆盖旧的佛塔。这座佛塔后来在清迈处于缅甸君主统治下时进行了翻修。

4. 乌钵苏（戒堂）

清曼寺的主殿位于佛堂的西南面。它是住在寺庙里的僧侣们举行宗教仪式的地方，所以参观者不允许进入主殿。一块泰文的石碑放在主殿的北门廊前。石碑的两面都有文字。它包含了清迈的建立历史，以及寺庙内进行的翻修和修复的详细记录。碑文的末尾提到了照看寺庙的人的名字。这一碑文是计算清迈成立确切日期的重要证据，原来清迈成立的日期是公元 1296 年 4 月 12 日，碑文还反映了清迈、帕

府和素可泰的关系，揭示了统治清迈的缅甸国王如何信奉佛教，领导寺庙多次修缮，并在那里建功立业。它还提到了那个时代普通人的名字。

5．Ho Trai

清曼寺的经库原本是一座两层楼的建筑。上层是用木头建造的，下层是用砖和灰泥建造的。然后，它被搬到了主殿后面的池塘里，翻修成了一座单层建筑，只有一层且是木头建造的。这座建筑是架空的，没有提供梯子，所以想要进去的人需要带上自己的梯子。

兰那人认为，既然贝叶经被认为是佛教存在的证据，那么刻贝叶经、准备包裹经文的布料、制作存放经文的经柜、建造佛塔，都会有助于佛教的传承。因此，许多经文和桑皮纸手稿被提供给寺庙。它们确实值得研究并应用于现代用途。

四、结论

对贝叶经、桑皮纸手稿、碑文等支持历史旅游的研究，源于这些文献的价值。更详细地说，它们记录了宗教教义、历史、文学、信仰以及科学和艺术的各个分支知识的著作。一般来说，在历史遗产旅游中，游客大多会了解历史的大局，欣赏建筑和艺术品的美。兰那贝叶经和桑皮纸手稿不仅包含佛陀的教导或仪式，而且还有许多有趣的知识或信息。这些信息可能会吸引曾经去过清曼寺的人重新参观。将这些文献中的信息公之于众，并将其用于清曼寺的游客讲座，可以提高游客对文字作为主要史料的价值和意义的认识，这些文字比口述历史更可信。

此外，这些文件的例子还包括记载"清迈律法"的经文、编年史、清曼寺庙清单、流星和地震的记录、兰那王国统治缅甸时清盛镇的布局图、马药配方、土火箭制作手册、植树手册、被指派照看清曼寺的人员名单，这是在兰那发现的已知最古老的巴利文中唯一已知的碑文，以及在 Phra Sae Don Khamani（Phra Kaew Kao）底座下的黄金表面上的碑文。

五、建议

本研究以贝叶经、桑皮纸手稿和碑文为研究对象，以这些文献中的信息为基础资料，为清曼寺的历史旅游提供支持。

研究者对如何进一步开展这项研究提出了几点建议：

1．本研究的结果应该用来指导清曼寺的游客，以此来检验本研究的结果。这是为了考察是否有可能利用贝叶经、桑皮纸手稿和碑文中的信息来支持历史旅游。

2．研究贝叶经、纸质手稿和碑文的方法和概念，也应当应用于其他寺庙和古迹的研究当中。

Reference:

[1] Jongrak N. Phruttikam khong Nak Thongtieo chao Thai thi Asai Yunai khet Krungthepmahanakon Lae Parimontol Tor Kantadsiijai Chaiborikan Boristnamtieo (Studying the Use of Travel Agencies by Thai Residents of the Bangkok Metropolitan Area).An Indepedent Study Submitted in Partial Fulment of the Master Degree of Business Adminstration, Faculty of Commerce and Accountancy, Thammasat University, Thailand, 2017.

[2] Kannakammakan truodsob lae Suebkhon Duang Mueang Lae Tamnan Puenmueang Chiang Mai. Chodmaihet Kantrodsob Lae suebkhon Duang Mueang Noppaburisrinakonchiangmai. Chiang Mai: So Saph Kanpim. Thailand, 1996.

[3] Penth H., Khrueathai P. and Ketprom S. Prachum Jaruek Lan-Na Lem 2 Jaruek Samai Phrachao Kawila. Chiang Mai: Khlang Khomun Jaruek Lan-Na, Instutute of Social Research, Chiang Mai University, Thailand, 1998.

[4] Upranukro J. Wai Phra 9 Wat: Kantongtieo Lae Pholkratop tor Sappayakorn Watthanatham (Nine Temples Merit Tour: Tourism and Its Impacts on Culture Resources). Master Degree Thesis of Cultural Resource Management Program, Graduate School, Silpakorn University, Thailand, 2014.

傣泰民族佛教文学的跨界交流

刀承华[①]

分布在我国德宏、西双版纳、临沧、普洱等地的傣族，分布在泰国、越南东北部、印度阿萨姆省的泰人，分布在缅甸东北部的掸族，以及分布在老挝的佬族等族群，是同源民族，统称傣泰民族。由于信仰佛教，傣泰民族各族群都拥有大量的佛教文学，而且这些族群的佛教文学从古至今一直发生着跨界交流关系，导致一些作品类型在这些族群中都有流传，而这些作品在同一国家同一地域的非佛教民族中却没有流传。本文试图就这一现象进行探讨。

一、傣泰民族佛教文学跨界流传的佛教作品类型

傣泰民族跨界流传的佛教文学作品类型为数不少，在此主要介绍如下几类典型作品：

（一）佛祖来历故事类型

这一类型的作品德宏傣族和耿马傣族称《白鹤》，西双版纳、泰国清迈、泰国中部、缅甸泰痕、老挝佬族等都称《白乌鸦》。这一类型作品讲述一对乌鸦的五颗蛋被风刮散，分别被母鸡、母黄牛、母乌龟、母蛇、狮子等捡到并珍藏，后来五颗蛋都生出一个男婴，男婴长大后成为佛祖。这个作品来源于印度《佛陀史》。

（二）螺蛳神童故事类型

这一类型的作品我国德宏傣族和泰国大泰称《白螺蛳阿銮》，泰国泰族称《金海螺》，缅甸掸族称《白螺蛳召阿銮》或《素湾纳——红螺蛳》，老挝佬族称《陶黑螺丝》，等等。作品内容为一个王后生下一颗螺蛳，国王恼怒之下将螺蛳放在竹排上任其顺水漂流。螺蛳被妖魔捡去，后来螺蛳变成一男孩，妖魔将其抚养。最后螺蛳神童回到人间，和公主成亲并当上国王。

（三）十二女故事类型

这一类型的作品我国德宏傣族称《十二位王妃的眼珠》，孟连傣族和泰国称《十二女》，缅甸掸族称《十二姐妹》或《占塔索帕》，等等。这个作品讲述一位

[①] 作者为云南民族大学教授。

国王已有十二位王妃，又在不知实情的情况下将变形为人类美女的妖婆娶为妃子，妖婆施计陷害十二位王妃，唆使国王挖下十二位王妃的眼珠，并把她们赶出王宫。第十二位王妃在山洞里生下一王子，王子长大后几经磨难，最后回到王宫，使妖婆原形毕露，得到应有的惩罚，王子继承了父亲的王位。

（四）帕树屯—婻玛诺娜故事类型

这一类型的作品通常称为天鹅处女型故事。我国德宏傣族称《婻忒罕》，西双版纳傣族称《召树屯》，泰国泰族称《帕树屯—婻玛诺娜》，缅甸掸族称《坤甘和蛹劳罕》或《树屯》，老挝佬族称《陶西吞》等。这个作品讲述七位仙女来到人间洗澡，第七位仙女与人间王子成婚，后王子出兵打仗，仙女被陷害欺辱，返回仙国。王子打仗归来得知妻子已返回自己家乡，便长途跋涉、历尽艰辛追寻，徒步行走一年零三个月零三天，到达妻子家乡，通过了岳父的种种难题考验，终于夫妻团聚。

（五）香发姑娘故事类型

各地区流传的这一类型的作品篇名相同，西双版纳傣族、德宏傣族、泰国泰族、缅甸掸族、老挝佬族等，都一律称《香发姑娘》。作品讲述头发芳香四溢的香发姑娘的爱情、婚姻和神奇曲折的身世。

（六）松帕敏和嘎西娜故事类型

这一类型的作品西双版纳傣族称《松帕敏和嘎西娜》，德宏傣族和缅甸掸族称《并机并尼》，泰国泰族称《沙姆阔》。这一类型的作品讲述身为王子的男主人公在邻国举办的招亲比武中获胜，和公主结为夫妻，彼此恩爱。夫妻外出游玩时凭借一段木头渡江，大浪将木头打断，夫妻离散。妻子上岸后被一位老婆婆收留，老婆婆建了一座亭子，后来夫妻在亭子里重逢，把一半财产赠与老婆婆，另一半财产布施行善，最后夫妻回国治理自己的国家。

二、傣泰民族佛教文学跨界交流的条件

任何现象的形成都具有其内在和外在的原因和条件，傣泰民族佛教文学跨界交流的现象亦不例外，其形成条件如下：

（一）共同的佛教信仰

佛教的传播是傣泰民族佛教文学相互交流的首要条件，也是佛教文学没有在同一国家、同一地域的非佛教民族中流传的原因。

公元前3世纪，佛教徒在印度华氏城举行第三次结集，佛教的"三藏经"亦即经藏、律藏、论藏在这次结集中真正实现了定型。此后，阿育王派僧团到斯里兰卡、缅甸等地传授佛教，于是，佛教传入了斯里兰卡等地，随后从斯里兰卡向中南半岛的泰国、缅甸、老挝、柬埔寨等国传播、普及，也传到了我国傣族地区。

佛教传入傣泰民族各族群的时间不一致。关于佛教传入中国傣族地区的时间专家们有不同看法。黄惠焜认为佛教传入傣族地区的时间是唐代；有专家认为在公元752年南诏成为吐蕃属国后傣族开始接受佛教；陈保亚、木境湖认为佛教北上入滇

的年代不能早于明代，至少傣族全民信仰佛教不会早于明代。尽管观点不一，但可说明佛教传入傣族地区的时间是相当久远的。

泰国是以佛教为国教的国家。早在公元3世纪，佛教就已经开始传入现今泰国领土上的林阳国、金邻国等孟人建立的小国，被孟人所接受，并得到普及、流行。13世纪，素可泰王国建立，其统治者为了巩固统治，加强中央集权，而大力提倡佛教。此后佛教在泰国的意识形态领域一直占据着主导地位，以至于曼谷王朝7世王在宪法中规定国王必须是佛教徒或佛教的护持者，泰国国旗上白色横条代表佛教，可见佛教在泰国神圣和重要的地位。

至于老挝，有专家认为老挝南部占巴塞著名的佛教古刹瓦普寺始建于10世纪以前。老挝国家图书馆的Dr. Boukhay Phengpha chanh认为，佛教于公元1357年传入老挝。[1] 黄兴球认为"佛教在14世纪的时候进入老挝地区。有两条路线：一是从柬埔寨经过老挝南部进入老挝，到达老挝的古都琅勃拉邦；另一条线路是从缅甸进入老挝北部的垄南塔地区"。[2]

缅甸是南传上座部佛教占主导地位的国家之一，"掸族在东吁王朝时期才基本全民信仰上座部佛教"，[3] 也就是说，在13世纪以后，南传上座部佛教已在掸族民众中普及、扎根。

佛教传入以后，在傣泰民族中发挥了促进文化交往的正功能。巴利语佛教经典"三藏经"随阿育王派到斯里兰卡传授佛教的僧团进入斯里兰卡，后由斯里兰卡传至信仰南传上座部佛教的傣泰民族各族群。这部佛教经典的《经藏》中的《小尼迦耶》包含的文学成分最丰富，其中的《法句经》《上座僧伽他》《上座尼伽他》[4] 和《佛本生经》堪称巴利语佛教文学的代表作。在傣泰民族社会家喻户晓的佛教文学首推佛本生经。在流传过程中，傣泰民族各族群的民众对佛本生经进行了本土化改造，以满足本族群民众的审美期待，于是具有族群特色的多样化的佛本生经在傣泰民族各族群之间出现了交叉传播、跨界交流的现象。

（二）彼此的文化认同

傣泰民族是同源民族，都来源于古越人，拥有共同的文化渊源。虽然随着历史的演进，傣泰民族分化成为不同的族群以后，生活在不同的国家，属于不同的政治实体，在不同的自然生态和人文生态中发展了各自的文化，但源自祖先的共同文化根基却具有很高的稳定性和继承性，牢固地存留在各自的文化中没有消失。比如傣泰民族各族群都在江河流域择地而居，传统的民居形式均为干栏式建筑；稻作文化是这些族群的共同文化特征之一；共同拥有文身、染齿等习俗；女性挽发髻、穿筒裙和窄袖短衫；都一律拥有灵魂崇拜，并形成了叫人魂、叫谷魂、祭田神、祭树

---

[1] Dr.Boukhay Phengpha chanh 2014年在首届国际贝叶文化研讨会上的发言。
[2] 黄兴球. 老挝族群论. 北京：民族出版社，2006：4.
[3] 周娅. 地缘文化及其社会构建. 北京：中国社会科学出版社，2016.
[4] 《上座僧伽他》（Theragatha）和《上座尼伽他》（Therigatha），Thera为"上座"之意，gatha为"偈颂"之意，"伽他"为gatha的音译，也可意译为《上座僧偈陀》《上座尼偈陀》。笔者注。

神等习俗；都一律崇拜寨神、勐神、祖先神、家神、天神、地神、山神、水神、树神等，并有相应的祭祀活动；节日习俗相同或相似，都有泼水节（宋干节）、进洼节、出洼节等，庆祝这些节日的时间大致相同，活动内容几乎一样。更为重要的是，共同的民族情感、民族记忆、民族意识、价值观念等共有意识，牢牢地存在于成员的思想中，致使傣泰民族的文化同质性十分显著。

另外，傣泰民族各族群的绝大部分居民都信仰南传上座部佛教，都有拜佛、听经、布施、做功德的习俗，都有轮回转世、善有善报恶有恶报、弃恶从善、为来世积德的宗教观念。宗教习俗和宗教观念的同一性是傣泰民族情感联结的重要因素之一。

文化的亲缘关系和宗教信仰的同一性，使傣泰民族各族群之间形成了很强的文化认同，佛教文学的跨界交流具有了强劲的内驱力，从而得以长久持续。

（三）语言的趋同和文字的使用

傣泰民族各族群是由远古时候的一个人类共同体分化而来的，就语言而言，在语音、词汇、语法、表达方式等诸多方面存在许多共同特点。语言的相同或相似，是傣泰民族佛教文学跨界交流的一个重要条件。

另外，傣泰民族各族群都拥有并使用自己的古老文字。文字的创制和使用，是文学得以保存和跨境、跨区域交流的重要因素之一。傣泰民族拥有以下几种古老文字：

德宏老傣文　字体呈方形，产生年代久远，明王朝设立的专门翻译各藩属及四境各少数民族语言文字机构"四夷馆"中的"百夷馆"，就是专门翻译德宏老傣文材料的。

西双版纳老傣文　亦称傣泐文，字体呈圆形，相传是一个名叫督因达的佛爷创制的，与泰国兰那文有渊源关系，明王朝设立的翻译机构"四夷馆"中的"八百馆"就是翻译西双版纳老傣文资料的。

傣崩文　字母呈圆体，亦称圆体傣文，主要在德宏瑞丽、耿马的部分地区使用。

金平傣文　又称傣端文，字母呈长形，主要在我国金平地区和越南岱族地区使用。

兰那文　泰语称"多檀"，意为"经文"，13世纪由泰国兰那的芒莱王之子创制（参考贺圣达《东南亚文化发展史》第234页），主要是用于记录佛经。

泰文　由泰国素可泰王朝三世王兰甘亨大帝在孟文和高棉文的基础上创制，后经历代学者的修改，成为现今全泰国通用的文字。

老挝布罕文　在老挝流行，用于改编佛教作品，记录非宗教性的文本。[1]

老挝文　现代通行的老挝文字。

泰痕文　字体圆形，主要在缅甸掸邦地区使用。

傣泰民族各族群都拥有并使用自己的文字，这使族群间跨界、跨区域的文学交

---

[1] 郭山，周娅. 贝叶文化与和谐周边建设. 昆明：云南大学出版社，2011：327.

流拥有了传播、交流的工具。

上述文字多与孟文有渊源关系,字形相似。老挝学者安纳托尔·派尔缇耶博士在其论文《泰文和老挝文贝叶经中的经典故事》中写道:"老挝文、泰阮文(泰润文)、泰泐文(西双版纳傣文)和泰艮(泰痕)文的字形几乎是相同的。如果你能够读懂其中一种文字,那么解码其他文字就会变得很容易,因为从一种文字到另外一种文字的变化很小。"文字的相同或相似,导致了文字的跨界、跨区域的交叉使用。与此同时,以文字为媒介的文学跨界交流具有了很大的便利条件。

语言、文字的趋同性,是傣泰民族佛教文学相互交流的强劲助力。

三、跨界交流的途径

傣泰民族佛教文学跨界传播主要有三种形式:书面传播、口头传播、文艺形式传播。传播的途径主要有以下几种:

(一)对佛教文学的翻译

随着佛教的传播,南传上座部佛教的巴利语经典如"三藏经"等传入傣泰民族地区。佛教僧侣对佛教经典进行了翻译,以方便傣泰民族群众阅读和理解佛法佛规,从而皈依佛教。

傣族专家刀永明在其论文《傣族文学与佛教》中写道:"佛寺给傣族人民培养了众多的知识分子。佛寺既是传教的地方,又是培养智力人才的学校……'康朗'是知识渊博的高级知识分子,他们当中,有的注释和翻译佛教经典、佛经故事,传播印度文化。"[1]傣泰民族译介佛教经典的方式有以下几种:

音译 即用本民族文字转写佛教经典原文。胡廷武在其论文《中国贝叶经的学术空间》里写道:"公元5世纪,印度高僧觉音来到斯里兰卡,用当地的僧伽罗文字母,把三藏经全部记录下来,之后上座部佛教传到之国,也纷纷创造和完善本国或本地区文字,用于记录巴利文佛教经典,这就是今天的僧伽罗文、泰文、缅文、柬埔寨文、老挝文和中国西双版纳贝叶经的初始。这种记录,实际上也就是音译。"[2]在德宏傣族地区,拜佛日里"贺路"(赕佛师)在佛寺为信众念诵的佛教训诫经文《五诫经》《毕杰少细》等,是用德宏老傣文将巴利语经文转写而成的。德宏傣族佛经《菩提扁细呀》《四无量》《苏巴坦》(经藏之一)、《威萨底》(经藏之一)、《阿塔散麻把尼提札》《吾巴立万纳苏》(经藏之一)、《布杂札布札立牙南》《板第路板谢》《布别杂嘎达蚌雅大》等是用德宏老傣文从巴利语转写而成的。

另有一种情形,是傣泰民族各族群用各自文字以音译方式互相转写佛教文学经典。德国老挝古籍专家哈拉德·汉德斯及老挝籍专家戴维·沃顿合著的论文《老挝贝叶经数字图书馆》中写道:"在老挝,与宗教有关的文本通常使用经文,而非宗

---

[1] 山茶编辑部.傣族文学讨论会论文集.北京:中国民间文艺出版社,1982:114.
[2] 郭山,周娅.贝叶文化与和谐周边建设.昆明:云南大学出版社,2011:26.

贝叶文化与区域文化遗产传承保护

教性的文本则由现代老挝文的前身老挝布罕文写成。有相当数量具有相同标题的作品既有经文的文本也有老挝布罕文文本。"①这里的"经文"即是兰那文。也就是说，佬族人用自己的文字转写兰那文佛教经典。

傣泰民族各族群之间互相转写经文的现象是很普遍的。

还有一种情形是为了便于阅读，增强转写文忠实原文的可信度，进行行对行、段对段、页对页的转写。阿尼尔·释迦长老在其论文《泰国的贝叶经抄本》中写道："在古代泰国，高棉文字作为学习和记录佛经的工具曾被广泛使用。这些贝叶经中所使用的语言为巴利语、巴利语—泰语、巴利语—高棉语、泰语—高棉语以及泰语。有些贝叶经里，甚至同时使用三种语言，例如在一部贝叶经中同时使用巴利语、泰语、高棉语。""兰那经文（兰那文）贝叶经多数是在泰国北部发现的。这些贝叶经使用巴利语、巴利语—兰那语和泰语—兰那语。""在泰国东北部发现的贝叶经多数是经文，使用的是巴利语、巴利语—泰东北语和泰北语。"②音译作品的习俗在泰国一直流传至今。《召门隆》（门隆王）、《玛卡瓦》（因陀罗神）等原文是用缅甸泰痕文书写，后有专家用泰文转写，单页为原文，双页为转写的泰文，逐行遵照原文转写。

注疏　亦即对原文进行注译。如西双版纳的《中阿含经》，有贝叶经和绵纸经两种形式，其内容结构中，一般是巴利语和当地傣语相结合，即前半段若是纯巴利语，后面一定紧跟着傣泐语解释。

阿尼尔·释迦长老在其论文《泰国的贝叶经抄本》中写道："泰国国家图书馆中收藏的贝叶经分为14类。分别是：1.巴利经典：由巴利三藏组成；2.注解部分：由对巴利经典进行的注评组成；3.次注疏部分：由对巴利经典进行的次级注评组成；4.次—次注疏：由对论藏的次—次注评组成；5.新次注疏：由对经藏的新的次注评组成；6.解译：由对巴利原典的解释说明组成；7.别论：由与巴利三藏相关的专论组成；8.专门的文学作品：由与巴利原典相关的专门的文学作品及其注疏和次注疏组成……"③

泰国阿育陀耶王朝时期译自巴利语的讲述佛祖前身行善布施的经典《大世词》，是一行巴利语一行泰文相间，听起来难以理解，也不连贯，于是帕昭松探国王下令再编一部同样内容的经典，一段巴利文一段泰文相间，这便有了《大世赋》。这也是注疏的一种方式。

意译　在老挝，维苏纳腊王时期（公元1502—1520年），国王将三藏经从巴利文译成老挝文。④傣泰民族其他族群也都有意译佛教文学的现象。

可见，翻译是使傣泰民族佛教文学以书面形式跨界交流的重要途径。

---

① 郭山，周娅.贝叶文化与和谐周边建设.昆明：云南大学出版社，2011：327.
② 郭山，周娅.贝叶文化与和谐周边建设.昆明：云南大学出版社，2011：316.
③ 郭山，周娅.贝叶文化与和谐周边建设.昆明：云南大学出版社，2011：315.
④ 贺圣达.东南亚文化发展史.昆明：云南民族出版社，1886：281.

（二）对佛教文学的再创作

傣泰民族佛教文学跨界交流的又一种方式是对佛教文学的再创作，典型例子有佛本生经等。傣泰民族的文人学士对原版的佛本生经进行了扩展、重构，使重构的作品符合本民族的欣赏习惯。如德宏傣族和缅甸掸族，就以佛本生经为题材创作了数百个阿銮故事，即讲述佛祖成正觉以前的各世经历的故事，如《五颗金乌鸦蛋》《白螺蛳阿銮》《十二位王妃的眼珠》《楠忒罕》《并机并尼》《酸鱼阿銮》《射星阿銮》等等。

在泰国，僧侣和民间作者们从佛本生经中选取材料，对其进行扩展和重构，赋予比原作更为曲折、精彩的情节，冠以佛本生故事之名，然后投入民间，使之成为受众面非常广阔的作品。泰国称通过这样一种扩展重构的方式而形成的佛本生故事为"本生经以外的佛本生故事"。故事集《班雅萨槎罗》是最为典型的"本生经以外的佛本生故事"。"班雅萨槎罗"的意思是"五十个佛本生故事"，相传是泰国北部兰那高僧帕拉铁拉模仿印度佛本生经或者借托佛祖转世经历而创作的，另有说法是多位民间作者所作，由后人收集成册。除《班雅萨槎罗》以外，在泰国民间还流传着许多不留作者姓名的"本生经以外的佛本生故事"。

老挝浩如烟海的古籍文献中，有相当一部分是佛本生经，早在1589年老挝的寺院里就创作出了6个佛本生故事，在老挝的佛寺里珍藏着模仿佛本生经创作的《五十个故事》的多个版本。

以佛本生经为蓝本创作的傣泰民族佛教文学，多以贝叶经或绵纸经形式呈现。这是傣泰民族佛教文学书面形式跨界交流的又一重要途径。

（三）佛经活动中的交流

傣泰民族各族群都有很成熟的佛经文化。傣族有向佛寺献经书的习俗，老百姓可出资请人抄写经书献给佛寺，傣语称"路厘"或"赕坦"。老百姓献的经书被珍藏在佛寺的经柜里，或置放于藏经阁中。傣族还有"混厘"的习俗，即在适当的时候，将所献的经书取出来，请念诵技巧娴熟的念者念诵，经书的主人请亲戚朋友听经。在拜佛的日子里，佛寺也会安排念者为拜佛群众念诵经典。丧家也会请人到家里念诵经文，为死者超度。上述活动所念的经书，有相当一部分是傣族佛教文学。村民们一旦听说某村某寨从哪里获得一部经书，人们都会争相借来抄写或诵读，甚至到地域相连的异国去借。国别的相异，阻止不了傣泰民族文学的相互交流。

泰国的泰蓬，在入夏期间佛爷为拜佛群众念经，然后向村民讲述佛本生故事；丧家办完丧事，要请人到家里给相帮们讲述佛本生故事以示感谢，帮助丧家排解失去亲人的悲伤；产妇生育孩子以后要在火塘边睡一个月，在这期间，产妇家要请故事讲述者来为产妇和探访者讲述佛本生故事，帮助产妇排解生产过程中的惊恐和不安，感谢探访者的关心和祝福。在泰国北部，入夏的日子里，人们常常相聚拿佛本生故事手抄本来念诵……丧家也常常找人来为参加葬礼的人们讲故事，有时采取口语叙述的方式，有时则是采取讲唱的形式。在泰国中部，男子出家仪式、献僧衣仪式、结婚庆典等活动，人们会在晚上聚在主人家听讲故事。[①]

类似这样的习俗在傣泰民族各族群中普遍流行。这种习俗，势必促进佛教文学传播。这是傣泰民族佛教文学口头形式交流的重要途径。

（四）文艺形式与新型媒体的结合

随着科学技术的发达，傣泰民族社会成为民族文化、佛教文化、现代文化并存，传统习俗和现代生活方式同在的社会，民众对精神文化的需求由单调型转向了多样型，致使族群间的佛教文学交流除了书面和口头两种形式以外，又出现了文艺形式和新型媒体相结合的交流形式。

傣泰民族为了满足民众的审美需求，将佛教文学改编成戏剧或影视剧搬上戏台或银幕荧屏，用于交流的新型媒介主要有光碟、广播、手机微信、互联网等。如傣族的《召树屯》（德宏称"嫲忒罕"）被改编成电影《孔雀公主》，制成光碟；《十二位王妃的眼珠》《嫲西拉》等等，被改编成傣戏制成光盘。泰国的《十二女》《帕树屯—嫲玛诺娜》《金海螺》《维莎圣銮》，以及掸族的《朗玉相过》等，也都被改编成电视剧，制成光盘。这类光盘在傣泰民族地区都有流传。另有一种传播方式是以讲故事的形式在手机微信上传播，如西双版纳的《白牛王公主》《召贺洛》等等。文艺形式和新型媒体的结合，使傣泰民族的佛教文学作品，能以一种便捷、直观、形象的审美形式呈现，满足各种年龄层次民众的审美欣赏需求，获得更为广阔的受众面，收到更为理想的跨界交流效应。

四、结语

综上所述，佛教的传播、相互间的文化认同、相近的语言和文字的使用，为傣泰民族各族群佛教文学的跨界交流提供了条件；傣泰民族各族群用自己的传统方式和现代方式进行着佛教文学的交流，促进了佛教文学由静态到动态的交流，导致傣泰民族各族群佛教文学类型的交叉共有，使这些族群的文学更加丰富充实，呈现出五彩缤纷的景象。

更为重要的是，傣泰民族佛教文学的相互交流，以及多个佛教文学类型交叉共有现象的产生，成为这些族群乃至于中国、泰国、老挝、缅甸等国家交流合作的重要桥梁，起到了文化的先导作用。傣泰民族分布地具有重要的战略地位。我国傣族聚居区西双版纳和德宏，是我国对外开放的重要门户之一，是联结东南亚、南亚的前沿；泰国、老挝、缅甸、越南都地处"一带一路"沿线。傣泰民族虽然居住在不同的国家，有国界分隔，但分布地却是基本相连或相近，有的村寨甚至分属两个国家，德宏瑞丽的银井寨就是典型例子，一半属于中国一半属于缅甸，寨中居民存在血亲或姻亲关系，在社会、经济、文化等方面一直保持着密切关系。可以说，地缘关系将傣泰民族联结在一起。从民族成分来说，泰国泰族和老挝佬族是各自国家

[①] Prakong Nimmanahaeminda. 民间故事研究. 曼谷：泰国朱拉隆功大学出版社，2008：77.

的主体民族，掸族是缅甸一个不可忽视的民族，越南泰人是越南人口最多的少数民族，约 120 万。这些族群的亲缘文化关系的联结、文学的交流，是"一带一路"在中南半岛地段举足轻重的因素和内容。

　　傣泰民族由于较高的文化同质性、宗教信仰的同一性，居住地的连接性，以及佛教文学的交流关系，在国际交往中的身份认同、文化认同、价值认同的心理诉求非常强烈，无论在文化方面，还是在经济贸易方面，彼此都能友好交往，和谐交流。因此，应挖掘傣泰族群关系的正面因素，利用其正面功能，进一步促进傣泰民族的文化文学交流，使之在"一带一路"倡议中发挥积极作用。

参考文献：

［1］黄兴球.老挝族群论.北京：民族出版社，2006.

［2］郭山，周娅等编.贝叶文化与和谐周边建设.昆明：云南大学出版社，2011.

［3］山茶编辑部.傣族文学讨论会论文集.北京：中国民间文艺出版社，1982.

［4］贺圣达.东南亚文化发展史.昆明：云南民族出版社，1986.

［5］Udomroongruangsri.兰那文学（泰文版）.曼谷：泰国朱拉隆功大学出版社，2003.

［6］Prakong Nimmanahaeminda.民间故事研究.曼谷：泰国朱拉隆功大学出版社，2008.

傣族贝叶文化世俗经典中的诗歌修辞研究

刀金平[①]

傣族是一个歌与诗的民族。傣族诗歌作为一种文学形式，不论是古拙简短的生产生活歌谣，还是温柔含蓄的情歌；不论是婉转哀伤的悲剧叙事诗，还是鸿篇巨制的创世史诗《巴塔麻嘎捧尚罗》、神话史诗《乌莎巴罗》和英雄史诗《章相》，无不反映着傣族人民各个历史时期的政治制度、经济结构、宗教信仰、伦理道德、礼仪风俗等，反映着傣族人民的思想和感情、价值观念与民族心理。据统计，流传于西双版纳傣族民间的世俗经典，其数量就有5000余部，其中表现传统文化艺术方面的诗歌，数量有2300余部。2017年起，西双版纳傣族自治州少数民族研究所开始整理、翻译的《中国傣族诗歌全集》，除去现代傣族诗歌（第十九篇现代诗篇）之外，所编纂的总目录中，即将整理翻译的诗歌作品就涵盖了18篇108集之多。

从类型上来讲，傣族诗歌可简单地分为古歌谣、情歌与叙事长诗。依此类推，古歌谣又分为劳动歌、生产歌、祭祀歌、祝福歌、习俗歌、儿歌等；情歌分为求爱情歌、失恋情歌、凤凰情歌等；叙事长诗分为创世史诗、神话史诗、英雄史诗、悲剧史诗等。

在傣族诗歌类作品中，具有代表性的、歌颂爱情的《召树屯》（汉译"孔雀公主"），悲剧叙事诗《娥波冠》（汉译"香发姑娘"），气势磅礴、诗句超万行甚至上十万行的《乌莎巴罗》《章巴细敦》（汉译"四棵桂花树"）、《兰嘎西贺》（汉译"十头魔王"）、《巴塔麻嘎捧尚罗》（汉译"傣族创世史诗"）、《章相》"五大诗王"，以及委婉动听的《叁敦浴》（汉译"花卉情诗"）、《叁喻》（汉译"隐语情诗"）、《叁丢勐》（汉译"韵律情诗"）、《叁帕》（汉译"转行情诗"）、《叁诺列》（汉译"鹦鹉情诗"）、《叁烘》（汉译"凤凰情诗"）等诗篇。诗歌中婉转动听的歌词，永不言弃的奋斗精神，气势磅礴的战争场面，不仅为傣族人民所熟识，更为傣族人民所热爱。

修辞手法方面，由于语言地域性、自身的传统文化特点以及受到南传上座部佛教文化的影响，傣族诗歌以其善用比喻、拟人、夸张、排比等特点，成为傣族诗

[①] 作者为西双版纳傣族自治州少数民族研究所所长，西双版纳傣族自治州贝叶文化研究中心主任，译审。

歌最具特征的语法表现形式，形成了具有独特性与鲜明特点的诗歌表现手法和文化特征。

本文仅就傣族诗歌中的修辞手法特点，做一个简单的介绍，意在使人们对傣族诗歌修辞手法的运用有一个初步的认识。

作为诗歌的一种表达形式与表现手法，傣族诗歌与汉族和其他少数民族的诗歌一样，在修辞手法方面也具有比喻、拟人、夸张、反问、借代、对比等表现手法，但其表现手法上也有自身的一些特点，主要表现在以下几个方面。

一、善用比喻

善用比喻，可以说是傣族诗歌的一个突出特点。正如《论傣族诗歌》作者，一位德高望重的祜巴勐（统管全勐佛教事务的大长老）在他的论著中所说："无论是祝福词、民间歌谣，或叙事诗，最显著的共同点之一，就是我们在讲叙事诗的特点时讲到的比喻手法。"这些比喻"把我们这绚丽多姿的叙事诗打扮得五彩缤纷，芳香四溢"。

首先，在审美观方面，正如汉族诗歌常以"善鸟香草，以配忠贞；恶禽臭物，以比谗佞"一样，傣族诗歌也常以宝石、孔雀、鲜花比喻正面人物，以秃鹰、怪鸟、魔鬼比喻反面形象。

其次，在语言运用方面，傣族诗歌常常用自然界的美来比喻、象征人物性格的美，以物喻人、婉转含蓄，把自己和理想、情操、祈望寄寓于自然界的各种美好事物之中，极富色彩的美。

我们不妨举几个例子了解傣族诗歌是如何运用比喻的表现手法来彰显诗句之美的。诗歌《召树屯》（孔雀公主）片段：

密密丛丛的树林里，

有一个镜子般的金湖碧波荡漾，

美丽的凤凰在那里栖息，

多情的金鹿望着水中的情郎。

……

静静的湖水、美丽的凤凰、多情的金鹿，勾勒出一幅色彩鲜明、意蕴美好的图画。这样的描写，使画面变活了，而且自然界中这些美好的事物，正是傣族人民理想、性格的最好象征。

再看看喃玛诺娜（孔雀公主）对召树屯唱的一首歌：

愿你像一棵椰子树，

树高根深，

我会天天坐在树下，

觉得快活凉爽。

……

贝叶文化与区域文化遗产传承保护

　　椰子树是亚热带特有的一种挺拔俊秀的树，用它比喻召树屯的英俊健美，是再恰当不过的了。愿椰子树"树高根深"，寄托着婻玛诺娜对召树屯的一片深情和对美好生活的憧憬。"我会天天坐在树下，觉得快活凉爽"，又隐喻了社会生活中傣族妇女同丈夫之间相濡以沫、长久相伴的关系。

　　召树屯在追赶婻玛诺娜的长途跋涉中，他是这样表达对婻玛诺娜的爱情忠贞的：

我死了也会化为一阵风，
要是她的门是朝北边开，
我就会吹进她的屋里，
要不然我会变为一朵白云，
飘到她的屋顶。
……

　　这些诗句是那样的富于情感，用傣族地区极富特色的自然景物，象征主人公的性格，抒发内心的感情，显得十分自然贴切。

　　再如《求爱情歌》片段：

男：美丽的菩提树啊，
　　叶子又嫩又青，
　　青嫩的叶子有千万片，
　　不知哪片是姑娘的心？

女：善良的小鸟啊，
　　夕阳已落下山岗，
　　你的孩子正在家里哭泣，
　　你的爱妻正在家里盼望，
　　你为何还在田野上飞翔？

男：池塘里的荷花啊，
　　你时时散发着幽香，
　　花瓣是你的面颊，
　　荷叶是你的衣裳，
　　阿哥想采一片荷叶带回去，
　　又怕把你损伤。

　　池塘里的荷花啊，
　　你时时散发着幽香，
　　泥土护着你的根基，
　　浮萍绕在你的身旁，
　　阿哥不如泥土也不如浮萍，
　　只得远远地向你张望。

女：阿哥啊阿哥，

你的歌声像泉水，

淙淙地流进了阿妹的心，

你的笑容像彩云，

轻轻地飘进了阿妹家的竹林。

……

正如我们看到的，在整首歌中，男女之间互相试探、询问，表达爱慕之情，不论是小伙"青嫩的叶子有千万片，不知哪片是姑娘的心"的求爱，或"阿哥想采一片荷叶带回去，又怕把你损伤……阿哥不如泥土也不如浮萍，只得远远地向你张望"的想求爱又不敢求爱的矛盾心情；还是姑娘"善良的小鸟啊，夕阳已落下山岗，你的孩子正在家里哭泣，你的爱妻正在家里盼望，你为何还在田野上飞翔"的探询，以及姑娘"阿哥啊阿哥，你的歌声像泉水，淙淙地流进了阿妹的心，你的笑容像彩云，轻轻地飘进了阿妹家的竹林"的接受求爱的心意。整个过程中，小伙把求爱的心隐藏在赞美对方的语言当中。同样的，姑娘也把接受求爱的心意，隐藏在赞美对方的语言中。双方温柔含蓄，既不显山不露水地倾诉了爱意，又表达了接受求爱的心意。正是采用了比喻（明喻）的表现手法，才使得言语、文采得到了升华、优美、含蓄、真挚、朴实的情感语言展露在人们面前。

再次，采用连环比喻，语言文句精练、优美。如《祝福歌》中老人为一对新人祝福的词句：

今天是日月星辰最闪亮的吉日，

今天是宇宙空间最晴朗的吉日，

今天，天神撒下谷种；

今天，仙女撒下鲜花；

今天，善良战胜邪恶；

今天，智慧放射出光辉；

今天，大象走出森林；

今天，金树结下金果；

今天，相亲相爱的人结为夫妇；

……

九宽十宽不如芭蕉叶宽，

九绿十绿不如粽子叶绿，

九尖十尖不如稻禾叶尖，

九音十音不如蝉叫的声音，

九象十象不如洁白的神象，

九天十天不如今天美好又吉祥。

该诗句采用了大量美好、形象的比喻和连环比喻，分别赞美婚礼的吉日及对新人的祝福。诗句看起来似乎很啰唆、烦琐，但经过字词的加工，比喻的应用，读起来朗朗上口，质朴、自然、优美，富于形象和色彩。

最后，比喻贴切，语言文句精练、简洁，具有韵律美。如诗歌《相勐宗布》的诗句：

无边的坝子翠绿如茵
淙淙的溪水
绕着竹楼人家
密密的椰树顶着蓝天
高高的佛塔挂满彩霞
……
还有对婻西里宗布的描写：
她有花朵的芬芳
她有金鹿的善良
她的名字像洒满阳光的翅膀
飞旋在一百零一个国家的土地上
……

这些优美的诗句，长诗的比喻用得十分出色。两段诗句中应用"翠绿如茵""顶着蓝天""挂满彩霞""花朵""金鹿""阳光"等一系列比喻，非常形象而又贴切地赞美了傣乡的美丽，表现出婻西里宗布美好的外貌和内心。读后使人如沐春风，感觉一种强烈的节奏感和韵律美。

又如傣族创世史诗《巴塔麻嘎捧尚罗》中的一段诗句：
英叭神累了
不想再操劳
躺在云层里
闭目静悄悄
……

这既是傣族民间的普通口语，又是明朗简洁的诗句；既让人一目了然，又包含着许多意境。以英叭神"躺在云层里"，"闭目"修饰"累了""不想再操劳"，不禁让人联想到傣族农民在田野里干了一天活计之后，累得筋疲力尽，躺在大树下闭目休憩的情景，文字精练简洁。

再如《拴牛魂歌》一段诗句：
公牛魂呀，母牛魂呀
大大小小的牛魂呀
田犁完了，秧栽完了
今天解下牛铃
今天扯下牛鼻绳

用金银线拴在你们的角上

保住你们的魂

让你们又肥又壮

恢复体力更健康

……

诗句尽管不长，但以其精练的语言，一言道明了给牛拴魂的目的、作用及意义。

二、巧用拟人

拟人，就是把事物人格化，把本来不具备人的一些动作和感情的事物变成和人一样。巧用拟人，可以说是傣族诗歌的另一个突出特点。诗歌拟人化的特点，在情歌中使用尤其广泛、频繁。如情歌《等待钟情的凤凰》：

男：金色的缅桂花哟，

　　开得又美又香。

　　缅桂花开在大树的枝头，

　　阿哥天天把你仰望。

　　金色的缅桂花哟，

　　你是待开放花蕾，

　　还是早已怒放？

　　蜜蜂可曾来采过蜜，

　　蝴蝶可曾落在你身上？

女：远方飞来的凤凰哟，

　　你仔细张开眼睛望望，

　　这朵缅桂是待开的花蕾，

　　这朵缅桂刚刚吐芳香。

　　风不曾拂过她的花瓣，

　　蜂不曾落在她的身旁，

　　缅桂不恋花蝴蝶，

　　只等待钟情的凤凰。

　　阿哥哟，

　　你为何不落在妹身旁？

又如《凤凰情诗》中的《铜凤凰传书》一诗：

　　铜凤凰啊铜凤凰，

　　你的聪慧超过天神帕雅英，

　　你的热忱帮助啊，

贝叶文化与区域文化遗产传承保护

使我感激泪尽,
……
今天我请你直接出面,
飞去找金凤凰,
把我的一片忠心,
贴在她的心上。
你的经验比小鹦鹉更丰富,
你的毅力比小鹦鹉更坚强,
完成任务更有保障。
你要穿过茫茫的森林,
飞过阡陌连倾的田野,
飞到金凤凰栖息的地方。

铜凤凰啊铜凤凰,
遇到逆风你要放平翅膀,
遇到大树你不要栖息,
狡猾的猎人会把你射伤;
戈当树的浆叶,
会粘住你的羽毛,
使你不能继续飞翔;
你要飞越祸害与灾难,
飞向金凤凰居住的地方。

当你快飞到她身边的时候,
你千万要仔细观望,
别的铜凤凰,
是否飞来和她做伴,
是否给她带来瓜果的芳香,
如果她已和别人成双,
你就赶快回到我的身旁。

如果金凤凰孤孤单单,
身边没有一只铜凤凰,
你就缓缓地飞到她的身边,
……

两首诗中的缅桂花、蜜蜂、蝴蝶、铜凤凰、金凤凰,从外表上看,它们是花、蜜蜂、蝴蝶和鸟，但却是拟人化了的花、蜂、蝶、鸟。在《铜凤凰传书》一诗中，铜凤凰、金凤凰实际上是一对傣族男女青年，它们具有含蓄、朴实的性格，美丽、优雅的容貌，对爱情的专一、为爱情不畏艰险的心理素质，是融勤劳勇敢、含蓄专一、优雅美丽、坚强无畏为一体的傣族典型青年的特征。

三、大胆应用张扬的夸张

应用张扬的夸张表现手法，也是傣族诗歌的一个突出特点。在傣族诗歌中，使用了大量的夸张表现手法。有的长诗中，尤其是神话史诗，引用的夸张写意，张扬得令人匪夷所思。如神话史诗《乌莎巴罗》在评价释迦牟尼佛祖的力量时，这样评价：

九百九十万头普通大象的力量
才等于一头吉利灭卡拉神象的力量
九百九十万头吉利灭卡拉神象的力量
才等于一位法轮王的力量

九百九十万位法轮王的力量
才等于四大天王中一位的力量
九百九十万位四大天王的力量
才等于一位帕雅英的力量

九百九十万位帕雅英的力量
才等于一位夜摩天王的力量
九百九十万位夜摩天王的力量
才等于一位乐变化天王的力量

九百九十万位乐变化天王的力量
才等于一位他化自在天王的力量
所有一切神灵的力量加在一起
才抵得佛祖一根指头的力气
……

诗歌中这样的描写和夸张，一方面或许就是为了强调和说明释迦牟尼佛祖的福德隆盛、法力无边；另一方面把释迦牟尼佛祖加以神化后，方能烘托出佛祖的伟大与杰出，在信众中树立起无比的威望。

在讲到勐迦湿抵抗妖兵入侵，讲到军队的数量时，诗歌中这样叙述道：
六国兵马由各自君王带领
浩浩荡荡连夜开赴战场

贝叶文化与区域文化遗产传承保护

他们带来的兵将哟
有六阿贺之多
……
九个勐的帕雅接到信札
立即调集强大兵马
日夜兼程马不停蹄
飞速赶往勐迦湿城

昆辛调集九百八十万士兵
从勐阿柯傣赶来
昆占调集九百八十万士兵
从勐布拔瓦帝赶来

昆松调集九百八十万士兵
从勐达腊兰拔赶来
昆达调集九百八十万士兵
从勐拉南赶来
……
支援勐迦湿的各路人马
全部齐集勐迦湿境内
人数有十八阿贺
……

这里,"阿贺"是一个数量词,据说是"一"后面有四十二个零。诗句中还列举了计算"阿贺"的一个简单方法,即把六十九捆如脸盆一样大的团花树木桩放在大道上,让众多的士兵踩过去,直到把团花树木桩被踩得粉碎,才相当于一阿贺。那么,诗句中讲到军队的人数达十八阿贺之多,从以上所举的例子中不难看出,十八阿贺的军队人数是何其的多。这样的夸张写意,在其他民族的诗歌中恐怕不多见。

在讲到帝释天的坐骑蔼罗筏孥时,这样夸张道:
神通广大的蔼罗筏孥
是一头威武巨象
拥有高超法力
它会变幻许多法术

它的背有五十由旬宽
有一百由旬长

它还会变出二十八个头
每个头上长有两颗长牙

蔼罗茂驽的长牙很奇特
每颗长牙上有七个花池
而且花池里还另有名堂
池里面都长有七株荷花

每株荷花有七片花瓣
每片花瓣上有七座宫殿
每座宫殿里有七个仙女
每个仙女有七个侍女
……

诗句中，一"由旬"大约四十里。对于巨象有多少牙、有多少花池和荷花、有多少花瓣和宫殿、有多少仙女和侍女，诗作者在计算后得出：有五十六颗牙，三百九十二个花池，两千七百四十四片花瓣，一万九千二百零八座宫殿，一十三万四千四百五十六个仙女，九十四万一千一百九十二个侍女。对一头大象，便能如此加以想象，以这样超现实的夸张表现手法，把一头大象刻画得神乎其神，又不失大象的本质，充分体现了傣族先民丰富的想象力。诗句通过对张扬的夸张的应用，以及运用丰富的想象力与不寻常之语，使人不禁浮想联翩，产生强烈的共鸣。

四、注重排比的引用

注重排比表现手法的引用，也是傣族诗歌的突出特点之一。如神话史诗《乌莎巴罗》序歌所唱：

听吧，各位父老乡亲
看吧，山泉水样明亮的眼睛
我手捧着一部金黄色巨著
我要吟唱一部动人的贝叶经

它是一个美丽而古老的传说
就像湄南荒河有多长说不清
它是一个稀奇古怪的故事
就像夜空中闪烁着的星星
……

我要讲述这个曲折的故事
让傣家人把善良和丑恶分清

贝叶文化与区域文化遗产传承保护

我要放声高唱这动听的歌
驱散罩在人们头顶上的乌云
……
傣家人对客人如同和煦阳光
傣家人的心肠像金鹿一样善良
傣家人如同蚂蚁觅食一样勤劳
傣家人像菩提树一样受人敬仰
……
湄南荒河两岸森林连成片
湄南荒河两岸宝藏取之不尽
湄南荒河两岸风光秀丽
湄南荒河两岸气候温润
……
再如赞美女主人公乌莎公主美丽的诗段：
年轻美丽的乌莎姑娘
她容貌盖世令人倾倒
她婀娜窈窕亭亭玉立
她身上的香味令人陶醉

姑娘本是莲花所生
姑娘本是莲花的女儿
姑娘比鲜花还美丽
姑娘浑身全是花香

姑娘身上的气味啊
再香的香水也比不上
姑娘身上的香型啊
集中了世间所有的花香
……

这样的表现手法，在傣族诗歌中多之又多。通过运用排比表现手法，使得诗歌文气贯通，语势加强，富有节奏感和旋律美，把作者的感情，抒发得淋漓尽致。

歌与诗，是语言发展的一种高级形式，是经过了艺术加工的更精练、更优美的一种语言表达方式。傣族诗歌，是傣族文学的一座高峰。它以优美、精练的文学语言和艺术表现形式，千百年来广泛流传于傣族民间，为傣族人民所喜爱。本人所阐述的观点，仅仅是傣族诗歌众多特点当中的一小部分，目的是对傣族诗歌的修辞手法做粗浅的探索，以起到抛砖引玉的作用。

参考文献：

［1］西双版纳傣族自治州民族事务委员会编.傣族文学简史.昆明：云南民族出版社，1988.

［2］云南少数民族文学丛书编辑委员会编.傣族古歌谣.北京：中国民间文艺出版社，1981.

［3］西双版纳傣族自治州少数民族研究所编.乌莎巴罗.深圳：深圳出版发行集团海天出版社，2011.

中国贝叶经传承与保护概况

张振伟[①]

一、中国贝叶经传承脉络

狭义的贝叶经指刻写在经过加工的贝叶棕叶子上的经文。贝叶经起源于印度。印度早期写本的书写载体主要是如桦树皮、沉香、棕榈叶等经过处理和加工的树皮和树叶,其中最为常见的是刻写在贝叶棕叶子上。贝叶棕梵语发音为 Pattra,[②]汉音译为"贝多罗树",其叶子简称贝叶,故这种经书通常称作贝叶经。贝叶经的制作过程包括采叶、水煮、磨光、裁割、烫孔、刻写、上色、装订八个环节。[③]贝叶经书写顺序从左至右、由上而下横向书写,刻写行数通常为五行、六行和八行三种。由于贝叶具有耐久性强,不怕潮湿,不易磨损,刻在上面的字迹长年不变的特点,[④]因此,除宗教典籍外,有价值的历史文献、医药典籍、天文历法、文学作品等也刻写在贝叶上。

"梵夹装"是与贝叶经密切相关又有不同的一个概念和典籍类型。所谓梵夹装,是古代中国人对从西域、印度传进来,用贝多罗树叶书写的梵文佛教经典两板相夹形式的一种称谓。或者说是古代中国人对从印度传进来的两板相夹形式梵文贝叶经的专门称谓。[⑤]后期也包括纸本书写的经文。梵夹装可以横向分为多个小种,如传统贝叶经、西北、草原丝绸之路沿线"梵夹装变种"形式,西藏地区(及蒙古地区)的"梵夹装变种"形式,清代宫廷梵夹装等等。[⑥]由于贝叶棕生长在热带,贝叶经制作区域受限,加之纸张的书写和使用较之于贝叶更为便利,因此纸质的梵夹装典籍不仅广泛存在于中国东部、西部、北部等温带地区,也广泛存在于印度、东南亚和云南省南部等贝叶棕生长的热带地区。

[①] 作者为云南大学西南边疆少数民族研究中心副研究员,博士。
[②] 黄惠焜."贝叶文化"十论.思想战线,2000(5).
[③] 这一制作技艺根据现代流传在云南省西双版纳傣族地区的贝叶经制作技艺整理而来,参见邓殿臣.谈谈"贝叶经"的制作过程.法音,1988(11).印度历史上的贝叶经制作技艺暂不可考。
[④] 艾温扁,征鹏.贝叶经——傣族文化的宝藏.思想战线,1981(2).
[⑤] 李致忠.中国书史研究中的一些问题——古书经折装、梵夹装、旋风装考辨.文献,1986(2).
[⑥] 周懿."梵夹装"装帧形制考——丝绸之路沿线梵夹装形制演变的相关问题.中国社会科学院硕士学位论文,2015.

贝叶经伴随佛教的对外传播而传播。印度佛教僧侣携带着贝叶经前往尼泊尔和中国新疆、西藏、汉地以及中亚、南亚等地区宣经传教，弘扬佛法。这些国家和地区的佛教徒也前往印度学习佛教，并带回大量贝叶经，或翻译为本国文字。从已发现的贝叶上可以看到，刻写在贝叶上的文字不限于梵文，还有巴利文、缅甸文、僧伽罗文、傣文、于阗文、回鹘文、吐火罗文、维吾尔文等种类的文字。

贝叶经从印度传入中国有久远的历史。东汉明帝（公元58—75年在位）时，僧人迦叶摩腾、竺法兰白马驮经入中土，并将其中的《四十二章经》译为汉文，这是由梵文翻译为汉文的第一部经典。白马送来的佛教经卷，就是印度的贝叶经。①从此以后，各个朝代不断有印度、西域等地高僧携带大量梵文贝叶经来到汉地译经讲学，弘法布教。汉地僧人也纷纷西行求法取经。其中唐代玄奘大师一人就从印度取回520函657部贝叶经。在现存的汉文大藏经中，将近1500部6000多卷佛教典籍译自梵文贝叶经，如果包括译后失传或未翻译的经典在内，传到汉地的梵文贝叶经至少在5000部以上。梵文贝叶经具体是何时传入藏地已无从考察，但7世纪在佛教传入藏地的同时，梵文贝叶经也随之而来。②贝叶经传入南传上座部佛教地区的时间也很难细考，但至迟公元15世纪，云南省南传上座部佛教地区已有确定的佛教寺院和佛教仪式活动记载。并且，云南省南传上座部佛教地区是中国境内少数还保存有贝叶经刻写与使用传统的区域。

二、中国贝叶经传承与保护现状

现存的中国贝叶经相对而言不太集中，在汉传、藏传、南传地区都有发现。在汉传佛教地区，原藏于河南省南阳市镇平县老庄镇杏花山菩提寺的一册贝叶经据传是唐代早期孤善本，为我国现存年代最早且保存完好的"贝叶经"之一，已被列为国家一级保护文物。一说该册贝叶经刻本内容为《楞严经》，③由其圆形梵文文字判断为印度南部地区所著。全夹共226叶，其中6叶残缺，叶长49厘米，宽5厘米，上下夹板为檀木制作，叶中有两个圆孔贯穿全册，叶周以金粉涂刷防护，横版书写，是标准的传统贝叶经形制装帧。④除此以外，杭州灵隐寺文物馆藏有一部梵文贝叶经，共有41张贝叶。方广锠教授研究认为，该贝叶经大约在北宋咸平三年（公元1000年）传入中国，原为北宋王朝所设立的译经院所有。据北京大学的萨尔吉教授研究，内容为《十事疏》，用尼泊尔钩体书写而成。山东青岛湛山寺收藏有近40多叶大小不一、年代不同的贝叶经。据介绍，大张贝叶经有3叶，约写于19世纪末；中型有3叶，经考证出于明代；小型贝叶30多叶，比较陈旧，破损严重，可能是唐宋时期的贝叶经。安徽九华山保存有2函贝叶经，1函内有10叶，1函内

---

① 张泽洪.贝叶经的传播及其文化意义——贝叶文化与南方丝绸之路.贵州民族研究，2002（2）.
② 李学竹.中国梵文贝叶经概况.中国藏学，2010（1）增刊.
③ 如果该刻本证实为《楞严经》，则可解决20世纪早期关于《楞严经》是否为中国人"杜撰"的争议，参见李学竹.中国梵文贝叶经概况.中国藏学，2010（1）增刊.
④ 周懿."梵夹装"装帧形制考——丝绸之路沿线梵夹装形制演变的相关问题.中国社会科学院硕士学位论文，2015.

贝叶文化与区域文化遗产传承保护

有73叶，1988年经国家文物鉴定中心鉴定为二级藏品，内容不详。成都宝光寺保存有一部《妙法莲花经》梵文贝叶经，叶数不详。四川峨眉山万年寺收藏有一部《华严经》梵文贝叶经，共246叶，据说系明代嘉靖年间暹罗国王所赠，用金泥书写在黝黑的贝多罗树叶上。浙江普陀山文物馆存有两种梵文经书贝叶经，叶数和内容均不详。福州雪峰寺收藏有一部梵文贝叶经，叶数和内容均不详。[1]

藏传佛教地区的贝叶经典籍非常丰富。由于西藏气候干燥，温湿适宜，西藏地区共保存有1000多函的贝叶经文献，共近6万页叶片，双面书写，近12万面，内容涵盖宗教、哲学、文学、艺术、医学、天文等学科。[2]大型寺院是藏传佛教地区贝叶经收藏的主要场所，其中在20世纪80年代，中国社科院的罗炤教授曾对布达拉宫、罗布林卡、哲蚌寺所藏的梵文贝叶经做了全面清查、整理、编号等工作。其中罗布林卡有60多函200多部经书，布达拉宫大约有200多函800多部经典，哲蚌寺只有1函213张贝叶。这三处加起来大概将近300函1000多部经典论著。[3]藏传佛教地区除贝叶经典籍外，还有大量的纸本梵夹装典籍。这些纸本梵夹装典籍在制作纸张时，使用了当地特殊的狼毒草韧皮为原料。使用这种原料制作的纸张，不惧虫蛀鼠咬，可千年不腐。

南传上座部佛教地区作为中国境内唯一还保存有贝叶经制作和使用技艺与传统的区域，贝叶经的保存和使用最为普遍。在云南省南传上座部佛教地区1600多所开放寺院中，有相当部分的南传上座部佛教寺院保存有数量不一的贝叶经。贝叶经或梵夹装典籍在部分南传上座部佛教宗教仪式中仍有使用。2008年，"贝叶经制作技艺"被列入国家第二批"非物质文化遗产"名录。从2002年以来，西双版纳州少数民族研究所对贝叶经古籍进行挖掘、收集、整理，共收集到经书400多部，其中贝叶经书150多部、绵纸经书200多部、唱本40多部。从中选择出具有代表性、流传面广、影响大的130部作为《中国贝叶经全集》的入选篇目。[4]从2006年至2010年，《中国贝叶经全集》100卷由人民出版社出版。除此以外，西双版纳地方政府不定期举办贝叶经刻写与传习活动，培养新的贝叶经制作技艺传承人。临沧市耿马县也对境内的贝叶经和南传上座部佛教典籍进行了收集整理，出版了《中国云南耿马傣文古籍编目》。

三、贝叶经文化保护与协调发展

贝叶经是佛教文化的重要载体，对贝叶经的研究，主要集中在贝叶经收藏和使用较集中的几所大学和研究机构，并具有鲜明的区域特色。其中，云南大学与西双版纳傣族自治州人民政府于2001年合作共建的"云南大学贝叶文化研究中心"

---

[1] 李学竹.中国梵文贝叶经概况.中国藏学，2010（1）增刊.
[2] 周懿.从梵夹装装帧形制演变看唐蕃古道的文化融合.西藏民族大学学报（哲学社会科学版），2016（1）.
[3] 李学竹.中国梵文贝叶经概况.中国藏学，2010（1）增刊.
[4] 岩香宰.《中国贝叶经全集》整理出版工作进展顺利.今日民族，2007（3）.

是国内较早的专门从事贝叶经收集整理研究的学术机构之一，主要研究对象为中国南传上座部佛教地区的贝叶经典籍。此外，北京大学"梵文贝叶经与佛教文献研究所"成立于2004年，隶属于北京大学外国语学院，以季羡林先生所开创的梵语、巴利语专业为依托，致力于整理研究珍贵的佛教原典文献，培养通晓梵语、巴利语的专业人才，它的主要研究材料来源于20世纪50年代民族文化宫从西藏地区收集的一批贝叶经典籍的照片。由"坦博艺苑"与兰州大学敦煌研究院共建的兰州大学贝叶文化研究中心也于2019年11月成立，它的主要研究对象是"坦博艺苑"收集的贝叶经典籍。西藏博物馆、西藏社会科学院、云南省社会科学院、西双版纳州民研所等机构也收藏有部分贝叶经，并有专业的研究人才队伍。由私人收藏家建立的"坦博艺苑"是贝叶经收藏的重要民间机构，据称拥有超过150万页的古巴利文、梵文、藏文贝叶经和佛学典籍。[1]

从中国贝叶经的传承与保护现状和已有研究来看，各级政府和相关研究机构构成了贝叶经保护和研究的主要力量。政府力量的介入，为贝叶经保护与贝叶文化的发展提供了直接的助力。这表现在各级非物质文化遗产名录的制定和非遗传承人的认定与支持上，还表现在以民族宗教事务委员会为代表的政府机构投入大量的人力、财力在贝叶经的收集、整理和翻译工作上。各相关研究机构也从与政府的合作中，获得了大量的贝叶经典藏资源和其他方面的研究支持，为持续开展研究提供了便利。

概括而言，中国贝叶经文化的保护和传承工作取得了一系列前所未有的成绩，包括贝叶经的整理、编目、翻译、出版、数字化等等，但在很多方面仍有进一步发展的余地。

首先，贝叶经研究与保护中的族际合作与国际合作应得到充分重视。现有的贝叶经重要保护机构和研究单位，各有传承脉络不同的贝叶经典籍收藏和研究对象，相互间交流合作较少。但在贝叶经典籍的整理、翻译和研究过程中，不同文字、时期的贝叶经的相互验证和比较，不同研究机构对彼此收藏的贝叶经的识读，可能会产生出人意料的成果。同时，在族际合作基础上扩大到与相关国家贝叶经保护及研究机构的合作，借鉴其他国家在贝叶经保护和研究中的经验，对贝叶经文化的进一步发展也能起到非常重要的作用。在这方面，德国与老挝国家图书馆的合作项目、尼泊尔国家档案馆与德国和印度的合作交流，[2]为国内开展相关工作提供了很好的借鉴。

其次，贝叶经的保护与发展应充分吸收当下计算机技术的发展趋势，进一步加强数据库建设，实现线上线下融合发展。数字化存储和数据库的建设与使用，能充分突破贝叶经典籍保存和使用方面的局限，使贝叶经这一特殊的佛教文化资源得到

---

[1] 中国教育电视台. 兰州大学参与共建贝叶经研究中心 让古文物"活"起来. http://www.centv.cn/p/342386.html.
[2] 徐亮. 尼泊尔国家档案馆的国际合作研究. 中国档案，2018（8）.

更广泛的阅读和使用。目前，在贝叶经的图像化处理与数据化应用方面，已经有了一系列的前期工作基础和技术储备，[①]能够为贝叶经典籍资源的数据化处理和使用提供相应的保障。当然，贝叶经作为特殊的佛教典籍文本与文化资源，在数据化处理的同时，作为民族文化的重要呈现形式和非物质文化遗产，也应发挥其在促进地方文化保护与产业化运作方面的积极作用。

中国贝叶经典籍的历史传承脉络源远流长，对中国佛教和社会文化产生了持续且重要的影响。现存的中国贝叶经典籍内容丰富，虽然在搜集、整理、识读、翻译、出版方面取得了一系列成绩，但距离全面整理和翻译出版还相距甚远，相关研究还有很大的发展空间。对贝叶经典籍的保护，需要各区域、民族、研究机构的通力合作。在贝叶经典籍的保存和利用中，应充分发挥计算机技术的重要作用。

中国贝叶经典籍内容宏富、涉及问题庞杂，对贝叶经传承和保护的研究，远非一篇文章所能涵括。本文仅列其梗概，作简单介绍之用。

---

① 钟卿，等.傣文贝叶经的图像增强与二值化方法研究.云南大学学报（自然科学版），2017（5）.

傣文贝叶经《佛祖巡游记》音译词的规范化

保明所[①]

一、引言

《中国贝叶经全集》共出版了100卷，《佛祖巡游记》为第1卷，2003年4月，由人民出版社正式发行。全书共11章，809页，50余万字。翻译所依据的贝叶经原件共11册，219片贝叶，双面刻写，合437页，每一页上刻有老傣文5行。该经原件是西双版纳傣族自治州贝叶文化研究中心的学者们从众多版本中遴选出来的，刻本保存完整，内容丰富细致。经书以贝叶原件的缩印、老傣文转写、国际音标、汉语直译、汉语意译、新傣文转写"六对照"的格式进行排版。《佛祖巡游记》的主要内容记述了佛祖在菩提树下修得正果，大彻大悟，心生慈悲；为普度众生，传播佛法，率众弟子持钵乞食，南行传教；以一切知智慧预测佛教未来5000年中各时期将会发生的各种福运和灾祸；并预言了西双版纳的山、水、寨、勐名称，西双版纳境内许多地名就来源于此书。

本文所讨论的音译词指的是在《佛祖巡游记》文本中，对照着傣文词语的发音，用语音相近的汉字对译过来的词语，即汉语译文中的音译词。它不同于借词中的音译词，即从外族语言中借来的词，在汉语词汇系统中具有一定的稳定性的词。此前尚无学者对此问题进行过个案研究。在民族古籍翻译成汉语的过程中，如何才能把原文本的信息准确全面地用汉语表达出来是衡量翻译质量高低的重要标志。从词汇层面来说，应尽可能采用意译才能更好地把原文信息传达出来，音译词过多而没有相应的注解，常常会给读者带来理解上的障碍。在《佛祖巡游记》的汉语译文中，音译词存在一些不规范的现象，已在一定程度上影响到了读者对原文本的理解。希望本文的研究成果对查阅该经文的读者有所帮助，为该书再版时提供一些参考。本研究在自建全文本词汇语料库基础上进行。

二、音译词不规范的类型

规范的音译词是前后一致的符合汉语表达习惯的形式。《佛祖巡游记》中不乏

[①] 作者为云南大学文学院副教授，博士。

贝叶文化与区域文化遗产传承保护

其例。如

傣文	音标	原译文
ᥛᥫᥒ	məŋ^{51}	勐
ᥛᥫᥒᥑᥣᥒ	məŋ^{51}xa:ŋ^{11}	勐康（地名）
ᥙᥢᥴᥚᥭᥴ	ba:ŋ^{13}fa:i^{13}	曼排（地名）①
ᥒᥤᥚᥤᥢ	ni^{33}pa:n^{51}	涅槃
ᥟᥣᥑᥢᥖᥣ	ʔa^{55}ra^{33}han^{55}ta:^{55}	阿罗汉

以上这些音译词的出现次数从 2 次到 200 余次不等，但都保持了前后的一致性，且符合汉语的表达习惯，属于规范的音译词。

不规范的音译词是相对于规范的形式而言的。判别音译词的不规范形式有两条标准。第一，看前后文的一致性。同一个词汇在同一文本中不同地方出现时，用来音译的形式（汉字）理应是一致的。如果前后文不一致，就判别为不规范的音译词。第二，看语义信息的传递是否通畅。若该音译词让以汉语为母语的读者理解起来有困难，且无相应的注解，则可判定为不规范音译词。依据这两条标准进行判别后发现，《佛祖巡游记》中不规范音译词，主要表现为三种类型。

（1）汉字使用的不规范。同一个词，在前后文不同地方出现时，用来译写的汉字不相同。如

傣文	音标	原译文	汉义
ᥚᥧᥣ	phja:^{51}	帕雅 / 叭雅	王
ᥗᥖᥧ	tha:^{51}tu^{55}	塔都 / 坦都	骨灰，舍利，遗骨
ᥖᥥᥝᥖᥣ	te^{51}va^{33}da:^{55}	丢瓦拉 / 丢丢拉	神灵，神仙
ᥟᥣᥔᥨᥒᥑᥭ	ʔa^{55}soŋ^{55}xai^{55}	阿松开 / 阿僧祇	阿僧祇
ᥛᥣᥞᥣᥐᥙ	ma^{33}ha:^{55}kap^{55}	麻哈嘎 / 马哈嘎	大劫
ᥔᥣᥰᥛᥙᥧᥖ	sa:^{55}ri^{33}but^{55}	萨利布 / 萨里布	舍利佛
ᥚᥐᥐᥝ	phak^{33}ka^{33}va:^{51}	帕嘎哇 / 帕噶哇	佛祖
ᥟᥢᥢᥖ	ʔa:^{55}nan^{51}ta^{33}	阿难 / 阿达	阿难陀
ᥑᥧᥢᥔᥦᥢᥖᥨᥒ	xu:n^{55}sɛn^{55}toŋ^{51}	昆先佟 / 昆先董	昆先董（地名）
ᥚᥧᥣᥟᥣᥔᥨᥐ	phja:^{51}ʔa^{55}sok^{55}	帕雅阿梭 / 帕雅阿所	阿育王
ᥐᥖᥥᥝᥣᥞᥨᥐ	ka^{33}te^{51}va^{33}lok^{33}	夏丢瓦罗 / 噶丢瓦罗	天界
ᥓᥨᥱᥐᥤ	jo^{51}ki^{51}	约仉 / 约几 / 哟仉 / 哟几	由旬（长度单位，传说一由旬等于一万六千米）
ᥛᥣᥞᥣᥬᥖ	ma^{33}ha:^{55}ra:t^{33}	麻哈拉 / 麻哈腊 / 麻哈兰	大臣

在同一文本之中，同一个词语的汉语音译形式应该是同一的，这样才符合规范。从上面的例子可以看出，《佛祖巡游记》中的许多名词，在进行汉语音译时，

---

① "勐"（地方）"曼"（寨子）已是傣族研究者常用的汉语词了。

使用了同音字或音近字来音译同一词语，大部分音译词出现了两个不同的译名，少部分出现了三个或四个不同的译名，难免会让读者产生误解。因此，我们认为这是一种不规范的音译词。

汉字使用不规范的音译词中，有少数是错别字。如

傣文	音标	原译文	正确词
ေစာ်	tsau[13]	名	召
ေစာ်	tsau[13]	台	召
ေတဝဒ	te[51]va[33]da:[55]	恙瓦拉	丢瓦拉
ြပ းမ ရ	phja:[51]maŋ[51]ra:i[51]	帕雅奔来	帕雅莽来

以上不规范音译词中，"名""台"与"召"，"恙"与"丢"，"奔"与"莽"都属形近而误，产生这类不规范现象的主要原因是校对不精。这类词数量很少，规范起来很简单，只要把错字改正过来就可以了。

（2）音译词与汉语中的词语不对应。在贝叶经翻译中，对译就是尽量在汉语词汇中寻找与傣语词语对等的词语。虽然傣汉两种语言之间的词语常常存在部分对应、零对应的情况，但寻找它们之间的对等词是对译的主要目标。历史上，汉语在翻译梵文或巴利文佛经的时候，一些专有名词已经有了固定的音译名称，这些名词的语义信息完整定型并得到了人们的普遍认可。在贝叶经的译文中，一些专有名词未用对等的汉语词汇进行对译，而是新造了另一个音译词，因而给母语为非傣语的读者造成了理解上的障碍。这种现象在贝叶经翻译中较为普遍。如

傣文	音标	原译文	对等词
ြပ အ ေသ	phja:[51]ʔa[55]sok[55]	帕雅阿梭	阿育王
ြပ အင	phja:[51]ʔin[55]	帕雅英	因陀罗，天帝
အ ေသင ၀	ʔa[55]soŋ[55]xai[55]	阿松开	阿僧祇
သ ရ ပ	sa:[55]ri[33]but[55]	萨利布	舍利佛
က ကသန သ	ka[55]ku[55]san[55]tha[33]	嘎古先塔	拘楼孙佛
သမ ဏ	som[55]ma[33]na[33]	松麻纳	沙门
က သ ပ	ka[55]sa[55]bap[55]	嘎萨巴	迦叶波佛
ကသ န ရ	ku[55]si[55]na:[51]ra:i[51]	古西纳来	拘尸那罗（佛祖涅槃之地）
ေက တမ	ko[51]ta[55]ma[33]	呙达麻	乔达摩
ေမ ၀ ေတ ဟ	məŋ[51]vi[33]te[51]ha[55]	勐韦碟哈	尾提诃（古印度小国名）
ေစာ ေက န က မ န	tsau[13]ko[55]na:[51]ka[33]ma[33]na[33]	召呙纳嘎麻纳	拘那含牟尼佛
ေပ သ သတ ေစာ	po[51]thi[51]sat[55]tsau[13]	波提先召	菩萨，大士
ေက သမ ပ	ko[55]sam[55]pi[33]	呙桑比	峤萨罗国

以上这些跟佛教的产生和传播具有密切关系的专有名词，原译文的词对汉语读者来说是难以理解的，若是译成汉语中的对等词，理解起来就容易多了。

（3）音译词与意译词并存。同一个词在文中有的地方用音译，有的地方用意

译。如

傣文	音标	原文音译	原文意译
ᨾᨠᨻᩊ	ma^{33}ka^{33}pha^{55}la^{33}	麻嘎帕腊	道，正果
ᨻᨧᩴ	pha^{33}tsau^{13}	帕召	佛祖，佛陀
ᨻᨷᩲ	pha^{33}ba:t^{35}	帕巴	脚印，足迹
ᨻᨿᩣ	pja:^{51}	帕雅	王，官
ᨳᨭᩩ	tha:^{51}tu^{55}	塔都	骨灰，舍利，遗骨
ᩅᩈᩣ	va^{33}sa:^{55}	瓦沙	佛历
ᨾᩉᩣ	ma^{33}ha:^{55}	麻哈	大
ᩁᨧ	ra:^{51}tsa^{33}	拉扎	大臣
ᩉᩴ	hɔ^{13}	伙	汉族
ᩈᨲᩥ	sat^{55}ti^{55}	萨帝	生灵，众生
ᨻᩅ	pha^{51}va^{33}	帕瓦	修行
ᨷᨳᨾ	ba^{55}tha^{55}ma^{33}	巴塔麻	起初
ᨾᩉᩣᨧᨲᩥᨿ	ma^{33}ha:^{55}tse^{55}ti^{55}ja^{33}	麻哈吉帝亚	大塔
ᨻᨠᩁᨶᩦ	bo^{55}kan^{55}xan^{55}ni^{33}	波给挖尼	荷花塘
ᩉᩪᩭ	hoi^{13}	回	箐
ᩈᩮᩁ	sɛn^{55}	先	十万

以上这些词语在《佛祖巡游记》中有两种翻译方式并存，就汉语的表达习惯来说，采用意译更便于理解和记忆。在音译与意译两种形式并存的词语中，极少数音译形式已为傣族研究者所熟悉，这一类词语的音译可算作规范的形式。如

傣文	音标	原文音译	原文意译
ᨷᩢ᩶ᩁ	ba:n^{13}	曼	村寨
ᨲᩢ᩶ᩁ	ta:n^{51}	赕	布施
ᨾᩮᩬᩨᨦ	məŋ^{51}	勐	地方，坝区
ᨧᩮᩢᩢᩣ	tsau^{13}	召	主，王
ᨶᩬ᩠ᨿ	nɔi^{11}	囡	小
ᨷᩢ᩠ᨶ	pan^{51}	版	千
ᨲᩫ᩶ᨾ	tham^{51}	坦	经典

在《佛祖巡游记》中，有少数一半音译一半意译的词语，如

傣文	音标	原译文	汉义
ᨻᨧᩴ	pha^{33}tsau^{13}	帕祖	佛祖
ᨻᨻᩩᨳᨧᩴ	pha^{33}put^{33}tha^{33}tsau^{13}	佛祖召	佛祖
ᨻᨿᩣᨿᩢᨠ	phja:^{51}jak^{33}	帕雅妖	妖王
ᨻᨿᩣᩋᩈᩰᨠ	phja:^{51}ʔa^{55}sok^{55}	王阿梭	阿育王
ᨻᨲᨳᨠᨲ	pha^{33}tat^{55}tha^{55}ka^{33}ta^{55}	佛达它嘎达	佛祖
ᨾᩉᩣᩋᨶᨲᨳᩮᩁ	ma^{33}ha:^{55}ʔa:^{55}nan^{51}ta^{33}then^{55}	麻哈阿难陀罗汉	阿难陀
ᨸᩮᩣᨳᩥᩈᨲᩴ	po^{51}thi^{51}sat^{55}tsau^{13}	波提先召菩萨	菩萨，大士

对于这类半音译半意译的词语，同样应尽量采用意译的方式更适合汉语的表达习惯。

三、音译词不规范的原因

（1）集体翻译的成果。集体译经是佛教史上的一个传统，少则数人，多则数十人。贝叶经的翻译也是如此，它是集体智慧的结晶。集体译经最大的好处是可以在较短时间内完成译经任务。不足之处是由于各人对原文的理解有细微差别，以及翻译风格不尽相同，难免会导致整体的译文质量有高有低。《佛祖巡游记》是汉译的第一部贝叶经，是一项开创性的工作，没有可借鉴的经验，翻译时由不同学者负责不同的章节，最后由一人统稿审定。由于译者在处理一些词语的时候所持的翻译理念有异，出现同一词语译写不规范的情况就不足为奇了。

（2）缺乏可查阅的大型双语词典。词典编纂是一项基础工作，非一朝一夕之功。傣语缺乏词典编纂的历史传统，第一部傣汉双语词典是刀世勋先生的《傣汉词典》（2002年），收词约2万条，主要为常用词。此书还远远不能满足贝叶经翻译的需要。贝叶经中大量的巴利语词、古语词、专有名词等无法从工具书中查到确切的汉语意思，这成为当时译经学者们最大的困难，只能先用音译的方式记录下来，所以《佛祖巡游记》中音译词较多。

（3）傣、汉两种语言系统中佛教词汇的对应关系沟通不畅。佛教是世界性的宗教，在许多国家和民族中具有悠久的历史，各国各民族都用自己的语言读经解经，形成了本国或本民族独特的佛教术语体系。佛教早在东汉就传入中原了，在漫长的发展中形成的汉语佛教理论有一套完整的术语体系，这套术语体系与梵文和巴利文的对应关系已被前辈时贤整理出来，成为佛教研究的重要部分，是佛教研习者共同遵守的一个规范。因此在把傣文贝叶经翻译成汉语时，傣文中的佛教术语体系应尽量与汉语的佛教术语体系对应，只有这样，才能准确地把贝叶经中所包含的信息准确地用汉语表达出来。在翻译《佛祖巡游记》的时候，由于对傣汉两种语言系统中佛教词汇对应关系的研究不够深入，许多用傣文记录的巴利语宗教词语没有准确地与汉语词语建立对应关系，译经者创造了一些音译词来记录这类词语，导致读者理解上的困难。

（4）缺乏音译词规范标准。由于《佛祖巡游记》是一部集体翻译的成果，不同学者在处理傣语中的疑难词汇的时候会用不同的方法，有的学者采用音译，有的学者采用意译，在音译的时候，同一个音有的用这个字记录，有的用那个字记录。也就是说对疑难词的翻译没有一个统一的标准，因此造成了文本中许多音译词不规范的现象。

四、音译词规范化的策略

音译词的规范就是要确立几条可操作的标准，把不规范的音译词按相应的标准

贝叶文化与区域文化遗产传承保护

确定下来。针对音译词的不规范现象，可采取以下措施进行规范。这里所讲的规范化策略主要是为《佛祖巡游记》再版时提供参考，也可为其他贝叶经的再版或翻译提供借鉴。

（1）统一音译词的书写形式。傣文属于拼音文字，字形与音节基本是一一对应的关系。汉语是表意文字，一个音节往往对应许多汉字。在音译的时候用哪些汉字来对译傣语的相应的音节应当制定一个明确的标准，并且贯穿始终。这样就可避免音译时汉字使用不规范的问题。

（2）尽量采用意译形式。"除了人名、地名、国名要用音译方式，以及不用音译就不能准确地表达原外来概念的以外，应尽量采用意译，因为意译更接近民族语言习惯，便于理解和记忆。"[①]在贝叶经的翻译中，能意译的词应尽量采用意译。在《佛祖巡游记》中，音译与意译并存的词语可采用意译替换音译的方式进行规范。半音译半意译的如能采用全意译的就采用全意译，不能全意译的就保留半音译半意译的形式。译文中的音译词如果汉语读者会产生理解困难的应尽量采用意译的形式进行替换，实在不能意译的词语，可采用注释的方法进行补充释义。因此，对文本中语义不易理解的音译词的语义探索就是一项重要的任务。许多音译难以理解的词汇，意译后就豁然开朗了，如

傣文	音标	原译文	意译
သာ ၃	sa:^{55}thu:^{51}	萨图	善哉
သုဝစိတ္တ	su^{55}tsa^{55}rit^{33}ta^{33}	苏扎利达	善行
သက္ကရာဇ်သမ်ပုတိဝပ်	sak^{55}ka^{55}ra^{33}tsom^{51}pu^{33}ti^{33}vap^{33}	沙嘎拉宗布提俚	南赡部洲
ဂန်သမယ	ʔe^{33}kaŋ^{55}sa^{55}ma^{33}jaŋ^{51}	厄刚夏马羊	（有）一次
သရီရ	sa^{55}ri^{33}ra^{33}	沙利腊	尸体
ပရိစဂ	ba^{55}ri^{33}tsak^{55}ka^{33}	巴利扎嘎	舍离
ပရမ	ba^{55}ri^{33}ma^{33}	巴拉麻	仁德
ကတေဝလောက	ka^{33}te^{51}va^{33}lok^{33}	戛丢瓦罗	天界
ဖျားစက္ကဝတ္တိ	phja^{51}tsak^{55}ka^{55}va^{33}ti^{55}	帕雅扎伽瓦帝	轮转王
မဟာဖုမ်	ma^{33}ha:^{55}phom^{51}	麻哈捧	大梵天王
ဖျားဝေသန္တရာ	phja^{51}ve^{51}san^{55}ta^{55}ra^{33}	帕雅韦先达腊	善施王子
ဇတဝန	pa:^{35}tse^{51}ta^{55}van^{51}	坝吉达日	祇园精舍
ဒီပင်္ကရ	ti^{33}baŋ^{55}kɔn^{55}	迪巴关	燃灯佛
အရိယမေတ္တေယျဇော်	ʔa^{55}ri^{33}ja^{33}me^{51}te^{55}jen^{51}tsau^{13}	阿利亚也呆佛	弥勒佛
ဖျားအိဿုန်	phja^{51}ʔai^{35}son^{55}	帕雅艾苏	水神

以上这些原译文中音译词通过意译后，与汉语中的词对应起来，理解起来就容易多了。但《佛祖巡游记》中的大部分音译词无法得知其确切的意义。如

---

① 黄伯荣，廖序东．现代汉语．北京：高等教育出版社，2011：265．

傣文	音标	原译文	汉义
ᥓᥣᥱᥓᥣᥴᥙᥨᥖ	ra:^{51}tsa^{33}but^{55}	拉扎布	—
ᥑᥣᥴᥣᥲᥐᥨᥛ	sa^{55}ra^{33}na:^{51}kom^{51}	萨拉纳贡	—
ᥑᥧᥖᥛᥣᥝᥖ	sut^{55}tha^{33}va:t^{33}	苏塔洼	—
ᥘᥨᥝᥞᥤᥱᥒᥤ	lo^{51}hi^{55}ni^{33}	罗希尼	—
ᥖᥛᥛᥣᥱᥣᥴᥘᥨᥝᥰᥙᥨ	tham^{33}ma^{33}ra^{33}so^{55}tsau^{13}	坦麻腊梭召	—
ᥐᥨᥴᥞᥤᥴᥐᥧᥖᥖᥣᥴᥘᥣ	dɔi^{55}si^{55}kut^{55}ta^{55}la^{33}	山西古达腊	—
ᥒᥣᥴᥚᥤᥰᥝᥣᥰᥝᥣᥴᥒᥣᥴᥐᥨᥢ	ʔa^{55}phi^{33}va^{33}va^{33}na^{33}kɔn^{51}	阿皮瓦拿贯	—
ᥛᥤᥐᥣᥴᥣᥴᥑᥣᥴ	mi^{51}ka^{51}ra:^{51}tsa:^{51}	米伽拉拉	—
ᥑᥣᥴᥙᥱᥓᥣᥱᥢᥴᥙᥣᥰᥒᥨᥴ	sa^{55}pe^{51}tsa^{33}na^{33}ba:^{55}jo^{51}	萨别扎拿巴呦	—
ᥛᥣᥱᥞᥣᥰᥑᥣᥴᥛᥤᥰᥖᥛᥴᥘᥨᥝᥰ	ma^{33}ha:^{55}sa:^{55}mi^{51}tha^{33}so^{55}	麻哈沙弥坦麻梭	—

贝叶经中的音译词大都源于巴利语词，国际上通行的罗马字母巴利文与汉语的对应关系是明确的，只要找出文本中傣文拼写的巴利语词与国际通行的罗马字母巴利语词的对应关系，就可准确地译为汉语的对应词了。这方面的研究前人已经做了不少工作（刀世勋 1982，张公瑾 2003，戴红亮 2015、2018），但还是有许多音译词还没得到很好的解释，有待进一步整理研究。

（3）编写贝叶经词典。在傣文贝叶经的整理、翻译、研究过程中，疑难词的释义是最大的困难。如果能够编写一部专门收录傣文贝叶经中疑难词的傣汉双语词典，供研究傣文贝叶经的学者们参考，那是一桩功德无量的事业。在贝叶经中，最难理解的词主要是巴利语借词，应作为词典收录的主要对象，在收录此类词的时候应多方求证其准确的意义，用傣文字母拼写的巴利语借词如何与国际上通行的罗马字母巴利文对应起来又是其中的重中之重。有的词语的对应关系明显，这类词语容易得到合理解释，而有的词语由于用傣文记录巴利语时发生了变异，其释义就有较大困难，需要仔细甄别考证。此外，一些古傣语的词和常用词的特殊用法也应该收录到词典中供人们查阅。实际上，若这样的词典编纂出来了，以上的许多问题也就迎刃而解了。可喜的是，2015 年西双版纳傣族自治州少数民族研究所编写的《傣汉词典》由云南民族出版社出版发行，其中收录了许多贝叶经翻译中常见的疑难词汇，这对贝叶经译文的校勘再版具有较大帮助。

五、结论

贝叶经的经就是经典的意思，经典就是要作为一种典范，一直流传下去，只有质量越来越好的文本才能成为流传的经典。贝叶经 100 卷出版了，但经文翻译质量的提升一直是摆在我们面前的一个重要课题。如何提升译文质量，从微观方面看，涉及语音、语法、语义、修辞等方面的问题；从宏观的方面看，涉及整个的傣族文化和佛教文化体系。这里对音译词的探讨只是一些初步的分析，往后对贝叶经其他方面的研究还有待我们更好地去探索。希望在贝叶文本数据库的支持下，对贝叶经经文的研究取得更大的进展。

参考文献：

［1］《中国贝叶经全集》编辑委员会.佛祖巡游记.北京：人民出版社，2010.

［2］黄伯荣，廖序东.现代汉语（增订五版）.北京：高等教育出版社，2011.

［3］戴红亮.基于语料库的现代傣语词汇研究.北京：中央民族大学出版社，2015.

［4］刀世勋.傣汉词典.昆明：云南民族出版社，2002.

［5］周荐.词汇学与词典学研究.北京：商务印书馆，2004.

［6］西双版纳傣族自治州少数民族研究所.傣汉词典.昆明：云南民族出版社，2015.

［7］周娅.《中国贝叶经全集》及其翻译校勘中的若干问题.昆明：云南大学出版社，2007.

［8］刀世勋.巴利语对傣语的影响.民族语文，1982（6）.

［9］张公瑾.傣文《维先达罗本生经》中的巴利语借词——以《十愿经》第一节为例.民族语文，2003（4）.

西双版纳傣文古籍翻译整理初探

陆云东[①]

西双版纳傣文古籍是傣族人民千百年来创造的丰富多彩的历史文化的积淀，是傣族人民宝贵的精神财富，也是中华民族灿烂文化的重要组成部分。本文根据西双版纳傣文古籍翻译整理现状，结合笔者从事10多年的傣文古籍翻译整理的工作实践，对目前傣文古籍翻译应遵循的原则和必备的素养提出几点看法。

一、翻译傣文古籍的意义

西双版纳傣文古籍《论傣族诗歌》中记载西双版纳傣文古籍有84000卷，但至今未能核实。据中央民族大学教授张公瑾先生分析，现在可查的南传上座部佛教巴利文经典大概有10000种，如果每种再分为10卷8卷，那么说傣文古籍有84000卷也不为过。根据西双版纳州少数民族研究所收集到的600多部傣文古籍来看，大部分傣文古籍还散落在民间，未能收集、整理、翻译出版，因此傣文古籍工作任务艰巨，任重而道远。

傣文古籍主要由两部分组成，一是用贝叶刻写的经书，用绵纸、桑皮纸抄写的经书。虽说是经书，但并不全是佛教经典。二是生产生活中的方方面面，历史上有价值的东西，都会记录在里面，包罗万象。除了形成文字的经书外，还有流传于民间的大量说唱文学、民间故事、神话传说等，这些都是保存于民间的活形态资料。翻译整理这些傣文古籍，可以让傣族的子孙后代了解傣族的过去，吸取民族文化精华，还可以多学科地研究傣族文化，了解傣族发展的历史进程，促进傣族繁荣昌盛。

西双版纳傣文古籍整理工作从20世纪80年代开始，至今不过40年，与几千年的汉文古籍整理相比，还是一门新学科。除了经验不足外，西双版纳傣文古籍本身的复杂性也增加了整理的难度。过去由于古籍办公室人员编制少，傣文古籍整理工作长期处于只收集，鲜有翻译出版的状况。现在的情况与过去相比已经发生了根本的变化。2001年，"首届中国贝叶文化研讨会"在西双版纳景洪市召开，来自全国各地的100多位专家学者对傣文古籍的研究进行了探讨，在此次会议上首次提出

[①] 作者为西双版纳州少数民族研究所/西双版纳州贝叶文化研究中心副译审。

了"中国贝叶经"这个概念,引起了世人的关注。专家学者们对编译、整理、出版傣文古籍即贝叶经提出了很好的建议和意见,由此促成了西双版纳州委、州人民政府决定编译、整理、出版《中国贝叶经全集》100卷。2005年《中国贝叶经全集》项目正式启动,州政府抽调了30多位专家学者加入编译、整理工作,并增加了州古籍办公室的编制。经过8年的努力《中国贝叶经全集》100卷全部得以出版发行。

通过编译、整理、出版《中国贝叶经全集》100卷,西双版纳州已培养出一支专业的傣文古籍翻译整理人才队伍。当傣文古籍翻译整理工作形成一定规模之后,只有展开理论研究和方法论的探讨,才能将古籍整理工作继续向前推进。由于傣文古籍卷帙浩繁,要从中选出一部部专著进行翻译整理,并加以出版,不仅需要理论作指导,而且要有一套严密的工作程序和先进的科学方法供翻译者遵循。因此,注重古籍翻译工作的同时,也要加强理论建设。从目前傣文古籍整理的工作上看,我们就是用汉文把傣文古籍的著述内容翻译出来,然后出版,为广大的读者和中外研究学者提供重要的少数民族历史文献资料。

近年来,很多学者著文指出,通过对傣族古代文化的研究,发现傣族传统文化本身就是一种绿色文化、和谐文化,它所倡导的天人和谐、社会和谐、人与人和谐的思想,与我们今天所进行的和谐社会的构建是一脉相承的。因此,傣文古籍工作必然对于增进我国民族团结、社会进步、边疆稳定繁荣将会起到积极的促进作用。由此可见,翻译整理傣文古籍是一项十分重要的文化建设工作。

二、翻译傣文古籍的基本原则

从事傣文古籍翻译工作也同其他民文翻译工作一样,必须遵循一定的原则。"信、达、雅"被视为公认的翻译工作基本原则,傣文古籍翻译也要遵循这一原则。笔者根据多年的傣文古籍翻译工作的实际,提出以下原则:

(一)真实性原则

对傣文古籍的翻译,真实性是必须首先保证的。这里讲的真实性其实就是"信",力求在古籍原文的基础上,以当地人最朴实的语言翻译出来,避免翻译过程中"文化转换""加工创造",要忠实于原著,以"信"为本。由于翻译者翻译能力不一,不强求一定要做到"达""雅",但"信"一定要做到。若翻译的内容不真实,不仅不能真实地揭示原著的内涵,不能向读者提供切实可靠的资料,而且会误导读者,使之得出错误的结论,那就贻害不浅了。切忌从个人的爱好为出发点,对那些自己不感兴趣或认为不重要,甚至认为是糟粕的东西,进行任意删改或加工,也许这些你认为不重要的部分,其中恰巧蕴含着具有重要价值的内容;或者现在看来是糟粕的东西,随着研究的深入,可能会在里面发现深层次文化的内涵或线索。

(二)尊重语言特性原则

由于傣汉两个民族有着不同的文化背景、不同的思维方式、不同的风俗习惯,其语言表达方式各有特点，都具有极强的语言表现力，因此在傣文古籍翻译过程中，用汉语翻译傣文古籍很难充分地将其原文中的语言特点表现出来。而这些语言特点又是傣文古籍中最生动、最细腻、最精彩、最富有傣族特色、最耐人寻味之处。所以，我们在翻译过程中，要尽可能地反映原文的语言特点，必要时充分利用备注等手段加以解释阐述。例如，傣族佛本生故事《玉喃妙》（意为花猫姑娘）是一部在西双版纳地区家喻户晓的故事。该书塑造了善良、诚实、执着、对爱情忠贞不渝的傣族青年形象，表达了傣族人民崇尚婚姻自由、崇尚真挚爱情、向往美好生活的高尚品德。书中主人公的一句经典对白为傣族群众世代传颂。主人公对爱情许下了这样的誓言："如果是叶子就拴在腰间；如果是花猫就嚼饭喂它。"按照傣族傣语发音和当时狩猎生活背景，傣族群众觉得相当的优美，而且句子很押韵，朗朗上口，所以它深受傣族群众的喜爱。但按照现代汉语来讲，算不上佳句，如果按照汉语的特点来翻译，舍去了叶子和花猫，改用汉语习惯用语如"海枯石烂"之类的形容词，那就会失去傣族的语言特点，傣族群众也无法感同身受。既要保留原文形式和特色，又要让读者理解其真正的含义，在翻译的时候，采取译后加注释是非常有必要的，例如，傣族谚语"秃鹰衔来，乌鸦叼去"，按照原文直译出来，可能读者不解其意，但可以加上注解，解释为，竹篮打水一场空。这样就既可以保留原文的特点，又可以让读者明白傣汉两种语言的表达方式和特点。

（三）实事求是原则

在傣文古籍翻译过程中，常常会遇到傣语古语、巴利语借词、布朗语借词、缅语借词、柬埔寨语借词等难度大的词语，此类词语有些深奥难懂，已经超出了翻译者所掌握的范围。在对这些词语暂时不理解，工具书又查不到的情况下，不应牵强地翻译，更不能凭个人主观意志随意删减，应在保留原文的前提下采取音译方式，以便留到今后研究破解。随意删减或妄加猜测、强行翻译，对古籍翻译工作来说都是极其严重的谬误。无论采取何种方式，必须把古籍的翻译情况如实表示出来，让读者知道，哪些问题尚有疑问，哪些地方还没有弄明白，让后来者去解决，或者让读者去探讨、钻研，这才是翻译工作者应具备的科学态度。

三、傣文古籍翻译整理者应该具备的素质

根据笔者10多年的傣文古籍翻译整理经验，要成为一名优秀的傣文古籍翻译工作者，必须具备一定的基本理论知识和专业技能，可归纳为以下几点：

（一）必须具备一定的思想修养

作为一名傣文古籍翻译整理者，首先要具有民族自豪感和责任感，也就是对历史悠久的傣族文化感到自豪，同时要有继承发扬民族文化的责任感和使命感。其次要认同傣族文化是中华民族文化的重要组成部分，56个民族的文化共同构成了灿烂的中华民族文化。要认识到翻译、整理、继承前人的文化遗产，是一项光荣而艰巨的工作，因而要有吃苦耐劳的精神，还要保持谦虚谨慎的态度和勇于探索的品质。

（二）具备一定的傣汉双语互译能力

掌握傣汉两种语言文字是做好傣文古籍翻译的必备条件，两者缺一不可。掌握两种语言文字的程度越高，翻译出来的作品质量就越高。在翻译傣文古籍工作实践中，有些人是高僧或是还俗的康朗，他们具有较高的傣语文字造诣，但汉语水平只相当于小学生，在翻译的过程中很吃力，翻译出来的作品甚至读不通顺。有些是高等院校毕业的高才生，虽然掌握了较高的汉语文字水平，但由于掌握的傣语文字的基础不扎实，掌握的傣语词汇量不大，特别是傣文古籍中涉及的傣古语、巴利语、佛教用语较多，在翻译过程中也很吃力，对所翻译的傣文古籍一知半解，所翻译出来的作品失去了真实性，没有达到"信"的要求，不能算作一部好的译作。所以作为一名合格的傣文古籍翻译者，必须具备驾驭傣汉两种语言文字的能力，而优秀的傣文古籍翻译者，必然是在工作实践中经过千锤百炼而磨炼出来的。

（三）具备深厚的多种文化修养

傣文古籍包罗万象，内容十分丰富，涉及宗教、历史、哲学、政治、经济、天文、历法、军事、医药、伦理道德、法律法规、文学艺术等等，可以说是傣族传统文化的集大成者，是傣族智慧的万有文库。因此，要做好博大精深的傣文古籍翻译工作，必须博览群书，具备诸多学科的知识。然而人的一生毕竟时间和精力有限，不可能做到样样精通。虽然不能做到面面俱到，但笔者在傣文古籍翻译实践中，总结出有几个方面的知识是必须具备的。一是要掌握基本的佛教基础知识（包括北传佛教和南传上座部佛教），因为傣文古籍中佛教经典所占比例较大，这就要求傣文古籍翻译工作者要多读佛教原著，了解佛教文化，尽量多掌握汉语言佛学知识和佛教专用词汇，这些都是从事傣文古籍翻译工作的基本功。二是要掌握大量的巴利语借词，因为任何体裁的傣文古籍都有巴利语的存在。如果不熟悉或不掌握巴利语，通读原文就很困难，要想翻译全文更是难上加难。三是要熟练掌握老傣文用于拼写巴利语借词的特殊格式，傣语称为"多发"，汉语可以解释为重叠字或合体字，它是声韵母相互代替、相互重叠的特殊书写方式。大多数人觉得老傣文难学，其实难点就在于对重叠字的认识。重叠字的声韵母，在上下和前后的位置相互代替，可谓千变万化。如果不能熟练掌握重叠字的拼读方法，不要说翻译傣文古籍，可能连读都很困难。重叠字的拼写和拼读方法，至今没有人系统地总结阐述过，一直以来都是约定俗成的，但只要认真下功夫探索，也能发现重叠字的一般规律。掌握了重叠字的拼读方法，最大的益处就是能通过各种工具书查找不懂的词语。因为傣文属拼音文字，读不出词的读音是无法查阅工具书的，这是傣文的特点。四是学习掌握基础泰文，学习泰文是为了查阅泰文词典等工具书。笔者在翻译傣文古籍实践过程中，常常遇到疑难词，特别是巴利语借词，查遍所有版本的《傣汉词典》也无法找到相应的词义，问遍了专家学者也找不到答案，转而查阅《泰汉词典》《泰巴汉南传佛学词典》，终于找到了词义解释。由此可见，查阅国内外的工具书是我们可以利用的手段，掌握一门或多门外语有时可以取得事半功倍的效果。

总之，傣文古籍翻译整理工作是一项艰深而浩大的工程，需要付出大量艰辛的劳动，甚至需要几代人不懈努力。从事傣文古籍翻译工作的同仁，肩负着历史使命和责任，应共同努力工作，为继承发扬民族传统文化而贡献力量。

参考文献：

[1] 包和平，王学艳.论民族古籍整理中的翻译问题.图书馆学刊，2005（4）.

[2] 秦家华，周娅，岩香宰主编.贝叶文化与民族社会发展.昆明：云南大学出版社，2007.

[3] 郭山，周娅，岩香宰主编.贝叶文化与傣族和谐社会建设.昆明：云南大学出版社，2008.

让贝叶文里的文字活起来

——德宏傣文古籍抢救保护翻译整理与开发利用

张 云[①]

为贯彻落实国务院办公厅国办发〔2007〕6号文件《国务院办公厅关于进一步加强古籍保护工作的意见》和云南省人民政府办公厅云政办发〔2007〕235号文件《云南省人民政府办公厅贯彻落实〈国务院办公厅关于进一步加强古籍保护工作的意见〉的通知》精神,经德宏州政府研究决定成立德宏州少数民族古籍抢救保护领导小组(德政办发〔2014〕38号文件《德宏州人民政府办公室关于成立德宏州少数民族古籍抢救保护领导小组的通知》),已选出200部有价值的傣文古籍翻译出版。

"十三五"期间,2017年6月向云南省民宗委申报德宏州少数民族古籍抢救保护项目,于2018年3月入选云南省民族文化"百项精品"项目。第一批下拨项目资金40万元。现已完成历史类5部、佛教类1部、文学类6部的老傣文图片制作、老傣文译现代德宏傣文、现代德宏傣文译汉文、汉文整理及编辑校对工作。该项目工作还在继续推进。

2019年5月,项目组邀请云南大学贝叶文化研究中心的三位专家指导该项目。专家组建议实现"三个提升":提升德宏傣族文化在全国少数民族传统文化中的"辨识度"和"文化形象";提升中国德宏傣族文化在整个东南亚尤其是傣泰民族文化圈中的文化势能;提升德宏少数民族文化服务于国家和云南省发展战略的文化支撑作用及人才创新力。挖掘古籍文献中可运用转化的内容,提升传统文化在当代的创新力和附加值。

一、目前德宏州傣文古籍状况

在长期的历史发展进程中,傣族人民积累了丰富而灿烂的物质文明和文化遗产,留下了大量的老傣文手抄经书,已翻译的历史类傣文古籍《萨缅帕拉吾》记载傣文经书传世84000部,其中"经藏"21000部、"律藏"21000部、"论藏"42000部,总称为"三藏经",并有一部五卷本贝叶经名为《别闷西版西甘》,专门讲述

[①] 作者为云南省德宏州图书馆副研究馆员。

这84000部佛经的由来传说。实际上有那么多吗？现已无从考证，但也说明了傣文经书数量之大。这些古籍经书有的刻写在贝叶上，称为贝叶经；有的抄写在绵纸上称绵纸经，有的写在桑皮纸上称为桑皮纸经，还有刻写在象牙片上的称为象牙片写经，写在象骨片上的称为象骨片写经，总称为傣文古籍经书。书写文字有圆形缅傣文、长方形德宏老傣文，内容包括宗教信仰、傣历、傣医、叙事长诗、民间故事、神话等。因此，德宏傣文古籍从书写文字和书写材质上看都是丰富多彩的。

目前德宏州收藏傣文古籍的基本情况为：德宏州档案馆181卷，德宏州民语委200卷，德宏州文化馆、德宏州图书馆200卷，芒市文化馆200卷，瑞丽市档案馆200卷左右，梁河县档案馆300卷，盈江县档案馆200卷，畹町文化馆150卷。全州有大小奘房592座，每座奘房都有傣文古籍经书存放。据不完全统计，大奘房菩提寺500卷，佛光寺300卷，五云寺350卷。德宏州傣学学会收藏200卷，民间傣族文化人方正午收藏78卷，金常玉收藏125卷。上述单位和个人所收藏的傣文古籍大多未翻译。

二、德宏傣文古籍的内容及其归类

德宏傣文古籍的内容十分广泛丰富，涉及傣族社会生活的方方面面，是德宏傣族社会历史和文化的见证物，是古代傣族人民智慧、才华和创造力的结晶。从内容上看，大致可分为以下几大类：

（一）历史类

现选出50部，如《嘿勐沽勐——勐卯古代诸王史》《银云瑞雾的勐卯果占璧简史》《勐卯果占璧王召武定》《思汉法王》《盈江简史》等是研究傣族历史，参考价值很高的傣文古籍。

（二）文学类

文学类傣文古籍文献占了傣文古籍很大的比重，有民间神话、创世史诗、民间传说、民间故事、叙事长诗、各种习俗歌等。现选68部，如《阿銮》故事系列、《纳纽光喊》《广母勐谢》《勇罕》等。

（三）佛学类

佛学类主要有"三藏经"，"三藏经"又分为"经藏""律藏""论藏"三部分，现选出32部，如《苏玛哈娃》《苏谢纳喊》《皮探玛亚门》等。

（四）礼仪类

中国是礼仪之邦，傣族是讲究礼仪的民族，所以礼仪类的傣文古籍文献的数量也不少，教育人们没有父母的血汗和母亲的哺育，自己就不会长大成人，父母的恩情是永远报答不尽的。教育人们尊老爱幼，教育妇女做媳妇的礼节，等等。现选出16部，如《贡纳巴底》《五种教育方法》《琐达坝大》等。

（五）天文历法类

傣族观天象，以地球绕太阳运行一周时间纪年，年为阳历，以月亮的一个圆缺周期时间纪月，月为阴历月，有星期，每星期7天，上述称为傣历。德宏州历史上由于受佛教文化的影响，也有用佛历和小历的。中华人民共和国成立后，傣族也随着使用公历。现选出两部天文历法类的傣文古籍准备翻译。

（六）语言类

有记载傣族语言文字的原始创作和发展历程的傣文古籍文献，从文字起源、语言、语法、文学改革等方面记述，现已选出4部待翻译。

（七）占卜类

占卜类傣文古籍有图表及其说明，内容涉及选择出殡日、建房日、做生意、购买货物（含牲畜）、讨亲、嫁女、建立村寨等，现选出18部，如《测算吉凶日》《倮嘎扎滴啥纳然》《占卦病因》等。

（八）医学类

傣族医学古籍是一份珍贵的医学遗产，位列四大少数民族医类之一，学问高深。如德宏的《傣医用药典》《八种致病原因》（导致生病的8种原因：1. 缺少运动；2. 心情不平静；3. 体内气血不畅；4. 体内三种不清新的浊体混合；5. 季节更替过快；6. 饮食与肠胃不合；7. 过度的体力消耗；8. 寿命本身所决定）。现已选有价值的16部，如《傣医傣药》《卫利亚苏哈》《盈江傣医傣药》，待翻译。

三、翻译研究出版傣族傣文古籍开发利用前景

（一）构建和谐社会的价值

我国是多民族的国家，民族地区和谐社会的构建，是至今我国"和谐社会"构建的一个重要课题。傣族是一个跨境民族，德宏傣族地区是各民族杂居的地区，又地处我国的边境。因此，和谐社会的构建是傣族地区现阶段发展的一个重要任务，傣文古籍对当今构建和谐社会具有典型的意义和积极的作用。首先，傣文古籍提倡人与自然的和谐，如傣族原始宗教提出："大地是母亲，森林是父亲，只有从父母那里才可以获得食物。"傣族认为："没有森林就没有水，没有水就没有田地，没有田地就没有粮食，没有粮食就无法生存。"所以傣族爱护森林，不随意毁坏森林。其次，傣文古籍中表现的系列伦理道德规范、礼仪、戒律等，都对人与人、人与社会的和谐起到不可低估的作用。如流传在德宏地区的《五种教育方法》，教育子孙说，道德修养好的人，经常教育子孙不嗜酒如命，不乱说乱讲，不打架斗殴，不吸食鸦片，不男盗女娼，勤勤恳恳种田地，用良心去做生意，不欺行霸市。上述傣文古籍，都可促进人与人、人与社会的和谐，可起到法律的辅助作用。所以说，傣族的傣文古籍具有构建和谐社会方面的作用、价值。

（二）文化产业开发价值

如前述德宏傣文古籍的内容及其归类，德宏傣文古籍包含历史、文学、佛学、礼仪、天文历法、语言、占卜、医学等多方面的内容，底蕴非常深厚，是一宗非常难得的宝贵文化遗产。德宏傣文古籍的文化产业开发价值有如下两方面：

1. 出版价值

德宏傣文古籍包含的内容丰富多彩，翻译整理出版这批傣文古籍是一个展示傣族贝叶文化的巨大工程，是傣族优秀文化对弘扬中华文化，为丰富世界文化做出的贡献。出版以广大群众为读者对象的文学故事、佛经故事、寓言故事，向广大读者和游客销售，让他们深度了解傣族优秀传统文化。

2. 影视创作题材价值

20世纪五六十年代，云南少数民族题材的电影曾经引起电影界的关注，并得到全国观众的喜爱，其中有在德宏拍的，反映傣族生活的《孔雀公主》《摩雅傣》《勐垅沙》等。其中《孔雀公主》就是由当时翻译的德宏傣文古籍文学类的《召树屯和喃木诺娜》改编创作成的影片，给观众留下了难以磨灭的美好印象。目前，云南省正大力开发文化产业，影视业也是其中重要组成部分，德宏傣文古籍可在影视创作中发挥不可取代的作用。德宏傣文古籍是影视创作取之不尽的源泉，大量的傣文古籍中的历史类、文学类、佛教类等经典为影视创作提供了很好的素质。如文学类阿銮系列故事《勇罕》《俄应》《京省勐晃》等，佛教类《佛祖故事》《述达麻哈黎班纳》等，历史类《萨缅帕拉吾》《芒市的传说》，等等，都可以拍摄成电影、电视剧，搬上银幕。

（三）旅游开发价值

德宏傣文古籍记载着一批风景名胜的传说、地名传说、节日传说、习俗传说。比如《云雾缭绕的勐卯》《泼水节的传说》等等。另有一些古籍意涵丰富、民族特色鲜明，这些文献都是可供旅游业开发利用的宝贵资源。将旅游景点和相关古籍文献结合起来，可以使景点有故事、有传说，赋予景点以灵魂，成为活的景点，让游客在实地进行旅游体验，丰富景点的内涵，建设富有民族特色和文化内涵的个性主题景点，以促进旅游业的发展。

（四）医药价值

傣族医药由于历史悠久，具有民族特色和地方特色，因此，傣族医药和蒙古族医药、藏族医药、维吾尔族医药一起被中华人民共和国卫生部列为"四大民族医药"。在傣文古籍中，有不少记载医药类的经典，如德宏的《傣医用药典》《八种致病原因》《德宏傣药验方集》等，这些医药经典，阐发了傣医药的基本理论，记录了草药采集、制作、用药配方、诊疗经验等内容。傣医药中大量使用的植物成分大多符合现代人"健康""安全""绿色生态"的用药心理。因此，充分认识傣族医药典籍的价值，可以将其中的验方与现代医药技术相结合，发挥傣医药的作用，治病救人，为人类做贡献。所以，傣文古籍中记载的医学理论，草药采集、制作、用药配方、诊疗经验等，都具有很高的研究价值。

（五）南传上座部佛教研究价值

南传上座部佛教主要流行于斯里兰卡、缅甸、泰国、柬埔寨、老挝和我国云南德宏、西双版纳、临沧、普洱等地，至今这几个地区大都信仰南传上座部佛教。云南的傣族、德昂族、布朗族、佤族等少数民族信仰南传上座部佛教的比较多，而傣族是信仰南传上座部佛教的主体民族，南传上座部佛教对傣族地区的政治、经济、文化有着深刻而巨大的影响，很有必要深入、系统地研究。要进行研究，须以傣文古籍佛教类文献入手，研究成果才能有根据，才有利于研究的深入开展。傣文古籍中有相当数量的佛教和与佛教有关的民间文学作品，佛教经典主要是"三藏经"，还有大量与佛教相关的如阿銮叙事长诗、阿銮故事以及佛祖巡游世界传法的故事。这些经典既是讲经，又是文学作品。另外，傣文古籍中的其他文献，历史类、法律类、礼仪类，也都涉及南传上座部佛教，是专家研究南传上座部佛教不可缺少的宝贵材料。所以，傣文古籍在研究南传上座部佛教方面有很重要的价值。

四、德宏傣文古籍传承、收集整理和研究的现状与存在问题

傣文古籍在过去曾经是具有活性形态的经典。因为过去，傣文古籍在傣族人民生活中发挥着重要作用。如佛经类的经典，人们在劳动生产之余必须去佛寺（奘房）学习和诵读；文学类的经典如阿銮故事系列叙事长诗等，过去更是得到广大傣族男女的喜爱，农闲时，傣族人都会聚到佛寺里，佛爷或长者为他们诵读。傣族有向佛寺献经书积功德的习惯，隔一段时间把献的经书拿出来诵读。这一习俗增加了傣文古籍活动特点，所以傣文古籍在过去的传承处于一种良性状态。而今，情形完全不同。随着改革开放和全球化、现代化的不断推进，近二三十年来傣族村寨发生着巨大的变化，在文化方面最明显的变化是电视进入千家万户，晚上和闲暇时人们都聚在电视机旁观看节目。加之互联网的快速发展以及QQ、微博、微信等社交工具的普及，人们的娱乐活动也更为丰富了。于是，人们没时间听故事，也没有人念诵傣族民间叙事长诗。现在佛经类的古籍只有僧侣诵读老人听经，中青年都不感兴趣。其他种类的傣文古籍也基本上很少有人了解和使用了。虽然今天傣族还有向佛寺献经书的习惯，但很少有人读。更为严重的问题是，能看懂老傣文古籍的人很少。所以，数以万计的珍贵傣文古籍基本上处于一种无人问津的状态。傣文古籍的传承面临着极大的危机。

五、傣文古籍研究成果转换

一是党的十八大、十九大给少数民族古籍抢救保护创造了良好的政策环境。云南省贯彻"保护为主、抢救第一、合理利用、加强管理"的方针，参与"中华古籍保护计划"和"十三五"国家古籍整理重点图书出版规划。

二是国家古籍保护中心颁布的《中国少数民族文字珍贵古籍入选标准（暂行）》将少数民族文字古籍中有历史、学术、艺术价值的少数民族文字珍贵古籍收录范围放宽至1949年。要求入选标准中列出了11大类少数民族古籍，其中傣文古籍排在第5位，此入选标准也证明了傣文古籍的重要价值。

三是德宏州组织人员开展傣文古籍翻译整理，同时又为《中华古籍总目·少数

民族卷·傣族卷》提供资料。傣文古籍通过登录云南省古籍保护中心平台，报送国家古籍保护中心平台，并登录国家古籍保护中心平台后编入《中华古籍总目》永载史册，传承下去。这也对贯彻落实党的十九大精神和省委、省政府关于繁荣发展少数民族文化的一系列文件精神，抢救、保护、传承云南省优秀少数民族传统文化，促进少数民族文化大发展、大繁荣，推进民族文化强省和民族团结进步、边疆繁荣稳定示范区建设以及实践国家"一带一路"倡议有非常重要的作用。

六、德宏州珍贵傣文古籍资料图片

①象牙片写经
书写材质：象牙片
佛教类
数量：12片

②象骨片写经
书写材质：象骨片
佛教类
数量：12片

③贝叶经
书写材质：贝多罗树叶
书写文字：圆形缅傣文
文学类

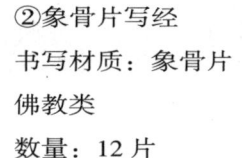

④桑皮纸经

书写材质：桑皮纸

书写文字：圆形缅傣文

历史类 　　　　　　　　　　　　天文类

⑤绵纸经

书写材质：竹制绵纸

书写文字：长方形德宏老傣文

礼仪类 　　　　　　　　　　　　天文类

⑥一部经书里面同时出现3种文字（圆形缅傣文、长方形德宏老傣文以及被当地人称为"巴利"的一种较少人能识读的文字），在民族古籍定级中被定为珍贵古籍

宗教类 　　　　　语言类 　　　　　　　圆形缅傣文

⑦印刷出版的傣文古籍经书

书写材质：现代纸张

书写文字：圆形缅傣文

民间故事

⑧占卜类

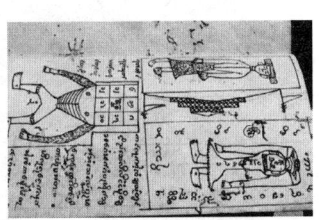

⑨咒术类

⑩ 装帧形式多种多样

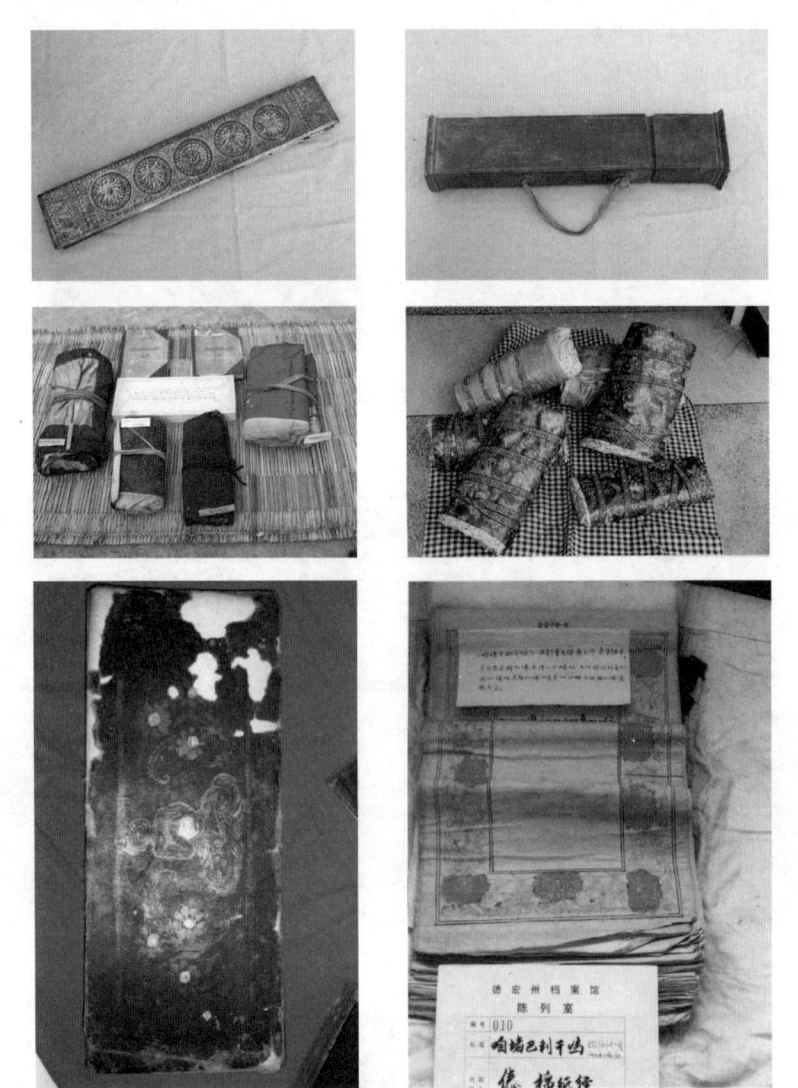

参考文献：

[1] 刀保尧主编.勐卯弄傣族历史研究.昆明：云南民族出版社，2005.

[2] 杨永生编著.傣族历史文化研究文集.德宏：德宏民族出版社，2007.

[3] 杨永生主编.勐卯弄傣文史籍译注.德宏：德宏民族出版社，2009.

[4] 何少林编著.中国傣族.银川：宁夏人民出版社，2011.

云南南部傣泐贝叶经的复兴、传播与发展[*]

Apiradee Techasiriwan[①] 文　王明姣[②] 译

傣族和贝叶经文化概况

云南省最南端（滇南）的西双版纳傣族自治州地区，旧时曾被称为傣泐王国，又叫作景龙金殿国，与兰那王国等毗邻（兰那王国中心区域位于今天泰国的北部地区，首府为现今的清迈）。傣泐地区历史上曾受兰那等邻近国家在政治、文化、传统、语言和典籍等方面的影响，其中之一就是佛经手稿文化的影响。

尽管有部分傣泐人认为他们的佛经手稿在一千多年前就已经存在，但其他学者认为傣泐的佛经手稿是从兰那的佛经手稿变迁而来的，于14世纪在兰那王国才得以发展。在提洛卡拉王统治时期（1441—1487年）传到西双版纳，彼时也是兰那王国的黄金时代及鼎盛时期，佛教蓬勃发展。此时，国王将王国的疆域往各个方向扩展，例如，向西扩展到掸邦，北至景龙。在扩展疆域的同时也将佛教以及用于记录佛法和佛陀教义的佛经手稿一并传到了现今西双版纳境内。

后来，傣泐人不仅用手稿记录佛法和宗教经典，例如，藏经、本生经、三藏经、圣物历史等，而且还用来记录世俗经典以及其历史、知识和文学，例如，在手稿上记录编年史、法律、民间故事、传统医学、仪式和巫术等。

贝叶经的复兴

1950年年初，中国政府对书面语言表达不完善的部分少数民族提出了规范少数民族书面语言的政策。因此，中国语言研究所、国家科学委员会和云南省民族事务委员会等相关政府部门一起合作，从1952年开始对傣族的语言及手稿进行观察和研究。他们把当地的傣文分为两类，即西双版纳傣文和德宏傣文，因两地傣文文字有所不同，所以也相应地制订了改良计划，包括制定一些政策，即删除多余字母和添加必要字符，以消除写作方式之间的重叠，同时也解决模棱两可的书写问题。至

---

[*] 本文为作者在《云南南部和老挝北部的泰泐手稿：在新近恢复的手稿文化中，旁体的作用和发展》一文中的部分文本基础上修改而成，2019年，于德国汉堡大学完成。（在编辑过程中略有删减——编者注。）

[①] 作者为泰国清迈大学社会研究所副研究员，兰那文字文化与民俗研究中心（CLCF）主任，博士。

[②] 译者为云南大学毕业的社会学硕士，现为云南省药物依赖防治研究所研究实习员。

贝叶文化与区域文化遗产传承保护

此，旧的傣泐文和拼写被新的傣泐文和拼写取代。该计划于 1955 年首次试行，先用于小学官方教材，后来逐渐扩大到报纸、杂志、教科书和印刷的传统傣泐文学作品上。

尽管如此，傣泐人对新傣泐文却持有不同的看法，部分傣泐人愿意使用，而其他人却觉得无法适应，因为新傣文不再反映词源，也不适合用来写巴利文。因此，西双版纳及其他地方仍在公开沿用老傣文。

然而，在 1966 年至 1976 年期间，大量的贝叶经遭到毁坏。那次危机（"文化大革命"）之后，傣泐人和其他少数民族得到中国政府支持，继续向世界展示他们自己的文化特色并一直延续至今。

贝叶经的传播

从傣泐文复兴伊始至今，在整个滇南地区，一些文人学者仍然活跃在贝叶经的手抄工作中，年龄大都已七八十岁，其中大多数人在"文化大革命"前就开始了手稿修复，并于 20 世纪 80 年代初再次继续这项工作，例如下面这几位：

Pò Saeng Nòi

Pò Saeng Nòi，又名 Pò Long Khan Kaeo，居住在大勐龙的曼飞龙。2012 年笔者见到他时，他已七十七岁。他从十四五岁时就开始了手稿修复生涯，当时他还是个新手，在贝叶上复刻了很多当地历史，初衷是为了给子孙后代保存勐龙和西双版纳的历史文化遗产。

（Techasiriwan 收藏）

Pò Saeng Sam

另一位是来自孟连的 Pò Saeng Sam，生于 1938 年，他在桑皮纸上复刻了许多历史文本手稿，以便将这些故事传递给年青一代。

此外，就历史手稿来说，文人记录者们往往更热衷于记录历史、旧习俗、仪式文书和民间故事，以及关于傣族的其他传统知识等，以抄录副

（Techasiriwan 收藏）

本的形式将它传承给年青一代。因此，手稿的记录被视为一种将传统，尤其是历史知识传承给年青一代，并使傣泐文化得以保存和延续的重要文化技术。

例如，手稿"泐西双邦/召十二邦"（西双版纳十二城邦的统治）是被记录在工业纸上的。由一位有着贵族背景的前政府公务员 Cao Maha Khanthawong（1925—2013年）对手稿进行了复刻。1986年退休后，他成为一名精通西双版纳历史文化的学者，他在工业用纸制成的笔记本上抄录了许多世俗文本。

手稿的序言分别提到了1950年年初在共产党领导下以及在"文化大革命"期间（1966—1976年）西双版纳的概况。一直到1982年之后，西双版纳才逐渐恢复稳定，政府逐渐允许当地人再次信奉自己的宗教和民族文化，少数民族的传统文学才开始复兴。自1984年后，文学专家们聚在一起通过整理现存的旧手稿和采访老年人，共同重建了一个传统的傣文学语料库。在这些新整理的手稿中，编纂者按主题进行归类：与宗教有关的故事被归类在"宗教"（sāsana）一栏下，而关于传统故事类的则被归类到"传统"一栏的标题下。

另一个例子是手稿"Nangsü Phün Moeng La"（勐腊志/勐腊纪事），1996年，由 Ai Chòi Cha Han 将贝叶经撰写在桑皮纸上并私人持藏。

在正文前页的一段简短文字（包括序言）中作者写道，由于在现存的手稿中找不到这一段特定纪事，所以，他决定去采访老年人和贵族，收集有关位于西双版纳东南部的勐腊地区的历史资料，他把这些资料整理到一起记录在手稿上，以便后人从中了解到勐腊的历史。最后，他还为自己手稿中出现的错字道歉。

值得注意的是，这些编撰者们做的不仅仅是复刻现存古老手稿中的文本，而且还将原稿中的文本与口述传统信息相结合，包括将自己通过采访得到的信息一起进行撰写。

傣族贝叶经的发展

在研究关于傣泐手稿论文集时，手稿的发展过程已然成为一个值得加以关注的重要问题。手稿的格式、布局、材料、副本、标点符号和手写体都随着时代的变化而发生相应的变化。通过研究，笔者发现自1950年1月中国共产党解放云南后，一部分手稿受到了现代印刷技术的影响。

笔者将论文中的傣族贝叶经大致分为三个时期，即

第一时期：1884—1949年，中国共产党在云南取得胜利以及传统召法制度（最高统治者被称作召片领）的结束（1950年）

这一时期的手稿特点似乎已经成为贝叶经的一种标准形式，即以桑树纸作为书写材料，用黑墨水书写文字，在页面顶部装订，而且手稿是用连续的文字书写，文本中没有标点符号，有时只用空格和（或）其他标点符号来分开段落和句子，在末尾插入空白行，以将末页（版权页）与正文分开。此外，抄录者会用特殊的符号标记文章或章节的开头和结尾，并采用方形框标记和突出关键词语。

贝叶文化与区域文化遗产传承保护

在 Phaya Saen Aeo Lai 时期

在 Cao Cheng Rai 统治时期

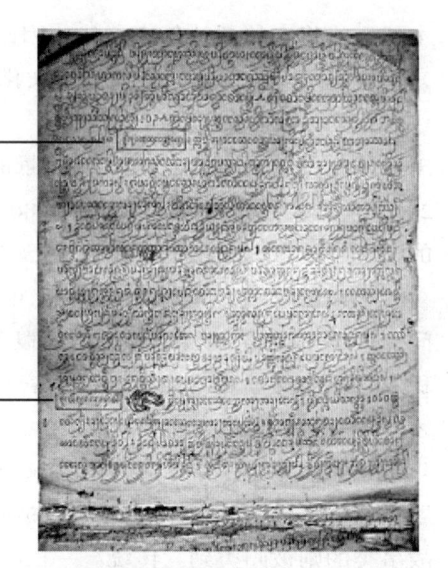

（1884年《勐泐志》云南大学收藏，昆明）

第二时期：1950—1966年，1966年后"文化大革命"爆发（大约此后的15年期间撰写手稿基本停滞）

这个时期的贝叶经与第一时期的贝叶经有很多共同点，但也有一些变化。第一，部分手稿材料是由工业用纸制成，用订书机装订而成。第二，手稿的布局略有不同，新段落的第一行是缩进的；但有些文稿依然像第一时期的文稿一样，段落开头没有空格或缩进。第三，使用了印刷书常用的标点符号和圆括号。第四，文本末尾标注了具体的公元时间，而且日期是按照阳历标注，而非沿用阴历的祖腊历（CS）系统。

第三时期：1980—2013年，改革开放后时期，标志着贝叶文化的复兴

在这一时期，原稿发生了明显的变化。反映了其受到了日益发展的现代印刷技术的影响。

（1966年 Phaya Coeng 时期：云南大学收藏，昆明）

相比之下，第一时期提到的两种手稿格式，其中一种在顶部进行装订，而笔者发现这一时期的部分手稿却像印刷书籍一样是在左侧装订的。

此外，笔者发现大量的手稿是用黑色墨水或圆珠笔写在工业纸上的。

另外，有些撰写员将文本抄录到由工业纸制成的笔记本上，如下面手稿所示。而且撰写员试图保留桑皮纸手稿上的一些古老特征，就像他们仍然会在封面页使用

短冒号，在文末使用冒号。

(《景龙十二位统治者》，Grabowsky 收藏，1986 年)

另外，部分信众通过把记载着宗教经文的经卷赊给寺庙来积攒功德。而在过去，资助人会雇用撰写员为他们制作手稿，但我发现有些手稿是用复印机复印出来的。

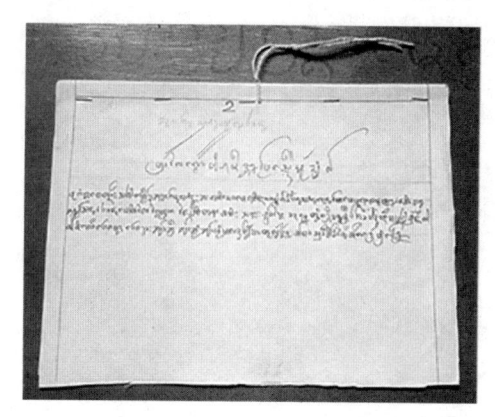

(Parami，景龙，Techasiriwan 收藏，2012 年)

另一个案例则是书写材料和写作方式混合的手稿。这是一份佛经手稿，封面和封底是用构树纸制作的，正文标题以及所有权声明（里面提及所有者的名字和收购年份）是手写的，但正文却非手写，而是用工业用纸打印而成的。最重要的是传统的旋风式装订方式让手稿看起来成为名副其实的复制品。

贝叶文化与区域文化遗产传承保护

（《景洪志/纪事》，景龙，Grabowsky 收藏，1999 年）

最后，笔者还发现了保存和复兴傣泐文学的尝试性实践。在昆明印刷出版的一本傣汉双语出版物中，发现了傣文文本的傣文字体不是打印的，而是用旧傣泐手写的，内容是有关云南省少数民族傣族的地方志、传说和习俗法的合集。

（昆明出版的《孟连宣抚司法规》，Techasiriwan 收藏，1986 年）

令人欣慰的是，从过去到现在，傣族贝叶文化在经历了多次变革、不同境遇和危机的情况下，仍被保存下来并延续至今，让他们宝贵的历史文化和知识得以代代相传。

（说明：参考文献略，详见书内本文的英文版）

西双版纳南传上座部佛教傣文经典传承与发展现状研究

康南山[①]

佛教讲求礼敬佛、法、僧三宝，如何将其中的法宝亦即佛教经典传承下来是每一位佛门弟子必须担当的责任。对于传承与发展西双版纳南传上座部佛教来说，佛教傣文传统经典的传承尤为重要。笔者从个人的经历入手，综合本人1983年出家至1997年还俗与1998年至今在云南省佛教协会工作掌握的情况，分析和总结了西双版纳南传上座部佛教傣文经典传承与发展现状，研判其趋势。本文还回顾了云南南传上座部佛教界为南传上座部佛教能更好地传承下去和适应中国社会，30年来的积极努力、付出及其效果。西双版纳南传上座部佛教发展的现状亦可从当地南传上座部佛教傣文经典的传承现状大致研判其全貌。

一、西双版纳南传上座部佛教傣文经典

西双版纳南传上座部佛教经典传统上传承下来的只有用兰那文（又译兰纳文）书写的经典，很少有泰文或缅甸文的。从泰国较早传入西双版纳的南传上座部佛教经典文字还有酸角文，傣语称为"多帕喊"（to¹phăk¹kham¹），但是西双版纳数百年来传播的南传上座部佛教宗派是花园派和红林派与兰那文书写的南传上座部佛教经典。这三个要素也是西双版纳南传上座部佛教的特点。

由于佛教经典书写的是兰那文，很多地方将之称为"多坦"（to¹ thăm⁴），意为佛经文字，以区别于其他傣文。兰那文是从兰那国13世纪下半叶，孟族建立的哈里奔猜古孟文脱胎出来的。[②] 兰那国南传上座部佛教寺院在弘扬佛教教义的过程中，为了能更为全面地记载和传授佛教教理教义，根据巴利语发音，以兰那文作为主要编写文字刻成佛经，形成兰那佛经文。在几代国王的支持下，完成了巴利三藏和很多佛本生经的兰那文书写。从13世纪初至15世纪都有记载南传上座部佛教经典几次分别传到琅勃拉邦和缅甸景栋再传入西双版纳。[③] 斯里兰卡僧团于1095年在清迈城建立了影响巨大的新宗派花园派（Wat Suondok，或 ni⁶ ka¹ya⁶son¹ dək²）。1530年在清迈城又创立了红林派（Wat Padaeng，或 ni⁶ ka¹ya⁶ba²dεŋ¹），相较于旧的宗派也

[①] 作者为云南省佛教协会副会长兼秘书长，云南民族大学博士研究生。
[②] 谢远章．泰傣学研究六十年．昆明：云南民族出版社，2008：139．
[③] Kang Nanshan. Theravada Buddhism in Sipsong Panna：Past and Contemporary Trends. RCSD, Faculty of Social Sciences, Chiang Mai University，2009．

称之为"锡兰新派",这两个宗派的祖庭至今仍保留着。这个宗派及其经典于1448年传播到现在缅甸的景栋,①随后就应该传入西双版纳了。兰那文经典的内容不仅是佛教教义教规,还有天文历法、医药、文学、法律法规、谚语、巫术等。兰那文传入西双版纳之后得到广泛使用,书写得到一定的发展,成为有自己特点的傣泐文。有人根据传播区域的不同,划分了三个区,并称呼泰北部使用的为"兰那文",在景栋一带的为"傣恳文",在西双版纳的为"傣泐文"。实际上这三种文字是同一种文字,只是在这三个区域的传播使用过程中书写方面有些变化而已。1961年至1963年,西双版纳改进了一种新的字体,称为新傣文,旧体兰那文(佛经文)称为老傣文。

兰那文(老傣文)书写比较灵活,这是其最大的特点,但也由于太灵活容易导致书写出现不规范,随意性太大,无统一的书写规范成了老傣文的缺点。兰那文具体有以下三种规则:一是相连的两个词,如果辅音字母相同而元音不同,可以只用一个辅音字母把元音都合并于这个辅音字母中,就成了一字读两个音即把两个字合并成一字,按这个规律可以把三个字、四个字甚至更多字合成一个字;二是固定的单体字,书写简单易懂,这种固定字可以用辅音字母和元音字母来解读;三是习惯用的多音字,一般作为符号用于历法和保护咒文、护身符等。

二、兰那文和经典的传统传承方式——布施佛经活动

西双版纳南传上座部佛教经典传承主要有三种传统方式:一是出家人和老人抄写佛经,再由信众礼请布施给寺院;二是由出家人(有时是老人)念诵给广大信众聆听;三是广大信徒听了之后再口口相传,把佛教教义传得更广。通过这些方式,南传上座部佛教经典才得以在西双版纳继续传承。为了把佛教发扬光大,西双版纳傣族制定了布施佛经的习俗。布施经书傣语叫"赕坦"($tan^4\ thăm^4$),这个活动对佛教的传承意义重大。布施佛经,从内容上分佛本生故事经和巴利经诵两种,从念唱的形式上分傣语唱诵和巴利语唱诵,从布施者形式上分全村寨集体布施和个体一户人家布施两种。

(一)抄写经书

抄写佛经是布施佛经活动的第一阶段。布施经书,一般情况需要新的经书,所以需请人抄写,邀请的对象一般是出家人,或"波章"(bo^5can^1,佛教活动领头人)、康南(kha^1nan^1,比丘以上还俗的男士)以及懂得佛经文的老人。抄写经书,需要对照旧的经书来抄写,同时,要根据整个佛寺布施经书的计划来成套地,如一整卷或一整部地完成抄写。例如,一部佛本生经有十册,如果一个人能抄写完这十册他可以一个人抄写。如果他抄不完,可以分给别人抄写。谁布施由谁出资礼请。

---

① The Padang Chronicle and The Jengtung State Chronicle (Translated). Center for South and Southeast Asian Studies, The University of Michigan, 1981.

布施经书的前一天，所有新抄写的经书需送到佛寺，布施者把抄写费用向抄写者礼请，抄写者把布施者的姓名写在封面上并写几句祝福语。布施者把即将捐赠的佛经带回家供奉一晚上，如果家里有人会念唱的，则可以在晚上念唱一遍；如果家中有出家僧人，便该请他晚上回家念唱一遍，家人坐着聆听。第二天下午或傍晚，所有人会把要布施的佛经全部布施到佛寺里，交给波章或者住持，分类、分部、分卷放好，以便按顺序请出家人念唱。

（二）念唱经书

念唱经书是布施经书活动的第二阶段。念唱经书时间一般是7至15天，出家人轮流在大雄宝殿的诵经庭里日夜念唱给信众听。第一天，老人们各自带着自己的铺盖在大雄宝殿里找位置铺好铺盖，准备聆听诵经。大殿中一般会划分男女区域和中老年区域，同性同龄人关系较好聊得来的，会将铺盖铺得相互靠近一点，方便互相照顾和闲聊，以及搭伙用餐。

布施的全部佛经集中到寺院后，首先由波章念诵供养经文，然后由出家人念诵祈福吉祥经。接着波章会根据老人们的意愿，按部、卷、册的顺序排好，然后礼请僧人到大雄宝殿中央已经备好的诵经庭里就座。僧人就座后，波章先念简单地恭请念诵的一句经文，然后出家人开始念唱，每册开头和结束时靠近诵经庭的几个老人负责敲打三次铓锣和吹响一下海螺，以表示一册经书的开始和结束。出家人念唱佛经时，要求：一是声音洪亮，让大雄宝殿内所有人都能听见。有了扩音器后，大雄宝殿外的人，甚至全村的人也能清晰听到念诵的声音；二是这种念唱很讲究调子，调子分好几种，西双版纳各地略有不同，与巴利语偈颂的调子不一样，佛本生故事绝大部分是傣语，穿插一些巴利语，傣语部分一般是前一句与后一句都是押韵的，念唱起来类似章哈调。所以，笔者认为这种不是诵经而是唱经。

出家人由波章邀请进大雄宝殿轮流念唱，一次念唱一册或两三册，有的甚至更多，具体根据法师的能力和嗓子的耐力，直到把本次布施的全部经书都念唱完。也可以请其他寺院的法师来帮念唱。念唱结束的前一天是庆祝的一天，家家户户都以美食供养寺院和孝敬在寺院听经的老人。晚上，寺院里敲锣打鼓，放孔明灯和火花，有时会举行文艺表演等活动。最后一天是滴水回向仪式，出家人诵经祝福回向给所有布施的信众，波章念诵所做的全部功德回向给信众，所有信众或各家各户代表滴水许愿所做的布施功德无量，生生世世有回报。至此，整个布施佛经活动全部结束。

（三）培养人才

布施经书活动是培养佛教人才的一个重要途径。西双版纳僧才的传统标准：一是修行好，严持戒律；二是能念诵、念唱信徒所需要的各种佛教仪轨的经文；三是能写一手好的佛经文字；四是有能力主持佛教活动；五是有能力教育广大信众正信正行。布施佛经活动是培养出家人修习傣文书法和了解佛本生故事最好的方式。决心出家的人，从进入寺院当预备和尚时就开始学习基础佛经。出家当小沙弥之后就

贝叶文化与区域文化遗产传承保护

得背诵更多的经文和读、写佛经文字。学会佛经文字后,开始抄写经书,大约抄写几十本佛经之后,书写兰那文的水平就自然提高了。一个人抄写上百册的佛经,他的书法水平和对经书语句的掌握程度就能达到很高的水平了。布施佛经活动对一个出家人来说既是动力也是压力——信众礼请僧人抄写,僧人不写则对不起信众,这是压力;抄写经文可以有收入(供养)和提高自己的书法水平,以及让自己更加熟悉佛经语言文字和内容,这是动力。布施经书活动时念唱佛经,也是培养僧才的一种非常有效的途径。一个出家人必须先学佛经文字和佛本生故事经,大概需要几个月甚至一两年之后才可以上台念唱。经验不足的年轻僧人上台念唱佛本生故事经是学习和锻炼的好机会,如果念错或念漏,台下老人可以立即给予纠正,这样久而久之,这些僧人自然而然就会逐步精通佛本生故事内容和掌握佛经语言文字了。

(四)满足信仰的需要

布施佛经,从广义上看,是传播佛教的一种重要途径;从狭义上看,是傣族信徒积德行善的信仰行为,是广大信徒修行的非常有效的方式。一般佛教信徒成家后,一对夫妇或一户人家每年要布施一本经书。布施佛经能积德,听闻佛经能够学习佛法,了解佛陀在过去世的菩萨道中所积下的功德,并理解佛教教义教规,感悟人生,积极行善积德,诸恶莫作。信众听出家人念唱佛本生故事经,也是一种极大的享受,感动时,大家都会流泪,甚至有些人会哭出声来;幽默时,大殿里会哄堂大笑。老年人听经时,需住在寺院里七天至半个月,这也算是一种住寺修行的有效方式,不需要回家做家务事,更不需到地里做农活,子女儿孙做好食物送到佛寺里孝敬。老人通过不断听佛本生故事经来提高自己对佛学的修养,通过了解佛本生故事之后可以向小孩子们讲佛经故事,让佛教教义、伦理道德传播得更为广泛。

布施佛经的第二种内容是布施巴利三藏,不过由于巴利三藏量很大,在西双版纳佛寺中大多数寺院经、律、论三藏不全,一般流传的是《前十五部论》和《后十五部论》,出家时间长的法师一般就学这些内容,大型佛事活动也是念这些经。布施巴利三藏也是布施《前十五部论》和《后十五部论》,或只是布施《前十五部论》。布施藏经就只布施一套,是全体村民共同布施的。如果一个人抄写要两到三年才抄写完,可以由几个人分工抄写。念诵藏经时,不是一个人念诵而是三五人甚至更多人围着同一本经书共同念诵,需要分好几组轮流念诵,周边村寨佛寺都会被邀请组成僧团来分担念诵任务。这种布施藏经活动中的经文念诵一般需要七天至半个月才能完成。

三、传承与发展的困境

20世纪80年代,在中国落实宗教信仰自由政策之初,西双版纳南传上座部佛教恢复过程非常活跃,发展很快。然而,到了20世纪90年代末南传上座部佛教放慢了脚步,努力在寻找方向。逐渐走向弱化,这几年更加明显。这种趋势是有原因的,笔者认为主要有以下几个方面:

全球化语境下，西双版纳社会多元文化日益明显。傣族从相对封闭的农耕社会转向现代化，走向城镇化，由农耕自给自足的生产方式转向市场经济。多元文化对傣族生产生活影响日益加大，傣族信众信仰观念也正在随着社会的变迁而变化。随着社会不断进步，经济迅速发展，西双版纳傣族与外界接触越来越频繁、深入，更多的人到国内发达地区，甚至出国旅游，思想逐渐开放。很多年轻人走出傣族村寨来到城镇，去沿海发达地区务工，甚至到国外学习工作，个别甚或远嫁到东南亚和欧美国家。多元文化的影响和融合，使傣族年轻人一方面学习经文的意识和兴趣逐渐淡化；另一方面他们需要学习的东西内容繁杂，学习压力大，故分身乏术。

多种文字同时使用是一个民族文化发展的很大障碍。傣族使用多种文字是阻碍傣族传统文化传播的主要原因之一，这是大部分傣族人共同意识到但又很难得到解决的问题。现在云南傣族使用的文字种类有六种：西双版纳老傣文（兰那文或佛经文）和新傣文、德宏老傣那文和新傣那文、傣绷文（也称圆体文）和傣端文（金平傣文）。西双版纳新傣文是1961年在中国社科院傅懋勣带领下，在景洪开始了改革傣文的工作，1963年完成改进工作并开始在西双版纳推行。西双版纳报纸是传播新傣文的主要媒体，之后编辑出版了很多新傣文书写的文学作品、专著、长诗等，新傣文在西双版纳广泛推广，并很快普遍使用。1980年西双版纳开始恢复信仰南传上座部佛教，由于傣族信仰的南传上座部佛教经典都是用老傣文（兰那文）记录的，佛教寺院自然而然又开始使用老傣文。由于南传上座部佛教傣文经典使用大量的巴利语，很多词语具有巴利语词根，而新傣文很难表达巴利语的真实含义，故其不能替代老傣文。所以，西双版纳傣族至今就一直新、老傣文两种文字并用。

1980年底，西双版纳佛教界就开始探索佛教现代化教育和中国化道路了。1988年，勐海县佛教协会在景真八角亭开办出家人学校，两年后以失败告终，又在勐海镇曼贺佛寺开办了几年。都应长老也在勐混佛塔寺办了几年，后来还是未能继续承办下去。1995年5月，经国家宗教局批准，云南上座部佛学院在西双版纳总佛寺正式挂牌成立，并于1995年9月开始招生，主要招收、培养州内及周边信仰南传上座部佛教的德宏、普洱、临沧、保山等地的学僧。2008年3月，佛学院迁入新址南连山勐泐大佛寺内，新址占地面积60亩，建筑面积8188.58平方米。截至2019年，佛学院招收了36个教学班级，共计招收1346名学僧，已毕业32个班级，共计毕业学僧1089名。为了走宗教中国化道路，积极引导南传上座部佛教与社会主义社会相适应，佛学院与国民教育学校联合办学，提高佛学院学僧的汉语文化水平，使学僧不仅掌握傣文和经文，也掌握汉语文化知识，把佛学院学僧培养成全面发展的僧才。学院于2005年3月开始与西双版纳职业技术学院联合举办"傣汉双语"中专班，由西双版纳职业技术学院的教师教授汉语课程，课程完全按照国民教育学校中专类的内容进行教学，佛学院的僧侣教师教授傣文和佛学。毕业后由职业技术学院颁发国家承认的中专学历。虽然做了很多努力，但培养出来的这些人才对南传上座部佛教的健康发展未能发挥出多少推动性的作用。

贝叶文化与区域文化遗产传承保护

现在西双版纳南传上座部佛教传承难的问题是缺乏人才，佛教人才不管是数量还是质量都很欠缺。十几年来，从僧人数量来看变化很大。据统计，西双版纳全州，2012年佛寺有593座，僧侣总数2475人，其中，比丘（比库）以上有712人；2018年年底，佛寺有598座，僧侣总数1978人，其中比丘（比库）以上有431人。僧侣人数中小沙弥数量的变化不能说明问题，但是比丘以上属于教职人员，六年时间内，人数从712人减少到431人，减少了281位。这个数字就说明了问题的严重性。在众多外界因素的影响下，出家人的数量逐渐减少，出家时间也越来越短，导致了南传上座部佛教人才匮乏。同时，在寺院学习方式也在当下发生了一定的转变，住持对小沙弥一对一的传统传承方式也变得作用有限，很多小沙弥出家几年，学到的佛教知识也极为有限。随着南传上座部佛教基础佛教院校教育工作的开展，部分年轻的南传上座部佛教僧侣进入佛学院接受较为正规的学习，但这类群体人数占总体人数非常少，并且在佛学院学习期间，更多时间是学习佛教理论和国民教育的内容，西双版纳南传上座部佛教传统内容如佛本生故事经、偈颂的念唱方法、兰那文（佛经文）以及傣族信众日常所需要的仪式念诵的经文等没有得到很好学习。这样既满足不了广大信众所需要的传统方式，也未能引导广大信众走向南传上座部佛教的新模式。

传统的经文抄写和经文念唱的能力变得越来越弱，佛教傣文经典传承人才逐步减少。在这样的背景下，佛寺的僧人已经满足不了广大傣族信众更高的精神需求，仅能满足信众对于基本仪轨的信仰需要。在农村大部分佛寺中，一寺仅一两个僧人和一个住持，未能形成僧团，佛教活动转向以仪轨为主要传承内容。信徒到寺院请求僧人做佛教仪式时，更喜欢请僧人做与自己生计有关的佛教仪式，比如祈福身体健康、生意兴隆、家人平安、出入平安等。信徒热心做与这些祈福内容相应的宗教仪轨，寺院住持认为做这些活动得到的供养更直接，因此也热心做这些佛教仪式，这些仪式丰富多彩，花样繁多，信徒有更多的选择。这就导致了佛教的核心教义难以在傣族信徒中传播和普及。

西双版纳傣文佛教经典传承难的问题也反映了传统与现代的矛盾。西双版纳老傣文（佛经文）的传播，几百年来一直是以传统方式传承下来的，至今未能采用现代化的传承方式。虽然很多经典和诵经先后使用了录音机、影碟机、录像机和电脑等现代音响设备和印刷体，这几年也开始通过网络手段传播，但是这些都是简单的内容和休闲的方式，没有更专业的方式系统地传播南传上座部佛教傣文经典。

四、中国南传上座部佛教经典中国化的启示

习近平总书记提出"坚持宗教中国化方向"，为中国五大宗教指明了未来的发展方向。中国南传上座部佛教更要坚持中国化方向，否则南传上座部佛教要在中国继续传承就更难了。笔者认为西双版纳南传上座部佛教要继续传承，关键还是南传上座部佛教经典是否能传承，这就需要我们在坚持中国化方向的指引下做好以下几

个方面的工作：

首先，要做好南传上座部佛教经典语言文字的传承。20世纪八九十年代，泰国北部和缅甸掸邦东部景栋市有人开发了兰那文（老傣文）蜡纸刻写油印体，后来又有人研究出兰那文的电脑输入法和印刷体。1994年至1996年期间，西双版纳有僧人前往泰国清迈学习佛经文电脑输入法，学成后回到西双版纳总佛寺，从事傣文电脑输入工作，为南传上座部佛教傣文经典的传播发挥了重要作用。后来西双版纳报社又研究出了另一种老傣文电脑输入法，起初字体拼写出现很多欠缺，经过几年的技术改进，也走向成熟且富于美感。以上这些做法都为西双版纳南传上座部佛教傣文经典的传承和发展奠定了很好的基础。未来要与时俱进，跟上现代印刷体、媒体和电子以及网络技术，甚至通过智能化技术和设备传承经典。

为了适应中国社会，走好中国化道路，南传上座部佛教经典文字也需要走向汉化。傣族是中华民族之一，汉字是中华人民共和国官方语言文字，未来只会越来越普及，将来使用这种语言文字书写南传上座部佛教经典会方便更多的人使用佛经。傣族中懂得傣文的人只可能会越来越少，那么读懂南传上座部佛教傣文经典的人也就会越来越少，与其让南传上座部佛教和傣文经典消亡还不如就让南传上座部佛教经典由傣文转换成汉文的经典，这样不仅让不懂傣文的傣族读得懂南传上座部佛教经典，还使其他民族也能读懂南传上座部佛教经典，以促进南传上座部佛教中国化进程，继续传承下去。历史上译成汉文的南传上座部佛教经典有《阿含经》《清净道论》《法句经》等，而《南传大藏经》先后由新加坡、中国台湾和大陆出版发行。西双版纳法住禅林大导师玛欣德长老十几年来做了大量的翻译和著述工作，翻译的有：（1）《阿毗达摩讲要》（上、中、下三集）；（2）《大护卫经》；（3）《比库巴帝摩卡》；（4）《增支部一集巴利》等；著述的有：（1）《生命的意义》；（2）《您认识佛教吗？》；（3）《如是师语》；（4）《上座部佛教修学入门》；（5）《上座部佛教止观禅修次第》等。这些都为中国南传上座部佛教汉文经典奠定了很好的基础。

其次，布施经书活动的优良传统需要继续传承，但是必须转变形式。传统形式和内容的布施经书活动已经不适应当代傣族社会；抄写经书，每家每户或每对夫妇一年供养一本经书对南传上座部佛教的传承也已经没有太大的意义；每本佛经都要由出家人念唱完的做法大多数情况下都难以备足各种条件。布施佛经的形式必须进行转换。比如，每户家庭或每对夫妇一年捐资印刷佛经或者请人刻写贝叶经等；举办讲经活动时，请高僧来讲经而不是按传统的方式念唱佛本生故事经；也可以适当购买汉文版的南传上座部佛教经典供养给寺院，年轻人包括出家人和在家人都可以学习。资金多的寺院，可以建藏经楼和讲经堂，提供讲经的场所，方便出家人讲经和信众听闻佛法。

再次，发扬在家居士群体参与念诵佛经的传统。近十余年，各地傣族村寨出现了一批批穿白衣的男女居士，这些居士是从传统的白衣居士提升的，他们经常组织到村寨寺院诵经，逐渐形成了居士诵经团。南传上座部佛教高僧认为居士诵经团有利于佛教传播，也有利于信徒安居乐业，培养他们乐善好施的精神，应该对白衣居士诵经团给予支持和引导。比如2017年和2018年的春节期间，在景洪大金塔寺举办居士偈颂比赛活动，来自西双版纳州各地的约几千位白衣居士参加了比赛。这样的居士群体对南传上座部佛教传承具有很大的潜力，应该给予大力支持并让其发挥更大的作用。

最后，佛教人才培养必须把传统与现代教育相结合。为了使南传上座部佛教更好地传播，在党和政府的关心支持下，南传上座部佛教界积极努力兴办现代佛学院校。云南佛学院西双版纳分院经过多年的办学已经有了一定基础，还需要继续研究办学模式和教学目标，提高教学质量。传统培养方式是为了暂时满足广大信教群众的需要，现代教育是为了引导未来广大信众的信仰方向，积极引导南传上座部佛教走中国化道路。

五、结语

在全球化和多元化的语境下，西双版纳南传上座部佛教傣文经典在传承方面虽然和传统的形式相比走向多样化、多渠道，但一方面由于西双版纳缺乏传承经典的专业僧才和缺少向广大傣族信教群众传播佛法的力量；另一方面由于傣族语言环境的变化，傣族信众接受传统傣语教育受限，傣族信众中能理解傣文佛教经典内容的人也越来越少了，因此，南传上座部佛教经典内容并没有得到真正的传承和发展。如今在社会快速发展、文化大融合的背景下，西双版纳傣族传统文化的传承不应该断裂，对此，西双版纳南传上座部佛教界未来要加大力度，采取多方式、多渠道开展人才培养，一定要重视南传上座部佛教傣文经典的传承，探索傣族传统文化，在南传上座部佛教中国化历程中找到新的发展之路，让傣族传统文化能与中华民族博大精深的传统文化融合发展，向世界展现新的生机与活力！

参考文献：

（一）英文参考书

[1] The Padang Chronicle and The Jengtung State Chronicle（Translated）. Center for South and Southeast Asian Studies，The University of Michigan，1981.

[2] Lester, Robert C. Theravada Buddhism in Southeast Asia. The University of Michigan Press，1973.

[3] Mangrai, Sao Saimong. The Padaeng Chronicle and the Jengtung State Chronicle. The University of Michigan Press，1981.

[4] Wyatt, David K. and Wichienkeeo, Aroonrut eds. The Chiang Mai Chronicle. Draft Edition 5，1995.

[5] Kang, Nanshan. Theravada Buddhism in Sipsong Panna: Past and

Contemporary Trends. RCSD, Faculty of Social Sciences, Chiang Mai University, 2009.

（二）汉文文献

[1] 黄凌飞.中国南传上座部佛教音乐的人类学研究.昆明：云南大学出版社，2015.

[2] 刘岩.傣族南迁考察实录.昆明：云南民族出版社，1999.

[3] 刘岩.南传上座部佛教与傣族文化.昆明：云南民族出版社，1993.

[4] 伍琼华，彭多意主编.中国南传上座部佛教资料辑录.昆明：云南大学出版社，2015.

[5] 谢远章.泰傣学研究六十年.昆明：云南民族出版社，2008.

[6] 郑筱筠.中国南传上座部佛教研究.北京：中国社会科学出版社，2012.

（三）傣文文献

[1] 景栋巴亮教派史（The Padaeng Chronicle of Chiang Tung）.缅甸掸邦景栋.

[2] 景栋史（The Chiang Tung Chronicle）. The Khobaka and Cultural Association of Chiang Tung. 缅甸掸邦景栋，2003.

[3] 清迈史. Hans Penth. The Chiang Mai Chronicle. Chiang Mai: Silkworm Books, 1996.

贝叶文化与区域文化遗产传承保护

贝叶经在斯里兰卡佛教文化中的传承

Wimal Hewamanage[①] 文 孙晓[②] 译

语言的使用是"智人"的显著特征，这也意味着拉丁语中"智人"一词的书面语要晚于口语的出现。例如，梵语中的 bahuśṛta（巴利语的 bahussata）一词，人们听到或学到的比较多，它被古印度语言学者采用，并验证了佛教口口相传的过程。在棕榈叶上刻写是南亚、东南亚国家最古老的传统之一。梵语中，棕榈叶被称为 tālapatra、tādapatra、tādipatra，在巴利语中则是 tālapaṇṇa。而在僧伽罗语中它被称为 Puskola，泰米尔语是 ola-leaf。在印度次大陆，人们发现了三种贝叶棕榈（talipot）：扇叶树头榈（talipot palm）、巨掌棕榈（palmyra palm）和龙塔棕榈（lonta palm），前两种棕榈已在斯里兰卡使用。这些贝叶经手稿以僧伽罗语、巴利语、泰米尔语刻写为主，也存在以梵语、缅甸语和泰语刻写的形式。它们精确地涵盖了巴利语学、佛学、僧伽罗语学、传统医学、占星术、烹饪等诸多内容。但本文着重于研究斯里兰卡贝叶经对佛教文化的重要性。W. A. De Silva 的 *Catalogue of Palm Leaf Manuscripts in the Library of Colombo Museum Vol.I* 一文以及 Ariya Lagamuva 撰写的 *Sri Lankave Puskola Poth Lekhana Kalāva* 一文是该领域的杰出作品。而 C. M. Austin De Silva 所撰写的 *Production of Books in Ancient Ceylon* 一文，也有助于更好地了解贝叶经手稿的制作过程。

斯里兰卡人相信，棕榈树最早是由 Śakra 神在斯里兰卡种下的，目的就是为了刻写佛陀的教义。守护精神的含义与棕榈树相关，后来与该国的僧侣联系在了一起。在将佛教引入斯里兰卡之前，原始宗教中所描述的树神形象与榕树、贝叶棕等树木有关。他们认为，依附在这些树木上的树神保护着人们和村寨里的日常生活。有超过 123 个村寨的名称中带有 tāla 或者 tal 的前缀（Lagamuva 2006：107）。同时，贝叶棕也因为其树形直立、寿命较长，被用作边界的标记树。在古代，斯里兰卡曾建有占地约 50 英亩的 Madilla 皇家棕榈公园，位于 Alavva 附近的 Galatara 村寨。

[①] 作者为斯里兰卡科伦坡大学孔子学院院长，武汉大学博士，斯里兰卡科伦坡大学佛学系佛教与巴利语高级讲师。
[②] 译者为云南大学发展研究院社会学专业 2018 届硕士。

斯里兰卡的贝叶经史及其与佛教的关系

斯里兰卡的贝叶经刻写史与印度的一样长。由于佛寺教育在该国教育领域中起着至关重要的作用,因此自公元前3世纪至今,它们被称为parivenas(僧伽罗语中为pirivena)。Mahaviharaya和Abhayagiriya是阿奴拉达普勒时期的著名中心。波隆纳鲁沃时期的Dimbulagala Alahana Pirivena,科特时期的Totagamuva Vijayaba Pirivena和Keragala Padmavati Pirivena,以及该国最后一个王朝康提时期的Asgiriya、Mallavatta、Niyamakanda Pirivenas,都是著名的教育中心。从一开始,僧侣对贝叶经的刻写就不仅仅包含了巴利语和佛教文化,还包括僧伽罗的文化和语法。诸如Gurulugomi、Vidyacakravarti、Devrada Dampasangina和Parakramabahu Ⅳ国王等也做出了贡献。

图书馆(僧伽语中为的potgula)是诸多公认的佛寺最重要建筑之一。国王Voharika Tissa和Ganthakara Pirivena在Mahavihara(大寺)内建造的房屋被命名为ganthapaṇṇika。著名评论员Buddhaghosa Thera在这里研究佛教经典,并继续他的评论者翻译项目,这里就好像图书馆一样(Lagamuva 2006:70)。在康提王朝,著名的佛寺被称为potgulvihāraya,如Ovala potgulvihāraya、Mahavela potgulvihāraya、Dematamaluva potgulvihāraya、Haguranketa potgulvihāraya。

伟大的Dutthagamani国王(公元前161—公元前137年)修建了佛法讲堂(dharmaśālā),并提供了檐篷、vijinipatas、讲道椅子和书籍。在国王生命的最后时刻,他还读了一本名为Puññapotthaka(功绩簿)的书(Geiger 1950:222)。公元前2世纪,Kakavanna-Tissa国王(公元前205—公元前161年)的弟弟Uttiya王子通过一位假装成和尚的小男孩,用贝叶(patra)将自己深沉的爱意传递给他的嫂子。Kakavanna-Tissa国王误认为这是Uttiya王子的老师Kalyanitissa Thera(法师)写的手书。趁着Uttiya不在,将Kalyanitissa Thera放进了油锅,随后岛上的第一次海啸发生了(Geiger 1950:147)。贝叶经刻写从公元前6世纪开始用于日常写作,然后在公元前3世纪由Arahant Mahinda(达阿罗汉)将佛教文化传入斯里兰卡后,用于记录宗教文化。

公元前5世纪到公元前1世纪,佛教借由口头传播、传承。瓦塔伽马尼国王统治时期(公元前29—公元前17年),佛教在斯里兰卡中部省份Aluviharaya(Aloka Vihara)首次被刻写在贝叶经上。此时,虽然没有得到王室的支持,但得到了当地领导人的帮助。在击败了统治当地14年的南印度侵略者之后,迎来了国王的第二任期。由于不稳定的政治权力和干旱、饥荒的暴发,一部分僧侣前往邻国印度,而一部分人则冒着生命危险在斯里兰卡保护法轮。了解到口头传播所遭遇的传承危机后,僧侣们决定将法轮和教义都刻写在贝叶经上。这一决定在世界宗教史上记上了浓重的一笔,记录了一系列的教科书、注释、教规,证实刻写机制在斯里兰卡得到了建立和完善。根据印度和斯里兰卡的记载,刻写贝叶经至少很明显是在这一重大事件发生之前几个世纪就已经开始了。例如 Nissankamalla 铭文（公元 1187—1196 年）中所述，有关捐赠和礼物的记录应该刻写在铜板上而不是贝叶经上，因为贝叶经的记载会被蚂蚁、老鼠破坏。因此，显然在此期间贝叶经已经是众所周知的刻写材料了。

据岛上关于佛教贝叶经刻写近代史的记载，在 19 世纪和 20 世纪举行的两次活动最具代表性。第一次是在代表《尼柯耶》、斋戒、阿玛拉普拉的著名僧侣领导下发生的。Valane Siddhattha Thera、Hikkaduwe Sumanagala Thera 和 Yatramulle Dharmarama 代表 Siam Mahanikaya，Lankagoda Dhirananda Thera、Randombe Dhammalankara Thera、Veligama Sumangala Thera 和 Vaskaduve Subhuti Thera 代表 Amarapura Mahanikaya，他们一起代表了宗教社会。Iddamalgoda Abeykoon Atapattu Mudiyanse Ralahami、来自 Ratnapura Saman Devalaya 佛寺的 Diyavadana Nilame 和 Batuvantudave Devarakshita 则代表了世俗社会。贝叶经刻写委员会于公元 1867 年在位于 Sabaragamuva 省 Ratnapura 区 Palmadulla Pirivena 的 Sudassana Dharmasala 成立，被定名为 Sudharmodaya Pirivena。第二次是 1981—1991 年在 Etipola Medhankara Thera 和 Ambanpola Ratanasara Thera 领导下于马塔莱的 Aluviharaya 举行的。所有这些都与贝叶经高度相关，近代史表明了斯里兰卡人对于贝叶经的热爱，尽管当时印刷机制已经很完善。

巴利语文献中包含了教规、注释、子注释、编年史、手册、语法书、词典等，由于贝叶经刻写委员会非常关注巴利语经典，因此它们全部被刻写在了贝叶经上。这些文献一直被刻写在贝叶经手稿上用以保存、传播，直至公元 1737 年引入印刷术为止。尽管如此，值得注意的是，直到 19 世纪初，贝叶经手稿依旧十分流行。不仅是在斯里兰卡，甚至是南亚、东南亚的佛教国家，都基于贝叶经手稿对上述主题进行学术编写。同理可知，从阿奴拉达普勒到康提时期的传统僧伽罗文学很可能是对巴利语文学的翻译或改编，或者至少引用了巴利语文学的主题。僧伽罗语经典作品 Siyabaslakara，为文学作品的创作提供了必要指导。

有关佛陀前世的文学作品必须用诗歌写成，而习俗、仪式等则用散文写成。对于戏剧，必须在诗歌和散文中都使用。因此，传统的僧伽罗文学不仅仅是该国的佛教文化，基于贝叶经手稿的传统僧伽罗文学则对专业性要求很高。一些佛教信徒对僧伽罗文献解读做出了极大的贡献。Gulugomi、Vidyacakravarti、国王 Parakramabahu Ⅳ 是典型代表。

斯里兰卡贝叶经的收藏

Suluvaga、Mahavaga、Smantapāsādikāva 和 Visuddhimaggatīkāva 是斯里兰卡迄今为止发现的最为古老的贝叶经手稿。斯里兰卡对于贝叶经手稿的收藏，在质和量上都处于国际前列。科伦坡博物馆图书馆藏 5000 多份贝叶经手稿，其中包括 2000 份 W. A. de Silva 的手稿、1200 份 Hue Nevil 的手稿和 261 份 Ananda Kumarasvami 的手稿。佩拉德尼亚大学藏有 4000 多份手稿，其中包括 De Seram 的手稿。科伦坡大学民族医学研究所也藏有 700 多份手稿。而奴戈沽达的 Jayawardhanapura 大学、Dalugama 的凯拉尼亚大学、国家档案馆、科伦坡国家图书馆和坎迪东方图书馆的藏书也极为重要。伦敦大英博物馆收藏了近 2469 份手稿，丹麦哥本哈根皇家图书馆收藏了 1000 份 Rusmas Rask 的手稿。阿姆斯特丹国家图书馆、慕尼黑国立博物馆、荷兰国家图书馆、法国国家图书馆、博德林图书馆以及牛津大学都藏有贝叶经手稿，其中大部分都是斯里兰卡的文化遗产（Lagamuva 2006：85）。它们的作用不仅仅是收集贝叶经，更是有利于形成足够的机制来保护、传承贝叶经，并为研究者研究提供基础材料。

贝叶经的制作

考虑到书籍生命力的经久不衰，为了制作和刻写而形成可读材料的贝叶经工艺也是一个漫长的制作过程。包括对棕榈叶的选择、煮沸、干燥、平滑和抛光、制件、打孔和装订。首先，选择未展开的贝叶嫩叶，小心地从主叶脉上取下并卷起。然后，将卷起的棕榈叶在大容器中煮沸，开锅后换小火继续煮沸几个小时。取出后，晾晒三天整。随后进行平滑和抛光，通常用杵将棕榈叶在光滑的圆木桶上反复碾压。由于叶片柔软且具有弹性，因此可以按照一定的尺寸将其制成长度 6—32 英寸不等、宽度 2—2.75 英寸不等。而后，用一根加热的铁棒在纸张一侧打两个孔，并用绳子穿过这两个孔将手稿绑扎起来。手稿的封面和封底都是用乌木、铁树、val-sapu、gammalu、波罗蜜树和 milla 等木材或金属制成。封面通常装饰有五颜六色的图案。

Panhida 和 ulkaṭuva 是贝叶经刻写的两种方式，第一种是训练有素的刻写师所使用的，第二种则被接受刻写训练的练习者所使用。练习者应使用 ulkaṭuva（方式）在粗糙的纸上（karakolaya）书写名为 guru-akuru（给老师的信）的字母，直到能够熟练地在棕榈叶上进行刻写。这种方式所使用的笔长约 4—6 英寸，呈圆形或正八边形，从上到下越来越细，由铜、铁或者黄铜制成。老师会从简单的字母、单词到句子逐步地培养练习者，使他们的刻写逐步美观而快捷。而刻写师所使用的工具，是一种更为专业的刻写笔。这种刻写笔约 10—20 英寸长，采用银制品和象牙进行装饰。笔杆采用金、银、铜、黄铜、铁或青铜制成，但笔针为钢制。其中，一支 14.4 英寸长的金笔是由国王纳兰德拉辛交给佛牙寺法王马哈加巴达·尼莱姆和迪亚瓦达娜·尼莱姆的。

佛教贝叶经手稿率先以梵语、巴利语或僧伽罗语开头，表示对佛陀的尊敬，如 namo buddhāya、namo tassa bhagavato arahato sammāsam buddhassa、Namah sri ghaṇāya、namah samanta bhadrāya 和 Namav muni saraṇa。手稿最开始的术语 "svasti" "svasti siddham" 和 "svasti śri" 的 "sva" 都有 "保佑你" 的含义。而手稿最后所写的 "siddhirastu" "śubhamastu" "kalyanamastu" 和 "arogyamastu" 同样有 "保佑你" "保佑你身体健康" 的含义。此外，作者和抄录者更喜欢提及他们

的宗教愿望，并祝愿所有生命体。下面来看一个实例：

　　Iminā puññakammena yāva buddho bhavāmahaṃ
　　Mahosadhova nānena joti siṭṭhīva bhoginā
　　Vessantarova dānena hotu mayhaṃ bhavā bhave
　　Imaṃ likhita punnena metteyya mupasaṃkami
　　Patitthahitvā saraṇe suppatitthāmi sāsane
　　Sabbe sattā sukhappattā averā ca anūmayā
　　Dīghāyukā aññamaññaṃ piyā papponti nibbutiṃ.

　　译文：通过善行所积累的功德，我能够成为一名佛陀
　　拥有Mahauṣadha一样的智慧，拥有Joti seṭṭhi一样的财富
　　拥有Vessantaro一样的慈悲，我可以得到从生活到生命的实现
　　通过写下这篇文章的功德，我得以见到佛祖
　　并得到他的庇护，加入Sasana（锡兰佛教精进会）
　　愿所有人都能够获得幸福，摆脱仇恨和妄想
　　获得长生，并在适当的时候得到涅槃（Silva 1938：xxi，由作者编辑）

　　实例中的所有内容均根据字母和经文等的数量进行计数，八个字母为一行，四行为一节经文，250节为一bhāṇavāra（aṭṭhakkharā ekapadaṃ-ekā gāthā catuppadā；gāthā eko mato gantho-gantho dvattiṃsa akkharo；Dvattiṃsakkharagāthānam-pannāsadvisatam pana；bhāṇavāro mato eko - aṭṭhakkhara sahassako）。这种格式是巴利文书写佛教手稿的独有特征。一卷手稿有3到1000页不等，但大多为50页至100页。佩拉德尼亚大学收藏的 *Jātaka Poth Vahanse* 手稿共两卷，分别为1055页和1263页。手稿中仅有两种标点符号：逗号、kākapāda（鱼尾纹形）和kundaliya（蛇形）。前者表示句子的结尾，后者表示段落的结尾。两节和三节kundaliya表示各节的结尾，两节或三节双kundaliya表示各章的结尾。（Silva 1938：xix）

　　书写贝叶经时，应遵循从左到右的书写规律，并且页面顶部的第一行是被称为"mavpeḷa"的母行，而其余部分则是被称为"darupeḷa"的子行。采用巴利语和梵语书写的手稿使用的是复合辅音，而采用僧伽罗语书写的手稿使用的则只是辅音。此外，这些字母被分为三种文体，即mulukuru——用于Ruhuna国家且收尾略有修饰、sihakuru——用于玛雅国家且字体圆润、gajakuru——用于Pihiti国家，但它们基本上是相同的。在手稿中，看不到单词之间的空格。

斯里兰卡贝叶经手稿的交换

　　在古代，佛教国家之间的贝叶经手稿交换是非常常见的。斯里兰卡现存贝叶经手稿中就有一些用缅甸语和泰语书写的巴利语手稿。法显（公元337—422年），一位中国的游僧，曾为寻找 *Vinaya*（《律》）一书，探访包括斯里兰卡在内的南亚、东南亚国家（公元399—412年）。因为印度没有《律》书，他曾在斯里兰卡

Abhayagiri 佛寺住了两年。随后，在 Mahisasaka 学校找到了《律》书的副本，并邀请斯里兰卡僧侣 Sanghavami 前往中国将其翻译成中文。后来，从这所学校脱离出来的一群人组建了 Dharmaguptikas 团体，这个群体就是至今在所有东亚佛教中依然被认可的《律》。公元 5 世纪末，两卷重要的斯里兰卡贝叶经——*Samantapāsādikā*（Vinaya commentary）和 *Vimuttimagga*（《解放之路》）被带到了中国，并翻译成中文。公元 5 世纪，第一卷由 Sanghabhadra 译为 Shan-jian-li-p'-ip'-osha，其中就包含了大正《中国大藏经》（T. 1648）。公元 6 世纪初，第二卷由 Sanghapala 译为 Cie-to-tao-lun（Guruge 2010）。

国王 Buvanekabahu Ⅵ（公元 1470—1478 年）时期，缅甸国王 Dhammacedi 派遣了 22 名僧侣携学生以及 Citraduta、Ramaduata 二位部长前往斯里兰卡交流。他们在 Kalyani 河的 Kalyānisīmā 接受了较高的祝圣礼，并带回了许多流传在暹罗和柬埔寨的巴利语贝叶经（Perera 1988：67，68）。此事被记录在缅甸佩贡的一处碑文上，并附着 1442 年从斯里兰卡带回的贝叶经书单。书单中共有 295 卷，其中包括唐格温和他的妻子捐赠给僧侣的书籍（Lagamuva 2006：144；Silva 1938：xxv）。后来，由于拉贾辛格一世国王的信仰向印度教转变以及 16 世纪缅甸与葡萄牙的冲突，致使诸多贝叶经被送回，斯里兰卡也失去了它的文化宝库。

流行的佛教文化与贝叶经

僧伽罗佛寺最常见的术语 pansala 一词，来源于 paṇṇasālā，在巴利语中表示用贝叶棕榈盖的茅草屋顶。一些僧侣仍在使用贝叶编制的雨伞，被称为 goṭu-atta。扇形棕榈 Palmyra-fan（vaṭāpata）是僧侣的象征，它们多用于佛教活动。佛牙游行是最受欢迎的佛教文化仪式之一，每年在康提举行，以纪念佛牙，祝愿国家繁荣与和平。直到现在，僧伽罗的 kendaraya 还被写在贝叶经中。

后缀 vahanse 被用来表示对某人的尊敬，常被用作僧侣、国王、神灵等的后缀，但在这里，同样表示对两卷贝叶经手稿的尊重。*Jātaka Poth Vahanse* 和 *Piruvānā Poth Vahanse* 分别由僧伽罗语和巴利语写成。它们是斯里兰卡佛教文化中最受尊敬的书籍，并至今沿用贝叶经版制。*Piruvānā Poth Vahanse* 是一本从 Paritta 诵经仪式中所使用的 Sutta Pitaka（经藏）中选取出的巴利语篇章合集。*Jātaka Poth Vahanse* 讲述了自 Jātakaṭṭhakathā 时期到 Kurunagala 时期 547 个关于 Gotama Buddha's former Bodhisattva life translated（摩佛陀前菩萨的生活阅历）的故事。至今，即使所有佛寺都不再藏有贝叶经，但这两卷贝叶经还在佛寺使用。他们用浮屠塔（dhātukaranḍuva）安葬佛陀或门徒的舍利。宗教活动中，这两本贝叶经被僧侣从舍利塔中取出，放在头顶上并且用 mutu-kuḍaya（pearl-umbrella 混元珍珠伞）做的伞遮挡着。由于 *Piruvānā Poth Vahanse* 的特殊性，作为唯一一卷以僧伽罗语命名的巴利语手稿，它甚至不同于为新手阅读和佛寺教育所印刷的现代巴利语书籍。它被用于整晚或七天举办的诵经仪式。*Catubhāṇavāra-pāli* 是该书的原名，但其僧伽罗语名称在巴利语系佛教徒中更为盛行。在僧伽罗文献的结尾，有一个附录，记录了后来流行的 parittas（诵经），甚至包含了一些 yantra（神秘图腾）和 mantras（神圣话语）。诵读 *Jātaka Poth Vahanse* 依然是一种受人尊敬的行为，其自身的风格被称为 vāsagam-šailiya，同时提高了听众的兴趣。

结 论

贝叶经自始至终都是斯里兰卡佛教文化的重要组成部分。它以巴利语经典、注释、子注释以及巴利语其他文献来充实。由于传统僧伽罗文学极大可能是从巴利语翻译或改编而来的，因此它们的主题几乎完全是佛教文化。*Siyabaslakara* 是僧伽罗文化的指向标，它促使诸多作者展现佛教主题，而非单纯的世俗表达。瓦塔伽马尼国王统治时期，佛陀开始在贝叶经上刻写文字，这是整个世界宗教史上最重要的事情之一。这是宗教教育完善概念和关键解释的第一次体验。*Jātaka Poth Vahanse* 和 *Piruvānā Poth Vahanse* 是斯里兰卡佛教文化中最畅销、最受尊敬、最广为人知的书籍，并至今沿用贝叶经版制。斯里兰卡对于贝叶经的保护也值得赞赏，国家图书馆、科伦坡博物馆图书馆、佩拉迪尼亚、基拉尼亚和斯里贾亚瓦德纳普拉科特大学图书馆在贝叶文化的保护和鼓励研究方面做出了杰出贡献。尽管印制工艺已十分普遍，但贝叶文化在斯里兰卡依然存在，一部分以传统家族为代表的年青一代依然维护着贝叶文化遗产。

傣民族医药古籍与师承教育模式探析

——以滇西应用技术大学傣医药学院为例

玉喃哈[①]

傣医药作为傣民族传统医药，据记载至今已有2500多年的历史，因其具备完整的理论知识、丰富的医药学价值而被列为我国四大民族医药之一。南传上座部佛教传入之前，当地人民善用药用植物医治常见病症，但未形成传统医药理论体系。13世纪随着佛教传入，我国云南省西双版纳傣族地区创造了经书文、文学、历法、法律、医学等应运而生。相对其他贝叶经而言，医药古籍经典的流传范围相对较小，因此搜集难度较大。师承教育是傣医药最重要的传承方式，民间傣医年事已高，傣医药文化的传承十分紧迫，若不及时采取措施拯救医药典籍，将会有更多精品典籍消失在民间。

一、傣医药古籍经典传承存在的问题

（一）傣医药古籍传承危机

傣医药古籍经典最早以贝叶经的形式记载、传播、学习和传承，由于"文化大革命"等原因，大规模贝叶经被烧毁或流失，现存的贝叶经医药典籍显得更为珍贵。近百来年，傣医药古籍多以纸经形式传抄，鲜少搜集到历史悠久的贝叶经医药古籍。贝叶经要比纸经更加经久耐磨。笔者在调研时得知：按照西双版纳傣族的传统习俗，民间傣医若无人传承其医术医技，亲属在其逝世后不会保存其遗物，会将其医书典籍、行医用具等，与其生前物品一同焚烧销毁。目前，西双版纳地区的傣医药传承人已进入青黄不接的发展阶段，随着老一辈民间傣医相继逝世，傣医药典籍的数量逐年减少，许多珍贵的医药文物已不复存在。傣医药正面临前所未有的传承危机，如不及时传承抢救，传统优秀医技和经方验方将会失传。

（二）傣医药古籍搜集难度较大

西双版纳傣族地区信仰南传上座部佛教的村寨历来都有赕坦（佛教供奉经书的一种仪式）的风俗习惯，但傣医药古籍不在赕佛经范畴中，笔者调研发现很多佛寺

[①] 作者为滇西应用技术大学傣医药学院讲师。

均无医药相关典籍。这也导致傣医药经典的流传范围窄、使用率较低，搜集难度较大。除此之外，有两种情况增加搜集难度：一是大部分民间傣医的家族传承意识极强，不愿轻易售卖祖传典籍；二是傣族尤其是傣族医者，对盗取医术行骗者防范意识很强，通过官方渠道或多次接触后，才能获取一些古籍相关信息。

（三）傣医药古籍市场价格虚高

受市场经济影响，已有商人察觉商机，搜集傣医药典籍进行贩卖，部分民间傣医及其家属意识到其价值。笔者在调研过程中发现，傣医药文献的收购价格日益攀升，项目组无法支付高昂价格，应用价值较高的典籍难以购买原版，更有傣医年事已高后，其亲属分割典籍导致古籍下落不明。

（四）傣医药古籍知识产权问题

贝叶经是佛教的产物，一方面，按照傣族传统，无论传抄、翻译、编写时都不能署名，因为傣族认为一切民族文化均不能占为己有，知识的共享意识颇强；另一方面，大多数民间傣医知识产权观念淡薄，一些经济效益较好的傣医不愿分享家传秘方，又不具备现代医药学知识，这会对后期的产品开发、研究工作造成一定阻碍。

（五）傣医药古籍开发力度不足

从事傣医药古籍文献研究的机构有西双版纳州傣医医院（西双版纳州民族医药研究所）、云南中医药大学、滇西应用技术大学等科研院所和高校。其中西双版纳州傣医医院和州民族医药研究所已合并为一个单位，主要由医院科研科负责从事相关工作，该单位起步较早，大部分古籍开发工作都由其牵头进行，遗憾的是仍未搭建数字化平台。

云南中医药大学近十年来在云南省西双版纳州、德宏州搜集到数十本傣医药古籍经典；滇西应用技术大学傣医药学院成立一年来，也搜集到将近十本傣医药古籍手抄本。两所高校的古籍仍处在图书馆或档案室馆藏状态，需进一步加强开发应用。

（六）傣医药古籍翻译难度大

云南省西双版纳傣族地区自古以来都由佛寺教育传承傣族传统文化，现有的学校教育与佛寺教育的冲突造成新一代傣族年轻人经书文识字率较低。翻译傣医药古籍文献不仅需要精通傣汉双语，更要了解巴利语（佛教语言）借词，掌握一定的医药类专业术语及翻译理论知识等。这对翻译者的知识技能要求极高，现有的翻译人才屈指可数，且都集中在西双版纳州民族医药研究所，承担科研、行政双肩挑工作，翻译的时间和精力难以保障。

二、傣医药人才院校培养模式

（一）傣医药院校培养及政策支持

滇西应用技术大学傣医药学院成立于2017年5月，学院设有傣医学、中药学、康复治疗学、护理学、中药资源与开发5个专业，在校本科生共有1021人。傣医学作为学院特色专业，2017年招生至今已有在校傣医学学生139名。

学院承担西双版纳州人民政府支持的"傣医药人才培养三年行动计划"项目，该项目将通过遴选傣医药学院优秀青年人才、设立傣医药师承项目、实施傣医药优秀僧才培训，组织开展傣医药古籍搜集、修复、整理、保存等项目，全方位培养傣医药人才。此外，学院"傣民族医药古籍搜集、整理、修复、翻译、保存"项目获云南省民宗委云南少数民族文化"百项精品"扶持，该项目将整理、修复和保存傣医药古籍、翻译出版精品著作并建立傣医药文献数据库。可见，学院十分重视古籍文献的传承，并将其融入人才培养的各个环节。

（二）傣医学专业课程设置

在课程设置方面，医药学傣语也作为专业基础课程开设，专业基础课程模块包括：傣医基础理论等课程；专业核心课程模块有：傣医药学史、傣医方剂学、傣医皮外骨伤科学等课程。作为应用技术型大学，傣医药学院开展多次认知实践、识药认药鉴药等教学活动，使学生更好地融入傣医药产业的大环境。傣医学专业学生要在掌握傣医基本理论、基础知识的同时熟悉中医、西医的临床诊断技术。

医药学傣语作为专业基础课程，使傣医学专业学生通过学习掌握西双版纳经书文及新傣文，能够使用国际音标注音，识记常用傣药及经方验方，能够借助工具书挖掘、搜集、整理、传承傣医经方验方，从事傣医药古籍文献的研究。

（三）本土学生可塑性

傣医药学院已有5名西双版纳籍傣族学生。考虑到傣医学专业的本土性特征，需加大政策力度，降分鼓励本地生源考生报考傣医学专业。在开展教学及科研工作时，本地傣族学生的优势非常明显，一是易于理解傣族传统文化系统内的傣医药特殊性，熟练掌握、运用、传承傣医药文化。二是语言文字方面的优势，云南省西双版纳傣族地区的民间傣医，年龄超过45岁的大都不能熟练使用汉语，掌握傣语和傣文无疑是传承傣医药的必要条件。三是个别学生来自傣医世家或有传承渠道，对傣医药抱有极大兴趣和学习热情。

（四）傣医药学院的文化传承优势

滇西应用技术大学傣医药学院鼓励师生开展与傣医药古籍文献相关的创新创业项目、社会实践活动等教学项目，通过寒暑假等空闲时间跟师系统学习傣医药古籍文献。西双版纳的地理区位有利于师生开展前期调研工作，学院科研团队已走访西双版纳州、德宏州约50名民间傣医及其传承人，定期与其保持联系，为输送优秀学生民间拜师做足准备。学院通过官方、民间等多种渠道，发动广大师生搜集、获取民间傣医及古籍经典的信息，保障传承工作有序进行。傣医学、中药学专业学生与搜集整理、翻译古籍文献相关性较大，经过长时间学习"实用傣语""医药学傣语"，熟悉傣汉双语、国际音标及傣医药专业名词术语，并且具备信息化技术手段，能初步完成傣医典籍的整理翻译工作。

三、师承教育与古籍开发有机结合

《中华人民共和国中医药法》第三十五条规定：国家发展中医师承教育，支持具有丰富经验与技术专长的中医医师以及中药专业技术人员在执业过程中带徒授业，传承中医药学术知识，培养中医药专业技术人员。傣医药主要依靠师承教育、院校教育来传承文化，两种教育模式各有长处，院校教育更为系统、科学、专业，而师承教育则更具针对性和特殊性，两者强强联合方能弥补短板，有机融合。

（一）傣医药古籍的传承途径

传承傣医药古籍经典的途径主要有以下三种：一是向古籍持有者直接购买、借阅扫描或形成手抄本复印件。二是通过拜师仪式由师傅将其当作拜师礼赠送学生，言传身教实践教学。三是可与云南佛学院西双版纳分院等联合，将优秀僧才遴选入古籍传承项目，借助南传上座部佛教信仰的力量，发挥僧才传统文化和傣文功底优势，共同完成医药古籍传承工作。笔者通过调研得知：民间傣医不愿意直接贩卖原版古籍，多数征得同意可抄写、复印或扫描，但如有学生愿意拜师学习，也愿意将古籍作为传承信物倾囊相授。

傣医药古籍的搜集工作并非一朝一夕就能完成，个别傣医失去行医能力后，傣医药典籍也不知去向，这无疑增加了搜集抢救工作的难度。尤其针对已无带徒精力的傣医，有关部门应借助自身的影响，动员傣医和亲属破除封建迷信思想，积极引导民间傣医捐赠或分享医药典籍，以防不法分子哄抬物价。必须和民间傣医建立稳固的情感联结，宣传文献典籍的医药学价值，转变其家族传承的固定思维，提高其共享、开发、研究的意识。

（二）遵循传统拜师习俗

傣医药学院拟开设"傣医药古籍研究"实践课程，遴选一批"医药学傣语"课程成绩优异的学生，开展傣族传统拜师仪式活动，跟师学习某一部傣医药经典著作，并与师傅共同整理、翻译傣文古籍文献，将其汇编成册。为确保傣医药经典翻译质量，需制定一套规范化的实践课程管理体系。首先，在西双版纳州内寻找愿意带徒传授医技并开发祖传医术典籍的民间傣医。其次，按照医学、药学、康复治疗学等专业分配学院专职教师负责监督师承学习进度，并从专业角度审定翻译作品。最后，有针对性地选拔2—3名学生，利用寒暑假等较长周期集中跟师学习，有计划地执行学习、整理、翻译古籍经典工作，共同完成后期编译，配合学院完成傣医药数字化平台建设工作。

（三）古籍开发知识产权归属问题

傣文古籍的产出形式一般可分为两大类：一是以著作形式出版，古籍持有者、师承学生、负责教师等均为编者，共同持有著作权与署名权，共享著作产生的经济利益。二是将开发价值较高的古籍经方验方转化为产品或专利，可采取一次性购买或院校、学生、古籍持有者三方共享专利共有权的方式。值得庆幸的是，不愿出售古籍的民间傣医均提出可以通过复印、扫描等形式分享古籍。在实施傣族传统医药实践活动数字化、信息化、文献化时，要征得傣族同胞同意，做好保密工作，对其民族信仰充分尊重。

（四）加大地方性知识研究，填补理论知识空白

据笔者调研统计得知：西双版纳傣族地区流传的医药学典籍80%以上均为药典类手抄本且年份约在100年以内。民间傣医在传抄医书时，并不严格按照原著抄写，会根据自身医学经验增加或修改其经方验方，导致民间流传的配方不一致。师承模式有利于师徒共同开发古籍，在民间、医院、院校反复验证其临床效果，证实某种经方验方的科学性。梳理古籍时，通过大规模整合同种配方，从中追寻其发展脉络，便于今后教学研究使用。傣医药的基础理论仍在不断发展完善，学生可将傣医在实践中传授的辨证思想、医技手法等归纳为理论知识，以此改善傣医药药方多，医技及理论知识匮乏的现状。

西双版纳地区的傣民族信仰南传上座部佛教和原始宗教，这在傣医药中也体现得十分明显，傣医药的基础理论"四塔五蕴"就是最典型的佛教知识。民间傣医不仅会用口诀接骨、止血、拔牙，而且还会给疑难杂症病人占卜测算。在民族地区要充分理解其传统文化的特殊性，在现代医学和传统医学中寻找平衡点，在培养学生的过程中适当灌输地方性知识，使其真正掌握傣医教育思想的内涵。目前的院校教育使傣医药过度中医化、西医化，深挖傣医基础理论，补充地方性知识教育，让傣医药回归特色和本色是当前傣医药教育的题中应有之义。

（五）傣医药古籍的数字化平台建设

云南中医药大学民族医药博物馆已逐步建立了信息数字化藏品，以图片、视频、音频、文字说明等进行数字化加工整理并收藏保管。西双版纳州傣医医院（西双版纳州民族医药研究所）已整理翻译出版20余部作品，但未搭建数字化平台，傣医药著作的传播和继承较为局限。

滇西应用技术大学傣医药学院正在搭建傣医药数据库，包括傣医药数据库、傣医药人才库和傣医药古籍资源库。傣医药学院现已具备信息化的人力、物力、财力，动员师生参与田野调查，传承古籍经典，汇集信息化数据。传统媒介具有局限性，无论是贝叶经、纸经都难以长期保存，信息化不仅突破传承障碍，而且能发挥信息化、智能化功能，提高傣医药的使用率和影响力。一旦完成傣药查询、药方查询在线诊疗等傣医药知识查询系统，将填补理论教学空白，推动教学及专业建设向纵深发展，起到科研反哺教学的作用。

四、结语

滇西应用技术大学傣医药学院搭建平台，结合院校培养与师承教育，联合民间傣医、院校教师、临床专家等多方导师之力，共同培养傣医药传承人，并对古籍进行整理、翻译、开发、临床研究等。在保护与传承医药典籍的同时，挖掘补充傣医

理论知识，进一步将傣药经方验方规范化，充分发挥学院科研优势加大地方性知识的调研，最终将研究成果纳入傣医药数据库，使傣医药古籍经典得到永久性保护与传承。

参考文献：

[1] 李和伟，王启帆，付宇，曹净植.《中医药法》视角下有关中医师承教育的思考.中医杂志，2017（21）.

[2] 黎冬梅，金玲钰，郭春，刘鑫，佟宇帆.试论我国傣医药知识产权保护现状及对策——以西双版纳傣族自治州为例.遗产与保护研究，2018（9）.

[3] 张强，江南，吴永贵.云南民族医药古籍数字化整理探讨.中国民族民间医药杂志，2015（2）.

[4] 周红黎.傣医古籍整理与保护研究.中国民族民间医药，2018（3）.

[5] 罗艳秋，保丽娟，吴永贵.傣族医药古籍资源的调查与定级研究.中国民族医药杂志，2009（10）.

[6] 赵婧琦.地方性知识的高等教育及其问题研究.内蒙古大学硕士学位论文，2019.

[7] 段忠玉，张超.傣医药文化传承与保护研究.医学与社会，2016（3）.

[8] 西双版纳州傣医医院.发展中的西双版纳州民族医药研究所西双版纳州傣医医药.中国民族民间医药杂志，2015（2）.

[9] 谷晓红，闫永红，林燕，高颖，刘铜华.坚持传承创新促进医教协同.中医教育，2016（3）.

DREAMSEA 项目概况及其抢救濒危手稿的经验介绍

周寒丽[1]

一、项目概况

东南亚是世界上文化最具多样性的地区之一，在450万平方千米的土地上，约6.37亿的人口（2016年的统计）中，[2]上千个不同文化背景和习俗的民族在此地居住已有上千年，并创造出不一样的历史和文明。对于文明的传承和传播，语言和文字功不可没，因此文字作为文明传承和传播的主要工具，被人们书写在不同的载体上，以供后来者学习并保存。

手稿简单而言，就是一种在物质媒介上经手写而成的文本。它是在印刷术尚未普及的地方或者印刷术广泛推广以前，人类社会用以保存和传播文化的重要手段，也是我们今天学习人类过去创造的文明，乃至了解现代社会的关键资料。

实际上，在东南亚海岛和大陆，至今仍有很多民族保持着传统的文化记录方式，他们不仅保存着数目可观的手稿，并且上了年纪的当地学者们还在不断地记录和传抄新的手稿。因此，手稿文化并非一种彻底死去的文化，手稿文化的研究和保护，不仅有学术意义，也有现实意义。但是在历史发展进程中，很多人不再对手稿感兴趣，并逐渐丢弃了这种传统的文化传播方式。当地人，尤其是年轻人认为，在智能化时代的今天，在纸质、贝叶、树皮、羊皮纸、竹子和金属等不同的物质材料上书写的文化传播方式已经"过时"了。这种看法的存在，导致了很多手稿被忽视、丢弃、烧毁或者扔掉。此外，由于缺少手稿保存的知识，加上大部分手稿没有被载入正在进行的研究中，因而手稿的破损和消失也意味着东南亚各民族异质身份的消失。

根据目前的调研情况，民间收藏的手稿总量上可能会超过机构收藏。然而不幸的是，很多私人收藏有各自的保管方式且其文本也不为人知，并从未在公众面前展示过，加之由于私人收藏带有很大不确定性：首先，大部分手稿已经有一定的年限了，由于东南亚地处热带雨林气候区，气候炎热潮湿，这种情况下很难保证手稿不被毁损；其次，由于大部分手稿是用非社会主流的文字书写，能看懂并可以继续传

---

[1] 德国汉堡大学亚非研究院东南亚语言与文化系博士研究生；普洱学院副教授。
[2] Report for Selected Countries and Subjects. World Economic. IM. Outlook Database, 2016.

抄的专业人员并不多，一旦收藏者（作者）去世，收藏者（作者）的家属会如何处理这些手稿也未可知，这些手稿也将会面临未知的命运。最后，东南亚不稳定的社会状况和政治冲突也会加剧对手稿的破坏。因此，民间手稿经常处于被破坏、毁灭和消失的潜在可能中。

出于保护东南亚文化多样性的目的，尽快开展对东南亚手稿的保护工作是非常迫切的。2017年Lisbet Rausing and Peter Baldwin慈善基金（ARCADIA）资助"东南亚濒危和具有影响力的手稿的数字化存储"（The Digital Repository of Endangered and Affected Manuscripts in Southeast Asia）项目对东南亚民间收藏的濒危和具有影响力的手稿进行数字化存储。该项目计划五年内完成，即到2022年完成240000帧的数字化存储。

二、项目实施的目的、范围和数字化存储的原因

东南亚是目前世界上文化形态最为多样化的地区之一，DREAMSEA项目致力于保护东南亚的手稿文化，并捍卫多元文化在东南亚的生存和发展。只要是来自东南亚地区，涉及自然科学、文学、历史和宗教等领域内的手稿（不管是何种书写材料）都是项目抢救和保护的对象。在完成数字化存储后，相关数据都会上传到网络数据库中，以供来自不同领域的学者进行学术研究。

项目目前签订协议的合作范围包括印度尼西亚、泰国、老挝、越南。印度尼西亚主要集中在巴厘岛和爪哇岛等地。值得一提的是，项目成员在爪哇岛发现了原著年份在100年左右，传抄年份在10年内的，用巴利语和线形文字书写在竹片上的手稿，其内容是关于当地民间的神话故事，精通巴利语的学者基本上都能阅读该手稿。说明巴利语自近现代以来，在此地仍有传播，这或许跟佛教曾在爪哇岛广泛流传有关。

此外，在东南亚主要选择了泰国、老挝和越南作为调查点。泰国的调查点集中在泰北地区，包括难府、南奔和清迈三个据点。老挝调查点主要集中在中部，即琅勃拉邦省。近日，老挝的手稿数字化已经完成，主要集中在佛教经典领域。越南主要集中在越南北部地区和南部占婆人的聚居区。关于被挑选进行数字化的手稿，其文本内所采用的语言，限于学术专家所精通文字的有限性和项目地区的手稿采用文字的普遍性，在泰国和老挝选取的手稿大部分都是Tham字（即兰那文，也叫傣泐文或老傣文）书写的文本。越南北部选择的是古代汉语书写的文本，南部选择的是占婆文字书写的文本。

尽管以前也曾有很多项目对东南亚各国的手稿进行过收集和数字化存储工作，但如此大规模的抢救工作尚属首次。濒危和具有影响力的手稿需要进行数字化存储，因为这是一种可以永久保存并不断复制手稿的方式。由于书写手稿的有机物，尤其是绵纸，在东南亚热带雨林气候下，都难以长期完好保存，所以，数字存储保证了手稿的完整性和连续性，同时也是向收藏者（作者）致敬。

三、项目运行方式

为了能顺利完成项目目标，DREAMSEA 对项目运行做了良好的架构。项目总部设在雅加达的国立伊斯兰大学，由总负责人、秘书（负责联络开会和财务支出）、摄影师和 IT 技术人员组成，主要负责项目协调、资金支配和网络维护。汉堡大学的印度尼西亚研究专家 Prof. Dr. Jan van der Putten 是海岛手稿文化的学术指导，也是项目的全局规划者。泰佬民族研究专家 Pro. Dr. Volker Grabowsky 作为大陆国家手稿文化的学术指导，主要负责老挝、泰国的手稿数字化，并对大陆国家的手稿抢救工作进行综合规划和指导。

每一个地区的项目小组主要由五个人组成，分别是学术专家、学术专家助手、摄影师、摄影师助手和当地向导。学术专家和助手要求精通英语，能跟项目负责人和联络人进行良好沟通，并具有一定的手稿文化的学术知识和摄影技术知识。摄影师和摄影师助手需要精通摄影设备的操作，能快速准确地拍摄出符合项目组要求的高质量图片，并精通电脑操作，把已经数字化的文件上传到网络数据库；雅加达的技术人员会在随后立即检查，如果不符合要求，则需要重新进行拍摄。因此为了避免做重复工作，每一份数据化了的手稿都必须达到项目组要求。当地向导则是项目在实际操作中的关键人物，如何获得可靠的信息，如何高效快速地搭建起与当地学者和收藏者直接沟通的桥梁，都离不开一个可靠并熟知当地社会规则的向导。

项目组为各地区小组提供专业的数字化设备，为了还原每一帧图片的真实面貌，项目组对图片像素、大小都有标准化规定。项目组采用的设备是目前世界上较为先进的拍摄器材，当然其操作也相当复杂。2019 年 5 月 17—18 日期间在泰国北部难府的 DREAMSEA 研讨会上，总部技术人员对与会的学者都进行了摄影设备操作的专业训练。由于海岛和老挝的手稿数字化项目已经完成，目前已经轮到泰国难府对本地的濒危手稿进行数字化处理，因此设备目前在难府，下一个点在南奔和清迈。

在对当地向导的选择上，则具有很大的灵活性，他们需要熟悉当地文化情况，或者当地的收藏者、学者或者手稿文字。除了食宿费、材料费和交通费以外，项目成员还有劳务补贴，由于项目的补贴是按天计算，并按照每组每天五个人的标准，有些地方聘请的向导不止一个，那么就需要学术专家进行分配，尽量保证公平公正。

项目给每一个目标点的时间是半年，大概需要集中进行拍摄的时间在一个月左右，如果需要数字化的手稿数量超出或者不足，时间可以前后调动。其工作流程大致如下：第一，先对当地的手稿分布情况进行调研；第二，学术专家召集成员开会，协调成员工作时间，制定田野计划；第三，小组成员下田野，根据实际情况和向导建议再开始拍摄。

四、实际操作

DREAMSEA 项目的工作流程为：手稿分布的调研、筛选手稿、数字化手稿、对

贝叶文化与区域文化遗产传承保护

数字化的手稿进行描述，以及后期的技术处理和上传到数据库。几乎每个小组都要按照此流程进行工作。

濒危手稿分布的调研和筛选手稿，是学术专家需要做的工作。实际上，在很多小组承接项目以前都已经有了基本的，甚至是详细的方向。因此该步骤并不需要标准化的作业。对筛选手稿进行数字化则有一定的标准，因为项目预算有限，时间有限，作为学者应该明白，不可能把全部收集到的手稿都进行数字化，只能优先处理那些重要的手稿。什么是重要的手稿，选择的标准第一是濒危，即未曾被政府或者其他机构数字化过，手稿的保存状况不乐观，手稿未来的命运不确定；第二是具有影响力，即该手稿具有一定的学术研究价值，或代表了当地的传统文化或者历史。当然如果当地手稿所存不多，或者时间宽裕，那么以上两点可以根据实际情况进行调整。

此外，每一本数字化的手稿，应该留下一个标签——"该手稿曾被 DREAMSEA 项目数字化保存过"，这样可以避免后来人做重复工作。

数字化手稿，则是摄影师需要完成的工作，这部分主要涉及硬件操作，拿到摄影设备的时候，会附有详细的指导说明。在数字化的过程中，学术专家可以从旁协助，遇到页码和内容等相关问题的时候及时向向导和收藏者请教。

数字化手稿主要用英文进行描述，此部分也非常重要，这决定着该手稿的收藏价值和后来人在学术研究领域的准确性。因此，DREAMSEA 项目组对此做了非常标准化的规定，如表一和表二。

表一　手稿基本信息

国别	
城市	
手稿名称	
手稿页数	
保管情况（保管历史和保管人历史）	
收藏名称	

表二　手稿元数据

1	DREAMSEA 项目编号	
2	书架号	
3	赞助者（收藏者）	
4	从右到左（书写方式）	
5	参考目录	
6	标题	
	a. 文本文字	

续表

	b. 罗马拼音文			
	c. 英文			
7	主题			
8	原作者			
9	抄写员			
10	数据输入的原始时间			
11	（手稿）原文的作者日期	年	月	日
12	西历的作者日期	年	月	日
13	原文的复制日期			
14	西历的复制日期	年	月	日
15	开始日期			
16	结束日期			
17	作者（写作）地点			
18	（手稿被）复制地点			
19	（手稿采用）语言			
20	（手稿采用）文字			
21	书写媒介（材料）			
22	手稿尺寸	长：	宽：	
23	水印			

如果手稿上没有相关信息内容，表格中的内容就不需要填。在完成收集手稿的数字化工作后，就要进行后期技术处理，即归档文件。这部分工作非常关键，同时也很容易出现差错，因为按照项目组要求，每一天都要建立一个文件夹，每完成一份手稿的数字化工作就必须要把其归入当天的子文件夹中，并在文件里附上该手稿的元数据。检查无误之后，再上传到项目的网络数据库。这样就算是完成了一份手稿的数字化工作，实现了手稿的永久保存。此外，项目在2022年完成之后会结集各地的手稿样本和介绍，出版一部分重要的和具有学术研究价值的文本。

五、结论

DREAMSEA项目已经实施近两年了，目前已经顺利完成了海岛国家的手稿数字化工作，老挝的手稿数字化也刚刚结束。这两地手稿数字化工作的成功完成，对于其他地区的手稿抢救工作具有很大的借鉴价值和指导作用。通过了解DREAMSEA项目的概况、立项原因、立项目标、实施范围、运行机制和实际操作，我们对DREAMSEA项目也有一个大概的印象。同时我们将继续关注DREAMSEA项目后续的手稿抢救工作，这对于我们未来进一步保护和抢救濒危的云南少数民族手稿提供了一个可借鉴的模式和一个可供学习的案例。

经典傣文的名称和使用分布初探

岩坎章拉[①]

一、经典傣文的产生与传播

在南传上座部佛教[②]诞生之初，由于巴利语[③]只有语言而没有文字，巴利三藏经典都是靠口头传承的。根据文献记载，佛陀入灭后，才出现使用斯里兰卡的僧伽罗文将巴利三藏经典刻在贝叶片上的现象，这标志着巴利经典正式开始文字化的进程。[④]

经典傣文的传播与南传上座部佛教的传播有直接的关系。张公瑾认为，古印度字母（婆罗米字母）的传播与婆罗门教和佛教的传播有联系。中南半岛泰、缅、老、柬等国和中国傣族、布朗族等都信仰南传上座部佛教，其使用的文字形式也都从婆罗米字母演化而来。婆罗米字母因不同走向而分为南北两系，传到中南半岛后又可分为两个系统，其一是南系的古代吉蔑文，其二是来自北系的古代孟文。古代孟文则演化为缅甸文和经典傣文。孟文、缅文、经典傣文，这三种文字从辅音字母、元音字母、元音符号和数字形式来看，都极为相似，可说明这三种文字之间的亲近渊源关系。[⑤]谢远章认为经典傣文脱胎于古孟文。据哈里奔猜纪年记载，公元663年，今清迈南边的罗斛国孟族公主占玛黛维，北上建立哈里奔猜国，哈里奔猜位于泰国的南奔府，在清迈的南边。这一王国在《蛮书》及《元史》中被称为"女王国"。[⑥]当时哈里奔猜国的南传上座部佛教十分盛行。一直到13世纪，兰那王国的芒莱王征服了孟族的哈里奔猜国，南传上座部佛教才为兰那王国所接受。较发达的孟族文化（包括佛教）在一定程度上促进了兰那王国的大发展。[⑦]兰那文（经典傣文）就以哈里奔猜的孟文字母为模本创造产生，并随着南传上座部佛教从兰那地区

[①] 作者岩坎章拉，僧名：都坎章。西双版纳傣族僧人，泰国清迈大学社会科学院族群关系与发展研究中心硕士研究生。
[②] "南传上座部佛教"，也称"上座部佛教"，统称"南传上座部佛教"，又因其使用巴利语作为佛典语言，所以也称为巴利语系佛教。主要流传在斯里兰卡、缅甸、泰国、柬埔寨、老挝、中国云南等地区。
[③] "巴利语"（Pali-Bhasa）：原意为圣典语、佛经语，为南传上座部佛教的经典用语。巴利语与梵语（Sanskrit）同属古印度语。
[④] 西双版纳傣学研究会.西双版纳傣教.昆明：云南民族出版社，2012.
[⑤] 刘岩.南传上座部佛教与傣族文化.昆明：云南民族出版社，1993：167.
[⑥] 谢远章.谢远章学术文选.昆明：云南大学出版社，云南人民出版社，2016：106.
[⑦] 谢远章.谢远章学术文选.昆明：云南大学出版社，云南人民出版社，2016：110.

传播到西双版纳（勐泐/勐泐王国），因此又称泐文或傣泐①文。②

兰那王国也就是当时泰国北部以清莱、清迈一带为中心的王国。1180年，傣族首领帕雅真在西双版纳的景洪一带建都时，兰那和西双版纳在政治上曾长期结为同盟，文化发展水平也可称并驾齐驱，相互间亦有姻亲关系。如兰那王国的缔造者芒莱王，其母亲则是西双版纳景洪王甸陇建仔的女儿，名为帖帕罕凯（Thep Phra Kham Khai）③，又名喃乌明庄勐（Nang O Ming Jom Muang）。基于这个背景，长期以来西双版纳与兰那人民之间一直存在着民间贸易、宗教联系和文化交流等密切的往来，特别是传统文化和民族民间文学经过长期的交流与融合，形成了具有共同特点的傣（泰）语族文化遗产。这一联系如今依然在民间文化交流方面扮演着重要的角色，同时也在中泰两国人民友好往来的外交事务上有着积极的促进作用。④

各地经典傣文的巴利辅音字母对照表

罗马马利 Roman Pali	兰那/泰北 经典文字 Tai Tham-lanna	傣泐经典 文字 Tai Tham-Tai Lue	傣痕经典 文字 Tai Tham-Tai Khun	老挝/伊普 经典文字 Tai Tham-Lao-Isan	罗马马利 Roman Pali	兰那/泰北 经典文字 Tai Tham-lanna	傣泐经典 文字 Tai Tham-Tai Lue	傣痕经典 文字 Tai Tham-Tai Khun	老挝/伊普 经典文字 Tai Tham-Lao-Isan
k					th				
kh					d				
g					n				
gh					p				
ṅ					ph				
c					b				
ch					bh				
j					m				
jh					y				
ñ					r				
ṭ					l				
ṭh					v				
ḍ					s				
ḍh					h				
ṇ					ḷ				
t					ṁ				

云南省西双版纳地区的佛教，主要是从泰国北部兰那地区经缅甸景栋传入，当它传入西双版纳境内后一般被称为"润派"佛教（Yong/Yuan Buddhism）。润派佛教是中国南传上座部佛教教派中传入最早、发展最快、流传区域最广的一个派系。正因此，这一南传教派目前在中国境内拥有的寺院、僧侣和信众数量最多，影响力

---

① "傣泐"，一般是指勐泐的傣族或后裔，傣泐族群以西双版纳为中心在历史上不断地往外迁徙，如今分布在中国云南省西双版纳及周边、老挝、缅甸掸邦、泰国北部。在越南的莱州省，以及美国还有少量的傣泐族群，傣泐是傣泰民族中分布较广的一个族群。
② 谢远章.谢远章学术文选.昆明：云南大学出版社，云南人民出版社，2016：112.
③ 何平."八百媳妇"——"兰纳王国"及其主体民族的政治、社会与文化.思想战线，2013（1）.
④ 谢远章.谢远章学术文选.昆明：云南大学出版社，云南人民出版社，2016：112.

比其他南传派别也较大。① 润派佛教主要使用的文字就是本文所指的经典傣文。经典傣文最初只有 41 个字母、8 个元音和 33 个辅音，与巴利语字母的读音和顺序完全一致，后在巴利字母的基础上又根据傣语特点增添了一些字母，通过发展和完善，其符合和适应当地民族语言的特征，成为目前可同时使用于佛教和世俗的经典傣文。

南传上座部佛教传入傣族地区之后，傣族将其早期的本土信仰纳入佛教文化体系当中，二者相互融合，形成了你中有我、我中有你的信仰现象。南传上座部佛教的传入，不仅给傣族带来了文字，而且通过寺院里以巴利三藏经典作为代表的诸多典籍和经书通过一代又一代的传承，积淀起浩瀚的南传上座部佛教和民族文化，成为中华文化中不可或缺的一部分。目前，佛教界用来记写巴利语佛典的文字有斯里兰卡的僧伽罗文、缅甸文、孟文、柬埔寨高棉文、泰国文、老挝文、国际音标和罗马字母等，此外，还有跨境流通使用的经典傣文。

二、经典傣文的名称、使用和分布

国内的傣族目前常见有五种傣文，如长体傣文（傣讷文、豆芽文）、圆体傣文（傣绷文、傣龙文）、金平傣文（傣端文、傣皓文）、傣泐文，其中傣泐文又可分为新傣文和老傣文，老傣文也即本文所指的经典傣文。每种傣文都有其自身的特点和价值，在傣族历史长河发展中都扮演着重要的角色。随着时代的发展进步，民族文字也逐渐进入现代印刷领域。新中国成立后，为了便于学习和印刷，以经典傣文为基础发展出了西双版纳新傣文，经典傣文在西双版纳曾一度停止使用，不过在孟连、澜沧、景谷、耿马、金平等地区一直延续使用。1980 年，我国宗教信仰自由政策得到恢复，傣族民众重拾佛教信仰，重建佛塔佛寺、重写佛经佛典等，在这种情况下，新傣文无法完全替代经典傣文来书写巴利语经典的局限日益凸显。于是 1986 年 5 月，在西双版纳州第六届第五次人民代表大会上，决定恢复使用老傣文（经典傣文）。此后，新老两种傣文同时使用，该决定一经通过，南传上座部佛教领域立即全面恢复使用经典傣文。其保存的大量历史文献，是傣族悠久文化的宝库，也是傣族社会发展的珍贵史料，特别是经典傣文佛典是国内较为完善和系统的南传巴利语系统的佛教经典，更有其特殊的价值。②

我国境内的经典傣文，有信仰南传上座部佛教的傣族、布朗族、德昂族、佤族、阿昌族和少数彝族等共同使用。同时，这一文字也在泰国北部和东北部、老挝、缅甸掸邦等地区使用，但不同国家和地区对其称呼有所区别，如在泰国北部称其为兰那文（Ark Son Lanna）、兰那经文（Tuo Tham Lanna）；泰国东北部地区称之为伊善经典文字（Tuo Tham Isan）；在老挝称为老挝经典文字（Tuo Tham Lao）或澜掌经典文字（Tuo Tham Lang Chang）；在缅甸掸邦的景栋称其为傣痕文（Tuo Tai

---

① 郑筱筠，梁晓芬. 中国南传上座部佛教教派发展的历史脉络探析. 世界宗教研究，2014（3）.
② 张公瑾. 傣族宗教与文化. 北京：中央民族大学出版社，2002：72—73.

Khun）或傣痕经典文字（Tuo Tham Khun），不过在景栋的周边地区，如大其力、勐永、勐养龙以及缅甸掸邦东部第四特区等，均称其为经典文字（Tuo Tham）。至今，该文字依然是当地的掸族（傣族）及其他民族在佛教领域所使用的主要文字。此外，该文字也通过傣族移民的跨文化传播，在美国落地生根。在美国科罗拉多州丹佛市约居住有 1200 余名祖籍为中国西双版纳和老挝的傣泐人，该州也是美国傣泐人最集中的地区，他们不仅在自己的社区里修建了佛寺佛塔，以南传上座部佛教信仰为中心来推动传统文化复兴，重构傣泐民族认同，①而且佛寺里的经书基本上都依然使用经典傣文。各个国家和地区所使用的经典傣文，它们之间差异微乎其微，在各地仍然可以通用。

根据笔者的观察，再结合实际的情况，该文字较为妥当的名称应为经典傣文，为何应称其为经典傣文？笔者的理由有以下几点：

第一，该文字的产生，早期是为了记录和传播巴利经典，至今仍然是我国南传上座部佛教和其他国家地区所使用的经典文字；第二，各个国家地区对其称呼都带有 Tham 一词，Tham 是源于巴利语的 Dhamma，有经典或佛经佛法之意，这也表明了该文字主要使用的群体是佛教信众，称为经典傣文，也是信众对其传承佛法的一种寄望；第三，该文字的发明创造及使用的最大群体是傣泰（Tai）民族，称其为经典傣文也较为贴切；第四，刘岩在 1993 年著的《南传上座部佛教与傣族文化》一书中已有用经典傣文这个名称的提法，以及西双版纳傣学研究会编著的《西双版纳佛教》一书中，关于傣文研究的介绍也使用了经典傣文的名称，意味着傣族内部的文人学者也接受及推崇这个名称；第五，于 2008 年 1 月 21—22 日在清迈西北大学（Payap University）召开的相关经典傣文（老傣文）国际会议上，中国西双版纳州民族研究所和州报社的代表出席了会议，就经典傣文国际码悬而未决的问题进行讨论，其中在纳入国际编码的名称上达成了共识，统一使用 Tai Tham Unicode。这一决定也得到来自中国其他地区、缅甸、英国、美国和泰国本地专家的认可。这里的 Tai 可指傣泰语民族的各个支系，Tham 是指经典或佛法，Tai Tham 可直译为经典傣文。

三、结语

综上所述，经典傣文是随着南传上座部佛教而传播开来的，首先它从一个在宗教领域的文字，逐渐发展为世俗社会所通用的民族文字。当它传播到各地，被不同族群使用时，又再次发生本土化的发展，文字名称与区域或族群名称形成关联。此外，各族群字母风格的差异所传递的信息是一个区域和族群的文化特色符号。这一符号回应的是族群之间的历史关系；从另一个角度来分析，也可发现共同使用经典傣文的傣泰各族群的社会发展脉络和文化分化过程。然而在文字的名称上，各个族群都以南传上座部佛教的历史文化为基础，把书写不同字母风格傣泰语民族，都归

---

① 郑晓云. 美国丹佛市傣泐人现状调查研究. 世界民族，2019（3）.

纳到经典（Tham）的文化圈，以维持族群间共同的文化记忆，构建文化共同体。

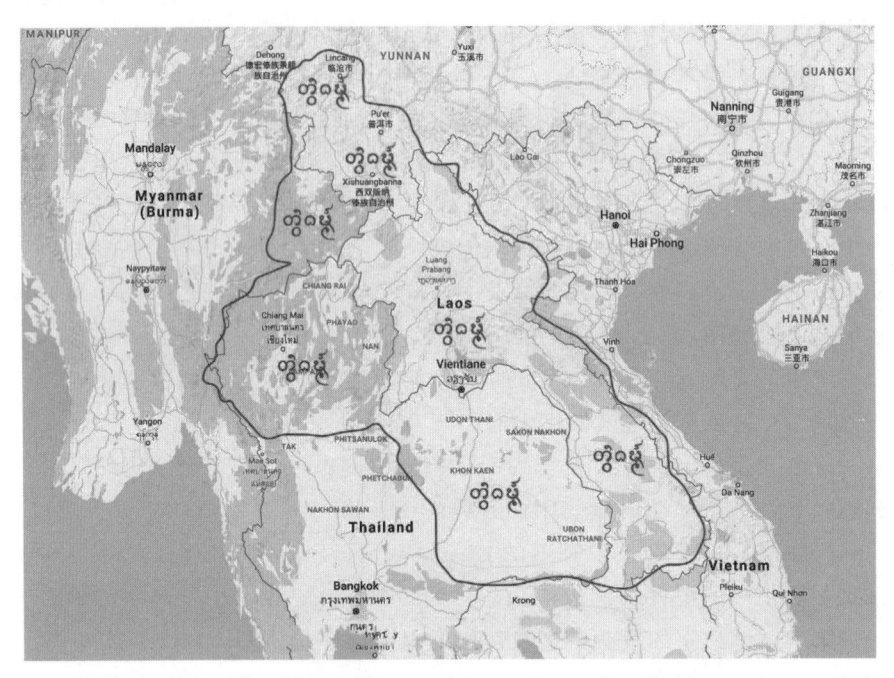

图1　经典傣文使用区域分布（图：岩罕保）

文字是民族文化在历史发展进程中的产物，它延续着一个民族与社会的历史记忆，在社会发展和文化传播过程中扮演着具有意义的角色。经典傣文所承载的贝叶文化，其在宗教、文化、教育、生态、经济等方面的价值不可估量。经典傣文是属于跨境跨族群使用的文字，它不但是研究我国南传上座部佛教和傣族文化史的宝贵资料，也是研究我国各民族文化关系发展史的珍贵文献，更是探寻我国与周边国家文化共性的一座桥梁。经典傣文的学习与研究，保护和传承，第一，有助于维系我国传统文化的多元性，使中华文化丰富多彩而有魅力；第二，对我国南传上座部佛教经典传承以及巩固南传上座部佛教在我国的良好发展有着重要的意义；第三，中国南传上座部佛教与东南亚佛教国家具有天然的纽带作用，在推动我国与东南亚文化交流和交往关系的发展上有着积极作用。彼此间族源相近、信仰相同、民心相

图2　泰国清迈大学大门，有泰文、经典傣文/兰那文（中间）、英文（图：岩坎章拉）

通，共享的文化记忆不仅能更好地巩固彼此的情谊，而且有助于推进各个方面的合作与可持续发展。

图3 中国云南佛学院大门，有藏文、中文、经典傣文（右）（图：岩坎章拉）

参考文献

［1］刘岩.南传上座部佛教与傣族文化.昆明：云南民族出版社，1993.

［2］张公瑾.傣族宗教与文化.北京：中央民族大学出版社，2002.

［3］谢远章.谢远章学术文选.昆明：云南大学出版社，云南人民出版社，2016.

［4］郑筱筠，梁晓芬.中国南传上座部佛教教派发展的历史脉络探析.世界宗教研究，2014（3）.

［5］何平."八百媳妇"——"兰纳王国"及其主体民族的政治、社会与文化.思想战线，2013（1）.

［6］郑晓云.美国丹佛市傣泐人现状调查研究.世界民族，2019（3）.

［7］玛欣德尊者.您认识佛教吗？.昆明：云南省佛教协会印行，2009.

［8］西双版纳傣学研究会.西双版纳佛教.昆明：云南民族出版社，2012.

巴利语系贝叶文化典籍的保存、保护与研究

——以西双版纳傣族自治州古籍保护中心为例

岩温宰香[①]　玉罕为[②]

一、引言

西双版纳州作为我国唯一的傣族自治州，历史悠久，具有深厚的民族文化底蕴，拥有我国珍贵的文化遗产——巴利语系贝叶文化典籍，且有较为丰富的勐泐[③]文化地方文献，其中有不少属孤本、善本、珍本。这些古籍不仅是西双版纳民族文化之精髓，更是中华民族宝贵的精神财富。当下，在"一带一路"倡议和中华文化走出去的时代背景下，以南传上座部佛教和巴利语系贝叶文化为中心的双向交往，能加强傣泐民族文化的交流与互动，促进"一带一路"民心相通和文化共融，从而促使跨族群的文化认同感得以加强。自 2002 年西双版纳州政府启动"抢救树叶上的傣族文化"行动以来，西双版纳州古籍保护中心积极开展相关古籍保护工作，取得了一些成效。以下，我们在汇报有关古籍保护工作进展的基础之上，探讨有关巴利语系贝叶文化典籍的保存、保护与研究等问题，并针对孤本、善本、珍本古籍的保护、修复和再生保护等问题再做进一步研讨与思考。

二、巴利语系贝叶文化典籍

巴利语系贝叶文化典籍，包括叶质形的贝叶经和纸质形的绵纸本两种文献典籍。其中叶质形的贝叶经是指用铁笔在贝多罗（梵文 Pattra）树叶上所刻写的佛教经文。后在传播和发展的过程中，贝叶经的名称还有"贝叶书""贝叶典籍"等。贝叶经书傣语称"坦姆兰"，佛教三藏经典、佛本生故事等主要记载在贝叶经里。绵纸本是指用蕨笔蘸墨在绵纸上书写的经文，书写的内容一般是关于世俗的文献典

[①] 北京师范大学民俗学博士生，中国文化志愿者暨"中国古籍保护协会文化志愿者联合会会员"。
[②] 云南省西双版纳州图书馆古籍保护中心主任，中国文化志愿者暨"中国古籍保护协会文化志愿者联合会会员"。
[③] "勐泐"，直译为汉语是"泐国"，因王都在澜沧江畔的"景陇"，被中国史籍翻译为"景陇国"或"景陇金殿国"。

籍，这种纸采用当地构树皮为原料制成，有宽面页式和折叠页式两种，只有少量的折叠本，才能转抄佛经经典。傣语称绵纸本为"宝咖拉沙"，折叠页式为"宝练"。傣族学者艾罕炳认为，傣族众多的民间故事、叙事长诗、民间歌谣、情歌、谚语祖训、俗语格言、谜语以及伦理道德、法律法规、天文历法、医药卫生、生产知识、咒符咒语等，均不得抄入贝叶经，而抄写在绵纸本里。针对相关对贝叶文化的错误解读，他在相关学术专著里对其进行了明确的定义。他认为，广义的贝叶文化是傣族传统"稻作文化""竜林文化"即"水文化"与南传上座部"佛文化"相融合的升华，是人们对傣族传统文化的一种象征性称谓，是傣族社会历史和文化的统称。说它是"贝叶文化"，是因为它保存于贝叶制作而成的贝叶经里及构树皮制成的绵纸书本里而得名。他认为，有的学者将贝叶文化说成是贝叶经或仅是佛教文化是不全面的，是狭义的。有的学者错认为傣族民间世俗的文化均可刻抄在贝叶经里，这种说法与事实不符，不能以讹传讹。[1]可见，贝叶文化包括刻写佛教经义的叶质"贝叶经"以及书写佛教经义和世俗文籍的纸质"绵纸经"。本文所要论述的巴利语系贝叶文化典籍即此叶质和纸质两种典籍样式。"作为傣族传统文化象征的贝叶文化，博大精深，源远流长，仅贝叶经、纸本经就有84000'康'（部）之多。它涵盖了佛学、历史、哲学、文学、艺术、天文历法、生态学、心理学、医药、伦理道德、风俗民情、生产生活知识等"类别。[2]

三、西双版纳傣族自治州贝叶文化典籍的收藏情况

西双版纳傣族自治州图书馆始建于1976年11月，总占地面积3500平方米，总建筑面积4036.88平方米。西双版纳傣族自治州古籍保护中心（以下简称州古籍保护中心）隶属于西双版纳傣族自治州图书馆古籍保护部，建设有150平方米的古籍阅览室和120平方米的古籍书库。从20世纪80年代开始，西双版纳傣族自治州政府就安排专人在当地的傣族村寨和佛寺四处收集散落民间的贝叶文化典籍；2002年，又启动了"抢救树叶上的傣族文化"行动，翻译整理出版了《中国贝叶经全集》100卷。

截至目前，州图书馆已在全州多个佛寺建立分馆，并由州图书馆出资改善古籍保护条件，有些古籍直接由佛寺委托州图书馆收藏、保存。由于一些刚建立分馆的佛寺收藏的大量经书还未登记造册，因此，州古籍保护中心计划于2020年前完成全州598个佛寺古籍经书的书目录入，并积极改善各佛寺古籍的保存条件。

四、贝叶文化古籍保护工作所面临的问题及对策

虽然州古籍保护中心在贝叶古籍保护工作中取得了一些成绩，但仍然存在起步

---

[1] 艾罕炳.西双版纳傣族赕文化.昆明：云南人民出版社，2010：2.
[2] 征鹏.新时期中国少数民族文学作品选集·傣族卷.北京：作家出版社，2015：1.

贝叶文化与区域文化遗产传承保护

晚、资金投入不足以及技术滞后、人才匮乏等问题。以下，我们进一步分析关于贝叶文化典籍在保存、保护和研究过程中存在的具体问题，并探讨解决这些问题的相应对策。

（一）充分认识贝叶文化的重要性及古籍保护的紧迫性，加大贝叶古籍的收集力度

当下，古籍的破坏、遗失以及流失海外等现象令人担忧。在傣族民间，有一些古老的习俗，有人去世的时候，家人会将其生前用过的所有物品包括其生前所收藏的全部经书一并焚烧给逝者，以表达对逝者的一种尊敬。在傣泐地区的佛寺和民众之中，很少有对古籍经文的保护理念，古籍收藏环境也极其简陋，一般都是摆放在缅寺佛塔的藏经阁或悬挂在自家的家神龛位上，时间久了，虫蛀、风化、霉烂等现象非常严重。许多寺院保存的古籍破旧了，他们会将其内容重新抄录在绵纸或刻写在贝叶上之后，将旧经书焚毁；有些很有价值的古籍，甚至会被一些国外商人以极低的价格买走，流失海外。由于以上种种原因，导致很大一部分古籍经文流失和损毁，给傣族文化造成了重大损失。古籍保护，时不我待！

目前古籍保护亟待解决的问题就是，第一，建立一套行之有效的制度，扩大图书馆外延，即将有价值的佛寺藏经阁或民间收藏，以及各文化部门如地方志、史志办等部门的古籍藏书纳入州图书馆管理范围，并对其进行目录编制、造册等科学的管理。同时，对这些机构的古籍收藏环境进行改造，使其具有更科学的收藏环境，以减少古籍收藏中存在的自然、人为破坏的因素。待时机成熟后，再逐步将这些古籍转移至州古籍保护中心进行统一收藏。第二，加强对古籍保护意识的宣传力度，动员全社会力量，宣传古籍保护工作的重大意义，使古籍保护的观念和意识深入人心。第三，调动一切积极因素，增加古籍搜集的力度和数量。在贝叶文化古籍的搜集过程中，仅凭州古籍保护中心的一己之力是远远不够的，公众参与程度的高低将直接影响到搜集工作的进程与质量。因此，应该积极拓展搜集渠道，鼓励全社会力量，比如地方史志办、政协以及相关文化部门参与贝叶古籍的收集活动，尽可能动员收藏者捐献出古籍经文。比如，利用傣族民间的"木价"礼仪[①]或置换方法（把新印刷的经文与古籍经文进行置换）等。第四，运用现代技术手段，建立古籍搜集网络和微信公众号，广泛征集古籍信息，扩大古籍搜集的深度和广度。第五，充分利用我国的相关法律法规，切断古籍倒卖这条利益链，杜绝古籍流失海外。

（二）培养一批高素质的从事贝叶文化研究和传承的工作队伍

研究中，我们发现很多有价值的贝叶经文因为没有被翻译成汉文、英文等文字而少有人知晓。甚至，有些贝叶古籍产生的历史时期、内容及其内在价值都很难进行最基本的鉴定。因此，古籍保护的相关人才培养和技术培训以及人才引进等工作，将成为今后一段时期内州古籍保护中心重要的工作任务之一。对贝叶文化古籍

---

① 一种让渡的礼仪，象征性地给对方一些钱财，让对方把物品转让给自己。

的发掘、利用等工作的首要任务应该是对经文的翻译，而翻译是一项艰深、繁杂的工作，需要加大力度挖掘和培养既精通汉文又懂新傣文、老傣文甚至懂泰语、老挝语、英语等语言的人才。但在西双版纳地区，虽然大部分傣族能听、说傣语，却不能读、写傣文尤其是老傣文，更不用说能看得懂掺杂着巴利文、泰文、缅文和老傣文的贝叶经文，这给贝叶文化的传承和发掘工作带来了极大困难。为此，建议州古籍保护中心到各大院校招聘相关专业的本科生、硕士生或博士生加入古籍保护队伍，让他们与当地的"渡彼"[①]"康朗"[②]"布占"[③]等通晓巴利语系的人员进行合作交流，实现优势互补，努力培养古籍翻译等相关人才。

（三）加快对贝叶古籍文献的修复工作，实现贝叶古籍的数字化管理

古籍文献资源的不可再生性和唯一性给古籍开发和保护增加了很大的难度，虽然古籍修复技艺已在2008年被列入第二批国家非物质文化遗产名录，但我国相关专业的古籍修复师严重匮乏，古籍修复的速度远远不及古籍折损、老化的速度。所以必须加大对古籍修复人才的培训、培养力度，建立古籍文献修复人才培养的长效机制，加快古籍修复工作进度，保护古籍文献的完整性。各收藏单位应该集中力量，有计划、有目标地对破损的古籍进行修复，尤其是对一些孤本和濒危古籍做好修复工作。在修复过程中，要不断改进技术，防止古籍文献进一步损坏。

由于贝叶文化典籍种类繁多，卷帙浩繁，博大精深，实现贝叶经的数字化转换，将极大方便文献的借阅、使用和管理，在充分挖掘其自身价值的同时，也能更好地保护这些古籍文献。因此，我们建议建立一整套对贝叶古籍的实体收集、修复、计算机数据录入等行之有效的管理制度，以从根本上解决"藏"与"用"的矛盾，减少对古籍文献的反复利用和二次破坏。同时，在建立古籍资料数据库时还可以利用网络实现资源共享，让更多的人能够在线查阅，为读者提供令人满意的古籍知识服务，以促进古籍文献的开发与利用，更好地满足人们对古籍资料的发掘、阅读和研究的需要。除此之外，应选派州古籍保护中心的工作人员和志愿者参加相关古籍修复、翻译等培训活动或演讲、展览等交流活动，努力学习、借鉴国内外先进经验，充分了解业内相关工作、技术的进展情况，不断提升自己的专业技能，逐步培养出一批具有较高水平的古籍保护专家、修复专家、整理专家、鉴定专家。

（四）加强贝叶古籍孤本、善本、珍本的保护、修复和再生保护工作

孤本、善本、珍本都是比较稀见或比较珍贵的文本，其文化内涵、传承及历史价值都是不可替代的。首先，应该对这些珍贵文本的档案进行实体开发。这里的

---

① 傣语，在当地翻译为"佛爷"。在南传上座部佛教信仰区域内，可以根据僧人的称谓来判断其在僧团中的地位，即僧阶制度各个级别的称谓。它代表着僧人在僧团中已经达到的修行程度和社会认可度。僧阶是按年龄、戒腊、学行来划分的，这只是一种荣誉，并不是一种特权。当僧人的年龄、戒腊和学行达到一定程度后，就可以由信众提出来，举行升座仪式，逐级晋升到上一个僧阶。

② 西双版纳傣语，还俗的"渡彼"。

③ 西双版纳傣语，也叫"波章"，是傣族村寨里的神职人员，一般由受过具足戒的出家僧人还俗后通过村民信众推选胜任。主要的工作职责是协助大佛爷做好宗教仪式或引导村民举行日常礼仪，是协调宗教与世俗事务的重要媒介。

贝叶文化与区域文化遗产传承保护

"档案实体"指的是有关这些文本的纸质档案、光盘档案、照片档案、实物档案等。"档案实体开发主要包括档案服务、档案编研和档案展览"[①],其中,档案服务是指基于这些文本档案所提供的档案信息查询、阅览、摘录和复制服务;档案编研是指在现有的这些文本档案资源基础上,汇编档案资料、参与这些文本研究等工作;档案展览是指按照一定规则系统地展示这些文本档案资源或其复制品的过程,展览形式可以分为固定展览、巡回展览、网上展览等。其次,还要注重对这些文本的内涵开发。例如,可以通过与其他部门合作,拍摄与之相关的影视作品等,以宣传开发的形式实现对其价值内涵的挖掘利用。让这些古老的文本得以最大限度地发挥其应有的价值,最大限度地实现其再生保护意义。

(五)让贝叶文化活起来,真正回归到老百姓的日常生活,为民众服务

在当今多元的文化环境下,贝叶文化如何面向未来、如何提升自己内在的创造力与自信力等,既是值得我们深思的问题,也是我们民族文化研究者永恒的课题之一。贝叶文化不是一种史前遗存的"活化石",它有别于那些考古性质的"文物"。它应该是全民族范围内由家庭、社会和寺庙等各个阶层综合传习和传承的傣家人自己的传统文化读本。但在汉语教育普及的当下,以贝叶作为文化传承载体的傣民族文化链出现了断裂。如何让贝叶文化更多地融入百姓生活中去,充分发挥其应有的积极作用,是我们各相关领域的工作者今后努力研究的课题。对此,我们认为可以借鉴傣族传统的对青少年的教育模式,通过经典学习诵读、贝叶经文刻写技艺培训和实例教学演示,以南传上座部佛教贝叶经和贝叶文化的集成、文化服务和动态传播为核心,提升其对当地社会文化发展和社区民众的影响力,形成地方社区民众、地方知识与文化传统以及地方公共文化空间的三位一体、和谐发展的文化模式。

五、结论

综合以上探讨,我们可以得出结论:巴利语系贝叶文化典籍的保存、保护与研究是一项长期持续的工作,还存在许多亟待解决的问题。这些工作仅依靠西双版纳州古籍保护中心工作人员的力量是远远不够的,还需要各级部门的大力支持,更需要社会各界人士的共同努力。因此,建议西双版纳州古籍保护中心在开展相关工作的同时,加强与档案部门、文化馆和博物馆等相关部门的合作,并就贝叶古籍保存、保护与研究等问题与他们进行合作交流,将抢救、记录、保护与研究的成果推向社会大众。通过讲座、展览、培训、研讨、出版物等形式,加强对贝叶古籍保护知识的宣传,增进公众对贝叶文化的了解和认同,促进贝叶古籍的利用和贝叶文化的传播,扩大贝叶文化的受众,提升贝叶古籍保存、保护与研究工作效率。

---

① 韩英,章军杰.论非物质文化遗产的档案资源开发.档案学通讯,2011(5).

参考文献：

[1] 艾罕炳.西双版纳傣族赕文化.昆明：云南人民出版社，2010.

[2] 万安伦.中外出版史.北京：高等教育出版社，2017.

[3] 艾罕炳.贝叶神韵.昆明：云南人民出版社，2009.

[4] 中国贝叶经全集编辑委员会编.中国贝叶经全集.刀正明，岩香，岩贯，刀金平等译.北京：人民出版社，2006.

[5] 征鹏.新时期中国少数民族文学作品选集·傣族卷.北京：作家出版社，2015.

[6] 万安伦，梁家楠.论贝叶经传入傣族及傣族贝叶出版的历史地位.中国出版，2019（9）.

[7] 杨庆，杨寿川.傣族贝叶典籍：世界珍贵的记忆遗产.云南民族大学学报（哲学社会科学版），2004（6）.

[8] 巫咏红.民族档案之瑰宝——傣族贝叶档案.西南民族大学学报（人文社科版），2005（4）.

[9] 罗英.傣族文化遗产简述.今日民族，2018（11）.

[10] 刘梦雪.我国古籍文献的保护与开发利用探讨.经济研究导刊，2019（14）.

[11] 郑筱筠.帕松列和帕祜巴升座的重大意义：兼论中国南传上座部佛教僧阶制度.中国宗教，2016（3）.

[12] 孤本、珍本与善本.新湘评论，2018（15）.

[13] 朱太岩.孤本·珍本·善本·述略.兰州学刊，1983（3）.

贝叶文化与区域文化遗产传承保护

西双版纳傣族贝叶文化载体

——贝叶棕现存情况调查

玉楠叫[①]

贝叶棕是佛教"五树六花"中的"一树",随着佛教传播到我国,贝叶棕从印度引种到我国云南西双版纳地区,至今约有700多年的种植历史。[②]南传上座部佛教因将经文刻写在贝叶棕叶片上形成贝叶经,信奉南传上座部佛教的西双版纳傣族人民同东南亚地区人民一样,很早就有用贝叶制"纸"记录自己的民族文化的历史。历史上贝叶棕在西双版纳的低海拔地区种植,如景洪市的勐龙、嘎洒、勐罕和勐腊县南部地区的傣族佛寺和村寨中都有广泛种植,贝叶棕已成为一种地理和民族文化的标记树。但随着经济社会的发展,纸张的大量运用,改变了傣族运用贝叶棕制册记录的习惯。

近年来,少数民族传统文化传承保护与生物多样性保护已成为一个重要的关注热点。西双版纳地区贝叶经是傣族贝叶文化的重要组成部分,也是国务院2008年6月公布的第二批国家级非物质文化遗产。贝叶棕是西双版纳傣族贝叶文化传承的重要载体和不可或缺的代表性植物,刻写的是"百科全书式"的傣族文化,[③]栽培保护贝叶棕对傣族文化传承以及与东南亚开展贝叶文化交流都具有重要意义。我国贝叶棕仅在云南西双版纳傣族自治州有零星种植,受栽培技术、传统观念制约及民间利用率低等影响,目前该地区贝叶棕濒临灭绝,其繁殖与保护应予以重视。

一、贝叶棕现存情况

贝叶棕主要生长在平均海拔1000米以下,常年日照充足和气候温热地区,它是棕榈科属,高大粗壮的常绿大型乔木,通常树高20—25米左右,树体高直、树冠如一把巨伞,原产印度、马来西亚、斯里兰卡等地,在我国主要生长在云南西双版纳地区。对西双版纳傣族而言,贝叶棕是集文化、经济、观赏于一体的不可多得的树种。据不完全统计,目前西双版纳州现存贝叶棕主干高2米以上的不足300株,

---
[①] 作者为西双版纳傣族自治州中共景洪市纪委、景洪市监委工作人员.
[②] 罗文扬,胡建湘,韩烨,等.贝叶棕生物学特性及繁殖栽培技术.安徽农学通报,2006(8).
[③] 岩罕炳.贝叶神韵.昆明:云南人民出版社,2009:68-71.

主要分布在勐罕镇傣族园、勐仑植物园、曼听公园以及零星分布在部分寺庙内，现有苗木储量不足 5000 株。从目前统计情况看，贝叶棕在西双版纳州活体数量已达到濒危等级，如不及时有效地对贝叶棕加以保护，在未来的 20—30 年内，贝叶棕将有可能在西双版纳这片土地上消失。

二、贝叶棕作为贝叶文化载体的价值

贝叶棕是西双版纳贝叶文化形成的重要载体，随着佛教传入中国后，传教僧人携带贝叶经与贝叶棕种子来到西双版纳地区，之后在西双版纳的土地上贝叶棕落地生根。南传上座部佛教僧人将经文篆刻在贝叶棕的叶子之上形成了贝叶经，贝叶棕成为最有名并能记载文化的植物之一。随着时代变迁和社会发展，贝叶棕承载着贝叶文化的融合、发展与传承延存至今。贝叶棕对贝叶文化的形成和发展，具有不可替代的作用，是西双版纳傣族"活态"文化[1]发展和复兴的重要传承载体。

什么是贝叶文化载体？或者说贝叶棕为什么会是贝叶文化形成不可替代的载体？就如甲骨文是因镌刻、书写于龟甲与兽骨上而得名的，具有固定的载体一样，贝叶文化也是以贝叶为传承载体的文化。据古书记载，从南传上座部佛教 500 个制度制定开始，书册上就有对贝叶棕的引种记录，至今已有千余年。追溯至南传上座部佛教传入西双版纳傣族地区之时，文字也随之传入，而当时贝叶就是承载和记录佛经的载体。信仰南传上座部佛教的西双版纳傣族先民，从贝叶经制作得到了灵感，经历千余年的历史发展，傣族人民不断改造、创新、发展用独有的民族特色工艺制作的贝叶纸，刻写了大量的文化书籍，据称有 84000 余部。[2]贝叶书册需经过砍叶、水煮、晒干、压平、刻字等工序制作，一般砍叶是在春季，后将叶片裁剪成宽约 5 厘米长条，用水汆煮一定时间；然后用刀轻刮去叶皮表面，等叶条自然晒干后切去两端头尾留下约 30 厘米的最佳部位，打孔装帧成册后用錾子笔刻写，最后涂上用特殊植物制成的墨汁，等墨汁渗入刻写好的字体凹陷部位后，用棉布轻拭后，所刻字体立即清晰呈现。[3]目前，西双版纳地区民间遗存有丰富的贝叶文化古籍。但贝叶典籍不等于就是佛经，虽然贝叶经主要功能是记录佛经，但我国的贝叶文化所包含的是有典型地域特点的傣族文化，它记录着傣族的政治、历史、经济、文化、天文、地理、科学、历法、法律、医药等。后期虽然出现了绵纸，有相当一部分的书籍被绵纸代替，但时至今日，贝叶仍然延续着古代承载文化的职能。贝叶所承载的文字或者说傣族人民把千余年来所积累总结出的文化写进贝叶中，这也就是为什么即使纸张代替了大部分的贝叶纸记载文字的功能，从贝叶典籍上沿用的"文化本体"依然叫"贝叶文化"。贝叶棕既是傣民族精神文化的象征、传统生活的现实反映，也是傣民族历史发展进程中依然存有"活体"的文化载体，它源于佛教信

---

[1] 周娅.一种珍贵的"活态"传统文化及其人文价值——论傣—泰民族贝叶文化，2007（1）.
[2] 李土荣，罗文扬，武丽琼，邓旭.贝叶棕的生长习性和应用.中国园艺文稿，2010（3）.
[3] 岩罕炳.贝叶神韵.昆明：云南人民出版社，2009：2.

仰、用于生产生活、记载历史文明、传承人文精髓，贝叶棕在傣民族文化体系构建中的地位牢固而不可撼动。

三、贝叶棕保护存在的问题

（一）受种植观念制约，民间鲜少培育和种植贝叶棕

贝叶棕傣语叫"Duo lang"，相传只有心诚的佛爷才能栽活它，由于傣族群众对贝叶棕心存敬畏，因此民间一般傣族群众不敢擅自培育和种植，多在佛寺附近可寻迹到少量贝叶棕。[①]西双版纳州勐海县佛教协会副会长、打洛镇勐景来佛寺（贝叶书院）住持都坎章针对贝叶棕的种植观念也提出了看法，他说："贝叶棕属于佛教的'五树六花'中植物，以前懂得贝叶棕种植方法和技巧的不多，所以一般群众都觉得只有佛爷或者村寨里德高望重的尊者才能种植成活，贝叶棕是神圣的植物。但如果抛开宗教的色彩，贝叶棕其实只是普通的植物，普通群众家中是可以种植的。现在景洪市勐罕镇也有少数村民开始种植贝叶棕。对于贝叶棕的保护，不能局限于僧人种植，应大力推广种植。"

（二）繁殖技术突破难，环境与气候对贝叶棕培育影响大

据初步走访调查，西双版纳地区的景洪市勐罕镇、勐龙镇、普文镇、景哈乡、大渡岗乡、嘎洒镇、景讷乡以及景洪城区内，勐腊县勐仑镇和磨憨镇等地都零星种植着贝叶棕。这些地区常年日照充足，气候温热，平均海拔均在1000米以下，适合贝叶棕正常生长、育苗。贝叶棕的生命周期长，一般50—80年才会开花，结果后随即死亡，因此在植物学中被称为"一次性花果植物"。[②]西双版纳州现存的母树比较少，母树受环境和气候的影响会出现坐果率低的情况，所以很难采到贝叶棕种子，且部分母树还存在只开花不挂果的现象。贝叶棕的种子属坚硬的椰蓉组织，发芽率极低，从种子到发芽需2至3个月。[③]种子含有一定量的糖分，在育苗中容易变质或被蚂蚁等昆虫啃食，中科院勐仑植物园记录贝叶棕种子育苗的出芽率不到40%。且贝叶棕在幼苗期生长特别缓慢，仅有2片到5片叶，前3年每年生长量不超过10厘米，易被其他植物遮阳，导致光照不足而死亡。另外，由于贝叶棕的种植缺乏科研单位对贝叶棕的育苗和推广的技术支撑，即使培育出幼苗，移栽技术不到位也很难成活。因其树种属直根系植物，根茎比较脆嫩，容易折断，出现移植成活率比较低的情况。因此，贝叶棕树种的发展受到制约。近年来，西双版纳州勐海县打洛镇勐景来佛寺曾先后3次从景洪市勐罕镇引种贝叶棕，但却都没能种植成活。

（三）经济价值有待挖掘，贝叶棕民间利用率不高

资料显示，贝叶棕叶片防腐防虫，制作成贝叶书写材料，可存百年。且其花朵、种仁、树干、髓心、根的汁液、幼株等都有其药用、食用等价值。"在西双版

[①] 罗文扬，胡建湘，韩烨，等.贝叶棕生物学特性及繁殖栽培技术.安徽农学通报，2006（8）.
[②] 胡建湘，韩烨，等.贝叶棕繁殖栽培技术初报.福建热作科技，1997（4）.
[③] 罗文扬，胡建湘，韩烨，等.贝叶棕生物学特性及繁殖栽培技术.安徽农学通报，2006（8）.

纳的500多座佛寺中，保留至今的贝叶文化经籍多达50000多部、2000多种，除了傣文刻写的以外，还有老挝文、缅甸、泰国文刻写。"[①]随着时间的推移，很多佛寺珍藏的古籍正在自然损毁，而贝叶纸制作技艺的传承也出现了令人担忧的局面。用于制作贝叶的贝叶棕数量逐渐减少，贝叶文化"载体（贝叶棕）"的生命危在旦夕。从目前来看，西双版纳本土的贝叶棕暂时只能提供少量的贝叶用于典籍刻写，其他的经济价值未曾受到挖掘与利用。以刻写贝叶来说，一般贝叶书册少的需要8—10片叶片，多的则会用到20片才能刻制成1册，刻制1部贝叶书册典籍可能就会用到50—60片及以上的贝叶。但贝叶棕生长周期很长，每年只抽叶8—9片，湿热季抽生很快，旱季很少抽新。西双版纳州景洪市普文大佛寺住持都三法说："现在普文的佛寺贝叶经已经留存很少了，去年损坏的大概有20多册，今年都重新抄录完成，但是一部分已经不是用贝叶刻写抄录的。"西双版纳州勐海县格朗和乡佛寺的都坎恩说："格朗和乡的佛寺已经没有贝叶刻制的经文典籍了，现在用的是傣绵纸和普通纸张抄录的经文典籍。"国家级非遗贝叶文化传承人西双版纳州景洪市勐罕镇傣族园曼将村贝叶文化传习所波空论大师也表示："现在年轻人几乎不愿学贝叶制作工艺技术，老刻经人又越来越少，人们对贝叶棕的保护意识更是薄弱。而部分僧侣和刻经人虽对于贝叶经的刻写和工艺是专业的，但是对于贝叶棕的种植和保护技术，了解甚少。"由于社会经济的发展淡化了保护意识，贝叶棕传统利用技术面临失传，所以现代利用率不高。

四、保护措施和对策建议

贝叶棕承载着西双版纳地区独具特色的民族文化体系，也是现在西双版纳州文化旅游、科普研究、生态保护、民俗文化具有民族地域特点的重要代表性文化元素。只有推动贝叶棕树种的培育保护，使其树种繁茂生长，才能滋养丰富和继续保护传承"贝叶文化"这一傣族非物质文化遗产。

（1）加大科研投入，加强贝叶棕繁殖技术的研究。建立"贝叶棕种质资源库"及种苗培育基地，以生物多样性保护为目的，与中国科学院西双版纳热带植物园或其他科研单位合作，建立信息档案系统和贝叶棕种质资源收集圃，避免现存的贝叶棕种质资源被浪费。积极推动贝叶棕生物学特性、繁殖技术研究，建立贝叶棕种苗培育基地，为贝叶棕及其他文化树种的推广种植提供充足的种苗准备。

（2）将贝叶棕纳入濒危珍贵树种名录，加强宣传力度，鼓励民间种植。通过政策引导和资金扶持，鼓励个人和企业参与贝叶棕的育苗和种植。探索通过地方政府采购的方式，结合"美丽乡村"建设，无偿地向适宜种植贝叶棕的寺院、村寨、公园、城市绿化区提供优质种苗，有意识地让西双版纳州少数民族村寨、佛寺及各

---

① 中国民主同盟西双版纳傣族自治州委员会编写.加强傣族文化传承载体——贝叶棕的保护建议.2019年4月22日，内部资料。

县市发展种植贝叶棕，进而推动贝叶棕"进村、入寺、驻城"，有效地增加贝叶棕数量。通过加强宣传力度，提高群众的保护和自愿种植贝叶棕的意识。

（3）提升利用率，搭建国际贝叶文化圈建设。贝叶文化这一类的非物质文化遗产需实现"活态"传承，贝叶棕的合理种植是"活态"传承的基本保障。以国家"一带一路"倡议为契机，加大与东南亚国家贝叶文化的专题交流，搭建与东南亚国家的文化交流平台。同时，通过打造"六国贝叶文化交流节"，充分挖掘推广边疆民族地区贝叶文化品牌和贝叶文化精品，推动贝叶文化融入当前经济社会发展的环境，实现其经济、文化价值。

中国南传上座部佛教典籍中的"赕"主题故事及其阐释

田玉玲[①]

"赕"为西双版纳傣语，是巴利语"dana"的音译，意为布施、供奉、供养，汉语通常译作檀那、布施、施舍、供养等。"赕"是十波罗蜜之首，包括物施、无畏施和法施三类。物施是一种外向的物质奉献，无畏施是一种内向的自我约束（持戒），而法施则隐含着虔信、领悟、践行和护持佛法之义。赕波罗蜜修行涵盖了普通信众的基本宗教实践：既要慷慨奉献、严格持戒，同时还要护持佛法，领悟佛法，戒除贪、嗔、痴三毒，过正命的生活。三者之中，物施外显易行，得到僧团与信众的全面推崇。法施可以通过赕献佛经、修缮寺塔、供奉佛像等物质赕奉方式实现，与物施有相似之处，也是中国南传上座部佛教地区常见的赕佛活动。

一、南传上座部佛教典籍中的"赕"主题故事

南传上座部佛教将佛陀视为修行的导师和榜样，南传上座部佛教典籍中的经藏、论藏部分主要包括佛本生、佛传，以及由此展开的各种佛教故事与论述。典籍中的"赕"主题故事以佛陀前世修行布施、佛陀住世应供、带领僧团传法布道故事为主。翻阅南传上座部佛教典籍，以"赕"为主题的故事俯拾皆是。走访中国南传上座部佛教寺院，随处可见大批以"赕"为主题制作的供奉品，其样式十分丰富，是中国南传上座部佛教艺术无法忽视的重要组成部分。

（一）佛本生中的"赕"主题故事

佛本生中的"赕"主题故事俯拾皆是，在《扎哩呀》《五十世轮回》《十世轮回》等佛本生故事汇编中，都有大量关于菩提萨尊者[②]修行赕波罗蜜的故事。其中，《十世轮回》是佛本生故事的节选本，共收录了菩提萨尊者十世轮回的本生故事。当菩提萨尊者第四世降生为涅蜜阑大王时，他终生慷慨布施，惠及众生。[③]菩提萨尊者第七世降生为尖达大王时，他积极慷慨布施，常常忙得连饭都来不及吃。[④]《瞿坛

[①] 作者为昆明学院副教授。
[②] 菩提萨尊者即菩萨，是佛陀在本生故事中的称谓。
[③] 中国贝叶经全集编辑委员会编.中国贝叶经全集（第5卷）.刀正明，岩香，岩贯，刀金平，等译.北京：人民出版社，2006：146.
[④] 中国贝叶经全集编辑委员会编.中国贝叶经全集（第5卷）.刀正明，岩香，岩贯，刀金平，等译.北京：人民出版社，2006：280.

出家》这样总结菩提萨尊者前549世修行的赕波罗蜜：

  菩提萨尊者还在世间时，祈祷多行善事，以圆满布施等三十波罗蜜①。经过五个时期，圆满地完成了五项布施。即不惜以世间所有财富成布施，乃至无数的食物和饮水；不惜以自己的身体器官成布施，捐献自己的肝、肺乃至耳、眼、血、肉和心脏；不惜以自己的生命去替别人而死，使人与动物从痛苦和苦难中得到解脱，拯救生灵，让他们得到幸福和快乐；不惜以自己心爱的儿女成布施，满足人们的心愿；不惜以自己的爱妻成布施奉献给他人。菩提萨圆满了自己的五项布施，按照清净道八十四道法完成自己的意愿，直到成为英明的维先达腊。②

  中国南传上座部佛教地区最有名的"赕"故事当数贝叶经《维先达腊》。③书中记载，维先达腊王子刚离开母腹就开始布施。④王子八岁时，他已经有强烈的做赕心愿，每年赕掉无数财物。一年，邻国久旱无雨，派出八位使者来向维先达腊求赕他那头"迈步走向何处雨水就会落下"的珍贵白象。维先达腊不仅爽快地答应了使者的要求，还专门为白象装饰了种种宝物，连同他自己的500名仆人和饲养白象的象师都一齐布施给使者。赕掉了给全勐带来吉祥和幸福的白象，百姓们十分愤怒，王子一家不得不离开王宫。沿途，王子先后赕掉了拉车的宝马、华丽马车。在森林修行期间，他又赕献了自己的一双儿女和王后。最终，虔诚的维先达腊功德圆满，得以和妻儿父母重新团聚，重返王宫。维先达腊王子一生精勤布施，圆满完成赕波罗蜜的修行，成为信众心目中布施圆满的象征。

  《维先达腊》是傣族地区流传最广泛的贝叶经典，各地流传着很多长短不一的版本。每年"赕坦"必赕《维先达腊》，僧侣要为信众全文念诵。佛寺里面随处可见各种相关的挂图和壁画，很多地方都有"赕白象""赕维先达腊""赕扎哩呀"等围绕这部经典展开的大型赕佛活动，象征供赕者如维先达腊一样虔诚做赕，已经功德圆满，来世得以转生天界。

  （二）佛传中的"赕"主题故事

  佛传故事是佛陀的本传，讲述悉达多王子出家修行、悟道成佛、传法布道直至寂静涅槃的故事。悉达多王子觉悟了最高智慧成为佛陀，由前世的供养人转变成现世的应供者，接受一切众生供养。因此，佛传不再讲述供赕故事，代之的是佛陀接受信众供养、普施法雨教化众生的故事。

  傣族地区流传的佛传故事主要有《瞿坛出家》《召西塔奥播》两种，前者故事完整，后者是傣族民间的地方版本，较为简略。《瞿坛出家》中与"赕"相关的

---

  ① 波罗蜜是佛教信徒修行的法门，包括赕、持戒等，共有十种，称为十波罗蜜，也可以把每种波罗蜜再细分为波罗蜜、近波罗蜜、至上波罗蜜三种，故十波罗蜜也可称为三十波罗蜜。参见中国贝叶经全集编辑委员会编.中国贝叶经全集（第11卷）.刀正明，岩香，岩贯，刀金平，等译.北京：人民出版社，2006：1428.
  ② 中国贝叶经全集编辑委员会编.中国贝叶经全集（第3卷）.刀正明，岩香，岩贯，刀金平，等译.北京：人民出版社，2006：43.
  ③ 维先达腊故事，汉译本译作《须大拿本生》《善施王子》等。
  ④ 中国贝叶经全集编辑委员会编.中国贝叶经全集（第2卷）.刀正明，岩香，岩贯，刀金平，等译.北京：人民出版社，2006：163.

故事情节十分丰富，诸如众天神朝贺王子降生、七步莲花、牧女赕糜、婆罗门赕茅草、商人赕饭团、频毗娑罗国王布施饭食、敕建竹林精舍等情节不仅在文本中有精彩描述，也常常出现在各地佛寺的壁画中。黄惠焜等人收集的《召西塔奥播》①简短概要，全文不足800字，没有记录详细的"赕"故事。除了这两部译成汉语的作品之外，其他贝叶经典籍中也零星记载着各种佛陀故事，赕佛情节也很丰富。诸如龙王供佛、采花供佛、猴象供佛、给孤独长老赕建邸园精舍等，对这两部佛传经典有所补益。

（三）其他佛教故事中的"赕"主题作品

其他佛教故事通常是由佛陀讲述，或与佛陀相关，其中也包含着大量的"赕"主题故事。《宋摩南富翁》是一部讲述因果业报的贝叶经，既有富翁宋摩南赕佛得福报的描述，②也有众人恶行恶报、不供赕变饿鬼等情节。③其实，这些故事描述并不详尽，也没有多少文学色彩，但恰恰是这种朴素平实、联系现实的讲述方式，却十分真实震撼，深刻地影响着广大信众，不断劝导众人供赕向善。

西双版纳地区流传的《佛祖巡游记》④吸收了大量当地的风物、地名传说，讲述佛祖与众僧所到之处，百姓纷纷供赕布施，佛祖为各地留下佛发、足印给信众建塔供养。佛陀还根据各地山川风物的特色及百姓的供赕行为，为各地村寨、山水命名。例如，苏塔瓦寨的村民用衣服和白布黑布铺地，迎接佛祖进村休息，当地得名"勐片朗片豪"。书中此类"赕"故事不胜枚举，多是各地百姓供赕时发生的种种趣闻琐事，充满世俗的情趣，拉近了佛教和信众的距离。

典籍中也有大量表现"赕"主题的民间传说故事，其基本模式为：主人公虔诚做赕——过上美满生活——更加虔诚地修行供赕。江应樑先生在《滇西摆夷之现实生活》中就记录了一个赕佛建塔得福报的故事。⑤修建佛寺佛塔是整个村寨，乃至整个区域的大事，是个人、家庭乃至一个村寨都难以完成的大赕，需要四邻八乡的参与支持。这类故事的广泛传播，无疑有力激发了广大信众赕塔建寺的热情，于是，一座座佛寺佛塔不断拔地而起。

（四）其他中国南传上座部佛教典籍中的"赕"主题故事

中国佛教典籍中夹杂着大量非宗教性的世俗文本，作者或历代的抄经人常常在其中加入一些与作品主题不甚相干的佛教故事，其中就有不少以"赕"为主题的故事。《沙萨纳芒鉴——古代罗纳塔王朝及佛教的传播》⑥一开篇，就接连讲述野猪、

---

① 云南省历史研究所编印. 西双版纳傣族小乘佛教及原始宗教的调查（内部资料）.1979：5.
② 中国贝叶经全集编辑委员会编. 中国贝叶经全集（第13卷）.刀正明，岩香，岩贯，刀金平，等译.北京：人民出版社，2006：356.
③ 中国贝叶经全集编辑委员会编. 中国贝叶经全集（第13卷）.刀正明，岩香，岩贯，刀金平，等译.北京：人民出版社，2006：313.
④ 中国贝叶经全集编辑委员会编. 中国贝叶经全集（第13卷）.刀正明，岩香，岩贯，刀金平，等译.北京：人民出版社，2006：207-208、212-213、287.
⑤ 江应樑. 滇西摆夷之现实生活.芒市：德宏民族出版社，2003：365-366.
⑥ 沙萨纳芒鉴——古代罗纳塔王朝及佛教的传播.杨光远译.昆明：云南民族出版社，2002.此书流传于德宏傣族地区，是一部记录王朝历史的典籍.

猴王、猎人、女妖以及夫妻赕佛的故事，每一个供赕者都因此获得无量功德。其中，夫妇赕佛的故事最为有趣：某天，一对夫妇赶路夜宿山洞。一道光芒预示佛祖即将降临。夫妻俩商量着轮流睡觉，不能错过了拜见佛祖。后半夜，妻子睡着了，而丈夫却一直没有入睡。天亮时分佛祖降临，男子竟然忘了叫醒妻子，一个人急匆匆跑去拜佛，他献上的野山芋变成了香喷喷的食物。佛祖预言他将成为威名赫赫的国王。妻子猛醒过来不见丈夫，便急匆匆地跑去寻找，俩人拉拉搡搡不停扭打，她脚踢到的泥土就变成了无数的鲜花、小旗、米花，散发出芳香的味道，变成了献给佛祖的赕品。由于她向佛祖赕献了大地的泥土，佛祖预言她将成为高贵的王后，并拥有无限的智慧和才干。这些故事往往篇幅短小，情节独立，与下文关联不大，多是作者或抄经人出于对赕的重视，及对赕佛故事的喜好，特别加入的。类似的情节、类似的处理手法在卷帙浩繁的佛教及当地的其他典籍中并不鲜见。

此外，当地的民间传说故事尽管并不直接讲述"赕"的故事，但常常强调故事主人公乐善好施，修行严谨，并因此过上了幸福美满生活。在这些作品中，"赕"不再是僵硬的教条，早已转化成为大众推崇的品行美德乃至正信生活，这既是南传信众日常生活的真实写照，也是"赕"思想在各类文本中的渗透和折射。

二、南传上座部佛教典籍对"赕"的阐释

赕是印度人布施出家修行者的一种古老传统。佛教创立以后，佛陀大力倡导信众做赕，并将其列为十波罗蜜①之首。

（一）"赕"的种类

南传上座部佛教宣称，菩萨及在家信众必须修行十波罗蜜方才能功德圆满，悟道成佛。因此，也将波罗蜜修行称为菩萨道，即菩萨成佛必须经历的修行。尽管原始佛教与南传上座部佛教并不强调菩萨思想，却十分重视波罗蜜修行。南传上座部佛教将波罗蜜分为十种②，赕波罗蜜排在首位，可分为物施、法施和无畏施三类。

1. 物施

物施包括外物施和内物施两种。外物施就是向僧团或有情众生布施身外的财物，内物施即布施自己的身体、器官乃至于生命。当然，普通大众最易施行、最常施行的就是外物施。因此，狭义的赕往往指的就是外物施。

南传经藏列举了信众可以布施僧团的十类物品，其实就是僧侣修行的生活必需品。③论藏则把布施分为六类，即色施、声施、香施、味施、触施和法施，其中前五类均为物施。色施，就是赕衣服、鲜花等各种具有色彩的物品；香施是赕檀香木等

---

① 波罗蜜也写作波罗蜜多，汉语通常译为"度"。
② 十波罗蜜即布施（赕）、持戒、出离、智慧、精进、忍辱、真实、决意、慈、舍。汉传佛教通常将其归纳为六种，称为六度，或六波罗蜜，分别是布施、持戒、忍辱、精进、禅定（禅那）、智慧（般若）。
③ （根据经藏的列举法）可以布施的外物有十种：食物、饮料、衣服、交通工具、香水、花与药膏、座位、床、住所和点灯的物品。详见［缅甸］明昆三藏持者大长老.南传菩萨道（上）之第十篇：什么是修行波罗蜜之详细与深入的方法？. http://www.fodian.net.

有香味的物品；味施就是赕各种美味的食品；触施是赕椅子、床、床单、被单等各种可以接触使用的物品。①可见，几乎所有可食、可用、可观、可感、可听、可闻的物品都可以供赕。在实际生活中，信众往往根据僧团、佛寺的实际需要及个人的经济能力做布施，并不囿于以上列举的物品。

2. 法施

法施是指以一颗无贪、无瞋、无痴与清净的心，"毫不模棱两可地教导真实法……协助尚未建立三皈依、持戒等之人建立这些德行。协助已建立这些德行之人更进一步地提升与净化它们……以讲座等方式来弘扬佛法是属于法施。佛陀说法施是至上的布施。"②

僧侣精通佛法，以各种方式为信众讲经说法，即是法施。普通信众也可以做法施，他们主要通过迎请高僧讲经说法、修缮佛像佛塔、抄写经典、赕献佛寺等方式进行法施。当然，一些学识渊博的学者或居士也可以直接讲经说法，为大众法施。傣族地区每年都有"赕坦"活动，信众纷纷请僧侣、波占或康南帮助抄写佛经赕进佛寺，并请僧侣为大众诵读宣讲，就是典型的法施。

3. 无畏施

"什么是无畏施呢？无畏施就是持五戒。当我们不杀生的时候，别人就不必担心被我们杀了。我们不偷盗，别人就不必时时刻刻提防着我们。我们不邪淫，别人就不必担心我们会强暴他的妻子。我们不妄语，别人就不必害怕被我们坑蒙拐骗。我们不饮酒，别人就不怕我们会佯装酒醉地胡搅蛮缠。"③可见，无畏施通常指的就是持戒，就是遵纪守法、持守戒律，既不伤及他人，也不危及自身，过正命的生活，这是佛教对普通信众的基本规范与要求。佛教信徒往往都具有平和、温柔、善良的性格，与无畏施思想的影响是分不开的。

此外，无畏施还有另一层含义，即维护社会安定，保护大众的生命安全。"当众生面临国王、盗贼、大火、敌人、野兽、龙、夜叉、阿修罗等的危害时，菩萨就会布施无畏予他们，保护与解救他们，甚至不惜舍去自己的生命。"④这种更高层次的无畏施，是国王、菩萨、英雄的勇敢作为，也是佛教所积极褒奖的积德善行。但是，佛教并不盲目拔高对普通民众的要求，把这种高危的行为加诸大众，而仅将这些英雄主义的行为作为对菩萨和国王的要求。这与儒家所倡导的"穷则独善其身，达则兼济天下"的思想是一致的。

（二）修行赕波罗蜜的宗教意义

功德福报是佛教吸引信众的重要思想，大量典籍中记载着修习赕波罗蜜所获的无量功德福报：财富、地位、幸福、和睦、声望、平安、健康、美貌等，世人苦苦

---

① ［缅甸］明昆三藏持者大长老. 南传菩萨道（上）之第七章：杂集. http://www.fodian.net.
② ［缅甸］明昆三藏持者大长老. 南传菩萨道（上）之第七章：杂集. http://www.fodian.net.
③ 济群法师. 十善业道经的启示. http://www.fodian.net.
④ ［缅甸］明昆三藏持者大长老. 南传菩萨道（上）之第七章：杂集. http://www.fodian.net.

追求的一切都因此美梦成真，还可以累积资粮，自饶益、饶益他，惠及无数来世。同样，出家僧侣修行十波罗蜜也有助益他们的宗教修持，助其早日觉悟得脱。佛教经藏、论藏对此均有不少论述。

南传上座部佛教同时强调，只有合理的赕才能获得最大的功德福报。佛教将供赕对象分为十四个层次，从畜生、家人直至伟大的佛陀，施主做赕的功德因为受施对象层次上升而依次提升。供赕给佛祖、僧侣可以获得最大福报。

同时，把布施分为善士施与非善士施两大类。所谓善士施，就是有戒行之人所做的良善布施，可以获得最大的功德福报。非善士施则与之相反，是无戒行之人所做的不完善的布施，只能获得较小福报，甚至根本不能获得福报。① 传统上，傣族都是以自己种植或采集的新鲜果蔬、粮食、鲜花赕佛，或用这些劳动产品换回的钱准备赕品。他们相信，只有赕奉这些最纯洁的劳动成果才能获得最大功德。善士施的思想，强化了信众供赕的热情和虔诚，规范了信众的供赕行为，对南传上座部佛教信众的实物供赕传统影响深远。由此，供赕人与应供者被调整到平等的位置，供赕人虔诚欢喜供养，应供者平和自然受供，这正是南传上座部佛教僧俗平等和谐、长久与共的重要原因之一，也是古代乡土社会人际互助的一种理想范式，对南传上座部佛教文化圈内各信教民族的社会文化生活都产生了深远影响。

此外，南传上座部佛教还强调供赕的必要性和迫切性。佛教认为，一切人间财富都是五欲的目标，不仅随时都可能丧失，还会招致其他的危险。只有尽早布施，才可能真正保全辛苦赚来的财富，才能把这些生不带来、死不带去的物品以功德福报的形式转移到来世。这也就是南传上座部佛教信众把功德视为来世的隐形银行，把供赕视为积极的储蓄行为的思想来源。②

赕波罗蜜的三种修行方式涵盖了普通信众宗教生活的基本规范——戒恶、行善、智慧。唯有戒恶的行善，才是真善。唯有以佛法为指导的智慧善行，才是最有益的善行，才能获得最大的功德。"赕"看似简单，易行能行，其实可深可浅、可多可少、可大可小，具有非凡的包容力。如果信众能够充分理解"赕"的意义和内涵，在日常生活中严格持守，不仅对宗教修行有利，对个人的身心修养有利，对人际和谐、生活幸福也大有裨益。"布施好品德，帮助众亲眷，行为无瑕疵，是为最吉祥。"③ 佛教信众信"赕"修"赕"，这是佛化社会"正命""吉祥"幸福生活的重要基础。

三、结语

中国南传上座部佛教典籍中何以出现大量的"赕"主题故事，及其大量的相关阐述，原因大致有三个方面：

---

① ［缅甸］明昆三藏持者大长老.南传菩萨道（下）之第一章：布施波罗蜜.http：//www.fodian.net.
② ［缅甸］明昆三藏持者大长老.南传菩萨道（下）之第一章：布施波罗蜜.http：//www.fodian.net.
③ 李荣熙译.吉祥经.http：//www.fodian.net.

（1）"赕"对南传上座部佛教僧团的发展具有重要作用。首先，"赕"是南传上座部佛教僧团最重要、最基本的经济来源，僧团的一切衣食用度都来自百姓供赕。其次，实物供赕为僧侣排除了俗世的种种干扰，有利于僧侣集中时间、精力进行宗教修行。再次，实物供赕大大增加了僧众接触交流的机会，有助于僧侣向信众传播佛教，推动南传上座部佛教向全民化方向发展。最后，实物供赕传统也大大降低了宗教的信仰门槛，降低了信众的宗教成本，使每个人都可以成为佛教信徒，有效扩大了佛教的信众群体。

（2）南传上座部佛教重视赕波罗蜜的修行，早期的南传上座部佛教经典本身就记录了极其丰富的"赕"主题故事。伴随着"赕"思想在中国南传上座部佛教地区的广泛传播，大量的"赕"主题故事也以多种形式在民间广泛传播，并逐步成为中国南传上座部佛教艺术的重要主题。

（3）频繁举行的赕佛活动成为信众日常生活的重要组成部分，也逐步成为佛教艺术的重要创作题材，由此产生了大批表现赕佛活动的作品，尤其在绘画作品中，常常可以看到拜佛、听经等与赕佛活动相关的场景。为赕佛活动而制作的各种物品更是不计其数。

在南传上座部佛教民族化、地方化进程中，表达"赕"思想的佛教典籍和相关制品广泛传播，积极推动了相关宗教思想与宗教实践不断延伸至信众的日常生活领域，各地信众频繁举行的供赕活动逐步发展成为一系列相对固定的赕佛活动，为供赕人提供了宗教功德、社会名望与宗教信心，也起到了教化年轻后辈的重要作用。赕佛活动的社区化、区域化还促成了"赕"的多重社会功能：整合社区资源、互助与分享、节日与集会、艺术展演等，将赕佛活动由个体、家庭活动转化成为集体、社区乃至区域性的大众活动，成为联系集体、社区、区域的重要纽带，不断维系、加固佛寺与民众、集体、社区、区域的联系。至此，赕佛活动已经不仅仅是个人、家庭的宗教需要，也成为集体、社区的现实需要。"赕"由最初个体化的宗教行为，发展成为大众化的集体宗教活动，进而演化成为南传上座部佛教地区不可或缺的、最鲜活丰富的民俗活动。

贝叶文化传承的村寨支持模式探寻

——基于西双版纳州三个傣族村寨的调研

玉万叫[①]　王明姣[②]

一、研究背景与问题提出

南传上座部佛教传入傣族地区后,与傣族文化融合发展,形成以南传上座部佛教为核心,包括原始宗教和傣族其他民间文化在内的傣族文化体系——贝叶文化。傣族是跨境跨国而居的民族,在与东南亚各国人民交往交流中,贝叶文化逐渐形成集民族性、宗教性、跨国性为一体的文化形态。随着"一带一路"倡议在东南亚实施,我国宣扬"文化自信"理念之际,贝叶文化的传承、保护和发扬更是受到了西双版纳政府部门的重视。西双版纳每个傣族村寨都有自身的运行体系和独立运行的文化场域,故有学者将傣族贝叶文化定位为村社文化[1]。

傣族贝叶文化相关文献可谓汗牛充栋,学者大多运用社会学研究方法对贝叶文化进行整体概括性描述和分析,以傣族村寨为研究单位来研究贝叶文化传承较为少见。针对傣族村寨贝叶文化研究,主要从傣族村寨文化体系、村寨文化变迁、村寨社区发展、村寨的某一文化角度等进行研究。村寨文化体系方面,曹成章在《傣族村社文化研究》一书中纵向探索傣族历史发展和文化特点,他认为,傣族社会文化是村社文化,并以村社文化这一概念来阐明傣族文化的性质和特点[1]。村寨文化变迁方面,主要表现为以文化变迁为主要线索,描述和解释某村寨傣族社会文化发展的动态性全貌[2],或以村寨为案例,探索傣族文化变迁的背景、表现和原因,并提出民族文化理性自觉的重要性[3]。村寨社区发展方面,罗阳在《云南西双版纳傣族社区与发展》中提出,傣族社区有自然和人文方面极其丰富的资源,社区的建设、发展应结合傣族的民族文化和环境资源[4]。此外,有些学者从村寨波章[③]体系[5]、传统权威组织"细梢老曼"[6]、竹楼的保护[7]等角度进行研究,然而鲜有学者从贝叶文化村寨传承支持模式方面研究贝叶文化。故本文将对此进行探讨。

[①] 作者为清迈大学社会科学学院社会学博士。
[②] 作者为云南省药物依赖防治研究所实习研究员。
[③] 波章是西双版纳傣族地区南传上座部佛教管理日常社会事务及组织宗教活动的在家众。

二、传统傣族村寨贝叶文化传承支持模式

"支持"是指一个事物对另一事物的支撑。学者们普遍认为:"弱势群体问题的根本症结之一是其所拥有的社会资源(包括财力、人力、物力、权力、能力等)整体匮乏。"[8]因此,"社会支持模式""社会支持网络"等概念应运而生,指人所处的社会或社会关系网络能给予包括财力、人力、信息等社会资本支持。少数民族传统文化相对于国家的主流文化和现代文化都处于边缘位置,某种程度而言是文化的"弱势群体",缺乏传承和发展所需的财力、人力、物力、权力以及能力等资源。贝叶文化脱胎于南传上座部佛教并深受傣族原始宗教影响,傣族社会的政治、经济、教育、宗教、民众等支持因子支撑着贝叶文化的传承。

(一)贝叶文化传承的传统村寨支持模式

南传上座部佛教在西双版纳傣族地区得到封建领主"召片领"的拥护和支持,经长期本土化融合,成为西双版纳傣族地区的主流宗教。南传上座部佛教与西双版纳傣族本土文化结合,最终孕育出贝叶文化,贝叶文化的传承和繁荣又依托于村寨的政治、经济、宗教、教育以及村民的参与。

首先,村寨头人依托贝叶文化承载的理念、思想、伦理对村寨进行治理,正向、主动地促进了贝叶文化的传承与发展。村民以贝叶文化思想内容为指导,通过宗教活动等从经济上逆向带动贝叶文化的传承与发展。以贝叶文化为核心的南传上座部佛教几乎完全依赖于世俗社会的供养,村寨供养佛寺并承担活动的开支以及上级行政组织的宗教开支[9]。原始宗教祭祀活动全由村寨支撑,出远门、结婚生子、上新房等都要拿出资金、美食供养召曼。①傣族村寨南传上座部佛教和原始宗教运行机制,为传承、发扬贝叶文化提供了保障,二者分工明确、各司其职,奠定了贝叶文化传承的宗教支持基础。

其次,傣族传统村寨中佛寺教育、家庭教育并行,为贝叶文化的传承提供了教育支持保障。佛寺教育是传统傣族社会最重要的教育方式,佛寺承担着传承贝叶文化的使命。每个傣族男子都要入寺为僧一段时间,随后带着从贝叶经里学到的贝叶文化知识重新融入世俗社会,将贝叶文化践行于世俗社会。女性则以家庭教育为主要受教育方式,由熟知贝叶文化的长辈辅导。村寨佛寺内外的教育为贝叶文化纵向传承提供了有力保障。

最后,傣族遵循佛陀的教导,行善积德、广做布施、虔诚敬佛,既接受眼前的现实,又追求来世"福报"。赕佛是傣族佛教信仰的表现之一,每家每户都要去佛寺供养,到佛寺里念经禅修。结婚生子、上新房等喜事,村寨生产活动等均按照贝叶文化教导的方式来进行。

---

① 召曼,傣语音译,原始宗教祭司之意,"丢拉曼"(寨神)在人世间的代理人。

（二）当今傣族村寨贝叶文化传承支持现状

西双版纳傣族村寨因传统文化积淀、地理位置、生态环境等的不同，呈现出不同的贝叶文化传承支持模式。故本文基于村寨经济支撑、村寨宗教运行机制、村寨教育传承、村寨人员参与四个方面进行分析。

1. 勐龙镇曼掌村模式——传统方式支持

曼掌村贝叶文化传承的支持模式以传统方式运行，未得到创新，如图1所示。

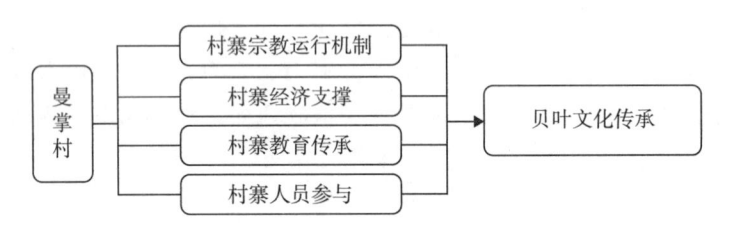

图1 曼掌村贝叶文化传承支持模式

首先，曼掌村对贝叶文化传承的支持表现在对宗教信仰的虔诚。佛寺得益于村民愿意花费护持佛法：2011年，曼掌村村民每户出2000元修建佛寺。村民积极供养佛寺，保证佛教活动的正常运行。原始宗教深入曼掌村村民生活各领域，村民至今依据传统，每年举行祭祀活动，出远门、上新房等都会拿出资金、美食供养召曼，传统习惯保证了原始宗教的运行。

其次，曼掌村宗教机制不变，佛教和原始宗教有序运作。波章在南传上座部佛教日常社会事务及组织宗教活动中起到连接世俗和神圣世界的作用。召曼每年定期召集村民进行丢拉曼、寨心的祭祀活动。佛教供养方式和内容虽逐渐简化，但活动依然定期开展。

再次，曼掌村的贝叶文化教育传承发生了转变。佛寺教育是贝叶文化传承的重要途径，曼掌村佛寺教育日渐式微。自20世纪90年代以来，鲜有男孩出家学习贝叶文化，2006—2016年间仅一位高僧住持管理佛寺。学校教育与佛教教育在曼掌村并行存在，2016年年底，曼掌村出家的6位小和尚以学校教育为主，仅用晚上或周末、假期来学习傣族文化，贝叶文化学习效果不佳。佛寺教育的衰落影响家庭代际间的贝叶文化传承。

最后，曼掌村传统文化活动参与者老龄化现象凸显。村民定期赕佛或祭祀，结婚生子、上新房、丧葬祭祀虽按照传统的方式进行，但以中老年人居多。按照傣族原始宗教理念，出远门、结婚生子时需向召曼留蜡条，这已成为老年人的专属。村寨的传统文化活动依旧开展，但随着社会的发展、不同文化的碰撞、佛寺教育的衰败、贝叶文化未进入学校教育系统等各方因素综合影响，年轻人正式学到的贝叶文化较少，对自身文化日渐疏离陌生。

贝叶文化在曼掌村传承至今，社会变迁情境下所受阻力愈来愈大。曼掌村的生产生活已经渐渐脱离贝叶文化体系，生产生活、物质文化的变化会引起村民的价值观、规范的变化。贝叶文化中蕴含的价值观、规范和观念对村民的影响势必会减弱，从而阻碍贝叶文化的传承。

2. 普文镇曼干纳模式——佛寺领协支持

曼干纳的贝叶文化传承支持方式与曼掌村大体相似，其区别在于佛寺起到领导带头的作用，如图2所示。

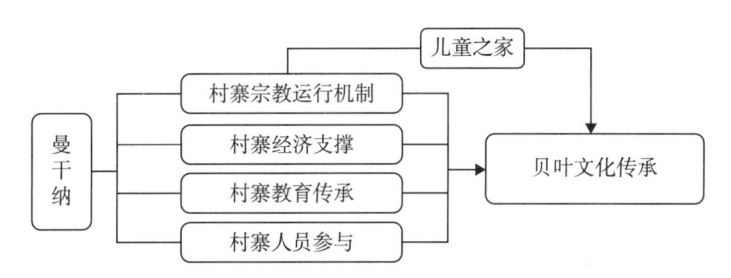

图2 曼干纳贝叶文化传承支持模式

曼干纳佛寺是"文化大革命"后普文镇唯一恢复的佛寺。佛寺虽已恢复，但并未恢复波章一职，佛教事务由住持都比三和佛教协会的老人协助完成。虽无召曼一职，但每年都比三和村子里的老人会带着村民定期在神龛和寨心前祭祀。原始宗教功能虽逐渐被佛寺所取代，但原始宗教信仰还是得以保留。曼干纳村村民与曼掌村村民相似，在宗教信仰领域都愿出资供养，一定程度上保障了贝叶文化的传承和发展。

自20世纪60年代以来，曼干纳50年无佛寺，村寨教育传承出现结构性断代，甚至中年人都不熟悉、了解贝叶文化。据都比三[①]所言："由于受外来文化影响早，部分年轻人傣话都讲得很困难。"[②] 2012年，在都比三的推动下曼干纳佛寺举办了第一期儿童夏令营，主要教授曼干纳以及附近其他傣族村寨的儿童傣文、礼佛、念经等，让儿童了解贝叶文化。自第一期儿童夏令营到笔者调研时，曼干纳佛寺共举行了10期夏令营，参与人数达300余人。2015年，由西双版纳州妇联授牌，在曼干纳佛寺成立了"儿童之家"，成为全镇青少年学习传统民族文化的主要场所。曼干纳佛寺"儿童之家"以儿童为主要受众，并将活动延伸到儿童的家长、村寨老人的身上，传授贝叶文化知识；斋戒日，都比三带领村里的中年男女在佛寺里念经。此外，在都比三的影响下，2017年初，常来参加儿童活动的普文镇11名男孩出家，其中3位来自曼干纳。

曼干纳以佛寺领导带头支持影响为基点，增加"儿童之家"支持因子，强化了村寨成员参与意识，营造了村寨的文化参与氛围，为促进"文化自觉"的觉醒起到了潜移默化的作用。

3. 打洛镇勐景来村模式——佛寺公司带头

相较前两个村寨，勐景来贝叶文化传承得益于勐景来佛寺和金孔雀旅游公司的

---

① 都比三于2010年担任曼干纳佛寺住持。
② 2017年1月5日于西双版纳州景洪市普文镇曼干纳佛寺对都比三进行采访，随后多次跟进访谈。

贝叶文化与区域文化遗产传承保护

共同努力,如图 3 所示。

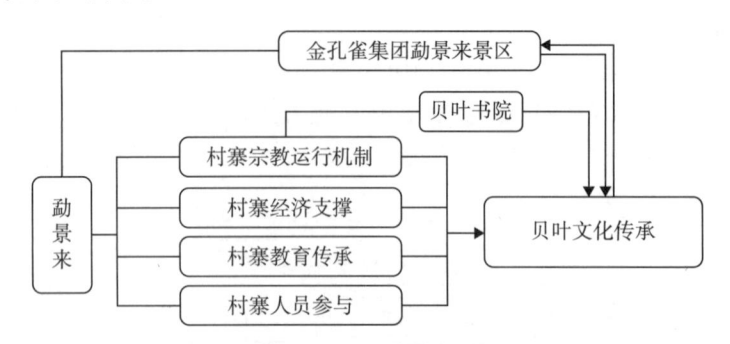

图 3　勐景来贝叶文化传承支持模式

勐景来贝叶文化传承支持模式中村寨宗教运行机制未变,驻勐景来的金孔雀集团鼓励村民参与,增加了勐景来村寨贝叶文化传承的支持因子。2003 年,金孔雀集团入驻勐景来便与村民签订遵守《村民暂行管理规定》的协议以保留干栏式建筑,违者罚款,促进了勐景来对传统傣式建筑的保护。为了吸引游客,公司在寨子里租用民居成立了酿酒、造纸、榨糖、竹编、制陶、打铁、织锦等 14 户傣族手工艺项目点,每月补助手工艺传承人 400 元,每户房屋租金 1500 元,且经营所得收入归传承人,以此激励村民学习传承本民族文化。勐景来景区 70% 的员工为本村村民,分别从事导游、绿化、手工等工作,从事经济活动即为践行文化参与。

勐景来几乎全村都是公共文化空间:傣式民居遍布全村,傣风壁画、傣汉双语的格言随处可见,村民可随处接触本民族文化,年轻人易习得贝叶文化。通过规划村寨传统建筑格局,推动手工艺项目点,制定规章制度约束村民破坏传统文化的行为等带动村民保护民族文化。与此同时,浓厚的文化氛围吸引众多游客增加经济利益。

除了带领村民经营日常的佛事活动外,在主持都坎章的推动下,成立的贝叶书院增加了勐景来贝叶文化传承模式的一个支持因子。书院定期举办文化传承班,传授青少年傣族传统文化知识;开办傣族文化课程;带领众僧挖掘整理宣传南传上座部佛教和傣族文化,向大众免费提供《贝叶格言》《释迦牟尼佛画传》《傣族经书文词典》等书籍的借阅;恢复傣族传统节日、风俗活动,提高村民的本民族文化自觉、提升文化自信。在贝叶书院的带领下,掌握佛经戒律的村民增加,每逢赕佛,村民能与僧人朗朗背诵经文;儿童与佛寺的亲近度增加,常看到儿童来佛寺与僧人交流。公司搭建文化场景,贝叶书院营造文化氛围,良性互动共同推动勐景来村贝叶文化传承。

(三)当今傣族村寨贝叶文化传承支持分析

西双版纳傣族村寨贝叶文化传承支持模式中,村寨宗教运行机制未变,而"村寨宗教运行机制"因子支持贝叶文化传承的强弱受村寨宗教领袖的意识影响;村寨经济支撑随村民收入的增加而增强,但村民会不断追求物质收入的增长而减少活动的参与;佛寺传统教育的衰弱影响家庭教育贝叶文化传承功能的发挥,且贝叶文化未能进入当地学校教育系统,傣族青少年通过正式的教育渠道学习贝叶文化的机会少。

"儿童之家""贝叶书院"填补了贝叶文化教育传承的真空地带,承担起傣族村寨儿童的传统文化教育和陪伴功能。村寨佛寺以公益形式对青少年儿童开展贝叶文化传承是佛寺教育和国家义务教育体制产生冲突的背景下一个新的发展方向。勐景来的传统文化氛围更为深厚,得益于公司的利益驱动模式。以旅游文化公司为主导的传统文化传承是文化保护的一条途径。但通过市场第三者来传承和保护村寨贝叶文化并非长远之计,村民是贝叶文化的中心载体,其要实现可持续发展需要村民的文化自觉。

三、加强贝叶文化传承的支持系统

(一)教育支持——重视贝叶文化传统教育功能

在傣族社会里,佛寺是傣族男孩学贝叶文化的"学校",家庭、村寨是傣族青少年习得贝叶文化的重要场所。"传统社会的文化所表现出高度同质性,意味着不需要把儿童从社区中隔离出来进行独立的训练"[10],儿童成长的生活情境能起到早期教育的作用。特别是对少数民族地区来说,学校教育内容和社区生活文化形成了二元结构。学校教育是现代教育的主导教育,受教育者在国家力量的强制下进入学校接受教育,传承国家主流文化,学校教育是文化再制的主要渠道,从一定程度而言,似乎尚未纳入学校教育的文化体系被排斥在主流文化外围。

佛寺历史上一直是傣族社会传统文化传承的教育场所,"教教合一"曾在傣族的传统教育中起到过重要的作用。西双版纳相关部门应认可并重视傣族佛寺教育,不只是把贝叶文化视为一种传统文化任其发展,而应给予相应的各类支持,协调佛寺教育和学校教育,重视贝叶文化的传统教育功能,做好连接学校教育与佛寺教育之间的工作。

(二)经济支持——扶持贝叶文化产业

文化产业是文化保护的内在需求和重要途径[11]。文化旅游虽吸引众多傣族民众参与,但傣族民众很少能进入文化旅游策划的核心部门,导致未能激发傣族民众文化主人公的意识。贝叶文化包含的傣族民间文化,特别是各类工艺都带有浓郁的地域特色,易形成产业链,且掌握制作核心技艺的是傣族民众,这样可促发民众的文化主人翁意识。贝叶文化经济支持的最终落脚点是通过经济发展促进傣族民众文化参与,当地政府可带动傣族民众发展傣族村寨合作社,促使村民学习,共同发展,促进贝叶文化的传承,共享经济成果。

(三)文化自觉——开展贝叶文化建设

文化自信的前提是文化自觉,文化自觉是文化保护的原生动力,村民以集体行动参与是文化自觉的第一步。社区营造指基于社区的文化和资源,通过动员社区人持续以集体的行动来处理共同的生活问题,促进社区人与人之间、人与环境、人与文化之间建立紧密的联系的过程,特别是促进社区人对自身文化的反思。以共同历史文化延续为核心,以产业经济发展为主线,促进社区文化和经济的发展。傣族村寨是一个有机的社区,村民互相认识,有共同的历史文化、宗教信仰和利益关系,这是开展社区营造的基础。傣族村寨许多正式或非正式的群众组织是开展社区营造的组织基础，如僧人、康朗、老庚组、老年协会、妇女小组等。通过政府或当地NGO的培育，开展群体活动，带领村民认识了解自身文化、运用文化，激发傣族民众的文化自觉；以传统文化为核心带动村寨经济发展，促发傣族民众自觉传承和保护贝叶文化。

四、结语

"一带一路"倡议的深入推进、"文化自信"理念的宣传，为贝叶文化的传承提供了政策支持，在政策指引下相信贝叶文化传承所需资源会增加，传承力度会增强。本研究对比三个不同村寨的支持模式发现不同的村寨因拥有不同的支持因素而产生不同的文化传承效果，进而提出应重视贝叶文化传统教育功能，扶持贝叶文化产业，开展傣寨文化建设以支持贝叶文化的传承与发展。笔者认为不同的贝叶文化支持因素改变而引起的文化变迁，增加何种支持因子、如何增加是未来研究贝叶文化传承的主要方向。

参考文献：

[1] 曹成章.傣族村社文化研究.北京：中央民族大学出版社，2005.

[2] 金少萍.西双版纳城子傣族村寨文化变迁的民族志研究.北京：知识产权出版社，2014.

[3] 郑晓云.社会变迁中的傣族文化——一个西双版纳傣族村寨的人类学研究.中国社会科学，1997（5）.

[4] 罗阳.云南西双版纳傣族社区与发展.成都：四川大学出版社，2007.

[5] 郑筱筠.试论中国南传上座部佛教的宗教管理模式.中国宗教，2011（1）.

[6] 伍琼华，闫永军.傣族村落中的传统权威组织——曼安村的"细梢老曼"与乡村秩序.云南民族大学学报（哲学社会科学版），2012（3）.

[7] 毕发钱，毕发明.西双版纳勐景来旅游村寨传统民居的保护研究.西部大开发·中国，2012（1）.

[8] 张友琴.社会支持与社会支持网——弱势群体社会支持的工作模式初探.厦门大学学报（哲学社会科学版），2002（3）.

[9] 郑筱筠.历史上中国南传上座部佛教的组织制度与社会组织制度之互动——以云南西双版纳傣族地区为例.世界宗教研究，2007（4）.

[10] 罗吉华.文化变迁中的文化再制与教育选择.中央民族大学硕士学位论文，2009.

[11] 丁智才.民族文化产业视域下边疆民族地区民族特色文化保护探析.湖北民族学院学报（哲学社会科学版），2006（4）.

贝叶经籍文化交流是德宏沿边开放先行先试的重要路径

李茂琳　熊甜芳　蒋潞杨[①]

一、德宏傣文贝叶经遗存简况

贝叶经，最早起源于古代印度。据专家考证，贝叶经是公元7世纪前后传入缅甸、泰国后，又传入我国云南德宏、西双版纳等西南边疆少数民族地区，目前发现存有贝叶经的国家有中国、印度、泰国、缅甸、老挝等。傣文贝叶经是我国珍贵的文化遗产，记载有佛教经典、天文历法、社会历史、医药、文学艺术等内容。

在德宏发现的贝叶经，有缅—巴利、德宏方形老傣文和圆形缅傣文等。据资料统计，德宏州收藏有贝叶经的单位有：德宏州档案馆共250片，初步鉴定年代为元代；梁河文物管理所共收有450片，年代为清代咸丰年间；瑞丽市档案馆收有600片，年代为清代；另盈江档案馆、盈江文物管理所、陇川县图书馆、德宏州民语委等单位也有部分收藏。德宏州大量的贝叶经及绵纸经、构纸经收藏在奘房里，大的奘房专门设有藏经房，部分贝叶经在私人手里，属私人收藏，还有部分贝叶经等傣文古籍经书散存于民间。目前德宏州图书馆民族古籍工作人员正在进行统计。德宏州的有些贝叶经内容非常丰富，价值连城，但原有多数贝叶经已流失国外，后来的贝叶经则只有一小部分流失国外。

古籍普查中发现德宏州的大多数贝叶经还未译成汉语，只知道刻写了佛教经典《三藏经》《召为善达纳》《召玉托达纳》《兰嘎西贺》《召树屯》及傣族的三大悲剧《线秀》《月罕佐与冒弄养》《娥并与桑洛》等。这些古籍形成了中华文化中极具特色的地方民族文化，成为傣族文化的百科全书。2007年7月，德宏州图书馆牵头对德宏州民族文学文献古籍进行普查，掌握了一批民族文学文献古籍。2008年以来，以勐巴娜西珍奇园为首的一些单位和个人又于缅北和民间搜集、收藏了30多函贝叶经文，其中多数被中央电视台鉴宝栏目认定为文物，颁发了证书。

[①] 李茂琳，德宏师范高等专科学校副教授；熊甜芳，德宏师范高等专科学校社科系讲师；蒋潞杨，德宏师范高等专科学校社科系助教。

二、贝叶经籍在德宏跨境文化交流中的作用

德宏师范高等专科学校于 2016 年 4 月与江晓林夫妇合作成立了江应樑傣族研究中心，中心成立仪式上，展出了江晓林先生收藏的一函斯里兰卡人制作赠与他的傣文贝叶经（图3）、德宏州原副州长板岩过先生捐赠的一函有 360 多片组成的贝叶经（图1）和一片民间贝叶卦签（图2），360 片贝叶经是他在德宏民间与缅甸北掸邦同胞中搜集到并收藏的，据德宏州图书馆与德宏傣学会特聘曾经在缅甸寺庙修行多年的经师僬所比达鉴别，360 片贝叶经年代最迟也应是清朝时制作的，系由至少 6 部经类混杂而成。而单片贝叶卦签是印度阿萨姆邦访问学者到德宏时所赠，这个卦签上有两个傣族原始崇拜的象征性图案和第二个时期傣文文字变革时期用的早期文字咒文，还间杂有巴利语咒文，是较早时期用竹片制作，用于原始宗教占卜的贝叶签。经师僬所比达称，佛教第五次结集后南传上座部佛教文化圈国家的缅、泰、老、柬诸国每年都会在缅甸集中做至少一次诵经大会，或举行单个国家自己的诵经会。不同国家和地区的僧人在这个时期进行佛法的交流与佛经的传送，有佛僧会携带传播佛音的贝叶经函参加诵经会与众僧侣交流。在德宏师范高等专科学校江应樑傣族研究中心展出的过程中，缅甸、泰国和老挝的参观者对此表示了极大的认同，同一个宗教的信仰为大家找到了进一步沟通的桥梁。

图 1　360 多片贝叶经函

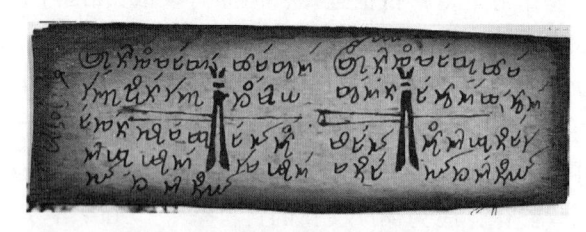

图 2　曾经在民间使用的贝叶卦签

图 3　来自斯里兰卡的贝叶经函

笔者曾在德宏州沈国去先生家里看到过一函缅甸曼德勒友人赠予，制作年代为中华民国时期的极为完整的贝叶经纪念品（见图4），贝叶经一面有彩色佛本生经故事，一面为傣语经文。沈先生的缅甸曼德勒友人是一名商人，这名商人在缅甸有很多民间制作贝叶经的高手朋友，他们多数都是利用空闲时间几乎无偿地为缅寺制作传世的贝叶经赕佛，在中缅民众的民间交流中，不仅有经济方面的往来，还有更多的文化上的交流，而贝叶经在类似的民间交流中起到了文化、情感纽带的作用。

据芒市三台山德昂族乡的民间民族文化传承人李腊翁回忆，他曾使用过从缅甸传入用贝叶制作的傣文经书，并曾用这类写经本进行听诵传唱。他用过的贝叶经后来在"破四旧"中被列为禁物。听他说，他的同仁，也曾于20世纪50—70年代用过贝叶制作的傣文经书。像他们一样见识过古本贝叶经的同胞，境内境外有数百人。

图4 来自缅甸的贝叶经函

曾经的古籍贝叶经仿佛是老人与境外同胞通连的心路，至今他和与他有同样经历的德昂同胞还念念不忘。

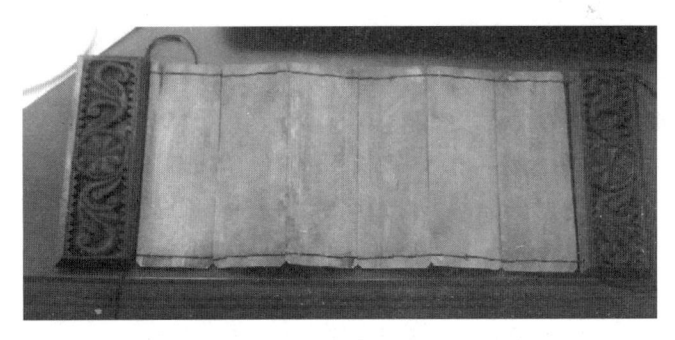

图5 出自瑞丽口岸古董店的贝叶经函

笔者曾于2010年4月出席云南省傣学会在西双版纳组织的国际傣学会，在与老挝学者闲谈时，曾咨询过其僧俗贝叶经使用情况。客人告诉我们，老挝将南传上座部佛教当作国粹和国人的精神家园，贝叶经使用和制作也很普遍，几乎成为传统文化的象征。笔者曾向西双版纳傣语文专家刀金平要了5株用植物园贝叶棕种子培育的用于制作贝叶经的贝叶棕，回芒市后交由芒市勐巴娜西风情园方××园艺师培育，现都已成活，但生长十分缓慢。德宏州傣学会的好多人知道有贝叶棕移植芒市后，都纷纷前去参观，一睹贝叶棕的风采。芒市勐巴娜西珍奇园将傣族的"五树六花"作为象征性佛教植物向前来观赏的寻路人推介，引起包括泰国、缅甸、马来

贝叶文化与区域文化遗产传承保护

西亚、斯里兰卡来访者极大的兴趣。人们将金碧辉煌的亚洲最大的勐焕大金塔和美丽的传说联想在一起，感到仿佛又回到了佛光普照的国度。这契合了南传上座部佛教文化圈各国人民的宗教情结，拉近了民族间的距离。李茂琳曾多次在瑞丽国家重点开发开放试验区中心城市瑞丽华丰商贸市场古董店看到沟通中缅与南亚贝叶文化的器物，每次去时看到的经本都不一样，曾买了一函现代制作的一面有本色佛本生经故事，一面为经文的贝叶经（图5），用作教具。在教学过程中，该贝叶经颇受德宏师范高等专科学校傣语班学生和应用缅甸语班学生的喜爱。在一定程度上拉近了不同国家不同民族学生间的情感。

在与德宏傣学会专家和缅甸、老挝、印度、斯里兰卡、泰国、柬埔寨、孟加拉国等国学者的交谈中，这些国家学者隐隐流露出对南传上座部佛教的宗教情感和对古籍贝叶经卷的珍视。有南传上座部佛教经历和国民主要信奉南传上座部佛教的东南亚诸掸国，在国际僧俗交流中，有史以来都几乎是无国界和无缝的对接。在中国西南主要流传南传上座部佛教地区与上述国家的交往中，共同的南传上座部佛教信仰和文化认同拉近了彼此的距离，促进了民心相通。

三、贝叶经与南亚东南亚国家互联互通的作用

贝叶经是傣族、德昂族等民族珍贵的文化遗产，是中华民族文化的瑰宝。德宏贝叶经刻本和更为大量的纸质抄本属巴利语系文献，主要是550个佛本生经故事、经典三藏和非经典文献，也间杂有傣族民间文学、历史、语言、医药、天文历法、法律、礼仪、占卜、咒术等类别。此外，还有许多非经典文献（包括大量的经典注释著作）。可以看到的是，傣族社会获得历史性的进步，文化上得到全面的发展，都受到了贝叶经深刻的影响。

由于傣族地区气候炎热，历史上战乱频繁，又没有完善的保藏设备，贝叶经佚失的情况十分严重，而现存的贝叶经多数是残缺不全的残片，只有各级图书馆和档案馆馆藏贝叶经稍微完整。从这些经籍来看，德宏作为南传上座部佛教文化圈内影响深远的区域文化边境属地，历史悠久，其贝叶文化不仅传承着自身及泰、老、掸、阿洪姆各国各地的文化精华，还积极吸取了汉文化和印度文化元素，成为包容各种文化的多元贝叶文化网状结构。

基于南亚和东南亚有关佛本生经故事和早期印度阿育王及后来的佛音时代，以及第三至第五次分别于斯里兰卡和缅甸举办的几次佛教结集，南传上座部佛教文化及其适应湿热地区气候的经典载体贝叶经已在东南亚、南亚各国人民心中烙下深深的印记。贝叶经不仅成为联结他们心灵的纽带，而且成为沟通经贸往来、互通友好、文字与文化传播、宗教交流和日常文化生活的必需品。

在近代，无论是东南亚南传上座部佛教文化圈诸掸国，还是中国西南边境的傣族、德昂族先民多用贝叶书写经书，从事佛教传播。德宏傣族与德昂族是信仰南传上座部佛教的两个世居民族，由于其具有悠久的历史和对佛教的较早接受，出于

对佛教文化辉煌历史的纪念,他们也曾将制作与使用贝叶经和传播贝叶文化作为对佛法的弘扬,但目前其制作工艺将面临消亡和失传的危险,所以必须尽快发掘、整理、拯救和保护贝叶文化。德宏州已计划出版"六对照"(贝叶经原件扫描图像、老傣文、新傣文、贝叶经汉语直译、意译、国际音标)贝叶翻译作品,但目前还只是一个初步的设想。

20世纪90年代前期至今,云南旅游业异军突起,发展至今,云南的旅游业发展水平一直保持在全国第6—8位、西南地区之首的位置。作为中国推向国际市场的重要旅游目的地,云南成为大量的外来游客文化消费、尤其是旅游文化消费的市场。毫无疑问,旅游市场是云南文化产业发展最广阔的平台。贝叶文化将在提升旅游形象、丰富旅游产品文化内涵、营造旅游地独特氛围和增加旅游纪念品的种类等方面为德宏地区旅游业的进一步发展产生巨大的推动作用。根据目前西双版纳和德宏旅游产品开发现状,完全可以考虑推出贝叶文化中所蕴含的包括"贝叶经的制作和刻写""学写傣文、学刻傣文贝叶经"体验、制作"微缩贝叶经""佛寺壁画和傣锦工艺品"藏品等潜在旅游产品,直至将来在傣族德昂族区域建立贝叶经博物馆,作为永久性文化旅游项目。我们还要从贝叶经中开发佛教(仪式)音乐,形成独特的风格、韵味和内涵,弘扬佛教音乐,在贝叶经中发掘傣族医药和德昂族医药来造福人类!

随着国家"一带一路"倡议的提出和实施,德宏是瑞丽国家重点开发开放试验区,作为孟中印缅经济走廊的先导区,如何走出去和引进来,加强与南亚和东南亚各国民间和国家的联系,增进区域内和区域外的互通互连将显得非常有必要。因此,可以考虑,在文化交往与学术交流中把贝叶文化和其中连带的传统制作工艺与植物引种及南传上座部佛教文化文创产品开发,作为先行走出去的项目来打造,先行建立一个以贝叶文化为核心的窗口。通过这个窗口拓展僧俗间的互通互联,达到多领域的延伸,从而将南亚和东南亚各国联结到同源异流的共同文化情结中来,实现各美其美,美人所美,美美与共的共同体的构建,然后升华到多领域的合作与建设中来,从心灵深处消除一些历史误会,从而达到互利双赢的目的,为人类做出各国应有的贡献。

中国—东南亚、南亚贝叶文化传承与保护国际研讨会综述

韩 帅[①]

2019年11月16—18日，由云南大学发展研究院、泰国清迈皇家大学艺术与文化办公室、云南大学贝叶文化研究中心（PLCRC，Palm-Leaf Culture Research Center，YNU）共同主办的"中国—东南亚、南亚贝叶文化传承与保护国际研讨会"（International Seminar on the Inheritance & Protection of Palm-Leaf Culture in China-Southeast Asia and South Asia）在云南大学东陆校区科学馆举行。来自泰国清迈皇家大学、泰国清迈大学、老挝国家图书馆、泰国玛希隆大学、斯里兰卡科伦坡大学、德国汉堡大学等的10名国际专家学者，以及来自中央民族大学、北京师范大学、云南省社科院、云南省民宗委（古籍办）、云南自然与文化遗产保护促进会、云南大学、云南师范大学、云南民族大学、昆明学院、普洱学院、滇西应用技术大学等高校与相关机构的专家学者，和来自德宏州图书馆、西双版纳州民族研究所暨西双版纳州贝叶文化研究中心、西双版纳州图书馆、勐海县打洛镇贝叶书院等单位和机构的贝叶文化传承与保护的实践者参加了本次会议。

本次会议包括主旨发言和交流发言两个部分。2019年11月16日上午，斯里兰卡科伦坡大学社会学院的Premakumara de Silva教授，中央民族大学戴红亮教授，老挝国家图书馆贝叶经数字图书馆项目负责人David Wharton博士，斯里兰卡科伦坡大学佛教系系主任、孔子学院院长Ven. Dr. Prof. Dhammajothi Thero教授，云南大学发展研究院副院长郭山教授，泰国清迈皇家大学贝叶经研究中心主任Direk Injan博士，云南大学贝叶文化研究中心主任、副研究员周娅博士做了主旨发言。此外，进行了两场交流发言，先后有26位发言人围绕着会议主旨议题，就"贝叶文化的历史源流与现状""贝叶文化遗产的现代价值""贝叶经制作技艺的传承与保护""贝叶典籍的数字化整理与保护"以及"中国—东南亚、南亚各国贝叶文化传承与保护的实践"等具体议题展开了深入交流与研讨。

一、贝叶文化的历史源流与现状

斯里兰卡科伦坡大学社会学院的Premakumara de Silva教授做了会议论坛的第

[①] 云南大学民族学与社会学学院2019级宗教学硕士研究生。

一场主旨发言。他指出，在斯里兰卡岛，土著人的悠久传统和传统知识最早是通过口耳相传保存下来的。贝叶被用来记录传统知识，并指导古代社会如何利用这些知识。斯里兰卡和南亚大部分国家/地区拥有广泛传播的贝叶经文化，超出了传统意义上书写材料的范围。贝叶经（puskola poth）仍然是公元5世纪到公元20世纪的整个南亚国家/地区的主要书写材料。

老挝国家图书馆贝叶经数字图书馆项目负责人 David Wharton 博士向我们介绍了他在云南、缅甸和印度东北部等地区发现的一些傣族语言群体所保有着的、独特的、前现代的、当地的傣族佛教文化和手稿文献的表达方式。在当下，古老的传统拼字法大多用于日益濒危的手抄本当中，并且仍然是少数专业抄写员的专属。这些群体在傣族文化和语言研究中受到的关注很少，在佛教研究领域基本上还不为人所知，因此迫切需要传承和记录他们濒临灭绝的文化与技艺。

斯里兰卡科伦坡大学佛教系系主任、孔子学院院长 Ven. Dr. Prof. Dhammajothi Thero 教授指出：古代手稿是人类从祖先那里得到的最重要的遗产之一。作为人类的一员，所有国家的人民都有责任把它们视为重要的文件，因为它们记录了人们在达到目前的生活状态之前所经历过的种种漫长旅程。这些手稿真实地描绘了不同国家所带来的有益的和灾难性的变迁。因此，这些资源作为信息的宝藏和灵感的来源，我们从中可以学习祖先的经验，得出深刻的见解，并发现通往更美好未来的道路。而目前更主要的目标是为了更好地维护和保存它们，以及使研究人员更容易获得它们。

泰国清迈皇家大学贝叶经研究中心主任 Direk Injan 博士向我们介绍了他以清迈市区清曼寺的贝叶经、纸质抄本、碑文等为研究对象所开展的相关研究。研究表明，在1835捆贝叶经、33份纸质抄本和4篇碑文中，记载了许多重要且有趣的资料。例如，清迈古城的庙宇名单（公元1873年）；清迈地区和清曼寺的重要历史事件（公元1296—1891年）；等。这些原始史料既可以用来丰富当地旅游业的历史，也可以用来提高公众对文献本身的认识。

二、中国—东南亚、南亚各国贝叶文化传承与保护的实践

云南大学贝叶文化研究中心主任、副研究员周娅博士在其主旨发言中提出：目前中国对于贝叶经这一文化遗产保护的实践类型包括形制性保护、传承性保护、制度性保护和研究性保护等，并且取得了一定的成绩。但由于诸多现实条件的制约，在保护范围、保护意识、保护合作以及保护技术性手段等方面的实践成效还十分有限。建议在巴利语系贝叶经保护和贝叶文化传承方面开展区域性国际合作，推动相关区域性联动机制的建立，采取如多国联合申报"世界记忆遗产"等具体措施，共同推动这一珍贵的区域人文资源在当代中国—东南亚、南亚地区的传承与保护。

德国汉堡大学博士生、普洱学院副教授周寒丽同我们分享了 DREAMSEA（东南亚濒危和具有影响力的手稿的数字化存储）项目的相关情况。该项目主要抢救的是

民间和宗教场所保存的手稿，并不涉及政府或者机构收藏。目前，该项目已经顺利完成海岛国家的六个地区和一个大陆国家（老挝）963份手稿，共42131帧的数字化存储工作。项目计划到2022年为止完成240000个页面的数字化存储。通过对该项目的综合介绍，并对其在手稿文化保护过程中的实际操作进行梳理，可以为我们在未来的手稿文化保护中提供一个良好借鉴。

泰国清迈大学Dr. Assoc. Prof. Apiradee Techasiriwan教授指出20世纪六七十年代，因特殊的历史原因，大批傣泐文手稿受到毁坏。自20世纪80年代初至今，中国政府与当地的傣泐学者一直在通力合作以复兴傣泐文及其手稿文化。中国对传统的傣泐手稿的影响是很大的，显而易见地表现为印刷技术和现代印刷风格对傣泐手稿的影响。伴随着这些影响因素傣泐手稿写作的支撑点、材料、格式、制作等都在变化和发展中。

斯里兰卡科伦坡大学Dr. Wimal Hewamanage博士向我们介绍了在斯里兰卡对贝叶的应用，其以佛教为中心，通过定性和定量的数据，揭示了佛教是如何丰富斯里兰卡贝叶文化的。

云南大学民族学与社会学学院影视人类学实验室主任张海同我们分享了他尝试用影像来书写贝叶经的制作技艺和信仰意义的宝贵经历。他用影像探讨并记录了当地贝叶经文化的保护、传播与传承的情况，试图在影像中发现异同，为两国在未来贝叶文化交流中提供更直观和具象的研究资料。

德宏州图书馆馆员张云同我们分享了德宏傣文古籍的保护整理开发工作的相关情况。她从傣族历史文化进程，德宏傣文古籍的基本状况，德宏傣文古籍的内容及其归类，翻译研究德宏傣文古籍开发利用前景，德宏傣文古籍的传承、收集整理和研究存在的问题，傣文古籍研究成果转换六个方面论述该项目的重要性。

西双版纳州图书馆玉罕为指出，傣族跨境而居，傣文古籍的保护也是对中华文明的一种传承，同时也促进民心相通，推动文化认同。东南亚各国的泰傣族群人口数量庞大，分布地区广泛，与我国边疆接壤面积大，如何保护好傣文古籍，助推"一带一路"倡议，是一个我们面临的新的命题。傣文古籍与东南亚傣族文化具有深厚的渊源，傣文古籍的修复是一件功在当代、利在千秋的重大工作。

西双版纳州综合信息办玉楠叫向我们介绍了西双版纳贝叶文化形成的重要载体贝叶棕的现状，由于贝叶棕对繁殖环境和栽培技术有一定要求，西双版纳地区贝叶棕逐渐减少，正面临灭绝的危险，贝叶棕亟待保护。

三、贝叶文化遗产的现代价值

云南大学发展研究院副院长郭山教授同我们分享了他对西双版纳傣族M村佛寺贝叶经存量、结构、来源及使用状况的田野调查，可以看到贝叶经典籍在傣族日常生活中，尤其是在涉及人生大事（如生老病死等等）的赕仪式时出现的频率很高。虽说普通傣族民众不能识读贝叶经，但贝叶经在当下傣家人心目中仍然是滋养心灵、安顿生活的一剂"良药"。

昆明学院田玉玲副教授指出，佛传故事是南传上座部佛教经典的重要组成部分，深入研究南传上座部佛教，深度挖掘南传上座部佛教故事内涵，对其当代价值再认识十分必要而迫切，以向更多人传播理性、自律、和谐的工作生活方式，与时代和谐发展要求相融互通，让佛教理念在当代社会发挥应有的作用。

云南民族大学硕士生范丽娇则从文本出发向我们介绍了西双版纳傣族贝叶经中部分经文关于生态和自然保护的论述，对傣族地区和谐的生态观有积极的作用和影响。探究贝叶经的生态文化内涵以及对傣族地区生态保护的影响，分析贝叶经生态保护理念，阐述贝叶经的现代化意义有与时俱进的重要历史作用。

滇西应用技术大学傣医药学院玉喃哈则向我们介绍了滇西应用技术大学傣医药学院在傣医药传承方面所做的工作：包括搭建平台结合院校培养与师承教育，联合民间傣医、院校教师、临床专家等多方导师之力，共同培养傣医药传承人并对古籍进行整理、翻译、开发、临床研究等。

北京师范大学博士生岩温宰香认为，以南传上座部佛教和巴利语系贝叶文化为中心的双向交往，能加强傣泐民族文化的交流与互动，促进民心相通和文化共融，从而促使跨界族群的文化认同感得以加强。

云南大学民族学与社会学学院张振伟副教授首先简要梳理了贝叶经和历史上所称的"梵夹装"典籍在中国汉传、藏传、南传上座部佛教地区的发展和传承脉络；其次指出在不同教派地区贝叶经记载文字存在较大的差异，对于文化的交流存在一定的障碍；再次在此基础上介绍了云南大学贝叶文化研究中心等几家有代表性的保护及研究机构；最后指出在贝叶经的研究及保护过程中，应该充分发挥不同教派和研究机构的作用、相互合作、共同参与，最终实现贝叶经研究的协调式发展。

四、其他

学者们还就贝叶经的语言和翻译问题，以及贝叶经和贝叶文化的历史、文化、艺术、民间信仰等方面做了交流。

中央民族大学戴红亮教授在其主旨发言中以《维先达腊》中的巴利语释读为例，分析了傣文古籍中两种巴利语形态的释读和对应问题。总体来看，傣文古籍巴利语识别主要存在以下几个方面的问题。一是研究基础薄弱，没有一部合适的傣文巴利语词典，往往需要借助其他语言的巴利语词典来作为重要的辅助工具。二是傣文转写巴利语时采用了复杂的转写规则，即使一一对应的借词，也需要一定的转写知识，更为重要的是，很多借词在转写时采用了特殊转写规则，这就使两者对应关系不明显。三是很多偈颂在口耳相传中出现了各种误读、误写和误抄，这就更使巴利语识读难度加大。四是缺乏综合性人才，傣文古籍巴利语识读需要懂巴利语、古傣文、缅甸语、泰语方面的专家，但这种多语种人才培养起来难度较大，需要专门的机构长期进行。傣文古籍巴利语识别不仅关系到傣文古籍整理质量和研究水平，也关系到对贝叶文化了解的深度和广度，是一项必须要处理的问题。因此文中提出了若干建议，希望能共同推动这项工作取得进展。

云南大学文学院副教授保明所博士则基于自建全文本词汇语料库对《佛祖巡游记》中音译词的不规范现象进行了探讨。先分析了音译词不规范的三种主要类型：一种是汉字使用不规范；一种是音译专名与汉语专名不对应；一种是音译与意译并存。接着探讨了产生不规范现象的主要原因：（1）集体翻译的成果；（2）缺乏可查阅的大型双语词典；（3）傣、汉两种语言系统中佛教词汇的对应关系沟通不畅；（4）缺乏音译词规范标准。最后提出了解决音译词不规范现象的策略：（1）统一音译词的书写形式；（2）尽量采用意译形式；（3）编写贝叶经词典。

云南省佛教协会副会长兼秘书长康南山先生通过分析南传上座部佛教贝叶经经典传入我国的过程，向我们介绍了在传播过程当中所产生的对于傣族人民来说极为重要的两种文字——新傣文和老傣文。同时详细阐述了这两种文字的产生过程及其区别。同时指出近年来由于西双版纳地区社会的发展和变迁，南传上座部佛教的经典和其所使用的文字的传承面临的挑战，并且在此基础上提出了他关于南传上座部佛教经典和文字传承发展的思考与建议。

泰国清迈大学硕士生、西双版纳州勐海县贝叶书院院长都坎章向我们介绍了经典傣文的产生与传播过程，同时探讨了经典傣文的名称和使用分布情况。他从各地的名称出发来作对比及分析，结合文字的特点，从中找出一个共同的名称；最后，尝试探讨经典傣文的使用分布情况，以便更好地帮助我们对其了解。

泰国玛希隆大学 Dr. Asst. Prof. Aphilak Kasempholkoon 教授发现，虽然研究结果表明泰国的大部分经文都用来记录宗教神圣的故事，但是贝叶经的另一部分还记录了重要的文本知识。有关贝叶经的性别文献记录还有一些保存在寺庙里，强调了经文的内容。为了使继承人一生幸福，佛教作为一种神圣的宗教有助于"仪式"的实现。

德国汉堡大学博士生 Sutheera Satayaphan 同我们分享了一部名为 Kāraked 的古老的暹罗舞蹈戏剧。这出戏剧大概是在大城府时期写的，一直演到18世纪曼谷时期早期。这出戏剧剧本是写在类似协奏曲或 leporello 手稿上的，手稿是由 Khòi 树的树皮制成的。尽管对暹罗戏剧手稿进行了大量的研究，但以前对 Kāraked 戏剧的研究却很少能被找到。本研究对这四部手稿进行考察，以反映戏剧及其自身所具有的手稿文化的特点。

云南民族大学副教授饶睿颖博士向我们介绍了南传上座部佛教文化圈的祜巴信仰。祜巴自19世纪以来一度被泰北地区信众赋予"东奔"也就是圣僧的称号。同时以敏锐的视角关注了祜巴信众群体当中的精英阶层的诉求。在此基础之上她向我们着重介绍了泰北祜巴群体中最具名望的两位祜巴：祜巴西唯差与祜巴温忠，通过他们的弘法事迹，探讨了泰北精英阶层对佛教传统信仰的回归与诉求。

云南省民宗委古籍办副译审依旺的首先向我们介绍了南传上座部佛教进入傣族社会并且发展壮大的过程，同时简要描述了贝叶经的产生和发展过程以及贝叶经的具体制作流程。同时在此基础上，从历史源流、文化内涵、艺术价值三个角度详细阐述了南传上座部佛教与贝叶经之间的关系：南传上座部佛教不但是贝叶经生存和发展的基础，而且构成了贝叶经丰富的文化底蕴和内涵，同时贝叶经本身也彰显了丰富的佛教艺术特色和价值，并认为贝叶经和南传上座部佛教之间是一种相辅相成、紧密联系的关系。

综上所述，本次会议是近年来在巴利语系贝叶经和贝叶文化研究领域举办的规模较大、辐射面较广、影响力较高的国际学术交流活动。会议召集了在中国—东南亚、南亚贝叶经与贝叶文化传承、保护及研究方面的多位卓有成就的专家学者以及来自贝叶文化传承与保护一线的实践者们，共同为如何更好地将贝叶文化这一古老而珍贵的文化活态遗产传承和保护下去这一核心议题进行了深入而富有成效的交流。对贝叶文化进行研究与保护合作，对于支撑云南大学面向南亚、东南亚建设世界一流高校，以及为中国"一带一路"倡议提供面向南亚、东南亚地区的文化着力点，促进区域内各国间文化交流与合作，有着重要的现实意义和价值。

——— 贝叶文化与区域文化遗产传承保护

会议总结及闭幕致辞

周　娅

各位会议代表，各位来宾，老师们、同学们：

大家好！

愉快的时光总是那么匆匆！经过短短一天半的时间，来自斯里兰卡、泰国、老挝、德国、英国及中国的学者相聚在云南大学东陆园中，为"中国—东南亚、南亚贝叶文化传承与保护"这个重要的人文社会科学议题，做了深入的探讨与交流。

首先，我想代表会议的主办方：云南大学发展研究院、云南大学贝叶文化研究中心以及泰国清迈皇家大学文化与艺术办公室，向不远数千里而来的各位国际友人和省外代表，致以衷心的感谢！对省内各兄弟院校、合作单位的同行，尤其是来自咱们西双版纳、德宏等地州市的同仁们，表示诚挚的谢意！感谢各位代表和嘉宾长期以来对我们贝叶文化传承、保护与研究工作所给予的支持和帮助。谢谢大家！

刚才，我们贝叶中心的合作单位——泰国清迈皇家大学贝叶经中心的主任 Dr. Direk Injan 博士已经对会议做了很好的点评总结。那么在会议闭幕之前，我也还想借此机会，再谈一点儿对这次会议的体会，作为对咱们会议的一点总结补充。

这次会议的成功举办，是在云南大学不断扩大对外学术交流与合作、不断提升国际化水平以及学校"双一流"大学建设相关工作的推动下所取得的一个成绩。2018 年 12 月，我们正是在对泰国清迈大学、清迈皇家大学等高校进行贝叶经和贝叶文化国际学术合作的过程中，形成了合作举办 2019 年这次会议的想法。所以从某种意义上说，这次会议也是我们贝叶文化研究的一次国际合作创新。但同时，这次会议也是对我们贝叶中心，历史上两次"贝叶文化国际研讨会"的传统的一种继承与延续。早在 2010 年和 2012 年，我们便分别在西双版纳和清迈两地，进行了两次国际研讨会，对贝叶经和贝叶文化进行国际交流与研究，也取得了一些实际的成效，推动了中泰双边在这个议题上的学术合作与地方贝叶文化的传承保护实践。

通过举办这样的学术交流活动，我们一边推动了从民间，到地方，到学术机构，到政府层面的对贝叶文化的进一步重视，一边我们也庆幸地交到了许多国际学界志同道合的好朋友。

比如刚才总结发言的 Dr. Derik Injan，以及他所在的贝叶经中心和 CMRU 文化与艺术办公室，长期致力于泰国北部兰那古文献的收集整理，以及贝叶经的传承与保护实践，为泰国的贝叶经传承与保护工作，包括保护技能培训、展览、贝叶经的数字化整理等方面做了大量实际工作。

又比如来自英国，在德国帕绍大学获得博士学位，却在老挝一待就是十多年的 Dr. David Wharton，他本人不仅会泰语、老挝语，而且他和他的导师，也是我们的老朋友——德国帕绍大学教授 Prof. Handius 一起，为老挝全国的贝叶经数字化保护提供技术指导与支持，并与老挝国家图书馆合作，建成了"老挝贝叶经数字图书馆"，为国内外读者提供数以万计的贝叶经数字化高清图片系统查询和元数据（meta-data）检索网络服务，为老挝的文化遗产保护做了重要的贡献。他本人至今仍致力于此，可谓"乐此不疲"地将他自己的大量精力贡献给东南亚国家的傣泰掸老族群及其抄本文化，他的学术研究覆盖老挝、缅甸、泰国、中国云南等地，这样的成就和学术专注力值得我们尊敬和学习！明天上午，我们还有 David 的精彩学术报告，希望大家都能来参加。

再比如我们贝叶中心的老朋友，这次遗憾因为他们学院主办一个重要学术会议而缺席了我们这个会议的德国汉堡大学的 Prof. Volker Grabowsky 教授。虽然他本人不能前来参会，但他的数位弟子，在座的来自泰国清迈大学的 Dr. Apiradee，周寒丽博士以及年轻的 Sutheera，都是正在傣泰族群历史文化以及贝叶经和抄本文化研究领域耕耘的青年学者，这既说明贝叶经与贝叶文化的研究在国际上有着重要的研究意义和价值，也说明该领域的研究常做常新，其学术生命力常青！

还有去年我们郭山院长带团访问斯里兰卡科伦坡大学而建立起学术交流与合作的科伦坡大学的相关研究机构和学者专家，包括 Dean & Prof. Premakumara de Silva，Ven. & Prof. Dhammajothi Thero 大长老以及年轻的毕业于我们武汉大学的 Dr. Wimal，他们的加入，提升了我们在中国—东南亚、南亚贝叶文化传承与保护方面的研究工作与南亚区域国家的国际交流与区域合作。我们也期待在不远的将来，与科伦坡大学在贝叶经与贝叶文化传承与保护研究方面的国际学术合作与交流工作取得突破与进展。期待下一步的合作。

我们昨天和今天发言的，除了很多作为贝叶文化相关领域的研究者、喜爱者和积极推动者以外，有很大一部分来自贝叶文化覆盖区域本土的中青年学者，其中的大多数就是傣泰民族，你们是贝叶文化传承与保护的最重要的资源"人"，你们是贝叶文化最不可替代的本土实践者、文化持有者、继承者、守护人，贝叶文化这一活态文化的生命常青，你们任重道远！

我们这两天的学术交流，涉及以下重要议题：

贝叶棕在自然环境中的种植保护，贝叶经经典文献抄本的传承与保护在各个相关国家的具体情况，贝叶经和贝叶文化历史、语言文字、识读和翻译、文学、艺术、社会习俗、信仰、刻写制作技艺、经济运用、传统医学价值、生态价值和观念、族际参与、传承困境、影像的网络的数字化等技术方面的抢救保护实践经验，以及对上述具体议题的相关观察、记录、认知、以跨国和不同地区之间的比较观察和研究，等等。

通过我们大家对上述重要议题方面的交流，我们形成了一些共识，同时更清晰地认知到：贝叶文化虽然具有活态文化资源价值，但它的遗产特质也十分明显，尤其它在现代社会背景下，承载贝叶文化的贝叶文献和纸质抄本在其形制、抢救保护等方面，都有着明显的濒危性和紧迫性；贝叶文化广博的文化意蕴和思想价值的现代继承与运用，也有待进一步地提升。所以需要我们从各个方面更多地积极推动和持续致力于对贝叶经和贝叶文化的传承与保护。

在这些思想的交流与碰撞中，我们有对于贝叶文化这项丰富的人文资源与人类文化遗产的深切热爱，也有对于它传承与保护现状的呈现与担忧；既有对它丰富内涵与文化外延的精彩学术交流与探讨，也有对如何继承和保护好这一珍贵文化资源的理性分析、建议与思考。

此外，大家也更加清晰地认识到，贝叶文化为人类保留了丰富的人文资源与共同记忆、族群智慧和地方知识，既有地域性、地方性、族群性等特征，更有跨族群、跨区域、跨时代的共同性和更高层面的价值——那就是对人类文明的记录、记忆、传播和传承。虽然我们现在对此所做的工作还十分有限，但是我们正在凝聚共识，也进一步知悉，我们要更加珍视和传承与保护好这份珍贵的人类文化遗产，要更加重视地方实践、民间力量和人才培养，要加强跨区域、跨国的国际合作。今后，我们如何保有贝叶文化的生命力，让它一直焕发既有神圣意蕴，又有现实的世俗光华与神采，在保护与传承中不断历久弥新，这是我们今后仍将继续不懈研究与实践的重要议题。

我想，我们这次的会议是务实的，切要的，更是内容丰富而意义深远的！

为期两天的"中国—东南亚、南亚贝叶文化传承与保护国际研讨会"即将闭幕。我们要感谢两位同声传译老师，他们一位是来自云南大学外国语学院的刘学军教授，一位是来自云南师范大学的刘德州教授，两位老师通过他们的辛勤而专业的工作，为会议提供了非常专业、精准的语言翻译支持，请大家一起向两位老师鼓掌致意！还要感谢我们的音响师王老师，还有我们各位年轻的来自云南大学发展研究院、云南大学民族学与社会学学院的各位会务组成员，他们都是非常优秀的硕士研究生，他们为保证会议顺利进行做了大量的前期准备工作和会议期间的会务工作，感谢他们！

最后，我再次代表主办单位，向在座所有参会代表、各位学者专家，以及来旁听我们研讨会的各位老师、同学对会议的参与和支持，表示由衷的感谢。希望我们大家能在不久的将来，可再在某时、某地一起聚首，分享我们对贝叶经和贝叶文化传承与保护的最新研究与实践成果。让我们期待那一时刻的早日到来。

也让我们一起成为贝叶文化的守护者和守望人！

谢谢！

Explorations of Lao Manuscript Culture: The Case of the Vat Maha That Collection

Volker Grabowsky[①]　Khamvone Boulyaphonh[②]

Vat Maha That Rasabòvòravihan or Vat Maha That, the "Monastery of the Great Stupa" is well known for its "Great Stupa" or "Pha Maha That"［the Great Stupa was built at the same time as the temple hall（sim）in 1548］. However, many locals call the monastery simply Vat That（"Monastery of the Stupa"）or, even more remarkably, Vat That Nòi（"Monastery of the Small Stupa"）, reflecting the fact that larger stupas were erected later at other monasteries in Luang Prabang, such as at Vat Xiang Thòng. Vat Maha That is located on a lower slope on Fa Ngum Road in the centre of the former royal capital and centre of Lao Buddhism. The town quarter attached to the monastery is called Ban Vat That. In the past, Vat Maha That was the main monastery of the group of monasteries situated in the lower（southern）part of Luang Prabang, the so-called *khana tai*（southern group）. Its location is also called *than müang*（the base of the city）. In 2017, three monks and twelve novices had ordained at Vat Maha That under the supervision of the abbot, Venerable Pha Vandi Vannatharo. The monastery is the focal point of the most important and impressive Lao New Year Festival, which is held every year in mid-April. Thus, Vat Maha That plays a crucial role in preserving an ancient tradition as part of Luang Prabang's Buddhist heritage. During the Lao New Year Festival, the famous *hae vò*（palanquin procession）starts at Vat Maha That in the south and follows the main road through the city centre, ending finally at Vat Xiang Thòng near the confluence of the Mekong and Khan rivers. In the procession, the most senior monk sits on a *vò*（palanquin）carried by strong men. Young monks, novices, younger girls in traditional dress and lay people also participate in the procession. On the way, lay people splash water over the monks and novices. This tradition exists only in Luang Prabang. However, the character of the procession has significantly changed and it has become intermixed with other processions, for instance, the procession of Miss New

---

[①] Doctor and Professor of Asia-Africa Institute, University of Hamburg.
[②] Doctor of Buddhist Archives of Luang Prabang.

Year (Lao: *nang sangkhan*). Thus, the original meaning of the *hae vò* has changed in terms of its significance, and monks and novices do not play the same central role as they did in former times[①].

The monastery was founded by King Say Setthathirat in 1548 and since then has been renovated and restored many times. During the twentieth century, Vat Maha That was regarded as the temple of the viceroy, the lord of the front palace (*Vang Na*), and his family. Thus, it was a monastery under royal patronage. At present, many buildings in this monastery have been registered by the UNESCO as part of the architectural heritage of Luang Prabang. Such constructions include, besides the Great Stupa itself, the temple hall (*sim*) and the three monk's abodes (*kuti*) in the lower part of the temple compound. Therefore, the structures and materials of these buildings are well preserved. Like every monastery in Buddhist Luang Prabang, Vat Maha That is an important intersection between the monastic community of monks and novices (the Sangha) and the community of lay-people in the surrounding town who support the Sangha with the necessities of life. The monastery is the centre of numerous community activities, such as religious rituals and festivals, social events, and lessons.

1. Introduction

In February 2017, the research team of the manuscript project of the Buddhist Archives of Luang Prabang visited the monastic library of Vat Maha That to examine the manuscripts. Though the team found most of the manuscripts to still be in good physical condition, in a number of boxes the manuscripts were already damaged by insects, some of them severely, and many manuscripts were not arranged properly. Moreover, most manuscripts do not have any inventory numbers, indicating that they had not been inventoried by the Preservation of Lao Manuscripts Programme run by the National Library and supported by the German Foreign Ministry in the 1990s, probably because these manuscripts were kept in the abbot's abode (*kuti*) and used exclusively by Sathu Nyai Phui Thirachitta Maha Thela during his lifetime.

Later, we learned from Lung Bunthan Philaphuangphet, the monastic master (*kwan vat*) of Vat Maha That, that these manuscripts had been kept in the abbot's *kuti* for years and, in 2015, were moved to the present library, where they are kept until the present. We realized that the whole corpus of manuscripts would eventually become endangered due to the particular situation of that monastery, which was characterized by the frequent

---

① For more information about the Lao New Year Festival: Pierre S Nginn. New Year Festival (Fifth Month Festival) // René de Berval. Kingdom of Laos. Saigon: France-Asia, 1959: 268–271; Hans Georg Berger. Het Bun Dai Bun: Laos-Sacred Rituals of Luang Prabang. London: Westzone, 2000: (no page number); Arne Kislenko. Culture and Customs of Laos. London: Greenwood Press, 2009: 147–150.

changes of abbots in recent decades as well as a lack of responsible individuals capable of safeguarding the collection. So far, the manuscripts have been kept in the monastic library, which is usually closed and without regular care. It is likely that insects (such as termites) will damage the manuscripts, as this happens in many of the monasteries of Luang Prabang. In the future, there is no guarantee that the manuscripts will be kept in this building. Therefore, we consider the manuscripts to be highly endangered.

For this reason, the Buddhist Archives decided to ask for permission from the monastery to bring the whole corpus of manuscripts to our Buddhist Archives at Sala Thammavihan in Vat Suvannakhili on January 18th, 2018. There we started to preserve and digitize the manuscripts with modest financial support from the Centre for the Studies of Manuscript Cultures (CSMC), University of Hamburg, until the end of August 2018. Due to time constraints we managed to conclude the inventory and digitization of only one-third of the whole corpus by August 31st, 2018. Later on, the preservation and digitization project was continued with the financial support of the Digital Repository of the Endangered and Affected Manuscripts in Southeast Asia (DREAMSEA) from September 2018 to June 2019. During the two parts of the project, a total of 3,467 documents were registered, which were either written by hand or typed in various scripts, mainly in Tham Lao, Old Lao, modern Lao, and Thai. The 1,541 manuscripts written in Tham Lao and Old Lao scripts were selected for digitization. At present, all the original manuscripts are kept at the monastic library in Vat Mata That, while the digital images of those digitized manuscripts are kept in different institutes and displayed on the DREAMSEA website[①].

2. The Manuscript Collection of Vat Maha That

Lao village communities as well as town quarters usually have a *vat* (ວັດ) as its cultural and spiritual centre. The *vat* is a Buddhist temple-monastery which is not only the place for the Sangha (the community of monks and novices) to live and meditate, but also a place for lay people to come together for festival celebrations, to take part in religious rituals, to search for spiritual experiences, and to seek the advice of highly respected monks in more worldly matters. The *vat* is a place where the Sangha and the laity come together to participate in mutually rewarding and meritorious activities. Besides that, the *vat* is an educational centre, which offers the teaching of the Dhamma, the fundamental truths revealed by the Buddha, as well as secular sciences[②]. In other words, it is a repository

---

① https://www.hmmlcloud.org/dreamsea/manuscripts.php?country=&tags=&city=&author=&library=&language=&projnum=0011&writingSupport=&title=&script=&searchType=1.

② The Lao temple-monastery (*vat*) as a social space and the interaction between Sangha and laity in the Lao context are discussed in Hayashi 2003: 101-111. See also Holt 2009 and Bounleuth 2016.

of traditional knowledge. It is at the very core of every Lao village community. While a *vat* determines the identity of a community, the members of that community have the obligation to maintain the *vat*.

The idea of a *vat* is still present in the mindset of the lay community, even when a village has no *vat*. This is evident from the requirement of the monks' presence in the performance of ritual ceremonies. In this case, it is necessary to invite monks from the *vat* of a neighbouring village. A religious ritual without the presence of monks and novices can hardly be imagined. In fact, the mere presence of the Sangha members adds a sacred meaning to non-religious ceremonies, such as a housewarming party, the inauguration of a hospital, or a wedding[①].

3. Variety of Genres and Themes

The manuscripts discovered and documented at the monastery of Vat Maha That are all written on palm-leaf, apart from less than a dozen paper manuscripts. The vast majority of these palm-leaf manuscripts contain one single text running over one palm-leaf fascicle, although others contain more than one, and some even run up to ten fascicles. However, many of the multi-fascicle manuscripts are not complete and have one or more missing fascicles. A number of manuscripts comprised of a single fascicle may have originally been part of a larger multi-fascicle manuscript, with the remaining fascicles having been lost. Some manuscripts are complete and in good physical condition while others are lightly or severely damaged with parts of the text missing.

In the 1990s, the Preservation of Lao Manuscripts Programme (PLMP) divided thousands of texts—86,000 texts written on 368,000 fascicles, of which about 12,337 texts are currently available for online research-into twenty categories (see http://www.laomanuscripts.net). Of these, the last two categories ("miscellaneous" *lai muat* and "undetermined" *bò dai cat muat*) are remarkable because they illustrate a peculiar feature of Lao manuscripts: specifically that some manuscripts, palm-leaf and paper manuscripts, contain various texts. Whereas the personal collection of manuscripts kept by Pha Khamchan Virachitto in his living quarters contained a high percentage of such multiple-text manuscripts, in particular among the mulberry paper folding books, they are rare in the Vat Xiang Thòng collection. Several secular or non-religious texts do not appear in any of the manuscripts from this collection, for example: customary law texts, philological and astrological treatises, and the wide field of secular literature, apart from a few folk

---

① This "Buddhization" of formerly non-Buddhist rites and rituals is best reflected in *Anisong* texts, which are generally known under the terms *Salòng* or *Sòng* in Lao. For a detailed analysis of *Anisong* manuscripts in a Lao cultural environment, based on the Pha Khamchan Virachitto's personal collection, see Bounleuth 2015a.

tales (*nithan* นิทาน). Texts related to white magic (*sainyasat* ไสยศาสตร์) and rites and rituals (*phithikam* พิธีกรรม) are as rare as medical treatises (*tamla ya* ตำฉลฯๆ ตำราขา). The collection contains several dozen chronicles; almost all of them have to be classified as "Buddhist chronicles" (*tamnan phutthasatsana* ตำนานพุทธศาสนา).

A significant number of manuscript-fascicles (414) contain texts from the Pali canon and thus can be classified as belonging to the categories of Vinaya, Suttanta or Abhidhamma. Of almost equal importance are the popular Jataka stories, dealing with the previous lives of the Buddha, representing one-fifth of the manuscripts of the Vat Xiang Thòng corpus. Besides the Jataka tales (398 manuscript-fascicles), *Anisong* (Pali: *ānisaṃsa*) texts (300 manuscript-fascicles) are featured most prominently in the Vat Xiang Thòng collection of manuscripts[①]. *Anisong* texts are generally known under the terms *Salòng* or *Sòng* in Lao. These popular texts, inscribed mostly on palm-leaf, mulberry paper and other kinds of paper, are used for performing sermons or preaching. These short homiletic texts, which rarely contain more than twenty folios, are about the rewards of merit or literally the "advantage" which a believer may expect to receive from performing a particular religious deed.

Table 1　Distribution of Texts of the Vat Maha That Collection According to Genres

Genre	ໝວດ	หมวด	No. of Fascicles	% of Total
General Buddhism	ທຳມະທີ່ວໄປ	ธรรมะทั่วไป	—	—
Vinaya Rules	ພະວິໄນ	พระวินัย	97	6.3
Suttanta Doctrine	ພະສູດ	พระสูตร	289	18.8
Abhidhamma Doctrine	ພະອະພິທຳ	พระอภิธรรม	28	1.8
Buddhist Tales	ນິຍາຍທຳມະ	นิยายธรรมะ	52	3.4
Jataka Tales	ຊາດົກ	ชาดก	398	25.8
Prayers	ບົດສູດມົນ	บทสวดมนต์	80	5.2
Anisong (Blessings)	ອານິສົງ	อานิสงส์	300	19.5
Rites and Rituals	ພິທີກຳ	พิธีกรรม	3	0.2
Monolingual Pali	ຄຳພິບາລີ	คัมภีร์บาลี	47	3.0
Buddhist Chronicles	ຕຳນານພຸດທະສາສະໜາ	ตำนานพุทธศาสนา	99	6.4
Secular Chronicles	ຕຳນານເມືອງ	ตำนานเมือง	25	1.6
Customary Law	ກົດໝາຍ	กฎหมาย	—	—

---

① As Arthid Sheravanichkul (2009 and 2010) has shown in his seminal study of gift-giving in the Thai and Lao world, the kind of gifts recommended in *Anisong* texts pertain to (a) giving alms to the Sangha (food and medicine, robes and cloth, ritual offerings such as flowers and lamps, sponsoring the construction of temple buildings, copying of religious texts); (b) producing objects of worship (images, stupas); (c) constructing public works (bridges, roads, hospitals, schools) and (d) giving gifts in ceremonies or festivals (celebrating a new house, funerals, the Buddhist New Year, etc.). The manuscripts of Pha Khamchan Virachitto's collections containing *Anisong* are analysed in Bounleuth 2015b and Bounleuth 2016: 130–136.

(Continued)

Genre	ໝວດ	หมวด	No. of Fascicles	% of Total
Didactics	ຄຳສອນ	คำสอน	61	4.0
Medical Treatises	ຕຳລາຢາ	ตำรายา	3	0.2
White Magic	ໄສຍະສາດ	ไสยศาสตร์	7	0.5
Folktales	ນິທານ	นิทาน	—	—
(Secular) Literature	ວັນນະຄະດີ	วรรณคดี	43	2.8
Proverbs	ຄຳສຸພາສິດ	คำสุภาษิต	1	0.1
Astrology	ໂຫຼາສາດ	โหราศาสตร์	5	0.3
Miscellaneous	ຫຼາຍໝວດ	หลายหมวด	—	—
Unclassified	ບໍ່ຈັດໝວດໃຫ້	บ่จัดหมวดให้	—	—
Total	ລວມທັງໝົດ	รวมทั้งหมด	1541	100

The large number of Jataka texts written on palm-leaf manuscripts is not surprising (See Table 1). This suggests that the Jataka stories, dealing with the previous lives of the Buddha, are not only well known to the Lao people of Luang Prabang, but also very popular. Among the many Jataka stories, the Vessantara Jataka is the most popular one. It tells the story of one of the Buddha's lives immediately before he was born as Sidhartha Gotama. The story is about the compassionate Prince Vessantara, who gives away everything he owns, including his children, thereby displaying the virtue of perfect generosity or *dana*. It is also known as the *Thet Mahasat* (Great Birth Sermon), familiar to Lao Buddhists under the name *Phavet* or *Phavetsandòn*. *Phavet* is also the name of a traditional festival, Bun Phavet, which is held sometime around the fourth lunar month of every year. The festival lasts two or three days, with the story of Prince Vessantara being recited all day on the final day of the festivities. The Jataka story, composed in verse form and comprising thirteen chapters or *kan* (ກັນຯ), is chanted aloud by monks and novices with years of experience preaching all of the chapters. The text combines Pali words and phrases with the respective Lao translation[①]. According to the tradition, three of them—Himmaphan, Thanakhan, Kumman—are usually divided into two volumes. As a consequence of this subdivision, the story of Prince Vessantara is composed and written on sixteen fascicles of palm leaves. However, many of the Jataka manuscripts from the Vat Si Bun Hüang collection comprise only one of the thirteen *kan*, not the complete text.

4. The Colophons

Colophons reveal a lot more about the background of the manuscripts, its production,

---

[①] The Vessantara Jataka, known among Lao Buddhists as *Phavet* or *Phavetsandòn*, is the last story of the Jataka, which is a series of 547 canonical tales recounting the past lives of the Buddha. See Bounleuth 2016: 110.

purpose and usage. Colophons appear at the end of the manuscript. They either directly follow the main text from which it is separated by a blank line or by smaller-sized letters (as in the last example), or they appear on the recto side of an additional folio. As Hundius (1990) indicates in his definition, the Tai-Lao manuscript tradition lacks a clear distinction between the writer or author of a manuscript and the copyist. Lao manuscripts usually use the terms *phu taem*, *phu khian*, *phu or phu litchana*[①] for denoting the scribe who would call himself *kha* ["serf (of the Buddha)"]. Besides, a number of colophons also mention a *phu sang*, literally the "maker" of a manuscript.

Some colophons of our corpus are scribal colophons (119 manuscripts). The vast majority of manuscripts with colophons (815), however, express the wishes of their sponsors and donors; 555 manuscripts or 45 percent of the total, do not have colophons at all and are almost all undated. While rather few manuscripts have colophons that are exclusively scribal, many more record the names of both the scribe and the persons who sponsored the making of the manuscript and donated it to the Sangha. In general, the intentions for making the donation and the wishes expressed in the colophons pertain to the principal monastic or lay supporters and the religious faithful (*mūlasaddhā*) who took the initiative of making the production of the manuscript possible (see Hinüber 2013).

The three wishes that seem evenly distributed over all periods are that the writing of the manuscript will eventually lead to *nibbāna* ("the splendid city, the peak of *nibbāna*"), that it will lead to obtaining merit (*puñña*) or rewards of merit (*phala ānisaṃsa*) either for the writer, the sponsor and donor, his family or other people, and that the copying of the manuscript and/or its sponsoring and donation to the Sangha will support (*kamchu*) the Teachings of Buddha (*sāsana*) to last for 5,000 years, counted from Buddha's entering of the *parinibbāna* (see Veidlinger 2006: 164-165). This basic purpose is grounded in the widespread belief among the Tai and Lao that the complete degeneration of the Buddha's Teachings will be reached after 5,000 years. Whereas the intention of the sponsor and donor to extend the lifespan of Buddhism is expressed as a standard phrase in almost all of the longer colophons, and even in most of the rather short ones, the wish to be reborn in the age of Buddha Metteyya (Ariya Maitreya) is reflected in a rather large number of colophons (altogether 17). This wish is expressed in different phrases. They are mostly written in the Lao vernacular (13 colophons), while four are in Pali. Some colophons just express the donor's wish to be reborn in the age of Buddha Metteyya and to meet him in person and ordain as a monk to become his disciple, as is expressed in the following example:

---

① From Pali: *likhita*, "written" "inscribed".

• May I reach the crystal city which is Nirvāna and may I be ordained at the residence (*samnak*) of Pha Ariya Metteyya (Maitreya), who will emerge in the world in the future. May this not be ignored. (ขอให้ผู้ข้าได้ถึงเวียงแก้วนิรพาน และได้บวชในสำนักพระแก้วองค์ชื่อว่าอริยเมตไตรย อันจักมาภายหน้า อย่า คลาดอย่า คลา) [BAD-22-1-0578, a *kot set* year but no year of an era given]

Others add the wish that the donor will also get the chance to enter the path (*magga*) towards enlightenment as an *arahant* through the teachings of Buddha Metteyya. This is expressed in the following examples:

• May the power of this merit support the sponsor of this manuscript to meet Pha Metteyya (Maitreya) who will emerge in the world in the future. May the power of this merit destin me to attain enlightenment in the institution of Pha Ariya Metteyya. After having finished reading, may I, the sponsor, attain Nirvana definitely. (ขออำนาจกุศลส่วนนี้จ งนำเอาตัวผู้สร้างธรรมส่วนนี้ ให้ได้พบพระ เมตไตรยองค์จักลงมาอุบัติในโลกภายหน้า ชอเดชะกุศลจงดลบันดาลให้ผู้ข้า ได้บรรลุอุดมธรรมในสำนักพระศรี [อริยเมตไตรย]) [BAD-23-1-0629, dated 23 April 1963]

• *Ariya mettaya santike anāgate arahanta magga. Nibbāna paccayo hotu me niccaṃ dhuvaṃ* (May I enlighten as Arahanta and achieve the Magga in the age of Ariya Metteyya. May this be a condition for me to reach Nirvāna). (ขอให้ผู้ข้าได้ถึงอรหันตมรรคญาณในสำนักพระศรีอริยเมตไตรยเจ้า อย่าคลาดอย่าเคลิ้ว ก็ข้าเทอญ นิพุพาน ปจุจโย โหตุ เม นิจจํ ธุวํ) [BAD-22-1-1154, dated 29 March 1826]

• *Anāgate metteyyo santike bhave pabbajetu daramānopi sattayo desetuṃ anukampāya* [In the future (let me) exist in the presence of Metteyya who (comes) with compassion to teach the suffering beings to ordain]. (อนาคเต เมตุเตยโย สนุติเก เภว ปพุพาเชตุ ทรมาโนปิ สตุตโย เทเสตุง อนุกมุปาย) [BAD-22-1-0282, dated 16 July 1766]

• *Iminā nussara sadhā nena yathayathabhave jāto tikkhapañño mātharitho surūpopātha saniyaṃ mathurasaro niyalo nuttasabbasampattinaṃ arahantā arahantī maggañānaṃ ariya mettayya santike anāgate kāle niccaṃ dhuvaṃ* [Remembering faith in such a manner, (let me) exist as someone endowed with sharp wisdom (...) obtaining constantly the greatest pleasure of Arahatship, the wisdom of the paths (*maggañānaṃ*), as an Arahat in the presence of the venerable Buddha Metteyya, forever in the future]. (อิมินา นุสุสร สธาเนน ยถ ยถ ภเว ชาโต ติกฺขปญุโญ มาถริโถ สุรูโปปาฐ สนิยํ มธุรสโร นิยโล นุตฺตสพฺพสมฺปตฺตินํ อรหนฺตา อรหนฺตี มคฺคญาณี อริย เมตุเตยย สนุติเก อนาคเต กาเล นิจฺจํ ธุวํ) [BAD-22-1-1082, dated 26 November 1938]

Colophons generally appear at the end of the main text, following it either directly or separated from it by a blank line. In quite a large number of cases, colophons, especially the lengthier ones, are written on a separate folio, sometimes in smaller letters and covering only the central parts of a folio. Colophons in manuscripts of religious content commissioned by sponsors to be donated to a monastery are highly formulized since they follow a similar pattern that is characteristic of Buddhist colophons from Laos and other areas of the Dhamma script cultural domain, including Northern Thailand (Lan Na), the Tai

Khün area of Chiang Tung and the Tai Lü speaking regions in southern Yunnan. Colophons usually provide information about the date that the manuscript was finished, while the date when the scribe started writing is rarely recorded. Thereafter, the scribe's name might follow, especially when the scribe is also the sponsor of the manuscript. However, in general it would be the names of the leading monastic or lay supporters (*mūlasaddhā*) that would feature prominently in the second section of the colophon, sometimes mentioning the copied text. Thereafter the *mūlasaddhā*, oftentimes a lay couple representing their extended family, would express the main objective of the donation of the manuscript, i.e., to ensure that the Teachings of the Buddha (*phuttha-satsana*) last until the end of 5,000 years. Other colophons are relatively long and may even run over more than one side of a palm leaf. Apart from the dating, the recording of the names of the scribe and principal sponsor, the mention of the motives and intentions for making the manuscript, the aspirations a scribe or sponsor/donor had for the good results of the acquired merit, some of the longer colophons also contain some personal expression, including biographical details. The concluding Pali phrase is optional and, in most cases, rather short. The structure of such colophons is analyzed in Table 2, discussing two samples which are from different periods and whose sponsors/donors came from different social backgrounds.

Table 2 Contents of Colophons

		BAD-22-1-0616	BAD-22-1-0839
	Era	BE 2491	CS 1220
Lunar Calendar	Year	*poek chai* (Year of the Rat)	*poek sagna* (Year of the Horse)
	Month	first lunar month	first lunar month
	Fortnight	fourth waning day	fourth waning day
	Day of the Week	sixth day of the week (Friday)	sixth day of the week (Friday)
	Zodiac Day	*poek si*	*huang mao*
	Corresponding to	AD 1914, June 11, Thursday	AD 1958, December 24, Friday
Time		*nyam kham* (time of the late evening drum, 16:30-18:00)	*nyam kòng doek* (time of the late evening drum, 19:30-21:00)
Initiator	Scribe	Saen Kumphon (at Ban Phon Sai)	—
	Sponsor/Donor	Saen Kumphon (at Ban Phon Sai)	Thit (ex-monk) Kaeo Sao (Ms.) Sopha I (Ms.) Pheng together with all of their male and female servants
	Title	*Thamma Rattana Sut* (Sutta Text)	*Lam Sut* (Sutta Text)

(Continued)

	BAD-22-1-0616	BAD-22-1-0839
Objective	To ensure that the good results of the benefits (*phala-ānisaṃsa*) derived from the making of the manuscript support the sponsor's father, Chan Suk, and his mother, Sao Nyathi, as well as several other relatives	To ensure the continuation of the Teachings of the Buddha until the end of five thousand years
Wish	As for myself, may I attain enlightenment and become one of the teachers of the world (i.e., the Buddha) in the future. Before I attain enlightenment as I am still moving in *samsāra* (cycle of rebirth), in any of my rebirth, may I be purified physically, mentally and with regard to my speaking, more than other human being. May I be saved from all kinds of diseases and dangers until I attain enlightenment as an omniscient person in the future	May all of us reach the three states of happiness with Nirvāna as the ultimate goal. May our wishes not be ignored. May all our wishes come true
Concluding Phrase (in Pali)	—	*Idaṃ dhammadānaṃ nibbāna paccayo hontu* (May my dhamma-gift be a condition to reach Nibbāna)

One of the most interesting colophons concerning the wishes and aspirations of a sponsor/donor is recorded in the relatively long colophon of manuscript BAD-22-1-0375, titled *Paet Mün*[①]. The principal initiator and the main sponsor of this manuscript was Pha Phui Thirachitta Maha Thera, the abbot of Vat Maha That, who dedicated it to his deceased parents, sibling, teachers and old friends who had already passed away. Thus, the benefits derived from the meritorious donation should affect an improvement of their actual state in the otherworld and pave their way to "the realm of heaven" (*sawan*). At the same time, the fruits of the merit should also help the donor, a high-ranking abbot, to achieve his ultimate goal: the successful attainment of Nibbāna. The manuscript is dated both according to the traditional style (see chapter above) and according to the international calendar: April 26th, 1983. The manuscript comprises three palm-leaf fascicles, each of which having colophons with identical wording (fascicle 1, f° 17 r-v; fascicle 2, f° 16 r-v; fascicle 3, f° 15 r-v). Its wording is quoted in full:

[①] *Paet Mün* means literally "Eighty Thousand" and is a short form of *Paet Mün Si Phan* ("Eighty-four Thousand") referring to the 84,000 Dhamma-Khaṇḍa (Dhamma Teachings), which is the traditional Theravada description of the complete Tipitaka canon.

ผูกต้น ลานที่ ๑๗ หน้า ๑-๒: คำนำของผู้สร้าง: วันอังคาร ขึ้น ๑๕ ค่ำ เดือน ๖ ปีกาไค้ (กุน) พ.ศ. ๒๕๒๖, จ.ศ. ๑๓๔๕ ตรงกับวันที่ ๒๖ เมษายน ค.ศ. ๑๙๘๓ หมายมีพระผุย ถิระจิตโต วัดพระมหาธาตุ ราชบวรวิหาร นครหลวงพระบาง ได้มีจิตศรัทธาสร้างหนังสือ ๘ หมื่น ผูก ๒ นี้ไว้กับพระพุทธศาสนา เพื่อถวายไว้เป็นศาสน สมบัติประจำวัดพระมหาธาตุ ราชบวรวิหาร นครหลวงพระบาง ขออุทิศกุศลแห่งธรรมทานนี้ไปให้แก่ผู้มีคุณทั้ง หลาย มีบิดามารดา ญาติกา ครูอุปัชฌา อาจารย์ และสรรพสัตว์ทั้งหลาย ผู้ล่วงลับไปสู่ปรโลกอันหาประมาณบ่ได้ อันเป็นเพื่อนเกิดแก่เจ็บตาย อันหาประมาณ บ่ได้ ถ้าหากทราบด้วยญาณวิธีใดแล้ว ของได้อนุโมทนา เพื่อสำเร็จ ประโยชน์สุขในคติภพนั้นเทอญ อีกประการหนึ่ง ขอผลนิสงส์แห่งธรรมทานนี้ จงเป็นอนุคามินีติดตามข้าพเจ้า ไปสัมปรายภพ ขอให้ได้ประสบมนุษยสมบัติ สวรรค์ สมบัติ และนิพพานสมบัติ ในอนาคตกาลด้วยเทอญ อิชฺชิตํ ปตฺถิตํ มยฺหํ ขิปฺปเมว สมิชฺฌตุ นิจฺจํ ธุวํ

Fascicle 1, folio 17 on the recto and verso sides: The sponsor's introduction is as follows. On Tuesday, the fifteenth waxing day of the sixth lunar month, a *kakhai* (kun) year, 2526 BE, 1345 CS corresponding to April 26th, 1983[①], Pha Phui Thirachitta Maha Thera, the abbot of Vat Pha Maha That Rasabòvòravihan in Luang Prabang had the religious faith to sponsor the making of the manuscript entitled 8 Mün, fascicle 2 to support the Teachings of the Buddha, for the property of Vat Pha Maha That Rasabòvòravihan in Luang Prabang. May I dedicate the benefits of this merit to all benefactors, including my parents, siblings, teachers and all other living creatures that were friends in birth, age, illness and death and have already died and stayed in the other worlds. If they acknowledge my dedication, they may rejoice and achieve blissful benefits in their worlds. Moreover, may the benefit of this merit support me to enter the realm of heaven. May I achieve human prosperity, heavenly prosperity and the successful attainment of Nirvāna in the future. May whatever I wish quickly come to be, may all my aspirations be fulfilled, constantly and certainly.

The relatively rigid structure of the Lao Buddhist colophon nevertheless leaves space for more personal expressions of the scribe who would add them either in a shorter colophon which is separated from the main (sponors's/donors's) colophon or as a final sentence being part of the main colophon. In the personal statements of scribes, we frequently find humble excuses of bad handwriting and misspellings, even by properly trained and experienced scribes. A striking example is the scribal colophon appearing at the end of the last of twenty fascicles of the manuscript entitled *Matthu Anulom* and dated August 29th,

---

① The corresponding date of the Gregorian calendar has been accurately calculated by the scribe.

1923. The scribe, ex-monk Man, begs for leniency as follows: "I am Thit (ex-monk) Man, the scribe. If any mistakes have been made, such as the omission of letters, the illegibility of my handwriting, and misspellings, I apologize to all Bhikkhu (monks), the Buddha, the Dhamma and the Sangha." [1] Occasionally the scribe would stress his lack of experience, being a novice both with regard to his monastic status and his being a beginner in the copying of texts [2]. Yet we even find the insufficient quality of the writing support, along with constraints of time as an excuse, such as in manuscript BAD-22-1-0647 (f° 15r): "My handwriting is not beautiful because the palm-leaves are not good, and I had to hurry in my writing. There are some mistakes, please consider." [3] Reflecting a special sense of humour with sexual allusions is the colophon of a monk-scribe complaining about his unfulfilled desire to touch a widowed laywoman whose physical attractiveness might have been on his mind while he was writing:

รจนาแล้วยามเทียง ขอให้ผู้ข้า[มี]รูปผู้ดีศรีผู้เกลียง แดกี้ข้าท้อน ชาติจะมาภายหน้า ขอให้ได้พบองค์สัพพัญญูเจ้า ตัว (หนังสือ) ไม่สวย อย่าได้หัวเราะ กระผมด้วย มือกระด้างไม่ได้คั่นนมสาวแม่ร้าง เขียนไว้ค้ำมูล (ชู) สาสนา หนังสือวัด หนอง เน้อ อ้ายจันทร์วัดหนอง เขียนเน้อ จบเท่านี้แล้ว

The writing of this manuscript was finished at noon (between 10: 30–12: 00 o'clock). May I be born as a good and intelligent person in my next lives. May I meet the Enlightened One. My handwriting is not so beautiful. Do not laugh at me. My hand is rough because it has never touched the breast of the widow girl. The making of this manuscript is to support the Teachings of the Buddha. The manuscript belongs to *Vat Nòng*. Ai Chan from *Vat Nòng* is the scribe.

5. Scribes, Sponsors and Donors

As mentioned above one tenth (119) of the colophons in the 1,220 manuscripts of the Vat Maha That corpus record the names of scribes, while the vast majority only state that the writing was accomplished at a certain date, directly followed by the names of the leading and initiating monastic or lay supporters (*mūla-saddhā*) and their intentions for sponsoring the making of the manuscript. With one exception (BAD-22-1-1082) all scribal colophons explicitly mention the scribe's name, and in many cases also his affiliation to a certain

---

[1] ข้าพเจ้าทิดมัน เป็นผู้รจนา เขียนเน้อ ตกกี้ดี เหลือกี้ดี บ่พอกี้ดี ตัว (หนังสือ) บ่ดีบ่งามกี้ดี ใส่ตัวอักษรผิดกี้ดี ข้าพเจ้าขออนุญาตนำพระภิกษุสงฆ์ ทั้งปวงกับพระพุทธเจ้า พระธรรมเจ้า พระสังฆเจ้า แดกี้ข้าเทอญ.

[2] See, for example, the colophons of manuscripts BAD-22-1-0176 and BAD-22-1-0596.

[3] เขียนบ่งามเน้อ ลานบ่ดี เขียนฟ้าวเต็มที บ่อนตกกี้มี บ่อนเหลือกี้ดี ค่อยพิจารณาเอาท้อน.

monastery (51), village or town quarter (11). Three-fifths of the known scribes were members of the Sangha, either abbots or other monks, and in some cases also novices. Two-fifths of the scribes were laymen of whom four are called *achan* ("learned man"), also often called by its short form *chan*, while most of the other lay scribes were former monks (*thit* or *khanan*) or novices (*xiang*).

Though most scribes were monks and novices, with former monks and novices making up the rest, the vast majority of sponsors/donors were lay people. Our analysis of the names of monasteries and home villages of scribes and sponsors/donors reveals that two-thirds (64 of 96) of the "leading monastic supporters" (i.e., monks and novices) were based at Vat Maha That itself (which was anticipated), while the remaining 32 principal monastic supporters came from 19 different monasteries. One third (33) of the 99 manuscripts recording the home villages, town quarters or places of residence of the "leading lay supporters" were sponsored by people living in the town quarter of Ban Vat That, which lies in the immediate neighbourhood of Vat Maha That. The only other place from which a substantial number of sponsors originated were Ban Hua Xiang (10) and, surprisingly, the Royal Palace (9) where the King of Luang Prabang resided and the Front Palace, the residence of the viceroy. The relatively large number of royal sponsors will be discussed in a section below. The most prominent principal monastic supporter was the Supreme Patriarch (Saṅgharājā) of Luang Prabang called *Phutthapanya* (Buddhapaññā) who sponsored the making of a palm-leaf manuscript consisting of twelve fascicles, which survived as a complete set. The manuscript, entitled *Visai Banha* (Pali: *Vijaya Pañhā*) is the story of King Sivirat and his minister Sonsai making military preparations to fight against King Sivijaya of Pharanasi (modern Benares). A young novice (*chua*) named Mi was hired as scribe. The karmic benefits derived from the production of this manuscript were asked to be transferred to the Supreme Patriarch's late elder brother, as is stated in the colophon (BAD-22-1-1160, fascicle 1, f° 25r) which is written in much smaller size than the main text in the central part of the leaf:

จุลศักราช ๑๒๒๒ ตัว ปีกดสัน เดือน ๖ ออก ๕ ค่ำ วัน ๓ มื้อเปิกเส็ค รจนาแล้วยามเทียงวัน หมายมีสังฆราช พุทธปัญญา มีใจใสศรัทธาสร้างวิไชยปัญหาไว้กับศาสนาพระโคตมะเจ้า ตราบต่อเท่า ๕๐๐๐ พรรษา ทานไปหาพี่อ้ายชื่อว่าทิดพรหมา อันสุระคต (สวรรคต) จุติไปสู่ปรโลกภายหน้า อันขอให้ไปบังเกิดเป็นญาณแก้ว ญาณคำ นำพีของข้าให้ได้ถึงสุข ๓ ประการ มีนิรพานเป็นทีแล้วก็ข้าเทอญ นิจจํ ธุวํ ธุวํ จัวมีเขียนเหลือผาหยา ขอให้ได้ดั่งคำมักคำปรารถนาแดก็ข้าทอน สาธุ สาธุ

In Culasakkarat (CS) 1222, a *kot san* year, on the fifth waxing day of the sixth

183

(lunar) month, the third day of the week (Tuesday), a *poek set* day[①], the writing of this manuscript was finished at noon between (10: 30–12: 00 o'clock). Saṅgharājā Phutthapanya had the religious faith to sponsor the making of this manuscript entitled *Visaiyabanha* to support the Teachings of Gotama Buddha to last until the end of 5,000 years. Dedicated to my elder brother named Thit (ex-monk) Phomma who has already died and has gone to the other world. May the benefit of this merit be a golden vehicle to transfer my older brother to reach the three states of happiness with Nirvāna as the ultimate goal. *Niccaṃ dhuvaṃ dhuvaṃ* (continuously and forever). (I) Chua (Novice) Miam the scribe writing beyond (my) wisdom. May my wishes and desires come true. *Sādhu sadhu* (Well done! Well done!)

In some rare cases, we have evidence of the ethnic or professional background of sponsors such, as in the colophon of manuscript BAD-22-1-0545, which mentions a Mae Thao (grandmother) Khün (แม่เฒ่าขึน) from Ban Pa Phai village (บ้านป่าไผ่) who was most probably a Tai Khün immigrant from the Chiang Tung area in the eastern Shan State of Myanmar. Another manuscript (BAD-22-1-1020) was written by an unnamed Lao scribe at Vat Chòm Si in Luang Prabang in the Lao variant of the Dhamma script. The manuscript, comprised of 57 folios, contains a bilingual text — *Sap Patimok* (Pali: Satta Pāṭimokkha, "Words of the Sangha Disciplinary Precepts") — written in Pali and Lao in accordance with the Nissaya system in which a Pali word or phrases are directly followed by a translation into the vernacular. The contents start from the beginning of the Patimokkha and run until the end of Pārājika, the Buddhist monastic code. In contrast to the general convention of the Lao manuscript culture of four lines written on each side of a palm leaf, this particular manuscript runs over six to eight lines. This is unusual even in the Northern Thai and Tai Lü manuscript cultures (five lines per side is the norm). The colophon states:

ลานที่ ๕๗ หน้า ๒: ศักราชได้ ๑๒๐๖ ตัว เดือนยี่เพ็ง ในเมืองหลวง แม่นเดือน ๔ เมืองอาลวกนครแล้วยาม กองแลงแล ปีกาบสีแล ข้าเผียกในวัดจอมสี เมืองหลวงแล แม่นหนังสือหม่อมอินทวงศา เมืองอาลวกนครราชธานี ศรีสุกพาวิพาตา มหานครหลวงแสนหวีฟ้า หอคำหลวงเมืองเชียงรุ่งแล เจ้าไทผู้ใดยืม ให้รักษาดี เอามาส่งเทอญ เจ้าจอมตนใดขออย่า (ข้อมูลขาดหาย)

Folio 57 on the verso side: In Culasakkarat (CS) 1206, on the full moon day of the second (lunar) month (according to the Lao calendar), in the capital city, in the fourth lunar month (according to the) Müang (Lü calendar) in the city of Alavakkanakòn, the

---

[①] 1222 Vaisakha 5 = Tuesday, 24 April 1860 which was indeed a *poek set* day.

writing of this manuscript was finished at the time of the sunset drum (between 13:30–15:00 o'clock), in a kap si year①. I copied (*phiak*) (this manuscript) at Vat Chòm Si, in the city of Luang (Prabang) from a manuscript belonging to Mòm (monk) Inthavongsa from the city of Alavakkanakhon Lasathani Sisuk Phaviphata Maha Nakhòn, Luang Saenwifa Hò Kham Luang Müang Xiang Hung (the full name of Xiang Hung or Chiang Rung, the capital of Sipsòng Panna)②. Those who borrow (this manuscript) shall take good care of it and send it back. Any monk may not fail... (missing text).

The Lao scribe claims that he obtained the master-copy used for producing his own manuscript from a monk called Mòm Inthavongsa who was based at Chiang Rung, the capital of Sipsòng Panna, and was most likely of Tai Lü ethnicity. We can assume that the master-copy was almost certainly written in the Tai Lü variant of the Dhamma script, in Pali and the vernacular Tai Lü language. The date recorded in the colophon is obviously the date when the writing of the original Tai Lü manuscript was accomplished by Mòm Inthavongsa and does not represent the date when the unknown Lao scribe made his own copy. It seems that the Lao scribe copied the first half of the colophon directly from the colophon of the master-copy but amended the lunar month from the "fourth" (according to calendar of Chiang Rung and Chiang Tung) to the "second", according to the Lao tradition. Here he made a slight mistake, as the Tai Lü calendar is only one month ahead the Lao calendar and not two like the Lan Na calendar of Chiang Mai. Therefore, the date in the colophon should represent the third lunar month of the Lao calendar with February 21st, 1845 as the day when the writing of the master-copy was accomplished. It is unclear, however, how the Lao scribe obtained the master-copy. It is most likely that a visiting monk from Sipsòng Panna—perhaps even the scribe himself—brought it to Luang Prabang, where he made his own "Lao version" at his home monastery Vat Chòm Si, which is located at the foot of the sacred hill, Phu Si, in the centre of the town of Luang Prabang.

Two manuscripts record the High Commissioner of the Siamese crown as the principal lay supporter, either together with his Lao wife (BAD-22-1-0482, dated January 6th, 1871) or alone (BAD-22-1-1205, dated September 17th, 1891). The second manuscript is highly interesting for several reasons. Firstly, it was produced less than two years before the Pak Nam incident of July 1893, when French "gunboat diplomacy" enforced the Siamese cession of all territories situated on the left bank of the Mekong river to French Indochina. The kingdom of Luang Prabang ceased to be a Siamese vassal state under the supervision of a High Commissioner sent by the government

---

① 1206 Pausha 15 = Wednesday, 22 January 1845. In fact, it should be the third lunar month of the Lao calendar leading to the following correction of the date: 1206 Magha 15 = Friday, 21 February 1845.

② It seems that the owner of the manuscript was a monk from Chiang Rung in Sipsòng Panna, most probably an ethnic Tai Lü.

in Bangkok and became a French protectorate. Secondly, the colophon reveals that the manuscript entitled Sipsòng Tamnan (Twelve Chronicles) was copied from a printed book (*nangsü phim*) published by the Siamese king. Thus, the original text was translated from the Thai language and script into Lao and written on palm leaves in the Lao variant of the Dhamma script. Finally, the date when the writing of the manuscript was finished is given both in the traditional Lao style, based on the "Minor Era" (*Chulasakkarat*) and the "Bangkok Era" (*Rattanakosin Sakkarat*), which starts with the founding of Bangkok (1782) as Year 1. The colophon (on f° 36 r-v) reads:

มหาศักราช ๑๒๕๓ ตัว ปีรวงเหม้า เดือน ๑๐ ออกใหม่ ๘ ค่ำ วัน ๖ รจนาแล้วยามเทียง วันที ๑๑ เดือนกันยายน รัตนโกสินทร์ศก ๑๑๐ หมายมีพระราชศรัทธา ท่านพระภัสดานุหลัก (รักษ์) ข้าหลวงใหญ่ มีศรัทธาธรรมะ คำเลือม ใส่ใน วรพุทธศาสนาเป็นอันยิงจึงได้สร้างสิบสองตำนาน ไว้กับศาสนาพระโคตมะเจ้า ตราบต่อเท่า ๕๐๐๐ พระพรรษา นิพพาน ปจุจโย โหตุ โน นิจุจํ ธุวํ ธุวํ ปรมํ สุขํ หนังสือข้าพเจ้าเพย ศรีสุทธีธรรม ได้ชอบทานกับ หนังสือพิมพ์ของพระบาท สมเด็จพระพุทธเจ้าอยู่หัว ได้ทรงสร้างแก่กรุงเทพมหานคร สร้างขึ้นมานั้นโดยแล้ว พระสงฆ์องค์ใดมีศรัทธาจะสร้าง จะเขียน จะสวด ขอให้รจนาตามพระคาถานี้เถิด

In Culasakkarat (CS) 1253, a *huang mao* year, on the ninth waxing day of the tenth (lunar) month, the sixth day of the week (Friday)[①], the writing of this manuscript was finished at noon time (between 10:30–12:00 o'clock). On September 11th in (year) 110 of the Rattanakosin Era (1892), Pha Phatsadanulak, the (Siamese) High Commissioner, had the most ardent religious faith to sponsor the making of this manuscript entitled *Sipsòng Tamnan* to support the Teachings of Gotama Buddha to last until the end of 5,000 years. *Nibbāna paccayo hotu no niccaṃ dhuvaṃ dhuvaṃ paramaṃ sukkhaṃ* (May this be a condition for us to reach Nirvāna, which is the greatest bliss, certainly). I am Chao Phia Sisutthamma, who reviewed this manuscript and compared it with the typed manuscript which was published by His Majesty the King in Bangkok. A monk who is devout and wants to sponsor, copy or chant, please make a copy of this manuscript.

The principal lay supporters who sponsored the making of manuscripts were mostly couples with the name of the husband mentioned first, followed by the wife's name. The couple would include their children (*luk* ลูก), grandchildren (*lan* หลาน), great-grand

---

① 1253 Bhadrapada 9 = Saturday, 12 September 1891.

children (*len* เหลน), or simply the "whole family" (*phanthavongsa* พันธุวงศา), as beneficiaries of the merit resulting from the donation. A large number of colophons (99 manuscripts total) mention a woman as the principal lay-supporter, either alone or together with her husband, whose name would be listed in second position. These women are recognizable by their titles *sao* or *nang* for younger or middle-aged women, *pa* ("aunt") for elderly women, or simply *mae-òk*, which means "laywoman". One is tempted to speculate that in cases where a woman was the only leading lay supporter, she was either an unmarried woman or a widow; in the latter case children and other family members would explicitly be mentioned as beneficiaries. The colophon of manuscript BAD–22–1–0573 (f° 11r) specifies the female donor's principal intention of merit transfer to her late husband as follows:

จุลศักราชล่วงแล้วได้ ๒๔๘๒ พรรษา ปีกัดเหม้า เดือน ๔ ออกใหม่ ๒ ค่ำ วัน ๑ (วัน) ทิตย์ รจนาแล้วบ่ายโมง ๑ หมายมี เจ้ามูลศรัทธา สาวที บ้านนอกวัดหัวเชียง มีใจใสศรัทธาพร้อมกันกับทั้งบุตรีบุตรา ญาติวงศาพีน้องได้ สร้างยังศัพท์ไชย น้อยผูกนี้ไว้กับศาสนาพระโคดมะเจ้า ตราบต่อเท่า ๕ พันพระพรรษานี้ แดกี้ข้าเทอญ ขอให้ส่วน บุญกุศลส่วนบุญอันนี้ไป รอดไปถึงทิดคุณ ผู้เป็นสามีที่จุติตายไปสู่ปรโลกภายหน้า ครั้นตกทีร้าย ขอให้ย้ายใส่ทีดี ครั้นถึงทีดีแล้ว ขอให้ดีกว่าเก่า ร้อยเท่าและพันที ครั้นบุญหากมีเมือภายฉุน ขอให้เอาตนเข้า (สู่เวียง) แก้ว กล่าวคือว่าพระอมตมหานิรพานนั้นแดกี้ข้า เทอญ สุทธินํ วตเมทานํ ปรมํ สุขํ สาธุ อนุโมทามิ

In BE 2482, a *kat mao* year, on the second waxing day of the fourth (lunar) month, the first day of the week, Sunday. The writing of this manuscript had been finished in the afternoon at 1:00 o'clock. Sao (Ms.) Thi from Ban Hua Xiang together with her children and all relatives had the religious faith to sponsor the making of this manuscript entitled *Sap Sai Nòi* to support the Teachings of Gotama Buddha to last until the end of 5,000 years. May this merit support Thit Khun, her husband who has already died to the other world. If he has been stuck in a place of suffering, please have him moved to a good place. If he has already been born in a good place, please let him enjoy happiness numerous times greater than previously. If he still has merit, may he enter the crystal city that is Nirvana, definitely. *Suddhinaṃ vatta me dhanaṃ paramaṃ sukhaṃ sādhu anumodhāmi* (This gift of mine has been properly offered) (Nirvana is the highest stage of happiness. Well done! We rejoice).

Perhaps the most amazing discovery of the Vat Maha That collection is the relatively large number of royalty acting as sponsors and donors of manuscripts. A total of thirty-two manuscripts can safely be identified as sponsored by members of the royal family. Three manuscripts alone have a "royal mother" (*pha lasamada* or *pha lasasonani*) as the principal royal sponsor. The colophon of one of these manuscripts (BAD-22-1-0032, f° 27r) records Sathu Thòngsi, the "mother of King Sisavang Vong, the King of Lan Sang Hòm Khao (Kingdom of the Million Elephants and the White Parasol) as the royal sponsor who dedicated the "fruits of merit" (phala-puñña) derived from the donation to her own parents (in October 1906). At least three further manuscripts were sponsored by incumbent kings. King Sisavang Vong (r. 1904–1959) sponsored two on the same day in the early period of his reign. The two single-fascicle manuscripts (BAD-22-1-0195 and BAD-22-1-0196) are put together in one manuscript-bundle (mat), protected by two not beautifully embellished wooden covers (mai pakap). Containing short texts entitled *Palami* (Pāramī) and *Unhatsavisai* (Uṇhassa-vijaya) respectively, the two manuscripts have colophons with identical wording indicating that their writing was accomplished on the same day: Friday, June 30th 1911.

ศักราช ๑๒๗๓ ตัว ปี (รวง) ไค้ เดือน ๘ ขึ้น ๔ คำ พร่าว่าไค้วัน ๖ รจนาแล้วยามกองแลง หมายมืองค์สมเด็จพระเจ้า สีสว่าง (วงศ์) ไค้มีใจใสศรัทธาสร้างลำปัญญาบารมีผูกนี้ ไปหาพ่อเก่าแม่หลัง ขอให้ไปรอดไปถึงจ่ายมบาลเจ้านี้ เทอญ ขอให้อยู่สุขสำราญใจทุกคำเช้าวันคืน พยาธิโรคาอย่าไค้มาผจญบังเบียด นิจจํ ธุวํ ๆ อห์ อรหนุโต โหมิ อนาคเตกาเล

In Culasakkarat 1273, a (*huang*) *khai* year, on the fourth waxing day of the eighth lunar month, the sixth day of the week (Friday)①, the writing of this manuscript was finished at the time of the sunset drum (between 13:30–15:00 o'clock). His Majasty King Sisavang (*Vong*) had the religious faith to sponsor the making of this manuscript entitled *Panya Parami* to dedicate to *phò kao mae lang* (his previous parents). May this merit reach the guards of the hells. May I be happy in daytime and nighttime. May I be prevented from all diseases constantly and certainly. May I become an arahant in the future (BAD-22-1-0196, f° 26v).

The most prolific royal sponsor of manuscripts was not a king of Luang Prabang but a viceroy (*uparat*). While viceroy Un Kham (r. 1872–1889) commissioned the making of three manuscripts in the early years of his reign, his son and successor Bunkhong (r. 1890–1921) is listed as the sponsor of at least nine manuscripts between 1895 and 1918, with four manuscripts donated on one day in November 1895 alone. Only one colophon (of manuscript BAD-22-1-380) mentions explicitly his name "Bunkhong", while the others call him either *Chao Maha Sivit Wang Na* ["Lord of the Great Life, (Head of the) Front Palace"] or by even more elaborate titles. Perhaps the most impressive

---

① 1273 Ashadha 4 = Friday, 30 June 1911.

joint sponsorship of Viceroy Bunkhong as principal royal initiator and his closest relatives is recorded in the colophon of a manuscript entitled *Munlanipphan* (Mūlanibbāna), "Foundations of Nibbāna" (BAD-22-1-0778, f° 34r):

จุลศักราช ๑๒๗๒ ตัว ปีกดเส็ด เดือน ๑๑ ขึ้นค่ำ ๑ วัน ๓ รจนามื้อก่ำเหง้า รจนาแล้วยามแตรใกล้เที่ยงวัน หมายมี อัครวร ประสิทธิ คัมภีรเศรษฐานคราอิสระหอคำฝ่ายหน้า และมเหสี และพระชนนี ทั้งราชบุตรา ราชบุตรี พระราชวงศานุวงศ์ สามัคคีมีพระราชศรัทธาเลื่อมใสในพระพุทธศาสนาเป็นอันยิ่ง จึงได้สร้างมูลนิพพาน โชฎก ศาสนาพระโคดมเจ้า เท่า ปัญจสหัสสา สุทินํ วตเมทานํ นิพพาน ปจฺจโย โหนฺตุโน นิจฺจํ ธุวํ

Folio 34 on the recto side: In Culasakkarat (CS) 1272, a *kot set* year, on the first waxing day of the eleventh (lunar) month, the third day of the week (Tuesday), a *ka mao* day[①], the writing of this manuscript was finished at the time of the forenoon horn (between 9:00-10:30 o'clock). Akkhavorapasitthikhamphila Setthanakkhara Itsara Hò Kham Fai Na (king), together with the queen and his mother, princes, princesses and all royal family members, had the most ardent religious faith to sponsor the making of this manuscript entitled *Chuntha Sukarikasut* to support the Teachings of Gotama Buddha to last until the end of 5,000 years. *Suddinaṃ vattame danaṃ nibbāna paccayo hotu no niccaṃ dhuvaṃ* (Well donated is our gift, Nirvāna is the greatest stage of happiness).

Although manuscripts were usually commissioned by members of the same family, the Vat Maha That corpus also contains several cases of joint sponsorship by persons from different families. Manuscript BAD-22-1-0933, entitled *Lam Chüang* (a popular epic about a pre-historical Tai king in the Upper Mekong basin) comprises nine extant fascicles, each of which was commissioned by different main sponsors. Moreover, some colophons provide interesting insights into the shared responsibility of different sponsors. While several colophons stress the sponsor's efforts to procure the palm leaves for the scribe, one manuscript's (BAD-22-1-0904) colophon (f° 66r) stresses that the principal monastic initiators — two senior monks — gave money to the unnamed scribe while a former novice looked for the writing material:

พุทธศักราชได้ ๒๕๑๒ ตัว ปีกัดเร้า เดือน ๙ แรม ๑๕ ค่ำ วันจันทร์ รจนาแล้วยามบ่ายโมงหนึง หมายมีสาธุ ใหญ่ผูย

---

① 1272 Asvina 1 = Tuesday, 4 October 1910.

贝叶文化与区域文化遗产传承保护

และสาธุพ่อบุตรดา เป็นผู้ออกทรัพย์ และเซียงพันเป็นผู้ช่วยออกใบลาน พร้อมกันมีใจใสศรัทธาสร้าง พระธรรมยมก (ยามุก) ผูกนี้ ไว้กับศาสนาพระโคตมะเจ้า ตรายต่อเท่า ๕ พันพระพรรษา ขอให้ได้ดั่งคำมัก คำปรารถนาแห่งฝูงข้าทั้ง ๓ แคก็ข้าเทอญ อิทัเม ธมุมทานิ อาสวกุคยาวห์ นิพุพาน สังขาตโหนุตุ อนาคเต กาเล นิพุพาน ปจุจโย โหนุตุ โน

In the Buddhist Era (BE) 2512, a *kat hao* year, on the fifteenth waning day of the eighth (lunar) month, a Monday[①], the writing of this manuscript was finished in the afternoon at 1:00 o'clock. Sathu Nyai (great monk) Phui and Sathuphò (monk) Da were the sponsors who donated money, and Xiang (ex-novice) Phan looked for the palm leaves. They had the religious faith to sponsor the making of this manuscript entitled *Nyamuk* to support the Teachings of Gotama to last 5,000 years. May all the wishes and desires of the three of us come true. *Idhaṃ me dhamma dhānaṃ āsavaka khayavahaṃ nibbāna saṅkhātaṃ hontu anāgate kāle nibbāna paccaya hotu no* (Giving the gift of the Dhamma is the condition for being released from defilements in the future, may this be a condition for us to reach Nibbāna).

Though manuscripts kept in a monastic repository belonged to that monastery, they were frequently borrowed for various purposes, either to be studied and copied by monks from a neighbouring monastery who lacked a specific text or to be used in Buddhist rituals and ceremonies outside the monastery's compound. This explains why the scribes admonished all borrowers of manuscripts to return them to their original place, as expressed in the following rather short colophons: "Those who borrow it, please give it back to Vat Sikoet monastery" (ใผยืมให้ส่งวันสีเกิดเน้อ, BAD–22–1–0007, f° 26v) and "This manuscript belongs to Vat Pha Maha That Rasabòvòravihan. Those who have borrowed it have to return it to its original place." (หนังสือวัดพระมหาธาตุราชบวร วิหาร ถ้าบุคคลผู้ใดยืมไปแล้วต้องให้เอามาส่งทีเดิม, BAD–22–1–0216, f° 15v). An interesting case is manuscript BAD–22–1–0004, which contains two different texts sponsored by two couples. The two main sponsors' colophons (ff° 51r and 52r) are preceded by a colophon of the manuscript's owner. One of the sponsors probably took it back later and kept it in his home (f° 50v), and his colophon is preceded by a brief scribal colophon directly following the end of the second text (f° 50r). These two colophons are quoted in full:

หมายมีธรรมปัญญาวัดธาตุ เป็นผู้รจนา ขอส่วนบุญอานิสงส์ผลบุญนำหลายๆ แคท้อน มูลเก่าลงหลาย ถ่ายได้ห้าใบเต็ม ส่วนของเพิ่นแล้ว บ่ตกบ่เหลือแล้ว

Thammapanya from Vat That, is the scribe. May I share much merits with you. The old

---

[①] 1331 Pratomashada 30 = Monday, 14 July 1969.

manuscript had lost much (text), (thus I) copied an additional five full leaves. Now (the manuscript) is fully completed.

มธุอนุโลมรวม มี ๒ ผูกต่อกัน ของหัวป้าแสนใหม่ปู่ ร่อมแจ (ซอยมุม) กำแพงวัดธาตุเน้อ โยคาจอมเจ้าตนใดก็ดี คนคฤหัสถ์ หญิงชายฝูงใดยืมไปฟังแล้ว กิจประโยชน์ ให้ส่งเจ้าของเก่าแดทอน สาธุๆ อนุโมทามิ ๓ ทีแล

Matthu Anulom Hòm, 2 fascicles are bound together. (This manuscript) belongs to Hua Pa Saen (and) Mai Pu, (their house is located) behind the corner of the wall (surrounding) Vat That. If any wandering monks, laymen or laywomen borrow (this manuscript) to recite it, they must return it to its original owner after having used it. Well done! Well done! I rejoice three times.

Occasionally we find ownership statements that help to identify the provenance of a manuscript which does not contain any paratextual information about the scribe and sponsor (s). The palm-leaf manuscript BAD-22-1-0482 (dated January 6th, 1871), of which only the first fascicles (*phuk ton*) of the Nitsai Chatuvik has survived, is a case in point. A brief ownership statement appears on the verso side of folio 8v. It is written in modern Lao script with a blue ballpoint pen, and reads "หนังสือสาธุจันทา วัดหัวเชียง", "the manuscript belongs to Monk Chantha from Vat Hua Xiang". This indicates that this fascicle—part of a larger codicological unit comprising several fascicles—originally belonged to Vat Hua Xiang in the lower (southern) part of the town of Luang Prabang. Most of the ownership statements, however, confirm the belonging of the manuscript to Vat Maha That itself. In other cases the ownership statement is written on a separate side of a leaf with a pink ballpoint pen. The following example is BAD-22-1-0152, a manuscript commissioned by abbot Chao Mòm Bunthan on December 31st, 1947. It is written both in Tham Lao script and in Roman characters.

In Roman script: Vat Phramahathat / Rasehabovoravihall (sic) / Luang-Prabang.
Thitapunya Bhikkhu Phra Bunthan Rathikun / Vat Phra Maha That Rasabòvòravihan / Phra Nakhòn Luang Phrabang

In Tham Lao script: ถิตะปุญญาภิกขุ พระบุญทันราธิกูล / วัดพระมหาธาตุราชบวรวิหาร / พระนครหลวง พระบาง
ได้สร้างนิยายพิมพารำไรไว้กับศาสนา / พระโคตมะเจ้า เท่า ๕๐๐๐ พรรษา นิพุพาน ปจุจโย โหตุ เม

(He) sponsored the making of the *Niyai Phimpha Hamhai* (manuscript) to ensure that the Teachings of Buddha Gotama will last 5,000 years. Nibbāna paccayo hotu me [May (this) be a condition for me (to reach) Nibbāna] .

6. Conclusion

Luang Prabang has maintained its fame and status as a centre of Lao Buddhism until the present date. The ancient and exceptional manuscript culture of Laos has survived colonial rule, war, and modernization in a globalized world. Unlike in many parts of the world, production of manuscripts did not stop during the 20th century in Laos, where traditional ways of writing have been preserved by monks and lay scribes until present times. The ancient manuscript mentioned above is also the first documentary evidence of the Dhamma (*Tham*) script in the Lao Kingdom of Lan Sang. This sacred script is a special feature of Lao literature. It originated in the neighboring northern Thai kingdom of Lan Na—probably as a derivative of the ancient Mon alphabet of Hariphunchai—in the late fourteenth century and made its way south through the Mekong river basin. As its name indicates, this script was used for the writing of the Buddhist scriptures and other religious texts.

Lao manuscripts were mostly inscribed with a stylus on rectangular cut and cured palm-leaf sheets varying in length. Each sheet had two holes; a cotton string was passed through the left one, making it possible to bind several palm-leaf sheets together as one bundle, or fascicle (*phuk*). Recent research estimates that more than ninety percent of Lao manuscripts are "palm-leaf books" (*nangsue bai lan*). According to traditional Buddhist beliefs, no matter whether they were written carefully or not, manuscripts should not be treated disrespectfully, or kept in a demeaning place. The texts that manuscripts contain, especially the ritual ones, should not have any insertions or other writing added to them. Any person who breaks this rule would lose the respect of devout Buddhists. The corpus of digitized manuscripts kept at the monastic repository of Vat Maha That is so far the largest ever conducted in the city of Luang Prabang. The impressive collection of palm-leaf manuscripts was the work of senior intellectual monks who appreciated the ancient manuscript culture of Laos. Notably, Sathu Nyai Phui Thirachitta Maha Thela (1925–2005), who served as the abbot of Vat Maha That from 1967 until his death in 2005, contributed much to the building-up of the unique manuscript collection at his home monastery. He was a passionate scribe, sponsor and collector of manuscripts.

The analyses of colophons recorded in these manuscripts reveal quite interesting features: Though the structure and content of the colophons of the corpus as a whole are hardly different from what we know from other Lao, Northern Thai or Tai Lü manuscripts which bear religious texts, some aspects are nevertheless astonishing, such as the relatively high percentage of women serving as principal lay supporters or the presence of royalty among the sponsors and donors of manuscripts. Moreover, several colophons also help to sharpen our understanding of the cooperation between scribes and sponsors/donors as well as different sponsors/donors in the making of a manuscript. Despite the fact that in recent years a lot of projects have been carried out to preserve, document, and digitize manuscripts in various parts of Theravada Buddhist Southeast Asia, still much has to be done to identify either physically or culturally endangered collections of manuscripts, both in monastic repositories and private collections. The authors hope that this article will help to raise awareness and speed up research in the diverse manuscript cultures of the Thai and Lao world, which constitute a most precious heritage of the people of the region.

References

(Ⅰ) Archival Mterials

[1] BAD-22-1-0004: *Matthu Anulom* (Conforming to the Daily Routine of the Buddha); palm-leaf manuscript; one fascicle of 56 folios; language: Lao, Pali; script: Tham Lao; CS 1293, a *huang mot* year (AD 1931).

[2] BAD-22-1-0007: *Ubpat* (Chanting for Warding off Calamities); palm-leaf manuscript; one fascicle of 27 folios; language: Lao, Pali; script: Tham Lao; CS 1223, a *huang hao* year (AD 1861).

[3] BAD-22-1-0032: *Matthu Anulom* (Conforming to the Daily Routine of the Buddha); palm-leaf manuscript; ten fascicles with a total of 279 folios; language: Lao, Pali; script: Tham Lao; CS 1268, a *hwai sanga* year (AD 1906).

[4] BAD-22-1-0152: *Ninyai Phimpha Hamhai* (The Story about Bimbā's Lamentations); palm-leaf manuscript; one fascicle of 30 folios; language: Lao, Pali; script: Tham Lao; BE 2490, a *moeng khai* year (AD 1947).

[5] BAD-22-1-0176: *Pannya Parami* (Paññā Pāramī); palm-leaf manuscript; one fascicle of 8 folios; language: Lao, Pali; script: Tham Lao; undated.

[6] BAD-22-1-0195: *Unhatsavisai* (Uṇhassavijaya); palm-leaf manuscript; one fascicle of 11 folios; language: Lao, Pali; script: Tham Lao; CS 1273, a *huang khai* year (AD 1911).

[7] BAD-22-1-0196: *Pannya Parami* (Paññā Pāramī); palm-leaf manuscript; one fascicle of 6 folios; language: Lao, Pali; script: Tham Lao; CS 1273, a *huang khai* year (AD 1911).

[8] BAD-22-1-0216: *Mangkhala* 38 (Part of the Discourse on Blessings); palm-leaf manuscript; one fascicle of 16 folios; language: Lao, Pali; script: Tham Lao; BE 2465, a *huang hao* year (AD 1922).

[9] BAD-22-1-0282: *Sap Mahavak*（Words of the Great Group—Part of the Abhidhamma）; palm-leaf manuscript; one fascicle of 48 folios; language: Lao, Pali; script: Tham Lao; CS 1128, a *hwai set* year（AD 1766）.

[10] BAD-22-1-0375: *Paet Mün*（Eighty Thousand）; palm-leaf manuscript; three fascicles with a total of 50 folios; language: Lao, Pali; script: Tham Lao; CS 1345 / BE 2526, a *ka khai* year（AD 1983）.

[11] BAD-22-1-0414: *Matsima Nikai*（Majjhima Nikaya）, palm-leaf manuscript; one fascicle（No. 14）of 26 folios; language: Lao, Pali; script: Tham Lao; CS 1205, a *ka mao* year（AD 1843）.

[12] BAD-22-1-0482: *Chatuvik*（Title of a Poem）; palm-leaf manuscript; one fascicle of 10 folios; language: Lao, Pali; script: Tham Lao; CS 1231（in fact: 1232）, a *kot sanga* year（AD 1870/1871）.

[13] BAD-22-1-0545: *Sòng Khao Salak*（Benefits Derived from Offering Food Distributed by Lottery Tickets）; palm-leaf manuscript; one fascicle of 8 folios; language: Lao, Pali; script: Tham Lao; CS 1308 / BE 2489, a *hwai set* year（AD 1946）.

[14] BAD-22-1-0573: *Sap Sai Nòi*（Words of the Small Victory）; palm-leaf manuscript; one fascicle of 11 folios; language: Lao, Pali; script: Tham Lao; BE 2482, a *kat mao* year（AD 1939）.

[15] BAD-22-1-0578: *Sai Luang*（The Great Victory）; palm-leaf manuscript; one fascicle of 8 folios; language: Lao, Pali; script: Tham Lao; a *kot set* year（no further date given）.

[16] BAD-22-1-0596: *Sap Phahung*（Sapta Bāhuṃ—Words of Eight Verses about the Buddha's Auspicious Victories）; palm-leaf manuscript; one fascicle of 6 folios; language: Lao, Pali; script: Tham Lao; BE 2492, a *kat pao* year（AD 1949）.

[17] BAD-22-1-0616: *Rattana Sutta*（Rattana Sutta—Discourse on the Triple Gems）; palm-leaf manuscript; one fascicle of 13 folios; language: Lao, Pali; script: Tham Lao; CS 1310 / BE 2490, a *kat pao* year（AD 1947）.

[18] BAD-22-1-0647: *Tamnan Nithan Vat Pha Kaeo Viang Din Dòi Tao*（The Chronicle of the Monastery of Vat Pha Kaeo Viang Din Dòi Tao）; palm-leaf manuscript; one fascicle of 16 folios; language: Lao, Pali; script: Tham Lao; CS 1281, a *poek chai* year（AD 1919）.

[19] BAD-22-1-0778: *Munlanipphan*（Mūlanibbāna）（Discourse on the Way Leading to Nibbāna）; palm-leaf manuscript; one fascicle of 16 folios; language: Lao, Pali; script: Tham Lao; CS 1272, a *kot set* year（AD 1910）.

[20] BAD-22-1-0839: *Ban Ton*（The Beginning Section）; palm-leaf

manuscript; one fascicle of 33 folios; language: Lao, Pali; script: Tham Lao; CS 1220, a *poek sanga* year (AD 1858).

[21] BAD-22-1-0904: *Yamuk* (Yamaka) (Book of Pairs); palm-leaf manuscript; one fascicle of 66 folios; language: Lao, Pali; script: Tham Lao; BE 2512, a *kat hao* year (AD 1969).

[22] BAD-22-1-0933: *Sapphahung* (Words of the *Bāhuṃ* Sutta or the Jaya Maṅgala Gāthā); palm-leaf manuscript; one fascicle of 8 folios; language: Lao, Pali; script: Tham Lao; BE 2515, a *tao chai* year (AD 1972).

[23] BAD-22-1-1020: *Sap Patimok* (Sapta Pāṭimokkha) (Words of the Basic Code of Monastic Discipline); palm-leaf manuscript; one fascicle of 57 folios; language: Lao, Pali; script: Tham Lao; CS 1206, a *kap si* year (AD 1844).

[24] BAD-22-1-1082: *Khutthakanikai* (Khuddaka-Nikāya) (Minor Collection); palm-leaf manuscript; 17 fascicles with a total of 139 folios; language: Lao, Pali; script: Tham Lao; CS 1200, a *poek set* year (AD 1838).

[25] BAD-22-1-1154: *Sap Khatha Thammabot* (Gāthā Dhammapada) (Words about the Buddha's Path to Enlightenment); palm-leaf manuscript; one fascicle of 147 folios; language: Lao, Pali; script: Tham Lao; CS 1187, a *hap hao* year (AD 1825).

[26] BAD-22-1-1160: *Visaiya Banha* (Vijeyya's Problem); palm-leaf manuscript; 12 fascicles with a total of 148 folios; language: Lao, Pali; script: Tham Lao; CS 1222, a *kot san* year (AD 1860).

[27] BAD-22-1-1205: *Bòk Tua Akkhara Hai Thük Nak Bao* [Telling the Correct Pronounciation of (Consonant and Vowel Letters)]; palm-leaf manuscript; one fascicle of 158 folios; language: Lao, Pali; script: Tham Lao; CS 1253, a *huang mao* year (AD 1892).

(Ⅱ) Books and Journals

[1] Arthid Sheravanichkul. *Than lae thanbarami: khwam samkhan thi mi tò kan rangsan vannakhadi thai phutthasatsana* ทานและทานบารมี: ความสำคัญที่มีต่อ การรังสรรค์ วรรณคดีไทยพุทธศาสนา [Dana and Danaparami: Significance in the Creation of Thai Buddhist Literature]. PhD dissertation, Chulalongkorn University, Bangkok, 2009.

[2] Arthid Sheravanichkul. Narrative and Gift-Giving in Thai Ānisaṃsa Texts // Skilling P, McDaniel J. Buddhist Narrative in Asia and Beyond. In Honour of HRH Princess Maha Chakri Sirindhorn on Her Fifty-Fifth Birth Anniversary. Bangkok, 2010.

[3] Berger, Hans Georg. Het Bun Dai Bun: Laos-Sacred Rituals of Luang Prabang. London: Westzone, 2000.

[4] Sengsoulin, Bounleuth. Manuscripts Found in the Abode of Pha Khamchan

at Vat Saen Sukharam // Volker Grabowsky, Hans Georg Berger. The Lao Sangha and Modernity: Research at the Buddhist Archives of Luang Prabang, 2005–2015. Luang Prabang: Anantha Publishing, 2015.

［5］Sengsoulin, Bounleuth. Buddhist Manuscript Culture in Laos on the Road to Modernity: Reflections on Anisong Manuscripts // Volker Grabowsky, Hans Georg Berger. The Lao Sangha and Modernity: Research at the Buddhist Archives of Luang Prabang, 2005–2015. Luang Prabang: Anantha Publishing, 2015a.

［6］Sengsoulin, Bounleuth. The Manuscript Collection of Abbot Sathu Nyai Khamchan at the Monastery of Vat Saen Sukharam (Luang Prabang, Laos). Manuscript Cultures, 2015b (8).

［7］Sengsoulin, Bounleuth. Buddhist Monks and Their Search for Knowledge: An Examination of the Personal Collection of Manuscripts of Phra Khamchan Virachitto (1920–2007). Abbot of Vat Saen Sukharam, Luang Prabang, PhD dissertation, Africa-Asia Institute, Universität Hamburg, 2016.

［8］Grabowsky, Volker and Hans Georg Berger. The Lao Sangha and Modernity: Research at the Buddhist Archives of Luang Prabang, 2005–2015. Luang Prabang: Anantha Publishing, 2015.

［9］Hayashi, Yukio. Practical Buddhism among the Thai-Lao: Religion in the Making of a Region. Kyoto: Kyoto University Press, 2003.

［10］Hinüber von, Oskar. Die Pali-Handschriften des Klosters Lai Hin bei Lampang in Nord-Thailand. Wiesbaden: Harrassowitz Verlag, 2013.

［11］Holt, John Clifford. Spirits of the Place: Buddhism and Lao Religious Culture. Honolulu: University of Hawaii Press, 2009.

［12］Hundius, Harald. The Colophons of Thirty Pāli Manuscripts from Northern Thailand. Journal of the Pali Text Society, 1990 (14).

［13］Khamvone Boulyaphonh and Volker Grabowsky. A Lost Monastery Rediscovered: A Catalogue of Lao Manuscripts Kept in the Abbot's Abode (kuti) of Vat Si Bun Hüang, Luang Prabang. Hamburger Sü dostasienstudien, New York and Luang Prabang: Anantha Publishing, 2017 (15).

［14］Kislenko, Arne. Culture and Customs of Laos. London: Greenwood Press, 2009.

［15］Nginn, Pierre S. New Year Festival (Fifth Month Festival) // René de Berval. Kingdom of Laos. Saigon: France-Asie, 1959.

［16］Veidlinger, Daniel M. Spreading the Dhamma: Writing, Orality, and Textual Transmission in Buddhist Northern Thailand. Honolulu: University of Hawaii Press, 2006.

(Ⅲ) Websites

[1] Digital Library of Lao Manuscripts (DLLM). http://www.laomanuscripts.net (last accessed on 6 May 2020).

[2] Digital Repository of Endangered and Affected Manuscripts in Southeast Asia (DREAMSEA). https://www.southeastasianarchaeology.com/2020/02/17/dreamsea-digital-repository-of-endangered-and-affected-manuscripts-in-southeast-asia/.

Palm-Leaf Manuscripts and the Dai People's Dan in Xishuangbanna

—Based on Field Investigation in M Village

Guo Shan[①]

Translated by Liu Yanxue[②]

M village is located in the east side of National Highway 214 from Menghai County to Lancang County, Xishuangbanna Prefecture, and is subordinate to Jingzhen village committee of Mengzhe town. As of November 2019, there are 359 people in 68 households, and with the exception of 7 Han people and 4 Blang people, all of them are Dai people. M village is a typical Dai village. In 2014, the repair of the village Buddhist temple was completed, and the manuscripts were more orderly preserved and kept.

1. The Basic Situation of the Palm-Leaf Manuscripts in the Buddhist Temple of M Village

According to records, in the past, "the written palm-leaf manuscripts mainly consisted of leaf-shaped and paper forms. The leaf-shaped form is the real palm-leaf manuscripts, which is called 'Tan Lan' in Dai language. It has four types, that is, four-line, five-line, six-line and eight-line per page. The first three are the most common specifications of the palm-leaf manuscripts. The paper one refers to the cotton paper script, and the term is Bo Ga La Sha in Dai language. There are two types, wide-page and double-folding, and the former is the most common." [③]

According to the author's field investigation in M village in November 2019, the manuscripts currently collected in the Buddhist temple of M village have been sorted out and described by the following aspects.

In terms of material, the specifications of the leaf-shaped carved version are still four-

---

[①] Doctor and Professor of Palm-Leaf Culture Research Center, Deputy Dean of the School of Development Studies, Yunnan University.
[②] Master Degree Candidate of Religion, School of Ethnology and Sociology, Yunnan University.
[③] Qin Jiahua, Zhou Ya. Collection of Palm-Leaf Culture. Kunming: Yunnan University Press, 2004: 12.

line, five-line, and six-line per page, and the specifications of the paper-shaped classics are also wide-paged, but the number is far more than the leaf shape. And the paper-based manuscripts, in addition to the traditional cotton paper manuscripts, and even the double-folded ones, have 16 copy paper manuscripts, printed folded ones, printed ones, duplicated ones, and copying and printing of books and other forms.

In terms of quantity, it can be divided into the following seven categories, namely: ① 44 copies of leaf-shaped block copy (letter); ② more than 780 volumes of cotton paper manuscripts; ③ 22 volumes of manual folds; ④ 66 volumes of folded books; ⑤ 45 volumes of printed books; ⑥ 38 volumes of copied manual books; ⑦ 64 volumes of copied and printed books, totaling more than 1,000 books (volumes).

In terms of time, 15 books (letters) of leaf-shaped manuscripts were written before the 1980s (i.e. reform and opening-up), and more than 240 volumes of cotton manuscripts were copied before the 1980s. The other books were produced and published after the reform and opening-up.

In terms of content, the leaf-shaped manuscripts are the most abundant in the "Tripitakas", slang for "Three Bidaga" in Dai language, and the Buddhist Story (jātaka) (represented by "Visendara"). Among them, there are seven "Tripitakas" and six "Visendara", and there is also "Nirvana Sutras", slang for "Niepanasu" in Dai language, "Paramita Sutras" (including ten Paramita Sutra, thousand sentences Sutra, hundreds of thousand Paramita Sutra, etc.), and "Recitation Sutras" (Mahabata, Mahamasa), etc. In addition to the contents of the leaf-shaped manuscripts, the manuscript of cotton paper "The Buddhist Story" is the most abundant. In addition, there are also "On Purity", slang for "Weisutiya", "Birth Date Sutra" (Tanmuzaida in Dai language), "Exorcism Sutra" (Luojiawuti), "Recitation Sutras" (Mahabatan, Zundasugalidasu), the Education Sutra (Tanmalaishuangluo) and so on.

It is worth mentioning that, in addition to the traditional palm-leaf manuscripts and manual cotton paper manuscripts, modern printing and publishing of the Buddhist Sutras of Theravada have entered the Buddhist temples in the village, and are gradually loved by people. The reading of printed Sutras is more "eye-saving", which means that printed Sutras are easier to identify during recitation, so they are easier to read and more popular.

2. On the Position of Palm-Leaf Manuscripts in the Dan Ritual from the View of "Suzaida"

In the local Dai vocabulary, "Su" is pronounced "she-m", which means baptism, introspection, internalization, and perfection. They say, "It is a stone. If you give it 'Su' day after day, it will become a treasure." The act of "Su" is very important in daily life, and the Dai people have always thought of "Su" throughout their lives. The explanation in the "Dai-Han Dictionary" is "doing merit to the birthday horoscopes to make life longer". The explanation given by the Great Buddha is "continuing and following". "Zaida" is Pali, meaning life, or something that a person brings with him once he is born. "Suzaida" literally means to continue life, so that life can be smooth and everything is fine. In their eyes, everything in the world has its own specific life. People who have been born have this kind of life, and families have this kind of life. Houses they built have this kind of life, including stockaded villages and Buddhist temples. In short, everything has this kind of life when it comes out and in the whole growth process, or with the passage of time, there will inevitably be deviations. Therefore, it is necessary to organize and correct it, so that it can continue to grow (or go) smoothly. Everyone has his own life course from birth to death. People believe that this is how life is affected, so "destination" is used to explain personal life events. When a person's daily life footprint coincides with a destined life course, that person's life path will "go right and go well", otherwise problems will occur. Therefore, people must make corrections and amends from time to time in their lives. "Su Zaida" is the Dan ritual of performing such corrections and amends. Frequent corrections can ensure that one grows better, does not go astray, and does not follow evil paths. Therefore, there is Dan ritual for the individual, called "Suzaidagun", Dan ritual for the family, called "Suzaidahen", Dan ritual for the village, called "Suzaidaman", Dan for the Buddhist temple called "Suzaidawa" and so on. As a result, this ritual is more frequent in Dai people's village, especially in the stockaded villages with large populations and large households, which are held almost every week after the Opening Festival.

The process of the "Suzaida" ceremony that the author observed during participating in the field survey in November 2019 is as follows:

This time, it was "Suzaidahen", which is a Dan for the family. The Dan's people are the couple of Ai Guang and their son Ai Xiang and daughter-in-law Yu Guangjiao. Before the ceremony, Ai Xiang had already set up the venue. Three pairs of bamboo stands were placed in front of the center of the rectangular house in order, and a pot and some snacks were placed at the rear.

Each person attending the ceremony brought a pair of wax strips, a scarf, and a little blessing gift money to the owner's home (Dan's people). After entering the house, put these items in a pot prepared by the host in advance, and then found a place to sit. The order of sitting is male first, female last, and the old first, and the young behind. Participants are all elderly people who have reached the age of "Ao Xing". Respondents told the author that these elderly people who have begun to "Ao Xing" can bring blessings to the host family.

At 2:00 pm, the preparations for the ceremony began. A buddha (short for the Great Buddha which called "Fo Ye") held a fan in front of everyone and sat in the front of the bamboo frame. The Bu Zhang and Kang Lang sat on the sides. There was a tea tray and a tea table in front of them. There were a few wax sticks, towels and a pair of burning candles in the tea tray, and wax sticks, towels, fruits, etc. on the tea table. Ai Xiang has slowly pulled the white thread "Maisu-mong"① (Maisumeng) used for the ceremony from the end of the candle, the palm-leaf manuscripts, etc. that were tied in front of the buddha ("Fo Ye"), and first made a few turns on the bamboo frame. Then lead the white thread outside the gate, so that the long white thread drawn from the buddha's hand connects the inside and the outside of the house.

When everything was ready, Bu Zhang announced that today's "Su Zaida" ceremony for the Ai Guang family is underway. Firstly, Bu Zhang led everyone to worship the buddha. In Dai language, it is called "su-ma-da-la". Then, Bu Zhang asked the buddha "gao-wen-dan" to explain that today do Dan for the Ai Guang's family. He hoped that the whole family would be in good health and everything would go well. Pleased the buddha to help them and so on. Bu Zhang read a paragraph, and everyone read the paragraph. After finishing reading, the buddha began to recite the Auspicious Sutra "Manggela", handing a white thread. At the beginning, the buddha recited a paragraph, and everyone would follow it. Then the buddha recited alone, and everyone listened. After the recitation, the buddha, the Bu Zhang and two Kang Langs discussed the chanter of five sutras, "Diba mangdasu" "Luojiawuti" "Sansongxidian" "Ya Ni" and "Zaiyasangjiaha". After allocating the Sutras, the buddha began to recite the first Sutra. The people in the full house were listening quietly. In some middle sections, Mie Tao who was sitting behind would take rice and scattered it towards the sky, and everyone cheered in unison. After the buddha finished chanting, Bu Zhang and two Kang Langs chanted the Sutras they had in their hands. In the process, the buddha would sprinkle water from the silver pot with bamboo sticks to everyone. The wax fire on the bamboo shelf cannot be extinguished. A Kang Lang took a few wax sticks and went out of the scene with a little money to get these things far away from the house. It means that the bad things in the house have been driven out.

When the above five sutras were all chanted, everyone cheered and sprinkled rice into the sky. Ai Xiang took off the white thread from the bamboo frame and closed the bamboo

---

① The white thread group dedicated to the Great Buddha is usually stored in Buddhist temples, and is used in rituals such as making sacrifices for the Dan people, avoiding evils and seeking blessings.

frame.

　　Next is "ya-nanm", that is, asking the buddha to chant sutras and drip water for Ai Guang's family. At this time, Ai Guang's family gathered around and sat in front of the buddha and Bu Zhang, and set up a wax bar in front of themselves. Bu Zhang first told the buddha "gao-wen-dan", and then the buddha recited a blessing speech to the Buddha, to the effect that today's Ai Guang's family makes "shem-zai-da" for their family. "We point on the wax bar, drop water, and hope the God in the sky (diu-wa-la) and the God underground (nang-tuo-la-ni) remember our offerings of Dan, and help to send these offerings to the place where they should go. We know that these goods can only reach the place to go through mountains and rivers. Please ask the gods to help us, so that these offerings can not be lost in the water, or melted in the fire. Finally, they can all be well delivered to the place to go. At the same time, we also ask the Buddha to make these wishes come true." Finally, the buddha recited the "Sutra of Returning" to the Buddha. At this time, the Ai Guang family took turns to drop clear water into the pot. At the end of the chanting, all the people followed him to chant a sutra. At this time, Bu Zhang stood up and walked in the room with a bowl in his hand to sprinkle water on the people. It is a symbol of the shower of Buddha. In the process of arranging chapters and chanting sutras, firecrackers were set off outside the house, which symbolizes to drive away all evils and dark things.

　　After the dripping was finished, the buddha drew the thread one by one for the four couples of Ai Guang and his son Ai Xiang. So far, the whole ceremony is over. It takes about 3 hours.

　　After the ceremony was over, the buddha, Bu Zhang and the old people ate upstairs, and the rest went downstairs to eat. The son Ai Xiang sent the bamboo frame to the big green tree in the village's Buddhist temple. Today's five Sutras, in addition to the "Sansongxidian" were placed on the host's home for the remainder, the rest of the commandments of the "Dibamangdasu" and the exorcism of "Luojiawuti" "Ya Ni" and the four books of "Zaiyasanjiaha" will be stored in the Buddhist temple.

　　The "Gamu" concept[①] of the accumulation of merits and virtues formed by the people in the Xishuangbanna Theravada Buddhism determines that the fakes worshipped by the rituals are an exchange with the gods and the Buddha. Dan or doing Dan—offering a sacrifice—is a symbol of a gift to the gods and the Buddha. When they receives this

---

[①] In the interpretation of the Dai in Xishuangbanna, "Gamu" was born of all the past actions, words and thoughts of a person. After the settlement of good (merit) and evil (bad) according to Buddhist morals, if the balance is good, a good "Gamu" is produced, and on the contrary, a bad "Gamu" is produced. See Tan Leshan. Theravada and the Economy of the Dai Village—A Comparative Study of Xishuangbanna, Southwest China. Zhao Xiaoniu's translation. Kunming: Yunnan University Press, 2005: 72.

gift owned by the heart (not a gift owned by the hand)[1], they will increase their good "Gamu", and get blessed. As Leach said, the ceremonial ritual made "the sacrifice erected a bridge between the divine and human realms, through which the power of god can reach the sacrifice himself."[2] The villagers all know that the amount of blessings depends on the quality and quantity of Dan the sacrifice has, that is, the merits. A villager said, "I do it to live good in the next life. ... A person has this life and his next one. He can live well in this life, and he can control it (that is, he can depend on his realistic and rational actions to control it). But when he could have a good life in the next life, he can't control. So they have to rely on the bless from the gods and Buddhas. The protection of the gods and Buddhas depends on the Dan in this life. Therefore, if you don't do Dan in this life, you will not live good in the next life." "How much you get depends on yourself. Anyway, you do more and get more, less and less. If you don't, you have nothing." For the Dan people, it is important to make the Dan, and it involves their reputation and social status. By doing Dan, the behavior of the person is judged by all members of society, thus gaining a reputation. The village members have more intimate relationships, reorganized or acquired new social relationships.

It can be seen from the entire ritual process that the whole process of Dan is actually a process of chanting the Sutras by the buddha, Bu Zhang and Kang Lang to the chanters and co-participants in the arranged, ritual-like space. In this space, buddha, Bu Zhang and Kang Lang are teachers. They are the intellectuals in the minds of Dai people and the educators in the village. A person of Dan is an educator who undergoes a process of awakening his past behaviors and adjusting his future behaviors throughout the ritual activities. For co-participants, it is process of being educated. The textbook used in this class is the palm-leaf manuscripts. It is in this sense that "the Sutras and the extended stories told by the monks to the villagers have made the rural temples a classroom for the morals of the people... It has also achieved the roles of Buddhist monks in enlightening the spiritual life of Buddhist rural communities in Southeast Asia with moral education, entertainment, and emotional exchange are inseparable."[3]

---

[1] In studying the social structure of Kachin in the highlands of Myanmar, Leach saw that Kachin people clearly distinguished between "heart-owned gifts" and "hand-owned gifts" in matters such as property and ownership Useless, but still makes the recipient obligated to the giver. See Edmund Leach. The Political Systems of the Highlands of Myanmar. Yang Chunyu and Zhou Yihong's translation. Beijing: Commercial Press, 2010: 139.

[2] Edmund Leach. Culture and Communication. Guo Fan and Zou He's translation. Shanghai: Shanghai People's Publishing House, 2000: 83-86.

[3] Song Lidao. Tradition and Modernity—A Changing World of Buddhism in the South. Beijing: China Social Sciences Press, 2002: 45.

3. The Palm-Leaf Manuscripts Commonly Used in the Daily Life Dan Rituals of the Dai People

In the daily life of local Dai people, the Dan is an important ritual activity, and the palm-leaf manuscripts are indispensable in these ritual activities. According to the buddha, Bu Zhang, and Kang Lang of M Village Buddhist Temple, the author records the palm-leaf manuscripts involved and used in various rituals as follows.

Sutras used to Dan the dead: Guides such as "Mahabatang" "Diewadudangdangha", Tripitaka "Sam Bittaka", the Paramita Sutras "Palami" "Vissuthiya" "Yelong" (Chinese translation for "Big Warehouse"), jātaka "Setthi Songkhao" (Chinese translation for "Rich Man's Food Delivery Story"), and Nirvana "Nippannasut" "Devadut Tangha" "Maha Vibak" (also written as "Moheweiba", translated as "Sutra on Great Retribution of Karma" "Anisong Katamboonyak" "Kannakavati" and so on.

Sutras used to Dan future (that is, Dan Mahabang): The jātaka "Visendara" is a must, and "Tripitaka" (Sudianda, Wei Nai, Apidama), Storiy Sutras such as "Malai" "Dimiyagongman" "Mahesata" "Mahaweibahuan" "Yelong", and the Exorcism Sutras "Luojiawuti", the Baltic Sutras "Balamixian'guo", "Balamibanjiang", the Commandment Sutras "Dibamendasu" and so on.

Sutras used to Dan Suzaida: "Ya Ni" is used in Daning house (Suzaidahen). It is said that chanting it can drive away bad things such as ghosts and snakes. "Sansongxidian"; "Zaiyasanjiaha" (also known as Butagunlong)—people think that ghosts are more afraid of it, so chanting it can drive away ghosts; the Commandments "Dibamangdasu" "Luojia wuti", are used in Daning family.

Daning the Birth (Haowuza): Combined with the birthday of the individual (Zai Da), copy the "Sutras" for the use of the traditional Tripitaka texts.

When Dan pagoda tower, recite "Diandata" "Nanhuanhao". The latter is used to pray for Granny of Valley God.

It can be seen that palm-leaf manuscripts are almost indispensable in the funeral activities in the local Dai villages.

4. Conclusion

These Sutras of the Buddhist temple in M village are all the offerings of the Dai believers in the village. Each time they accumulate several Sutras for the Buddhist temple in the village, the existing stock is formed over time. In the author's interview with the village, the villagers said that most believers could not understand and read these Sutras, but when the buddha and Bu Zhang recite, they know the basic content and can follow the recitation. When asked why they didn't understand but still to Dan these books, they answered very clearly that it was a custom of their family. When asked how the villagers know which palm-leaf manuscripts should be Dan since the villagers couldn't understand, the villagers' answer was that they could ask Bu Zhang or Kang Lang. Which Sutras the Dan people should Dan are determined by the "Zai Da" at birth (equivalent to the birth date of the Han people), and Bu Zhang, Kang Lang, etc. can look at their "Zai Da" and guide the villagers when to do ritual and which Sutra to Dan.

Because of the well-known reasons, although the number of ordinary Dai people who can read and write the palm-leaf manuscripts is not large, the "weight" of the palm-leaf manuscripts in the mind of the Dai family is still not underestimated, and we have reason to compare it to a "good medicine" used by the Dai family in daily life to nourish their soul and settle down their lives.

The Study on Palm-Leaf and Sa Paper Manuscripts to Support the Information for Tourism: A Case Study of Chiang Man Temple, Muang District, Chiang Mai

Direk Injan [1]

1. Introduction

Chiang Man Temple is located inside Chiang Mai's old city wall area. It is an important historical site as the first temple built under the order of King Mangrai, after the establishment of Chiang Mai in 1296. The temple's noteworthy art objects and architectures include Chedi Chang Lom, Main Wihan, Ho Trai (scripture depository) in the pond, Phra Sae Tang Khamani (Phra Kaew Khao or Crystal Buddha), Phra Sila (stone buddha image), a stone inscription about the founding of Chiang Mai, and paintings that depict King Mangrai's biography.

In the present, Chiang Man Temple is a historical tourist attraction included in the Chiang Mai travel plan for tourists, and is visited by both Thais and foreigners. Nevertheless, it is interesting that behaviors of the two groups of tourists differ, and affect how they visit temples and religious sites. On one hand, Thai tourists tend to travel without tour guides and seldom study about the places before visiting them. They will learn from reading information signs, brochures, or other forms of media since they are more interested in spiritual practices, like making merits, and paying respect to Buddha images to pray for good fortune, rather than history. On the other hand, foreign tourists will study about the places to plan their trips. They might also visit the places in travel plans supervised by tour guides, which gives them more opportunity to learn about important facts in comparison to Thai tourists. This phenomenon results in how non-local Thai tourists do not revisit religious sites, and how foreign and Thai tourists who learn about the places themselves or from tour guides will know important information about history and art that are

---

[1] Academic coordinator of Officer of Art & Culture, Chiang Mai Rahabhat University, Thailand.

already widely available.

"Encouraging people to revisit a tourist attraction" is a challenge for those who make profit from the places as they have to impress tourists, or come up with ways to make the tourists interested enough to come back in the future. Most of the time, the focus is on convenience and novelty, like the Tourism Authority of Thailand's "nine royal temples tour" travel plan for Bangkok. In this travel plan, tourists are guided to visit important temples in Rattanakosin Island. Most people might have already visited them on various occasions, but this travel plan is a one-day trip that focuses on paying homage to Buddha images. This concept is now widespread all over Thailand. For instance, in Chiang Mai, there is a "nine main temples inside the old city wall area of Chiang Mai" travel plan, and a "nine temples in Chiang Mai" travel plan.

The "nine temples in Chiang Mai" plan (because paying homage to Buddha images is believed to influence lives) includes visiting Chiang Man Temple (for stability), Duang Dee Temple (for good fortune), Chedi Luang Temple (for greatness), Phra Singh Temple (for "lion-like" power and influence), Chai Phra Kiat Temple (for prestige), Muen Lan Temple (for wealth), Dab Phai Temple (for protection from dangers), Muen Ngoen Kong Temple and Mor Kham Tuong Temple (for affluence). This travel plan is an example of how tourists can be encouraged to revisit tourist attractions. However, Chiang Man Temple have many appeals. People might show interests in the academic aspect, or appreciate the beauty of art objects, or want to learn about the history. There is also a new trend of tourism that use the history, name of the temple, and related stories to attract the general public into visiting Chiang Man Temple.

The main objective of this research is to synthesize important information about Chiang Man Temple from the data gathered from palm-leaf manuscripts, Sa paper manuscripts, and inscriptions that can be featured to promote Chaing Man Temple as a tourist attraction. The information will be utilized in creating learning centers, or supporting historical tourism. The written texts are used as primary historical sources since they are considered credible, and are interesting in a certain aspect.

2. Objectives

(a) To study history-related information and the importance of palm-leaf manuscripts, Sa paper manuscripts, and inscriptions from Chiang Man Temple in Muang District, Chiang Mai.

(b) To utilize the information obtained from palm-leaf manuscripts, Sa paper manuscripts, and inscriptions in supporting historical tourism in Chiang Man Temple, Muang District, Chiang Mai.

3. Methodology

3.1 Area Scope and Population Scope

This research focused only on studying palm-leaf manuscripts, Sa paper manuscripts and inscriptions that are stored in Chiang Man Temple, Muang District, Chiang Mai. The studied documents consist of 1,835 palm-leaf manuscripts, 33 Sa paper manuscripts and 4 inscriptions.

3.2 Content Scope

From the collected contents, the study was done only on the written texts found in palm-leaf manuscripts, Sa paper manuscripts, and inscriptions in the aspects of history, state of society, and knowledge that could be applied in tour guides' lectures on Chiang Man Temple, or contents that represent the value and importance of the documents.

3.3 Knowledge Synthesis Method

(a) Important and interesting information from palm-leaf manuscripts, Sa paper manuscripts, and inscriptions in Chiang Man Temple, Muang District, Chiang Mai were selected and collected. The texts were then transliterated and translated into Thai.

(b) Contents and important points were categorized by date of documentation.

(c) Information that can be used in supporting historical tourism was gathered and arranged to demonstrate the importance of historic sites and antiques in Chiang Man Temple, Muang District, Chiang Mai.

4. Results

Evidences show that Chiang Man Temple, located in the area inside the old city wall area in Muang District, Chiang Mai, is the first temple built after Chiang Mai was established as the capital city under the rule of King Mangrai, the first king of Chiang Mai, in 1296. The widely available version of the temple's history is concise, and mainly focuses on art objects and architectures like the Main Wihan and its gilded paintings that depicts King Mangrai's biography, Chedi Chang Lom, Phra Sae Tang Khamani (Phra Kaew Khao), Phra Sila, and the inscription about the founding of Chiang Mai. However, the information from palm-leaf manuscripts, Sa paper manuscripts, and inscriptions were not featured in the temple's information for tourists.

Chiang Man Temple currently stores many palm-leaf manuscripts, Sa paper manuscripts, and inscriptions. The documents has been inspected and listed. There are 1,835 palm-leaf manuscripts, 33 Sa paper manuscripts, and 4 inscriptions. Many of them have been studied, transliterated, and translated, but most of the information is only available and recognized in academic circles.

4.1 Important and Interesting Palm-Leaf Manuscripts, Sa Paper Manuscripts, and Inscriptions Found in Chiang Man Temple

Most of the palm-leaf manuscripts owned by Chiang Man Temple provide contents about Buddhist teachings and ceremonies, but some of them provide contents about history, legends, laws, astrology, superstitions, astronomy, linguistics, poems, local ceremonies, and knowledge like folk medicine formulas and local wisdom. Moreover, there are post faces and additional passages not intended by the writers to be main contents of the scriptures. However, they provide interesting information on history, knowledge, and state of society of the time they were written. The scriptures are currently stored in the Ho Trai (scripture depository) and the Ubosot (ordination hall).

4.1.1 Important and Interesting Palm-Leaf Manuscripts

Samanakatha, Monk written in 1870, referenced two editions (1868 and 1870) of the rules and restrictions for the monks and novices governed by the Chiang Mai Monk Council. It states that monks who resided in the sub-districts' main temples were ordered to transcribe *Samanakatha* and send the copies to their subordinate temples. This document provides the lists of elder monks who governed Chiang Mai, the temples governed by Chiang Mai Monk Council, as well as duties and rules of monks and novices from the time it was written.

Mangraidhammasat Law, copied in 1874, contains ancient laws and teachings that are claimed to be what King Mangrai legislated as rules for governing the state. It discloses the legislation, punishments, economy, society, and roles of people in different social classes.

List of Temples in Chiang Mai, written in 1874, contains the list of 98 temples inside Chiang Mai's city wall area, and 61 temples outside the wall. It discloses the number and names of temples at the time (Today, only 38 temples inside the city wall area remain).

Transliteration of Chiang Man Temple's stone inscription, written in 1874, contains the transliteration of the stone inscription about the founding of Chiang Mai, which was written in Fakkham script. The abbot of Chiang Man Temple transliterated the text into Tai Tham script to inform King Inthawichayanon, one of Chiang Mai's rulers, about the construction of Chiang Man Temple's Ubosot.

The Chiang Mai Annals contains summarized records of important events, along with date and time. For example, there are the dates of deaths of rulers of Chiang Mai and Lamphun, obituaries of elder monks in Chiang Mai, coronations of Chiang Mai's rulers, and the army's two attacks on Kengtung, Myanmar; and one on Vientiane, Lao.

4.1.2 Important and Interesting Sa Paper Manuscripts

Most of the Sa paper manuscripts in Chiang Man Temple have contents about prayers and traditional Lanna ceremonies, and are stored in the abbot's parsonage. The following paragraphs are examples of interesting manuscripts.

Khatha (Incantations) collection provides Pali incantations, written in Tai Tham scripts, used in praying for various results. For instance, there is Khatha Sek Som Poi, which will grant the prayer's affections from elders. There are also a Khatha that will help a person win a woman's heart when written on betel leaf, Khatha Fu Thoi Kham Ja that will help a person win a case when they write it on a piece of wood and skip over it, and Khatha Sek Nam Lang Na that will grant the prayer's affections from others and compliance from enemies.

Textbook of horse care and horse medicines provides instructions on how to use herbs as medicines for horses to improve their health and cure their illnesses. There are formulas for medicines that nourish horses and keep them healthy, and medicine that treat horses with bloody mucus in stool. There is also a manual for physiognomy of horses.

Fire ball and sky rocket formula book is a duplicate of the sky rocket manual written by a monk from Dok Khamtai District, Phayao. It provides the formula, measurements of bamboo stalks used for making rockets, and an instruction on how to set off a rocket.

Auspicious tree planting manual provides guidelines on how to plant different species of trees, according to directions, for good fortune. It also contains advice on the species of trees that should not be planted near a house, and the trees that would bring bad fortune if grown in the wrong direction and should be cut down.

Layout plan of Chiang Saen town is a Phab Sa manuscript that contains the layout plan of Chiang Saen town in which the names of city gates, temples, and important places were specified. It is presumed that the layout plan had been drawn before Chiang Saen became an abandoned town. It is considered an important historical source that illustrates the geography of Chiang Saen town at the time it was drawn.

Record of astronomical phenomena and earthquakes contains the dates of when astronomical phenomena, which is meteor in this case, happened. Illustrations of the meteors' positions are included. The record also shows that two earthquakes have occurred.

4.1.3 Important and Interesting Inscriptions

Inscriptions in Chiang Man Temple are found on various surfaces including stone tablet, base of a bronze Buddha statue, gold surface, and wood surface. They provides information on the history of Chiang Mai, as well as renovations and restorations of historic sites and antiques in Chiang Man Temple.

● Stone Inscription about the Founding of Chiang Mai, and The Construction and Renovation of Chiang Man Temple (1571)

The inscription in Fakkham script was created in 1571, but it provides the information about the founding of Chiang Mai, which took place in 1296. Dates and times, and names of people related to the event are mentioned in detail, along with a record on many renovations that took place in Chiang Man Temple. Also, the names of people assigned by the rulers of Chiang Mai to look after the temple are mentioned at the end of the inscription. Around 68 families are said to had served the role.

- Inscription on the Base of the Standing Buddha Statue in Alms-bowl Attitude (1465)

The Standing Buddha statue in Alms-bowl Attitude is enshrined in Wihan Phra Kaew of Chiang Man Temple. It is the oldest known Buddha statue in Lanna area. At the statue's base, there is an inscription of the date of the statue's creation in Tai Tham script, Pali incantations, and names of elder monks and faithful ones who took part in the creation. This inscription is significant for being the oldest inscription in Tai Tham script found on bases of Buddha statues in Chiang Mai.

- Phra Sila Inscription (1790)

Phra Sila is a Buddha statue carved out of stone, in a form of style, in the style of Southern India's Pala Empire. The statue is now enshrined in a model of Khitchakut Mountain, inside Wihan Phra Kaew of Chiang Man Temple. A lacquered and gilded wooden frame was made for the statue. The inscription in Tai Tham script on the frame mentions that King Kawila, the first king of Chet Ton Dynasty, his wives, and his relatives created the frame in 1790 to dedicate the merits to other family members, and wished to be blessed by the results of merits. This inscription provides important data like the names of King Kawila's relatives. Another significance is how the "Ye Dhamma" incantation in Pala script (Pallawa) was inscribed. The script is presented in only two inscriptions found in Chiang Mai. Another inscription in said script is found on the Buddha's footprint marquetry, also restored during the reign of King Kawila, displayed in Chiang Mai National Museum.

- Inscription on the Base of Phra Sae Tang Khamani or Phra Kaew Khao (1873)

Phra Sae Tang Khamani is a Buddha statue carved out of clear quartz crystal. The legend says that King Mangrai brought this statue from Hariphunchai to Chaing Man Temple in 1296. The inscription under the base states that King Inthawichayanon made a golden base and a golden tiered umbrella for the enshrinement of the statue in 1873.

4.2 Utilization of Information from Palm-Leaf Manuscripts, Sa Paper Manuscripts, and Inscriptions in Supporting Historical Tourism

Details about the palm-leaf manuscripts, Sa paper manuscripts, and inscriptions in Chiang Man Temple in term of their ages, numbers, contents, and other interesting details can be used as supporting data for the descriptions of architectures, art objects, and history-related information that has been studied before. This can help raise the public's awareness of the importance and values of ancient documents, and how practical use of them can be made in the present day.

4.2.1 The Main Wihan

The Main Wihan of Chiang Man Temple was built in the style of typical Lanna architectures. The principal Buddha image is enshrined here along with models of Khitchakut Mountain and stupas. One outstanding feature of the Main Wihan is the gilded paintings on red background that depict the life and works of King Mangrai, with descriptions written in Tai Tham scripts. The paintings were designed and painted under the lead of those who governed the temple, for the 700th anniversary of Chiang Mai's establishment in 1996 (gilded artworks were popular in Shan state, Myanmar). The paintings depict the content recorded in palm-leaf manuscripts about the Legend of Chiang Saen, Folklore of Chiang Mai, Legend of Prachao Liab Lok, and the Chiang Man Temple's stone inscription, which are all documents found in Chiang Man Temple.

4.2.2 Wihan Phra Kaew

A model of Khitchakut Mountain was built for the enshrinement of Phra Sae Tang Khamani (Phra Kaew Khao) and Phra Sila in Wihan Phra Kaew. According to the Folklore of Chiang Mai, Chiang Man Temple's edition, King Mangrai brought Phra Sae Tang Khamani from Haripunchai. There is an inscription about the creation of golden base and golden tiered umbrella during the reign of King Inthawichayanon, Queen Thip Keson, Prince Ratchaphakhinai, and Princess Ubonwanna in 1873. The inscription was carved by pounding lines of small holes to create the shapes of alphabets. In addition, Phra Sila is mentioned in the Legend of Phra Sila, Chiang Man Temple's edition, where it is said to be created after 7 years, 7 months, and 7 days that followed the end of the Buddha's lifetime, by King Ajatashatru of Rajgir, India. The statue was then brought to, and enshrined in Lampang until 1476, when King Tilokaraj brought the statue to Chiang Mai and had it enshrined there. Another significant feature of Phra Sila is the inscription in Pala script (ancient Indian script) on the statue. Wihan Phra Kaew is also shelter the bronze standing Buddha statue in Alms-bowl Attitude with an inscription in Tai Tham scripts on its base. It is the oldest known inscription in Tai Tham script (inscribed in 1465).

4.2.3 Chedi Chang Lom

Chedi Chang Lom, the oldest stupa in Chiang Man Temple, is located behind the Main Wihan. It was built in the Lanna-Sukhothai style, with "lotus-shaped" base and 15 elephant sculptures around the stupa. The Inscription of Chiang Man Temple stated that the original stupa was built by King Mangrai alongside the construction of the temple. After that, a new stupa was built to cover the old one, during the reign of King Tilokaraj. The stupa was then renovated when Chiang Mai was under the rule of Burmese monarchs.

4.2.4 Ubosot

The Ubosot (ordination hall) of Chiang Man Temple is located at the southwest of the

Main Wihan. It is a place for monks who resides in the temple to perform religious rites so visitors are not allowed inside the wall of the Ubosot. A stone inscription in Fakkham scripts is placed in front of the Ubosot's northern porch. There are texts on both sides of the stone tablet. It contains the history about the founding of Chiang Mai, and detailed records of renovations and restorations carried out in the temple. Names of people who look after the temple are mentioned at the end of the inscription. This inscription is an important evidence used for calculating the exact date of when Chiang Mai was founded, which turned out to be April 12th 1296. The content reflects the relationship between Chiang Mai, Phayao, and Sukhothai; and discloses how Burmese Kings who ruled Chiang Mai uphold Buddhism, led multiple renovations in the temples and made merits there. It also mentions the names of common people in that era.

4.2.5 Ho Trai

The Ho Trai (scripture depository) of Chiang Man Temple was originally a two-storied building. The upper level was built of wood and the lower level was built of bricks and plaster. Then, it was moved into the pond behind the Ubosot and renovated into a single-storied building with only the level built of wood. The building is on stilts and there is no ladder provided so people who want to go inside it need to bring their own ladders.

Lanna people believed that inscribing palm-leaf manuscripts, preparing cloths for wrapping the scriptures, making trunks or cabinets for storing the scriptures, and building Ho Trai would help upholding Buddhism since palm-leaf manuscripts are considered the proof of Buddhism's existence. As a result, many scriptures and Sa paper manuscripts were offered to temples. They do deserved to be studied and applied into modern uses.

5. Conclusion

The study on palm-leaf manuscripts, Sa paper manuscripts, and inscriptions to support historical tourism stems from the concept of the value of these documents. To elaborate, they records writings on religious teachings, history, literature, beliefs, and various branches of science and art. Generally, within historical and heritage tourism, tourists will mostly learn the big picture of history, and appreciate the beauty of architectures and art objects. The information from ancient documents like palm-leaf manuscripts, Sa paper manuscripts, and inscriptions should be presented to tourists as well because they are a novelty, more interesting, and more credible than oral history.

The information from palm-leaf manuscripts, Sa paper manuscripts, and inscriptions in Chiang Man Temple can be effectively used as references and give more details on the history of Chiang Man Temple. The importance of these documents can be described as the following paragraphs.

Palm-leaf manuscripts in Chiang Man Temple provide the history of the founding of

Chiang Mai, construction and renovations of Chiang Man Temple in different time periods, and the history of important antiques. Examples include Transliteration of Chiang Man Temple's stone inscription, Notices from the Chiang Mai Monk Clergy, List of Temples in Chiang Mai, and the Chiang Mai Annals. Additionally, some of the scriptures contain the ancient laws legislated by King Mangrai, and details about the route from Phra That Doi Suthep Temple to downtown Chiang Mai. There is also a story about the renovation of Phra That Doi Suthep Temple during the reign of King Inthawichayanon which was written in a certain form of verse by Phaya Phromwohan, a royal poet.

Sa paper manuscripts in Chiang Man Temple provide contents about local knowledge and rituals such as record and illustrations of meteors in 1882 and 1883; record of the earthquakes and aftershocks in 1884; the layout plan of Chiang Saen, which is presumed to be drawn when Chiang Saen was under the rule of Myanmar; textbook of horse care and medicines; tree planting manual; sky rocket manual, and incantations collection.

Inscriptions in Chiang Man Temple with historical significance includes stone inscription in Fakkham script located in front of the Ubosot, created in 1518, which provides the history of Chiang Mai's founding and Chiang Man Temple; oldest known inscription in Tai Tham script on the base of Buddha statue, created in 1456; inscription of Pali incantation in Pala script, which is found on only two items in Chiang Mai: Phra Sila and the Buddha's footprint model (at Chiang Mai National Museum), and the inscription in Tai Tham script on the back side of the wooden frame that mentions its creation led by King Kawila, King of Chiang Mai, in 1790, and inscription in Tai Tham script about the creation of golden base and tiered umbrella for the statue is found under the base of Phra Sae Tang Khamani (Phra Kaew Khao), which was inscribed in 1518, during the reign of King Inthawichayanon who governed Chiang Mai.

Lanna palm-leaf manuscripts and Sa Paper manuscripts contain very significant and interesting contents not only Buddha's teaching or literatures, but there are many interesting knowledge or information for other people that can use as the attraction point for revisit tourist. The information might tempt people who used to visit Chiang Man Temple to revisit and be interested in valuable manuscripts and inscriptions. Making the information from these documents accessible, and using them in lectures on Chiang Man Temple for tourists can help raise visitors' awareness of values and significance of written texts as primary historical sources, which are more credible than oral history. Furthermore, Examples of these documents include the scripture that recorded the Mangraithammasat Law, annals, list of temples in Chiang Mai, record of meteors and earthquakes, layout plan of Chiang Saen town from the time Lanna Kingdom was under the rule of Burmese monarchs, formulas of medicines for horses, sky rocket manual, tree planting manual, list of people who were assigned to look after Chiang Man Temple, the only known inscription in Pala script (ancient Indian script) found in Lanna, the oldest known inscription in Tai Tham script on the base of Buddha statue (1465 CE), and the inscription on the gold surface under the base of Phra Sae Tang Khamani (Phra Kaew Khao).

6. Suggestions

This research focused on studying palm-leaf manuscripts, Sa paper manuscripts, and inscriptions in order to use information from these documents as preliminary data to support historical tourism in Chian Man Temple. The researcher has several suggestions on how to further this study.

(a) The results of this study should be tested by using them to guide tourists in Chiang Man Temple. This is to see if it is possible to accomplish in using the information from palm-leaf manuscripts, Sa paper manuscripts, and inscriptions to support historical tourism.

(b) The process and concept of using information from palm-leaf manuscripts, Sa paper manuscripts, and inscriptions should be applied in studies on other temples or historic sites.

References

[1] Jongrak N. Phruttikam khong Nak Thongtieo chao Thai thi Asai Yunai khet Krungthepmahanakon Lae Parimontol Tor Kantadsiijai Chaiborikan Boristnamtieo (Studying the Use of Travel Agencies by Thai Residents of the Bangkok Metropolitan Area). An Independent Study Submitted in Partial Fulment of the Master Degree of Business Administration, Faculty of Commerce and Accountancy, Thammasat University, Thailand, 2017.

[2] Kannakammakan truodsob lae Suebkhon Duang Mueang Lae Tamnan Puenmueang Chiang Mai. Chodmaihet Kantrodsob Lae suebkhon Duang Mueang Noppaburisrinakonchiangmai. Chiang Mai: So Saph Kanpim. Thailand, 1996.

[3] Penth H., Khrueathai P. and Ketprom S. Prachum Jaruek Lan-Na Lem 2 Jaruek Samai Phrachao Kawila. Chiang Mai: Khlang Khomun Jaruek Lan-Na, Institute of Social Research, Chiang Mai University, Thailand, 1998.

[4] Upranukro J. Wai Phra 9 Wat: Kantongtieo Lae Pholkratop tor Sappayakorn Watthanatham (Nine Temples Merit Tour: Tourism and Its Impacts on Culture Resources). Master Degree Thesis of Cultural Resource Management Program, Graduate School, Silpakorn University, Thailand, 2014.

Precious Regional Cultural Heritage

—Palm-Leaf Scriptures and Palm-Leaf Culture: Inheritance and Protection Practice and Cognition from China

Zhou Ya[①]

Translated by Liu Dezhou[②]

1. Introduction

With the deepening of globalization and with the increase of the depth, width and frequency of capital flows and economic, social and cultural exchanges in the world, geographical boundaries are becoming ambiguous; local characteristics are disappearing; regional cultural features are declining. They objectively trigger a worldwide phenomenon of "cultural folding" which is against cultural diversity, that is, the cultural phenomenon that a large number of regional traditional cultures bearing historical information are impacted, dissolved or even eliminated by more powerful global modern culture with accelerating rate[③].

For nearly half a century, the precious "palm-leaf culture" in China, South Asia and Southeast Asia has been undergoing this process. "Palm-leaf culture" takes Pali palm-leaf classics (including inscribed scriptures and various paper manuscripts) as its core, takes people's Buddhist belief and related cultural customs as its denotation, and serves as an important part of human civilization and world cultural diversity. At present, in the above mentioned areas, palm-leaf culture still has the characteristics of both freshness and heritage. Its freshness means that some regions still have a certain scale and existing cultural resources. (For example, there exist a large number of palm-leaf classics, inscribed

---

[①] The director of the Palm-Leaf Culture Research Center of Yunnan University, doctor and associate researcher of Institute of Ethnology and Sociology of Yunnan University, expert member of Yunnan Intangible Cultural Heritage Protection and Research Base, deputy secretary general of Yunnan Religious Society.

[②] Professor of School of Foreign Languages and Literature, Yunnan Normal University.

[③] Zhou Ya.Introduction to Some Core Issues and Values of the Studies on Dai and Thai Ethnic Groups—Review of Zheng Xiaoyun's "Collected Essays on Dai and Thai Ethnic Groups" .Journal of Hubei University (Philosophy and Social Science Edition), 2020(2): 165-166.

scriptures and copies. At the same time a certain amount of new palm-leaf inscribed scriptures and paper manuscripts are being produced.) And a series of traditional culture and customs and activities associated with it continue to exist. But at the same time, in many areas of the region, a large part of the cultural system has become "heritage". Its manifestations are that various kinds of social factors that traditionally supported the cultural system have melt down or disappeared. To a large extent, palm-leaf culture has lost its traditional functions, and it has shown a lot of antipathetic societal adaptability problems in the modern society. For example, it is less perceived/used by people, or is regarded as "useless" etc.

In China, palm-leaf scriptures and palm-leaf culture's becoming heritage rapidly is particularly prominent. This is firstly caused by the rapid development of industrialization in China, since 1980s and the rapid modernization of the vast cities and villages. In addition, compared with other countries with Theravada Buddhism as the mainstream culture, some ethnic groups in China believe in Theravada Buddhism and they are represented by Dai ethnic group. Their inheritance of palm-leaf culture is inevitably impacted by the mainstream Chinese culture (Han culture), which further intensifies the historization of palm-leaf culture. Over the past decade, the ethnic groups represented by Dai ethnic group, have taken the inheritance and revival of "palm-leaf culture" as an important way to maintain their ethnic identity and cultural identity. In addition to the efforts of the folk, Chinese government also attaches great importance to the protection of splendid traditional ethnic culture, and provide preferential policy and funding support for ethnic language education, preservation of ancient books and documents, and intangible cultural heritage protection for the inheritance and protection of ethnic traditional culture heritage. To some extent, these measures have played a positive role.

However, the most thought-provoking problems are endogenous problems—local Dai and related ethnic groups' young people's "free choice" in face of globalization, modernization and dramatic social changes. Few of them are willing to be committed to learn inscribing palm-leaf scriptures or learn palm-leaf scriptures and culture in Buddhist temples. Most young people actively choose to "seek" / "hug" modern urban life. Most of them and their parents also approve of modern national education. They only regard palm-leaf scriptures and palm-leaf culture as the traditional (obsolete) culture that can be learned or "experienced occasionally" in their spare time. This situation reflects the current living conditions and social values of the Dai youth in China, and poses a great challenge for the inheritance and protection of palm-leaf scriptures and palm-leaf culture in the local society.

It can be said that the trend of accelerating historization of palm-leaf scriptures and palm-leaf culture is inevitable. We need to have a clearer and deeper understanding of its cultural form and heritage value, so as to do a good job in the inheritance and conservation of this precious regional cultural resources[①] at the present stage.

2. Precious Regional Cultural Heritage—Palm-Leaf Scriptures and Palm-Leaf Culture

Palm-leaf scriptures are important media and representations of world Buddhist history and civilization.During the spread and development of Buddhism, early word-of-mouth spread of Buddhism lasted for hundreds of years. After that, Buddhist doctrines were recorded on the media, which were the media foundations for Buddhism to break through its locality and spread to larger regions and even to the world in ancient times.The palm-leaf scriptures were the main media of the Buddhist scriptures in this long period of time. As one of the world's three major religions, Buddhism is widely practiced and has about 500 million believers worldwide, accounting for about 7% of the world's population[②]. Considering the technical dimensions of religious demography in some of the world's largest Buddhist cultures, the actual number of people worldwide who believe in Buddhism may be close to 1 billion. Based on the global population of 7.585 billion, it should account for about 13% of the world's total population.Therefore, Buddhist civilization is an important part of human civilization.The palm-leaf scriptures and palm-leaf culture have also become important symbols of Buddhist culture, especially of Theravada Buddhism culture.

In China, palm-leaf culture is regarded as a characteristic ethnic culture in the southwest frontier area of China. Palm-leaf scriptures in China can be divided into Sanskrit scriptures and Pali scriptures.Among them, the spread and translation of Sanskrit palm-leaf scriptures in China had been relatively frequent since the Han Dynasty and reached their peak in the Tang Dynasty. After that, they gradually declined in central China due to the emergence, spread and popularization of Chinese Buddhist scriptures.Nowadays, Sanskrit palm-leaf scriptures have mostly become collections of Buddhist temples, collectors or collection institutions in the mainland of China and the inscribing, making, transmission and inheritance of palm-leaf scriptures have early become extinct.However, the making, inscribing, use and inheritance of Pali palm-leaf scriptures and many related cultural phenomena are still alive and preserved in southern and southwestern parts of Yunnan province where Dai people live and Pali Buddhism (Theravada Buddhism) is spread.Therefore, in China, "palm-leaf culture" is also regarded as a regional characteristic ethnic culture.Its geographical scope roughly includes the Dai inhabited areas

---

① Palm-leaf scriptures and palm-leaf culture in this paper have the implications of "cultural resources" and "cultural heritage" — The author.

② According to data of Pew Research Center's *The Changing Global Religious Landscape*, released on April 5, 2017.

of Xishuangbanna, Dehong, Lincang, Pu'er, Baoshan and other places in southwest and south Yunnan province.The ethnic groups that believe in Theravada Buddhism include Dai, Theravada Blang, Deang, Achang, Yi and Va. Among them, Dai ethnic group is the representative group of this culture.

To sum up, we can form the following basic cognition about "palm-leaf scriptures and palm-leaf culture":

First, the relationship between palm-leaf scriptures and palm-leaf culture. Palm-leaf scriptures are the core and representation of palm-leaf culture. Without palm-leaf scriptures, it is hard to be called the real "palm-leaf culture".

Second, "palm-leaf culture" has a broad sense and a narrow sense.Broadly speaking, palm-leaf culture should include all kinds of social and cultural events related to palm-leaf scriptures and the spread of Buddhism in world history.In a narrow sense, palm-leaf culture is a cultural system that includes the spread, production, inscribing, use, copying, various rituals, customs and activities centered on the inheritance of palm-leaf scriptures (or even paper manuscripts) in relevant ethnic groups.

Third, palm-leaf culture is a transnational and trans-regional culture.Given the fact that current human use, inscribing, production, inheritance and protection practices are mainly concentrated in the Pali Buddhism regions, we can say that palm-leaf scriptures and palm-leaf cultures are the common cultural resources and heritage for China and Southeast Asian and South Asian countries.

Fourth, palm-leaf culture in China has the dual attributes of living cultural resources and cultural heritage.In China, palm-leaf culture is mainly distributed in south and southwest Yunnan province and it is represented by the Dai inhabited areas.In this region, due to local differences, the palm-leaf scriptures and palm-leaf culture have the characteristics of living cultural resources, but they also show the attributes of cultural heritage to some extent.

Fifth, palm-leaf culture has world-class cultural heritage taste and value. Over a long history, palm-leaf scriptures and culture spread along with Buddhism all over the world.They reflect and symbolize Buddhist civilization and they have transnational, cross-regional, cross-ethnic groups, cross-language, cross-time and cross-space features and "world-class" taste of culture, high-grade and even world-class human cultural heritage value.

3. The Cultural Heritage Value of Palm-Leaf Scriptures and Palm-Leaf Culture

Palm-leaf culture is symbolized by palm-leaf scriptures.The core carriers of palm-leaf culture are palm-leaf scriptures (inscribed palm-leaf scriptures), followed by paper manuscripts.However, since there are many mixed records of the two, it is difficult to distinguish them completely.So many Chinese scholars refer to them collectively as "palm-leaf scripture classics" or "palm-leaf cultural classics", while international scholars refer to them collectively as "manuscripts".They not only reflect and symbolize Buddhist civilization, but also carry the history and traditional culture of many ethnic groups in the region.

3.1 The Value of Buddhist Cultural Heritage

Palm-leaf scriptures are Buddhist scriptures inscribed on palm leaves made through a special craft with iron pens manually.The palm-leaf scriptures are generally divided into Pali scriptures and Sanskrit scriptures, which are the source text scriptures of world Pali Buddhism (Theravada Buddhism) and Sanskrit Buddhism (Mahayana Buddhism) respectively.As the main writing medium and important symbolic carrier of Buddhism, the emergence of palm-leaf scriptures expanded the spreading areas of Buddhism, increased the spreading rate and efficiency of Buddhist culture, and laid a foundation for Buddhism to become a world religion.In this sense, palm-leaf scriptures themselves are the world's precious Buddhist cultural heritage.

Pali palm-leaf scriptures are the spreading carrier of Pali Buddhism.The distributing scope, "palm-leaf cultural region", includes most part of or parts of Sri Lanka, India and Nepal in South Asia, and Myanmar, Thailand, Laos and Cambodia in Southeast Asia, and Dai inhabited areas in south and southwest Yunnan province. Pali is a vernacular Indian language used by the Buddha in his teachings.Before the emergence of text carriers such as palm-leaf scripture, Buddhism was spread by word of mouth in Pali.In the first century, palm leaves began to be used as a carrier in Sri Lanka by using Sinhala to spell Pali Buddhist scriptures.Since then, Theravada Buddhism has maintained the tradition of inscribing and recording Buddhist scriptures in Pali.With the spread of Theravada Buddhism, different countries adopted their own languages to spell Pali and to record and preserve Buddha's Teaching. "Historic information" in the ancient texts of palm-leaf scriptures truly reflects Buddha's teachings and Buddha's doctrine. Palm-leaf scriptures play a unique and irreplaceable role in spreading Buddhism to more countries and wider regions, making palm-leaf scriptures become the symbol of "Dharma" among Tripitaka (Buddha, Dharma and Sangha).

Nowadays, a large number of palm-leaf scriptures and paper manuscripts are still preserved in Buddhist temples in China, Southeast Asian countries and South Asian countries and some are collected in cultural organizations, museums and folk organizations. Some of them have a history of more than 100 years, and are the precious historical memory and Buddhist cultural heritage of mankind in the region and the world at large.

3.2 The Value of Ancient Writing System Database and Ancient Documents

Another important heritage value of Pali palm-leaf scriptures is their preservation of ancient writing system. "Ancient writing system" here refers to the script recorded in the palm-leaf scriptures, which have been passed down for hundreds or thousands of years in the country/region/ethnic group.In China, for example, historically, "a considerable portion of the Buddhist scriptures were transcribed by Dai monks into Dai scripts on the basis of the pronunciations of the sources texts, and parts of them were translated into Dai languages." [1] However, with the change of times and society, these scripts are now rarely understood, thus showing features of heritage or "being ancient" nature.For example, in Xishuangbanna, the scripts used to inscribe palm-leaf scriptures is known locally as "old Dai (Tai) Lue script". Since the simplification reform in 1950s and 1960s, they have been replaced by a relatively simple "New Dai (Tai) Script".Because New Dai Script is really easier to learn, and "bilingual teaching" in the ethnic education system for ethnic groups adopts "New Dai Script", "Old Dai (Lue) Script" which is beautiful and charming but difficult to learn, has gradually faded out of Dai people's social life. However, due to some limitations of the New Dai Script, the folk people could not write and transcribe Buddhist classics, especially the palm-leaf scriptures with the New Dai Scripts. As a result, the "Old Dai Script", which still exists in the inscribed versions of the palm-leaf scriptures, has become the database to retain and record the Old Dai Script.

Such a situation also exists to a certain extent in other parts of the region.As far as writing systems or scripts are concerned, palm-leaf culture also shows remarkable diversity due to users' differences in country, users' ethnic group and place.For example, there are many types of scripts used to record Buddha's teachings in Pali palm-leaf scriptures and paper manuscripts.If divided according to modern countries, these scripts are from Sri Lanka, Myanmar, Thailand, Laos, Cambodia, China and other countries.From the perspective of historical view, the main recorded languages include Sinhalese, Khmer, Burmese, Lanna script, Dai script etc. The ethnic groups involved with its inscribing and inheritance include Sinhalese in Sri Lanka, Khmer in Cambodia, Shans in Myanmar, Laotian in Laos, Thais in Thailand and Dai in China.Even within an ethnic group, there may be a variety of scripts. For example, in China, the scripts used by Dai people to inscribe the palm-leaf scriptures or palm-leaf classics are divided into Xishuangbanna script (Dai Lue script), Dehong Dai script (Daina script), Gengma and Ruili Dai script and Jinping Dai script (Daiduan script). Among them, Dehong Dai script and Jinping Dai

---

[1] The Writing Group. A Brief History of Dai Ethnic Group (Revised Edition) .Beijing: The Ethnic Publishing House, 2009: 305.

script only have ancient paper manuscripts, rather than palm-leaf scriptures[1].

In terms of historical value, if preserved in proper condition, inscribed palm-leaf scriptures can be preserved for hundreds of years, even more than one thousand years.But most of the palm-leaf cultural regions have tropical climate and some areas had frequent wars in history.In addition, damage and crack problems caused by worms and improper air seasoning affect the actual preservation time of palm-leaf scriptures. Over-400-year-old inscribed palm-leaf scriptures have been found in Thailand. In Thailand, Myanmar, Laos and other countries, some palm-leaf scriptures are more than two or three hundred years old. In China, due to the impact of the "Cultural Revolution" in the second half of 20th century and the custom of replacing old scriptures with new ones in Dai temples, most of the palm-leaf scriptures were made after the 18th century[2].

In any case, the palm-leaf scriptures in China, Southeast Asia and South Asia are databases of variety of ancient writing systems, and are precious ancient books and documents containing a great deal of historical information and precious traditional culture of ethnic groups.

3.3 Ethnic Traditional Culture, Collective Memory and Local Knowledge Value

Palm-leaf classics not only include Buddhist content on inscribed palm leaves, but also include a large quantity of secular content on paper manuscripts, such as astronomy, calendar, medicine and medical knowledge, local laws and regulations, local history, technology and techniques, ethics and moral, and literature such as poetry, legends and aphorisms.They constitute local knowledge and collective memory in the traditional culture of ethnic groups, contain their "cultural genes", spiritual temperament and values of different ethnic groups, and play an important role in the formation of ethnic group identity and local culture.In China, Southeast Asia and South Asia, a large number of palm-leaf cultural classics have all of the above characteristics.

Chinese Dai palm-leaf cultural classics are regarded as "the encyclopedia of traditional Dai culture". Its rich contents involve almost every aspect of production and life in Dai society. This article takes Dai medicine as an example. Dai medicine, Mongolian medicine, Tibetan medicine and Uygur medicine, are known as "China's four ethnic medicines". Dai medicine has a systematic medical theories and rich practical experiences, and has distinct ethnic and local characteristics. It is one of the important components of traditional Chinese medicine.In the history of Dai ethnic group, most of the theories and practical experiences of medicine were recorded in the palm-leaf classics

---

[1] Zhang Gongjin. A Study on the Editions of Ancient Books in Dai Literature. The Ethnic Publishing House, 2018: 63.
[2] Zhang Gongjin. A Study on the Editions of Ancient Books in Dai Literature. The Ethnic Publishing House, 2018: 64.

and handed down to the people for hundreds of years.In Xishuangbanna, there is an inscribed medical book of the palm-leaf scripture called "Wannabatwei" ("the Book of Medicine"), which contains not only abundant prescriptions, but also pathological explanations.

The time when this palm-leaf scripture was written is unknown.The present version was copied in the year of 1289 in Dai calendar (1927) and it is a very precious Dai medical book[①]. Nearly a thousand prescriptions are collected in the paper manuscript of *Danghaya* (*Pharmacopoeia*). Two other manuscripts, including *Medical Book* and *Principles of Medical Science*, demonstrate the medical theory and dialectical thought of Dai ethnic group on diagnosis and treatment of diseases.These medical books are available in a variety of forms and formats in the local area. They are systematic and complete records of traditional Dai medicine and principles of medical science, and they are valuable classics of Dai ethnic group and local knowledge.Some of them have been used in the Dai ethnic group's modern medicine industry, and have a lasting influence and value on the Dai ethnic group's social life.

3.4 The Superimposed Value of "Cultural Heritage"

Palm-leaf culture is vast and plentiful and the culture itself also includes some contents of precious local cultural heritage, or they are deeply related to local cultural heritage in terms of contents.Thus it presents superimposed value of "heritage within heritage". For example, palm-leaf classics contain a lot of ancient art and skills.In addition to making skills of palm-leaf scriptures, production techniques of Buddha Statues, production techniques and procedures of Dai drums are included in paper manuscripts of palm-leaf cultural classics. For example, the name of Volume 75 of *Complete Works of Chinese Palm-Leaf Scriptures* is "Rules and Other Things about Making Big Drums and Buddha Statues" .Its source text is a 19-line double-sided paper manuscript. Materials, instruments and ritual procedures for making big drums and Buddha statues are clearly documented in the manuscript. In addition, the paper of many paper manuscripts is also the technical product of "intangible cultural heritage". For example, the paper making technology of Mangtuan Village, Mengding town, Gengma county was listed in the *National Intangible Cultural Heritage List* in 2008[②]. In 2006, "Dai Zhangha" (Dai traditional art form) was included in the first batch of *National Intangible Cultural Heritage List*, and many of Zhangha's songs originated from palm-leaf classics.

These local knowledge and traditional ethnic skills reflect the collective consciousness

---

① The Writing Group. A Brief History of Dai Ethnic Group (Revised Edition) .Beijing: The Ethnic Publishing House, 2009: 338.
② Zhang Gongjin. A Study on the Editions of Ancient Books in Dai Literature. The Ethnic Publishing House, 2018: 64.

and cognition of Dai people in authentic life, such as cosmology, ecology and values, as well as their individual or group activities, skills and practices, and they carry Dai people's ethnic psychology and precious collective memory.

Most of these "heritages among heritages" in the palm-leaf classics have the attributes of intangible cultural heritages, which are worthy of attention, protection and inheritance. Nowadays, these local knowledge and ethnic skills are only known and mastered by a few people, and they are handed down and practiced through master-apprentice relationship, which leads to the situation that some masters do not have successors. If we do not pay attention to the protection of texts and the inheritance of people, these valuable local knowledge and cultural experience will not be sustainable.

4. Palm-Leaf Scriptures and the Inheritance and Protection of Palm-Leaf Culture—the Practice in China

Palm-leaf scriptures and palm-leaf culture are of great significance and value to present the unique geographical advantage and cultural diversity charm of Yunnan province. Yunnan province has a special geographical position connecting China, Southeast Asia and South Asia, and it is also the place where Mahayana, Tibetan and Theravada Buddhism meet and merge. So Yunnan province is an converging "cultural node" of the three branches of the world Buddhist civilization. The existence of palm-leaf scriptures and "palm-leaf culture" over thousands of years show that they have strong vitality and cultural power. They were not only involved with all aspects of social production and life in the region in the past, but also has inexhaustible cultural creativity and social benefits for the cultural industry in the region today. For example, in China, palm-leaf culture has been deeply involved in the cultural industries in Xishuangbanna and Dehong, providing sources for the development of local economic and cultural industries, such as films and television industry, tourism industry, pharmaceutical industry, cultural and museum industry, cultural creation, arts and crafts industries etc.

In order to better reflect the important humanistic value of its regional cultural ties, we need to make a phased summary and cognition of its inheritance and protection practices.

Generally speaking, the protection and inheritance of palm-leaf scriptures and palm-leaf culture can be divided into two aspects: First, the protection of "palm-leaf scriptures", namely substantive protection of the palm-leaf scriptures and palm-leaf classic manuscripts (including paper manuscripts), improving and upgrading the existing preservation condition, and adopting digital technology for protection. Second, protection of "palm-leaf culture", namely, the local people's implementation of the inheritance and protection of customs relevant to palm-leaf culture in the region, including inheritance and protection of the folk palm-leaf scriptures making and production techniques, inheritance practices of scripture offering ceremonies, adopting all kinds of resources and power to promote indigenous people's perception of the value of these customs and identity, promoting the inheritance and protection of these customs and ceremonies in the region.

China, together with Southeast Asian countries and South Asian countries, is committed to the inheritance and protection of palm-leaf scriptures and palm-leaf culture, precious regional cultural heritages. At present, in China, the protection practice can be divided into four categories: form protection, inheritance protection, institutional protection and research protection.

4.1 Form Protection

Form protection refers to physical and material protection of palm-leaf scriptures and all kinds of paper manuscripts, including protective gathering, sorting, collection and maintenance of palm-leaf classics and literature. Subjects of the protection practice are mainly archives departments, cultural centers and museums, agencies of ancient documents (ancient document office and libraries, etc.), as well as Buddhist temples and folk cultural elites (religious affairs personnel, folk intellectuals and collectors who have higher traditional culture education on Dai ethnic group, such as Buddhist temple monks, Kang Lang/Bu Zhang/He Lu/An Zhang etc.). For example, in Xishuangbanna, there are a large quantity of collection of palm-leaf scriptures and paper manuscripts in the prefecture archives, prefecture museums, prefecture libraries and other institutions. Staffs of Dehong Prefecture Library were heavily involved in the collation and preservation of local ancient manuscripts. At present, the palm-leaf classics in Dehong prefecture are mainly paper manuscripts, with only a small amount of ivory manuscripts, elephant bone manuscripts and palm-leaf manuscripts. In recent years, nearly 4,000 books (volumes) of palm-leaf classics have been collected and sorted out in Mangshi where the prefecture government is located, while other manuscripts are scattered in cultural institutions and Buddhist temples in Ruili, Lianghe, Yingjiang and Wanding etc.

4.2 Inheritance Protection

Inheritance protection refers to the "living" inheritance and protection mechanisms of palm-leaf scriptures and palm-leaf culture performed by local government departments and non-governmental forces, including growing and cultivation of Talipot palms, protection and inheritance of inscribing and production techniques of palm-leaf scriptures, encouraging folk inheritance or restoration of traditional customs in order to increase the real use of palm-leaf scriptures, as well as spread of the content of palm-leaf scriptures and culture.

The main reason why it is difficult to inherit palm-leaf culture is that a series of social factors supporting the cultural system are eliminated or have disappeared with social changes. In the traditional Dai society, Buddhist temples were schools and palm-leaf scriptures were the teaching materials. Palm-leaf scripture had significant educational functions and practical functions in the traditional society. Therefore, they were an important link in the operation of Dai society; inscribing and making palm-leaf scriptures were routine, and there was no need for inheritance and protection.However, with social changes, the modern national education system has replaced the traditional education, and the functions of palm-leaf scriptures have been largely eliminated, and the inheritance of the palm-leaf scriptures, which have lost their practicability, has become a "big problem".

Therefore, in order to truly achieve protection and inheritance, it is necessary to jointly improve and alleviate the current "endangered" situation from the aspects of "market" demand, educational function, value perception, benefit and reward. Many prominent senior monks of Theravada Buddhism in China, such as lay Buddhist Dao Shuren, Kruba Venerable Han Ting, Kruba Venerable Deng Dai, Venerable Mahindra and younger monks such as Dubikanzhang from Mengjinglai Temple, Menghai county, have made a lot of beneficial practice to promote palm-leaf scriptures and palm-leaf culture of the traditional culture education, and to adapt to the contemporary social development. They have organized a lot of activities, such as public speaking, organizing palm-leaf scriptures inscribing skills study activities within Buddhist circles and folk elites, performing cross-border lecture communication and "Tamazaga" chanting activity, translating Pali Buddhist scriptures into Chinese and establishing "palm-leaf college", all of which have vigorously promoted the protection of palm-leaf scriptures and their spread in the Dai society.

4.3 Institutional Protection

Institutional protection refers to the practice of obtaining resources, especially financial support, by applying for cultural protection projects established by Chinese government agencies at all levels, so as to promote the cultural inheritance and protection of palm-leaf scriptures and palm-leaf culture.For example, relevant inheritance activities and the inheritors of "Intangible Cultural Heritage List of China" established by the Ministry of Culture and Tourism of China are provided with special financial support each year.This form of protection is mainly organized and operated by the "vertical management system" of the Department of Intangible Cultural Heritage of the Ministry of Culture and Tourism, its subordinate provincial departments of culture and tourism, as well as the municipal (county) level cultural tourism bureau and its subordinate cultural centers.

In 2008, after the application of "Dai Script Palm-Leaf Scriptures Inscribing and Writing Skills" was approved, the inheritors and inheritance training activities receive corresponding "state funding" each year.For example, Dehong prefecture took the compilation and translation of ancient books as an important work during "the 13th Five-Year Plan" of the prefecture government, and applied to Yunnan Provincial Ethnic and Religious Affairs Commission for "100 Excellent Works Project" of Yunnan province. At present, the project has received a special fund (400,000 *yuan* in the first phase) and the project is implementing now.

The recognition and support obtained from the institutional level of the state and governments at all levels stimulate the recognition and subjective initiative of the folk towards palm-leaf culture, which effectively guarantee and promote the local and folk inheritance and protection practices.

4.4 Research Protection

Research protection refers to promoting the protection and inheritance of palm-leaf classics and palm-leaf culture through cooperation with universities and research institutions. For example, from 2002 to 2006, funded by Toyota Foundation, professor Yin Shaoting, from Department of Anthropology, Yunnan University, cooperated with professor Tang Li to collect, collate, video, record and compile Dai ancient texts in Dehong, Xishuangbanna, Gengma, Menglian and published the results in *China Yunnan Dai Ancient Texts Catalog*. This mainly belongs to early research protection of Dai ancient texts, especially paper manuscripts of ancient texts. Another example is the cooperation between the People's Government of Xishuangbanna Prefecture and Yunnan University to establish "Palm-Leaf Culture Research Center" to collect, collate, select proper versions, translate and compile palm-leaf scriptures and paper manuscripts within the territory of Xishuangbanna in ten years. Then "Six Contrast" between photocopy of the original, the original old Dai scripts, international phonetic signs, Chinese literal translation, Chinese free translation and new Dai scripts' free translation are adopted for the publication of *The Complete Works of Chinese Palm-Leaf Scriptures* (100 volumes), so that more people will know and understand the content of palm-leaf scriptures. By way of researching and writing the application, Palm-Leaf Culture Research Center helped to make "Dai Palm-Leaf Inscribing Techniques" listed in the second batch of "Intangible Cultural Heritage List of the People's Republic of China". The center have held several domestic and international seminars on palm-leaf culture, objectively promoting domestic and international agencies and non-governmental forces to reach local consensus and international cooperation consensus on the protection and inheritance of palm-leaf scriptures and palm-leaf culture.

The above four types of protection practices play a certain role in promoting the inheritance and protection of palm-leaf scriptures and palm-leaf culture in China. However, due to the constraints of many practical conditions, the practical effects of protection scope, protection awareness, protection cooperation and technical means of protection (such as digital protection) are still very limited, and there are regional differences in protection efficiency.Especially in terms of technical means, it still needs to be further improved.

Recently, the digitization of ancient Tibetan manuscripts in China has been accelerated, and a large number of precious Tibetan ancient manuscripts have realized "cloud reading". As a province that has prominent culture diversity, rich ethnic cultural resources and ethnic ancient manuscript resources, Yunnan province should increase its technical and financial investment in digitization of ancient manuscripts, support digitization of ancient manuscripts, including ancient palm-leaf scriptures and documents and "cloud storage" "cloud reading" "cloud query" "cloud space" etc. As for digital protection of Dai ancient manuscripts, Ancient Manuscripts Office of Yunnan Provincial Ethnic and Religious Affairs Committee, Intangible Cultural Heritage Division of Yunnan Provincial Department of Culture and Tourism, Yunnan Provincial Museum, Anthropology Museum of Yunnan University and Palm-Leaf Culture Research Center have made some concrete practices.But in general, these are small-scale sporadic practice with little investment; there is no systematic and holistic consideration and no "top-level design".In the long run, some experiences and cognition accumulated in the early stage of these work have laid a certain foundation for future digitization and cultural protection practice at the national government level.

At the same time, while promoting digital and technical protection, we should also understand and deal with the relationship between people and technology in the process of inheritance and protection of palm-leaf culture. Digital protection is only one aspect of cultural inheritance and protection of palm-leaf culture. Humanism, represented by palm-leaf culture, should not and will not be covered up by technicism. Digitization is only one technical facet of protection content, memory and form. It can not replace the inheritance and continuity of inscribing and making tradition of palm-leaf scripture in the folk. It can not replace the spirits of the people who internalize palm-leaf culture into common ethnic culture; it can not replace those precious human cognition, skill experience, spirits, values and other "collective ideas" formed in long periods of time in traditional society. Technology is the "tool", and people are "fundamental". The former is "art", while the latter is "Tao". As a result, those derived from the traditional folk should get more attention. Traditional folk custom and ceremony are closely related to "donating scriptures" and inheritance and the practice of palm-leaf scriptures/culture should get more attention and practice. Only in this way can the "market demand" for the traditional inscribing and production of palm-leaf scriptures be formed within the Dai society, and then the production and consumption of the inscribing and production of palm-leaf scriptures will be generated, so as to ensure the benign development of the folk endogenous mechanism of inheritance and protection of palm-leaf culture.

5. Conclusion

Under the impact of globalization, some regional cultures are being rapidly dissolved, or even buried or abandoned by times.This kind of "cultural folding" phenomena against "cultural diversity" largely occurred in 20th century.Along with the development of society and progress of science and technology, palm-leaf scriptures, which have been widely dispersed in Southeast Asia, South Asia, and southwestern part of China for hundreds of years, may have lost their practical value to a great extent. However, because of skills of making palm-leaf scriptures and the profound cultural content in palm-leaf scriptures, they have not only become an important part of human Buddhism civilization, but also record and carry ethnic groups' beliefs, collective rituals, values and spiritual pursuit, and become the collective memory and cultural genes of different social groups. Therefore, although the practicability and cultural functions of palm-leaf scriptures/culture are dissolved, and the process of becoming heritage is accelerating in nearly half a century, thankfully, in some regions of Dai-Thai-Shan-Lao regions of China and Southeast Asian and South Asian countries, including Xishuangbanna (China), Chiang Mai (Thailand), Kengtung (Myanmar) and Assam (India), we can find a lot of palm-leaf scriptures and paper manuscripts; palm-leaf scriptures inscribing techniques are still inherited; people still regard palm-leaf scriptures and palm-leaf culture as one of the most important manifestations of their "traditional" culture.

Just like what Dr. David Wharton, researcher at EFEO and technical director of Digital Documentation of Manuscript Cultures of Digital Library of Lao Manuscripts, said, we have to recognize that manuscripts are part of a rich and intangible culture that is disappearing even faster than the manuscripts themselves[1]. In the face of globalization and modernization, the speed of palm-leaf scriptures/culture becoming heritage and their degree of "being endangered" need attention and action of various parties.

As the inheritance and protection of palm-leaf scriptures and palm-leaf culture are important cultural phenomena of mankind across countries and regions, the cultural departments of relevant countries and regions should attach great importance to them. It is suggested to establish a regional cooperation mechanism for cultural cooperation

---

[1] Dr. Wharton's speech at "International Seminar on the Inheritance and Protection of Palm-Leaf Culture in China and South and Southeast Asia", which was held in Yunnan University in 2019.

and protection among countries by taking the opportunity of The Belt and Road Initiative. Consensus reached through mutual trust and cooperation will give a stronger impetus to the inheritance and protection of palm-leaf scriptures and palm-leaf culture in various countries.

By 2020, China has surpassed Italy to become the country with the largest number of world heritage sites in the world. Culture and tourism departments of China have accumulated considerable experiences of applying for cultural heritage list. In the process of promoting the construction of The Belt and Road Initiative, we can work with the countries along the Belt and Road to establish cooperation mechanism on inheritance and protection of common cultural heritage and application for heritage list on bilateral or multinational basis. We can share advanced experiences of China on "applying for heritage protection"; we can promote cultural cooperation and people-to-people exchange within the region. For example, by jointly applying for world cultural heritage, we can promote substantive cooperation among China, Southeast Asian and South Asian countries for the protection of regional cultural heritage. In this regard, palm-leaf scriptures and palm-leaf culture, as important cultural heritages in the region, may provide a good option for China, Southeast Asian countries and South Asian countries to jointly apply for "Memory of the World" projects.

A Study on the Inheritance and Development of Dai Scriptures of Theravada Buddhism in Xishuangbanna

Kang Nanshan[①]
Translated by Liu Dezhou[②]

Buddhism stresses obeisance to three Buddhist treasures, Buddha, Dharma and Sangha. It is the responsibility of every Buddhist to inherit and pass down Dharma, Buddhist scriptures. For the inheritance and development of Theravada Buddhism in Xishuangbanna, inheritance of traditional Dai classics of Buddhism is particularly important.Based on the author's personal experience, including the period of time when he was a monk in 1983, resumed secular life in 1997, and began to work in the Buddhist Association of Yunnan province since 1998, the author analyzes and summarizes the status quo and development trend of the inheritance and development of Dai scriptures and classics of Theravada Buddhism in Xishuangbanna.This paper also reviews the positive efforts, contributions and effects of Theravada Buddhism circles in Yunnan in the past 30 years for better inheritance and adaptation of Theravada Buddhism to Chinese society.The present situation of the development of Theravada Buddhism in Xishuangbanna can also be roughly judged from the present situation of the inheritance of Dai scriptures of Theravada Buddhism.

1. Dai Scriptures of Theravada Buddhism in Xishuangbanna

Among Theravada Buddhist scriptures in Xishuangbanna, only those written in Lanna script have been inherited, and few scriptures in Xishangbanna were written in Thai or Burmese. Some of the early Theravada Buddhism scriptures introduced from Thailand into Xishuangbanna were written in to¹phăk¹kham¹ in Dai language. However, Wat Suondok sect and Wat Padaeng sect are the sects of Theravada Buddhism that have been preaching Buddhism in Xishuangbanna for hundreds of years and their scriptures are written in

---

[①] The vice president and secretary general of the Buddhist Association of Yunnan province, and a doctoral candidate of Yunnan Minzu University.
[②] Professor of School of Foreign Languages and Literature, Yunnan Normal University.

Lanna script. These three elements are also the characteristics of Theravada Buddhism in Xishuangbanna.

  Buddhist scriptures are written in Lanna script, which is called to^{1}thăm^4 in many places, meaning "characters of Buddhist scriptures" to distinguish it from other Dai scripts.Lanna script was derived from the ancient Mon of Hariphunchai founded by the Mon people in the second half of the 13th century①. In the process of preaching Buddhist teachings in the Theravada Buddhism temples in Lanna Kingdom, in order to record and teach the Buddhist teachings more comprehensively, on the basis of Pali pronunciation, Lanna script was adopted as the main script for editing and inscribing Buddhist scriptures, hence the formation of Lanna Buddhist scriptures.With the support of several generations of kings, the Lanna version of Pali Tripitaka and many volumes of Jataka were written. It was recorded for several times that Theravada Buddhism scriptures were introduced to Luang Prabang and Jengtung (Myanmar) before being introduced to Xishuangbanna from the early 13th century to the 15th century②. In 1095, Sri Lanka Sangha set up a new influential sect called the Wat Suondok or ni^{6}ka^{1}ya^{6}son^{1}dɔk^2 in Chiang Mai city.In 1530, another sect Wat Padaeng, or ni^{6}ka^{1}ya^{6}ba^{2}dɛŋ^1 was founded in Chiang Mai city, and the sect is also called "New Ceylon Sect". Ancestral temples of the two sects are still preserved.This sect and its scriptures were spread to Jengtung (Myanmar) and then to Xishuangbanna in 1448③. Lanna scriptures not only included Buddhist doctrines and canons, but also included astronomy, calendar, medicine, literature, laws and regulations, proverbs, sorcery, etc.Lanna script was widely used after its introduction to Xishuangbanna, and its writing undertook development and became Dai Lue script with its own characteristics. Some people divided it into three kinds according to its distributing areas. The script used in northern Thailand is called "Lanna script"; that used in the area of Jengtung is called "Khün"; and the script in Xishuangbanna is called "Old Tai Lue (Dai) script". They actually belong to the same script, but there are some variations in the process of writing.From 1961 to 1963, Xishuangbanna reformed its writing system and adopted a new script, which is called New Tai Lue Script, and the old Lanna script (Buddhist scripture script) is called Old Tai Lue script.

  Lanna script (Old Tai Lue script) is quite flexible in writing, which is also its most important characteristic.However, just because of its flexibility, it leads to non-standard writing, too much arbitrariness and non-uniform writing, which are the disadvantages of

---

① Xie Yuanzhang.60 Years' Studies on Thai and Dai Studies. Kunming: Yunnan Ethnic Publishing House, 2008: 139.
② Kang Nanshan. Theravada Buddhism in Sipsong Panna: Past and Contemporary Trends. RCSD, Faculty of Social Sciences, Chiang Mai University, 2009: 13-15.
③ The Padang Chronicle and The Jengtung State Chronicle (Translated). Center for South and Southeast Asian Studies, The University of Michigan, 1981: 38.

Old Tai Lue script. Lanna script has the following three rules: First, for two neighboring words, if their consonants are the same while their vowels are different, all the vowels can be integrated under one consonant. In this way, if two words have the same consonant and different vowels, they can be combined into one word. Similarly, three words, four words, even more words may merge into one word. Second, fixed single words are easy to read and easy to understand.They can be interpreted by their consonants and vowels. Third, polyphonic words are often used as symbols in calendar, protective incantations and amulets etc.

2. Traditional Inheritance of Lanna Script and Classics—Buddhist Scripture Alms

There are three main ways of the traditional inheritance of Theravada Buddhism classics in Xishuangbanna. First, monks and the elderly copy Buddhist scriptures, and then the believers request for scriptures alms giving to temples.Second, monks (sometimes the elderly) recite scriptures to believers. Third, the vast number of believers spread the Buddhist teachings more widely orally after listening to the teachings.In these ways, Theravada Buddhist classics are continuously inherited in Xishuangbanna.In order to promote Buddhism, Dai people in Xishuangbanna developed alms giving custom of Buddhist sutra.Scripture alms giving is called $tan^4thăm^4$ in Dai language, which is of great significance to Buddhist inheritance.In terms of content, alms giving of Buddhist sutra is divided into Buddha Jataka alms and Pali sutra recitation alms, and recitation is further divided into recitation in Dai language and Pali language. In terms of alms givers, they can be divided into village collective alms givers and individual family alms givers.

2.1 Copying Scriptures

Copying Buddhist sutra is the first stage of Buddhist sutra alms.Sutras to be donated are generally new sutras, so they have to be copied by monks, or Bo Zhang (bo^5can^1, the leader of Buddhist activities), Kang Nan (kha^1nan^1, former Bhikkhus and monks with higher positions who have resumed secular life) and old people who know the sutras well. When people copy sutras, they have to use old sutras for reference. At the same time, copying activities depend on the alms plan of the entire Buddhist temple, copying one volume after one volume, or one set after another. For example, Buddha Jataka include ten volumes.If one person can complete copying the ten volumes, he can copy them by himself. If he can't finish it, he could share the copying task with others.Whoever gives alms will invite others to copy the sutras at his expense.

On the day before alms giving, all new copied sutras are sent to the Buddhist temple. The alms giver offers the cost of copying respectfully to the copier (s). Then the copier write the name of the alms giver on the preface of sutras with some blessing words. The alms giver brings home the Buddhist sutras for one night's worship. If someone in the family can chant them, he can chant the sutras once in the evening.If the family have a monk, they will ask him to come home and chant the sutras once, while family members sit and listen to the chanting. On the following afternoon or evening, all the Buddhist sutras are offered to Bo Zhang or the abbot in the Buddhist temple and all sutras are arranged orderly according to categories, series, volumes, so that monks can chant them in turn.

2.2 Chanting Scriptures

Chanting scriptures is the second stage of the alms giving activity.It usually takes 7 to 15 days. Monks take turns to chant the scriptures for faithful believers in the chanting court of the main hall day and night. On the first day, old people bring their own bedding to the main hall and find a place to lay the bedding, making preparation to listen to the chanting. The main hall floor is usually divided into male area, female area, old people's area and middle-aged people's area. Peers of the same gender tend to have better relations and communication. Therefore, their bedding are closer for the convenience of taking care of each other and small talk, as well as group dinner.

After all the Buddhist sutras for alms are gathered in the temple, they are chanted first by Bo Zhang and then by the monks to recite sutras to pray for good luck. Then, according to the wishes of the old people, Bo Zhang will arranged the sutras into different categories, series and volumes. Then, the monks will be invited to sit in the reciting court which is in the center of the hall. After the monks are seated, Bo Zhang begins with reciting a simple and respectful sentence from the sutra, and then the monks begin to chant. At the beginning and the end of each volume, several old men near the reciting court beat their Mang gongs three times and blow the conch once to signify the beginning or the end of a volume.When monks chant Buddhist sutras, they are required to chant with loud and clear voices, so that everyone in the hall can hear them. After the appearance of megaphones, the people outside the main hall, even the whole village, can hear the chanting clearly. Second, this kind of chanting attaches importance to tunes. The tunes are divided into several kinds and they are slightly different from each other in different parts of Xishuangbanna. Different from Pali gathatunes, Jataka sutra is mostly chanted in Dai script, mixed with some Pali expressions. Dai sentences are often rhymed; their chanting sounds like "Zhangha" tune (traditional Dai singing tune) .Therefore, the author thinks that this is more singing sutra than chanting sutra.

The monks are invited by Bo Zhang into the main hall in turn to sing sutras, once a volume, two volumes, three volumes, and even more. It depends on the master's ability and endurance.The ceremony will not stop until all the donated sutra are sung. Monks or masters from other temples can be invited to help with the singing too.The day before the end of the singing/chanting is a day of celebration. Every family offer good food to the temple and to the old people who listen to the scriptures in the temple.In the evening, the temple play drums and gongs, fly Kongming lanterns and light fireworks; sometimes cultural and art performances and other activities are organized.The last day is the dripping water and bestowing merits ceremony. Monks chant scriptures to bestow merits to all the believers for their alms. Bo Zhang recites all the merits done back to the believers.All the believers and family representative script water and make vows of doing boundless alms, so that they lives have merits returned generation after generation.At this point, the whole activity of Buddhist sutra alms is over.

2.3 Cultivating Talents

The activity of sutra alms is an important way to cultivate Buddhist talents. The traditional standards of monk talents in Xishuangbanna are as follows. First, good practice and strict discipline. Second, being able to recite and sing all kinds of Buddhist ritual scriptures required by believers. Third, being able to write good Buddhist scripts. Fourth, the ability to host Buddhist activities. Fifth, being able to educate the masses of believers to hold upright belief and behaviors.The activity of Buddhist sutra alms is the best way to train the Monks to practice Dai script and understand Buddha Jataka.Those who are determined to become monks begin to learn the basic sutra from the moment they enter a monastery as a prospective monk.As a novice monk, he has to recite more scriptures and read and write sutras.After learning the sutras, he begins to copy them. After copying dozens of volumes of sutras, his level of writing Lanna script is improved. After copying hundreds of volumes of sutras, his calligraphy and mastery of the sutras can reach higher level.

Buddhist sutra alms is both a driving force and pressure for monks. When the believers ask monks to copy scriptures, if the monks can not copy, they will feel sorry to the believers, that is pressure to them. Copying scriptures can bring income (offering), improve their calligraphy skills and become more familiar with the language and content of the sutras, which is the motivation. Reciting and singing sutras at alms activity is also a very effective way to train monks. One monk has to learn the script of Buddhist sutra and Buddha Jataka first. It may take several months, or even one or two years before he can sing or chant on the stage.It is a good opportunity for the inexperienced young monks to learn and practice Buddha Jataka on the stage. If they have mispronunciation or omission, the old people in the audience can immediately correct them. In this way, over time, the monks will gradually master Buddha Jataka and improve their linguistic capacity in Buddhist sutras.

2.4 Fulfilling the Need of Faith

In a broad sense, Buddhist sutra alms is an important way to spread Buddhism.In the narrow sense, it is an act of faith for Dai believers to accumulate virtue and do good deeds, and it is a very effective way for them to cultivate themselves. Buddhist scripture alms can accumulate virtues. By listening to Buddhist scriptures, people could learn the dharma, understand the merits and virtues accumulated by the Buddha in the path of Bodhisattva in past generations, understand the Buddhist teachings and rules, understand the life, do good deeds and accumulate virtues, and do nothing evil.It is also great enjoyment for the devotees to hear monks chant and sing Buddha Jataka. In the process, when they are moved, they may shed tears, and even cry out. When they hear something humorous, they may burst into laughter.When old people listen to the sutras, they need to live in the temple for seven days to half a month, which is also an effective way to practice Buddhist conduct in the temple. They do not need to go home to do housework, not to do farm work in the fields, and their children and grandchildren prepare food to send to the temple for them.The old people constantly listen to Buddha Jataka to improve their cultivation of Buddhism. After understanding Buddha Jataka, they can tell their children the stories in Buddhist sutras, so as to spread Buddhist teachings and ethics more widely.

The second kind of Buddhist sutra alms is alms of Pali Tripitaka.However, because Pali Tripitaka contains too many volumes, most of the Buddhist temples in Xishuangbanna do not have a complete version. "The First 15 Abhidharma" and "The Second 15 Abhidharma" are usually circulating in Xishuangbanna.The monks generally study these treatises.In most Buddhist activities, it is these Adhidharma that are chanted or sung. If Abhidharma is to be offered, only one set is offered, and it is offered by the whole village. It takes two or three years for one person to copy, so it can only be done by several people. When reciting Abhidharma, rather than one person recites the sutras, three or five or more people recite them together around the same sutras, which requires several groups in turn. Buddhists in surrounding villages are invited to form a Sangha to share the recitation task. The recitation of Abhidharma usually takes seven days to half a month.

3. The Dilemma of Inheritance and Development

In the 1980s, when China began to implement the policies in protecting freedom of religious belief, Theravada Buddhism in Xishuangbanna was very active and developed rapidly.By the late 1990s, however, development of Theravada Buddhism was slowing down and trying to find its direction.Over the past decade, its weakening development trend has become more obvious and clearer in recent years. There are reasons for this trend. The author believes that the following are the main reasons:

In the context of globalization, social multiculturalism in Xishuangbanna is increasingly evident.Dai ethnic group is changing from a relatively closed farming society to a modernized and urbanized society, and from a self-sufficient farming production mode to a market economy. Pluralistic cultures influence the production and life of Dai people day by day. Dai people's belief and ideas are also changing with social changes. With continuous social progress and rapid economic development, Dai people in Xishuangbanna have more and more frequent and in-depth contact with the outside world, and more and more people go to developed areas in China, or even travel abroad, gradually broaden their minds.Many young people leave Dai villages and go to towns and cities, work in the developed coastal areas, and even study and work abroad.Some even get married and live in Southeast Asia, Europe or the United States.Due to the influence and integration of diverse cultures, Dai youth have gradually lost their awareness and interest in studying Buddhist sutras on the one hand. And on the other hand, they have to learn a lot of things, so they have more learning pressures and they cannot be in two places at once.

The simultaneous use of multiple writing systems is a huge obstacle for the development of an ethnic group's culture.The use of multiple scripts is one of the main factors hindering the spread of traditional Dai culture, which is the consensus of most Dai people and it is difficult to solve. Now Dai people in Yunnan province use six types of writing systems: Xishuangbanna Old Dai (Tai) script (Lanna script or Buddhist scripture script), New Dai (Tai) script, Dehong Old Dai (Tai) script, Dehong New Dai (Tai) Script, Old Shan Writing Script and Dai character [Jinping Dai (Tai) script]. In 1961, under the leadership of Fu Maoji from Chinese Academy of Social Sciences, the reform of Dai script was started in Jinghong. In 1963, the reform was finished and the New Dai script began to be used in Xishuangbanna. Newspapers in Xishuangbanna were the main media to spread the New Dai script. After that, many literary works, monographs and long poems were written and published in New Dai script. The New Dai script was widely promoted in Xishuangbanna and was soon widely used.In 1980, Xishuangbanna began to restore Theravada Buddhism belief. As scriptures of Theravada Buddhism of the Dai people were written in Old Dai script (Lanna script), the Buddhist temples naturally began to use Old Dai script again. Because of the large number of Pali linguistic structures used in the scriptures of Theravada Buddhism, many words have Pali roots, and the New Dai script is difficult to express the true meaning of Pali language. So it cannot replace the Old Dai script.Therefore, Dai people in Xishuangbanna have been using New Dai script and Old Dai script at the same time.

At the end of 1980, the Buddhist circles in Xishuangbanna began to explore the path of modern Buddhist education and Sinicization of Buddhism.In 1988, the Buddhist Association of Menghai county opened a monk school in Bajiaoting, Jingzhen, which failed two years later. Then a monk school was opened in Manhe Buddhist Temple in Menghai Town, which lasted for several years. Venerable Du Ying started a school in Menghun Buddhist

Temple which existed for a few years before it failed. In May 1995, with the approval of National Religious Affairs Administration of China, Yunnan Theravada Buddhist College was formally established in Xishuangbanna General Buddhist Temple and began to enroll and train monk students from Dehong, Simao, Lincang, Baoshan and other places in September 1995. In March 2008, the college moved to the new site of Nanlianshan Menglue Buddhist Temple, which covers an area of 60 *mu* (4 hectares) and has a building area of 8,188.58 square meters. By 2019, the college had enrolled 1,346 monk students in 36 classes, and 1,089 monk students in 32 classes have graduated from the college.

In order to adopt sinicization and actively guide Theravada Buddhism to adapt to the socialist society, the Buddhist College cooperates with national education schools to run the college, improve monk students' Chinese culture so that monk students not only master Dai script and Buddhist scriptures, but also learn Chinese culture, and become all-round students. In March 2005, the Buddhist College and Xishuangbanna Vocational and Technical College jointly organized "Dai-Chinese bilingual vocational classes" .In the classes, teachers from Xishuangbanna Vocational and Technical College teach Chinese courses and these courses are the same as those taught in vocational secondary schools of national education system. Monk teachers from Buddhist College come to give Dai script courses and Buddhism courses. Students of the classes graduate with technical secondary school diplomas which are recognized by the country. Although a lot of efforts have been made, the cultivation of these talents has not played an important role in promoting the healthy development of Theravada Buddhism.

At present, one of the problems of Theravada Buddhism inheritance in Xishuangbanna is lack of talents, and Buddhist talents are in short supply both in quantity and quality. Over the past decade, the number of monks has changed a lot. According to statistics, in 2012, there were 593 Buddhist temples and a total of 2,475 monks in Xishuangbanna prefecture and 712 of them were Bhikkhus. By the end of 2018, there were 598 Buddhist temples with a total of 1,978 monks, of whom 431 were Bhikkhus. Change in the number of novice monks is not significant, but the number of monks with the rank of Bhikkhus and above, who belong to teaching staffs, fell from 712 to 431 in six years, a decrease of 281.These figures illustrate the seriousness of the problem. Under the influence of many external factors, the number of monks are gradually decreasing and their time of serving as monks becomes shorter and shorter, leading to the shortage of talents in Theravada Buddhism.

At the same time, the way of learning in temples has also undergone a certain change. The traditional one-to-one inheritance between the abbot and novice monks is rare. Many novice monks have been monks for several years, but their knowledge on Buddhism is very limited.With the implementation of basic Theravada Buddhism education in the Buddhist college, some young Theravada Buddhist monks can go to Buddhist college for more formal learning, but the overall number of this group is small. During their studies in the Buddhist college, most of their time is spent on learning Buddhism theories and contents of national education. The traditional content of Theravada Buddhism, such as Buddha Jataka sutra, chanting methods of gatha, Lanna script (Buddhism scripture script) and ritual scripture chanting that Dai people need, are not well learned. The result neither meets the need of the majority of believers for traditional rituals, nor leads the believers to the new model of Theravada Buddhism.

The monk students' ability to copy and chant traditional sutra is becoming weaker and weaker, and the number of talents who can inherit the Buddhist sutras in Dai script is gradually decreasing. In this context, the monks in Buddhist temples can no longer meet the higher spiritual needs of the majority of Dai believers, but only meet their needs for basic rituals. In most of the Buddhist temples in the countryside, there are only one or two monks and one abbot in each temple. Therefore, they cannot form Sangha. Buddhist activities gradually focus on inheritance of rituals. When believers come to a temple and ask the monks to do Buddhist rituals, they prefer to ask the monks to do Buddhist rituals related to their livelihood, such as praying for good health, prosperous business, safe family, prosperity and safe trips. Believers are keen to do religious rituals related to these prayers. The abbots of temples believe that doing these activities will lead to more direct offerings. Therefore, they are also keen to do these Buddhist rituals. The rituals are colorful and various, and believers have more choices. As a result, the core teachings of Buddhism are difficult to spread and popularize among Dai believers.

The difficulty of inheriting Dai Buddhist classics in Xishuangbanna also reflects the contradiction between tradition and modernity. Old Dai script (Buddhist sutra script) in Xishuangbanna has been passed down in the traditional way for hundreds of years, and it has not been inherited in modern ways so far. Although many classics and sutra reciting activities use modern audio equipments such as tape recorders, DVD players, video recorders, computers, and Internet has been adopted for its spread in recent years, these are simple and leisure ways of spreading contents. There are not professional and systematic ways to spread Theravada Buddhism and Dai scriptures.

4. Insights on Sinicization of Chinese Theravada Buddhism Classics

Chinese president Xi Jinping proposes to "adhere to the orientation of sinicization of religions" and this points out the future development direction of China's five major religions. Chinese Theravada Buddhism should stick to the direction of sinicization. Otherwise it will be more difficult for Theravada Buddhism to continue its inheritance in

China.The author believes that the key to continuous inheritance of Theravada Buddhism in Xishuangbanna is to inherit Theravada Buddhism scriptures, which requires us to do well in the following aspects under the guidance of adhering to the direction of sinicization.

First of all, we should do a good job of inheriting the script of Theravada Buddhism. From 1980s to 1990s, some people in northern Thailand and Jengtung, Shan State of Myanmar developed Lanna script (Old Tai script) wax paper mimeograph, and later some people developed Lanna computer input method and printing fonts. From 1994 to 1996, monks from Xishuangbanna went to Chiang Mai, Thailand, to learn the computer input method of Buddhist sutras, and they returned to General Buddhist Temple of Xishuangbanna to do Dai script's computer input work, which plays an important role in the dissemination of Dai Buddhist scriptures in Xishuangbanna. Later, Xishuangbanna Newspaper Office developed another computer input method of Old Dai Script. At the beginning, there were many defects in font spelling. After several years of technical improvement, it has become mature and beautiful. All the above practices have laid a good foundation for the inheritance and development of Dai script of Theravada Buddhism in Xishuangbanna.In the future, we should keep pace with the times and keep up with modern printing technology, media, electronic technology and network technology, and spread scriptures and classics through smart technologies and devices.

In order to adapt to the Chinese society and adopt sinicization, Theravada Buddhist script need to move towards writing scriptures in Chinese. Dai ethnic group is one of the Chinese ethnic groups and they are citizens of the People's Republic of China. Chinese language is the official language of China, which will become more and more popular in the future. Writing Theravada Buddhist scriptures and classics in Chinese will be convenient for more people. The number of Dai people that can understand Old Dai script is likely to be less, and those who can read Dai Theravada Buddhism script will be less too.It will be better to write Theravada Buddhism scriptures in Chinese than to write Theravada Buddhism scriptures in Dai script and perish. This not only help Dai people who don't know Dai script to understand Theravada Buddhism scriptures, but also enable other ethnic groups to read and understand Theravada Buddhism scriptures, which will promote inheritance and sinicization process of Theravada Buddhism.

Historically, scriptures of Theravada Buddhism that were translated into Chinese include *Agama Sutra*, *The Path of Purification* and *Dhammapada*.*Theravada Tripitaka* have been published in Singapore and China. In the past ten years, Mahinda Bhikkhu, grand master of Dhammavihārī Araññā, has published a large number of translations and works on Buddhist scriptures, including: (1) *Essentials of Abhidama* (First Part, Middle Part, Second Part); (2) *Mahà Parittà*; (3) *Bhikkhu Patimokkha*; (4) *First Part* of *Aṅguttaranikāye—Pali*. His works include: (1) *The Meaning of Life*; (2) *Do You Know Buddhism?*; (3) *These Are Master's Teaching*; (4) *Introduction to Studies on Theravada Buddhism*; (5) *Sequence of Theravada Buddhism Meditation*. All these laid a good foundation for the Chinese scriptures of Theravada Buddhism.

Secondly, the good tradition of sutra alms needs to be continued, but the form must be changed. Traditional forms and contents of alms activities no longer adapt to the contemporary Dai society. Copying and offering one sutra a year for each household or each couple does not have great significance for the inheritance of Theravada Buddhism now. The conditions of having every scripture chanted or sung by monks are difficult to meet in most cases. The form of sutra alms must be changed. For example, every family or every couple can donate money to print Buddhist sutra or have sutra inscribed into palm-leaf scripture. When expounding the sutras, senior monks can be invited to expound sutras, instead of reading and singing Buddha Jataka in the traditional way. It is also feasible to purchase some Chinese versions of Theravada Buddhist scriptures and offer them to temples, so that young people, including monks and family members, can study them. Temples with adequate funds can build Tripitaka Pavilions and lecture halls, providing places for monks to preach and for believers to hear Dharma.

Thirdly, encourage lay Buddhists to participate in reciting sutras. Over the past decade, groups of men and women lay Buddhists dressed in white appeared in Dai villages. These lay Buddhists are promoted from the traditional householders. They often organize chanting-sutra activities in the villages or temples and have gradually formed sutra chanting groups. The eminent monks of Theravada Buddhism believe that the lay Buddhists' chanting groups are conducive to the spread of Buddhism, and conducive to the believers to live and work in peace and contentment, and conducive to cultivate their benevolence. So support and guidance should be provided to the lay Buddhists' chanting groups in white. For example, during the Spring Festival of 2017 and 2018, gather competitions were held at Jinghong Golden Pagoda Temple, and several thousands of white-clothes lay Buddhists from all over Xishuangbanna prefecture attended the competitions. They have great potential for the inheritance of Theravada Buddhism, so they should be strongly supported to play a greater role.

Fourthly, the cultivation of Buddhist talents must be combined with modern education. In order to spread Theravada Buddhism better, under the care and support of the party and the government, Theravada Buddhism community has made great efforts to set up modern Buddhist Colleges. After many years of running the college, Xishuangbanna Branch of Yunnan Buddhist College has laid a good foundation. However, it needs to continue to study college-running model and teaching objectives etc. to improve teaching quality. The traditional cultivating model is to meet the needs of the majority of believers temporarily, while modern education is to guide the direction of future faith of the believers, and it is necessary to actively guide the road of sinicization of Theravada Buddhism.

5.Conclusion

In the context of globalization and diversification, the inheritance of Dai script of Theravada Buddhism in Xishuangbanna has adopted more diversified and multiple channels than traditional forms. However, on the one hand, Xishuangbanna is lack of professional Buddhist talents and lack of strength to spread Buddhism among Dai believers. On the other hand, due to the change of the Dai script environment, Dai believers' chance of receiving traditional Dai script education is limited; the number of Dai believers who can understand Dai Buddhist scriptures is also becoming smaller. Therefore, the contents of the Theravada Buddhist scriptures have not been truly and adequately inherited and developed. Now under the background of rapid social development and cultural integration, cultural and traditional inheritance of Dai ethnic group in Xishuangbanna should not be broken. Therefore, Xishuangbanna Theravada Buddhism circles should make greater efforts to adopt multiple modes and multiple channels to carry out the cultivation of talents. We must attach importance to inheritance of Dai scripts of Theravada Buddhism scriptures, explore traditional culture of Dai people, find new development ways in the course of sinicization of Theravada Buddhism, so that traditional culture of Dai ethnic group will integrate and develop with the extensive and profound traditional Chinese culture to show the world new vigor and vitality of Dai people's traditional culture.

References

(Ⅰ) English References

[1] The Padang Chronicle and The Jengtung State Chronicle (Translated). Center for South and Southeast Asian Studies, The University of Michigan, 1981.

[2] Kang Nanshan.Theravada Buddhism in Sipsong Panna: Past and Contemporary Trends. RCSD, Faculty of Social Sciences, Chiang Mai University, 2009.

[3] Lester, Robert C. Theravada Buddhism in Southeast Asia. The University of Michigan Press, 1973.

[4] Mangrai, Sao Saimong. The Padaeng Chronicle and the Jengtung State Chronicle. The University of Michigan Press, 1981.

[5] Wyatt, David K. and Wichienkeeo, Aroonrut. The Chiang Mai Chronicle. Chiang Mai: Silkworm Books, 1995.

(Ⅱ) Chinese References

[1] Huang Lingfei.An Anthropological Study on Chinese Theravada Buddhism Music. Kunming: Yunnan University Press, 2015.

[2] Liu Yan. A Survey on Dai Ethnic Group's South Bound Migration. Kunming: Yunnan Ethnic Publishing House, 1999.

[3] Liu Yan.Theravada Buddhism and Dai Culture.Kunming: Yunnan Ethnic Publishing House, 1993.

[4] Wu Qionghua, Peng Duoyi. Collection of Chinese Theravada Buddhism Documents. Kunming: Yunnan University Press, 2015.

[5] Xie Yuanzhang. 60 Years' Studies on Thai and Dai Studies.Kunming: Yunnan Ethnic Publishing House, 2008.

[6] Zheng Xiaoyun.Studies on Chinese Theravada Buddhism. Beijing: China Social Sciences Press, 2012.

(Ⅲ) References in Dai Script

[1] The Padaeng Chronicle of Chiang Tung. Chiang Tung, Shan State, Myanmar.

[2] The Khobaka and Cultural Association of Chiang Tung. The Chiang Tung Chronicle. Chiang Tung, Shan State, Myanmar, 2003.

[3] Hans Penth. The Chiang Mai Chronicle. Chiang Mai: Silkworm Books, 1996.

Heritage of Palm-Leaf in Sri Lankan Buddhist Culture

Wimal Hewamanage[1]

1. Introduction

Language is a noteworthy characteristic of Homo sapiens which means wise man in Latin and its written form came to be used later than oral tradition. Sanskrit terms like *bahuśrta* (*bahussata* in Pali), more heard or extremely learned, was utilized for scholars in ancient Indian languages and it proves stage of oral tradition. Using palm-leaf for writing is one of the oldest traditions in South and Southeast Asian counties. Palm-leaf is called in Sanskrit, *tālapatra*, *tādapatra*, *tādipatra*, and in Pali it is *tālapaṇṇa*. *Puskola* is its Sinhala form and ola-leaf is its Tamil term. Talipot palm, palmyra palm, and lonta palm are three varieties of talipot or palm-leaf which is recognized in the Indian sub-continent and the first two have been used in Sri Lanka. Many palm-leaf manuscripts are available in Sinhala, Pali, and Tamil and also several in Sanskrit, Burmese, and Thai in the island. They cover precisely Pali language and literature, Buddhism, Sinhala language and literature, indigenes medicine, astrology, cookery, etc., but this research paper is centered on simply the importance of palm-leaf culture in the island toward Buddhism. W. A. De Silva's *Catalogue of Palm Leaf Manuscripts in the Library of Colombo Museum Vol. I*, and *Sri Lankave Puskola Poth Lekhana Kalāva* written by Ariya Lagamuva are outstanding work on the field. Article "Production of Books in Ancient Ceylon" composed by C. M. Austin De Silva are also useful to aware the process of preparing palm-leaf manuscripts.

Sri Lankans believe that a palm tree was first planted in Sri Lanka by the god Śakra to write the Buddha's teachings. The concept of guardian spirit was associated with palm trees and later on, it was linked with the Buddhist monks in the country. Before introducing Buddhism to Sri Lanka the concept of tree god depicted in folk religions associated trees like banyan and Palmyra. They believed that gods who lived in these trees protected people and village life. There are more than 123 village names with prefixes *tāla* or *tal* (Lagamuva

---

[1] Senior lecturer in Pali & Buddhist Studies, Department of Buddhist Studies, University of Colombo, Sri Lanka. He is also a PhD of Wuhan University.

2006: 107). At the same time the palm tree is used as a border marking tree considering its erect shape and longevity. In the ancient time there were royal palm parks. Madilla palm-park located in Galatara village near to Alavva exists with about 50 acres.

2. Palm-Leaf History of Sri Lanka and Its Relevance to Buddhism

History of writing in Sri Lanka is as long as Indian history. Since the monastery has played a key role in the sphere of education in the country monasteries are identified as *parivenas* (*pirivena* in Sinhala) from the third century BC to date. Mahaviharaya and Abhayagiriya were well-known centers during the Anuradhapura period. Dimbulagala Alahana Pirivena in the Polonnaruwa period, Totagamuva Vijayaba Pirivena and Keragala Padmavati Pirivena during the Kotte period, and Asgiriya, Mallavatta, Niyamakanda Pirivenas in the Kandyan period, the last kingdom of the country, are well-known education centers. From the beginning, palm-leaf writing was conducted by monks not only on Pali and Buddhism but also most of the classical Sinhala literature and even Sinhala Grammar. Lay authors like Gurulugomi, Vidyacakravarti, Devrada Dampasangina, and king Parakramabahu IV also contributed.

Library, *potgula* in Sinhala, is one of the foremost buildings of many recognized monasteries. The building called "ganthapaṇṇika" built in the Mahavihara premises by King Voharika Tissa and Ganthakara Pirivena where the great commentator Buddhaghosa Thera studied the Canon and continued his translation project on commenters seemed like libraries (Lagamuva 2006: 70). In the Kandyan kingdom, there were well-known temples called "potgulvihāraya"; Ovala potgulvihāraya, Mahavela potgulvihāraya, Dematamaluva potgulvihāraya, and Haguranketa potgulvihāraya are a few of them.

The great king Dutthagamani (161BC–137BC) built Dharma preaching halls (*dharmaśālā*) and offered canopies, *vijinipatas*, preaching chairs and books. The book called *Puññapotthaka* (merit book) was read at the final moments of the king's life (Geiger 1950: 222). During the second century BC prince Uttiya, the brother of king Kakavanna-Tissa (205BC–161BC) utilized palm leaves to send his message of esoteric love to his sister-in-law, the queen through a young boy disguised as a monk. History of the island records the first experience of tsunami associated with this story (Geiger 1950: 147). Palm-leaf was used from the sixth century BC for daily writings and then it was transferred to religious writings after introducing Buddhism to Sri Lanka by Arahant Mahinda in the third century BC.

Buddhism was transmitted from generation to generation from the fifth century BC to the first century BC as an oral tradition and it was first written on palm leaves at Aluviharaya (Aloka Vihara), in the central province of Sri Lanka during the reign of king Vattagamini

Abhaya (29BC–17BC) without royal support but with the help of a local leader. That occurred the second tenure of the king after defeating South Indian invaders who ruled for 14 years. Because of unstable political power and the period of drought and famine, several monks went to neighbouring India and some risked their lives being in the country to protect the Dhamma. Having understood the danger of depending only on oral tradition monks decided to commit the Dhamma both Pali Canon and commentaries into writing on palm-leaf. This remarkable writing project, ever signed in the religious history, of the canon and commentaries which existed with a series of texts, proves that writing mechanism had been a well-developed and established system in the country. Considering the Indian and Sri Lankan accounts it is very clear that writing had started at least a few centuries in advance of this great event. As depicted in the Nissankamalla inscription (1187–1196) records about donations and gifts should be written on copper plates instead of palm-leaf because palm-leaf accounts were destroyed by ants and rats. Hence, it is very clear that during this period palm-leaf was a well-known material used for writing.

Considering the recent history of the island regarding Buddhist palm-leaf writing two events which was held in the nineteenth and the twentieth centuries are more useful. The first has occurred under the leadership of well-known monks who represented Nikayas, Siyam, and Amarapura. Valane Siddhattha Thera, Hikkaduwe Sumanagala Thera, Yatramulle Dharmarama represented Siam Mahanikaya while Lankagoda Dhirananda Thera, Randombe Dhammalankara Thera, Veligama Sumangala Thera, and Vaskaduve Subhuti Thera represented Amarapura Mahanikaya. Iddamalgoda Abeykoon Atapattu Mudiyanse Ralahami, Diyavadana Nilame of the Saman Devalaya temple in Ratnapura and Batuvantudave Devarakshita represented lay society. The writing council was held in 1867 at the Sudassana Dharmasala in Palmadulla Pirivena, and today it is identified as Sudharmodaya Pirivena located in Ratnapura District, Sabaragamuva Province. The second was held from 1981–1991 at Aluviharaya, Matale under the leadership of Etipola Medhankara Thera and Ambanpola Ratanasara Thera. All those projects were highly linked with palm-leaf culture. The most recent event states the interest of palm-leaf culture among Sri Lankans, even though the printing mechanism is well-developed.

Though above councils pay much attention to Pali canons, Pali literature existing with canon, commentaries, sub-commentaries, chronicles, handbooks, grammar books, dictionaries, etc. all of them are composed on palm-leaf. This literature had been maintained as palm-leaf manuscripts until the introduction of the printing mechanism in 1737. Nevertheless, it should be noted here that the tradition of palm-leaf manuscripts was much popular until the beginning of the 19th century. Academic editions are made on the above subjects based on palm-leaf manuscripts not only in Sri Lanka but also in South and Southeast Asian Buddhist countries. At the same way, classical Sinhala literature from Anuradhapura to Kandyan period are most probably translations or adaptation of Pali literature or theme of the treatises at least quoted from Pali literature. The Sinhala classic, *Siyabaslakara* provides necessary guidance for literary work states.

The Buddha's former lives have to be written in verse and the customs, rituals, etc. in prose. For drama, etc. has to be used both verse and prose. Hence, classical Sinhala literature is nothing but Buddhist culture in the country. Demands of the academic editions of classical Sinhala literature which is based on various palm-leaf manuscripts are very high. Several lay Buddhists provided sufficient contribution to Sinhala Buddhist literature Gurulugomi, Vidyacakravarti, Parakramabahu IV are few examples.

3. Sri Lankan Palm-Leaf Collections

Suluvaga, Mahavaga, Smantapāsādikāva, and Visuddhimaggatīkāva are the oldest palm-leaf manuscripts found in Sri Lanka. Sri Lanka has both qualitative and quantitative remarkable heirship of palm-leaf manuscripts within and outside of the country. The Museum Library, Colombo has more than 5,000 manuscripts including 2,000 of W.A. de Silva collection, 1,200 of Hue Nevil collection, 261 of Ananda Kumarasvami. The University of Peradeniya has more than 4,000 manuscripts including De Seram collection and Institute of Indigenes Medicine, the University of Colombo has 700 manuscripts. Collections of the University of Jayawardhanapura in Nugegoda, the University of Kelaniya in Dalugama, National Archives, National library in Colombo and Oriental Library in Kandy are also very essential. There are nearly 2,469 manuscripts of Hue Nevil collection of British Museum in London, and 1,000 manuscripts of Rusmas Rask in Royal Library Copenhagen, Denmark. National Library Munich Aziastische Orjks Museum in Amsterdam, Netherlands, National Library of France in Paris, Collection of Bodlean Library, and Oxford have also existed with palm-leaf manuscripts and also most of them are Sri Lankan cultural heritage(Lagamuva 2006: 85). Their role is not merely collecting palm-leaf but there is sufficient mechanism to protect them for the next-generation and provide appreciable support for post-graduate research based on manuscripts.

4. Preparing Palm-Leaf Manuscripts

Formulating palm-leaf manuscripts for writing and preparing as a readable material with consideration for the longevity of books is a long processes. It includes selecting palm-leaf, boiling, drying up, smoothing and polishing, making pieces, punching holes, and binding. Tender leaf of the Talipot palm which is unopened is selected first and removed from its rach is carefully and rolled up. Then, the rolled palm-leaf is boiled in a large vessel and kept for a couple of hours over a slow fire. It takes three consecutive days, both day and night to dry up. Next step is making them smooth and polished and for that leaves are repeatedly run over smooth wooden cylinder, generally is used a pestle. Since leaves are softer and flexible they are made into pieces according to the conventional sizes with length varying from 6 to 32 inches and width from 2 to 2.75 inches without of wasting. Utilizing a heated iron rod the papers are punched generally in two places and manuscripts are tied up by passing a cord through those two holes. Covers of the manuscripts, front and back is made of either wood such as ebony, ironwood, *val-sapu*, *gammalu*, jack and *milla* or metal. Covers are decorated usually with colorful designs.

Panhida and *ulkaṭuva* are two instruments to use for writing; the first is the stylus which was used by well-trained writers and the second style was used by trainers. Trainers should write given letters named *guru-akuru* (teacher's letters) by his teacher on rough paper (*karakolaya*) by using *ulkaṭuva* (style) until familiar with writing on palm-leaf. Style is about four to six inches long, circular or octagonal shape and thin from top to bottom which is made of copper, iron, or brass. Students are gradually trained from simple letters, words to sentences to write beautifully and speedily. The stylus was used by professional writers and it is an advanced tool than the style. The styluses are most probably 10–20 inches long and much decorated with silver and ivory. Stylus is made of gold, silver, copper, brass, iron, and bronze but its pointer is made of steel. The gold stylus, 14.4 inches long, was given by the king Narendrasinghe to Denigama Nilame who held the post of Mahagabada Nilame and Diyavadana Nilame of the Temple of Tooth relic.

Buddhist palm-leaf manuscripts start with a Sanskrit, Pali or Sinhala sentence which presents the respects to the Buddha such as *namo buddhāya*, *namo tassa bhagavato arahato sammāsam buddhassa*, *Namah sri ghaṇāya*, *namah samanta bhadrāya*, and *Namav muni saraṇa*. The very first page says the term "svasti" or "svasti siddham" or "svasti śri", or "sva" which means bless you. At the end of the manuscripts it says "siddhirastu" "śubhamastu" "kalyanamastu" and "arogyamastu" which also means bless you and bless you a healthy life. Further, authors and copyists preferred to mention their religious aspirations and add wishes to all beings. For an instance:

Iminā puññakammena yāva buddho bhavāmahaṃ
Mahosadhova nānena joti siṭṭhīva bhoginā
Vessantarova dānena hotu mayhaṃ bhavā bhave
Imaṃ likhita punnena metteyya mupasaṃkami
Patitthahitvā saraṇe suppatitthāmi sāsane
Sabbe sattā sukhappattā averā ca anūmayā
Dīghāyukā aññamaññaṃ piyā papponti nibbutiṃ.

Through the merit of this good act, may I become a Buddha

In wisdom a Mahauṣadha, in wealth a Joti seṭṭhi

In charity a Vessantara, may I attain from life to life.

Through the merits of writing this, may I meet the Buddha Metteyya

And obtain his refuge and join the Sasana

May all beings attain happiness rid themselves of hatred and delusion

Obtain long life and in due course attain Nibbana (Silva 1938: xxi and edited by the author).

All contents are counted according to the number of letters and verses etc. Eight letters are a line, four lines are a verse, and 250 verses are a bhāṇavāra (*aṭṭhakkharā ekāpadaṃ-ekā gāthā catuppadā; gāthā eko mato gantho-gantho dvattiṃsa akkharo. Dvattiṃsakkharagāthānam-pannāsadvisataṃ pana; bhāṇavāro mato eko-aṭṭhakkhara sahassako*). This accountability is a unique characteristic of Buddhist manuscripts precisely written in Pali. Manuscripts exist with 3 to 1,000 pages, but most of them are 50 to 100 pages. Manuscript of the *Jātaka Poth Vahanse* in the University of Peradeniya Collection exists with two volumes; 1,055 and 1,263 pages respectively. Only two punctuation marks; comma and *kākapāda* (crow's feet) and *kundaliya* (serpent shape) have been used above manuscripts. The former denotes the ending of sentences and latter denotes ending of paragraphs. Double and triple *kundaliya* marks conclusion of the sections and two or three double *kundaliya* denotes chapter ends (Silva 1938: xix).

Writing should be followed from left to right on the palm-leaf and the first line of the top of the page named "mavpeḷa" mother line and rest are "darupeḷa" children line. Manuscripts written in Pali and Sanskrit languages were used compound consonant, but in Sinhala manuscripts mere consonants used. Further, the letters are divided into three styles namely, mulukuru, letters used in Ruhuna country with more ends, sihakuru used in Maya country with round and gajakuru used in Pihiti country, but they are fundamentally same. Spaces in between words cannot be seen in the manuscripts writings.

5. Exchange Sri Lankan Palm-Leaf Manuscripts

Sharing with Buddhist kingdoms of palm-leaf manuscripts was common in the ancient time. Several Pali manuscripts written in Burmese and Thai characters are available among Sri Lankan palm-leaf collections. Faxian (337–422), a Chinese monk traveler, visited South and Southeast Asia including Sri Lanka (399–412) to find Vinaya books. Then, there were no Vinaya books in India so he came to Sri Lanka and stayed for two years in the Abhayagiri monastery. He found a copy of the Vinaya of the Mahisasaka School and invited Sanghavami, a Sri Lankan monk, to go to China to translate it into Chinese. Afterwards, a group that broke away from this school came to be known as Dharmaguptikas and that is the Vinaya which is valid up to date in all East Asian Buddhist Sangha. At the end of the fifth century, two major Sri Lankan works; the *Samantapāsādikā* (Vinaya commentary) and the *Vimuttimagga* (Path of Liberation) were taken to China and translated into Chinese. The first was translated as Shan-jian-li-p'-ip'-osha by Sanghabhadra in the fifth century and it includes in the Taisho Chinese Tripitaka (T. 1648). The second was translated as Cie-to-tao-lun by Sanghapala at the beginning of the sixth century (Guruge 2010).

During the time of the king Buvanekabahu Ⅵ (1470–1478) Burmese king Dhammacedi sent twenty-two monks with their pupils and two ministers named Citraduta and Ramaduata for higher ordination. They received higher ordination at Kalyānisīmā which was located in the Kalyani River and went back to Burma with many Pali books and also those were spread in Siam and Cambodia as well (Perera 1988: 67, 68). It is recorded in an inscription at Pegun, Myanmar a name list of books that was brought from Sri Lanka in 1442. There are 295 books and this list contains books donated to monks by Taungdwin and his wife (Lagamuva 2006: 144; Silva 1938: xxv). Later on, Sri Lanka lost its literary treasures because of the conversion to Hinduism of the king Rajasinghe Ⅰ and the onslaught of the Portuguese in the sixteenth century Burmese supported the reestablishment of higher ordination in the Island and sent back many Pali books (Guruge 2010).

6. Popular Buddhist Culture and Palm-Leaf

The most common term for the monastery in Sinhala, *pansala* is derived from *paṇṇasālā* in Pali which means thatched with leaves that is nothing but palm leaves. Some monks still use palm leaves, named *goṭu-atta*, prepared suitably as umbrellas. Palmyra-fan (*vaṭāpata*) is a symbol of monks which most probably used all religious activities. A stylus (*panhinda*) is brought by peramunerala (chief secretary) of the tooth relic procession, one of the most attracted Buddhist cultural ceremonies which is annually held in Kandy to respect to the Buddha's tooth relic to wish prosperity and peace of the country. Until very recently horoscopes, *kendaraya* in Sihala were written on palm-leaf.

The suffix, vahanse points out the respect towards someone and it is utilized as a suffix to monks, kings, gods, etc., but here the same respect has given for two manuscripts; *Jātaka Poth Vahanse* and *Piruvānā Poth Vahanse* respectively composed in Sinhala and Pali. They are the most respected books in Sri Lankan Buddhist culture which still prefer to use palm-leaf books. The *Piruvānā Poth Vahanse* is the book of collection of Pali discourses selected from the Sutta Pitaka used in *Paritta* chanting ceremony. *Jātaka Poth Vahanse*, comprises of 547, and presents the Gotama Buddha's former Bodhisattva life translated from Pali *Jātakaṭṭhakathā* during the Kurunagala kingdom. At present, though there are no more palm-leaf books in all temples these two books are with them. They are reposed with the casket (*dhātukaranḍuva*) which deposits remains of the Buddha's or disciples. During the religious activities, these books are much respectfully brought from the monastery under the shade of a special umbrella, *mutu-kuḍaya* (pearl-umbrella), kept on the head. Since writing style of the *Piruvānā Poth Vahanse*, one and only Pali manuscript with Sinhala name, differs even from modern printed traditional Pali books used for special training providing for young novices to read and chant in monastery education. It is utilized during the paritta chanting ceremonies held throughout the whole night or seven days. The *Catubhāṇavāra-pāli* is the original name of the book but Sinhala name is much popular than that of the Pali name among lay Buddhists. An appendix is added at the end of the Sinhala text with popular later parittas and even some *yantra* (mystical diagrams) and *mantras* (sacred utterance). Reading the *Jātaka Poth Vahanse* is still a respectful act with its own style called *vāsagam-śailiya* while improving listeners' interest.

7. Conclusion

Palm-leaf culture is an essential part of the Sri Lankan Buddhist culture from the very beginning to date. It has been enriched directly with Pali canon, commentaries, sub-commentaries and rest of the literature written in Pali. The classical Sinhala literature is also nothing but Buddhist because they are most probably translations or adaptations from Pali to Sinhala or their themes were completely Buddhist. The Siyabaslakara, a guide book of the Sinhala literary work, has motivated writers to present Buddhist themes rather than mere worldly expressions. Writing on palm-leaf, the words of the Buddha during the reign of the king Vattagamini Abhaya was one of the most important events throughout the religious history of the world. This is the first experience as a project that completed whole primary words and its key interpretations of the religious teacher in the world. The well-known term to be used for the temple in Sinhala called *pansala* derived from Pali term *paṇṇasālā* with the sense of is thatched with palm-leaf. Palmyra-fan called *vaṭāpata* in Sinhala is a symbol of monks and palm-leaf umbrella *goṭu-atta*, are still popular among forest dwelling monks. *Jātaka Poth Vahanse* and *Piruvānā Poth Vahanse* are most popular, respectful and well-known two books by all Buddhists, and are still used in as palm-leaf manuscripts in every temple in the country. Protection of palm-leaf is also appreciable and the National Library, Colombo Museum Library, Peradeniya, Kelaniya and Sri Jayawardhanapura University Libraries are providing a remarkable contribution to protect them and motivate post-graduate students for research. Though the printing mechanism is very popular and developed palm-leaf culture is still alive in the country and there are some traditional families which maintain the ancient heritage on behalf of the next generation.

References

[1] De Silva, C.M.A. Production of Books in Ancient Ceylon Education in Ceylon, A Centenary Volume. Colombo: Ministry of Education and Cultural Affairs, 1969.

[2] De Silva, W.A. Catalogue of Palm Leaf Manuscripts in the Library of the Colombo Museum, Volume 1.Colombo: Ceylon Government Press, 1938.

[3] Gunawardana, V. D. S. 2003 Siyabaslakara Deepani, Colombo 10. Samayawardhana Book Shop (Pvt) Ltd.

[4] Guruge, Ananda W. P. Sri Lanka's Role in the Spread of Buddhism in the World Public Lecture under the Auspices of the Royal Asiatic Society of Sri Lanka, the first in a series of lectures to mark the 2,600 Sambuddhatva Jayanti, Colombo, November 15, 2010. http://www.urbandharma.org/udharma14/srilankahistory.html.

[5] Lagamuwa, Ariya.Sri Lankave Puskol poth lekhana kalāva, Battaramulla, Department of Cultural Affairs, 2006.

[6] Wikramagamage, Candra. Dehiwala: Buddhist Cultural Centre, Mahāvaṃsa, Volume 1, 2012. Perera, H R. Buddhism in Sri Lanka: A Short History. Kandy: Buddhist Publication Society, 1988.

The Revival, Transmission and Development of Tai Lü Papsa Manuscripts in Southern Yunnan[①]

Apiradee Techasiriwan[②]

1. General Information of Tai Lü and Tai Lü Manuscript Culture

In the area of Dai Autonomous Prefecture of Xishuangbanna in the far south of Yunnan province, the People's Republic of China was the Tai Lü kingdom, named *Hò Kham Chiang Rung*. During that times, they were invaded and occupied repeatedly by the neighbors namely Burma, Lan Na kingdom, etc. (In the present-day, the center of the Lan Na kingdom is situated in the upper northern region of Thailand with Chiang Mai as capital.) These have had various effects on Tai Lü not only the politics and government but also the culture, tradition, language, and manuscripts.

One of the important influence of Lan Na was the Dhamma script, although some of Tai Lü people believe that their script came into being more than 1,000 years ago, but other scholars presume that it is a variant of the Dhamma script which developed in the fourteenth century in the kingdom of Lan Na, then spread to Xishuangbanna during the reign of King Tilokaraja (1441–1487), which was the golden age and strongest of Lan Na and the flourishing of Buddhism. In the period, the king extended the boundaries of the kingdom toevery direction, for instance, expanded west to Shan and north to Chiang Rung (Xishuangbanna). The consequence of the situation was Buddhism also brought to Xishuangbanna together with Dhamma script using for writing "Dhamma" or Buddha doctrine on manuscripts.

Then, Tai Lü people has used the script for recording not only Dhamma or religious texts, such as Sutta, Jātaka, Tipitaka, history of sacred objects, etc. but also secular

---

[①] This paper is developed from a part of the author's dissertation entitled, "Tai Lü Manuscripts from Southern Yunnan and Northern Laos: The Function and Development of Paratexts in a Recently Revived Manuscript Culture", the University of Hamburg, Germany, 2019.

[②] Head of the Centre of Research in Lan Na Writing Culture and Folklore (CLCF) and a researcher of Archive of Lan Na Inscriptions, Social Research Institute, Chiang Mai University.

texts or their history, knowledge and literature, such as chronicle, law, folktales, traditional medicine, rituals, magic, etc. on manuscripts.

2. The Revival

In Yunnan in early 1950, Chinese policy of standard is the written languages of the ethnic groups were suggested to some of the ethnic groups who had imperfections in their written language. Therefore, in 1952 Chinese government sector in Yunnan (The Language Research Institute, National Science Council of China and the Commission of Ethnic Affairs of Yunnan) collaborated to observe and research the state of languages and scripts of the Dai ethnic group. They divided the dialects into two groups, namely Xishuangbanna dialect and Dehong dialect, as the scripts are different in shape. Therefore, a plan for the improvement of the scripts was hatched. The plan consisted of several policies, namely: to remove excessive characters and adding other necessary characters to eliminate overlap between the writing systems and to clarify ambiguous writing. Therefore, the old Tai Lü script and orthography were replaced by a new Tai Lü script and orthography. The plan was tested for the first time in 1955 for producing official documents for teaching in primary school, and was later extended to newspapers, magazines, textbooks and the printing of works of traditional Tai Lü literature.

However, the Tai Lü had different opinions about the new script. Some people agreed to continue to use the new script while others felt uncomfortable because the new script no longer reflected the etymology and unsuitable for writing Pali texts. Therefore, the old script is still publicly used throughout Xishuangbanna and other places.

Nevertheless, during 1966–1976, a large number of Tai Lü manuscripts were destroyed. However, after the crisis, the Tai Lü and other ethnic groups were given the chance to express their cultural particularities once again by the Government of China until the present day.

3. Transmission

Since the revival until now, throughout southern Yunnan area, there are several lay scribes still active in manuscript production. The majority of them in their seventies and eighties.

Po Saeng Nòi (Moeng Long)
(Collection of Techasiriwan)

Many of them had already started their scribal career before the "Cultural Revolution" and continued this work again in the early 1980s. For example, Po Saeng Nòi, also known as Po Long Khan Kaeo, lives in Ban Foei Lung (เมิงโลง Moeng Long). When I met him in 2012, he was already seventy-seven years old. Po Saeng Nòi started his career as a scribe at the early age of fourteen or fifteen when he was still a novice. He has copied a lot of local history on papsa because he wants to preserve the historical and cultural heritage of Moeng Long and Xishuangbanna for future generations.

The another case is Pò Saeng Sam of Moeng Laem. He was born in 1938. He has copied a lot of historical text manuscripts on mulberry paper for transmitting the stories to young generations.

Moreover, in the case of historical manuscripts, the scribes often express their desire to record the history, old customs, ritual texts and folktales, and any other kind of traditional knowledge of Tai Lü, in order to pass these on to the young generations in paratexts on the manuscripts such as colophons and prefaces. Therefore, the writing of manuscripts is seen as an important cultural technique to transmit traditional, in particular historical, knowledge to young generation and ensure that Tai Lü culture will be survive and continued to exist.

Pò Saeng Sam (Moeng Laem)
(Collection of Techasiriwan)

For example, the manuscript *"Cao sipsòng pang"* (The twelve reigns of the rulers of Xishuangbanna), is written on industrial paper. It was copied by Cao Maha Khanthawong (1925–2013), a former government employee from an aristocratic background, who became a productive scribe after retirement and a scholar most knowledgeable in the history and culture of Xishuangbanna, in 1986. Cao Maha Khanthawong copied numerous secular texts on notebooks made of industrial paper.

The preface of this manuscript refers to the situation after Xishuangbanna came under the leadership of the Communist Party in early 1950 and during the "Cultural Revolution" (1966–1976) until after 1982, the situation in Xishuangbanna normalised and the local population was again allowed to practice its religion and ethnic culture. The traditional literature of the ethnic groups was revived. After that in 1984, literary experts came together to reconstruct a corpus of traditional Tai Lü literature by collating old extant manuscripts and interviewing elderly people. In these newly arranged manuscripts, the compilers organized the contents by themes; the stories related to religion were grouped together under the label "religion" (*sāsana*), whereas the stories about traditions were placed under the title "traditions".

The another example is the manuscript "*Nangsü Phün Moeng La*" (The Chronicle of Müang La), Tai Lü manuscript written on mulberry paper, written and owned by Ai Chòi Cha Han, Moeng La, 1996.

The short paragraph comprising the preface appears on the first page of the manuscript before the beginning of the main text. Here, the scribe explains that there are no extant manuscripts to be found of this particular chronicle. Therefore, he decided to interview elderly people and noblemen to collect information about the history of Moeng La, a district situated in the southeastern part of Xishuangbanna. He compiled these data and wrote on the manuscript for future generations might get informed about the history of Müang La. Finally, he apologizes for his miswritings.

It is worthy to note that the scribe did not just copy his text from an older extant manuscript but combined written sources with oral traditions, including own interviews.

4. The Development of Tai Lü Manuscripts

While studying the Tai Lü manuscripts in my corpus, the development of the manuscripts is one important issue that is clearly evident. I found that the format, layout, materials, paratexts, punctuations and script of the manuscripts of each period have changed. Through my research, I identified several Tai Lü manuscripts in Yunnan that were influenced by modern printing technology introduced by the Chinese authorities after the Communist Party of China rose to power in Yunnan in January 1950.

I divided the Tai Lü manuscripts in my corpora roughly into three periods:

Period One (1884–1949): The Communist victory in Yunnan and the end of the traditional *cao fa system* (1950);

Period Two (1950–1966): The beginning of the "Cultural Revolution" (1966), which lasted for fifteen years, during which manuscript production came to an end;

Period Three (1981–2013): The start of the reform period marking the revival of Tai Lü manuscript culture.

4.1 Period One: 1884–1949

The characteristics of the manuscripts from this period seem to be of a standard form for Tai Lü manuscripts; that is, mulberry paper is used as writing support and the text is written in black ink, the manuscripts are bound at the top of mulberry paper and the concertina form, moreover, the content is written in continuous script without inter punctuation, even though sometimes phrases or sentences are separated by space and/

or punctuation and a blank line is inserted to separate the colophon from the main text. Furthermore, the scribes used special symbols mark the beginning and the end of a text or chapter. Rectangular frames are also placed around certain key words within the text.

(In the period of Phaya Saen Aeo Lai)

(In the period that Cao Cheng Rai is a ruler)

Chronicle of Moeng Long, **1884** (Collection of Yunnan University, Kunming)

4.2 Period Two: 1950–1966

The manuscripts in this period quite still exhibit the same features as the first period; however, some manuscripts show some changes. For example, firstly, the material of the manuscript is made of industrial paper and bound by staples. Secondly, the layout of the manuscript is slightly different. The first line of a new paragraph is indented; nonetheless, some paragraphs in the same text still begin without spacing as is the case with the manuscripts of the first period. Thirdly, punctuation and round brackets, like used in printed books, are used in the manuscript. Fourthly, the colophon at the end of the text specifies the Common Era and dates the manuscript in accordance to the solar calendar instead of the older Cūḷasakaraja (CS) system which

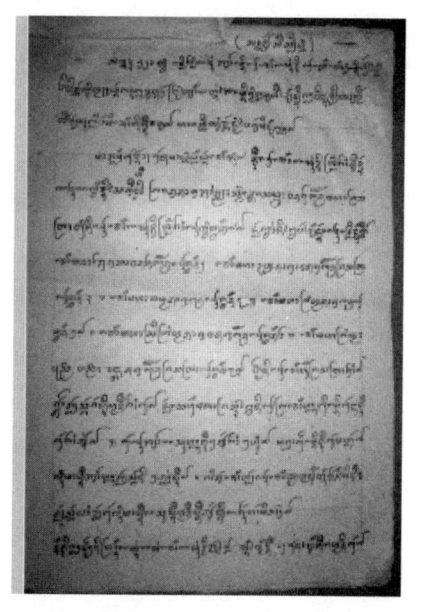

Chronicle of Phaya Coeng, **1966** (Collection of Yunnan University, Kunming)

according to the lunar calendar.

4.3 Period Three: 1980–2013

Many of the manuscripts from this period have changed markedly. Through these changes, we can clearly observe the growing influence of modern printing technology.

In contrast, one of the two standard formats of manuscripts mentioned in period one whereby the manuscripts are bound at the top, but I have found some manuscripts from this period which are bound on the left-hand side, like printed books.

Moreover, I found that a large number of manuscripts were being written on industrial paper in black ink and/or by ball point pen.

Furthermore, some of the scribes copied text to a notebook made of industrial paper as illustrated by manuscript. However, the scribe tried to preserve some old fashioned characteristics that appear in mulberry paper manuscripts; that is, they still provides a short colophon on front cover folio and a colophon at the end of the text.

The Twelve Reigns of Rulers, Chiang Rung, 1986 (Collection of Grabowsky)

Moreover, manuscripts containing religious texts are used as objects by lay-people to make merit by donating these to monasteries. In the past, sponsors needed to hire scribes to produce manuscripts for them, but I found some manuscripts are produced by a photocopying machine.

Parami, Chiang Rung, 2012 (Collection of Techasiriwan)

Another case is a hybrid manuscript with regard to both its writing support and the writing methods applied. Only the front and back cover folios are made from mulberry paper and only the title of the text and a statement of ownership mentioning the owner's name and year of acquisition are written by hand. However, the main text is not handwritten but printed in the Dhamma script on industrial paper. Nonetheless, the traditional whirlwind binding makes the manuscript appear to be a genuine reproduction.

***Chronicle of Ceng Hung*, Chiang Rung, 1999** (Collection of Grabowsky)

Finally, I have found attempts to preserve and revive Tai Lü literature. Some Tai Lü texts have been produced in a bilingual Chinese-Tai publication printed in Kunming. The edited texts are a collection of local chronicles, legends and customary law of Dai ethnic group in Yunnan province. They are not printed in Tai Lü script font for computer but it's the handwritten in the old Tai Lü (Dhamma) script.

***The Laws of Moeng Laem Long Golden Palace* published in 1986 in Kunming**
(Collection of Techasiriwan)

It is very pleasure that, even though, since the past until now, the Tai Lü manuscript culture has passed several changes, situations and crises, it has been still preserved and existed until present-day by young generations for transmitting their precious histories and knowledge from old generations to future generations.

References

(Ⅰ) In Western Languages

[1] Techasiriwan, Apiradee. Localising Tai Lü and Tai Khün Manuscripts in Space and Time Through Colophons // Tracing Manuscripts in Time and Space through Paratexts. Berlin/Bostan: Walter de Gruyter, 2016.

[2] Techasiriwan, Apiradee and Grabowsky, Volker. Note on Tai Lue Wooden Buddha Image Inscriptions and Buddhist Manuscript Colophons from Northern Laos. Aséanie, No. 33, 2014.

[3] Borchert, Thomas. Worry for the Dai Nation: Sipsongpannā, Chinese Modernity, and the Problems of Buddhist Modernism. The Journal of Asian Studies, 2008, 67(1).

[4] Chamberlain, James R. A Critical Framework for the Study of Thao Houng or Cheuang in ตำนานเกี่ยวกับท้าวฮุ่งท้าวเจือง: มิติทางประวัติศาสตร์และวัฒนธรรม (Chronicle of Thao Houng Thao Cheuang: In History and Cultural Perspecive). Bangkok: Thai Khadi Research Institute, 1995.

[5] Daniels, Christian. The Formation of Tai Polities Between the 13th to 16th Centuries: The Role of Technological Transfer. The Memoirs of the Toyo Bunko, 2000 (58).

[6] Davis, Sara L. M. Song and Silence: Ethnic Revival on China's Southwest Borders. Chiang Mai: Silkworm Books, 2005.

[7] Diana, Antonella. Re-Configuring Belonging in Post-Socialist Xishuangbanna, China. Andrew Walker (ed.), in Tai Lands and Thailand: Community and State in Southeast Asia Singapore and Copenhagen, NUS Press and NIAS Press, 2009.

[8] Diller, Anthony. The Tai Language Family and the Comparative Method // Proceedings of the International Conference on Tai Studies. Bangkok: Institute of Language and Culture for Rural Development, Mahidol University, 1998.

[9] Gedney, William. The Lue Language: Glossaries, Texts and Translations. Ann Arbor: University of Michigan Press, 1999 (1964).

[10] Grabowsky, Volker and Techasiriwan, Apiradee. Tai Lue Identitites in the Upper Mekong Valley: Glimpses from Mulberry Paper Manuscripts. In Aséanie, 2013

(31).

[11] Grabowsky, Volker and Wichasin, Renoo. Chronicles of Chiang Khaeng: A Tai Lü Principality of the Upper Mekong. Honolulu: Center for Southeast Asian Studies. University of Hawaii, 2008.

[12] Hartmann, John F. Linguistic and Memory Structures in Tai-Lue Oral Narratives. Canberra: Research School of Pacific Studies. The Australian National University, 1984.

[13] Hasegawa Kiyoshi. Cultural Revival and Ethnicity: The Case of the Tai Lue in the Sipsong Panna, Yunnan Province // Hayashi Yukio and Yang Guangyuan. Dynamics of Ethnic Cultures Across National Boundaries in Southwestern China and Mainland Southeast Asia: Relations, Societies, and Languages. Chiang Mai: Ming Muang Printing House, 2000.

[14] He Shaoying, et al. Inheritance of Dai Culture and the Preservation of Dai Park in Xishuangbanna // Don McCaskill, et al. Living in a Globalized World: Ethnic Minorities in the Greater Mekong Subregion. Chiang Mai: Mekong Press, 2008.

[15] Iijima, Akiko. Preliminary Notes on "the Cultural Region of the Tham Script Manuscripts". Senri Ethnological Studies, 2009 (74).

[16] Kato, Kumiko. Muang Polities in Sipsongpanna: A Comparison of the Categories of Land and People among the Muang. The Journal of the Faculty of Letters Nagoya University, History, 1994 (40).

[17] Lemoine, Jacques. Tai Lue Historical Relations with China and the Shaping of the Sipsong Panna Political System // Anne Buller. Proceedings of the International Conference on Thai Studies. The Australian National University, Canberra, 3-6 July, 1987.

[18] Liew-Herres, Foon Ming and Grabowsky, Volker. An Introduction to the Tai Lü Sources of the History of Moeng Lü (Sipsòng Panna). Aséanie, 2004 (14).

[19] Liew-Herres, Foon Ming; Grabowsky, Volker and Wichasin, Renoo. Chronicle of Sipsòng Panna: History and Society of a Tai Lü Kingdom. Chiang Mai: Silkworm Books, 2012.

[20] Moerman, Michael. Ethnic Identification in a Complex Civilization: Who are the Lue? American Anthropologist. New Series, 1965, 67 (5) Part 1.

[21] Sethakul, Ratanaporn. Tai Lue of Xishuangbanna and Müang Nan in the Nineteenth Century // Andrew Turton. Civility and Savagery: Social Identity in Tai States. Richmond, Surrey: Curzon, 2000.

[22] Rosenberg, Klaus. A Preliminary Study in the History of Khun Chüang. Paper presented at the International Conference on Thai Studies, Bangkok, 22-24 August 1984.

[23] Wyatt, David K. and Wichienkeeo, Aroonrut. The Chiang Mai Chronicle. Chiang Mai: Silkworm Books, 1995.

[24] Xiaobing Li. China at War: An Encyclopedia. California: ABC-CLIO, LLC, 2012.

(Ⅱ) In Thai

[1] Apiradee Techasiriwan อภิรดี เตชะศิริวรรณ. พัฒนาการอักษรและอักขรวิธีในเอกสารไทลื้อ (The Development of Tai-Lue Scripts and Orthography). MA thesis. Chiang Mai University, 2003.

[2] Cia Yaencong (alias Yanyong Chiranakhon) เจีย แยน จอง (ยรรยง จิระนคร). คนไทไม่ใช่คนไทย แต่เป็นเครือญาติชาติภาษา ("Tai" Does not Mean "Thai" but an Ethno-Linguistic Family). Bangkok: Sinlapa-watthanatham, 2005.

[3] Dhida Saraya ธิดา สาระยา. ประวัติศาสตร์สิบสองพันนา (The History of Xishuangbanna). Muang Boran Journal, 1989, 15 (3).

[4] Isara Yanatan อิสรา ญาณตาล. บทสำรวจเบื้องต้นเกี่ยวกับการฟื้นฟูอักษรไทลื้อในสิบสองพันนา (Revival of the Tai Lü Scripts in Xishuangbanna: A Preliminary Survey) // Saraswadee Ongsakul and Yoshiyuku Masuhara. Studies of History and Literature of Thai Ethnic Groups. Bangkok: Amarin, 2001.

[5] Kato, Kumiko and Isra Yanatan. คาโต้ คุมิโกะ และ อิสรา ญาณตาล. สถานภาพปัจจุบันของเอกสารพับสาในสิบสองพันนา (Present State of Papsa Documents in Xishuangbanna) // Saraswadee Ongsakul, Yoshiyuku Masuhara. Studies of History and Literature of Thai Ethnic Groups. Bangkok: Amarin, 2001.

[6] Natcha Laohasirinadh ณัชชา เลาหศิรินาถ. สิบสองพันนา: รัฐจารีต (Xishuangbanna: A Traditional State). Bangkok: The Foundation for the Promotion of Social and Humanities Textbooks Project, 1998.

[7] Prakong Nimmanahaeminda ประคอง นิมมานเหมินท์. มหากาพย์เรื่องท้าวบาเจือง: การศึกษาเชิงวิเคราะห์ (The Thao Ba Jueng Epic: An Analytical Study). PhD dissertation. Chulalongkorn University, 1987.

[8] Prasert na Nagara ประเสริฐ ณ นคร. ที่มาของอักษรไทยล้านนาและไทลื้อ The Origin of Lan Na and Tai Lü Scripts//Assembled Documents of the Conference Lan Na and Xishuang banna Cultures: Continuity and Change. Center for the Promotion of Arts and Culture Chiang Mai University and the Toyota Foundation, 1986.

[9] Sarassawadee Ongsakul สรัสวดี อ๋องสกุล. ประวัติศาสตร์ล้านนา (Lan Na History). 2nd edition. Bangkok: Amarin, 1996.

[10] Sumitr Pitiphat and Samerchai Poolsuwan สุมิตร ปิติพัฒน์ และ เสมอชัย พูลสุวรรณ. คนไตในชื่อเหมา มณฑลยูนนาน สาธารณรัฐประชาชนจีน: ประวัติศาสตร์การเมือง สังคมและวัฒนธรรม (Tai in Suemao, Yunnan, People's Republic of China: History of Political, Social and Cultural). Bangkok: Thai

Khadi Research Institute, Thammasat University, 2003.

［11］Tao Sü Sin. ตาว ซื้อ ซิน. สภาพการณ์ภาษา หนังสือ และ การศึกษา ของชนชาติไทสิบสองปันนา（The Situation of Language, Manuscripts and Education of Xishuangbanna Tai Ethnic Group）//Assembled Documents of the Conference Lan Na and Sipsòng Panna Cultures: Continuity and Change. Center for the Promotion of Arts and Culture Chiang Mai University and the Toyota Foundation, 1986.

［12］Term Meetem เทิม มีเต็ม. พุทธศาสนาในยูนนาน（Buddhism in Yunnan）. Bangkok: Watana Panit Publishing Co.Ltd. 1986.

［13］Thawi Sawangpanyangkun ทวี สว่างปัญญางกูร. ตำนานพื้นเมืองสิบสองพันนา（Xishuangbanna Chronicle）. Chiang Mai University Library, 1986.

［14］Thongthaem Nartchamnong ทองแถม นาฎจำนง. ถิ่นฐานของชาวไตในสิบสองพันนา（Tai Settlement Areas in Xishuangbanna）. Warasan Müang Boran, 1989, 16（3）.

［15］Yanyong Churanakhon and Ratanaporn Setthakul ยรรยง จิระนคร, รัตนาพร เศรษฐกุล. ประวัติศาสตร์สิบสองพันนา（A History of Xishuangbanna）. Bangkok: Amarin, 2001.

Let the Words of Palm-Leaf Living

—Rescue, Protection, Translation, Arrangement, Development and Utilization of the Ancient Dai Books

Zhang Yun[1]

Translated by Tian Weiwei[2]

In 2007, the General Office of the State Council issued the document No. 6, *The Opinions of the General Office of the State Council on Further Strengthening the Protection of Ancient Books*, and the General Office of the People's Government of Yunnan Province issued the document No. 235, *The Notice of the General Office of the People's Government of Yunnan Province on Implementing the Opinions of the General Office of the State Council on Further Strengthening the Protection of Ancient Books*. In order to implement the spirit of the documents, it was decided to establish the Leading Group of Rescue and Protection of Dehong Prefecture's Ethnic Ancient Books after the study of the People's Government of Dehong Prefecture in 2014, and it concurrently issued document No. 38, *The Notice of the General Office of the People's Government of Dehong Prefecture on Establishing the Leading Group of Rescue and Protection of Dehong Prefecture's Ethnic Ancient Books*. At present, 200 valuable ancient Dai books have been compiled, translated and published.

During the Thirteenth Five-Year Plan, the project has been declared to National Ethnic Affairs Commission of the Yunnan Province in June 2014. In March 2018, the project was selected into the Top Hundred Projects of Yunnan Province. The first batch of funds has been allocated, which is 400,000 *yuan*. Part of work on this project—the photo production of ancient Dai, the translation from ancient Dai to Dai, the translation from Dai to Chinese, and the collation and editing of these translations—has been completed now, including five historical books, one Buddhist books, and six literary books. In addition, other work on this project is continuing.

---

[1] Associate researcher librarian of Dehong Prefectural Library, Yunnan Province.
[2] Master, Major of Religion 2016, School of Ethnology and Sociology, Yunnan University.

1. The Current States of the Ancient Books in Dehong Prefecture

The Dai people accumulated rich and splendid material civilization and cultural heritages in the long history of development process, and left a large amount of manuscripts written by the old Dai. According to the record of the historical ancient book *Sa Mian Pa La Wu*, there are a total of 84,000 Dai scriptures, and they are collectively referred to as *Tripitaka*, of which there are 21,000 volumes of *Sutranta-pitaka*, 21,000 volumes of *Vinaya-pitaka*, and 42,000 volumes of *Abhidharma-pitaka*. And there is a five-volume palm-leaf scripture called *Bie Men Xi Ban Xi Gan*, which also specifically tells the origin and legend of these 84,000 Buddhist scriptures. Are there actually so many Buddhist scriptures? Although we can't verify it now, the records of ancient books can still indicate the quantity of the Dai scriptures. Some of these ancient scriptures are written on the palm's leaves and called Palm-Leaf Scripture, some of them are written on cotton paper and called Cotton Paper Scripture; some of them are written on mulberry paper and called Mulberry Paper Scripture; some of them are also written on ivory tablets and called Ivory Tablet Scripture, and some of them are written on elephant bone tablets and called Elephant's Bone Tablet Scripture, all of which are collectively referred to as the ancient Dai scriptures. These scriptures are written in circular Dai script and rectangular ancient Dai script. The contents include religious beliefs, Dai's calendar, medicine, long narrative poems, folk stories, myths, and so on. Therefore, from the perspective of the languages and materials of writing, the Dai ancient books are both full of variety.

The following is the current collection of ancient books in Dehong: the Archives of Dehong Prefecture has collected 181 volumes; the Working Committee of Ethnic Language of Dehong Prefecture has collected 200 volumes; the Cultural Center of Dehong and the Library of Dehong Prefecture have collected 200 volumes; the Cultural Center of Mangshi has collected 200 volumes; the Archives of Ruili has collected 200 volumes; the Archives of Lianghe has collected 300 volumes; the Archives of Yingjiang has collected 200 volumes; the Cultural Center of Wanding has collected 150 volumes. There are 592 Buddhist temples in the whole prefecture, and each Theravada Buddhist temple has collected many Dai ancient scriptures. According to incomplete statistics, there are 500 volumes in Puti Temple, 300 volumes in Foguang Temple, and 350 volumes in Wuyun Temple. The Dai Academy of Dehong Prefecture has collected 200 volumes, and the Dai's intellectuals have also collected some ancient books, including 78 volumes collected by Fang Zhengwu and 125 volumes collected by Jin Changyu. Most of the ancient books collected by the above units or individuals have not been translated.

2. Content and Classification of Dai Ancient Books in Dehong

The contents of the Dai ancient books are very extensive, which covers all aspects of the Dai people's social life. These ancient books are not only a witness of the society, history and culture of the Dai people in Dehong, but also a crystallization of the wisdom, talent and creativity of the ancient Dai people. In terms of content, the Dai ancient books can be roughly divided into the following categories.

2.1 History

Now we have selected 50 Dai ancient books, such as *The History of Ancient Kings in Meng Mao*, *A Brief History of the Misty Meng Mao*, *The King Zhaowuding of Meng Mao*, *The King Sihanfa*, *A Brief History of Yingjiang*, etc., which are very valuable in studying the history of the Dai.

2.2 Literary

Literary books account for a large proportion in the Dai ancient books, including folk myths, folk creation epics, folk legends, folk stories, long poems of folk stories, various custom songs and so on. And we have selected sixty-eight from these literary ancient books, such as *Series of Stories about Aluan*, *Na Niu Guang Han*, *Guangmu/Pagoda Meng Xie*, *Yong Han* and so on.

2.3 Buddhism

The Buddhist books mainly include the *Tripitaka*, which are divided into three parts: *Sutranta-pitaka*, *Vinaya-pitaka*, *Abhidharma-pitaka*. And we have selected thirty-two from them, such as *Su Ma Ha Wa*, *Su Xie Na Kham*, *Pi Tan Ma Ya Men* and so on.

2.4 Etiquette

China is a nation whose people value etiquette highly, and the Dai people also value etiquette highly, so there are a lot of Dai ancient books about etiquette in the area of Dehong's Dai. These ancient books educate people that without the blood and sweat of their parents, they would not grow up as adults, and the kindness of parents can never be repaid. In addition, ancient books also educate people to respect the old and to love the young, and teach women about the etiquette of wife. And we have selected sixteen from these ancient books, such as *Gong Na Ba Di*, *The Five Educational Methods*, *Suo Da Ba Da* and so on.

2.5 Astronomy and Calendar

After observing the astronomical phenomena, the Dai people made their own calendar based on those phenomena. The period of time that the earth orbits the sun is defined as one year, which is also called solar calendar. The period of time that the moon firstly changes from a new moon to a full moon and then changes from a full moon to a new moon is defined as one month which is also called the lunar calendar. This calendar also has weeks, and it defines every 7 days as a week. The calendar described above is also known as the Dai calendar. In the history of Dehong Prefecture, the Buddhist calendar and Chula Calendar (小历) were also used in Dai people's life because of the influence of Buddhist culture. After the establishment of the People's Republic of China, the Dai people also uses the Gregorian calendar. Two ancient books of astronomy and calendar have been selected for translation.

2.6 Language

Some Dai ancient books record the original creation and development process of the Dai in terms of the origin, language, grammar, literary reform and so on. Four of them have been selected for translating.

2.7 Divination

There are diagrams and descriptions in the ancient books of divination, which involve the selection of funeral day and building day, business, purchase of goods, marriage, establishment of village, and so on. Eighteen books have been selected, such as *How to Divine the Lucky and Unlucky Days*, *How to Divine the Causes of Diseases* and so on.

2.8 Medicine

The ancient medical books of Dai are a precious medical heritage. Dai medicine is listed in one of the four medicines of the major ethnic groups and is regarded as profound learning. For example, *Eight Causes of Diseases* records the eight causes that can lead to illness: ① lack of exercise; ② lack of calmness in the mood; ③ stagnant movement of Qi (气) and blood in the body; ④ mixture of three kinds of stale thing in the body; ⑤ the seasons changes too quickly; ⑥ unsuitable and irregular diet; ⑦ excessive physical exertion; ⑧ the limit of life itself. Sixteen valuable ancient books, such as *The Dai Medicine*, *The Dai Medicine in Yingjiang* have been selected for translating.

3. The Prospects of Developing and Utilizing the Dai Ancient Books

3.1 The Value in Constructing a Harmonious Society

China is a multi-ethnic country. The construction of a harmonious society in ethnic areas is an important issue for the construction of a harmonious society in China. The area of Dai in Dehong is an area where various ethnic groups living together, and it is located in the southwest border of China. And the Dai is also a transborder ethnic group. Therefore, the construction of harmonious society is also an important task for the development of the Dai's region at the present stage. The Dai ancient books have typical significance and positive effect on constructing harmonious society nowadays. First of all, the Dai's ancient books advocate harmony between human and nature. For example, the primitive religion of Dai believes that the land is our mother, the forest is our father, and we can only get food from our parents. Dai people believe that there is no water without forests, no fields without water, no food without fields, and no life without food. Therefore, Dai people protect the forests and do not destroy the forests at will. The series of ethics, morals, norms, etiquette, commandments, etc. shown in the Dai ancient books, have played an inestimable role in the harmony between human and society. For example, *The Five Educational Methods*, the book is widely popular in Dehong, which educates children and grandchildren to abide by disciplines and rules, not to addicted to drinking, not to talk nonsense, not to fight, not to abuse opium, not to be thief and prostitutes, not to oppress the fellow of same trade and dominate the market, but to work hard and do business with conscience. The aforementioned Dai ancient books can play an important role in supporting law and promoting harmony between people and society. Therefore, it can be said that the Dai ancient books have the function and value in constructing harmonious society.

3.2 The Value in Developing Cultural Industries

As has been argued, the contents of the 200 Dai ancient books are very extensive, including history, literature, Buddhism, etiquette, astronomy, calendar, language, divination, medicine, etc. which is a rare and precious cultural heritage. The Dai ancient books has two values in developing cultural industries.

3.2.1 The Value in Publishing

The 200 Dai ancient books in Dehong contain various contents. It is not only a huge project to show the palm-leaf culture, but also the inheritance and promotion of Chinese culture by the Dai's excellent culture, which can contribute to enrich the world culture. We can publish literary stories, Buddhist stories and allegorical stories for people, sell them to readers and tourists, and make readers or tourists deeply understand the Dai's excellent traditional culture.

3.2.2 The Value in Film and Television Industry

In the 1950s and 1960s, films of ethnic groups in Yunnan once attracted the attention of the film industry and the love of the whole country, including *The Peacock Princess*, *Mo Ya Dai*, *Meng Long Sha*, which were taken in Dehong and reflected the life of Dai people. Among them, *The Peacock Princess* is a film based on *Zhao Shu Tun & Nan Mu Nuo Na*, one of the translation of the Dai literature, which left an indelible and wonderful impression on the audience. At present, Yunnan province is vigorously developing the cultural industry. The film and television industry is also an important part of it. And Dai ancient texts can play an irreplaceable role and be an inexhaustible source in the creation of film and television. A large number of classics about history, literature and Buddhism can provide us with useful materials for the creation of film and television, such as series of stories about Aluan (including *Yong Han*, *E Ying*, *Jing Xing Meng Huang* and so on),

The Story of Buddha's Life, *Shu Da Maha Nibanna*, *Sa Mian Pa La Wu*, *The Legend of Mangshi* and so on, all of which can be filmed into movies or TV series and put on the screen.

3.3 The Value in Tourism

The Dai ancient books record a number of legends about scenic attractions, toponym, festivals and customs, such as *The Misty Meng Mao*, *The Legend of the Water-Splashing Festival* and so on. In addition, there are other ancient books with varied connotations and distinctive ethnic characteristics, which can provide valuable resources for the development and utilization of tourism. Combining scenic attractions of the relevant ancient books and literatures, we could turn the rigid attractions into vivid attractions with stories, legends, and souls. This measure can allow tourists to experience by themselves in the field, which can be beneficial to improve the connotation of the attractions, build the thematic attractions with ethnic characteristics and cultural connotations, and promote the development of tourism.

3.4 The Value in the Medical Industry

Due to its long history, the Dai's medicine has ethnical characteristics and local characteristics, therefore, the Dai's medicine, the Mongolian medicine, the Tibetan medicine, and the Uyghur's medicine have been listed as Four Traditional Medicine of Ethnic Groups by the National Health Commission of the PRC (the People's Republic of China). Among the ancient books of Dai, there are many medical classics, such as *The Pharmacopoeia of Dai's Medicine*, *Eight Causes of Diseases*, *The Prescriptions of Dai's Medicine in Dehong* and so on. These medical classics record the basic theory of Dai's medicine, the ways of harvesting herbs, the drug-processing of herbal medicine, prescriptions and clinical practices. Most of the herbs in the Dai's medicine are in accordance with the modern people's health of psychology, safety, and ecology. Therefore, we should fully understand the value of Dai's medical classics, combine the prescriptions in these classics with modern medical technology, play the active role of the Dai's medicine, treat patients, and contribute to medicine of human. In summary, it is worthwhile to study these Dai's medical classics that record the medical theories, the ways of harvesting herbs, the drug-processing of herbal medicine, prescriptions and clinical practices.

3.5 The Value in Studying Theravada Buddhism

Theravada Buddhism is mainly popular in Sri Lanka, Myanmar, Thailand, Cambodia, Laos, and some places in Yunnan, China (including Dehong, Xishuangbanna, Lincang, Simao and other places). The Dai, Deang, Blang, Va and other ethnic groups in Yunnan believe in Theravada Buddhism. Dai ethnic group is the main ethnic group that believes in Theravada Buddhism. Theravada Buddhism has a profound and huge influence on the politics, economy and culture in the Dai's region. Therefore, it is necessary to study deeply and systematically. And if we want to study the topics that related to Theravada Buddhism, we must start from the Buddhist literature written in Dai, so that the results of research are well-founded and credible, which is conducive to further research. There are a considerable number of Buddhist and Buddhist-related folk literary works in Dai ancient books. The Buddhist books mainly include the *Tripitaka*, which are divided into *Sutranta-pitaka*, *Vinaya-pitaka*, and *Abhidharma-pitaka*. There are also a lot of long narrative poems about Aluan, stories about Aluan and stories about Buddha preaching around the world, which are all related to Buddhism. These classics are not only Buddhist scriptures but also literary works. In addition, other literatures in the Dai ancient books also refer to Theravada Buddhism, such as historical literatures, legal literatures and etiquette literatures, which are indispensable materials for experts to study Theravada Buddhism. To sum up, Dai ancient books are greatly valuable in the study of Theravada Buddhism.

4. The Present Situation and Existing Problems on the Inheritance, Collection and Research of the Dai Ancient Books

In the past, Dai ancient books were classics with dynamic forms. Because Dai ancient books play an important role in the life of Dai people, the Dai people must go to Theravada Buddhist temple to study and read the Dai Buddhist scriptures in their free time. Literary classics such as the long narrative poems about Aluan have been loved by the majority of the Dai men and women in the past. During the agricultural lack-season, the Dai people will gather in the Theravada Buddhist temple, and Theravada Buddhist monks or the elders will read for them. The Dai people have the custom of sacrificing Buddhist manuscripts to Theravada Buddhist temple for the purpose of building merit and virtue, and after a period of time, they usually take these manuscripts out again for reading. This custom adds to the dynamic characteristic of the Dai ancient books. Therefore, the Dai ancient books were in a state of benign inheritance in the past. However, the situation is completely different today. With the continuous advancement of reform and opening up, globalization and modernization, Dai villages have undergone great changes. The most obvious change in culture is that TVs are installed in millions of households, and people usually watch TV programs at night and during leisure. In addition, the popularity of Internet, especially some social tool like QQ, Microblog and WeChat have enriched people's entertainment and social activities. As a result, people have no time to listen to the story, and no one chants the long folk narrative poems anymore like before; now only the elder listen to and monks chant the Buddhist scriptures, and young people are not interested in it. Although the Dai people still have the custom of sacrificing manuscripts to Buddhist temples today, few people can chant them. Other kinds of ancient books of the Dai ethnic group are also rarely understood and used. The worse problem is that few people can understand and write the ancient Dai. All in all, tens of thousands of precious Dai ancient books are now largely unattended, and inheritance of them is facing a great crisis. To solve this problem, it is necessary to solve the problem of funding for the rescue and protection of ancient books.

5. Transformation of the Achievements in Researching the Dai Ancient Books

Firstly, the 18th and 19th National Congress created a good policy environment for rescuing and protecting the ancient books of ethnic groups. Dehong Prefecture resolutely implements the policy of "taking the protection and rescue of it as the first priority, using it correctly and moderately, and strengthening management of it", and has taken practical actions to participate in Plan for Protecting Chinese Ancient Books and Plan for Compiling and Publishing Chinese Ancient Books during the Thirteenth Five-Year Plan.

Secondly, the National Center for the Protection of Ancient Books promulgated *The Criteria of Selecting the Precious Ancient Books Written by Chinese Ethnic Groups' Language* (*Provisional Version*), which stipulated that the scope of collecting the precious ancient books of ethnic groups with historical, academic, and artistic values written by ethnic groups' languages was relaxed to 1949. The Criteria lists eleven categories of ancient books, among which the Dai ancient books are ranked the fifth. The Criteria also proves the historical status and quantity of the Dai ancient books.

Thirdly, the 200 Dai ancient books translated by us also provide information for the *Chinese Ancient Books: Volumes of Dai*, which has been reported to the National Center of Protecting Ancient Books by the Yunnan Province's Center of Protecting Ancient Books. These 200 Dai ancient books have been written into the annals of history and can be passed down forever. It is also the implementation of the spirit of the 19th National Congress and the spirit of series of documents of the Party Committee of Yunnan Province and the People's Government of Yunnan Province. Rescuing, protecting and inheriting the superior traditional cultures of our ethnic groups, which can promote the great development and prosperity of ethnic groups' cultures, advance the construction of the strong ethnic cultural province, national unity and the Frontier Prosperity and Stability Demonstration Zone. In addition, it also has a very important significance on the Belt and Road Initiative.

6. Introduction about the Precious Dai Ancient Books in Dehong Prefecture（Please refer to the attachment）

Attachment: Introduction about the Precious Dai Ancient Books in Dehong Prefecture

① Ivory Tablet Scripture

The Material of Writing: ivory tablets

Quantities: 12

② Elephant's Bone Tablet Scripture

The Material of Writing: elephant's bone tablets

Quantities: 12

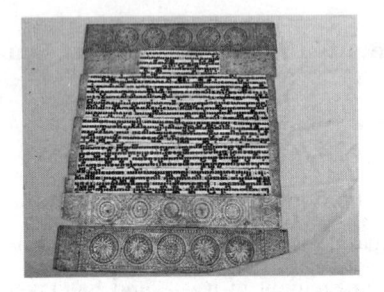

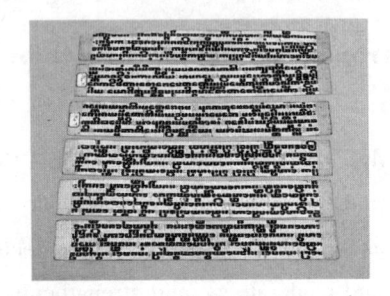

Buddhist Ancient Books

③ Palm-Leaf Scripture

The Material of Writing: palm leaves

Language: Circular Dai

Literary Ancient Books

④ Mulberry Paper Scripture

The Material of Writing: mulberry paper

Language: Circular Dai

Historical Ancient Books 　　**Ancient Books about Astronomy**

⑤ Cotton Paper Scripture

The Material of Writing: cotton paper made by bamboo

Language: Rectangular Old Dai

Ancient Books about Etiquette 　　**Ancient Books about Astronomy**

⑥ There are three kinds of languages in a Buddhist manuscript at the same time, and it has been classified as a precious ancient book in the classification of ancient ethnic books (Pali, circular Dai, rectangular Old Dai)

Religious Ancient Books 　　**Ancient books about Language** 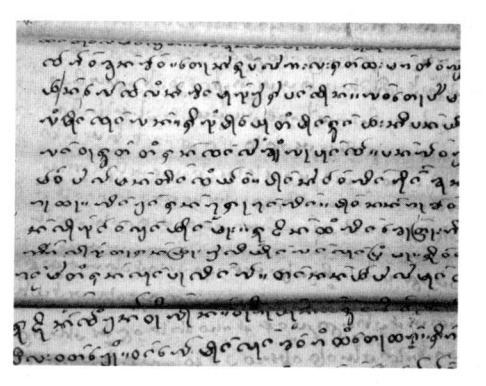　　**Circular Dai**

⑦ The Tai Ancient Scriptures that have been Printed and Published

The Material of Writing: modern paper

Language: Circular Dai

Folk Stories

⑧ Ancient Books about Divination

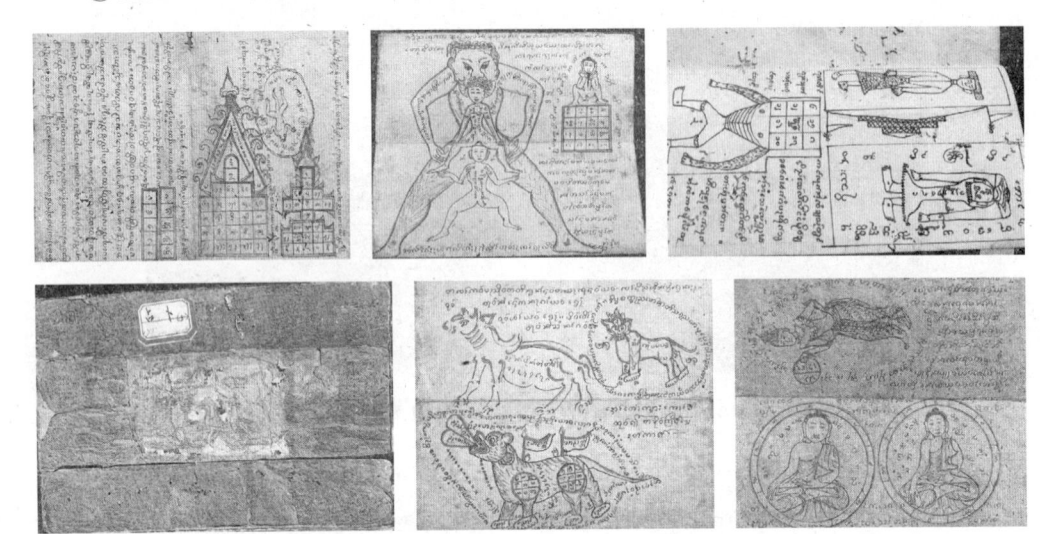

Ancient Books about Divination

⑨ Ancient Books about Incantation

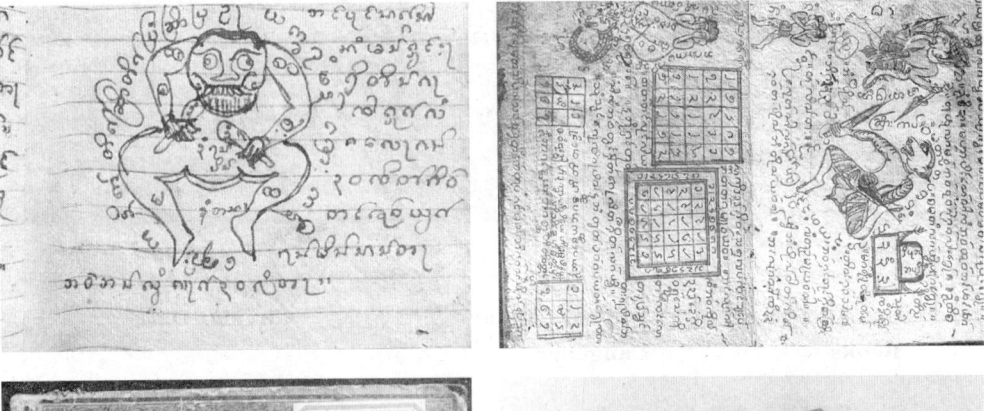

Ancient Books about Incantation

⑩ Various Forms of Binding and Layout

Various Forms of Binding and Layout

A Preliminary Study on the Names and Distribution of Tai Tham

Yankan Zhangla[1]

1. The Origin and Dissemination of the Tai Tham

At the birth of Theravada Buddhism[2], the Pali Tipitaka or the Buddha's teachings were orally transmitted given the fact that there was not yet written language. According to the historical records, the written system of Pali Tipitaka was first inscribed in Sri Lanka Sinhalese on palm leaves after Buddha's nirvana[3].

The spread of Tai Tham script is related to the development of Theravada Buddhism in Xishuangbanna. Zhang (2002) suggested that the introducing of Indian ancient script (Brahmi script) is related to the spread of Brahmanism and Buddhism in Thailand, Myanmar, Laos, Cambodia and other countries in the vast region of Southeast Asia, as well as the Dai[4] and Blang are as in southwestern China. The scripts of these countries and regions were strongly influenced by the Brahmi system, which evolved from Brahmi letters used in ancient India. The Brahmi alphabet developed into two systems consisting of the Northern one and the Southern one. It further developed into two systems in Southeast Asia: the ancient Khmer script in the south and the Mon script in the north. The ancient Mon script then evolved into Burmese and Tai Tham. Considering the same root, Mon, Burmese and Tai Tham have very similar consonants, vowels, diacritics and numerical forms. Therefore, it is clear that the three scripts are closely related to each other (Liu 1993: 167). Xie articulated that Tai Tham evolved from ancient Mon script. In 663, the Lawoe Kingdom was founded by the Mon. The Mon princess Cammadevi moved further north and established Haripunchai Kingdom, which located in nowadays Lamphun province of

---

[1] Graduate student, Center for Ethnic Studies and Development (CESD), Faculty of Social Sciences, Chiang Mai University, Thailand. This article is part of the master's thesis of the author, in Ethnicity and Development program, Faculty of Social Sciences, Chiang Mai University, Thailand.

[2] Theravada Buddhism, also known as the "Southern Buddhism" in Chinese, and because it uses the Pali language as the Buddhist canon language, it is also known as the Pali Buddhism. Mainly spread in Sri Lanka, Myanmar, Thailand, Cambodia, Laos, Yunnan province of China and other regions.

[3] Dai Lue Studies Association of Xishuangbanna. Xishuangbanna Buddhism. Kunming: Yunnan Ethnic Publishing House, 2012: 32.

[4] "Dai" is the name of one of 56 ethnic groups in China. "Tai" is a linguistic category, referring to language-related groups. "Thai" refers to the language and citizens of the Kingdom of Thailand.

northern Thailand. The kingdom was also documented as a kingdom controlled by a female ruler（女王）in Chinese historical records, such as *The Man Shu*（《蛮书》）and *History of the Yuan Dynasty*（《元史》）（Xie 2016: 106）; Theravada Buddhism was popular in the Kingdom.In the 13th century, King Mangrai became the first king of Lanna Kingdom and conquered Haripunchai Kingdom. Theravada Buddhism was adopted by King Mangrai as the state religion of Lanna Kingdom. To some extent, the relatively developed Mon culture (including Buddhism) promoted the development of the Lanna Kingdom. Lanna script originated from the Mon script（Xie 2016: 110）. The Lanna script was brought to Muang Lue, today's Xishuangbanna when Theravada Buddhism expanded from Lanna to Muang Lue and it has been known as the Lue or Dai Lue script till contemporary（Xie 2016: 112）.

The Lanna Kingdom was once centered around Chiang Rai and Chiang Mai in current northern Thailand. Since 1180 after the Dai Lue king Phaya Cheung built his capital in Chiang Rung, today's Jinghong district of Xishuangbanna, the Kingdom allied with the Lanna Kingdom politically through tight cultural connections and marriage alliance. Many cases vividly demonstrate this league. For example, the mother of King Mangrai, the founder of Lanna Kingdom, was Thep Phra Kham Khai or Nang O Ming Jom Muang. She was the daughter of Tao Long Kean Jai who was the King of Jinghong and the ruler of Xishuangbanna（He 2013）.For a long time, people of the two kingdoms had kept close interactions in trade, religion and culture. In particular, after a long period of exchange and integration of traditional culture and ethnic literature, they also formed the cultural heritage of the Dai/Tai language with common characteristics. This connection still plays a vital role in exchanging cultures, and in promoting the foreign affairs between China and Thailand（Xie 2016: 112）.

Theravada Buddhism in Xishuangbanna was mainly spread from Lanna via Kengtung（Chiang Tung）. When it was introduced into Xishuangbanna, it was generally referred as Yong Buddhism.Yong Buddhism was one of the earliest, fastest growing and most widespread schools of Theravada Buddhism in China. Currently it has the largest number of monasteries, monks and lay Buddhists in China. It is also more influential than other schools（Zheng, Liang 2014）.The main classic script used in Yong Buddhism is Tai Tham.Tai Tham originally consisted of 41 letters with 8 vowels and 33 consonants. It has the same pronunciation and order with Pali letters. Subsequently some letters had been added according to the characteristics of the Dai Lue language on the basis of the Pali letters, Tai Tham became a script that can be used in both Buddhism and the secular domains at present.

贝叶文化与区域文化遗产传承保护

Table 1　Pali Consonants of Tai Tham in Various Regions

罗马马利 Roman Pali	兰那/泰北经典文字 Tai Tham-lanna	傣泐经典文字 Tai Tham-Tai Lue	傣痕经典文字 Tai Tham-Tai Khun	老挝/伊普经典文字 Tai Tham-Lao-Isan	罗马马利 Roman Pali	兰那/泰北经典文字 Tai Tham-lanna	傣泐经典文字 Tai Tham-Tai Lue	傣痕经典文字 Tai Tham-Tai Khun	老挝/伊普经典文字 Tai Tham-Lao-Isan
k					th				
kh					d				
g					n				
gh					p				
ṅ					ph				
c					b				
ch					bh				
j					m				
jh					y				
ñ					r				
ṭ					l				
ṭh					v				
ḍ					s				
ḍh					h				
ṇ					ḷ				
t					ṁ				

Since Theravada Buddhism was introduced into the Dai Lue region, the Dai Lue integrated their aboriginal beliefs into the Buddhist cultural system. The import of Theravada Buddhism not only brought classic written words to the Dai Lue people, but also preserved and spread Buddhist cannons. One of the important example is that the Pali Tipitaka as well as scriptures has been inherited through generations in monasteries in Xishuangbanna. It is precisely because of this script, Theravada Buddhism was accumulated into a magnitude Dai Lue culture, and became an indispensable constituent of Chinese culture. At present, besides the documentation of the Pali Buddhist scriptures in the written system such as Sri Lanka's Sinhalese, Burmese, Mon, Cambodian Khmer, Thai, Laos, International Phonetic Alphabet and Roman alphabet, the Tai Tham is the only existing Chinese ethnic script system recording the Pali Buddhist tradition in China (see Table 1). It is circulated across multiple borders of China and the neighboring countries and has become the most significant carrier of Theravada tradition in these regions.

2. Names and Distribution of Tai Tham

Nowadays, there are five types of Dai or Tai scripts in China, such as Bean/Long script of Dai Nue, Round script of Dai Peng, Dai Duan script of White Dai in Jinping, Honghe, and Dai Lue script. Dai Lue can be divided into the new and the old scripts, of which the old script is Tai Tham. Each Dai script has its own characteristics and value.

They have played important roles in the development of the long history of the Dai ethnic group. The Dai scripts was gradually created as one font in the modern printing system. After the establishment of People's Republic of China, a new Dai Lue script based on the old Dai Lue script in Xishuangbanna was invented to facilitate the learning and printing of the language. Although the old Dai Lue (Tai Tham) was once gave way to the new Dai Lue in Xishuangbanna, it had been continued to be used in Menglian, Lancang, Jinggu, Gengma and Jinping, etc.

Since the early 1980s when religious policy was restored in China, the limitation of the new Dai Lue script in representing the Pali scriptures became acute when the Dai people regained their Buddhist beliefs. The insufficiency of the new Dai Lue script increasingly apparent in the process of the rebuilding of Buddhist temples and the rewriting of the Buddhist scriptures, so on and so forth. Finally, when Fifth Assembly of the Sixth National People's Congress in Xishuangbanna was held in May 1986, a resolution to restore the use of the old Dai Lue (Tai Tham) was discussed. Since then, both the new and the old scripts were legally adopted as official ethnic scripts of Xishuangbanna. Once the resolution was adopted, Theravada Buddhism in Xishuangbanna fully restored the use of Tai Tham as the voluminous historical documents. The traditional Tai Tham scrip is the treasure-house of the history of the Dai ethnic group. It recorded the social development and vicissitudes of the Dai Lue. In particular, the classical Buddhist scriptures written in Tai Tham has special value, because it is the most comprehensive and systematic Buddhist canons of the Pali tradition in China (Zhang 2002: 72-73).

The Tai Tham in China is used primarily by many ethnic groups in Yunnan, such as the Dai, the Blang and the Deang. Some Va people, Achang people and few Yi people who believe in Theravada Buddhism also utilize the script. Although it is also used in northern and northeastern Thailand, northern Laos and Shan State in Myanmar, the naming of Tai Tham is different across different countries and regions. Tai Tham is referred as Ark Son Lanna and Tuo Tham Lanna in northern Thailand, Tuo Tham Isan in northeastern region of Thailand, Tuo Tham Lao or Tuo Tham Lan Chang in Laos, Tuo Tai Khun or Tuo Tham Khun in Kengtung, and other parts of Shan State of Myanmar such as Thakhilek, Muangyong and Muangyangluang in the surrounding areas of Kengtung. It is referred as Tuo Tham in the 4th Special Region in the Eastern Shan State of Myanmar. Currently, the script remains as the main classic language of Buddhism used by the local Shan/Tai and other ethnic groups. In addition, Tai Tham is still used by the Dai Lue immigrants who moved to the United States. Approximately 1,200 Dai Lue people originally from Xishuangbanna of China and Laos are currently living in Denver, Colorado of the United States. Most Dai Lue are concentrated in this area in the United States. To revive their traditional culture and reconstruct their specific Dai Lue identity, the Dai Lue living in the United States till practice Theravada Buddhism and built Buddhist temples in their own communities (Zheng 2019). The Buddhist scriptures are still largely written in Tai Tham. The script used in various countries and regions varies very little and could be communicated across borders without difficulties.

According to the author's observation and his analysis of actual situations, the onomatology of the script as Tai Tham is explained by the following reasons:

First, the early development of the script aimed to record and disseminate the Pali teachings. Tham is the major language used by Theravada Buddhism in China and other countries. Second, Tham is a common word used in various countries and regions. It is originated from the Pali language "Dhamma", which means Buddhist sutras. This word explicitly indicates that Buddhist believers are the main groups who were using this script. When the Buddhist followers named it as Tai Tham it also carries their wish of inherited Dhamma. Third, The Tai people is the only and largest ethnic group who invented and are still utilizing the script. Therefore, to name the script as Tai Tham is more appropriate. Fourth, Tai Tham (经典傣文) was used by Liu Yan in his book *Theravada Buddhism and Dai Culture* as early as in 1993[①]. This word is used in the book of *Xishuangbanna Buddhism* compiled by Dai Lue Studies Association of Xishuangbanna as well. These usages of Tai Tham in the introduction of Tai script studies suggest that Tai scholars acknowledged and promoted the usage of Tai Tham[②]. Fifth, international academics and experts agreed to use Tai Tham as an international unicode. For example, an international conference on Tai Tham (old Tai script) was held on January 21–22, 2008 at Payap University. Academics and experts from China, Myanmar, the United Kingdom, the United States and Thailand were invited to participate in the meeting. The situation of Xishuangbanna was represented by the Institute of Ethnic Research and the Official News Agency of Xishuangbanna. They used the Tai Tham as a common expression to discuss the longstanding issues of the Unicode of Tai Tham. The Tai here refers to the various branches of the Tai or Dai ethnic group. Tham refers to the Buddhist scriptures and teachings of Buddhism. Tai Tham therefore can be translated directly as the classic Tai script.

3. Conclusion

To sum up, the Tai Tham script spread with Theravada Buddhism. First of all, it gradually developed from a script in the religious field to an ethnic script commonly used in secular society. When it spread to various places and was used by different ethnic groups,

---

① Liu Yan. Theravada Buddhism and Dai Culture. Kunming: Yunnan Ethnic Publishing House, 2019: 166–168.
② Dai Lue Studies Association of Xishuangbanna. Xishuangbanna Buddhism. Kunming: Yunnan Ethnic Publishing House, 2012: 148–150.

it was localized. Therefore, the names of the script associated with the name of the region or the ethnic group. In addition, the message conveyed by the differences of the alphabet style of each ethnic group is a regional and ethnic cultural symbol. This symbol responds to the historical relationship between ethnic groups. From another perspective, it can also be found that Tai Tham enabled the social development of the script and cultural differentiation process of various Dai/Tai ethnic group. However, in the names of the characters, each ethnic group is based on the history and culture of Theravada Buddhism. Conversely, the different alphabet styles of Dai/Tai people summarize the cultural circle of Tai Tham. The script helped maintaining the common cultural memory and structing the cultural communities among the ethnic groups.

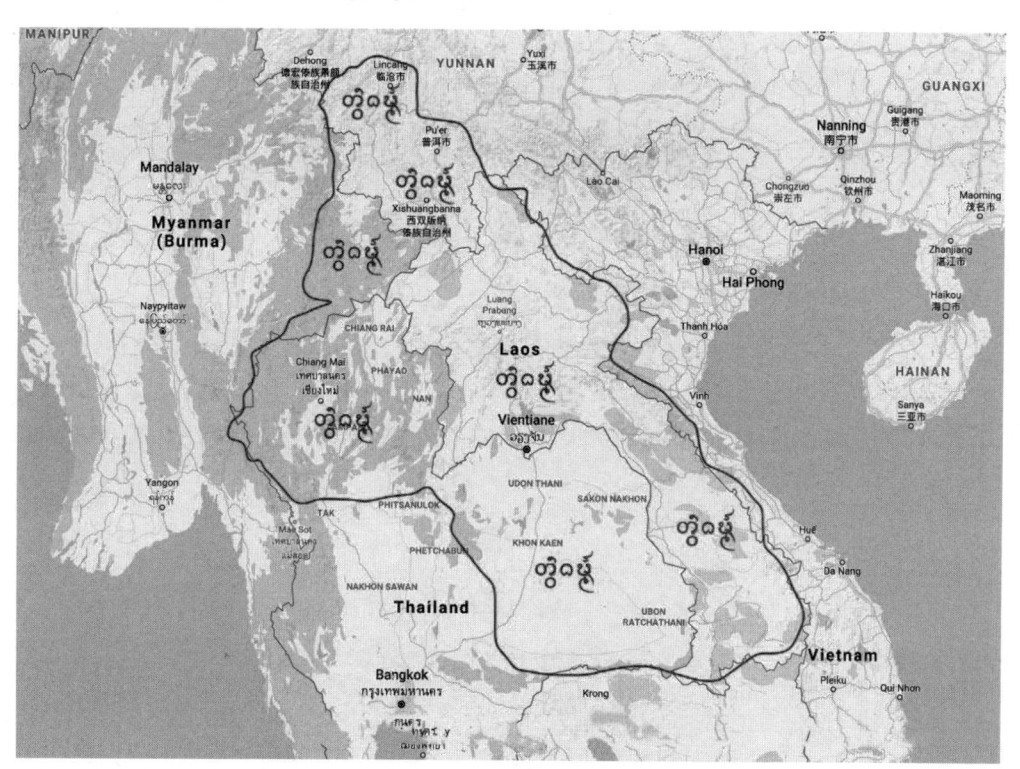

Figure 1　Distribution of Tai Tham（Taken by Ai Kham Pao）

Tai Tham script is a product of ethnic culture in the process of historical development. It inherits the historical memory of the Tai/Dai ethnic group and social development. It also plays a significant role in the process of cultural transmission. The palm-leaf culture carrying Tai Tham is invaluable in inheriting religion, culture, education, ecology and economy, etc. Furthermore, Tai Tham is a cross-border script among many cross-border ethnic groups. It is valuable not only in the study of the history of Theravada Buddhist and Dai culture, but also in the study of the historical and cultural relations among various ethnic groups in China and beyond. The research on the protection and inheritance of Tai Tham can help maintaining the plurality of the traditional culture of China on the one hand, and enriching the color and charisma of Chinese culture on the other hand. Therefore. It is of great significance to inherit the Buddhist classics and consolidate the development of Theravada Buddhism in China. Theravada Buddhism in Yunnan Province of China shares natural nexus with Southeast Asian Buddhist countries. It plays a positive role in promoting cultural exchanges and interactions between China and Southeast Asia. With similar ethnic ancestor, common religion, shared cultural memory, the maintenance and the flow of the Tai Tham scripts can not only strengthen the mutual friendship, but also promote cooperation and sustainable development in many aspects between China and Southeast Asia.

Figure 2　The Side Gate of Chiang Mai University, Thailand〔Three scripts on that, Thai (above), Tai Tham/Lanna (middle), and English (below) (Taken by Yankan Zhangla)〕

Figure 3　The Main Gate of Yunnan Buddhist College, Kunming, Yunnan Province, China［Three scripts on that, Tibetan（left）, Chinese（middle）, and Tai Tham（right）（Taken by Yankan Zhangla）］

References

［1］Liu Yan. Theravada Buddhism and Dai Culture, Kunming: Yunnan Ethnic Publishing House, 1993.

［2］Zhang Gongjin. Religion and Culture of the Dai. Beijing: China Minzu University Press, 2002.

［3］Xie Yuanzhang. Selected Works of Xie Yuanzhang. Kunming: Yunnan University Press, Yunnan People's Publishing House, 2016.

［4］Zheng Xiaoyun, Liang Xiaofen. Analysis of the Historical Context of the Development of Theravada in China. World Religion Studies, 2014（3）.

［5］He Ping. "Babai Xifu" — "Lanna Kingdom" and the Politics, Society and Culture of Its Main Ethnic Group. Thingking, 2013（1）.

［6］Zheng Xiaoyun.The Investigation and Research on Current Situation of the Dai Lue in Denver County and City, USA. World Nation, 2019（3）.

［7］Venerable Maxinde（Mahinda）.Do you know Buddhism? Kunming: Printed by the Buddhist Association of Yunnan Province, 2009.

［8］Dai Lue Studies Association of Xishuangbanna.Xishuangbanna Buddhism. Kunming: Yunnan Ethnic Publishing House, 2012.

The DREAMSEA Project, an Overview: Critical Work in the Preservation of Endangered Southeast Asian Manuscript Cultures

Zhou Hanli[1]

1. Project Overview

With an area of 4,500,000 square kilometers and a population of 637 million (2016 statistics)[2], Southeast Asia is one of the most culturally diverse regions in the world. Innumerable groups with distinct cultural backgrounds and customs have flourished in Southeast Asia for millennia. Over time, this variegated cultural heritage has created a wide diversity of histories and civilizations. Language and writing are indispensable for the inheritance and dissemination of civilization. Therefore, as the main tool for this transmission of cultural knowledge, the written word has long been recorded on different forms of carefully prepared organic matter for the benefit of future generations.

In short, a manuscript is a handwritten text on a physical medium. The manuscript production was a critical mode for the preservation and spread of cultural ideas before the proliferation of typography. In the modern times, manuscripts are critical source material for contemporary scholars to study past civilizations and their influence on the present societies.

In fact, in both insular areas and mainland of Southeast Asia, many ethnic groups still maintain traditional cultural records. In addition to the preservation of past manuscripts, older local scholars continue to record and copy new manuscripts. Therefore, manuscript culture is far from being "dead". The importance of the research and protection of manuscript cultures has both academic and practical significance. However, in the course of historical development, many people are no longer interested in manuscripts, and this traditional mode of cultural transmission has been gradually abandoned. The locals,

---

[1] PhD candidate, University of Hamburg, Germany.
[2] Report for Selected Countries and Subjects. World Economic. IM. Outlook Database, 2016.

especially young people, believe that nowaday, words written on paper, shellfish, tree bark, parchment, bamboo, metal, etc. are "outdated". The existence of this view has led to many manuscripts being ignored, discarded, burned or thrown away. In addition, due to the lack of knowledge of manuscript preservation and the fact that most of the manuscripts have not been included in ongoing research, the damage and disappearance of manuscripts also means the disappearance of the heterogeneous identities of Southeast Asian ethnic groups.

According to the current research situation, the total number of manuscripts in folk collections may exceed that of institutions. Unfortunately, many private collections have their own storage methods and their texts are unknown. Many of these collections have never been shown to the public. In addition, private collections tend to vary in their storage techniques, thus potentially jeopardizing the lifespan of the perishable material on which the manuscript has been written. Due to the hot and humid tropical climate of Southeast Asia, it is difficult to ensure that manuscripts are not damaged in self-storage scenarios. Furthermore, since most manuscripts are written using obscure scripts, the number of professionals who understand and can accurately copy these lesser-known writing systems is dwindling. Once the collector (or author) dies, it is up to the inheriting family to deal with the manuscripts, thereby presenting an uncertain fate for a potentially important cultural archive. In addition, unstable social conditions and political conflicts in Southeast Asia can also lead to the destruction of folk collections of manuscripts, further exacerbating the already precarious state of manuscript culture.

In order to protect the cultural diversity of Southeast Asia, it is an urgent task to preserve as many extant manuscripts as possible. In 2017, The Lisbet Rausing and Peter Baldw in Charity Fund (so-called ARCADIA) funded The Digital Repository of Endangered and Affected Manuscripts in Southeast Asia (DREAMSEA for short). The project is planned to be completed within five years, that is, to complete the digital storage of 240,000 frames by 2022.

2. The Purpose and Scope of the Project Implementation and Reasons for Digital Storage

A critical motivating factor for the project implementation is the vast cultural diversity of Southeast Asia. The DREAMSEA project is committed to protect the manuscript cultures of Southeast Asia and ensure the survival and development of these multicultural traditions. As long as they are from Southeast Asia, manuscripts (regardless of the writing material) in the fields of natural sciences, literature, history, and religion are all targets for preservation. After the digital storage is completed, the relevant data will be uploaded to the network database for academic research by scholars from different fields.

The scope of cooperation currently signed by the project includes these countries: Indonesia, Thailand, Laos, and Vietnam. The Indonesian study is mainly concentrated in Bali and Java. It is worth mentioning that the DREAMSEA project members found the original manuscripts on the island of Java about 100 years old and copied them within 10 years of their discovery. The Pali manuscripts, mainly concerning local folktales and myths, were written in linear text on sections of bamboo. It shows that the Pali language has spread here since pre-modern times, which may be related to the wide spread of Buddhism on Java Island.

In addition, Thailand, Laos, and Vietnam were selected as the survey sites on the Southeast Asian mainland. Thailand's investigation sites are concentrated in the northern region, including Nanfu, Lamphun and Chiang Mai. The Laos investigation site is mainly concentrated in the central part, namely: Luang Prabang Province. Recently, the digitization of Lao manuscripts has been completed, mainly in the field of Buddhist classics. The Vietnamese survey will be mainly concentrated in the northern and southern Cham districts. As to the manuscripts selected for digitization, because the academic experts mainly focus on several scripts such as Tham, Thai, Lao and Bali etc. the collections will focus on these manuscripts. Most of the manuscripts selected in Thailand and Laos are written in the Tham (also known as Lanna) script. In northern Vietnam, texts written in ancient Chinese were selected; while in the south, texts written in the Cham script were selected.

Although many projects have previously collected and digitally stored manuscripts from Southeast Asian countries, this is the first time that such a large-scale preservation effort has been carried out. Endangered and influential manuscripts need to be stored digitally in order to keep and copy the manuscript permanently. Due to the perishable nature of the organic matter on which the manuscripts are typically written, especially cotton paper and etamine, efforts towards the preservation of these manuscripts is a race against time. Finally, digital storage guarantees the integrity and continuity of the manuscript, and acts as a tribute to the collector (or the author).

3. The Project Operation Mode

In order to successfully complete the project goals, DREAMSEA has a solid framework for project operation. The project is headquartered at the National Islamic University in Jakarta. It consists of a general manager, secretaries (responsible for liaison meetings and financial expenses), photographers and IT technicians. And it is mainly responsible for project coordination, capital control and network maintenance. Dr. Jan van der Putten, an Indonesia research expert at the University of Hamburg, is the academic director of the island manuscript culture and the global planner of the project. Dr. Volker Grabowsky, a senior researcher on Tai cultures and languages, is the academic guide for the manuscript culture studies of the mainland countries. He is mainly responsible for digitizing the manuscripts of Laos and Thailand, and comprehensively planning and guiding the manuscript preservation work of the mainland countries.

The project team in each region is mainly composed of five people, namely: an academic expert, an academic expert assistant, a photographer, a photographic assistant and a local guide. The Academic expert and his/her assistant are required to be proficient in English, be able to communicate well with project leaders and liaisons and to have sufficient technical knowledge of photography and photographic technology. The photographer and his/her assistant need to be proficient in the operation of photographic equipment, be able to quickly and accurately take high-quality pictures that meet the requirements of the project team, and be proficient in computer operations, uploading the digitized files to a network database. Therefore, in order to avoid the duplication of work, every recorded manuscript must meet the requirements of the project team. The local guide is the key person in the actual operation of the project. The ability to obtain reliable information and efficiently build a bridge to communicate directly with local scholars and collectors is critical for a guide who is familiar with the local culture and social protocols.

The project team provides the regional teams with professional digital equipment. In order to restore the true appearance of each image, the project team has established standardized parameters of resolution and size to apply to each frame. The equipment used by the project team is currently the most advanced photographic equipment available, so the proper use of it requires some training. On May 17-18, 2019, at the DREAMSEA seminar in Nan Province, Northern Thailand, the technical staff at the headquarters conducted professional training on the operation of the photographic equipment for the participating scholars. Since the manuscript digitization projects of the insular regions and Laos have been completed, the next phase will take place in Thailand's Nan province. Therefore, the equipment is currently in Nan province, and will be subsequently relocated to Lamphun and Chiang Mai, once the project in each respective locality is completed.

There is flexible in the selection of local guides. First of all, you need to be familiar with the local cultural situation or the local collectors, scholars or manuscripts texts. In addition to room and board, materials, and transportation, the project members also have labor subsidies. Project subsidies are calculated on a daily basis and based on the standard of five people per group per day. However, due to the nuances of the situation at hand, there is occasionally the necessity to hire more than one guide. Therefore, it is the responsibility of the overseeing experts to ensure that all project participants are compensated fairly according to their contribution.

The time allocated to each target point for the completion of the project is half a year, and the time needed to focus on shooting is about one month. If the number of manuscripts to be digitized is higher or lower than previously anticipated, the time frame can be adjusted. The working process is roughly as follows: first, the local manuscript distribution is investigated; second, academic experts convene members to meet, coordinate members' working hours, and formulate field plans; third, group members enter the field according to actual conditions and guidance.

4. The Operation

The work-flow of the DREAMSEA project is as follows: survey of manuscript distribution, screening of manuscripts, digitization of manuscripts, description of digital manuscripts, and subsequent technical processing and uploading to the database. Almost every team will follow this process.

First of all, due to limited project budgets and limited time, scholars should understand that it is impossible to digitize all collected manuscripts. We can only prioritize manuscripts that are deemed to be of particular importance. What does constitute an "important" manuscript? The selection criteria for determining relative importance are as follows:

Is the manuscript endangered? The manuscript has not been digitized by the government or other institutions, continued preservation of the manuscript is not optimistic, and the future fate of the manuscript is uncertain.

The manuscript has a certain academic research value, or it represents local traditions, culture or history.

Of course, if there are not many local manuscripts, or time is abundant, the above two points can be adjusted according to actual conditions. In addition, every digital manuscript should be marked with the note: "This manuscript has been digitally saved by the DREAMSEA project", so as to avoid later people from doing duplicate work.

The digitization of the manuscript is the primary responsibility of the photographer. This aspect of the project mainly involves the operation of hardware. When the photography equipment is obtained, detailed instructions will be attached. In the process of digitization, academic experts can assist from the side. The guide or the collector can be consulted if issues such as page numbers or content are encountered.

The digital manuscript is mainly described in English in the database. These descriptions are very important, as they determine the collection value of the manuscript for later scholars who seek to study these collections. Therefore, the DREAMSEA project team has made very standardized rules for this, as shown in Table 1 and Table 2.

Table 1　Information about the Collection

Country	
City	
Name of Collection	
Number of Manuscript	
Custodial History	

Table 2　Manuscript Metadata

1	DREAMSEA Project Number	
2	Shelf Mark	
3	Sponsor	
4	Right to Left	
5	Catalog Reference	
6	Title	
	a. Native Script	
	b. Roman Script	
	c. In English	
7	Subject Matter	
8	Author	
9	Copyist	
10	Type Date in Origin	
11	Authorship Date in Native Script	Year:　Month:　Date:
12	Authorship Date in Gregorian	Year:　Month:　Date:
13	Copying Date in Native Script	Year:　Month:　Date:
14	Copying Date in Gregorian	Year:　Month:　Date:
15	Begin Year Date	
16	End Year Date	
17	Place of Authorship	
18	Place of Copying	
19	Language	
20	Script	
21	Writing Support	
22	Manuscript Paper Dimension	Height:　Width:　(in cm)
23	Watermark	

If there is no relevant information in the manuscript, the content in the form does not need to be filled. After the digitization of the collection of manuscripts is completed, the post-technical processing, i.e. archiving the files is necessary. This part of the work is very critical, and it is easy to make mistakes. According to the requirements of the project team, a folder must be created every day, and every completed digital work of the manuscript must be put into the subfolder of that day. The manuscript metadata must then be attached to the related file. After checking, it is uploaded to the project's network database. Therefore, once the digitization of a manuscript is completed, the permanent preservation of the manuscript is achieved. As a continued effort, the project will collect manuscript samples and introductions after the 2022 completion date and will publish further important academic research texts.

5. Conclusion

The DREAMSEA project has been underway for almost two years. At present, the manuscript digitization of insular Southeast Asia has been successfully completed, and the digitization of manuscripts in Laos has just ended. The resultant database of digitized manuscripts from these two cultural domains has a strong reference value and can be used as a guide for further manuscript preservation work in other regions. By understanding the overview of the DREAMSEA project, the reasons for its establishment, the objectives of the project, the scope of implementation, the operating mechanism and the actual operation, the benefits of such an undertaking should be self-evident. Furthermore, the follow-up manuscript preservation work of the DREAMSEA project will provide an instructive model for future protection and digitization efforts of manuscripts from endangered ethnic groups in Yunnan, China.

Buddhism and Sexology Literature: The Observances from Thai Palm Scripts[①]

Aphilak Kasempholkoon[②]

1. Introduction

According to Buddhism, sensuality seems a cause of suffering that wise men should be abandoned; like a verse mentioned in *Nibbedhika Sutra* that "sensual passion originated by male's imagination is counted as lust (so-called '*kama*' in Pali), which is a kind of worldly complicated emotion, so wise men should eliminate such feeling".

The idea that sexual desires particularly appear in male's mind accords with a Buddhist teaching about female's tribulations, such as the following statement from a Buddhist canon:

"Listen to me, all disciples! There are five things that bring about women's sufferings with which no men have to face: ① they, in the age of puberty, have to leave their family to their husbands' houses, whereas men have not to; ② they have menstrual period, whereas men have not; ③ they have to get pregnant, whereas men have not; ④ they have to bear children, whereas men have not; ⑤ they have to sensually please men, whereas men have not."

In *Agganna Sutra* or Buddhist Cosmology said that when the cosmic system had not completely formed after the great chaos, the "neutral beings" called *Abhassara Brahmas*[③] with bright star-like radiant bodies came down to earth, where was in the timeless darkness of the aqua-galaxy with no sun, moon or any zodiacal stars. Later the delicious edible matter, which seemed like buttermilk, called *nguan-din* occurred. As soon as partaking

---

① This article is a partial fulfillment of the research entitled "Thai Sexology Literature in Central Thailand: Thai Sexual Instructional Books" belonging to the research serial project entitled "Thai Sexology Literature in Central Thailand: Knowledge from the Unknown" funded by Thailand Research Fund in fiscal year 2016 under the supervision of Professor Sukanya Sujachaya. At the beginning, I would like to thank Professor Sukanya Sujachaya: the supervisor of the research serial project, Mr.Bunteuan Srivaraphot, Professor Dr. Somphon Phongthai, Professor Dr. Samoechai Phunsuwan and Miss Niphatphon Phengkaeo, for the expert advices, comments and beneficial sources to enlighten the study, as well as Mr. Damrongsak Bunsu, Mr. Prawit Sangmi and Mr.Atthaphong Bunsang for the manuscripts.

② Assistant Professor, Ph.D. Faculty of Liberal Arts, Mahidol University, Thailand.

③ The *Abhassara Brahmas* are the sixth-classed divine beings dwelling within eight great eras in approximate in the world of "Concrete-Self Brahma" for the consequence of their Pranita Dhyana Meditation.

that, the Brahmas lost their radiances as well as the sun, the moon and all stars took place.

Then the ex-divine beings automatically differentiated by ones' skin colors; ones with better skins discriminated others so that the *nguan-din* was replaced by edible mushroom-shaped matters called *Krabi-din*, coconut-shaped matters called *khrue-din* and the sudden-sprung rice as the result of discrimination. After consuming, gender identities, male and female, occurred. It has been said in the mythological canon that "with each sexual organ, men and women started interested in each other, then each couple aroused by lust copulated for the first time." Consequently, couples had to perform the intimate activities in private areas.

"Listen, Vasettha and Bharadvaja! At that pastime, if ones saw whoever copulate in the improper area, they threw dust, ashes or cow excrement to the couple and oppressively blamed those wicked persons to get misery. Such deed turned to be customarily behavior. Today in some places people still throw such dirty stuffs at the wicked prisoners but do not know the exact reason why they do that.

Vasettha and Bharadvaja, from the similar behavior I've just said about, if anyone committed the intercourse in the public space, they could not meet others' faces for a few months so that houses has been built in order to hide those private affairs."

The stories of sexual behavior are not only found in *Agganya Sutra*, but also in the other chapters of *Tipitaka*. For example, in the commentary parts of *Alambusa Jataka*, the story of a girl whose breasts were opened up to seduce a hermit, and *Nalinika Jataka* narrating about a princess disguising as a hermit to deceived another hermit that "her sexual organ" had been bite by a bear in order to allure him to have an affair with her.

All stories mentioned in the aforesaid expresses that from Buddhist aspects sex and sensuality are regarded important for mankind leading to the idea that monastic disciples are not permitted to have the intercourse, whereas lay persons should considerably control ones' desire.In ancient society men have been concerned as the ones who can be aroused, whereas women are the arousing objects and have to be "passive", as well.

After surveying ancient manuscripts in Thailand, some sexology literature has been found in monastery. Therefore, the relationship between sexology and Thai folk Buddhism sounds very interesting.

2. Thai Sexology Literature

In spite of the importance for sustaining our species, sex and sensuality were strictly concealed in traditional societies, so the books of sexology are secretly hided in restricted social spaces. Especially in Thai society, this obscene topic is smoothly hidden in rituals, traditions and both royal and folk arts. Considerably, comparing with "Karma Sutra" of the Indian and "the bedside books" of the Chinese, the Thai, who have absorbed both civilizations for a very long time, tend to have own books of carnal instruction.

There are a great deal of carnal knowledge, which were secretly kept as the Thai's obscene subjects, found from these field works. Concerning from the orthography and style, it can be assumed that the books are not older than the reign of King Rama Ⅳ. Some of them are stored in monastic areas, and some belong to private collections. The analytical document has been gathered from eight books written on Thai scrolls, palm scripts and paper notebooks, which are as follows.

(1) *Secular Nirvana* (a palm script from Trat province)

(2) *The Book of Male's Sexual Disability Treatment* (a paper notebook with national emblem)

(3) *The Book of Male's Sexual Disability and Sexology* (a paper notebook)

(4) *Kamin the Hermit's Book of Physiognomy* (Mr. Prawit Saengmi's palm script)

(5) *The Book of Sexual Amusement* (a manuscript lasted from Thonburi period)

(6) *The Book of Proper Periods for Intimate Affairs* (a manuscript lasted from Chachuengsao province)

(7) *The Book of Thai Folk Martial Art* (Mr. Prawit Saengmi's palm script)

(8) *The Book of the Appearances of Female Sexual Organ* (a paper notebook from Angthong province)

All in the aforesaid can be regarded as interesting (but obscene) information. This article, studying from the eight secret manuscripts, will be revealed the Thai's intangible knowledge towards sexology, especially to academically define, describe and examine the literal device together with the relation between sexology and other sciences since the kind of works is considered as Thai Textbook Literature.

There are some examples of Central Thai Sexology Literature as follows.

Kamin the Hermit's Book of Physiognomy: a man inhabited in Chachoengsao Province owns this 35-sheet Thai-ancient-letter palm script. The first part mentions the auspicious and inauspicious appearances of males and females (The first two page have been outworn, though). The second part, using digit symbol coding, alphabetical coding, religious coding and maps of female sexual anatomy, mentions female appearances and sexual preferences. The third part narrates the background story of the book: *Kama Deva* (God of Love) came to *Karmin the Hermit* to learn how to have most satisfying sensual activities with each kind of woman. The fourth part consists of calculating foretell for women's sexual preferences. The last part consists of how to calculate a woman's ascendant to foretell her sexual preferences.

Figure 1 Kamin the Hermit's Book of Physiognomy

This manuscript, which has been composed during King Rama Ⅲ to King Rama Ⅳ's period, can be counted as one of the most descriptive sexology books found in Thailand.

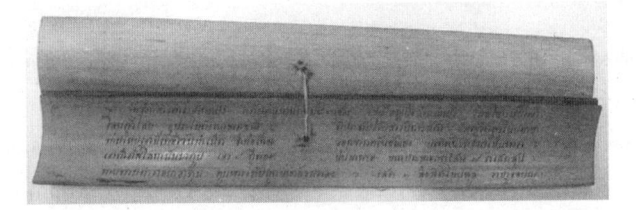

Figure 2 The Manuscript of *Secular Nirvana*

Secular Nirvana: a 28-sheet Thai-ancient-letter palm script belongs to Wat Phai Lom Temple in Trat Province. The first palm sheet is inscribed that "This is the complete version of *Secular Nirvana*", whereas the last sheet mentions about the contributor of this book "I, Mr. Rung the Actor, donate this duplicate manuscript of *Secular Nirvana* for men's sakes in the future." According to the quote, this palm script is rewritten from the previous completed version under the contribution of Mr. Rung the Actor. Without any traceable evidence of writing period, at least a stanza in its introductory part imparts that "As a lion seal for royal members". It can be predicted from the excerpt, which was a popular sentence during the reign of King Rama Ⅲ, that this book was written at that time.

At the beginning, *Secular Nirvana* describes in verse about how to "foretell" the appearance of each woman's sexual organ from her ascendant. Later, it is told in prose about "sensitive" parts of women's bodies, how to have affairs and the appearances of female organs.

The Book of Sexual Amusement: Assistant Professor Aphilak Kasempholkoon (the researcher) received a 37-sheet Thai scroll from a man inhabited in Thonburi District of Bangkok. After reading its white pencil-line booklet, the outworn document without the last sheet mentions "sexual postures" with Thai formularies for sexual problem remedy. Nevertheless, the last part of this book consists of mantras. One of the example is a sacred words to summon divine beings.

Figure 3 *The Book of Sexual Amusement*

3. "Secular" and "Sacred" Pleasure: Buddhism in Thai Sexology Literature

Interestingly, in the old days, most of Thai sexology books were not counted as "secular works" but the "religious ones" (at least they contains some aspects involving with Buddhism). It is possible that the writers once experienced the monkhood, while the expression as "Buddhist texts" signified perceptional ideas of people in those days. According to the study, some relations between Buddhism and Thai sexology have been revealed. Here are the main points.

3.1 The Use of Buddhist Terms

In *Secular Nirvana* the Buddhist term nirvana is found in the sentence "Either a man or a woman, whoever does like what was taught in this book, even in the next one hundred years, they will find the way of happiness like being in heavenly nirvana".

Despite the word "nirvana" literally means the supreme enlightenment or freedom from all sins (including sexual desire), it has been figuratively used here to compare with sensual happiness in general.

In *The Book of Thai Folk Martial Art* the words "*kama guna*" (desires) and "*panca khandha*" (five self-elements) are used, as well:

Desires, with five self-elements,

As the multiplicand of number five;

Before being distributed by nine

Form the fraction for all to find.

As for Buddhism, desires (*kama guna*) are concerned as "sources of pleasure and lust" composing of sight, sound, odor, savor and feeling, while five self-elements (*panca khandha*) means the composition of self: body, feeling, perception, thought and consciousness.

The use of the two term did not only show the author's Buddhist background knowledge but also his elaborate comprehension of "love and sex"; eroticism is composed of concrete and abstract features aroused by the five sensational sources mentioned in the aforesaid.

In *Kamin the Hermit's Book of Physiognomy*, a Pali word "*bindu*" is used in some paragraphs.

The word *bindu* here refers to sexual implantation, not its denotation meaning "a drop, a dot or a spot" like a drop of water, a dot under a letter or a spot decorated on ones' eyebrows (so-called *tilaka* in Sanskrit). It is used among Buddhist monks in order to define a dot, not smaller than a bedbug nor bigger than a peacock feather, painted in only indigo, brunette or obsidian colour on one end of a robe. The *bindu* is the remarkable blotch to remind all monks to wear the robe only for covering the bodies, not for beauty. If the mark is not made on one's robe before being worn, he will be accused of having an intermediate offence named *pācittîya*. This round-shaped blotch is marked just once on a robe; the repetition is not needed. While making a *bindu* blotch, the Pali mantra "*Imam bindukappam karomi*" should be recited. Comparing to the implantation that destroy women's virginity, the word *bindu* here figuratively refers to sexual intercourse.

3.2 The Use of (Pseudo) Buddhist Mantras

Interestingly, (pseudo) mantras have been added into some of the manuscripts. No matter how the hybrid Pali spells can be literally translated, the word "*kama*" (love, pleasure) is used to express the relevance to the local-Buddhist carnal matters. For the same result, the word "*svāha*", which is usually said as the incantatory word after casting the mantras, as well.

Here is an example from *Kamin the Hermit's Book of Physiognomy*:

A) *Om namo kāmadeba ya lākara svahā mapat*—From the dawn to the early morning, *kāma* (the most sensitive parts of women's bodies) are on the breasts. From the early morning to the midday, *kāma* are on the arms; hold your partner's. In the midday is on top of the head; press your palm at that point after touching her hair. In the afternoon is on the abdominal part; pinch it. In the dusk is on the chin; pinch it, as well. In the evening is in the navel; press there. In the midnight are on the palms, press her hands and all fingers. When the cocks start crowing is on the legs; squeeze the both. Before dawn is in the eyes; press hers.

B) Fantastically, here is the formulary for greatest fun. If you have the kind of passion, press the banana roots then wrings some water out for drinking and cleaning your face in order to increase your feeling. If a girl meets a man who know this medicine, she cannot leave him. Before making the recipe, recite this mantra three times

(*Ommakāmatikāma ommakāmatikāma māskavasiddhi āgatta chanchansvāha*).

Another example, the mantra for asking for good children, comes from *Secular Nirvana*, so Pali words connecting to father, mother and children are found: "Knowing which parts of the women's bodies become the most sensitive ones within a day, the proper touch satisfies your partner. Here is the mantra for two good children—Mātā pitu puttam danam."

3.3 The Reference of Buddhist Sacred Places and People

The Book of Male's Sexual Disability and Sexology mentioned "Takkashila" in the sentence "Would like to join the enjoyment in the school of Master Dishapamoksha, a headmaster of Takkashila." The city named Takkashila locates in Panjab State in the northwest of India. According to ancient Buddhist and Brahmin text, this place was famous for having various kinds of schools for almost all bodies of knowledge and seemed as important as the biggest university with several campuses or the old Indian educational centre. Many historical people graduated from schools here; for examples, King Pasendi (King of Kosala who was one of the main supporters of the Buddha during his lifetime), Jivaka Momārabhacca (the Buddha's personal physician), Angulimāla Thera (the serial killer known from collecting of the victims' thumbs who converted to be a Buddhist saint), etc.

Nevertheless, The (Royal) Recipe for Health-Deterioration Treatment elaborates on dvattimsākara (the 32 complements of human's bodies), so-called Mahā Purisa Lakshana (the specific appearances of the Buddha) by referring to Buddhist religious persons: if one has 30 complement, he will be one of the both principal disciples; whoever has only 10, he will become the Buddha's parent.

4. Connotation and Denotation Meanings in Thai Sexology Literature

According to the aforesaid, to inscribe some of the carnal knowledge as palm scripts, to keep the books of sexology in monasteries, to insert (pseudo) mantras and to use Buddhist terms like nirvana or *bindu* reflect the obvious influences of Buddhism towards Thai sexology literature, even though they mention sexual amusement.

4.1 Sacred-Making of Sexology Books

Apart from using some distinctive features of (local) Buddhism in order to elevate the books to credibly become "religious canons", the phenomenon reflects that the ancient Thai regarded "sexual activity" as an element of sacred procreation ritual for good descendants in required. The sexology literature, thus, goes further than its basic purpose as being "ritual literature".

4.2 Relation between "Sexual Pleasure" and "Religious Serenity"

Although sexual desire is regarded from the Buddhist aspect as suffering and becomes excessive for priests, almost all men temporally become ordained, and then come back to their secular lives. Because of the youth hormones, some monks break the law of sexual avoidance, so that there are many allegories in the *Tipitaka Canon* about men who could not resist their strong lust and deserved retribution.

After leaving monkhood, some learnt men who still needed sensual pleasure and their own good descendants composed Thai sexology literature with "Buddhist features" to show the relationship between "sacred" and "secular" ways, as if the great intimacy bringing the couples' pleasure is "the nirvana for laypersons". This idea reflects the Thai Buddhists' carnal knowledge: the figurative comparison between sexual fulfillment and religious nirvana; as in the folk song below:

Man, I've heard your metaphor,
Thai's similar the Buddha's;
Of sacredness-profanity,
To be balanced in our lives.
If all ignored the worldly world;
All of us would become insane;
Both aspects are necessary,
For love only leads to the flaws.

(Chareon Uppathamphanon; North People's Boat Songs Vol.2)

5. Concluding Remarks

On the one hand, considering from the Buddha's aspects, "sexual desire" is accepted as a common behavior for lay persons so that the supreme sensual pleasure (so-called kamachanda or secular nirvana) leads to both physical and mental anxiety as well as entices them from spiritual attempt of being enlightened (nirvana) so that the Buddha encouraged all disciples to avoid sensuality, especially did not allow any monastic disciples to involve with this secular activities. On the other hand, lay persons try their best way of having supreme pleasure, since they believe that it will bring happiness for couples and families in order to bear good offspring. Thus, secularity and sacredness are considered in the same level in real life.

References

[1] Chareon Uppathamphanon. North People's Boat Songs Vol.2. Bangkok:

Ratchareon, 1938.

[2] Niphatphon Phengkeao. Narratives towards Power. Bangkok: Sukkhaphapchai, 2012.

[3] Books of Secular Nirvana. Manuscript found in Phra Vimalamedhacarya's Library of Wat Phailom Temple, Trat Province, written in Pali-Thai on non-decorative palm scripts.

[4] Sukanya Phatthrachai. Retortion Songs: The Wisdom of Thai Folks. Bangkok: Text Book Project, Faculty of Arts, Chulalongkorn University, 1997.

[5] Sukanya Sujachaya. Revelation of Sexology Literature. Nakhon Phathom: Faculty of Liberal Arts, Mahidol University, 2018.

[6] Suphaphon Makchaeng. Kama Sutra: The Lesson for Laypersons. Ayupavara: The Commemoration to the 60th Anniversary of Assistant Professor Thanit Chakharatphong. Bangkok: Department of Eastern Languages, Faculty of Arts, Chulalongkorn University, 1994.

[7] Rit Rueangrit. Brahmajata the Complete Astrological Book and King Rama I's Book of Physiognomy. Bangkok: Liangchiang Chongcharoen.

[8] Aphilak Kasempholkoon. Secular Nirvana: Thai Sexology Book. Bangkok: Arts and Culture, 2012.

Kāraked: The Overlooked Siamese Dance-Drama Play Manuscripts

Sutheera Satayaphan[①]

1. Introduction

There are a number of manuscripts preserved at the Manuscript and Inscription Group, National Library of Thailand. Among those manuscripts, there is a collection belonging to a genre of performances called *Klòn Bot Lakhòn*, or dance-drama verses. Surveying the corpus of manuscripts reveals that there are four books of the dance-drama verses, listed in alphabetical order from the first letter of the Thai language (*kò kai* ก) to the last (*hò nok-hook* ฮ). *Kāraked* (การะเกด) is found in the first book.

Bot Lakhòn Nòk, titled *Kāraked*, is shown in the one of fourteen dance-drama story lists considered as dance-drama plays from the Ayutthaya Period[②]. There is no obvious evidence indicating the original date but it is believed that the story has been well-known since the late Ayutthaya period (Prince Damrong 1950).

This play was probably known among the people in the early period of Bangkok as well. However, there are only four extant manuscripts of *Kāraked* kept in the National Library at the present time, two of which contain different stories. Interestingly, although scholars in the field of Thai literature have attempted to investigate many of these pieces of literature, *Kāraked* has been overlooked. Therefore, this paper aims to study these four manuscripts thoroughly in order to present *Kāraked* as play manuscripts. The results reveal the texts, contents and components found in each manuscript, which will complete existing knowledge of manuscript cultures in Thailand.

2. *Lakhòn Nòk*: The Dance-Drama of Siamese People

There were no records of Siamese dance-drama until Simon de La Loubère (1969: 49), a French diplomat, arrived in Siam in 1687. He described a kind of Siamese

---

① PhD candidate, University of Hamburg, Germany.
② The Ayutthaya period covers 1350 to 1767. Nonetheless, the historical evidence of *lakhòn*, or dance-drama, was not discovered until the seventeenth century (Rutnin 1996).

performance in his description of the travel. In that work, the term *Lacone* was described as "a show or a poem intermix with epic and dramatic story. The stories are about histories in verse, serious, and sung by several actors. One of them sings the historian's part, and the rest those of personages which the history makes to speak; but they are all men that sing, and no women."

The description of the *Lacone* of La Loubère is closely related to a characteristic of *Lakhòn Nòk*, which is performed by men only. The pattern of the plays is a dramatic poem, called *Klon Bot Lakhòn*, which has a particular rhyme. The term *Lakhòn*, however, refers not only to a dance-drama, but also to all kinds of Siamese performances as well as contemporary TV dramas.

Lakhòn Nòk broadly means the dance-dramas performed outside the royal court, in contrast to *Lakhòn Nai*, which was performed inside the palace. Prince Damrong (1955: 7), the earliest Thai intellectual, noticed that the dance was comparable to *Lakhòn (nora) chatri* in Siam. After his survey of dance-drama, he found that the *Lakhòn chatri*, a well-known Southern performance, had presumably been adjusted from the *Lakhòn Nòk*, or folk dance-drama in Ayutthaya. Therefore, both *Lakhòn Nòk* and *Lakhòn (nora) chatri* have similar traditions. Prince Damrong also demonstrated that *Lakhòn chatri* was an original Ayutthayan *Lakhòn Nòk*.

3. *Lakhòn Nòk* in the Early Bangkok Period

After the fall of Ayutthaya Kingdom in 1767, most of the court dancers were captured and sent to Burma and settled there. Some dancers fled to other provinces. The plays performed in the Ayutthaya Kingdom were largely lost.

During the Thonburi period (1767–1782), the King of Thonburi attempted to reunify the country. For example, he established himself as a king and a founder of a new dynasty. Culturally, he made an attempt to restore traditional performances within the royal court, in particular *Khon* and *Lakhòn*, by continuing the traditions of Ayutthaya. For example, *Tamnan Lakhòn Inao* (Damrong 1955: 125), or the Legend of the Inao dance-drama, explains how the King of Thonburi re-established court performances by summoning female dancers from Nakhon Sridhammaraj and other provinces to Thonburi in 1969. He established the court dance-drama by having the former dancers become teachers and by following Ayutthaya traditions. For the plays of *Lakhòn*, there were some extant Ayutthaya court plays, some of which were incomplete. The King of Thonburi had also rewritten some parts such as the Thonburi version of *Ramakien*.

For *Bot Lakhòn Nòk*, Prince Damrong (1955: 129–130) pointed out that there was no record of the number of plays during that time. But 14 titles of plays were kept in the National Library, namely *Kāraked*, *Kāwi*, *Chaidat*, *Pikulthong*, *Pimsawan*, *Pinsurivong*, *Manohra*, *Mong-Pā*, *Maneepichai*, *Sangthong*, *Sangsinchai*, *Suwannasingha*, *Suwannahong* and *Sowat*. Moreover, there were five plays from undetermined periods titled *Kraithong*, *Kobut*, *Chaichet*, *Phrarot* and *Sinsurivong*. These five plays were believed to be written before the reign of King Rama Ⅱ (1809–1824).

In the reign of King Rama Ⅰ (1782–1809), the king had a policy of restoring the nation's culture, including performances. By doing so, he invited the royal members and intellectuals to write and revise particular pieces of literature. The king had supervised and written some parts of the works himself, as shown in his editions of *Ramakien*, *Unarut*, *Da-Lang* and *Inao*. Prince Damrong also pointed out that *Ramakien* and *Unarut* were completely supervised by the king whereas *Da-Lang* and *Inao* were edited from the incomplete versions.

As for dance-dramas, they were performed in the Ayutthaya tradition. The female-dance troupe still performed only in the royal court. For the outer dance-drama, a male troupe of *Nai Boonyang* appeared in the *Tamnan Lakhòn Inao* (1955: 137). *Nai Boonyang* was the master of outer dance-drama and also the head of a famous troupe. By performing *Lakhòn Nòk*, his troupe could afford to build a temple called "*Wat lakhòntham*", which means a temple built by a troupe.

Performances and works of literature had been advanced particularly in the reign of King Rama Ⅱ. Not only the royal court, but the outer dance-drama plays were also written by the king himself. It has been shown that a royal court female troupe performed the outer plays which were written by King Rama Ⅱ. The king had rewritten some parts of the plays, in particular the episodes suited for dancing. The outer dance-drama plays for the royal troupe had five titles, namely, *Sangthong*, *Chaichet*, *Maneepichai*, *Kraithong* and *Kawi*. Moreover, one play written by King Rama Ⅲ (1824–1851), while he was still Prince Chedsadabodin (1813–1824), was *Sangsinchai*. These plays were subsequently called the royal outer plays.

The royal court dance-drama declined during the reign of King Rama Ⅲ because of his disfavour. During that time, the royal court dance-drama plays were not performed. By contrast, private troupes sponsored by aristocrats and the outer troupes were still practiced and danced. Particularly among the nobility, the dance was practiced widely. Notwithstanding the splendour of the royal dance in the previous reign, the nobility dared not have their own troupes. The dance-drama troupes were forbidden to have possessions by the royal convention.

The fact is that King Rama Ⅲ did not prohibit dancing; he only disliked the royal dance-drama, as shown in the 1855 proclamation of King Mongkut (Chanvit, 2005: 77–

78), who announced that "King Rama Ⅲ disliked the royal court performance; he blamed others who danced. However, there were still private troupes of noblemen." In this case, Prince Damrong (1955: 157) explained that *Lakhòn* was a kind of theatrical entertainment from former times. In royal ceremonies, tradition dictated that *Lakhòn* must be performed although there were other kinds of amusements shown.

Contrarily, the outer dance-dramas were more popular among villagers and widely performed. There were many private troupes owned by villagers performing the outer dance-drama, for instance "*Lakhòn Cao Krab*", or the Cao Krap troupe.

The dance-drama reemerged in the reign of King Mongkut (1851–1868). According to a royal proclamation of 1855 (Chanvit 2005: 78), the king allowed people to establish a female troupe. For this reason, the outer dance-drama which had been exclusively performed by men could now be performed by women. Performing with actors and actresses made the performances more interesting and, moreover, troupes could gain considerable income and profits from the audiences. Among the people, the *lakhòn nòk* was very popular and private *lakhòn nòk* troupes were in high demand. Due to the rising income of private troupes, an official decree on the taxation of *lakhòn* was subsequently announced (Rutnin 1996: 100).

Even though *lakhòn* was allowed to be performed independently, it still followed traditional styles and texts derived from Ayutthaya. For the outer plays, some texts, however, were altered in the early Bangkok period as the plots had mostly centered around Ayutthaya. The stories of the plays could come from any tales except the royal plays such as *Ramakien*, *Inao* and *Unarut*, as well as the royal texts of King Rama Ⅱ.

4. *Kāraked*: A Concise Literary Background

The story of *Kāraked* is well-known among Northeastern Thai people. According to *The Encyclopaedia of Thai Cultures: Northeastern Volume 1* (2012: 191), *Kāraked*, or *Kālaked* in the Northeast, could be found in houses and monasteries. The manuscript was originally written on a palm leaf in *Tai nòi* script and kept at *Sawang-arom* monastery in Amphoe Mueng. It was later transcribed into modern scripts in 1976 and published by Sirichai Publishing, Ubon Ratchathani province. However, the manuscript of *Kāraked* was composed in the form of *Klòn-an* or *Klong-sarn* (กลอนอ่าน, โคลงสาร), which is a Northeastern prosody to be read among people.

In the manuscript, the author's name, Somdet Ku, not the scribe's, appears at the end of the text. Potchanee Pengplien (2012: 191) assumed that the author was a monk given the title *Somdet*, which indicates high-ranking monks. The author was a poet from Vientiane, Laos. Furthermore, the year 1738 also appears at the end of text. That year falls in the reign of King Siribunyasarn of Vientiane. It is also noted that before King Siribunyasarn ruled Vientiane, Souringa Vongsa had been the king (1633–1698), the reign in which Lan Xang experienced the apex of literature. Thus, the author may be a poet who lived in the reigns of King Souringa Vongsa and King Siribunyasarn (1760–1781).

Compared with Siam's history, the reign of King Siribunyasarn of Vientiane falls within the reigns of King Ekkathat of Ayutthaya and King Taksin of Thonburi (1768–1782). At that time, Ayutthaya was invaded by the Burmese and capitulated. Seven months later, Phraya Tak attempted to reunify the country by gathering people and armed forces. After he ascended the throne, he expanded his power by invading neighbouring cities. In 1779, Vientiane was invaded by Siamese forces. According to *A History of Laos* (1997), precious sacred items such as the Emerald Buddha image were brought to Bangkok. Simultaneously, hundreds of Lao families were forced to resettle in the north of Bangkok. It is possible that *Kāraked* was retold among these emigrants and later spread to Siamese people.

Although there is no historical record of how the *Kāraked* text was transmitted to central Thailand, Thai scholar Sujit Wongthes (1981) suggested that Laos possibly obtained *Kāraked* from Ayutthaya given the extant the *Bot Lakhòn Nòk* manuscripts. There is also an Ayutthaya nursery rhyme that contains *Kāraked* references. Furthermore, Tawat Punnotok (1980) added that due to the domination of Burma after 1571, the Lanna influence on the Northeast of Siam had declined. The Northeastern people began to receive cultural influences from Ayutthaya rather than Lanna, allowing the story of *Kāraked* to travel from the central to the northeast of Thailand. The origin of *Kāraked*, however, is still not concluded.

5. Synopsis of *Kāraked*

Kāraked is a well-known folktale, particularly in the Northeast of Thailand. The hero of the story is Thao Kāraked, the son of Thao Surivonggednuraj, ruler of Varanasi. When Kāraked had grown up, he went to a stable and there he saw a horse, Maneekab, which had a good appearance. After he rode the horse, it suddenly soared into the sky and took him to several cities. Eventually, he arrived at an ogres' town ruled by Thao Pheemon. The ruler had a beautiful daughter named Maleechan. One day, while Maleechan was wandering in the royal garden, Kāraked accidentally saw her. He hid himself from the servants and followed her into the castle. He stayed hidden until he was alone with Maleechan, and then he showed himself. Maleechan immediately fell in love with him. Then Kāraked slept with her and some servants informed the ogre king of their relationship. Thao Pheemon was so angry that he ordered soldiers to make and install a magical bow at the castle door to kill Kāraked. When Kāraked arrived at the castle, he and his horse were shot by the magical bow and were killed.

After their deaths, their bodies were floated on the river for several days. Thao Suban, or the Karuda, found them and brought them to a hermit's dwelling. The death of Kāraked caused Indra's seat to be hard and uncomfortable, and Indra immediately knew that Kāraked was in danger. He then came down to the dwelling and uttered a magical mantra and gave a glass bow to the hermit to give to Kāraked. After that, the hermit chanted the mantra, and Kāraked was revived and went back to Maleechan's castle. He stayed with her for several days by transforming himself into a garland on Maleechan's head.

Later, Kāraked fought with Thao Pheemon, Maleechan's father, and all the ogres were killed. A few moments later, Kāraked shot the magical glass bow to revive them. Thao Pheemon dreaded the power so he gave his city to Kāraked. However, Kāraked did not rule that city and went instead back to Varanasi with Maleechan.

On their way back to Varanasi, Kāraked and Maleechan conquered many brutal ogres. Finally, he was crowned king of Varanasi, and Kāraked ruled his city with righteousness.

6. The Characteristic of the Play Manuscript *Kāraked*

***Kāraked* volume 1**: Manuscript No. 30, literature section, the manuscripts and inscription group at the National Library of Thailand.

Title: *Bot Lakhòn Kāraked Lem 1*

Provenance: Sub Lieutenant Suk gave it to the library

The play was written on a greyish leporello manuscript by graphite. Considering the paratext, the librarian's label demonstrates that this manuscript was given by Sub Lieutenant Suk (นายร้อยตรีสุก) on March 25, Rattanakosin era 126, 1907.

This manuscript contains the play episode of "Thao Montha held the bow-lifting contest for matching a guy for his daughter until Nang Sai-yut meets Phra Kāraked". The text begins with the introduction of a city where the ruler, Thao Montha, had a beautiful daughter named Nang Sai-yut. Thao Montha sent messages to others cities to inform them that he would hold a bow-lifting contest. The man who was able to lift the royal bow would marry his daughter, Nang Sai-yut.

Indranin, or Indra, a guardian god residing in a glass-castle in heaven, knew of the contest and he brought the news to Kāraked by whispering it to him while he was sleeping. After Kāraked woke in the morning, he remembered his dream and he rushed to the hermit's dwelling. The hermit gave him a magical staff and glass shoes. The staff had a magical power which meant that anyone pointed to with the top of the staff would die whereas those pointed at with the bottom of the staff would be revived. Those who wore the shoes would be able to fly.

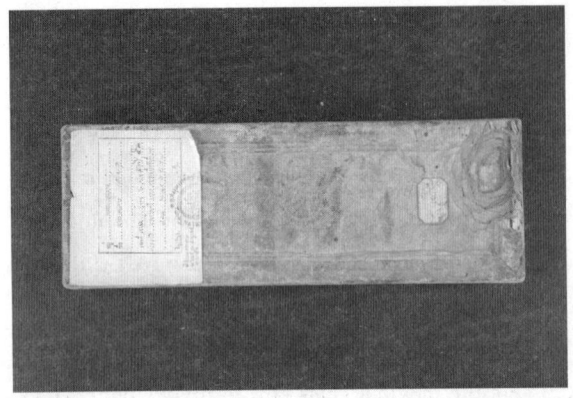

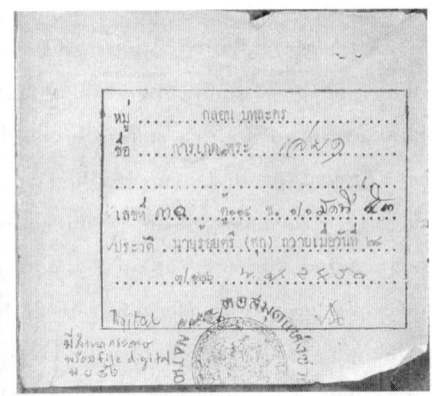

Figure 1 Manuscript No. 30, the Cover of the Manuscripts Mentioning the Former Owner

After Thao Montha had ordered his minister to send the messages, the news reached the kings of other countries, or *Kasat Roi-et*, which means a hundred kings, such as Phra Jampee of Krung Sri, Phra Jampa of Kabilphat, Phra Benchamas of Pha-ging, Phra Bancheun of Virat, Chao Malee of Chiang Mai and Daoreung of Phama (or Burma). All the kings were eager to attend the bow-lifting contest.

At the contest, all kings, including Kāraked, arrived together. Nobody could lift the bow except Kāraked. The hundred kings were jealous so they sent a challenge to Kāraked. Because of his talent and power, Kāraked bravely fought the other kings and won. The hundred kings yielded. Thao Montha realised that Kāraked was brave and suitable for his daughter and he prepared a date for the wedding ceremony. Kāraked went to Nang Sai-yut's room and stayed with her in secret.

There was an ogre city called Himavant, ruled by Pudtan, son of Thao Tantawan. One day he visited a forest. While he was standing on the top of a hill, he saw troops of the hundred kings. With doubt, Pudtan approached and spoke to the troops. The hundred kings told him about the contest for Nang Sai-yut. Happy with the news, Pudtan went back to his city and sent a message to Thao Montha asking for Nang Sai-yut's hand in marriage.

Thao Montha refused Pudtan's request, resulting in Pudtan preparing his troops to attack Thao Montha's city. When the news of Pudtan's troops spread, Kāraked volunteered to resolve the situation. He fought with Pudtan's troops and prevailed. Pudtan was killed.

Thao Tantawan, Pudtan's father, angry, asked his relatives and alliances to battle against Kāraked several times. At the end of the manuscript, Kāraked was kidnapped by an ogre named Prayong. Nang Sai-yut was distressed and went looking for him. The text of this manuscript ends here and neither the next chapter nor other manuscripts have been found.

Figure 2　Manuscript No. 30, Page 4, Presenting Different Handwriting on One Page

In this episode, the content of the play emphasizes the bow-lifting contest, the battle between Kāraked and the ogres, and the lamenting scene of Nang Sai-yut. In the *Lakhòn Nòk* tradition, emotional scenes such as battles and lamenting scenes were hugely popular.

Examining the plot, it is obvious that the motif of bow-lifting is similar to Ramakien's episode "Phra Rām Lifts the Bow". It may be concluded that the play might be influenced by some parts of Ramakien as the motif was well-known among the populace.

In terms of the physical condition, the manuscript is written in graphite in different handwriting, indicating that the manuscript was written or even copied by more than one scribe. Considering the scripts, they are somewhat untidy so the scribes may be common people. The characters and orthography are similar to the present scripts so this manuscript might not be so old.

According to the manuscript, there is only the librarian's label on the cover that contains the background of the manuscript. The text begins after the symbol "◎", which is called a *Fongman* (ฟองมัน) in Thai. The *Fongman* symbol appears at the beginning of each section whereas the symbol "ฯ" or *Paiyannoi* (ไปยาลน้อย) in Thai is used to indicate the end of each section. Moreover, there are accompanying songs inserted above the symbol *Paiyan* "◎".

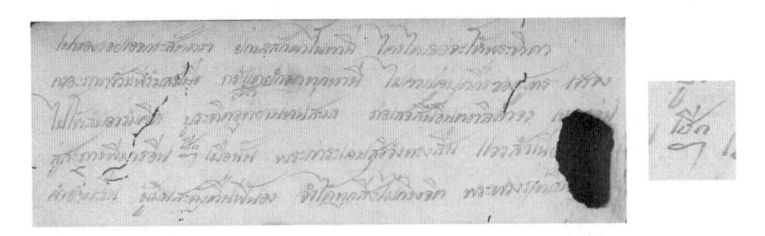

Figure 3 Manuscript No. 30, Page 5, Showing the Accompanying Song

The accompanying songs, in Thai called *Phleng Na Phat*, which literally means songs indicating the actions of the characters, are put above the symbol at the end of each part. The song indicates the action of the main characters, emotions or a sign of a change of setting. In this manuscript, there are songs that scarcely appear in others dance-drama manuscripts, such as *Hò-Hae* (ห้อแห่), which was inserted in the military mobilisation or the procession scene, and *Cao-Sen* (เจ้าเซ็น), which represents the character who was an Arabian King.

The songs inserted in each scene also hint at the period of the play. For instance, the song *Merican* (เมริกัน) is inserted in the scene of King Bancheun of London marching an army. The *Merican* song is assumed to be a song played with *Klong Marican* (กลองมริกัน), a bass drum brought to Bangkok by an American missionary. Thanit Yupho (1967: 48) explained that a troupe played the bass drum in the dance-drama, or Lakhòn titled *Phra Aphai Manee*, the episode of "Usaren and Nanglawengwanla Marched an Army", which was performed in the reign of King Chulalongkorn (1868–1910). For this reason, this *Kāraked* manuscript was probably written during that period.

Additionally, there is a note from the scribe indicating when to conduct a performance such as *Bok bot* (บอกบท), which means "to tell the lines". The paratext *Bok bot* was inserted during the scene in which the character Thao Jampee was reading the message from Thao Montha.

***Kāraked* volume 2**: Manuscript No. 31, literature section, the manuscripts and inscription group at the National Library of Thailand.

Title: *Kāraked Bot Lakhòn Lem 2*

Provenance: The original copy of the library

The play is written on a black leporello manuscript in white chalk. The scripts are orderly and have the same handwriting throughout the manuscript. The date and the scribe are unidentified. The former provenance is not recorded.

The text starts with a paratext demonstrating the title of the play which is "the first page of *Kāraked* first volume". Then, the play begins by introducing the hero, *Kāraked*, and his horse. He is riding his horse and travelling to a city garden. There, he saw a beautiful girl named Malithong among the servants and immediately fell in love with her.

At that time, a forest spirit saw the event. The spirit would like to pair Kāraked with Malithong so he hid Kāraked from the servants and brought him to Malithong's castle. At night, Kāraked revealed himself to Malithong. She was startled. Kāraked attempted to console and seduce her. Finally, she spent the night with him and became his wife. In the morning, Kāraked heard his horse calling him. He woke and told Malithong that he would come back in the evening.

He visited her in secret for several days until a servant noticed. The servant informed the ogre king, Malithong's father, Sri Phimon. The king was angry and ordered his minister to make and install a magical bow at the castle's door. At night, Kāraked went back to the castle unaware. He and his horse were shot by the magical bow and died. Malithong was shocked and fainted.

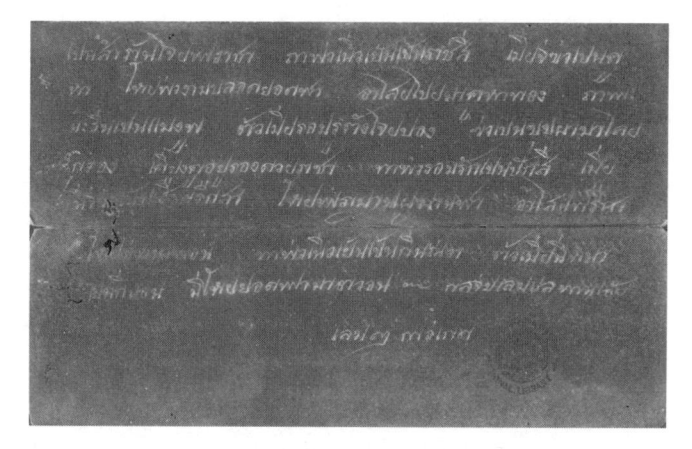

Figure 4　Manuscript No. 31, Showing a Scribal Paratext Indicating that the Manuscript Ends Here

The next morning when the ogre king learned of the death of Kāraked, he was extremely angry for he had nearly killed his daughter. He commanded the soldiers to leave the bodies of Kāraked and servants outside the city. In deep mourning, Malithong floated the bodies down the river.

The text of the manuscript ends with the lamenting scene. At the last folio, there is a scribal paratext indicating that "It is finished already, Volume Ⅱ *Kāraked*" (as seen in the circle below):

For the composition of the manuscript, it is found that there are two types of paratexts, namely, the librarian's paratext and the scribal paratext. The librarian's paratext appears as a label written by the librarians. It gives the title and some brief information about the manuscript. The scribal paratext can be found throughout text, such as the accompanying songs. However, the accompanying songs are inserted above the symbol " ◎ ", or the *Fongman*. As for the *Paiyan* symbol, it is rarely found in this manuscript.

Figure 5　Manuscript No. 31, Presenting a Scribal Paratext Specifying the Action Tunes or Accompanying Songs above a Specific Symbol of Siamese Poetry

Kāraked volume 3: Manuscript No. 32, literature section, the manuscripts and inscription group at the National Library of Thailand.

Title: *Kāraked*, *Phra. Lem 3*

Provenance: The original copy of the library

Figure 6　Manuscript No. 32, Presenting the Scripts in a Folio, Is Similar to Manuscript No. 31

The play is written on the black leporello manuscript in white chalk. The scripts are quite orderly. The handwriting is similar to manuscript No. 31 and the content continues from that manuscript. It is assumed that manuscripts 31 and 32 contain the same story but have different chapters; however, the content derives from similar literature.

The text continues the lamentation of Malithong. After the bodies of Kāraked and his horse were floated, they were found by Suban, a king of birds. Suban flew them to a hermit's dwelling. At that time, a Naga named Kudomsommit was ordained as a hermit. The

Naga lit the bonfire to revive Kāraked and his horse.

During the recovery, Kāraked had stayed with the hermit, serving and learning. One day, the hermit gave him a sword. He bid the hermit farewell and flew his horse to Malithong's castle. When she initially saw Kāraked, she was in doubt. After Kāraked explained what had happened to him, she understood and stayed with him in secret. Unfortunately, her servants found out that Kāraked had returned. They informed the ogre Sri Phimon, who ordered the troops to catch Kāraked. When the ogre's troops sieged the castle, Kāraked put Malithong on the horse and together they fled.

The content continued until Kāraked and Malithong arrived at a small hut in the city of King Iyara and slept there. After an ogre servant told King Iyara about them, the king moved his troops to the hut. He went in there and immediately fell in love with Malithong. The manuscript ends here. As for the composition of the manuscript, the appearing paratext is similar to manuscript No 31, particularly the accompanying songs. In addition, there is a short sentence written on the last folio stating *"the end of chapter"* by the scribe.

***Kāraked* volume 4**: Manuscript No. 33, literature section, the manuscripts and inscription group at the National Library of Thailand.

Title: *Kāraked*

Provenance: Received from the Ministry of Education, 30 June 1937

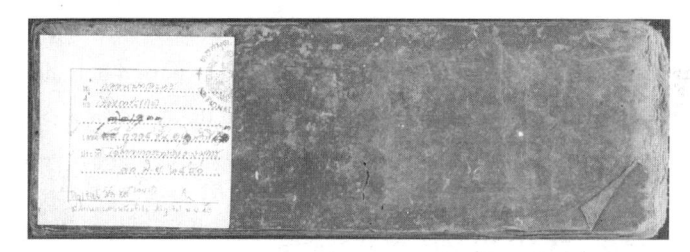

Figure 7 Manuscript No. 33, the Label on the Front Cover Presenting a Concise Detail about the Manuscript

Like the previous manuscripts, this one is also written on a black leporello manuscript in white chalk. The details about the original date and the scribe are not given. The handwriting is rather untidy.

The text begins with the scene describing the amusements at the cremation of Khun Thong. At that time, the Khun Thong's mother, Grandma Jamjee, learned that he had died. She was extremely sad and suddenly died.

Nom Phuang, who was Khun Thong's wife, prepared Khunthong and grandma Jamjee's cremation. She had realised Jamjee's last words that she had wanted her grandson, Kāraked, to be ordained as a novice. So Nom Phuang allowed Kāraked to be ordained. After that, Kāraked followed his preceptor to stay and learn at the temple, Wat Singha.

One day, the novice Kāraked was missing his mother and he asked his preceptor if he could leave the monkhood. He went back to his palace and ascended the throne. He then told his mother that he liked a girl named Chuichay, who was a daughter of grandmother Thong. They lived near Singha temple.

Kāraked proposed to Chuichay and she accepted. After he received her mother's permission to marry, they rode a horse back to his palace. After their marriage, Kāraked sought a hermit in order to learn from him. Unfortunately, the dwelling had been burnt and the hermit had fled, forcing Kāraked back to his palace.

The text ends here. There is a folio which contains a list of names, the monetary unit and a list of groceries left. Unfortunately, the messages are rather unclear.

Examining the text in the manuscript, the plot is different from the others. Although the hero has the same name, Kāraked, the character's traits are completely different. In this manuscript, Kāraked is not courageous, a common characteristic of heroes. As for the other characters, they had common names while in the other plays the names of the characters usually imitated royal names.

As for the paratext, apart from the accompanying songs, some sections contain folk songs or traditional Thai games such as *Phong-Phang* (โพงพาง) , *Ta-Ke-Ta-Khong* (ตะเข้ตะโขง) and so on. Moreover, after investigating the manuscript, an old song like *Chuichay* (ฉุยฉาย) is found in the scene of *Chuichay*, where a heroine picked flowers in a garden. It is believed that the song was transmitted from the Ayutthaya period.

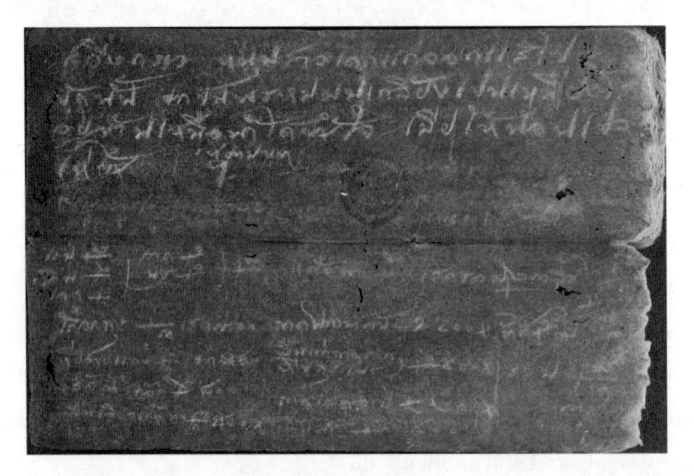

Figure 8   Manuscript No. 33, the Last Page Showing a List of Groceries and the Monetary Unit, but It Is Rather Blurred

Although manuscript No. 33 is eponymous labelled *Kāraked*, revising the manuscript thoroughly reveals another label titled *Chan yaowapoj* and *Phraya Jingjo*. Upon investigating the corpus of *Bot Lakhòn* further, manuscript No. 33 contains the story of *Jingjo*, or *Chan yaowapoj*, written by Mora. It reveals that this manuscript does not belong to the *Kāraked* play but is another play manuscript written in the year 1884.

7. Notes on *"Kāraked"* Manuscripts

7.1 The Characteristic of Manuscripts

Kāraked has four manuscripts preserved in the National Library of Thailand. One is on a greyish leporello manuscript (No. 30) and the others are on black leporello manuscripts (Nos. 31, 32 and 33). The greyish one was written in graphite with different handwriting that is rather untidy. As for the black manuscripts, they are written in white chalk; two of them contain the same handwriting, which is fairly organised but not the royal scribe's handwriting. The other black manuscript is written in untidy handwriting.

Manuscripts No. 31 and No. 32 are assumed to have been copied by the same scribe, considering the script's character and handwriting. However, it is not possible to determine the exact scribe, as in the others. After examining the manuscripts of *Bot Lakhòn Nòk*, it is found that the names of the scribes and dates scarcely appear in the manuscripts. Therefore, it is difficult to specify the scribe or the origin of the manuscripts.

7.2 The Text and Contents

These manuscripts were entitled *Kāraked* due to the name of the main character. However, the plots of the stories are varied. The text in the black leporello manuscripts (Nos. 31 and 32) are of the same story but different chapters. As for manuscripts No. 30 and No. 33, the texts are totally different.

Examination reveals that the text in manuscripts No. 31 and No. 32 were altered from the folktale called *Kāraked*, popular in the Northeast of Thailand. In particular, the character of a magical horse and a magical staff are rather popular motifs in Thai and Lao folktales. The magical horse is a necessary helper of the hero while the magical staff, used to kill or revive people, is made from a tree called *Maneekote*, which appears in several Lao stories.

Manuscript No. 30 contains a text the origin of which is unknown. Nonetheless, the plot of the text is somewhat similar to other plays of the era. For instance, the bow-lifting contest is widely found in Thai plays, such as in *Ramakien*, an inner court play. Therefore, the text of *Kāraked* in manuscript No. 30 may have borrowed the scene from others plays.

The text in manuscript No. 33 is completely different. The settings in the story change quite swiftly. The chapter shown in the manuscript has never appeared anywhere else; therefore, the origin of the chapter cannot be determined. Moreover, the names of the characters in these manuscripts are different, as shown in Table 1.

Table 1　The Names of the Characters in These Manuscripts

No. of Manuscript	Manuscript No. 30	Manuscript No. 31	Manuscript No. 32	Manuscript No.33
Hero	Kāraked	Kāraked	Kāraked	Kāraked
Heroine	Sai-yut	Malithong	Malithong	Chuichay
Magic/Helpers	Magic Stick and Glass Shoes	Horse Named Maneekab and a Glass Bow	Horse named Maneekab and a Glass Bow	-

7.3 The Paratext

The four manuscripts in which the paratexts appeared contain notable accompanying songs indicating the actions of the characters or the moods of the settings, for example, *Choet* (เชิด), which represents the fast action or the battle scenes, or *Oad* (โอด), which represents the sad scenes or the mourning. The accompanying songs can also roughly indicate the writing date of the manuscript, as presented in manuscript No. 30.

8. Conclusion

This study has examined a number of overlooked manuscripts in which the interesting texts are found. Investigating the manuscripts of *Kāraked*, it can be concluded that the *Kāraked* play has three different versions. The origin of the first version, manuscript No.30, cannot be specified but the plot is quite similar to other plays of the same period. Therefore, it is possible that the author of this version imitated a plot found in other plays. The second version, manuscripts No. 31 and No. 32, also cannot be determined. There are two different arguments: one states that it probably derives from the Northeastern tale told by Lao emigrants in the late Ayutthaya period or the early Thonburi period due to the migration of Laotians to Siam; the second argues that the story of *Kāraked* has its origin in the Ayutthaya period and originates in the Northeast and South of Siam.

The origin of the last version, manuscript No. 33, cannot be determined as well. The plot of this version is completely different from any other plays.

As for the characteristics of the manuscripts, the details about the dates and the scribes are not found. Apart from the text, there are paratexts concerning accompanying songs. The manuscripts in which those songs are contained are specifically play manuscripts. Additionally, the paratext in manuscript No. 33 also represents a list of names, the monetary unit and a list of groceries. This type of information is also found in other *Bot Lakhòn Nòk* manuscripts such as *Phra Rot-Meri*. The details of the groceries indicate that the manuscripts undoubtedly belonged to common people and were used among them.

To conclude, irrespective of whether or not the *Kāraked* play manuscripts were performed or not, versions of them were known among the people for a period of time. The name *Kāraked* was possibly familiar among the audiences. Investigating the manuscripts reveals that the origin of the folk dramatic plays could be traced back to the late Ayutthaya period, or even to the Thonburi period. A discussion of the transmission of the text is still needed.

References

(Ⅰ) Books

[1] Bung-On Piyaphan. The Lao in Early Bangkok. Bangkok: The Foundation for the Promotion of Social Science and Humanities Textbooks Project, The Thailand Research Fund, 1998.

[2] Chanvit Kasetsiri. Collected Proclamations of King Mongkut (2nd ed.). Bangkok: Toyota Thailand Foundation, 2005.

[3] Damrong Rajanuphab, Prince. *Bot Lakhòn Nok* of the Ayutthaya Era: Manora and Sang Thong (บทละครนอกครั้งกรุงเก่าเรื่องนางมโนห์ราและสังข์ทอง). Bangkok: Phimthai, 1919.

[4] De La Loubère, Simon. The Kingdom of Siam. London: Oxford University Press, 1969.

[5] Martin Stuart-Fox. A History of Laos. Cambridge: Cambridge University Press, 1997.

[6] Mattani Mojdara Rutnin. Dance, Drama, and Theatre in Thailand. Tokyo: The Center for East Asian Cultural Studies for UNESCO The Toyo Bunko, 2013.

[7] Saowalak Anantasant. The Ayudhya LaKhòn Nòk Manuscripts (บทละคอนนอกสมัยกรุงศรีอยุธยา). Master Thesis, Chulalongkorn University, 1972.

[8] Terry E. Miller, Jarernchai Chonpirat. A History of Siamese Music Reconstructed from Western Documents, 1505-1932. Crossroads: An Interdisciplinary Journal of Southeast Asian Studies, Volume 8, Number 2. Northern Illinois: Northern Illinois University, 1994.

[9] Thanit Yupho. Kruen Dontri Thai (Thai Classical Instruments) (เครื่องดนตรีไทย). Bangkok: Sivaporn, 1967.

[10] The Encyclopaedia of Thai Cultures: Northeastern Volume. 1. Bangkok: The Foundation of the Encyclopaedia of Thai Cultures, Siam Commercial Bank, 2012.

(Ⅱ) Manuscripts

[1] Manuscript No.30. Klon Bot Lakhòn subsection, Literature section, "Kāraked, Phra volume 1". The Manuscript Collection, The National Library of Thailand (White

Khòi paper, Thai Scripts, Thai Language, Graphite, 62 pages).

[2] Manuscript No.31. Klon Bot Lakhòn subsection, Literature section, "Kāraked, Phra volume 2". The Manuscript Collection, The National Library of Thailand (Black Khòi paper, Thai Scripts, Thai Language, White chalk, 43 pages).

[3] Manuscript No.32. Klon Bot Lakhòn subsection, Literature section, "Kāraked, Phra volume 3". The Manuscript Collection, The National Library of Thailand (Black Khòi paper, Thai Scripts, Thai Language, White chalk, 49 pages).

[4] Manuscript No.33. Klon Bot Lakhòn subsection, Literature section, "Kāraked". The Manuscript Collection, The National Library of Thailand (Black Khòi paper, Thai Scripts, Thai Language, White chalk, 57 pages).

An Analysis of Ancient Books of Dai Medicine and the Education Mode of Teach-Inheritance

—A Case Study of Dai Medical College of Applied Science of West Yunnan

Yu Nanha[①]
Translated by Wang Mingjiao[②]

Dai medicine, as the traditional medicine of Dai ethnic group, has been recorded for more than 2,500 years, and it is one of the four major ethnic medicines in China because of its complete theoretical knowledge and rich medical value. Before the introduction of Theravada Buddhism, the local people used medicinal plants to treat common diseases, which did not form a theoretical system of traditional medicine. Along with the introduction of Theravada Buddhism in the 13th century, the Dai ethnic group region of Xishuangbanna in Yunnan Province, created scripts and nurture the literature, calendar, law, medicine and other cultures. Compared with other palm-leaf scriptures, the spread range of ancient medical classics is relatively small and very difficult to collect, so that teach-inheritance education becomes the most important way of inheritance of Dai medicine. However, the inheritance tasks of Dai medical culture is very urgent on account of the aging of folk Dai medical doctors. More ancient Dai medical classics will disappear in the folk forever if not done in time.

1. Problems in the Inheritance of Dai Ancient Medical Books

1.1 The Crisis of Inheriting Dai Ancient Medical Books

The Dai ancient medical classics were first recorded, spread, studied and passed on in the form of palm-leaf scriptures. Large-scale palm-leaf scriptures have been burned

---

① A lecturer of Dai Medical College of Applied Science of West Yunnan.
② Master of Sociology, Research Assistant of Yunnan Institute for Drug Abuse.

down or lost in Laos, Myanmar or Thailand because of the political and historical reasons during the "Cultural Revolution" period, so that the existing ones become more precious. Over the past hundred years, Dai ancient medical books have been mostly copied in the form of paper scriptures, and rarely collected of palm-leaf scriptures classics with a long history, although palm-leaf scriptures are more durable than paper ones. During the investigation, the author learned that if no one inherits their medical skills or techniques, their families will not keep their relics after their death, and will burn and destroy their medical books, medical tools and other articles according to the traditional Dai customs in Xishuangbanna. At present, the inheritance of Dai medicine in Xishuangbanna has entered the stage of lacking of new generations ready to take over from elder ones. With the aging and increase death of the older generation of folk Dai doctors, the number of related books has been decreasing year by year, and many precious medical relics have disappeared. The inheritance of Dai medicine is facing unprecedented crisis, and the excellent traditional medical skills, classical prescription and proved recipe will be lost to the world if they are not handed down and rescued in time.

1.2 The Collection Difficulties in Dai Ancient Medical Books

The village residents in the Dai ethnic group region of Xishuangbanna that believe in Theravada Buddhism constantly have the custom of Dan Tham Long (a ritual of worship of Buddhist scriptures). The author found the Dai ancient medical books are not in the category of Buddhist scriptures and can not be found among Buddhist temples collections. This also leads the Dai medical classics to a status of narrow range of spread, low utilization rate and more difficult to collect. In addition, there are two situations to increase the collecting difficulties: one is that most folk Dai doctors have a strong sense of family inheritance and do not want to easily sell their ancestral classics; the other is that Dai people, especially doctors, have a strong sense of prevention of medical fraud, so that some related information of ancient books can only be obtained through official channels or multiple contacts with the owners.

1.3 The Artificially High Market Price of Dai Ancient Medical Books

Affected by the market economy, some businessmen have detected business opportunities and collected related Dai medicine books for sale, and some folk Dai doctors and their families have also realized their value, so that the price of purchasing Dai medical literature is rising day by day during the course of investigation and research. Finally, the project team can not afford it and it is also difficult to purchase the original version of the books with high application value. Moreover, the families and relatives of those aged Dai doctors will divide those books as family property, which leads to the mess and missing situations.

1.4 Intellectual Property Rights of Dai Ancient Medicine Books

The palm-leaf Scripture is a product of Buddhism, and according to the tradition of Dai ethnic group, it cannot be signed signatures when it is copied, translated and written. Their knowledge sharing consciousness is quite strong, and they believe that all ethnic cultures belong to everyone. However, the intellectual property concept of most folk Dai medical doctors is weak. Some doctors do not want to share the secret recipe handed down from ancestors because of the good economic returns. The worst part is that they do not have the modern medicine knowledge, which will cause some obstacles to the later product development and research work.

1.5 Inadequate Development of Dai Ancient Medical Books

The institutions engaged in the research work of Dai ancient medical literature include Institute & Hospital of Traditional Dai Medicine of Xishuangbanna Dai Autonomous Prefecture, Yunnan University of Chinese Medicine, West Yunnan University of Applied Science and other scientific research institutes and universities. Thereinto, the Institute of Traditional Dai Medical and the Hospital of Traditional Dai Medicine of Xishuangbanna Dai Autonomous Prefecture have been merged earlier into one hospital, which is mainly responsible for related works by the scientific research department of the hospital and lead the most of the ancient book development work. The only deficiency is that a digital platform has not been established yet.

In the past ten years, Yunnan University of Chinese Medicine has collected dozens of ancient Dai medical classics in both of Xishuangbanna and Dehong in Yunnan province. And the Dai Medical College of West Yunnan University of Applied Science has also collected nearly ten copies of related books since its establishment. Unfortunately, the ancient books of these two universities are still in the library or archives, and still need to be further developed and applied.

1.6 Translation Difficulties in Dai Ancient Medical Books

Since ancient times, Dai culture has been inherited by Buddhist temple education in Xishuangbanna Dai Autonomous Prefecture of Yunnan Province. The conflict between existing school education and Buddhist temple education has resulted in a low literacy rate of the new generation of Dai in classics. It has a high demand on translators' knowledge and skills to translate the Dai ancient medical books. They not only need to be proficient in the bilingualism of Dai and Chinese, but also need to understand the borrowed words of Pali (Buddhist language), to master certain professional terms of medicine and the knowledge of translation theory, etc. But there are only a few available translators, all of whom are undertaking both scientific researches and administrative tasks in the Institute of Traditional Dai Medicine of Xishuangbanna Dai Autonomous Prefecture, therefore, the time and energy for translation is difficult to guarantee.

2. Cultivation Mode of Dai Medical in Colleges and Universities

2.1 Cultivation & Policy Support in Dai Medical Colleges and Universities

The Dai Medical College of West Yunnan University of Applied Science was established in May 2017. It has 5 specialties in Dai medicine, traditional Chinese medicine, rehabilitation therapy, nursing and traditional Chinese medicine resources & development, which with a total of 1,021 undergraduate students. As a specialty of college characteristics, 139 Dai medical students have been rolled since 2017.

The institute undertakes the "Three-Year Action Plan of Cultivating Dai Medical Personnel" supported by the government of Xishuangbanna. The project is put into effect in all directions through selection of outstanding young talents from Dai Medical College, the establishment of teach-inheritance, the implementation of training for outstanding Dai medical monks, and the organization to collect, repair, organize and preserve Dai ancient medical books. In addition, the college's project of "Collection, Collation, Restoration, Translation and Preservation of Dai Ancient Medical Books" was supported by "100 Fine Works" of Yunnan National Bureau of Religious Affairs. The project will be sort out through organization, repair and preservation of Dai ancient medicine; translating and publishing fine works; and establishing a database of Dai medical literature. It can be seen that the college attaches great importance to the inheritance of ancient books and documents, and integrates them into all aspects of talent cultivation.

2.2 Course Setting of Dai Medicine Specialties

In the aspect of curriculum, the Dai language of medicine is also offered as the basic course of specialty. The basic course of specialty includes the basic theory of Dai medicine, etc. The core curriculum includes Dai medicine history, Dai medical prescription, the dermasurgery and orthopedics & traumatology (external skin and bone injury) of Dai medicine, etc. As an applied science university, Dai Medical College has set up many teaching activities, such as cognitive practice, drugs recognition and identification, so that students can better integrate into the environment of Dai medical industry. It also requires students are familiar with the clinical diagnosis technology of traditional Chinese medicine (TCM) and western medicine while mastering the basic theory and knowledge of Dai medicine.

"Dai Language in Medicine" is a basic medicine course for students majoring in Dai medicine. It requires them to master both of Xishuangbanna scriptures and new Dai language, to be able to use the international Phonetics, to memorize the commonly used Dai medicine and prescriptions, and to use reference books for the purpose of digging, collecting, sorting out and inheriting the prescription of Dai medical classics. The ultimate goal of this course is to train talented researchers engaged in the literature studying of Dai ancient medicine.

2.3 The Plasticity of Local Students

There are 5 Dai students from Xishuangbanna in Dai Medical College. Considering the local characteristics of Dai medicine major, it is necessary to increase policy support to reduce the score and encourage local students to apply for a permit of Dai medicine major examination. In the process of carrying out teaching and scientific research work, the advantages of local Dai students are very obvious. First, it is easy for them to interpret the particularity of Dai medicine in the system of Dai traditional culture, and to master, use and inherit Dai medicine culture skillfully. Second, the locals have the advantages of language and characters. Most folk Dai doctors in Xishuangbanna Dai Autonomous Prefecture of Yunnan Province, who are over 45 years old, can not skillfully use Chinese, but to master Dai language and Dai scriptures is undoubtedly necessary for the inheritance of Dai medicine. Third, some students are from Dai medical family or have inheritance channels, and have a great interest in Dai medicine studying.

2.4 Cultural Inheritance Advantage of Dai Medical College

Dai Medical College of West Yunnan University of Applied Science encourages students to carry out teaching projects such as innovative and entrepreneurial projects and social practice activities related to Dai ancient medical books and literature, and systematically study with teachers in their spare time such as summer and winter vacations. The geographical location of Xishuangbanna is conducive to teachers and students to carry out preliminary research work. The college's scientific research team has visited about 50 folk Dai doctors and their inheritors in Xishuangbanna and Dehong, and regularly kept in touch with them to make the outstanding students apprentice. Through various channels, including official and folk ones, the college mobilized teachers and students to collect and obtain information on the Dai medical classics, which effectively guarantee an orderly manner of inheritance work. Students majoring in Dai medicine and traditional Chinese medicine (TCM) have a strong correlation along with contribution on collecting, sorting out and translating works. After a long period of training on a solid foundation in "Practical Dai Language" and "Dai Language in Dai Medicine", and familiar with Dai-Chinese bilingualism, international phonetic alphabet and terminology of Dai medicine specialized terms, students can preliminarily complete the reorganization and translation works on the basis of information technology means.

3. The Integration of Teach-Inheritance Education & Ancient Classics Development

According to the article 35 of the *Law of the People's Republic of China on Traditional Chinese Medicine*, China shall develop the education for TCM practitioners, supports TCM physicians and TCM technical personnel with rich experiences and technical expertise to teach students in the course of medical practice, and to pass on academic knowledge, cultivate TCM professionals and technicians. Dai medicine mainly relies on teach-inheritance education and college education to inherit culture. Both types of education models have their own strengths. College education is more systematic, scientific and professional, while teach-inheritance education is more targeted and special. Therefore, we shall adopt one's strong points while overcoming one's weakness.

3.1 Inheritance Ways of Dai Ancient Medical Classics

There are three main ways to inherit the Dai ancient medical classics. First, they can be purchased directly from the holders, and be borrowed to scan or to make a manuscript copy. Second, they can be inherited as a master's gift to students through the master worship ceremony. Third, we can cooperate with Xishuangbanna Branch of Yunnan Buddhist Institute to select outstanding monks into the inheritance project, and leverage the strength of the Buddhist beliefs in Theravada Buddhism to give full play to the advantages of the traditional culture and Dai culture, and jointly complete the inheritance work of Dai ancient medical classics. According to the author's investigation, folk Dai doctors are unwilling to directly sell their original ancient medical books, but most can be copied in handwritten, copied or scanned with their consent, if there are students willing to worship them as teachers, they are willing to teach them the knowledge of ancient medical books.

There is a long way to go to collect Dai ancient medical books. In fact, some related books are disappeared after Dai doctors lose their ability to medical practice, which undoubtedly increases the difficulty of collecting and rescuing work. We should use the influence of the relevant departments to mobilize Dai doctors and their relatives to break down the feudal superstition and actively guide them to donate or share their medicine books, so as to prevent illegal bidding up prices, especially for those doctors who have no energy to train an apprentice. It is necessary to establish sufficient emotional connection with folk Dai doctors, inculcate the medicinal value of related literature and classics, change the fixed thinking of their family inheritance, and improve their consciousness of sharing, developing and studying on Dai ancient medical books.

3.2 Follow the Traditional Teacher Worship Customs

Dai Medical College intends to set up a practical course on the study of the Dai ancient medical books, select a group of students with outstanding achievements in the course named Dai Language in Medicine, and also carry out the activities of the Dai traditional teacher worship ceremony to study a certain medical book from the master, organize and translate the Dai ancient books literature with the master, and compile them into volumes. In order to ensure the translational quality of Dai medical classics, a set of standardized practical curriculum management system is formulated. First of all, look for the folk Dai practitioners in Xishuangbanna, who are willing to teach medical skills and develop ancestral medical classics. Secondly, full-time teachers of the college assigned to supervise the progress are responsible for supervising the progress of teach-inheritance and reviewing translation works from a professional perspective in accordance with majors such as medicine, pharmacy, and rehabilitation therapy, etc. Finally, select 2-3 students in a targeted manner to study with teachers/masters during winter and summer holidays and other long periods of time. Plan to study, sort out, and translate ancient classic works, complete the post-compilation together, and cooperate with the college to complete the construction work of digital medical platform.

3.3 Ownership of Intellectual Property Rights in Ancient Books Development

The output forms of Dai ancient books can generally be divided into two categories. First, they are published in the form of works, and the holders, inheritors of ancient books and teachers in charge are all editors, who jointly hold copyright and the right of authorship, and share the economic benefits of works. The second is to convert the valuable classic prescriptions of the ancient books into products or patents which can be purchased at one time or the three parties can share the patent rights. Fortunately, folk Dai doctors who are unwilling to sell their own ancient books have proposed that they can share through photocopying and scanning. In the implementation of digitization, information and documentation of Dai traditional medicine practice activities, it is necessary to seek the unification of Dai compatriots, keep confidentiality, and fully respect their national beliefs.

3.4 Increase Local Knowledge Research to Fill the Theoretical Knowledge Gap

According to the author's investigation and statistics, it is known that more than 80% of the medical classics circulating in Xishuangbanna are pharmacopoeia manuscripts within 100 years. When folk Dai doctors copied medical books, they would add or modify prescriptions based on their own experiences instead of strict accordance with the original texts, which resulting in inconsistent prescriptions. The model of teach-inheritance jointly develops ancient books, and repeatedly verifies their clinical effects in folks, hospitals, colleges and universities to verify the scientificity of a certain prescription. When sorting out ancient books, the same formula is integrated on a large scale to trace its development context, which is convenient for teaching and research use in the future. The basic theory of

Dai medicine is still under developing and improving. Students can summarize the dialectical thoughts and medical techniques taught by Dai medicine in practice into theoretical knowledge, so as to improve the current situation that Dai medicine has many prescriptions and lacks of medical technology and theoretical knowledge.

Dai people in Xishuangbanna believe in Theravada Buddhism and primitive religion, which is also very obvious in Dai medicine. The basic theory of Dai medicine named "Sita Wuyun" (the theory of four elements and five skandhas) is the most typical knowledge of Buddhism. Folk Dai doctors not only use mouth skills to set a broken bone, stanch bleeding, pool out a tooth, but also give divination and calculation to patients with complicated diseases. In ethnic groups' regions, it is necessary to fully understand its particularity of traditional culture, find a balance between modern medicine and traditional medicine, properly inculcate local knowledge in the process of cultivating students, so that they can truly grasp the connotation of Dai medical education thought. The current college education has excessively transformed the Dai medicine into the TCM and western medicine. Therefore, the first priority is to deep-digging the basic theory of Dai medicine, supplement local knowledge education and lead a revival of Dai medicine in characteristics and true qualities.

3.5 Digital Platform Construction for Dai Ancient Medical Books

Traditional Chinese Medicine Museum in Yunnan University of Chinese Medicine has gradually established a digital collection of information, where the information is digitally processed and stored in pictures, videos, audios and text descriptions, etc. Institute & Hospital of Traditional Dai Medicine of Xishuangbanna Dai Autonomous Prefecture has compiled, translated and published more than 20 works, but has not set up a digital platform yet, so the dissemination and inheritance of Dai medical works is relatively limited.

The college is setting up a database related to Dai medicine, including Dai medicine database, Dai medicine talent pool and Dai medicine ancient book resource database. Dai Medical College now has the manpower, material resources and information technology to mobilize teachers and students to participate in field research, inherit the classics of ancient books, and collect information data. Traditional media has limitations. Both palm-leaf and paper scriptures are difficult to preserve for a long time. Informatization not only breaks through the inheritance barriers, but also can play an informatization and intelligent function to improve the utilization rate and influence of Dai medicine. Once the medical knowledge query system such as the search for Dai medicine and the online diagnosis and treatment of pharmacy prescriptions completed, it would fill the gap in theoretical teaching, promote the development of teaching supplement and professional construction to further development, and achieve the role of scientific research and nurturing teaching.

4. Conclusion

The Dai Medical College of West Yunnan University of Applied Science has set up a platform to combine the colleges and universities training and teach-inheritance education, and to combine the efforts of various tutors such as folk Dai doctors, college teachers and clinical experts to jointly train Dai medical inheritors and organize, translate, develop and conduct clinical research on ancient books. While protecting and inheriting the classics of Dai medicine, it is necessary to explore and supplement the theoretical knowledge of Dai medicine, further standardize the prescription, give full play to the scientific research advantages of the college and increase the investigation of local knowledge, and finally incorporate the research results into the database of Dai medicine, so that the classics of Dai ancient medical books can be permanently protected and inherited.

The Village-Based Preserve-Support Model for the Dai Palm-Leaf Culture

—The Study of Three Dai Villages in Xishuangbanna

Yu Wanjiao[①]　Wang Mingjiao[②]

1.Introduction

A culture system of the Dai ethnic group, called palm-leaf culture has been formed and constructed by melting Theravada Buddhist culture as the core and including primitive religion and other folk cultures of the Dai ethnic group together, after Theravada Buddhism was introduced to the Dai ethnic group area.

Dai ethnic group mainly live along the borderlines between China and Southeast Asian countries. It benefits Dai people to communicate and integrate easily with different ethnic groups along the borderlines. They share similar cultures, beliefs, and religions. Consequently, palm-leaf culture becomes a culture form characterized by ethnicity, religion, and trans-nationality. Xishuangbanna local government departments have valued the development and inheritance of palm-leaf culture, since The Belt and Road Initiative has been carried out in Southeast Asian countries, because palm-leaf culture has played an auspicious role in providing a cultural field for mutual learning and mutual understanding among people living there.

Literature related to Dai palm-leaf culture is abundant, but most scholars analyze the forming process, function, and sub-fields of palm-leaf culture, few researchers take Dai villages as analytical units to study the inheritance of palm-leaf culture. For those who study on Dai villages, they tend to pay attention to describe the cultural system of a Dai village, village cultural change, village community development, and a certain cultural perspective of the village. As to culture system, Cao Chengzhang described in his work: *A Study on Dai Village-Based Culture*, asserts Dai culture can be seen as village-based culture, and

---

[①] A PhD in Social Sciences from the Faculty of Social Sciences, Chiang Mai University.
[②] An intern researcher at Yunnan Institute for the Prevention and Treatment of Drug Dependence.

uses this concept to illustrate the nature and characteristics of the Dai culture[①]. For village cultural change, it is treated as the main clue to describe and explain the dynamic picture of village culture development[②]; some take villages as cases to explore the background, performance, and reasons for the palm-leaf cultural changes and put forward the importance of rational consciousness of ethnic culture[③]. Regarding to village community development, Luo Yang in the book *Dai Community and Development in Xishuangbanna of Yunnan Province* points out that Dai communities have abundant natural and cultural resources, so the construction and development of the communities should be combined with the Dai culture and environmental resources[④]. Besides, some scholars study from the perspectives of village Bo Zhang[⑤] operating system[⑥], traditional authoritative organization including four key elders[⑦], protection of traditional household[⑧], etc. However, few scholars discuss palm-leaf culture based on preserve-support model based on villages' resources. Every Dai village in Xishuangbanna has its own operating system and independent cultural field, and considering of the concept "village-based culture" put forward by Cao, this paper will focus on three villages to explore how to protect and inherit palm-leaf culture.

2. Preserve-Support Model for the Palm-Leaf Culture in Dai Villages

The definition of support is that one thing is stood up by other things. Generally, scholars argue that "One of the fundamental crux of the problems vulnerable groups face is lacking social resources (including finance, human, material, power, and ability, etc.)"[⑨]. Concepts, such as "social support model" and "social support network" have been created to cope with such problems, because these concepts are considered to be able to offer ideas to provide social support to vulnerable people. The traditional cultures of ethnic groups are marginal compared to the mainstream culture of a country and modern culture, due to a shortage of resources to be inherited and developed. Palm-leaf culture belongs to

---

① Cao Chengzhang. A Study on Dai Village-Based Culture. Beijing: Minzu University of China Publishing House, 2005.
② Jin Shaoping. An Ethnographic Study on the Cultural Changes of City Village and Dai Ethnic Group Villages in Xishuangbanna. Beijing: Intellectual Property Publishing House, 2014.
③ Zheng Xiaoyun.Dai Culture in Social Change: An Anthropological Study of Dai Village in Xishuangbanna. Chinese Social Sciences, 1997 (5).
④ Luo Yang. Dai Community and Development in Xishuangbanna of Yunnan Province. Chengdu: Sichuan University Publishing House, 2007.
⑤ Bo Zhang is the representative of Theravada Buddhism in the Dai ethnic region of Xishuangbanna who manages daily social affairs and organizes activities that related to Buddhism.
⑥ Zheng Xiaoyun. A Study on the Religious Management Mode of Theravada Buddhism in China. Chinese Religion, 2011 (1).
⑦ Wu Qionghua, Yan Yongjun.Traditional Authoritative Organization in Dai Villages: "Xishaolaoman" in Man'an Village and Village Order.Journal of Yunnan Minzu University (Social Science), 2012 (3).
⑧ Bi Faqian, Bi Faming. Research on the Protection of Traditional Dwellings in the Tourist Village of Mengjinglai, Xishuangbanna. Western Development · China, 2012 (1).
⑨ Zhang Youqin. From Social Support to Social Support Network: Towards a Practice Pattern of Social Support for the Disadvantaged. Journal of Xiamen University (Social Science), 2002 (3).

marginal culture in China, but it is supported by Dai villages to develop and prosper. That is why it is necessary to study on the politics, economy, education, religion and people of the Dai region of Xishuangbanna.

2.1 The Preserve-Support Model for Palm-Leaf Culture Inheritance in Traditional Dai Villages

After long-term localization and integration, Theravada Buddhism has become the most important religion supported by feudal lards in the Dai ethnic group area of Xishuangbanna. The combination of Theravada Buddhism and local indigenous culture finally nurtured palm-leaf culture, whose inheritance and prosperity depend on the support from villages' politics, economy, religion, and education, etc.

First, the notions, ethics, and values of palm-leaf culture have been used by villages' leaders to govern and manage villagers, which actively promote the inheritance and development of palm-leaf culture. Guided by values from the culture, Dai people live peacefully and engage in their own economic activities. Therevada Buddhism—the core part of palm-leaf culture—relies almost entirely on the merit-making of secular society. Villages finance Buddhist temples and bear the expenses of religious activities of higher administrative levels[①]. Primitive religious rituals are held by villages, if someone will leave the village for quite a long time, get married, give birth to children, or move to a new house, they will treat Zhaoman, the representative of primitive religion in a Dai village with some amount of money or food which again facilitate the maintenance and development of primitive religious. These two kinds of religions cooperate smoothly and make a clear division to pave the foundation of religious support for the inheritance of palm-leaf culture.

Second, the juxtaposition of monastery education and family education in villages acts as an educational guarantee for the development of palm-leaf culture. Monastery education is the most crucial educational method to take responsibility to inherit and transmit palm-leaf culture. Nearly every young man in Dai traditional society became a novice or monk for a while to learn Theravada and local knowledge, and then reintegrated secular society again with the knowledge he learned in a monastery. For females, they were cultivated with values of palm-leaf culture by family or other institutes. Both kinds of education in villages provided a strong guarantee for the vertical inheritance of palm-leaf culture.

Third, Dai people follow the Buddha's teachings, do good deeds and accumulate virtues, make extensive alms-giving, and worship Buddhism sincerely. They not only accept the present reality, but also pursue "blessing" for the afterlife. Merit-making is one

---

① Zheng Xiaoyun. The Interaction between the Organization System and the Social Organization System of Southern Buddhism in China: A Case Study of Dai Ethnic Group in Xishuangbanna of Yunnan Province. Studies in World Religions, 2007 (4).

of the performances of the Dai Buddhist faith. Every person would go to the Buddhist temple to do offerings.

2.2 The Preserve-Support Model for Palm-Leaf Culture Inheritance in the Present Time

Nowadays, different Dai villages in Xishuangbanna present various palm-leaf culture preserve-support modes due to the accumulation of traditional culture, geographical location and social environment. This paper will analyze the three different preserve-support modes according to economic support, religious operating mechanisms, education inheritance and village personnel participation of villages.

2.2.1 The Preserve-Support Model Based on Traditional Style

The preserve-support model for palm-leaf culture in Manzhang village is run in a traditional way without innovation (See Figure 1).

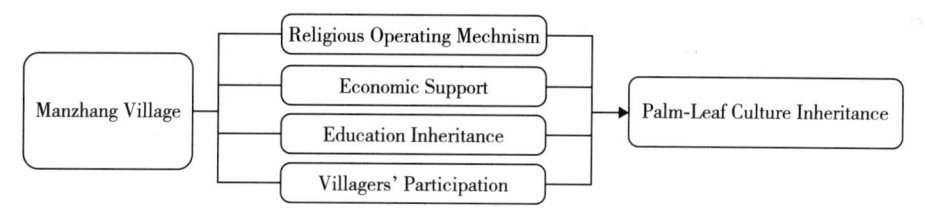

Figure 1　The Palm-Leaf Culture Preserve-Support Model of Manzhang Village

The first support for the inheritance of palm-leaf culture in Manzhang village is villagers' devotion to Buddhism. Villagers actively and generously support and ensure the normal life and operation of the temple by money or something else. For example, every household in this village donated 2,000 *yuan* to repair the temple in 2011. Primitive belief has stretched into every corner of normal life and traditional rituals are still held every year.

Second, religious operating mechanisms keep the same. Bo Zhang, the represent of Theravada Buddhism in the village manages Buddhist affairs orderly. Zhaoman practices his own role in primitive relevant rituals and activities such as offering to the god of the village. Although forms of these rituals tend to be simplified, these rituals are still held every year.

Third, education inheritance has been changed in this village. Monastery education becomes weaker and weaker. Since 1990s, few boys have chosen to become novices, and there was just an abbot managing temple without other monks or novices. To date, school education and monastery education co-exist in Manzhang village, but the six novices whose ordinations were held at the end of 2016 focus on schooling and just spend evenings, weekends or vacations on learning their own traditional culture, so palm-leaf culture learning effect is not good. The weak monastery education poses a negative influence on the inheritance of palm-leaf culture through the family education system.

Fouth, traditional culture activities in Manzhang attracts almost the elderly. Rituals and other forms of religious activities are also held regularly, but nearly the elders take part in them without youngsters. In this changing society, youngsters are unwilling to join in traditional activities, plus no course about palm-leaf culture provided in school, they increasingly alienate their own culture.

The resistance under the context of social change for palm-leaf culture to inherit has been increasing since the preserve-support pattern keeps the same without innovated intervene in Manzhang village. The production and life of Manzhang village has gradually separated from the palm-leaf culture system which will cause villagers' values and notions deviating from the culture and pose a threat to continuously inherit palm-leaf culture.

2.2.2 The Preserve-Support Model Guided and Assisted by the Temple

The palm-leaf culture preserve-support model of Manganna village in Puwen town is similar to that of Manzhang. The difference is that the Buddhist temple playing a guided and assisted role in Manganna (See Figure 2).

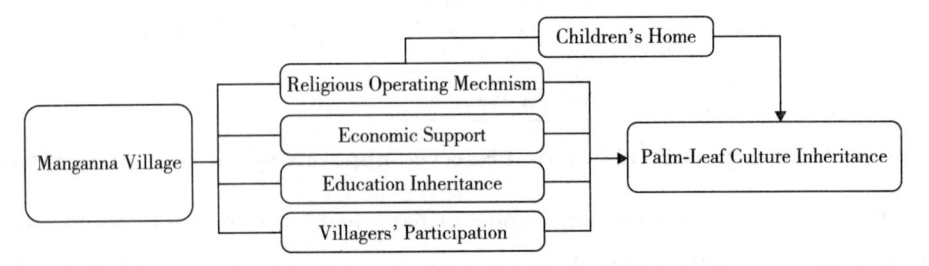

Figure 2 The Palm-Leaf Culture Preserve-Support Model of Manganna Village

Manganna temple is the only temple recover from the damage caused by the "Cultural Revolution" in Puwen town, but positions for Bo Zhang and Zhaoman no longer exist in this village. To date, all Buddhist affairs or activities are managed and assisted by the abbot Phra Sanfa and the elders respectively. For example, they lead villagers to worship village god shrine and village heart shrine every year. The latter affairs generally belong to the realm of primitive religion and Buddhist relevant people rear participant in. In this village, some roles of primitive religion have been replayed by Theravada, but primitive religious belief is still preserved. Similar to villagers of Manzhang, people in this village are willing to donate religious activities to promise the development and inheritance of palm-leaf culture to some extent.

Since the 1960s, there had been no temples and no monks/novices in this village until Phra Sanfa volunteered to be the abbot and rebuilt this monastery a few years ago. Palm-leaf culture has little influence in this area and middle and aged people are not familiar with traditional culture. Phra Sanfa pointed out that "influenced early by outside culture, some young people have difficulty in speaking their own Dai language now". In 2012, guided by the abbot, monastery of Manganna held the 1st children summer camp to provide classes like reading Dai scripts, Buddhist rituals and chanting for teenagers from Manganna and the vicinity. To date, 10 camps have been held for teenagers to cultivate affection for local knowledge and culture, and attract nearly 300 people to attend. In 2015, awarded by the Xishuangbanna Women's Federation, a "Children's Home" was established in Manganna Buddhist Temple, becoming the main place for young people in the town to learn the traditional ethnic culture. The "Children's Home" is targeted at providing traditional culture-related courses for children, and extends to organize activities to children's parents and the elderly in the village. For example, based on activities in Children's Home, Phra Sanfa often leads middle-aged people in the village to recite Buddhist scriptures. Influenced and moved by ideas and behaviors of Phra Sanfa, 11 boys in Puwen town, 3 of whom are from Manganna chosen to become novices to formally learn and inherit palm-leaf culture.

Villagers have paid much attention to cultural inheritance as well as creating a cultural atmosphere now, which profit from the endeavor of temple and Children's Home.

2.2.3 The Preserve-Support Model that Co-Uphold by the Monastery and the Company

Compare to the two aforementioned villages, the inheritance of palm-leaf culture of Mengjinglai village in Daluo town are benefited from the co-construction of Mengjinglai Temple and Golden Peacock Tourism Company (See Figure 3).

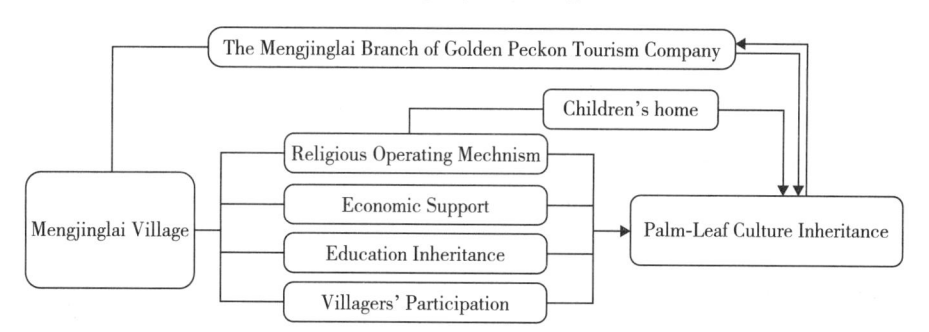

Figure 3 The Palm-Leaf Culture Preserve-Support Model of Mangjinglai Village

The religious operating mechanism keeps unchanged in this village. At the same time, one branch of Golden Peacock Tourism Company located in Mengjinglai encourages villagers to participant in cultural activities which adds the supporting factor for cultural development in this village. Since this branch began to settle in Mengjinglai in 2003, *The Provisional Management Regulations for Villager*s has been signed by the branch and villagers to preserve traditional local-style buildings and any sabotage are prohibited. In order to attract tourists and preserve traditional culture, the branch rents 14 villagers' houses to set up house-based Dai handcraft projects, including brewing, traditional paper making, sugar pressing, bamboo weaving, pottery, iron making, and brocade, and subsidizes 400 *yuan* per month for handicraft inheritors and 1,500 *yuan* for house rent. These projects motivate villagers to learn and inherit palm-leaf culture. 70% of employees in the Mengjinglai tourist zone are from this village, who are working for tour guides, greening, and manual work, while practicing cultural participation.

To cater to tourists' interest, the whole village has been designed and constructed into a cultural zone. Nearly all houses are Dai traditional style; murals pictured Dai histories or myths are in every corner; and motto brands written with both Dai and Chinese scripts can be seen everywhere. In this context, teenagers easily absorb and get familiar with palm-leaf culture. At the same time, the strong cultural atmosphere attracts many tourists to come and increase economic profits for villagers and the company.

The palm-leaf college has been established in the village's temple by villagers under the encouragement from the abbot Phra Khamzhang to provide a public learning zone for villagers. Some cultural inheritance classes and courses have been regularly organized by the college to offer opportunities for children, teenagers, and other villagers to learn traditional knowledge of the Dai ethnic culture. The abbot often leads monks and novices to collect and disseminate Theravada and Dai traditional culture, and freely handsel some books such as *Palm-Leaf Mottos*, *Biography of Shakyamuni* and *Dictionary of Dai Tham Script* that written, proof read and published by members of the college to the public. With the help from the palm-leaf college, more and more villagers mastered the commandments of the Buddhist scriptures. In important Buddhist days, sounds of village reciting Buddhist scriptures can be heard from the temple. The temple has become a significant place for children to learn and play. In Mengjinglai, it can be seen that a strong palm-leaf cultural atmosphere is attracting, benefiting from jointly promotion by the company and the palm-leaf collage.

2.3 Analysis of the Preserve-Support Model for Palm-Leaf Culture Inheritance Nowadays

Based on the research of the above three villages, village religious mechanisms in three villages are continuously operating but influenced by the consciousness of village religious leaders. The economic support of religious affairs increases with the increase of villagers' income, but villagers are inclined to spend more time on economic activities signifying less time can be paid to cultural participation. Family traditional culture education is negatively affected by the weakness of monastery education, and fewer accesses for Dai youngsters to get informal palm-leaf culture classes. The "Children's Home" and "the Palm-Leaf Traditional Acadamy" in two villages take responsibility to give traditional culture education for Dai children to fill the vacuum zone of educational inheritance of palm-leaf culture. This kind of public-welfare education given by village monasteries can be an alternative form to provide local knowledge and traditional culture courses for teenagers under conflict between Buddist monastery education and the national compulsory education system.

Mengjinglai village has a strong cultural atmosphere, which means that cultural protection can be guided by companies aiming to get profit from cultural tourism. However, it is not a long-term plan to inherit and protect the palm-leaf culture by a third party. Villagers are the key carriers of palm-leaf culture, and cultural awareness of villagers should be emphasized to develop the culture.

3. Suggestions for Improving Preserve-Support Model for the Dai Palm-Leaf Culture

3.1 Appreciate the Traditional Educational Function of Palm-Leaf Culture

In traditional Dai society, boys learned palm-leaf culture in monasteries, while families and villages provided palm-leaf related knowledge for other people. "The culture of traditional society was highly homogeneous, meaning that children needed not to be isolated from the community for independent training" [1], so the life field of children plays an early education-offering role for children. However, in modern times, particularly for ethnic groups, dual cultural structures exist between the content of school education and community life resulting in unsustained development of indigenous culture. Schooling is a principle form of modern education and the main channel for cultural reproduction. Educatees enter schools to receive education under the state power to learn modern knowledge and inherit the mainstream culture of the country.

Monasteries have always been important educational places to inherit palm-leaf culture of Dai. Relevant governmental departments in Xishuangbanna should recognize, sustain and give corresponding support to monastery education, coordinate the tension, resolve the conflicts and manage daily works between school education and monastery education.

3.2 Support the Cultural Industry of the Dai Palm-Leaf Culture

The cultural industry is the inner demand and important way of cultural protection [2]. Nowadays, cultural tourism in Xishuangbanna is the main cultural industry that has partly embodied palm-leaf culture and attracted the participation of many Dai people, but few Dai people can join in the core strategic department of cultural tourism, failing to stimulate cultural consciousness of the Dai people. Dai folk culture which includes handicraft has been a part of the palm-leaf culture. Handicrafts are characterized by palm-leaf culture and

---

[1] Luo Jihua. Cultural Reproduction and Educational Choice in Cultural Change. Minzu University of China, 2009.
[2] Ding Zhicai. A Study on the Protection of Ethnic Culture in Border Areas from the Perspective of the Ethnic Cultural Industry. Journal of Hubei Minzu University (Social Science), 2006 (4).

easily formed an industrial chain. Most Dai people master and are professional in handicrafts-making. If what they are skilled at or proficient in can bring them economic profit in turn, they can boost their cultural protagonist consciousness to protect and inherit their own culture. The final goal of economic support for the inheritance and development of palm-leaf culture is to increase economic profit for villagers from cultural activities attracting Dai people participation by setting up culture cooperatives.

3.3 Launch the Village-Based Cultural Construction of the Dai Palm-Leaf Culture

It is the key step of culture consciousness that Dai people collectively participant in culture construction and this culture consciousness is the intrinsic primordial power of cultural protection. Village-based cultural construction is centered on the continuation of common history and culture, with economic development of cultural industry as the main line. By mobilizing villagers to continue to collectively deal with issues of cultural protection, cultural heritage and cultural development, cultural construction can promote villagers to rethink about past, present and future of their own culture and relationship between human beings and culture as well. Dai villages are organic communities, where villagers know each other and have common history, religious belief and interest—which is the cultural foundation of village-based cultural construction. Besides, there are many formal or informal grass-root groups in Dai villages, such as peer groups, senior citizen associations and women groups constituting organizational basis for cultural construction. The government or local NGOs can assist villagers to learn their own culture, carry out cultural construction, cultivate cultural industries, stimulate the cultural consciousness of the Dai people, and promote the Dai People consciously inherit and develop palm-leaf culture.

4. Conclusion

The in-depth promotion of The Road and Belt Initiative and the propaganda of the concept of "cultural confidence" have provided opportunities for the inheritance of palm-leaf culture. In this environment, more resources will be provided to protect and inherit palm-leaf culture. This research finds that different villages generate different effects of cultural inheritance due to different preserve-support modes. Relevant methods—appreciate the traditional educational function, support the cultural industry, and launch the village-based cultural construction—have been proposed to enhance the inheritance and development of palm-leaf culture. The author believes that the preserve-support model is worth studying more details and much deeper in order to find out which way and how can be best to produce indigenous culture.

Possession of Palm-Leaf Based Ritual Knowledge: An Overview of Palm-Leaf Manuscript Traditions in Sri Lanka

Premakumara de Silva[①]

1. Introduction

In the island of Sri Lanka the long-established practices and traditional knowledge of indigenous communities in the earliest times were preserved through oral traditions and then in inscriptions (sellipi) or stone carving. The Sinhalese had a written alphabet as early as the second century BC and there are inscriptions still around written in that script. When I say "inscription", I mean writing on a stone. Palm-leaf manuscript tradition was used to document the traditional knowledge and know how available with the ancient society including traditional medicine, rituals, religion, culture, indigenous technology, health traditions and so on. Sri Lanka and most of the countries in South Asia equipped with a widely spread manuscript culture, exceeding limits of a mere writing material. These palm-leaf manuscripts are invaluable source containing a great deal of indigenous knowledge and wisdom, which were acquired by our ancestors within thousands of years as a result of experiments and experiences. Palm-leaf manuscripts (*puskola poth*) remained as the dominant writing material throughout South Asian countries dating back to the 5th century BC. Palm-leaf manuscripts commonly known as palm-leaf writing prepared using traditional technological process incorporated with cultural practices, the tender leaves of Palmyra palm (Borassus flabelliformis) utilizing for those purpose. There were books written on palm leaves too. The oldest available book belongs to the 12th century and were mostly written by Buddhist priests, and later by lay people as well.

2. A Synoptic History

This system of writing on palm-leaf was continued up to the end of the 19th century. And

---

[①] Senior Professor & Dean of the School of Arts, University of Colombo, Sri Lanka.

we must not forget one more thing here. Even now the horoscope of a person and the amulets for children when they are sick are drawn on these leaves. Large amount of information related to traditional medicine, cultural practices, astrology, agriculture, and ancient technology can be found by studding these palm-leaf manuscripts still available in Sri Lanka. At present due to several factors such as humidity, termites, rats, and human activities such as negligence, selling to foreigners as antiques and aesthetic objects these manuscripts are perished very quickly and the writing on palm-leaf manuscripts and associated traditional technological and cultural activities will be completely disappeared in the near future (Peiris 2018). Due to the above facts writing on palm-leaf manuscripts and associated traditional technological and cultural activities will be completely disappeared in the near future. In Sri Lanka, most of the indigenous knowledge and suitable practices written in these palm-leaf manuscripts is a valuable resource for the modern development of the nation. In order to safeguard this ancient tradition of palm-leaf manuscript writing it is necessary to revitalize this ancient tradition by disseminating the technical know-how of producing such manuscripts and also by redefining its potential uses in the contemporary society.

During the latter part of the 1st Century BC Buddhist monks passed on the Dhamma-teaching of the Buddha through oral tradition on palm leaves. This is the first recorded event where palm leaves had been used for writing[1]. While the native physicians put down their numerous prescriptions and indigenous curing procedures on palm leaves to preserve and protect them from extinction and to be used by generation to generation. Like Buddhist monks and native physicians, local ritual specialists also preserve their ritual knowledge through palm leaves traditions[2]. There is an extensive but mostly unpublished collections of these differing types of texts in multiple archives such as in temples, private collections, in government archives and in foreign museums (Godakumbura 1980; Liyanaratne 1983).

Apart from that there are hundreds of ritual texts collected by Hugh Nevill (1955)[3]

---

[1] The historical role of Buddhist monk of textual production in Sri Lanka is very important and they preserved and transformed the Dharma through acts of production, translation, commentary, anthropology, and recitation (Berkwitz 2009).

[2] Obeyesekere (2013) found out that palm-leaf manuscripts written by "local intellectuals", mostly literate villagers, on imagined or real historical events or *vitti*. These manuscripts are for the most part unpublished and broadly known as *vitti* pot, "books on past events". In addition to *vitti* pot there are related texts such as *bandaravaliyas* or histories of aristocratic families that are simply a Sri Lankan version of family genealogies that are found in many cultures but here put down in writing. They provide us invaluable information on the history and social organization of the new post-fifteenth century kingdoms of Kotte and Kandy supplementing the better-known historical chronicles. Other such work is known as *kadaim* pot or boundary books that delineate the boundaries of the imagined nation, the provinces and the districts contained therein.

[3] Hugh Nevill was a British civil servant. He served in Ceylon for nearly 30 years. He was born in June 1848; the exact place in England isn't known. He arrived in Ceylon (Sri Lanka) late in 1865. He served as a private secretary to the Chief Justice and was then an appointed secretary to the Prison Commission. After that, he often served as an Acting District Judge of Matara, for example, for about two months, or as an Acting Police Magistrate of Balapiti Modera. He died in France, at Hyere, in October 1897. His collection of manuscripts was about 2,227 palm manuscripts, and there were 932 poetical writings. Among them, 911 of them were published in three volumes in 1953 by P. E. P. Deraniyagala, the Director of National Museums, in Colombo. And they are in the Ceylon National Museums Manuscript Series.

who was a trained Indologist working in Ceylon for the British colonial powers, and his work is perhaps the most fruitful one in a historical perspective. Nevill collected ritual texts, many from the southern (Dondra) region and investigated their year of composition and their relation with wider South Asian literate traditions. His collection included about 931 ritual texts out of 2,227 palm-leaf manuscripts collected from various parts of Sri Lanka (Deraniyagala 1954, 1955; Kariyawasam 1989). Out of 931 manuscripts, for example, about 500 deal with the traditional rituals in which the various deities are praised and the demons propitiated. Some manuscripts describe various rituals which are unknown today[①].

3. The Focus

This paper examines possession of ritual knowledge particularly astrological ritual knowledge as Bali Tovil (planetary rituals) of traditional ritual specialists in low-country tradition in Southern Sri Lanka. The ethnographic data upon which this article is based was collected among the Berava or drummer caste in southern province of Sri Lanka and archival materials related to the subject under study. The drummer caste, although ranked low in the caste hierarchy, are nonetheless the carriers and custodians of a substantial body of ritual knowledge and skills based in their oral and palm-leaf traditions. This paper is focused on the oral and palm-leaf based knowledge mechanisms that enable groups of ritual specialists to come together to perform the highly elaborate rituals of exorcism and healing for which the south of the island is famous. The performance of such rituals sees the integration of an extraordinary range of knowledge and skills, including drumming, dancing, comic acting, sculpting, singing, recitation and drawing of yantra (amulets). I will give more information on this later. Crucial to this ritual tradition is the aspiration to reproduce acts, recitations, sequences and performances as faithfully as possible from occasion to occasion. There is also assumed repetition between rituals: a healing ritual performed today is believed to be essentially the same as the one performed last week and the week before. On a grander scale, repetition takes place across generations of ritual specialists, each bringing their knowledge and skills to bear in order to create the same ritually charged space at different points across time.

3.1 Sri Lankan Ritual Specialists (Aduro) and Their Knowledge and Skills in Manuscripts Traditions

The "Tovil system" makes reference to the southern traditions which include both

---

① The Colombo National Museum Library has an impressive collection of over 2,400 manuscripts, as well as a helpful catalogue. The University of Peradeniya Library also has a large collection, but it lacks a published catalogue.

the Yak Tovils: Mahasona, Samayama, Sanni Yakuma, Rata Yakuma and Maha Kalu Kumare Samayama as well as the Shanti Karmaya rites: Suniyama, Deva Tovil, Gammaduva, Gara Yakuma and the Bali Yage—as well as the less elaborate pidenis. The gods offered to in a Shanti Karmaya rite are superior to the demons and spirits in the Yak Tovils. Most of such traditional ritual practices in which the various deities are praised and the demons propitiated has been continued in both oral and manuscripts traditions in various rituals specialist's traditions in Sri Lanka. The traditions are perceived by the Aduro to have developed from the same source, the yage/homa sacrifice rituals of the Indian *Irsis* (seers) about 3000 years ago. The first yage/homa ritual was performed in Sri Lanka by visiting Indian Brahmins. In regard to ritual work, the traditions preserved by the Adura communities living in these regions have evolved in dialectics with distinct religious cults-social power centres. As Reed (2002) worked in Kandy and Simpson (1998) worked in Galle, their works reveal some interesting differences between the contemporary situation for the up-country and low-country traditions.

The Gurunanse or chief aduro (senior teachers) teach their students dance, songs, mask postures/dance, mantra, mask carving, acrobatics, drumming, Ayurvedic medicine, ritual decorations (gokkole), comedy dialogue, cosmology/the pantheon, diagnosis, astrological knowledge and curing procedures as well as all of the "guru mustis" teacher secrets. Such a vast verity of knowledge and skills were transmitted from generation to generation with the system of teacher-pupil relationships (Simpson 1997: 47) [1].

3.2 Manuscripts Traditions in Bali Tovil or Planetary Rituals

The belief in the good and evil influence of the planets according to the time and place of one's birth is quite widespread in Sri Lanka. The first thing done at the birth of a child is to cast the horoscope, which has to be consulted subsequently at all the important events of his or her life. When a calamity like a serious illness comes upon such a person, the horoscope would inevitably be consulted, and if the person is under a bad planetary influence, the astrologer would recommend some kind of propitiatory ritual (De Silva 2000; Kemper 1979, 1980). This could be a minor one like the lime cutting ritual (*dehi-käpīma*) or a major one like a *Bali* ceremony, depending on the seriousness of the case. If it is a *Bali* ceremony, he might also recommend the specific kind of Bali suitable for the occasion. Astrology is important for the Sri Lankans in any stage of life, and the Bali Tovil rituals

---

[1] Amongst the Berava ritual specialists there were formal systems of apprenticeship in which individuals claimed to have been taught by particular teachers (aduro). This relationship involved a period of residence for a boy in the teacher's house, a kinship connection with the teacher, an exchange of gifts and a life-long debt on the part of the pupil.

(planetary rituals)[①] are modelled on the basis of astrological knowledge of the powers of the planets' gods (De Silva 2000).

Bali Tovil or offering ceremonies performed to alleviate the misfortunes believed to arise as a result of passing through a bad astrological period or *apala kcālaya*, meaning literally "a fruitless period". The objective of these rituals is to bless and fortify an individual at a time when the auspicious protection of the planets is weak and vulnerability to malign influences is correspondingly high. The way this is achieved is through the making of numerous offerings to Buddha, deities and demons in the course of a night-long ceremony.

Most of the astrological knowledge of Bali Tovil traditions were drawn from traditional classical text books or manuscripts[②]. There are fifteen such texts listed here.

(1) *Yagalankaraya*

(2) *Rathnalankaraya*

(3) *Posijanalankaraya*

(4) *Somigunaalankaraya*

(5) *Chandralankaraya*

(6) *Mahabali nidhanaya*

(7) *Wessanthara Mangallaya* (folk-lore fiction)

(8) *Subhasiri Mangallaya*

(9) *Ranakekulu Mangallaya* (recently found in Hatharaliyadda)

(10) *Chandrawatharaya* (singing of lord Buddha)

(11) *Maha Sirasapadaya* (head to feet blessing poems)

(12) *Nawaguna Shanthiya* (blessing poems)

(13) *Maha Yamaka bandana Atakuru Sirasapadaya*

(14) *Lokarathna Malaya*

(15) *Daru Uthpaththiya* (Jinadasa 2009, 2010)

These text books were written in a mixture of Languages of Sinhala, Pali and more Sanskrit. According to the astrological explanation figure and formation of each Bali (figure) is described in the palm-leaf manuscript. These fifteenth-century compositions were often cited by informants as providing the model recitations upon which Bali Tovil, as they are performed today, are based.

[①] Bali is the ceremony wherein the presiding deities of the planets (*graha*) are invoked and placated in order to ward off their evil planetary influences. The belief in the good and evil influence of the planets according to the time and place of one's birth is quite widespread in Sri Lanka (De Silva 2000).

[②] The Bali Tovil is believed to have originated in North India at the time of the Buddha. The setting for the events that gave the ritual its genesis, as revealed by informants both in conversation and in the poems sung throughout the ritual, is the mythical city of Visāla Mahā Nuvara, the capital city of the Liccavi kings. Whatever the actual historical connections between the Bali and this particular place and time, the Bali is given a powerful legitimacy by the very fact of its location in an ancient and more established Buddhist mythological tradition (Simpson 2004).

In addition to that numerous amulets charts (yantras) and astrological signs are also drawn on it along with details of the person concerned. Yantra Drawings on palm leaves, which have traditionally been in the custody of ritual specialists known as kattadiralas/ aduro, have not been conserved by them with care, and our inheritance is fragmentary. The Aduro is a priest who practices rituals of healing and rituals of revenge, and is a folk artist as well who prepares yantras according to prescribed rules and consecrates him with prayers and magic in conditions (Paul Wirz 1954; G. Obeyesekere 1969, 1984; Kapferer 1983, 1997; David Scott 1994; De Silva 2000) The term "yantra" (amulet) is derived from the sanskrit "yantr", "to bind", from the root "yam", and is the general term for idols, figure drawings, pictures, or geometrical designs used in rituals. Models for yantras are in ancient palm-leaf manuscripts which belong to the tantric tradition. Some of these documents have been irretrievably lost. Some forms are undeciphered, some symbols are unrecognized and consequently some aesthetic and philosophic values remain uninterpreted.

According to Peiris (2018) the yantra drawing constitutes a unique artistic tradition. It is a confession of the frailty of the human condition and at the same time proof of man's readiness to defend himself; it is a testament of belief and like all ritual art, a manifestation of man's craving for the transcendent. There is a world view expressed in art, and yantra art is no exception. The drawings are linked to myths and through them to ancient astronomy, astrology, numerology and other occult arts which formed the system of metaphysical thought of the ancient and medieval world. Yantra drawings are charms used for protective and curative purposes and for soliciting boons. They are also used in sorcery (huniyam, kodivina), and anti-sorcery rites (Suniyama) for ritual specialists perform sorcery and claim to direct spirits to harm or destroy enemies or perform as a protective ritual (Kapferer 1997).

Yantras offer a variety of motifs and design elements. Ananda Coomaraswamy was of the view that Sinhala art showed more of the characteristics of early Indian art than did any Indian art surviving on the mainland of India at the beginning of the 19th century. He claimed to have identified several archaic design elements in Sinhala art related to the Egyptian, Assyrian and Hellenistic elements of very early Indian art. He also identified certain other elements which he thought might have been derived from the art of the pre-Sinhala inhabitants of the island. Some of the design elements in the yantras may well be indigenous to Sri Lanka, but only future comparative research will be able to establish this [Coomaraswamy 2003 (1907)]. The illustrated palm-leaf manuscripts of ritual priests may contain useful information on this aspect, as some rituals originated in very early times. The most likely areas for fruitful investigation will be representations of clay images, leaf altars and leaf screens which are lineal descendants of the earliest forms of iconography and ritual decoration used in the remote past. These were used chiefly in the conciliation of arboreal deities in vegetative fertility rites.

According to Peiris (2018), although we borrowed many cultural elements from India, they were changed in the process of adaptation and reinterpreted. Some fragmented figures are suggestive of surrealism with its exploration of the irrational, the unconscious and the dream. Distortion and other expressionist traits are prominent. The drawings belonging to this category work at the subconscious level and have the power to surprise and disturb. Some forms look like psychotic art, the products of fractured states of mental health. The artist has created his own universe when he competed with reality in his depiction of man's struggle against death.

Apart from palm-leaf drawings as I also discussed previously there are ritual poems written in palm-leaf tradition and such poems were ritually chanted in the Bali Tovil system in Sri Lanka (De Silva 2000). According to Kapferer (1983) there are five different kinds of kavis (poems) used during the rituals: "the Asirivada kavi, which relates aspects of the myth's relation to the demons and praises their powers and also the powers of the deities; the Ambun kavi, which tells how the offering baskets and other ritual structures are made; the Yadini kavi, which is basically similar to the Asirivada kavi, and which tells of the ancestry and origin of the demons; the Atacona kavi, which calls the demons from the eight directions; and the Sirasapada (head to foot) kavi, which is principally curative and is sung to remove the illness from the patient" (Kapferer 1983: 198). The kannalauva (summoning verses) shares the positive protective quality of set kavis-verses of blessing. Kannalauva (summoning verses) addresses super-naturals dwelling in "other worlds" and is performed with the purpose of attracting their attention. It should be noted that kannalauva verses are frequently recited at the start of any offering act of the Tovil rite as before presenting the offering one must have attracted the super-naturals' attention. In the poems and songs recited throughout the rituals of Bali Tovil and healing performed in southern Sri Lanka, descriptions of the objects passed on by the gods to the ancient sages (*reśi*) are given such as the golden rice pounders, the jewelled cockerels, and the drums sixteen miles long. Needless to say, rituals performed using the more earthly counterparts of these objects are not quite as efficacious as the incredible events upon which they were founded.

The extensive details concerning preparations, construction of offerings trays and the manner of performance of the ritual is given in fifteen ritual texts that I have listed before. Crucial in this respect is the centerpiece of Bali rituals, a floral altar (*mal baliya*) containing 9, 25 or 81 squares, into which offerings are placed for the planets and various other deities and demons. For example: Hugh Nevill collections of (1956) *Sinhala kavi*

Vols I , II & III Colombo National Museum using a translation of a poem he claimed to be in excess of 200 years old palm-leaf manuscript, provides us with the following description: The altar was made of plantain stems, a cubit and four finger widths square, and a square enclosure made around it. Nine kinds of leaves, rice of nine colours, nine kinds of flowers, betel, and nine offerings were taken for the offering. The nine coloured rice is for the twelve rasi or zodiacal signs, and the colours are red, white, yellow, smoke or grey, black, blue, golden and blue-black. The offerings for the planets are to be placed in their special directions, etc.

Careful and detailed prescriptions such as these are the ones believed to have been formulated by the sages in ancient India. With divine inspiration, the *rei*—also referred to as Brahmins (*bamuno*) and "the ancient teachers" (*poranäduro*)—first made these offerings and passed the instructions on to their descendants as a means of combatting affliction. The stories related above refer to the origin of the floral altar (*mal baliya*). However, there is another set of stories that tell of the origin of the clay images constructed in many of the larger Bali ceremonies. By following the instructions of the sages as they are believed to have come down in poems and stories transmitted primarily in an oral mode and then palm-leaf written mode, it is believed that victims in the present can be cured.

4. Conclusion

Palm leaves are one of the earliest forms of writing media in the world, used for over two thousand years with the earliest known palm-leaf manuscript written in 5th century BC. These manuscripts are found primarily in South and Southeast Asia, including South India, Nepal, Sri Lanka, Myanmar, Thailand, Indonesia, and Cambodia, where they serve not only as vehicles of textual information, but also as art, protective charms, religious offerings, gifts, and objects of worship. Though a large number of palm-leaf manuscripts are religious and ritual texts, they also cover subjects ranging from astronomy, art and architecture, to medicine and mathematics, etc. The production of palm-leaf manuscripts rose as written text came to slowly replace oral tradition around the 5th century, but rapidly declined from the 18th century onwards as handmade paper succeeded palm-leaf as a writing medium. Wider use of the printing press in the 19th century rendered the transcriptions almost obsolete. Palm-leaf manuscripts, although no longer commonly produced, continue to play an active role in shaping contemporary history and culture and reveal important information about cultures and religions of the Sri Lanka past. The existence of palm-leaf manuscripts has brought significant insight into the cultural, religious, political, and intellectual histories of Sri Lanka, and is an invaluable product of our history and preservation of such knowledge must be putting into place without much delay.

This paper has investigated the nature of ritual knowledge and skill presented in palm-leaf tradition in Sri Lanka, particularly traditions that preserve among the people belong not to the great tradition but the little or subaltern tradition. Contemporary ritual performers or aduro claim legitimacy by having been taught by particular teachers who in turn were taught by particular named teachers such that a performer's knowledge and skills can be traced back in the form of a line or pedigree referred to as a *paramparāva*. In such a formulation, ritual performance is apt to take on the character of a kaleidoscope with varying levels of knowledge, skill and competence being brought together to create distinctive ritual tradition in country like Sri Lanka.

References

[1] Coomaraswamy, Ananda K. Mediaeval Sinhalese Art. New York: Pantheon, 1956.

[2] Deraniyagala, P.E.P. Sinhala verse: (Kavi) Ceylon National Museums manuscript series: Ethnology Volumes 4-5 of Manuscript series, Ceylon Department of National Museums Part 1 of Sinhala verse: Ceylon. Department of National Museums, 1954.

[3] De Silva, Premakumara. Globalisation and the Transformation of Planetary Rituals in Southern Sri Lanka International Centre for Ethnic Studies. Colombo, 2000.

[4] Godakumbera, C. E. Sinhalese Literature. Colombo: Apothecaries. 1955.

[5] Kapferer, Bruce. The Feast of the Sorcerer: Practices of Consciousness and Power. Chicago: University of Chicago Press, 1997.

[6] Kapferer Bruce. A Celebration of Demons. Bloomington: Indiana University Press, 1983.

[7] Pieris L. S. D. Yantra Drawings on Palm Leaf. Sri Lanka: The National Trust, 2018.

[8] Obeyesekere, Gananath. Boundary Books and Immigration Myths: The Work of Topographia in Kandy Period Palm Leaf Manuscripts // Home and the World: Essays in Honour of Sarath Amunugama. Colombo: Siripa Publishers, 2010.

[9] Jinadasa, M. P. K. Bali Abum Kavi Potha-2 (Book of the Traditional Lyrics that Explain the Methods of Creating Bali Figures-02). Colombo: Godage & Brothers Publishers, 2009.

[10] Jinadasa, M. P. K. Bali Abum Kavi Potha-1 (Book of the Traditional Lyrics that Explain the Methods of Creating Bali Figures-01). Colombo: Godage & Brothers Publishers, 2010a.

[11] Simpson, B. On the Impossibility of Invariant Repetition: Ritual Tradition and

Creativity among Sri Lankan Ritual Specialists. Anthropology and History, 2014, 13 (3).

[12] Somadasa, K.D. Catalogue of the Hugh Nevill Collection of Sinhalese Manuscripts in the British Library. London: The British Library, 1987–1995. 7 vols Wirz P. Exorcism and the Art of Healing in Ceylon E.J. Brill, Leiden, 1954.

Some Observations of the Inheritance and Protection of Tai Buddhist Manuscript Cultures [1]

David Wharton [2]

1. The Ongoing Crisis and Disappearance of Tai Manuscript Cultures

Tai manuscript cultures have been in decline since the first half of the 20th century and are now facing an existential crisis. It is unlikely that most will survive for another generation except amongst the Shan, where there is currently a grassroots movement for their preservation and revival, and other smaller Tai ethnic groups for whom manuscript traditions are still an important feature of their cultural identity. For the majority of Tai communities, and certainly within Thailand and Laos, this is no longer the case [3], and it is likely that their manuscript cultures will disappear and that the manuscripts which do survive will be in major collections such as national or university libraries rather than in Buddhist temples.

During my training as a monk in the Thai forest tradition, I was taught to respect Dhamma books by not placing them on the floor but always in an elevated position. Today we routinely see jumbled piles of manuscripts which have been discarded on the dusty floors of temples as though they are rubbish. It is shameful that this cultural heritage which has been handed down for generations is now treated with such disrespect, but to witness such a lack of respect for the written teachings of the Buddha by monks living within temples throughout the region is truly disgraceful. It is an unfortunate sign of the systemic ignorance and neglect of what was once a fundamental and revered feature of Tai cultures. I often hear lame excuses for this, such as "well, the monks can no longer read the manuscripts", but there are no good excuses for this situation. The bottom line is that we should be doing better. On the

---

[1] This written paper elaborates on themes presented as one of the keynote speeches at the "International Seminar on the Inheritance and Protection of Palm-Leaf Culture in China, Southeast Asia and South Asia" held at Yunnan University, 15–18 November 2019.

[2] Research Associate, École française d'Extrême-Orient.

[3] There are, of course, counter examples where manuscript cultures continue under local leadership, but I am speaking here of the overall picture throughout the Tai societies of the region.

whole, the monks and lay people who are the primary local custodians of Tai manuscript collections are failing miserably and we are ignoring the consequences.

This stark assessment comes from over 15 years of experience working with Tai manuscript collections in Laos, Northern Thailand, Northern Myanmar and Southwest China, while based at the National Library of Laos and through my doctoral studies at the University of Passau. The invaluable work of previous large-scale survey projects, such as in Northern Thailand and Laos [1], can also be used as a baseline to assess the extent of manuscript degradation and loss over the intervening years. I will take Northern Thailand as the main example here, since it is the area of which I have the most first-hand experience and for which Chiang Mai University's Preservation of Northern Thai Manuscripts Project (1987–1991) catalogued the manuscript holdings of approximately 120 temples. Of these, during numerous field visits undertaken from 2013 onwards, I've witnessed whole collections which have been lost due to fire or water damage, collections which have been almost entirely eaten by termites, badly damaged by rodents, covered in dust and the excrement of birds or bats or rats, and which have simply "disappeared" with apparently no knowledge amongst local monks and lay people of how this took place. And of course there is also considerable trade in manuscripts, and I've visited a temple where a monk sold the manuscripts and the chests and then ran away when the local lay people informed the police. I estimate that up to 50% of the manuscripts catalogued in Northern Thailand during previous surveys may have been lost over the past 30 years [2], and this trend is continuing apace. I've recently heard reports of entire manuscript collections in both Northern Thailand and Laos which were stolen, and the manuscripts thrown away by the roadside because the thieves were only interested in selling the storage chests. And in late 2019 we discovered that the entire manuscript collection of a large temple in Vientiane had simply "disappeared". The list is endless, and this invaluable feature of Tai cultural heritage is being decimated.

This is not meant as a criticism of previous preservation projects. On the contrary, they were very successful and have been rightly praised. But the reality is that no externally funded project with a limited timeframe is able to provide a sustainable long-term solution to this crisis [3]. It is also an unintended and unforeseen outcome of the policy of leaving manuscripts *in situ* and of not removing them for safekeeping even when the signs are that

---

[1] Of these, Chiang Mai University's Preservation of Northern Thai Manuscripts Project (1987–1991) and the National Library of Laos' Preservation of Lao Manuscripts Programme (1992–2004) are the largest.

[2] The true figure will only be known once a thorough survey is undertaken using the previous records as a baseline. I hope that my estimate is incorrect and that the true figure is less, but this is my honest assessment based on visits to many temples in each of the eight northernmost provinces of Thailand over a number of years. In Laos we have been attempting to secure funding for several years now in order to begin a systematic re-survey of collections catalogued during the 1990s which would reveal the extent of such losses.

[3] That is, unless it were a project to simply collect manuscripts for safekeeping elsewhere, which is not being proposed here and would in any case only hasten the disappearance of local manuscript cultures. See below for further discussion of this option.

they will not be protected locally.

2. The Urgent Need to Work on "Manuscript Cultures" Rather Than "Manuscripts"

I'm encouraged by the fact that the title of this seminar is about "manuscript cultures" rather than only "manuscripts". By this I mean everything from the making of the palm-leaf or paper supports to the production and use of manuscripts, including traditional recitation styles, etc. Manuscript cultures throughout the region have been threatened in many ways over a number of decades now, which has led to a lack of transmission of their scribal cultures. In fact, this process began with the introduction of the printed book, long before access to modern electronic media such as television and the Internet, which have only accelerated the decline. In some areas traditional scripts have also been reformed for modern use, which has had an added negative impact on traditional manuscript use. So it is important to remember that local cultures themselves, of which manuscripts are one component, are in crisis, and this directly results in the kind of neglect described above. Of course, these are forces which are beyond our control, and no one I know is suggesting that we all go back to the days of listening to manuscript recitation instead of using the Internet. But it is an unfair competition, and one which local manuscript cultures are losing.

For many years now there have been projects to survey, catalogue, and to digitise manuscripts, but the related cultures of which they are a part receive little attention. Meanwhile, local manuscript cultures are disappearing even faster than the manuscripts themselves. They are also the only way we can truly understand the manuscripts from a local perspective. So are there ways to maintain and promote manuscript cultures? Or at least to document them before they disappear, in addition to digitising manuscripts?

Much of my own work at the National Library of Laos has also focused on the digitisation of large monastic manuscript collections and in making them available online through digital libraries. But at the same time, I've been personally making audio recordings of manuscript recitation over the past decade and have been designing projects to integrate audio and audio-visual documentation of traditional recitation and other aspects of manuscript cultures with the vision of developing online repositories of manuscript cultures rather than of manuscripts alone. In addition to safeguarding a digital record of endangered manuscript cultures, the results can be used in the teaching and study of these traditional knowledge and skills. In addition, the pre-modern scripts found in many online manuscript collections are no longer in everyday use and allowing users to listen to a recording while viewing the digital images will greatly assist in the study of the texts and in learning to read the scripts. I am convinced that we are missing an invaluable opportunity every time a project is designed or funded to only digitise manuscripts, often involving significant travel and meetings with local resource persons whose knowledge of, and skill in reading, the manuscripts is left undocumented. So while manuscript digitisation is very valuable, I strongly recommend that manuscript cultures should be an integral part of such projects.

3. Whose inheritance is this?

The title of this seminar is about the "inheritance and protection" of manuscript cultures, which begs the question: "whose inheritance is this?" Tai manuscript cultures have been maintained by many generations of local scholars and scribes, monastic and lay, over the past 500–600 years, but as outlined above this is largely no longer the case. This lack of local care and responsibility makes a huge difference to the survival or not of countless manuscript collections and their related cultures. So who has inherited them? Some of course are in private possession, and they are inherited by younger generations within a family who sometimes take good care of them but quite often have no interest. In such cases, the new owners are apparently free to do as they wish with them, which may include their intentional destruction, sale, or simply allowing them to decay through neglect. There may be laws on the protection of cultural heritage under which such private items are also covered, but it appears that they are rarely if ever enforced in such cases. The situation should be very different, of course, in temple collections, where the monks are the custodians (but not the owners) of the manuscripts. This is significant, because they do not have the right to sell or destroy the manuscripts in their temples. But at the same time the responsibility of monks to take care of manuscripts in their temple repositories is not clearly defined or implemented, and there are once again no consequences for those who neglect the manuscripts to the point that they are destroyed. This is an unfortunate situation, since strong leadership from monks in caring for manuscripts makes a huge difference to their survival. However, in many cases today, monks cannot take care of their temples in general, never mind manuscript collections which they never use and for which they have apparently no interest or respect.

Other stakeholders include government ministries and departments responsible for cultural heritage, national and local libraries, universities, and of course international projects who wish to digitise manuscripts for their overseas online collections, often without any attempt to address such local issues. The fundamental problem here is that in fact no one is taking responsibility. And of course, to be fair, no one has asked the local custodians such as monks and lay temple officials to formally agree to take care of the manuscripts under their care. They have inherited these collections as part of the contents of their local temples, but without any explicit understanding of what this entails or the knowledge required to take responsibility for them. Some manuscript preservation programmes have made efforts to train local monastics and lay people, but the results have mostly been short-lived and there is no institutional memory or apparatus for sustaining such work.

4. What does "protection" mean in this context?

The word "protection" also appears in the title of this seminar, but what does it mean in this context? What or who are we protecting the manuscripts from? Does protection mean conservation and preservation work so that manuscripts are stored safely? Unfortunately, as outlines above, this is an ongoing task rather than something that is undertaken during a limited project timeframe and then "completed". It is never completed. Even where there have been successful large-scale, long-term manuscript preservation programmes such as in Northern Thailand and in Laos, the funding comes to an end and so does the work. When we evaluate their success in the long-term, it becomes clear that even though they achieved a great deal, they can only temporarily alleviate the need for an ongoing commitment. I've visited a number of repositories where with good intentions the local custodians thought the best way to protect manuscripts was to lock the repository doors, only to discover years later that most of the collection had been eaten by termites.

So what should be done when local monks or lay owners either do not (or do not know how to) take care of manuscripts in their custodianship? The policy in Northern Thailand and Laos to never remove manuscripts from their locations and to train local custodians in manuscript preservation was a very good one at the time, but over the past 25–30 years there has been a generational change in the custodians who were trained, and thousands of manuscripts have been lost. I am doubtful whether any amount of additional training would help in many of the temples I have visited. But then what is to be done when local monks and lay temple officials are complicit in the loss of manuscripts through neglect? By and large this question is completely ignored and yet it is the main cause of manuscript degradation and loss. So are there situations where manuscripts should be removed and placed in the care of other custodians (perhaps in the closest collection which is well-maintained)? There are no easy answers to these questions, but they do need to be considered if we are to attempt to stem the tide of manuscript loss. Unfortunately, this situation is compounded by the general shift in funding opportunities over the past 15 years in favour of low-level funding for externally led manuscript digitisation and away from support for local institutions engaged in long-term preservation work, which means that even periodic external interventions are no longer possible.

5. A Comprehensive Model for Future Preservation Efforts

There is no easy answer to the questions raised above and local solutions will need to be sought within their own contexts. But there are some key lessons and features which may help future preservation and documentation efforts to be more comprehensive.

Firstly, we must stop thinking within only the narrow scope of manuscript digitisation and broaden our efforts to include manuscript cultures. We have to realise that the manuscripts are a part of rich local intangible cultures which are disappearing even faster than the manuscripts themselves. When working in the field, such documentation is very rewarding and much more interesting than the monotonous triggering of camera shutters to digitise thousands of frames of manuscript images. It is also essential to enrich our understanding of the manuscripts themselves and to document their recitation styles, etc. And yet it is not a component of the vast majority of manuscript digitisation projects.

Secondly, the widespread surveying and cataloguing of manuscript cultures is a potentially important tool in their preservation, ideally as national or provincial databases maintained by institutions such as national libraries. Without such records we have no way of knowing what is endangered or lost, and no foundation for taking appropriate action. The National Library of Laos, for example, plans to re-survey manuscript collections throughout the country using existing catalogues (of some 86,000 manuscripts) from 25 years ago as a baseline in order to reveal the extent of manuscript loss over this period. The existing catalogues are limited to manuscript collections, but the new data will be part of a more comprehensive "national database of manuscript cultures". This will build on the existing manuscript catalogue data to include conservation and preservation data (including issues that need to be addressed, and dated photographic record of storage conditions, causes of the causes of manuscript degradation and loss, etc.), records of microfilming or digitisation, records of where manuscripts are still produced and recited, and contact details of local resource persons. Large-scale manuscript surveys have also been conducted for Tai manuscripts in Northern Thailand, in Yunnan province, China, and are currently ongoing for Tai manuscripts in Shan State, Myanmar. These could be used in similar ways to record and to help efforts to safeguard manuscript cultures for future generations, and to promote their study.

Thirdly, we should re-assess our reliance upon external funding for projects with limited timeframes. Over the past four years, I've witnessed a very different approach in Shan State, Myanmar, where there is a network of monks and scribes who are working on manuscript survey, cataloguing, and preservation, but without such external project funds. This is taking place because it is led by highly respected senior monks which inspire respect and pride in Shan manuscript culture as well as the required financial and volunteer support. Although I greatly admire this model, I'm told that there is little chance of its success elsewhere, and in fact I don't know of any senior monks outside of the Shan State who have taken a similar interest in their manuscript cultures. At the same time, it has to be acknowledged that in some countries there are very wealthy temples and if a fraction of their funds could be used for such work—and remember the manuscripts are largely stored within the temples too—then it could be very beneficial. In the past, similar local movements to revitalise manuscript cultures have been successful in parts of Northern Thailand and elsewhere in the region, but the current trend is to depend upon external funding for time bound projects and with very little involvement from local temple communities. Even though it may not be possible on a large scale, I'd like to hope that there may still be some monks and some temples where there is an interest, and which could be encouraged and supported to protect manuscripts and to promote manuscript cultures. But this will not be widespread and will of course depend upon the continued leadership of such monks. Otherwise, any comprehensive efforts will require collaboration between local custodians and national or provincial institutions (such as government departments, national libraries, and universities) with long-term commitments and the internal resources for large-scale management of programmes for the preservation of manuscript cultures. This is in contrast to the current trend to fund only small external projects to digitise manuscripts for online collections overseas, which when witnessed from within Southeast Asia often appears counter-productive to the longer-term preservation of local manuscript cultures which needs to be undertaken by local institutes with a long-term commitment on the ground.

Lastly, we must also answer the questions: who are the custodians of the manuscripts? What are their responsibilities? This also entails addressing the dilemma of whether *in situ* preservation is viable in cases where the neglect of local custodians is leading to the loss of manuscripts. This is not easy, since *in situ* preservation must always be the first option, but experience over the past 30 years has shown that in many cases it has failed and will continue to fail. A related question then is who will make such decisions? Hopefully hard evidence from surveys revealing the extent of manuscript loss (such as planned in Laos) will stimulate renewed national-level debate of policies and practices for the future preservation of Tai manuscript cultures.

6. Conclusion

The above description of the crisis facing Tai manuscript cultures does not make for pleasant reading. But I strongly feel that we need to raise awareness of its severity and the urgent need to act if we are to address it. We may then make an informed decision as to the best way to proceed. It seems inevitable that the Tai manuscript cultures of the region will be largely lost within this generation or the next, except in isolated cases. Perhaps the best we can do is therefore to focus preservation efforts on such cases where there is a good prospect of survival (as in Shan State and elsewhere), and to do the best we can to document other manuscript cultures through manuscript digitisation and audio-visual recordings while the opportunity still remains. The current efforts led by overseas funding and institutions, mostly focused on small-scale manuscript digitisation for their online collections, are not designed for and do not claim to be addressing this crisis. There are no easy answers, and they will be different for different local contexts. But if we choose not to act and simply let the current trend of neglect take its course, then within a generation there will be no more opportunities to do so. I hope that this paper will serve to stimulate reflection about this precious inheritance and our collaborative action to protect and preserve it.

An Overview of the International Seminar on the Inheritance & Protection of Palm-Leaf Culture in China, Southeast Asia and South Asia

Han Shuai[①]

The International Seminar on the Inheritance & Protection of Palm-Leaf Culture in China, Southeast Asia and South Asia was held at the Science Museum of Donglu Campus of Yunnan University on November 16–18, 2019. It was sponsored by the Research Institute of Development of Yunnan University, the Office of Arts and Culture of Chiang Mai Rajabhat University, Thailand and the PLCRC (Palm-Leaf Culture Research Center, Yunnan University).

The meeting consists of the keynote speeches and the exchange speeches. On the morning of the 16th, Prof. Premakumara de Silva from the School of Social Sciences of University of Colombo; Professor Dai Hongliang of Minzu University of China; Dr. David Wharton, Project Manager of the Palm-Leaf Manuscripts Digital Library of the Lao National Library; Ven. Dr. Prof. Dhammajothi Thero, head of the Department of Buddhism and Dean of the Confucius Institute of University of Colombo, Sri Lanka; Professor Guo Shan, Vice Dean of the Institute of Development, Yunnan University; Dr. Direk Injan, Director of Palm-Leaf Manuscripts Research Center of Chiang Mai Rajabhat University, Thailand; and Dr. Zhou Ya, Associate researcher and Director of Palm-Leaf Culture Research Center of Yunnan University, delivered keynote speeches. In addition, two exchange speeches were held during the two days, and 26 conference papers were discussed focusing on the topics of the meeting. This seminar makes an in-depth exchange and discussion on the historical origin and present situation of palm-leaf culture, the modern value of palm-leaf cultural heritage, the inheritance and protection of the production skills of palm-leaf manuscripts, the digital arrangement and protection of palm-leaf classics and the practice

---

[①] Master degree candidate of Religion, School of Ethnology and Sociology, Yunnan University.

of inheritance and protection of palm-leaf culture in China, Southeast Asia and South Asian countries.

1. The Historical Origin and Present Situation of Palm-Leaf Culture

Prof. Premakumara de Silva, School of Social Sciences, University of Colombo, Sri Lanka, delivered the first keynote speech of the seminar. He pointed out that the long traditions and traditional knowledge of indigenous people were first preserved through oral traditions on the island of Sri Lanka. The tradition of palm-leaf manuscripts is used to record traditional knowledge and to guide ancient societies on how to make use of this knowledge. Sri Lanka and most countries in South Asia have widely spread palm-leaf manuscripts culture, which goes beyond the scope of traditional writing materials. Puskola poth is still the main writing material for all South Asian countries dating back to the 5th century BC.

Dr. David Wharton, Project Manager of the Palm-Leaf Manuscripts Digital Library of the Laos National Library, introduced the unique expression of pre-modern, local Dai Buddhist culture and manuscripts preserved by some Tai language groups he found in Yunnan of China, Myanmar and northeast India. At present, the ancient traditional spelling is mostly used in the increasingly endangered manuscripts and is still exclusive to a small number of professional scribes. These groups have received little attention in the study of Dai culture and language and are basically unknown in the field of Buddhism, so there is an urgent need to examine and record their endangered culture and skills.

Ven. Dr. Prof. Dhammajothi Thero, dean of the Confucius Institute and head of the Department of Buddhism at University of Colombo in Sri Lanka, pointed out that ancient manuscripts are one of the most important legacies that human beings have received from their ancestors. As a member of humanity, it is the responsibility of the people of all countries to regard ancient manuscripts as important documents, as they record the various and long journeys that people have experienced before reaching their current state of life. These manuscripts truly depict the beneficial and catastrophic changes brought about by different countries. Therefore, these resources serve as the treasure trove of information and the source of inspiration to learn from the experiences of our ancestors, to gain insights and to prepare for the path to a better future. At present, the main goal is to better maintain and preserve them and to make them more accessible to researchers.

Dr. Direk Injan, Director of the Palm-Leaf Manuscripts Research Center of Chiang Mai Rajabhat University, introduced his research on the palm-leaf manuscripts, paper manuscripts and inscriptions of the Chiang Mai Temple in Muang District, Chiang Mai. The research shows that many important and interesting materials are recorded in 1835 bundles of palm-leaf manuscripts, 33 paper manuscripts and 4 inscriptions, such as the the list of temples in the ancient city of Chiang Mai (1873), the important historical events of Chiang Mai area and Chiang Mai Temple (1296–1891) and so on. These original historical materials can not only be used to enrich the history of local tourism, but also can be used to raise public awareness of the literature itself.

2. The Practice of Inheritance and Protection of Palm-Leaf Culture in China, Southeast Asia and South Asia

Dr. Zhou Ya, director and associate researcher of the Palm-Leaf Culture Research Center of Yunnan University, put forward that the practical types of protection of this cultural heritage in China include formal protection, inheritance protection, institutional protection and research protection, and these protections have made some achievements. However, due to the constraints of many practical conditions, the practical results in the scope of protection, awareness of protection, protection cooperation and technical means of protection are still very limited. It is suggested that we should carry out regional international cooperation in the protection of the palm-leaf scriptures in Pali language family and inheritance in palm-leaf culture, promote the establishment of relevant regional linkage mechanisms and take specific measures such as multinational joint declaration of World Memory Heritage. We should jointly promote the inheritance and protection of this precious regional human resource in contemporary China, Southeast Asia and South Asia.

Associate Prof. Zhou Hanli of Pu'er College, who is also a doctoral student at the University of Hamburg in Germany, shared with us about the DREAMSEA project, the Digital Repository of Endangered and Affected Manuscripts in Southeast Asia. The project mainly rescues manuscripts preserved in folk and religious places and does not involve government or institutional collections. At present, the project has successfully completed the digital storage of 42,131 frames of 963 manuscripts from six regions of the island country and one continental country (Laos). The project plans to complete the digital storage of 240,000 pages by 2022. Through a comprehensive introduction of the project and combing its actual operation in the process of cultural protection of manuscripts, it can provide a good reference for us in the cultural protection of manuscripts in the future.

Dr. Assoc. Prof. Apiradee Techasiriwan, Chiang Mai University pointed out that a large number of Dai manuscripts were destroyed due to special historical reasons in the 1960s and 1970s. Since the early 1980s, the Chinese government and local Dai scholars have been working together to revive the culture of Dai and its manuscripts. China has a great influence on the traditional Dai manuscripts, which is obviously reflected in the influence of printing technology and modern printing style on Dai manuscripts. With these influencing factors, the supporting points, materials, format and production of Dai manuscript writing are all changing and developing.

Dr. Wimal Hewamanage from University of Colombo in Sri Lanka introduced the application of palm leaves in Sri Lanka. He reveals how Buddhism enriches Sri Lankan palm-leaf culture through qualitative and quantitative data centering on Buddhism. Palm leaves are widely used in daily Buddhist activities in Sri Lanka. it is not only used as writing material, but also used in roof covering, umbrella making and so on.

Mr. Zhang Hai, director of the Film and Television Anthropology Laboratory of the School of Ethnology and Sociology of Yunnan University, shared with us his valuable experience in trying to use images to write the making skills and belief significance of the palm-leaf manuscripts. He used images to explore and record the protection, dissemination and inheritance of local palm-leaf manuscripts culture, trying to find similarities and differences in the images, so as to provide more intuitive and concrete research materials for the future cultural exchanges between the two countries.

Zhang Yun, associate researcher librarian of Dehong Prefecture Library, shared with us the relevant situation of the protection and development of Dehong Dai ancient books. She discussed the importance of the project and introduced the Dehong Dai ancient books from 6 aspects: the historical and cultural process; the basic situation; the contents and classifications; the translation and studies; the inheritance, collection and the problems in research; and transformation of the research results of Dai ancient books.

Mrs. Yu Hanwei from Xishuangbanna Library pointed out that the Dai people live across borders, and the protection of Dai ancient books is also a kind of inheritance of Chinese civilization, which also promotes the connection between the hearts and minds of the people of The Belt and Road Initiative and brings cultural identity. The Dai people in Southeast Asian countries have a large population, a wide distribution area and a large border area with China. How to protect Dai ancient books and promote the construction of The Belt and Road Initiative is a new proposition that we are faced with. There is a deep relationship between Dai ancient books and Dai culture in Southeast Asia. The restoration of Dai ancient books is an important work that contributes to the present age and benefits for a thousand years.

Ms. Yu Nanjiao from Xishuangbanna Comprehensive Information Office introduced to us the current situation of Corypha umbraculifera, an important carrier of the formation of palm-leaf culture in Xishuangbanna. As Corypha umbraculifera has certain requirements for breeding environment and cultivation techniques, Corypha umbraculifera in Xishuangbanna area is gradually decreasing and is facing the danger of extinction. Corypha umbraculifera is in urgent need of protection.

3. Modern Value of Palm-Leaf Cultural Heritage

Dr. & Prof. Guo Shan, deputy dean of the Institute of Development of Yunnan University, shared that we can see that the palm-leaf manuscripts appear frequently in the daily life of the Dai people, especially in the rituals involving life events (such as birth, aging, sickness and death, etc.) through the field investigation on the stock, structure, source and use of the palm-leaf manuscripts in the Buddhist temple of the Dai village M in Xishuangbanna. Although ordinary Dai people cannot read the palm-leaf manuscripts, it is still a good medicine to nourish the soul and settle down in the eyes of the Dai people.

Dr. Tian Yuling, associate professor of Kunming College, pointed out that Buddhist stories are an important part of Theravada Buddhism classics. It is very necessary and urgent to deeply study and excavate the connotation of Buddhist stories and to re-recognize its contemporary value, in order to spread to more people a rational, self-disciplined and harmonious way of work and life, integrate with the requirements of the harmonious development of the times and let the Buddhist concept play its due role in the contemporary society.

Ms. Fan Lijiao, a master's degree student of Yunnan Minzu University, introduced from the text that there are some scriptures on ecology and nature protection in the palm-leaf manuscripts of the Dai in Xishuangbanna, which play a positive role and influence the harmonious ecological view of the Dai area. She focus on the ecological and cultural connotation of the palm-leaf manuscripts and its influence on the ecological protection of the Dai area, and analyzes the concept of ecological protection, as well as its modern significance and the important historical role of keeping pace with the times.

Ms. Yu Nanha, School of Dai Medicine, West Yunnan University of Applied Technology, introduced the work done by the School of Dai Medicine in West Yunnan University of Applied Technology in the inheritance of Dai medicine. It also included the construction of the platform combined with college training and teacher education. They train Dai medicine inheritors and organize, translate, develop, and clinical research the ancient texts together with the efforts of folk Dai doctors, college teachers, clinical experts and other mentors.

Mr. Ai-Wen Zaixiang, a doctoral student at Beijing Normal University, believes that the two-way communication between Theravada Buddhism and Pali palm-leaf culture can strengthen the cultural exchange and interaction of the Dai-Tai ethnic groups and promote people's connection and cultural integration of The Belt and Road Initiative, so as to strengthen the sense of cultural identity of cross-border ethnic groups.

Dr. Zhang Zhenwei, associate researcher from the School of Ethnology and Sociology of

Yunnan University, introduced several representative protection and research institutions, such as the Palm-Leaf Culture Research Center of Yunnan University, and then points out that different sects and research institutions should give full play to their own role in the process of research and protection. They should cooperate with each other, participate together, and finally realize the coordinated development of palm-leaf manuscripts research.

4. Others

Dr. & Professor Dai Hongliang from Minzu University of China analyzed the interpretation and correspondence of two Pali forms in Dai ancient books taking the interpretation of Pali in *Visandra* as an example. Generally speaking, the recognition of Pali in Dai ancient books mainly has the following problems. First of all, the research foundation is weak and there is no suitable Dai Pali dictionary, so it is necessary to use Pali dictionaries of other languages as an important auxiliary tool. Secondly, when use Dai language to transliterate Pali language, it uses complex rules of transliteration. Even one-to-one corresponding loanwords also need some knowledge of transliteration. More importantly, many loanwords adopt special rules of transliteration, which makes the corresponding relationship between the two not obvious. Thirdly, many praises have been misread, miswritten and miscopied in spoken Language, which makes it more difficult to read Pali. Fourthly, there is a lack of comprehensive talents, and the reading of Pali in Dai ancient books requires experts to understand Pali, ancient Dai, Burmese and Thai, but this kind of multilingual talents are difficult to cultivate and need to be carried out by special institutions for a long time. The recognition of Pali language in Dai ancient books is not only related to the quality and research level of Dai ancient books, but also related to the depth and breadth of understanding of palm-leaf culture, which is a problem that must be dealt with. His paper also puts forward a number of suggestions, hoping to jointly promote the progress of this work.

Dr. Bao Mingsuo, Associate Professor of School of Arts, Yunnan University, discussed the non-standard phenomenon of phonetic translation in the *Journey of Buddha* based on the self-built full-text lexical corpus. His paper first analyzes the three main types of non-standard transliteration words: the non-standard use of Chinese characters, the non-correspondence between transliteration proper names and Chinese proper names, and the coexistence of transliteration and free translation. Then it discusses the main reasons for the irregularities: ① the achievements of collective translation; ② the lack of large bilingual dictionaries that can be consulted; ③ the poor communication of Buddhist words in Dai and Chinese language systems; ④ the lack of standard standards for transliterated words. Finally, the paper puts forward some strategies to solve the non-standard phenomenon of transliterated words: ① unifying the writing form of transliterated words; ② adopting free translation as far as possible; ③ compiling a dictionary of palm-leaf manuscripts.

Mr. Kang Nanshan, vice president of the Buddhist Association of Yunnan Province, introduced two languages that are very important to the Dai people—the new Dai script and the old Dai script—by analyzing the process of the introduction of the Theravada Buddhism palm-leaf manuscripts into our country. At the same time, the production process and differences of the two characters are described in detail. At the same time, it points out the challenges facing the inheritance of Theravada Buddhism scriptures and characters due to the social development and changes in Xishuangbanna in recent years, and on this basis, puts forward his thoughts and suggestions on the inheritance and development of Theravada Buddhism scriptures and characters.

Ven. Du Kanzhang, a master of Chiang Mai University in Thailand and dean of Palm-Leaf Academy (a local Dai traditional academy) in Menghai County, Xishuangbanna, introduced the emergence and spread of the classical Dai scripts, and discussed the name and distribution of the Tai Tham. By showing the diverse names of the scripts in various regions, his article compares the characteristics of the scripts. He compares and analyzes the names of different places, combined with the characteristics of the text, to find a common name. Finally, he tries to explore the distribution of the use of classical Dai, in order to help us better understand it.

Ms. Sutheera Satayaphan, a Thai doctoral student from the University of Hamburg in Germany, shared with us an ancient Siamese dance drama *Kāraked*. The play was probably written during the period of Ayutthaya and lasted until the early period of Bangkok in the 18th century. The play was written on a similar concerto or leporello manuscript, which is made from the bark of the Khòi tree. Although a great deal of research has been done on the manuscripts of Siamese dramas, the previous studies on *Kārraked* dramas have rarely been found. This study examines these four manuscripts in order to reflect the cultural characteristics of drama and other manuscripts.

Dr. Rao Ruiying, associate professor of Yunnan Minzu University, introduced Krupa, a unique cultural phenomenon in the cultural circle of Theravada Buddhism. She payed close attention to the demands of the elites among the Krupa believers from a keen perspective. On this basis, she emphatically introduced the two most famous Krupas in northern Thailand Kruba Krupa Siwichai and Krupa Bunchum, and through their deeds of promoting the Dharma, she discussed the returns and demands of the elites in northern Thailand to the traditional belief of Buddhism.

Ms. Yiwangdi, associate professor of the Ancient Books Office of Yunnan Provincial Ethnic and Religious Affairs Committee, first introduced the process of Theravada

Buddhism entering the Dai society and its development, and briefly described the emergence and development process of the palm-leaf manuscripts as well as the specific production process of the palm-leaf manuscripts.

  This conference is a large-scale, wide-ranging and influential international academic exchange activity held in recent years in the field of palm-leaf manuscripts and palm-leaf culture of the Pali language family. The meeting convened experts and scholars who have made great achievements in this field to discuss how to inherit and protect the ancient and precious cultural heritage of palm-leaf culture better. Carrying out research and protection cooperation on palm-leaf culture is of great practical significance and value in supporting Yunnan University to build a top university in South and Southeast Asia, and providing a cultural focus for South and Southeast Asia for The Belt and Road Initiative. It is of great practical significance and value to promote cultural exchanges and cooperation among the countries in the region.

Conference Summary and Closing Speech

Zhou Ya[1]

Translated by Chen Qian[2]

Distinguished delegates, distinguished guests, teachers and students,

Good morning!

Happy time is always so quick! After a short period of one and a half days, scholars from Sri Lanka, Thailand, Laos, Germany, Britain and China gathered in the Donglu Campus of Yunnan University has comes to a contemporary end of our in-depth discussions and exchanges on the important humanities and social science topic of "Inheritance and Protection of the Palm-leaf Culture of China, Southeast Asia and South Asia".

First of all, on behalf of the organizers of the conference—the Development Research Institute of Yunnan University, PLCRC (Palm-Leaf Culture Research Centre) of Yunnan University and the Office of Culture and Art of Chiangmai Rajabhat University, I would like to extend my heartfelt thanks to all the international friends and representatives from outside the province who have come from thousands of miles away. I would like to express my sincere thanks to the colleagues from colleges and universities and cooperative units, especially those from Xishuangbanna, Dehong and other prefectures. I would like to thank all the representatives and guests for their support and assistance to our heritage, protection and research work. Thank you!

Just now, Dr. Direk Injan, director of the Palm-Leaf Manuscript Center from Chiangmai Rajabhat University, our partner from Thailand, has made a good summary of the meeting. Before the end of the meeting, I would also like to take this opportunity to say a little more about the experience of the meeting, as a supplementary summary and conclusion to our conference.

First, the success of the conference is a result of Yunnan University's continuous expansion of international academic exchanges and cooperation, ongoing promotion of

---

[1] Doctor and Associate Researcher, Director of PLCRC (Palm-Leaf Culture Research Center), Yunnan University.
[2] Master degree candidate of Religion, School of Ethnology and Sociology, Yunnan University.

its internationalization level, and the related work of the university's "Double First-Class" construction. In December 2018, we formed the idea of co-hosting this conference in the process of conducting international academic cooperation with universities such as Chiangmai University and Chiangmai Rajabhat University. Therefore, in a sense, this conference is also an international cooperation innovation in our research of palm-leaf culture.

At the same time, this conference is also a continuation of the two international conferences which lasts the international exchange tradition of our Palm-Leaf Culture Research Center (PLCRC), on palm-leaf culture research and cooperation. As early as 2010 and 2012, we held two international seminars in Xishuangbanna and Chiangmai respectively to conduct international exchange and research on the palm-leaf manuscripts and palm-leaf culture, and achieved some practical results, which promoted the academic cooperation between China and Thailand on this issues and the inheritance and protection practice of local palm-leaf culture.

Through holding such academic exchange activities, we had not only promoted the further attention to the palm-leaf culture from the civil society, to the local government and academic institutions, but also fortunately made many like-minded friends in the international academic community as follows.

Dr. Derik Injan just summarized the speech that he and his center of palm-leaf manuscript and Office of Culture and Art CMRU, long-term commitment to the north of Thailand collecting of ancient Lanna literature, as well as the inheritance and protection work for Thailand palm-leaf manuscripts, including the protection skills training, exhibition, digitization and so on, have done a lot of practical work of great value.

Dr. David Wharton comes from England and has a doctorate in University of Passau in Germany. He stayed in Laos for ten more years and he can speak Thai and Lao. He and his teacher Prof. Handius in University of Passau provide the instruction and support to the palm-leaf digital protection in whole Laos. They cooperate with Lao National Library to establish the "Lao Palm-Leaf Digital Library" and provide foreign readers palm-leaf manuscripts digital high definition picture system and meta-data retrieval network. Make some important contributions to the protection of Lao cultural heritage. He enjoyed pay more attention to Southeast Asian countries and their cultures. What's more, his academic research covers Laos, Myanmar, Thailand, Yunnan China and other places. We should study and respect the achievements and academic focus. At last, we will hold an academic report of David in tomorrow morning and we are looking forward to your attendance.

Another one of our old friend in palm-leaf center, Prof. Volker Grabowsky, was absent our meeting because of the important academic meeting in University of Hamburg. Although he can't attend the meeting this time, his students Dr. Apiradee, Dr. Zhou Hanli and Sutheera who work hard in the research area of history, palm-leaf scriptures and culture of the Dai-Tai ethnic groups are here. It not only shows that the research on the palm-leaf scriptures and the palm-leaf culture has an important research significance and value in the world, but also shows that the research in this field is persistent.

The other relevant research scholars and experts from University of Colombo, who developed academic exchange and cooperation with our dean Prof. Guo Shan last year, are including Dean & Prof. Premakumara de Silva, Ven. & Prof. Dhammajothi Thero and Dr. Wimal. Their participation improved our ability to inherit and protect the palm-leaf culture in China, Southeast Asia and South Asia. We are looking forward to make a progress in the international academic cooperation and exchange which is on the inheritance and protection of palm-leaf scriptures and palm-leaf culture. I'm looking forward to the next step of our cooperation.

In these two days there are many researchers related to the palm-leaf culture, and there are many scholars and practitioners from the area covered by palm-leaf culture. Most of them are Dai and Tai ethnic groups who are the most important people to inherit and protect the palm-leaf culture. The living of palm-leaf culture needs to be inherited and protected by you.

Our academic exchanges in these two days involve the following important topics:

The protection of palm-leaf culture in the natural environment; the situation of the inheritance and protection of the copy of palm-leaf scriptures in each relevant country; history, language, reading and translation, literature, art, social customs, beliefs and protection skills of palm-leaf scriptures and palm-leaf culture, as well as relevant observation, recording, cognition, comparative observation and research between different countries and regions on the above issues.

Through this discussion, we have reached a consensus and we recognized that although palm-leaf culture has the value of living cultural resources, its heritage traits are also very obvious. Especially under the modern background, the copies of the palm-leaf literature are in danger. Cultural deposits and modern inheritance and application of ideological value are promoted step by step. So we need to promote the inheritance and protection of the palm-leaf scripture and palm-leaf culture.

In the communication and collision of these thoughts, we have the love to the palm-leaf culture. What's more, we also have the worries about the palm-leaf culture. Both connotation and cultural extension of the wonderful academic communication and the way to inherit and protect this precious cultural resource are discussed in the meeting.

In addition, we know that palm-leaf culture preserves the memory, ethnic wisdom and local knowledge to human. It not only has the regional, local and ethnic characteristics, but also has the similarity in different area and higher level value, that's the records, memory, dissemination and inheritance to the human being. However, our work on this is still very limited.

We are trying to make an agreement and know more clearly. We should inherit and protect this valuable cultural heritage. We should pay more attention to local practice, folk power, personnel training and the international cooperation. In the future, how to keep the vitality of palm-leaf culture, and how to make it shine continuously in inheritance and protection are the important topics that we will continue to study and practice in the future.

In my opinion, this meeting is practical and important which is also rich in content.

"The International Seminar on the Inheritance & Protection of Palm-Leaf Culture in China, Southeast Asia and South Asia" is coming to an end temporarily. We should appreciate the two simultaneous interpreters, Prof. Liu Xuejun and Prof. Liu Dezhou, who come from Yunnan University and Yunnan Normal University. Also we should appreciate our sound engineer Mrs. Wang and many excellent members from Development Research Institute of Yunnan University and the School of Ethnology and Sociology of Yunnan University. They made lots of preparations to ensure the smooth progress of the meeting. Thanks!

Finally, I stand for the sponsor unit to express appreciation to all the representatives, scholars and experts, as well as teachers and students who attend this meeting and support the meeting. Hope we can meet together in the future and share our practice results and latest researches of protecting and inheriting the palm-leaf culture. Let us look forward to that moment.

Let us become the guardians of the palm-leaf culture!

Thanks!

后　记

在 2001 年编者刚接触贝叶经和贝叶文化时，网络的普及程度和影响力还不像现在这么无孔不入。21 世纪的头 20 年，世界各地的人们都经历了电子化、网络化、智能化等现代科技生活方式的深度现代化与全球化冲击。在当下这个连纸媒都濒危的"大而快"的大众媒体时代，"小而慢"的文化事项正被迫加速其"文化折叠"的速率，最终或许会在人类的现代文明中逐渐被消解，再也消失不见！编者和云南大学"中国—东南亚、南亚贝叶经与贝叶文化传承与保护"的团队成员，以及近 20 年来持续在该领域有联络、合作和保护实践的国际国内学者专家、地方文化精英，都在尽可能地为让贝叶经和"贝叶文化"能继续在这个时代存续与传承创造各种条件，通过组织开展研讨、出版研究文集等学术活动，推动相关各国的民间组织、机构、个人和学界等沟通信息、分享前沿实践进展、交流经验，促成各方达成对贝叶经和贝叶文化进行保护与传承的共识与合作。尽管力薄，但我们仍共识性地认为且相信：贝叶经和贝叶文化其文化本体中所蕴含的智识能量与智慧是超越了时空并且还将继续助益人类生存和文明发展并继续跨越时空的。

本次"中国—东南亚、南亚贝叶经与贝叶文化传承与保护"研讨会是云南大学"一流大学"建设创新团队项目的国际学术活动和阶段性研究成果。在云南大学贝叶文化研究中心与泰国清迈皇家大学、斯里兰卡科伦坡大学等高校研究机构的高效合作和努力推动以及中外学者的积极参与和支持下，这次会议得以顺利和成功举办。与会代表或是来自中国、泰国、老挝、斯里兰卡、德国和英国相关高校或研究机构的专家学者，或是长期在中国、东南亚、南亚区域从事巴利语系贝叶经和贝叶文化保护与传承的公共文化机构（包含地方文化机构和基层社区乃至佛寺等）的管理者和实践者，以及民间人士代表。从民间保护与传承主体，到专业机构的数字化技术专家和学术研究推动者，一定程度上代表了目前中国—南亚、东南亚区域巴利语系贝叶经和贝叶文化传承与保护实践的民间主体。然而，文化遗产的保护工作是一个庞大的体系，特别是跨国的区域性文化遗产保护，更需要各国政府相关部门取得共识并建立相应机制来协同进行。今后，我们希望看到包括国际组织、各级政府和相关部门等在内的更多文化遗产保护主体能更多地关注、支持并引导这一有意义

贝叶文化与区域文化遗产传承保护

的文化遗产保护与传承的集体行动,从而为中国—东南亚、南亚区域贝叶经与贝叶文化遗产的传承与保护做出更多更加有效的、更加实质性的推动作用与贡献。

感谢本次会议的合办单位泰国清迈皇家大学艺术文化办公室主任 Suchanart Sitanurak 女士和学术协调员、清迈皇家大学贝叶经研究中心主任 Derik Injan 博士;感谢贝叶文化研究中心的特聘研究员 Volker Grabowsky 教授、David Wharton 博士等对本次会议的支持。

衷心感谢云南大学校党委书记林文勋教授、原副校长杨泽宇教授、李晨阳教授等校领导对我们贝叶文化研究中心研究工作的长期关心和支持;感谢云南大学社科处杨绍军处长以及张剑源、陈小华副处长和原副处长范俊老师对我们提供的具体指导和帮助;感谢云南大学国际合作与交流处杨伟处长、沈芸副处长及钱均老师对会议的支持和帮助;感谢云南大学发展研究院和民族学与社会学学院诸位领导以及各位同仁的关心和鼓励。

感谢我们云南大学"中国—东南亚、南亚贝叶经与贝叶文化保护与传承"创新团队的成员:饶睿颖博士(云南民族大学副教授)、保明所博士(云南大学人文学院副教授)、张振伟博士(云南大学西南边疆研究中心副教授)、甘友庆博士(云南大学历史与档案学院副教授)和张海博士(云南大学影视人类学实验室主任)等诸位同仁;感谢彭多毅教授和与我们长期紧密联系合作的西双版纳贝叶文化研究中心及版纳州民研所的刀金平所长、岩香(原)所长、陆云东老师等同事,以及康南山、康南叫、康南坎章、康南罕、玉汪的、张云、玉罕为等贝叶文化传承实践的精英。共同的学术志趣将我们凝聚在一起。今后希望我们这个学术共同体能继往开来,继续为贝叶经和贝叶文化的保护、传承与研究贡献绵薄之力。

感谢以下毕业或就读于云南大学发展研究院以及民族学与社会学学院的硕士研究生:陈丹、袁子媚、饶晋铭、王明姣、孙晓、刘艳雪、李小辉、陈潜、韩帅等诸位同学,其中的几位也参与了本文集部分论文的翻译工作。韩帅同学还参与了初期统稿工作中的格式规范编辑工作。会议的成功顺利举办离不开你们的努力和奉献,感谢你们!

本文集亦是《贝叶文化论集》(2004年)、《贝叶文化与民族社会发展》(2007年)、《贝叶文化与傣族和谐社会建设》(2008年)、《贝叶文化与和谐周边建设》(2011年)等"贝叶文化研究系列丛书"的新集。在此,我们也要向长期支持我们研究成果出版工作的云南大学出版社蔡红华副社长、责编张丽华老师等一并表示衷心的感谢!

本文集编撰期间,正值新型冠状病毒疫情在全球范围内的暴发和肆虐。疫情虽无情,但在这次灾难中人们面对疫情相互帮助,彼此扶持,共享最新临床实践经验与科技研究成果的务实合作,必将为人类对抗和最终战胜病毒起到决定性的作用。其中显示出的"人类命运共同体"的集体行动与共同价值观念,进一步推动了"全球化"和"人类命运共同体"的深化。我们相信,这样跨国家、跨区域、跨族群在超国际体系的全球层面上务实深入的交流与合作，也必将推动全球人文领域的交流与合作大幅发展提升。它将进一步唤起人类群体对共同文化遗产的珍视，激发某种全球范围内普世性的"人类文化自觉"，从而促进全球社群对人类文化多样性和共同文化财富的共同守护，尽可能地保存和留住人类文化根脉，并让其成为人类共同体文化的基因库和"诺亚方舟"，勇敢地共同应对已来和未来……